EMPLOYMENT DISTRIBUTION BY MAJOR INDUSTRIAL SECTOR, 1900-1994
(DATA DISPLAYED GRAPHICALLY IN FIGURE 2.3 ON TEXT PAGE 31)

Year	Agriculture	Goods-producing Industries*	Nongovernment Services	Government Services
1900	38.1%	37.8%	20.0%	4.1%
1910	32.1	40.9	22.3	4.7
1920	27.6	44.0	21.4	6.0
1930	22.7	42.1	28.1	7.1
1940	18.5	41.6	31.1	8.8
1950	12.1	41.3	36.4	10.2
1960	6.6	41.4	38.8	13.2
1970	3.8	39.8	40.5	15.9
1980	3.5	35.9	43.9	16.7
1994	2.8	30.1	51.6	15.5

*Includes transportation and public utilities.
Sources: U.S. President, *Economic Report of the President* (Washington, D.C.: U.S. Government Printing Office, 1996) Table B-42; and U.S. Bureau of Labor Statistics, *Employment and Earnings*, 42, no. 1 (January 1995), Tables 1, 14.

TABLE 2.4 TOTAL AND LONG-TERM UNEMPLOYMENT RATES, SELECTED EUROPEAN AND NORTH AMERICAN COUNTRIES, 1979 AND 1990

	Overall Unemployment Rate		Long-Term Unemployment Rate	
	1979	1990	1979	1990
Belgium	7.5%	8.7%	4.6%	6.1%
Canada	7.4	8.1	0.2	0.5
Denmark	6.2	9.5	2.2	3.2
France	6.0	8.9	1.8	3.4
Germany	2.9	4.9	0.8	2.3
Ireland	7.1	13.7	2.7	9.2
Italy	7.8	11.1	4.0	7.9
Netherlands	3.5	6.4	1.3	3.1
Norway	1.9	5.2	0.1	1.0
Spain	8.6	16.3	2.6	8.8
Sweden	1.7	1.5	0.1	0.1
United Kingdom	4.5	5.9	1.3	2.1
United States	5.8	5.5	0.2	0.3

Modern Labor Economics

The Addison-Wesley Series in Economics

SIXTH EDITION

Modern Labor Economics
Theory and Public Policy

Ronald G. Ehrenberg
School of Industrial and Labor Relations
Cornell University

Robert S. Smith
School of Industrial and Labor Relations
Cornell University

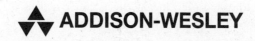

▲▲ ADDISON-WESLEY

An imprint of Addison Wesley Longman, Inc.

Reading, Massachusetts • Menlo Park, California • New York • Harlow, England
Don Mills, Ontario • Sydney • Mexico City • Madrid • Amsterdam

Executive Editor: John Greenman
Developmental Editor: Lori Jacobs
Text Design and Project Management: Interactive Composition Corporation
Cover Designer: Kay Petronio
Art Studio: Interactive Composition Corporation
Electronic Production Manager: Eric Jorgensen
Manufacturing Manager: Hilda Koparanian
Electronic Page Makeup: Interactive Composition Corporation
Printer and Binder: RR Donnelley & Sons Company
Cover Printer: The Lehigh Press, Inc.

Library of Congress Cataloging-in-Publication Data

Ehrenberg, Ronald G.
     Modern labor economics : theory and public policy / Ronald G. Ehrenberg, Robert S. Smith. — 6th
ed.
          p.   cm. — (The Addison-Wesley series in economics)
     Includes bibliographical references and indexes.
     ISBN 0-673-98013-8
     1. Labor economics.   I. Smith, Robert Stewart.   II. Title.   III. Series.
HD4901.E34   1996   96-33528
331—dc20   CIP

ISBN 0-673-98013-8

12345678910—DOC—99989796

Brief Contents

Detailed Contents

Preface

Modern Labor Economics: Theory and Public Policy has grown out of our experiences over the last three decades in teaching labor market economics and conducting research aimed at influencing public policy. Our text develops the modern theory of labor market behavior, summarizes empirical evidence that supports or contradicts each hypothesis, and illustrates in detail the usefulness of the theory for public policy analysis. We believe that showing students the social implications of concepts enhances the motivation to learn them and that using the concepts of each chapter in an analytic setting allows students to see the concepts in action. The extensive use of detailed policy applications constitutes a major contribution of this text.

Overview of the Text

Modern Labor Economics is designed for one-semester or one-quarter courses in labor economics at the undergraduate or graduate level for students who may not have extensive backgrounds in economics. Since 1974 we have taught such courses at the School of Industrial and Labor Relations at Cornell University. The undergraduate course requires only principles of economics as a prerequisite, and the graduate course (for students in a professional program akin to an MBA program) has no prerequisites. We have found that it is not necessary to be highly technical in one's presentation in order to convey important concepts and that students with limited backgrounds in economics *can* comprehend a great deal of material in a single course. However, for students who have had intermediate microeconomics, we have included ten chapter appendixes that discuss more advanced material or develop technical concepts in much greater detail than the text discussion permits.

After an introduction to basic economic concepts in Chapter 1, Chapter 2 presents a quick overview of demand and supply in labor markets so that students will see from the outset the interrelationship of the major forces at work shaping labor market behavior. This chapter can be skipped or skimmed by students with strong backgrounds in economics or by students in one-quarter courses. Chapters 3 to 5 are concerned primarily with the demand for labor, while Chapters 6 to 10 focus on labor supply issues.

Beginning with Chapter 11, the concepts of economics are used to analyze several topics of special interest to students of labor markets. The relationship between pay and productivity is analyzed in Chapter 11, and the earnings of women and minorities—encompassing issues of discrimination—are the subject of Chapter 12. Chapter 13 uses economic concepts to analyze collective bargaining in the private and public sectors. Chapter 14 offers an analysis of the growth of earnings inequality over the past fifteen years, and it serves the dual role of both investigating an important current phenomenon and reviewing many key concepts presented in earlier chapters. The final chapter treats the macroeconomic issue of unemployment.

In addition to the use of public policy examples and the inclusion of technical appendixes, the text has a number of important pedagogical features. First, each chapter contains two or more boxed examples that illustrate an application of that chapter's theory in a nontraditional, historical, business, or cross-cultural setting. Second, each chapter contains a number of discussion or review questions that allow students to apply what they have learned to specific policy issues. To enhance student mastery, we provide answers to the odd-numbered questions at the back of the book. Third, updated lists of selected readings at the ends of chapters refer students to more advanced sources of study.

Changes in the Sixth Edition

Those familiar with previous editions will find three major changes in the sixth edition. First, *international comparisons* are now incorporated into virtually every chapter, reflecting the growth of a truly global economy and the heightened interest of labor economists in analyzing labor markets and policies in a comparative framework. Our increased emphasis on international comparisons is based on the belief that economic theory is applicable across cultures and that students can better understand labor markets in their own countries by knowing how markets and institutions function elsewhere.

Second, virtually every chapter has been significantly trimmed with an eye toward sharpening the exposition and reducing the book's length. We have, however, maintained our practice of providing comprehensive and up-to-date citations to the professional literature on the topics we treat.

Third, several chapters have been substantially reorganized. The most prominent changes have been made in the labor demand chapters, especially Chapters 3 and 4, in which monopsonistic models are given more prominence. These changes reflect questions about the effects of minimum wage laws in the United States and elsewhere, as well as what we perceive to be growing interest among economists in building more complexity into their models of employer behavior. Monopsonistic models are also discussed in the chapters on mobility (Chapter 10), pay and productivity (Chapter 11), and discrimination (Chapter 12). Other prominent changes are the expanded treatment of general and specific training in Chapter 5, the new policy applications contained in Chapter 6 (especially the analysis of the Earned Income Tax Credit), and the inclusion of the signaling model in the body of Chapter 9. The chapters on public sector labor markets and on inflation have been eliminated, with some of their material incorporated into Chapters 13 and 15, respectively.

Accompanying Supplements

Two supplements enrich this sixth edition of *Modern Labor Economics*. The first is a study guide prepared by Professor George Kosicki of the College of the Holy Cross. For each chapter in the text the study guide offers (*a*) a brief summary of the major concepts, with numerical examples when appropriate; (*b*) a review section with multiple-choice questions; (*c*) a problems section with short-answer essay questions; (*d*) an applications section with problems and questions related to policies or labor market issues; (*e*) answers to all questions and problems; and (*f*) one or more newspaper articles that illustrate concepts central to the chapter.

A test bank by Robert M. Whaples of Wake Forest University offers 500 multiple-choice questions for teaching. It is included with an instructor's manual that outlines the major concepts in each chapter, presents answers to the even-numbered review questions in the text, and contains two suggested essay questions per chapter (with answers).

Acknowledgments

Enormous debts are owed to four groups of people. First are those instrumental in teaching us the concepts and social relevance of labor economics when we were students: Frank Brechling, George Delehanty, Dale Mortensen, John Pencavel, Orme Phelps, and Mel Reder. Second are the generations of undergraduate and graduate students who sat through the lectures that preceded the publication of each new edition of *Modern Labor Economics* and, by their questions and responses, forced us to make ourselves clear. Third are Patricia Dickerson, who patiently typed the many revisions incorporated into the sixth edition, and Nancy Tenney, our copyeditor for the past four editions, whose careful attention to detail has benefited all readers.

Fourth, several colleagues have contributed, both formally and informally, to this sixth edition. We appreciate the suggestions of the following people:

John Abowd
Cornell University

John Addison
University of South Carolina

George Berger
University of Pittsburgh at Johnstown

Francine Blau
Cornell University

George Boyer
Cornell University

Leonard Carlson
Emory University

Ted Chiles
Auburn University at Montgomery

Gary Fields
Cornell University

Robert Gitter
Ohio Wesleyan

Paul Grimes
Mississippi State University

James Henderson
Baylor University

Lee Husky
University of Alaska at Anchorage

Robert Hutchens
Cornell University

George Jakubson
Cornell University

Lawrence Kahn
Cornell University

Gary Keener
Heidelberg College

Thomas Kneisner
Indiana University

Alan Krueger
Princeton University

Peter Mattila
Iowa State University

Bruce McClung
Southwest Texas State University

Naci Mocan
University of Colorado at Denver

Robert L. Moore
Occidental College

Stephen Nuen
Utica College of Syracuse University

Walter Oi
University of Rochester

John Pencavel
Stanford University

Steven Pischke
Massachusetts Institute of Technology

Daniel Rees
University of Colorado at Denver

Tim Schmidle
Cornell University

Jeremy Schrauf
SUNY at Albany

Edwin Sexton
Virginia Military Academy

Robert Singleton
Loyola Marymount University

Richard W. Stratton
University of Akron

Leslie Stratton
University of Arizona

Robert Whaples
Wake Forest University

Laura Wolff
Southern Illinois University

Buhong Zheng
University of Colorado at Denver

Ronald G. Ehrenberg
Robert S. Smith

Introduction

Economic theory provides powerful, and often surprising, insights into individual and social behavior. At a purely scientific level, these insights are interesting because they help us understand important aspects of our lives. Beyond this, however, government, industry, labor, and other groups have increasingly come to understand the usefulness of the concepts and thought processes of economists in formulating social policy. This theory of behavior is simple yet compelling, and provides a systematic approach to the analysis of economic problems.

This book presents a comprehensive and understandable application of economic analysis to the behavior of, and relationship between, employers and employees. The aggregate compensation received by U.S. employees from their employers was $3,660 billion in 1994, while all *other* forms of personal income that year—from investments, self-employment, pensions, and various government welfare programs—amounted to $2,040 billion. The *employment* relationship, then, is one of the most fundamental relationships in our lives, and as such it attracts a good deal of legislative attention. A mastery of the fundamentals of labor economics is thus essential to an understanding of a huge array of social problems and programs, both in the United States and elsewhere.

As economists who have been actively involved in the analysis and evaluation of labor-related policies adopted or considered by the government, we obviously believe labor economics is useful in understanding the effects of these policies. Perhaps more important, we also believe policy analysis can be useful in teaching the fundamentals of labor economics. We have therefore incorporated such analyses into each chapter with two pedagogical purposes in mind. First, we believe that seeing the relevance and social implications of concepts studied enhances the student's motivation to learn. Second, using the concepts of each chapter in an analytical setting serves to reinforce understanding by permitting the student to see them "in action."

The Labor Market

There is a rumor that a former U.S. Secretary of Labor attempted to abolish the term "labor market" from departmental publications. He believed it demeaned workers to regard labor as being bought and sold like so much grain, oil, or steel. True, labor is somewhat unique. Labor services can only be rented; workers themselves cannot be bought and sold. Further, because labor services cannot be separated from workers, the conditions under which such services are rented are often as important as the price. Put differently, *nonpecuniary factors*—such as work environment, risk of injury, personalities of managers, perceptions of "fair" treatment, and flexibility of work hours—loom larger in employment transactions than they do in markets for commodities. Finally, a host of institutions and pieces of legislation that influence the employment relationship do not exist in other markets.

Nevertheless, the circumstances under which employers and employees rent labor services clearly constitute a market for several reasons. First, institutions have been developed to facilitate contact between buyers and sellers of labor services. This contact may come about through want ads, union hiring halls, employment agencies, placement offices, or plant personnel offices.

Second, once contact is arranged, information about price and quality is exchanged. Employment applications, interviews, and even word-of-mouth information from friends illustrate this kind of exchange in the market for labor.

Third, when agreement is reached, some kind of *contract* is executed covering compensation, conditions of work, job security, and even duration of the job. At times the contract is formal, such as with collective bargaining (union–management) agreements. At other times the agreement is unwritten and informal, with only an implied understanding between the parties based on past practices and experience. Nonetheless, it is often useful to think of the employment relationship as governed by a contract.

Labor contracts typically call for employers to compensate employees for their *time* and not for what they produce. Relatively few workers receive piece-rate wages or commissions, in which compensation is computed directly on the basis of output. The vast majority are paid by the hour, week, or month. They are paid, in short, to show up for work and (within limits) to follow orders. This form of compensation requires that employers give careful attention to worker motivation and dependability in the selection and employment process.

The end result of employer–employee transactions in the labor market is, of course, the placement of people in jobs at certain rates of pay. This allocation of labor serves not only the personal needs of individuals but the needs of the larger society as well. Through the labor market, our most important national resource—labor—is allocated to firms, industries, occupations, and regions.

Labor Economics: Some Basic Concepts

Labor economics is the study of the workings and outcomes of the market for labor. More specifically, labor economics is primarily concerned with the behavior of employers and employees in response to the general incentives of wages, prices, profits, and nonpecuniary aspects of the employment relationship, such as working conditions. These incentives serve both to motivate and to limit individual choice. The focus in economics is on inducements for behavior that are impersonal and apply to wide groups of people.

In this book we shall examine, for example, the relationship between wages and employment opportunities, the interaction between wages, income, and the decision to work, the way general market incentives affect occupational choice, the relationship between wages and undesirable job characteristics, the incentives for and effects of educational and training investments, and the effects of unions on wages, productivity, and turnover. In the process, we shall analyze the employment and wage effects of such social policies as the minimum wage, overtime legislation, pension reform regulations, safety and health regulations, welfare reform, payroll taxes, unemployment insurance, immigration policies, and antidiscrimination laws.

Our study of labor economics will be conducted on two levels. Most of the time we shall use economic theory to analyze "what is"; that is, we shall explain people's behavior using a mode of analysis called *positive economics*. Less commonly, we shall use *normative* economic analysis to judge "what should be."

POSITIVE ECONOMICS

Positive economics is a theory of behavior in which people are typically assumed to respond favorably to benefits and negatively to costs. In this regard, positive economics closely resembles Skinnerian psychology, which views behavior as shaped by rewards and punishments. The rewards in economic theory are pecuniary and nonpecuniary gains (benefits), while the punishments are forgone opportunities (costs). For example, a person motivated to become a surgeon because of the earnings and status surgeons command must give up the opportunity to become a lawyer and must be available for emergency work around the clock. Both the benefits and the costs must be considered in making this career choice. Likewise, a firm deciding whether to hire an additional worker must weigh the wage and salary costs against the added revenues or cost savings made possible by expanding its workforce.

SCARCITY　The most all-pervasive assumption underlying economic theory is that of resource *scarcity*. According to this assumption, individuals and society alike do not have the resources to meet all their wants. Hence, any resource devoted to satisfying one set of desires could have been used to satisfy another set, which means that there is a cost to any decision or action. The real cost of using labor hired by a government contractor to build a road, for example, is the production lost by not devoting this labor to the building of an airport or to the making of some other good. Thus, in popular terms, "There is no such thing as a free lunch," and we must always make choices and live with the rewards and costs these choices bring us. Moreover, we are always constrained in our choices by the resources available to us.

RATIONALITY   The second basic assumption of positive economics is that people are *rational* in the sense that they have an objective and pursue it in a reasonably consistent fashion. When considering *persons,* economists assume that the objective being pursued is *utility maximization;* that is, people are assumed to strive toward the goal of making themselves as happy as they can (given their limited resources). Utility, of course, encompasses both pecuniary and nonpecuniary dimensions. When considering the behavior of *firms,* which are inherently nonpersonal entities, economists assume that the goal of behavior is *profit maximization.* Profit maximization is really just a special case of utility maximization in which pecuniary gain is emphasized and nonpecuniary factors are ignored.

The assumption of rationality implies a *consistency* of response to general economic incentives and an *adaptability* of behavior when those incentives change. These two characteristics of behavior underlie predictions about how workers and firms will respond to various incentives. Rationality cannot be directly proven, however, and even totally habit-bound or unthinkingly impulsive people might be forced to alter their behavior in predictable ways if the resources at their command changed.[1] Thus, while we shall maintain the assumption of rationality throughout this text, this assumption is not absolutely necessary to the derivation of at least *some* of the behavioral predictions contained herein.

THE MODELS AND PREDICTIONS OF POSITIVE ECONOMICS

Behavioral predictions in economics flow more or less directly from the two fundamental assumptions of scarcity and rationality. Workers must continually make choices, such as whether to look for other jobs, accept overtime, seek promotions, move to another area, or acquire more education. Employers must also make choices concerning, for example, the level of output and the mix of machines and labor to use in production. Economists usually assume that, when making these choices, employees and employers are guided by their desires to maximize utility or profit, respectively. However, what is more important to the economic theory of behavior is not the *particular* goal of either employees or employers; rather, it is that economic actors weigh the costs and benefits of various alternative transactions in the context of achieving *some* goal or other. For example, when analyzing race or gender discrimination (see Chapter 12), economists frequently assume that employers are maximizing *utility,* not profits.

---

[1]Gary Becker, "Irrational Behavior and Economic Theory," *Journal of Political Economy* 70, no. 1 (February 1962): 1–13.

One may object that these assumptions are unrealistic and that people are not nearly as calculating, as well-informed about alternatives, or as amply endowed with choices as economists assume. Economists are likely to reply that if people are not calculating, are totally uninformed, or do not have any choices, then most predictions suggested by economic theory will not be supported by real-world evidence. They thus argue that the theory underlying positive economics should be judged on the basis of its predictions, not its assumptions.

The reason we need to make assumptions and create a relatively simple theory of behavior is that the actual workings of the labor market are almost impossibly complex. Millions of workers and employers interact daily, all with their own sets of motivations, preferences, information, and perceptions of self-interest. A detailed description of the individual outcomes and the processes that determine them would clearly be of limited feasibility and usefulness. What we need to discover are general principles that provide useful insights into the labor market. These principles could not be expected to predict or explain behavior with the same accuracy as the laws of physics predict the movement of an object through space, because we are dealing with human beings capable of making choices. Nevertheless, we hope to show in this text that a few forces are so basic to labor market behavior that they alone can predict or explain many of the outcomes and behaviors observed in the labor market.

Anytime we attempt to explain a complex set of behaviors and outcomes using a few fundamental influences, we have created a *model*. Models are not intended to capture every complexity of behavior; instead, they are created to strip away random and idiosyncratic factors so that the focus is on general principles. An analogy from the physical sciences may make the nature of models and their relationship to actual behavior clearer.

Using calculations of velocity and gravitational pull, physicists can predict where a ball will land if it is kicked with a certain force at a given angle to the ground. The actual point of landing may vary from the predicted point because of wind currents and any spin the ball might have—factors ignored in the calculations. If 100 balls are kicked, none may ever land exactly on the predicted spot, although they will tend to cluster around it. The accuracy of the model, while not perfect, may be good enough to enable a football coach to decide whether to attempt a field goal or not. The point is that we usually just need to know the *average tendencies* of outcomes for policy purposes. To estimate these tendencies we need to know the important forces at work, but we must confine ourselves to few enough influences so that calculating estimates remains feasible. (A further comparison of physics and positive economics is contained in Example 1.1.)

To really grasp the assumptions and predictions of economic models, it is necessary to consider a concrete example. Suppose we begin by asserting that, being subject to resource scarcity, workers will prefer high-paying jobs to low-paying ones *if* all other job characteristics are the same in each job. Thus, in pursuit of their own well-being, they will quit low-paying jobs to take better-paying ones for which they qualify if they believe sufficient improvement is likely. This principle does not imply that workers care only about wages or that all are equally likely to

---

EXAMPLE 1.1

Positive Economics: What Does It Mean to "Understand" Behavior?

The purpose of "positive" economic analysis is to analyze, or understand, the behavior of people as they respond to market incentives. But in a world that is extremely complex, just what does it mean to "understand" behavior? We have illustrated the nature and use of models with an example from physics, so it is interesting that physicists—who analyze the behavior of matter and energy—have also wondered what it means to understand the world. One theoretical physicist put it this way:

> We can imagine that this complicated array of moving things which constitutes "the world" is something like a great chess game being played by the gods, and we are observers of the game. We do not know what the rules of the game are; all we are allowed to do is to *watch* the playing. Of course, if we watch long enough, we may eventually catch on to a few of the rules. *The rules of the game* are what we mean by *fundamental physics*. Even if

we know every rule, however . . . what we really can explain in terms of those rules is very limited, because almost all situations are so enormously complicated that we cannot follow the plays of the game using the rules, much less tell what is going to happen next. We must, therefore, limit ourselves to the more basic question of the rules of the game. If we know the rules, we consider that we "understand" the world.*

If the behavior of nature, which does not have a will, is so difficult to analyze, understanding the behavior of people is even more of a challenge. Since people's behavior does not mechanistically follow a set of rules, the goal of positive economics is most realistically stated as trying to discover their behavioral *tendencies*.

*Richard Rhodes, *The Making of the Atomic Bomb* (New York: Simon & Schuster, 1986), 33.

---

quit. Workers obviously care about a number of employment characteristics, and improvement in any of these on their current job makes turnover less likely. Likewise, some workers are more receptive to change than others. Nevertheless, if we hold these other factors constant and increase only wages, we should clearly observe that the probability of quitting will fall.

On the employer side of the market, we can consider a similar prediction. Firms need to make a profit to survive. If they have high turnover, their costs will be higher than otherwise because of the need to hire and train replacements. With high turnover they could not, therefore, afford to pay high wages. However, if they could reduce turnover enough by paying higher wages, it might well be worth incurring the high wage costs. Thus, both the utility-maximizing behavior of employees and the profit-maximizing behavior of firms lead us to expect low turnover to be associated with high wages and high turnover with low wages, other things equal.[2]

---

[2]In this example the expected relationship between wages and worker/firm behavior is clear-cut. While this is often the case, the expected relationship is not always that clear. We shall see examples of this later on—especially in Chapter 6.

It is important to note several things about the above predictions:

1. The predictions emerge directly from the twin assumptions of scarcity and rationality. Employees and employers, both mindful of their scarce resources, are assumed to be on the lookout for chances to improve their well-being. The predictions are also based on the assumptions that employees are aware of, or can learn about, alternative jobs and that these alternatives are open to them. If any of these assumptions is invalid or inappropriate, the predictions would not be consistently borne out by observed behavior.

2. The prediction of a negative relationship between wages and voluntary turnover is made holding other things equal. The theory does not deny that job characteristics other than wages matter to employees or that employers can lower turnover by varying policies other than the wage rate. However, holding these other factors constant, we should observe the predicted negative relationship if the basic assumptions are valid.

3. The *assumptions* of the theory concern *individual* behavior of employers and employees, but the *predictions* are about an *aggregate* relationship between wages and turnover. The prediction is *not* that all employees will remain in their jobs if their wages are increased, but that *enough* will remain for turnover to be cut by raising wages. The test of the prediction thus lies in finding out if the predicted relationship between wages and turnover exists as one looks at aggregate data from firms or industries.

Careful statistical studies suggest support for the hypothesis that higher pay reduces voluntary turnover. One study, for example, estimated that a 10 percent increase in wages, holding all other job characteristics constant, would reduce a firm's quit rate by 3 percent.[3]

NORMATIVE ECONOMICS

Understanding normative economics begins with the realization that there are two kinds of economic transactions. One kind is entered into voluntarily, because all parties to the transaction gain. If Sally is willing to draw blueprints for $10 per hour, for example, and Ace Engineering Services is willing to pay someone up to $11 per hour to do the job, both gain by agreeing to Sally's appointment at an hourly wage between $10 and $11; such a transaction is mutually beneficial. The role of the labor market is to facilitate these voluntary, mutually advantageous transactions. If the market is successful in facilitating *all* possible

---

[3]Ann Bartel, "Wages, Nonwage Job Characteristics and Labor Mobility," *Industrial and Labor Relations Review* 35, no. 4 (July 1982): 578–589.

mutually beneficial transactions, it can be said to have produced a condition economists call *Pareto* (or "economic") *efficiency*.[4] (The word *efficiency* is used by economists in a very specialized sense to denote a condition in which all mutually beneficial transactions have been concluded. This definition of the word is more comprehensive than its normal connotation of cost minimization.) If Pareto efficiency were actually attained, no more transactions would be undertaken voluntarily, because they would not be *mutually* advantageous.

The second kind of transaction is one in which one or more parties *lose*. These transactions often involve the redistribution of income, from which some gain at the expense of others. Transactions that are explicitly redistributional, for example, are not entered into voluntarily unless motivated by charity (in which case the donors gain nonpecuniary satisfaction); otherwise, redistributional transactions are mandated by government through tax and expenditure policies. Thus, while markets facilitate *voluntary* transactions, the job of government is often to make certain transactions *mandatory*.

Any normative statement—a statement about what *ought* to exist—is based on some underlying value. Government policies affecting the labor market are often based on the widely shared, but not universally agreed upon, value that society should try to make the distribution of income more equal. Welfare programs, minimum wage laws, and restrictions on immigration are examples of policies based on *distributional* considerations. Other labor market policies are intended either to change or to overrule the choices workers make in maximizing their utility; the underlying value in these cases is frequently that workers should not be allowed to place themselves or their families at risk of physical or financial harm. The wearing of such personal protective devices as hard hats and earplugs, for example, is seen as so *meritorious* in certain settings that it is required of workers even if they would choose otherwise.

Policies seeking to redistribute income or force the consumption of meritorious goods are often controversial, because some workers will feel worse off when they are adopted. These "losers" will be either those from whom income is transferred or those who are forced to consume some good they would not otherwise have chosen. These transactions must be governmentally mandated because they will not be entered into voluntarily.

Economic theory, however, reminds us that there is that class of transactions in which there are no losers. Policies or transactions from which all affected parties gain can be said to be "Pareto-improving" because they promote Pareto efficiency. These policies or transactions can be justified on the grounds that they unambiguously en-

---

[4]Pareto efficiency gets its name from the Italian economist Vilfredo Pareto, who, at the turn of the century, insisted that economic science should make normative pronouncements only about unambiguous changes in social welfare. Rejecting the notion that utility can be measured (and therefore compared across individuals), Pareto argued that we can only know whether a transaction improves social welfare from the testimony or behavior of the affected parties themselves. If they as individuals regard themselves as better off, then the transaction is unambiguously good—even though we are unable to measure *how much* better off they feel.

hance social welfare; therefore, they can be unanimously supported. Policies with this justification are of special interest to economists, because economics is largely the study of market behavior—voluntary transactions in the pursuit of self-interest.

A transaction can be unanimously supported when

a. All parties affected by the transaction gain;
b. Some gain and no one else loses; or
c. Some gain and some lose from the transaction, but the gainers fully compensate the losers.

When the compensation in *c* takes place, case *c* is converted to case *b*. In practice, economists often judge a transaction by whether the gains of the beneficiaries exceed the costs borne by the losers, thus making it *possible* that there would be no losers. If the losers sustain losses that the gainers could not possibly compensate, then the transaction could never be beneficial to all and the principle of unanimous consent is obviously violated. However, when the compensation of losers is *possible* but does *not* take place, there are in fact losers! Many economists, therefore, argue that compensation *must* take place for a government policy to be justified on the grounds that it promotes Pareto efficiency.

As noted above, the role of the labor market is to facilitate voluntary, mutually advantageous transactions. Hardly anyone would argue against at least some kind of government intervention in the labor market if the market is failing to promote such transactions. Market failure can occur for several reasons, as discussed in the following paragraphs.

IGNORANCE   First, people may be ignorant of some important facts and thus led to make decisions that are not in their self-interest. For example, a worker who smokes may take a job in an asbestos-processing plant not knowing that the combination of smoking and inhaling asbestos dust substantially increases the risk of disease. Had the worker known this, he or she would probably have stopped smoking or changed jobs, but both transactions were "blocked" by ignorance.

TRANSACTION BARRIERS   Second, there may be some barrier to the completion of a transaction that could be mutually beneficial. Often such a barrier is created by laws that prohibit certain transactions. For example, as recently as two or three decades ago, many states prohibited employers from hiring women to work more than 40 hours per week. As a consequence, firms that wanted to hire workers for more than 40 hours a week could not transact with those women who wanted to work overtime—to the detriment of both parties. (Society as a whole also suffers losses when transactions that are not mutually beneficial are mandated by government, as illustrated in Example 1.2.)

Laws can also block transactions in other ways. Consider, for example, a firm that is willing to offer overtime work to its production workers at rates no more than 10 percent above their normal wage. Some workers might be willing to accept overtime at the 10 percent premium. However, this transaction, even though

EXAMPLE 1.2

Normative Economics, Positive Economics, and the War of 1812

The advocacy of mutually beneficial transactions underlying *normative economics* has a very practical social value in the labor market: it assures a *voluntary* allocation of workers to jobs. When compulsion is necessary to fill certain jobs, society suffers the costs of recruiting and retaining unwilling workers. Sometimes these costs can be very large, as the British learned from their "impressment" of seamen in the early 1800s.

The British navy had long followed a policy of paying its ordinary seamen considerably less than they could obtain on British merchant ships. Because of the difficulties caused by these low wages in recruiting and retaining sailors, Britain's navy resorted to the often-brutal impressment of merchant seamen during times of war. Those choosing to become British merchant seamen, therefore, faced the risk of being forced to serve in the navy against their will. This risk was especially high during the war-torn years around 1800.

During this time, American merchant ships were offering seamen wages that were roughly double the wages offered on British merchant ships—and therefore much more than double the wages offered by the British navy. As one might predict from this chapter's illustrative model of *positive economics*, high wages offered by the Americans caused many British seamen to choose work on board American ships. Moreover, many opted to become naturalized U.S. citizens in the hope of avoiding impressment.

Not recognizing the rights of its subjects to change citizenship, and facing substantial shortages of naval recruits, Britain began stopping American merchant ships on the high seas and carting off seamen who were suspected of being British. This capture and impressment of sailors employed on American ships angered the United States and was one of the principal causes of the War of 1812. Truly, then, its low naval wages in fact imposed very high opportunity costs on Great Britain!

SOURCE: Michael Lewis, *A Social History of the Navy, 1793–1815* (London: George Allen and Unwin Ltd., 1960).

desired by both parties, could not legally be completed in most instances because of a law (the Fair Labor Standards Act) requiring almost all production workers to be paid a 50 percent wage premium for overtime. In this case, overtime would not be worked and both parties would suffer.

Another barrier to mutually beneficial transactions may be the expense of completing the transaction. Unskilled workers facing very limited opportunities in one region might desire to move to take better jobs. Alternatively, they might want to enter job-training programs. In either case, they might lack the funds to finance the desired transaction.

PRICE DISTORTION   A special barrier to transaction is caused by taxes, subsidies, or other forces that create "incorrect" prices. Prices powerfully influence the incentives to transact, and the prices asked or received in a transaction should reflect the true preferences of the parties to it. When prices become "decoupled" from preferences, parties may be led to make transactions that are not socially beneficial or to avoid others that would be advantageous. If it costs $4 to grow a bushel of wheat, for example, but government subsidies permit it to be bought for $3, these subsidies induce resources worth $4 to be converted to uses in which they are valued at $3! Likewise, if plumbers charge $15 per hour, but their customers must pay an additional tax of $5 to the government, customers who are willing to pay between $15 and $20 per hour and would hire plumbers in the absence of the tax are discouraged from doing so—to the detriment of both parties.

NONEXISTENCE OF MARKET A fourth reason why transactions that are mutually beneficial may not occur voluntarily is that it may be impossible or uncustomary for buyers and sellers of certain resources to transact. As an illustration, assume that a woman who does not smoke works temporarily next to a man who does. She would be willing to pay as much as 50 cents an hour to keep her working environment smoke-free, and he could be induced to give up smoking for as little as 25 cents an hour. Thus, the potential exists for her to give him 35 cents an hour and for both to benefit. However, custom or the transience of their relationship might prevent her from offering him money in this situation, in which case the transaction would not occur.

NORMATIVE ECONOMICS AND GOVERNMENT POLICY

The solution to problems that impede the completion of mutually beneficial transactions frequently involves government intervention. When law creates the barrier to a transaction, the "intervention" might be to repeal the law. Laws prohibiting women from working overtime, for example, were repealed in recent years as their adverse effects on women became recognized.

In other cases, however, the government might be able to undertake activities to reduce transaction barriers that the private market would not undertake. Below, we cite three examples that relate to the barriers created by lack of information or restrictions on choice. Finally, we conclude with a brief discussion of the trade-off society faces between the goal of a more equitable distribution of income and the goal of achieving Pareto efficiency.

PUBLIC GOODS First let us take the case of the dissemination of information. Suppose that workers in noisy factories are concerned about the effects of noise on their hearing, but that ascertaining these effects would require an expensive research program. Suppose, further, that a union representing sawmill workers considers undertaking such research and financing the project by selling its findings to the many other interested unions or workers. The workers would then have the information they desire—albeit at some cost—which they could use to make more intelligent decisions concerning their jobs.

The hitch in the scheme is that the union doing the research may not have any customers *even though* others find the information it produces valuable. As soon as the union's findings are published to its own members or its first customers, the results can easily become public knowledge—and thus available *free* from newspapers or by word of mouth. Other unions may be understandably reluctant to pay for information they can get free, and the union doing the research ends up getting very little, if any, reimbursement for its expenses. Anticipating this problem, the union will probably decide not to undertake the research.

Information in this example is called a *public good*—a good that can be consumed by any number of people at the same time, including those who do not pay for it. Because nonpayers cannot be excluded from consuming the good, no potential customer will have an incentive to pay. The result is that the good never gets produced by a private organization. Because the government, however, can *compel* payment through its tax system, it is natural to look to the government to produce public goods. When information on occupational health hazards is to be produced on a large scale, the government is likely to have to be involved.

CAPITAL MARKET IMPERFECTIONS An example of a second type of situation in which the government might have to step in to overcome a transaction barrier involves a case in which loans are not available to finance job training or interregional moves, even though such loans might give workers facing a very poor set of choices access to better opportunities. Such loans are not typically provided by the private sector because they are not backed (secured) by anything other than the debtor's promise to pay them back. Banks cannot ordinarily afford to take the risks inherent in making such loans, particularly when the loan recipients are poor, because a number of defaults could put them out of business (or at least lower their profitability). This lack of available loans to finance worthwhile transactions represents a "capital market imperfection."

The government, however, might be willing to make loans in such situations even if it faced the same risk of default, because enabling workers to move to areas of better economic opportunity could improve overall social welfare and strengthen the economy. In short, because society would reap benefits from encouraging people to enter job-training programs or move to areas where their skills could be better utilized, it might be wise for the government to make the loans itself.

ESTABLISHING MARKET SUBSTITUTES A third type of situation in which government intervention might be necessary to overcome transaction barriers occurs when a market fails to exist for some reason. In the example above, a smoker and a nonsmoker were temporarily working next to each other, and their transitory relationship prevented a mutually beneficial transaction from taking place. A solution in this case might be for the government to impose the same result that a market transaction would have generated—and require the employer to designate that area a nonsmoking area.

In each case, when government does intervene, it must make sure that the transactions it undertakes or imposes on society create more gains for the beneficiaries than they impose in costs on others. Since it is costly to produce information, for example, the government should do it only if the gains are more valuable than the resources used in producing it. Likewise, the government would want to make loans for job training or interregional moves only if these activities enhanced social welfare. Finally, imposing nonsmoking areas would be socially desirable only if the gainers gained more than the losers lost.

EFFICIENCY VERSUS EQUITY   The social goal of a more equitable distribution of income is often of paramount importance to political decision makers, and disputes can arise over whether equity or economic efficiency should be the prime consideration in setting policy. One source of dispute is rooted in the problem that there is not a unique set of transactions that are Pareto efficient. There are, in fact, a *number* of different sets of transactions that can satisfy our definition of economic efficiency, and questions can arise as to which set is the most equitable.

To understand the multiple sets of efficient transactions that are possible, we return to our example of the woman willing to draw blueprints for $10 per hour. If Ace Engineering Services is willing to pay up to $11 per hour for blueprints, and Sally is willing to work for $10, their agreement on her employment at an hourly wage of, say, $10.50 would be beneficial to both parties. However, the same can be said for an agreement on wages of either $10.25 or $10.75 per hour. Which agreement is most equitable?

The disputes that can arise over which "Pareto-improving" agreement is most equitable often center on the parties' *initial endowments of resources.* Suppose that Sally is so wealthy she does not really "need" to work, and that Ace's offices are in a hard-to-reach location. In this event, her bargaining position will be relatively strong, and the agreed-upon wage will be closer to $11. With a different set of initial conditions, however, Sally might have voluntarily agreed to a wage closer to $10.

If we observe that Sally and Ace have agreed to $10.25 per hour, for example, two opinions are possible. Some might be content that a mutually beneficial transaction has occurred, but others might conclude the outcome is unfair and that Sally did not gain *enough.* Once the parties have agreed upon $10.25, however, policies to change the agreement—perhaps by changing the parties' resource endowments—will be viewed by those holding the former opinion as violating the criteria for judging a transaction as Pareto-improving (because one party will lose). Thus, while some may argue that a given policy is designed to choose *among* Pareto-efficient agreements, others may see the same policy as giving up efficiency to obtain more equity.

The second source of dispute over equity and efficiency is rooted in the problem that, to achieve more equity, steps *away* from Pareto efficiency must often be taken.[5] Minimum wage laws, for example, block transactions that parties might be willing to make at a lower wage; thus, some who would have accepted jobs at less than the legislated minimum are not offered any at all because their services are "priced out of the market." Similarly, the welfare program is currently structured

---

[5]See Arthur Okun, *Equality and Efficiency: The Big Trade-Off* (Washington, D.C.: Brookings Institution, 1975), for a lucid discussion of the trade-offs between efficiency and equity.

so that recipients who find paid work receive, in effect, a zero wage—a price distortion of major proportions, but one that is neither easily nor cheaply avoided (as we will see in Chapter 6).

Normative economics tends to stress efficiency over equity considerations, not because they are more important, but because they can be analyzed more scientifically. For a transaction to be mutually beneficial, all that is required is for each party individually to feel better off. Hence studying voluntary transactions (that is, market behavior) is useful when taking economic efficiency into account. Equity considerations, however, always involve comparing the welfare lost by some against the utility gained by others—which, given the impossibility of measuring happiness, cannot be scientifically done. For policy decisions based on considerations of equity, society usually turns to guidance from the political system, not from markets.

Plan of the Text

With this brief review of economics in mind, we turn now to the specific subject-matter areas of labor economics. The study of labor economics is mainly a study of the interplay between employers and employees—or between demand and supply. Chapter 2 presents a quick overview of demand and supply in the labor market, allowing students to see from the outset the interrelationship of the major forces at work shaping labor market behavior. This chapter contains many concepts that will be familiar to students who have a background in microeconomics.

Chapters 3–5 are concerned primarily with the demand for labor. As such, they are devoted to an analysis of employers' incentives and behavior. In tracing out the implications of this behavior for public policy, however, workers' supply behavior must also be taken into account. It is largely for this reason that the basic concepts of demand and supply are first treated together in Chapter 2.

Chapters 6–10 contain analyses of various aspects of workers' labor supply behavior. They address issues of whether to work for pay (as opposed to consuming leisure or working at home without pay), the choice of occupations or jobs with very different characteristics, and decisions workers must make about educational and other investments designed to improve their earning capacities. Like the earlier "demand" chapters, these "supply" chapters necessarily incorporate aspects of behavior on the other (employer) side of the labor market.

Chapters 11–15 address special topics of interest to labor economists, including the effects of institutional forces in the labor market. Chapter 11 analyzes how the compensation of workers can be structured to create incentives for greater productivity. Chapter 12 analyzes wage differentials associated with race, gender, and ethnicity. The labor market effects of unions are dealt with in Chapter 13, and Chapter 14 summarizes what economic theory contributes to our understanding of wage differences by looking at the contemporary issue of growing earnings inequality. The final chapter of the text focuses on the topic of unemployment.

Each chapter presents theoretical concepts that are then utilized in analyses of social or public policy issues, including those in other countries. Each is also spiced with boxed examples designed to illustrate a key point in some interesting historical, cross-cultural, or "applied" context. At the end of all chapters is a set of review questions that test student understanding; answers to odd-numbered questions are at the back of the book. Selected references and extensive footnotes are provided for those who want to go beyond what can be offered in this text.

REVIEW QUESTIONS

1. Using the concepts of normative economics, when would the labor market be judged to be at a point of optimality? What imperfections might prevent the market from achieving this point?
2. Are the following statements "positive" or "normative"? Why?
   a. Employers should not be required to offer pensions to their employees.
   b. Employers offering pension benefits will pay lower wages than they would if they did not offer a pension program.
   c. If further immigration of unskilled foreigners is prevented, the wages of unskilled immigrants already here will rise.
   d. The military draft compels people to engage in a transaction they would not voluntarily enter into; it should therefore be avoided as a way of recruiting military personnel.
   e. If the military draft were reinstituted, military salaries would probably fall.
3. Child labor laws exist at both the federal and state levels of government in the United States. These generally prohibit children from working until age 14 and restrict younger teenagers to certain kinds of work that are not considered dangerous. Reconcile the prohibitions of child labor legislation with the principles underlying normative economic analysis.
4. What are the functions and limitations of an economic model?
5. In Chapter 1 a simple model was developed in which it was predicted that workers employed in jobs paying wages less than they could get in comparable jobs elsewhere would tend to quit and seek the higher-paying jobs. Suppose we observe a worker who, after repeated harassment or criticism from her boss, quits an $8-per-hour job to take another paying $7.50. Answer the three questions below:
   a. Is this woman's behavior consistent with the economic model of job quitting outlined in the text?
   b. Is there any way we can test to see whether this woman's behavior is consistent with the assumption of rationality?
   c. Suppose that the boss in question had harassed other employees but that this woman was the only one who quit. Can we conclude from this that economic theory applies to the behavior of some people but not to others?
6. A few years ago it was common for the laws in many states to prohibit women from working more than 40 hours a week. Using the principles underlying normative economics, evaluate these laws.
7. Suppose the federal government needs workers to repair a levee along a flood-prone river. From the perspective of

normative economics, what difference does it make whether able-bodied citizens are compelled to work (for pay) on the levee or whether a workforce is recruited through the normal process of making job offers to applicants and relying on their voluntary acceptance?

8. "Government policies as frequently prevent Pareto efficiency as they enhance it." Comment.

SELECTED READINGS

Friedman, Milton. *Essays in Positive Economics.* Chicago: University of Chicago Press, 1953.

Hausman, Daniel M. "Economic Methodology in a Nutshell." *Journal of Economic Perspectives* 3 (Spring 1989): 115–128.

McCloskey, Donald. "The Rhetoric of Economics." *Journal of Economic Literature* 21 (June 1983): 481–517.

McNulty, Paul J. *The Origins and Development of Labor Economics.* Cambridge, Mass.: MIT Press, 1980.

Statistical Testing of Labor Market Hypotheses

This appendix provides a brief introduction to how labor economists test hypotheses. The discussion is intentionally kept simple and presumes that the reader has no previous background in statistics. To provide a concrete example, we will discuss how one might attempt to test the hypothesis presented in Chapter 1 that, other things equal, one should expect to observe that the higher the wage a firm pays, the lower will be the voluntary labor turnover among its employees. Put another way, if we define a firm's quit rate as the proportion of its workers who voluntarily quit in a given time period (say a year), we expect to observe that the higher a firm's wages, the lower will be its quit rate, holding *other* factors affecting quit rates constant.

A Univariate Test

In testing the above hypothesis, an obvious first step is to collect data on the quit rates experienced by a set of firms during a given year and match these data with the firms' wage rates. This type of analysis is called *univariate* because we are analyzing the effects on quit rates of just one other variable (the wage rate); the data are called *cross-sectional* because they provide observations across behavioral units at a point in time.[1]

---

[1]Several other types of data are also used frequently by labor economists. One could look, for example, at how a given firm's quit rate and wage rate vary over time. Observations that provide information on a single behavioral unit over a number of time periods are called *time-series* data. Sometimes labor economists have data on the behavior of a number of observational units (e.g., employers) for a number of time periods; combinations of cross-sectional and time-series data are called *panel* data.

Table 1A.1 contains such information for a hypothetical set of ten firms located in a single labor market in 1993. For example, firm A is assumed to have paid an average hourly wage of $4 and to have experienced a quit rate of 40 percent in 1993.

The data on wages and quit rates are presented graphically in Figure 1A.1. Each dot in this figure represents a quit-rate/hourly-wage combination for one of the firms in Table 1A.1. Firm A, for example, is represented in the figure by point *A*, which shows a quit rate of 40 percent and an hourly wage of $4, while point *B* shows the comparable data for firm B. From a visual inspection of all ten data points, it appears from this figure that firms paying higher wages in our hypothetical sample do indeed have lower quit rates. Although the data points in Figure 1A.1 obviously do not lie on a single straight line, their pattern suggests that, on average, there is a linear relationship between a firm's quit rate and its wage rate.

Any straight line can be represented by the general equation

$$Y = a + bX \qquad (1A.1)$$

Variable *Y* is the *dependent variable,* and it is generally shown on the vertical axis of the graph depicting the line. Variable *X* is the *independent* or *explanatory* variable, which is usually shown on the horizontal axis.[2] The letters "a" and "b" are the *parameters* (the fixed coefficients) of the equation, with "a" representing the intercept and "b" the slope of the line. Put differently, "a" is the value of *Y* when the line intersects the vertical axis ($X = 0$). The slope, "b," indicates the vertical distance the line travels for each one-unit increase in the horizontal distance. If "b" is a positive number, the line slopes upward (going from left to right); if "b" is a negative number, the line has a downward slope.

If one were to try to draw the straight line that best fits the points in Figure 1A.1, it is clear that the line would slope downward and that it would not go through all

TABLE 1A.1

Average-Wage and Quit-Rate Data for a Set of Ten Hypothetical Firms in a Single Labor Market in 1993

Firm	Average Hourly Wage Paid	Quit Rate	Firm	Average Hourly Wage Paid	Quit Rate
A	$4	40%	F	$8	20%
B	4	30	G	10	25
C	6	35	H	10	15
D	6	25	I	12	20
E	8	30	J	12	10

[2]An exception occurs in the demand and supply curves facing firms, in which the independent variable, price, is typically shown on the vertical axis.

FIGURE 1A.1

Estimated Relationship Between Wages and Quit Rates Using Data from Table 1A.1

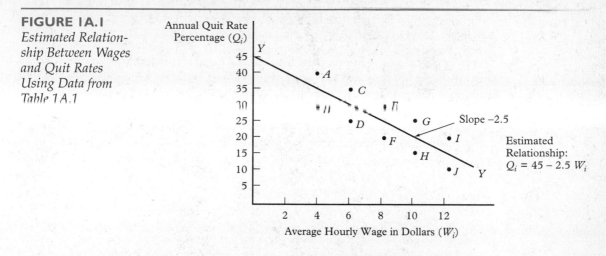

ten points. It would lie above some points and below others, and thus it would "fit" the points only with some error. We could model the relationship between the data points on the graph, then, as follows:

$$Q_i = \alpha_0 + \alpha_1 W_i + \epsilon_i \qquad (1\text{A}.2)$$

Here Q_i represents the quit rate for firm i, and it is the dependent variable . The independent or explanatory variable is W_i, firm i's wage rate. α_0 and α_1 are the parameters of the line, with α_0 the intercept and α_1 the slope of the line. The term ϵ_i is a random *error term*; it is included in the model because we do not expect that the line (given by $Q_i = \alpha_0 + \alpha_1 W_i$) will connect all the data points perfectly. Behaviorally, we are assuming the presence of random factors unrelated to wage rates that also cause the quit rate to vary across firms.

We seek to estimate what the true values of α_0 and α_1 are. Each pair of values of α_0 and α_1 defines a different straight line, and an infinite number of lines can be drawn that "fit" points *A–J*. It is natural for us to ask, "Which of these straight lines fits the data the best?" Some precise criterion must be used to decide "which line fits the best," and the procedure typically used by statisticians and economists is to choose that line for which the sum (in our example, across all firms) of the squared vertical distances between the line and the individual data points is minimized. The line estimated from the data using this method, which is called *least squares regression analysis*, has a number of desirable properties.[3]

Application of this method to the data found in Table 1A.1 yields the following estimated line:[4]

---

[3] These properties include that, on average, the correct answer for α_1 is obtained, the estimates are the most precise possible among a certain class of estimators, and the sum of the positive and negative vertical deviations of the data points from the estimated line will be zero. For a more formal treatment of the method of least squares, see any statistics or econometrics text. A good introduction for the reader with no statistical background is Larry D. Schroeder, David L. Sjoquist, and Paula E. Stephan, *Understanding Regression Analysis: An Introductory Guide* (Beverly Hills, Calif.: Sage Publications, 1986).

[4] Students with access to computer software to estimate regression models can easily verify this result.

$$Q_i = 45 - 2.5W_i$$
$$(5.3) \quad (.625)$$

(1A.3)

The estimate of α_0, the intercept of the line, is 45 and the estimate of α_1, the slope of the line, is -2.5. Thus, if a firm has a wage rate of \$4/hour, we would predict that its annual quit rate would be $45 - 2.5(4)$, or 35 percent. This estimated quit/wage relationship is drawn in Figure 1A.1 as the line YY. (The numbers in parentheses in the equation will be discussed later.)

Several things should be noted about this relationship. First, taken at face value, this estimated relationship implies that firms paying their workers *nothing* (a wage of zero) would be projected to have *only* 45 percent of their workers quit each year $(45 - 2.5(0) = 45)$, while firms paying their workers more than \$18 an hour would have negative quit rates.[5] The former result is nonsensical (why should any workers stay if they were paid nothing?) and the latter result is logically impossible (the quit rate cannot be less than zero). As these extreme examples suggest, it is dangerous to use linear models to make predictions that take one outside the range of observations used in the estimation (in the example, wages from \$4 to \$12). The relationship between wages and quit rates cannot be assumed to be linear (represented by a straight line) for very low and very high values of wages. Fortunately, the linear regression model used in the example can be easily generalized to allow for nonlinear relationships.

Second, the estimated intercept (45) and slope (-2.5) that we obtained are only estimates of the "true" relationship, and there is uncertainty associated with these estimates. The uncertainty arises partly from the fact that we are trying to infer the true values of α_0 and α_1—that is, the values that characterize the wage/quit relationship in the entire population of firms—from a sample of just ten firms. The uncertainty about each estimated coefficient is measured by its *standard error,* or the estimated standard deviation of the coefficient. These standard errors are reported in parentheses under the estimated coefficients in equation (1A.3); for example, given our data, the estimated standard error of the wage coefficient is .625 and that of the intercept term is 5.3. The larger the standard error, the greater the uncertainty about our estimated coefficient's value.

Under suitable assumptions about the distribution of ϵ, the random error term in equation (1A.2), one can use these standard errors to test hypotheses about the estimated coefficients.[6] In our example, we would like to test the hypothesis that α_1 is negative (which implies, as suggested by theory, that higher wages reduce quits) against the "null hypothesis" that α_1 is zero and there is thus no relationship between wages and quits. One common test involves computing for each coefficient a *t statistic,* which is the ratio of the coefficient to its standard error. A heuristic rule, which can be made precise, is that if the absolute value of the *t statistic* is greater than 2, the hypothesis that the true value of the coefficient equals zero can be rejected. Put another way, if the absolute value of a coefficient is at least twice the size of its standard error, one can be fairly confident that the true value of the

---

[5]For example, at a wage of \$20/hour the estimated quit rate would be $45 - 2.5(20)$, or -5 percent per year.

[6]These assumptions are discussed in any econometrics text.

coefficient is other than zero. In our example, the *t statistic* for the wage coefficient is $-2.5/.625$, or -4.0, which leaves us very confident that the true relationship between wage levels and quit rates is really negative.

Multiple Regression Analysis

The discussion above has *assumed* that the only variable influencing quit rates, other than random (unexplained) factors, is a firm's wage rate. The discussion of positive economics in Chapter 1 stressed, however, that the prediction of a negative relationship between wages and quit rates is made holding *all other factors constant*. As we will discuss in Chapter 10, economic theory suggests there are many factors besides wages that systematically influence quit rates. These include characteristics both of firms (e.g., employee benefits offered, working conditions, and firm size) and of their workers (e.g., age and level of training). If any of these other variables that we have omitted from our analysis tend to vary across firms systematically with the wage rates that the firms offer, the resulting estimated relationship between wage rates and quit rates will be incorrect. In such cases, we must take these other variables into account by using a model with more than one independent variable. We rely on economic theory to indicate which variables should be included in our statistical analysis and to suggest the direction of causation.

To illustrate this procedure, suppose for simplicity that the only variable affecting a firm's quit rate besides its wage rate is the average age of its workforce. Other things held constant, older workers are less likely to quit their jobs for a number of reasons (as workers grow older, ties to friends, neighbors, and co-workers become stronger, and the psychological costs involved in changing jobs—which often requires a geographic move—grow larger). To capture the effects of both wage rates and age, we assume that a firm's quit rate is given by

$$Q_i = \alpha'_0 + \alpha'_1 W_i + \alpha'_2 A_i + \epsilon_i \tag{1A.4}$$

A_i is a variable representing the age of firm i's workers. Although A_i could be measured as the average age of the workforce, or as the percentage of the firm's workers older than some age level, for expositional convenience we have defined it as a *dichotomous* variable. A_i is equal to 1 if the average age of firm i's workforce is greater than 40, and it is equal to zero otherwise. Clearly theory suggests that α'_2 is negative, which means that whatever values of α'_1, α'_2, and W_i pertain (that is, holding all else constant), firms with workforces having an average age above 40 years should have lower quit rates than firms with workforces having an average age equal to or below age 40.

The parameters of equation (1A.4)—that is, the values of α'_0, α'_1, and α'_2—can be estimated using *multiple regression analysis,* a method that is analogous to the one described above. This method finds the values of the parameters that define the best straight-line relationship between the dependent variable and the set of independent variables. Each parameter tells us the effect on the dependent variable of a one-unit change in the corresponding independent variable, *holding the other independent variables constant.* Thus, the estimate of α'_1 tells us the estimated effect on the quit rate (Q) of a one-unit change in the wage rate (W), holding the age of a firm's workforce (A) constant.

The Problem of Omitted Variables

If we use a univariate regression model in a situation calling for a multiple regression model—that is, if we leave out an important independent variable—our results may suffer from "omitted variables bias." We illustrate this bias because it is an important pitfall in hypothesis-testing and because it illustrates the need to use economic theory to guide empirical testing.

To simplify our example, we assume that we know the true values of α'_0, α'_1, and α'_2 in equation (1A.4) and that there is no random error term in this model (each ϵ_i is zero). Specifically, we assume that

$$Q_i = 50 - 2.5W_i - 10A_i \qquad (1A.5)$$

Thus, at any level of wages a firm's quit rate will be 10 percentage points lower if the average age of its workforce exceeds 40 than it will be if the average age is less than or equal to 40.

Figure 1A.2 graphically illustrates this assumed relationship between quit rates, wage rates, and workforce average age. For all firms that employ workers whose average age is less than 40, A_i equals zero and thus their quit rates are given by the line $Z_0 Z_0$. For all firms that employ workers whose average age is greater than 40, A_i equals 1 and thus their quit rates are given by the line $Z_1 Z_1$. The quit-rate schedule for the latter set of firms is everywhere 10 percentage points below the one for the former set. Both schedules indicate, however, that a \$1 increase in a firm's average hourly wage will reduce its annual quit rate by 2.5 percentage points (that is, both lines have the same slope).

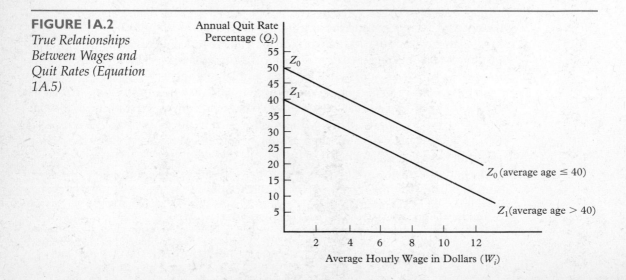

FIGURE 1A.2

True Relationships Between Wages and Quit Rates (Equation 1A.5)

Now suppose a researcher were to estimate the relationship between quit rates and wage rates but ignored the fact that the average age of a firm's workers also affects the quit rate. That is, suppose one were to omit a measure of age and estimate the following equation:

$$Q_i = a_0 + a_1 W_i + \epsilon_i \tag{1A.6}$$

Of crucial importance to us is how the estimated value of a_1 will correspond to the true slope of the quit/wage schedule, which we have *assumed* to be -2.5.

The answer depends heavily on how average wages and the average age of employees vary across firms. Table 1A.2 lists combinations of quit rates and wages for three hypothetical firms that employ older workers (average age greater than 40) and three hypothetical firms that employ younger workers. Given the wage each firm pays, the values of its quit rate can be derived directly from equation (1A.5).

It is a well-established fact that earnings of workers tend to increase as they age.[7] On average, then, firms employing older workers are assumed in the table to have higher wages than firms employing younger workers. The wage/quit-rate combinations for these six firms are indicated by the dots on the lines $Z_0 Z_0$ and $Z_1 Z_1$ in Figure 1A.3,[8] which reproduce the lines in Figure 1A.2.

When one estimates equation (1A.6) using these six data points, one obtains the following straight line:

$$Q_i = 57 - 4W_i \tag{1A.7}$$
$$(5.1)\ (.612)$$

This estimated relationship is denoted by the line XX in Figure 1A.3. The estimate of a_1, which equals -4, implies that every dollar increase in wages reduces the quit rate by four percentage points, yet we know (by assumption) that the actual

---

TABLE 1A.2
Hypothetical Average-Wage and Quit-Rate Data for Three Firms That Employ Older Workers and Three That Employ Younger Workers

	Employ Older Workers $(A_i = 1)$			Employ Younger Workers $(A_i = 0)$	
Firm	Average Hourly Wage	Quit Rate	Firm	Average Hourly Wage	Quit Rate
k	$ 8	20%	p	$4	40%
l	10	15	q	6	35
m	12	10	r	8	30

---

[7] Reasons why this occurs will be discussed in Chapters 5, 9, and 11.

[8] The fact that the dots fall exactly on a straight line is a graphic representation of the assumption in equation (1A.5) that there is no random error term. If random error is present, the dots would fall *around*, but not all *on*, a straight line.

FIGURE 1A.3

Estimated Relationships Between Wages and Quit Rates Using Data from Table 1A.2

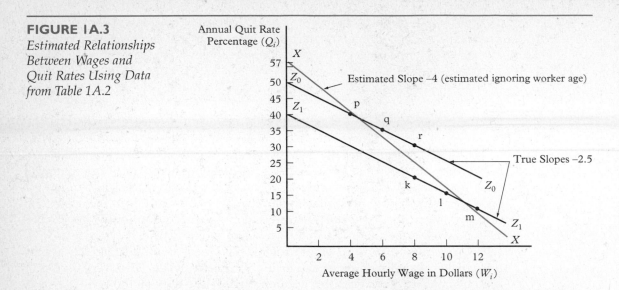

reduction is two and a half percentage points. Our estimated response overstates the sensitivity of the quit rate to wages because the estimated equation ignored the effect that age has on quits.

Put differently, quit rates are lower in high-wage firms *both* because the wages they pay are higher *and* because high-wage firms tend to employ older workers, who are less likely to quit. By ignoring age in the analysis, we mistakenly conclude that quit rates are more sensitive to wage changes than they actually are. Therefore, by omitting from our model an important explanatory variable (age) that both affects quit rates and is associated with wage levels, we have obtained the wrong estimate of the effect of wages on quit rates.

This discussion highlights "the other things held equal" nature of most hypotheses in labor economics. In testing hypotheses, one must control for other factors that are expected to influence the variable of interest. Typically this is done by specifying that the dependent variable is a function of a *set* of variables. This specification must be guided by economic theory, and one reason for learning economic theory is that it can guide us in testing hypotheses about human behavior. Without a firm grounding in theory, analyses of behavior can easily run afoul of omitted variables bias.

Having said this, we must point out that it is neither possible nor crucial to have data on all variables that could conceivably influence what is being examined. As emphasized in Chapter 1, testing economic models involves looking for *average* relationships and ignoring idiosyncratic factors. Two workers with the same age and the same wage rate may exhibit different quit behaviors because, for example, one wants to leave town to get away from a dreadful father-in-law. This idiosyncratic factor is not important for the testing of an economic model of quit rates, because having a father-in-law has neither a predictable effect on quits (some fathers-in-law are desirable to be around) nor any correlation with one's wage rate. To repeat, omitted variables bias is a problem only if the omitted variable has an effect on the dependent variable (quit rate) *and* is correlated with an independent variable of interest (wages).

2

Overview of the Labor Market

Every society—regardless of its wealth, its form of government, or the organization of its economy—must make basic decisions. It must decide what and how much to produce, how to produce it, and how the output shall be distributed. These decisions require finding out what consumers want, what technologies for production are available, and what the skills and preferences of workers are; deciding where to produce; and coordinating all such decisions so that, for example, the millions of people in New York City and the isolated few in an Alaskan fishing village can each buy the milk, bread, meat, vanilla extract, mosquito repellent, and brown shoe polish they desire at the grocery store. The process of coordination involves creating incentives so that the right amount of labor and capital will be employed at the right place at the required time.

These decisions can, of course, be made by administrators employed by a centralized bureaucracy. The amount of information this bureaucracy must obtain and process to make the millions of needed decisions wisely and the number of incentives it must give out to ensure that these decisions are coordinated are truly mind-boggling. It boggles the mind even more to consider the major alternative to centralized decision making—the decentralized marketplace. Millions of producers striving to make a profit observe the prices millions of consumers are willing to pay for products and the wages millions of workers are willing to accept for work. Combining these pieces of information with data on various technologies, they decide where to produce, what to produce, whom to hire, and how much to produce. No one is in charge, and while market imperfections impede progress toward achieving the best allocation of resources, millions of people find jobs that enable them to purchase the items they desire each year. The production, employment, and consumption decisions are all made and coordinated by price signals arising through the marketplace.

The market that allocates workers to jobs and coordinates employment decisions is the *labor market*. With over 131 million workers and over 6 million employers in the United States, thousands of decisions about career choice, hiring, quitting, compensation, and technology must be made and coordinated every day. This chapter will present an overview of what the labor market does and how it works. For those students who may already have mastered microeconomic theory, this chapter can provide a review of basic concepts.

The Labor Market: Definitions, Facts, and Trends

Every market has buyers and sellers, and the labor market is no exception: the buyers are employers and the sellers are workers. Because there are so many buyers and sellers of labor services at any given time, the decisions that are made in any particular case are influenced by the behavior and decisions of others. For example, when other employers are increasing compensation, a firm may decide to do likewise to remain competitive in its ability to attract and hold workers. Likewise, a current or prospective teacher may choose to go into another occupation if he or she discovers that teachers are having a difficult time finding jobs.

The *labor market* is thus composed of all the buyers and sellers of labor services. Some of these participants may not be active at any given moment in the sense of seeking new employees or new jobs, but on any given day thousands of firms and workers will be "in the market" trying to transact. If, as in the case of doctors or mechanical engineers, buyers and sellers are searching throughout the entire nation for each other, we would describe the market as a *national labor market*. If buyers and sellers only search locally, as in the case of secretaries or automobile mechanics, the labor market is a *local* one.

Some labor markets, particularly those in which the sellers of labor are represented by a union, operate under a very formal set of rules that partly govern buyer–seller transactions. In the unionized construction and longshoring trades, for example, employers must hire at the union hiring hall from a list of eligible union members. In other unionized markets, the employer has discretion over who gets hired but is constrained by a union–management agreement in such matters as the order in which employees may be laid off, procedures regarding employee complaints, the compensation schedule, the workload or pace of work, and promotions. The markets for government jobs and jobs with large nonunion employers also tend to operate under rules that constrain the authority of management and ensure fair treatment of employees. When a formal set of rules and procedures guides and constrains the employment relationship *within* a firm, an *internal labor market* is said to exist.[1]

---

[1]P. Doeringer and M. Piore, *Internal Labor Markets and Manpower Analysis* (Lexington, Mass.: D.C. Heath, 1971). A more recent analysis of internal labor markets can be found in Michael L. Wachter and Randall Wright, "The Economics of Internal Labor Markets," *University of Pennsylvania Law Review* 29 (Spring 1990): 240–262.

In many cases, of course, labor market transactions are not made within the context of written rules or procedures. Most transactions in which an employee is changing employers or newly entering the market fall in this category. Written rules or procedures generally do not govern within-firm transactions—such as promotions and layoffs—among smaller, nonunion employers. While jobs in this sector of the labor market can be stable and well-paying, many are not. Low-wage, unstable jobs are sometimes considered to be in the *secondary labor market*. We will discuss the concept of secondary labor markets in greater detail in Chapters 11 and 12.

When we speak of a particular "labor market"—for taxi drivers, say—we are using the term loosely to refer to the companies trying to hire people to drive their cabs and the people seeking employment as cabdrivers. The efforts of these buyers and sellers of labor to transact and establish an employment relationship constitute the market for cabdrivers. However, neither the employers nor the drivers are confined to this market; both could simultaneously be in other markets as well. An entrepreneur with $100,000 to invest might be thinking of operating either a taxi company or a car wash, depending on the projected revenues and costs of each. A person seeking a cabdriving job might also be trying to find work as an electronics assembler. Thus, all the various labor markets that we can define on the basis of industry, occupation, geography, transaction rules, or job character are interrelated to some degree. We speak of these narrowly defined labor markets for the sake of convenience, and doing so should not suggest that people are necessarily or permanently locked in to markets that are independent of other markets.

THE LABOR FORCE AND UNEMPLOYMENT

Figure 2.1 highlights some basic definitions concerning labor market status. The term *labor force* refers to all those over 16 years of age who are either employed, actively seeking work, or expecting recall from a layoff. Those in the labor force who are not employed for pay are the *unemployed*.[2] People who are not employed and are neither looking for work nor waiting to be recalled from layoff by their employers are not counted as part of the labor force. The total labor force thus consists of the employed and the unemployed.

The number and identities of people in each labor market category are always changing, and as we shall see in Chapter 15, the flows of people from one category to another are sizable. As Figure 2.1 suggests, there are four major flows between labor market states:

---

[2]The official definition of unemployment for purposes of government statistics includes those who have been laid off by their employers, those who have been fired or have quit and are looking for other work, and those who are just entering or reentering the labor force but have not found a job as yet. The extent of unemployment is estimated from a monthly survey of some 60,000 households called the Current Population Survey (CPS). Interviewers ascertain whether household members are employed, whether they meet one of the aforementioned conditions (in which case they are considered "unemployed"), or whether they are out of the labor force. A useful summary of recent (1994) changes in the CPS is found in Sharon Cohany, Anne Polivka, and Jennifer Rothgeb, "Revisions in the Current Population Survey Effective January 1994," *Employment and Earnings* 41, no. 2 (February 1994): 13–35.

FIGURE 2.1
*Labor Force
Status of the U.S.
Adult
Population, 1994*

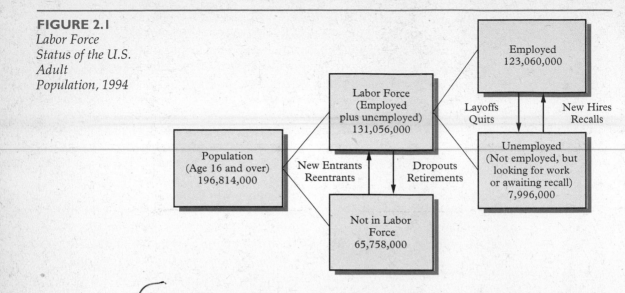

1. Employed workers become unemployed by voluntarily *quitting* or *being laid off* (being involuntarily separated from the firm, either temporarily or permanently).
2. Unemployed workers obtain employment by *being newly hired* or *being recalled* to a job from which they were temporarily laid off.
3. Those in the labor force, whether employed or unemployed, can leave the labor force by *retiring* or otherwise deciding against taking or seeking work for pay *(dropping out)*.
4. Those who have never worked or looked for a job expand the labor force by *newly entering* it, while those who have dropped out do so by *reentering* the labor force.

In 1994 there were over 131 million people in the labor force, representing 67 percent of the entire population over 16 years of age. An overall *labor force participation rate* (labor force divided by population) of 67 percent is substantially higher than the rates around 60 percent that prevailed prior to the 1980s, as is shown by the data in Table 2.1. This table also indicates the most important fact about labor force trends in this century: *labor force participation rates for men are falling while those for women are increasing dramatically.* These trends and their causes will be discussed in detail in Chapters 6 and 7.

The ratio of those unemployed to those in the labor force is the *unemployment rate.* While this rate is crude and has several imperfections, it is the most widely cited measure of labor market conditions. When the unemployment rate is around 5 percent in the United States, the labor market is considered *tight,* indicating that jobs in general are plentiful and hard for employers to fill and that most of those who are unemployed will find other work quickly. When the unemployment rate is higher—say, 7 percent or above—the labor market is described as

TABLE 2.1
Labor Force Participation Rates by Gender, 1950–1994

Year	Total	Men	Women
1950	59.9%	86.8%	33.9%
1960	60.2	84.0	37.8
1970	61.3	80.6	43.4
1980	64.2	77.9	51.6
1994	66.6	75.1	58.8

SOURCES: 1950–1980: U.S. President, *Employment and Training Report of the President* (Washington, D.C.: U.S. Government Printing Office), transmitted to the Congress 1981, Table A–1.

1994: U.S. Bureau of Labor Statistics, *Employment and Earnings* 42, no. 2 (February 1995), Tables A–1, A–2.

loose, in the sense that workers are abundant and jobs are relatively easy for employers to fill. To say that the labor market as a whole is loose, however, does not imply that no shortages can be found anywhere; to say it is tight can still mean that in some occupations or places the number of those seeking work exceeds the number of jobs available at the prevailing wage.

Figure 2.2 displays the overall unemployment rate during this century (the data displayed graphically in Figure 2.2 are contained in a table inside the front cover). The data clearly show the extraordinarily loose labor market during the Great Depression of the 1930s and the exceptionally tight labor market during World War II. However, when we look at long stretches of nonwar years, excluding the years of the Great Depression, two interesting patterns emerge. First, the average unemployment rate has clearly risen: it was 4.4 percent in 1900–1914, but in the most recent nonwar periods it was 5.3 percent (1954–1965) and 6.9 percent (1973–1994). Second, in recent years the unemployment rate has fluctuated less than it did in 1900–1914. In the years from 1900 to 1914, the average yearly change in the unemployment rate was 1.9 percentage points; in contrast, from 1954 to 1965 and from 1973 to 1994 it was 0.8 percentage points. The labor market, then, would appear to be more stable now than it was at the turn of the century, but it operates with proportionately more unemployment. Chapter 15 will present a more detailed analysis of the determinants of the unemployment rate.

INDUSTRIES AND OCCUPATIONS: ADAPTING TO CHANGE

As we pointed out earlier, the labor market is the mechanism through which workers and jobs are matched. Over the years in this century, the number of some kinds of jobs has expanded and the number of others has contracted. Both workers and employers have had to adapt to these changes in response to signals provided by the labor market. One way to capture the extent of employment transactions that labor markets must facilitate is to compare the number or distribution of jobs

FIGURE 2.2

*Unemployment Rates
for the Civilian Labor
Force, 1900–1994
(detailed data in table
inside front cover)*

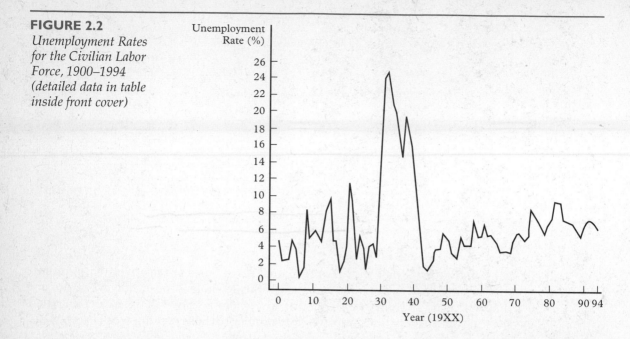

across sectors at different points in time. As we will see, the changes these "snap-shots" reveal are dramatic; however, they do not capture the full extent of move-ment that goes on between points in time. For example, from 1972 to 1986, roughly 11 percent of all manufacturing jobs were destroyed each year by plant closings and employment contractions, while another 9 percent were newly created yearly by plant expansions and openings.[3] Yearly snapshots revealed a 2 percent job loss, but this was just the net result; "gross" job movements during that period were about five times greater.

An examination of the industrial distribution of employment from 1900 to 1994 reveals the kinds of changes the labor market has had to facilitate. Figure 2.3, which graphs data presented in a table inside the front cover, discloses a major shift: *agricultural employment has declined drastically while employment in service in-dustries has expanded.* Goods-producing jobs increased roughly proportionately to the increase in total employment during the first seven decades, but their share fell sharply after 1970. The largest employment increases have been in the service sector. Retail and wholesale trade, which increased from 9.2 percent of employ-ment in 1910 to 20.9 percent in 1994, showed the largest increases in nongovern-ment services. However, the largest percentage increase has been in government employment, which almost quadrupled its share of total employment over the 94-year period. Some describe this shift in employment from agriculture to services as a shift from the *primary* to the *tertiary* sector (manufacturing being labeled the *secondary* sector). Others describe it as the arrival of the "postindustrial" state.

---

[3]Steve J. Davis and John Haltiwanger, "Gross Job Creation, Gross Job Destruction, and Employment Reallocation," *Quarterly Journal of Economics* 107, no. 3 (August 1992): 819–863.

FIGURE 2.3
*Employment
Distribution
by Major Industrial
Sector, 1900–1994
(detailed data in table
inside front cover)*

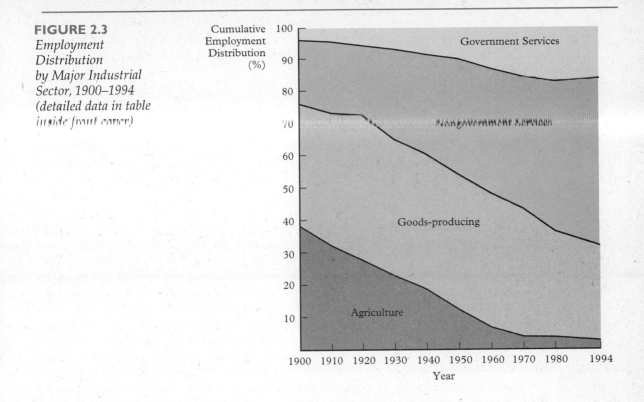

The combination of shifts in the industrial distribution of jobs and changes in the production technology within each sector has also required that workers acquire new skills and work in new jobs. Just since 1970, for example, the number of skilled craft and repair jobs has fallen from 13.2 percent to 11 percent of total employment, while opportunities for less-skilled operatives and laborers have declined from 22.7 to 14.5 percent of all jobs. Meanwhile, jobs for managers and administrators rose from 8 percent to 13.3 percent of the total, and those in sales increased from 7 to 12 percent.[4]

Labor markets must work very effectively if changes in the industrial and occupational distribution of employment are to occur without long delays or undue hardship. In the decade of the 1990s, the labor market is facing yet another daunting task: facilitating job matches for a labor force that is undergoing striking demographic change. From 1992 to the year 2005, for example, the number of white male workers is projected to increase by about 10 percent, while the number of women and black workers is expected to rise by 25 percent and the number of Hispanic and Asian workers by 64 and 81 percent, respectively. Put somewhat differently, of the net additions to the labor force from 1992 to 2005, it is projected that 59

[4]U.S. Bureau of the Census, *Statistical Abstract of the United States* (Washington, D.C.: U.S. Government Printing Office, 1974 and 1995): Table 571 (1974), Table 649 (1995).

percent will be women and 58 percent will be minorities.[5] The consequences of these changes for employer recruiting and management strategies, job training, the occupational mix, and the structure of compensation may be immense.

THE EARNINGS OF LABOR

The actions of buyers and sellers in the labor market serve both to allocate and to set prices for various kinds of labor. From a social perspective, these prices act as signals or incentives in the allocation process, a process that relies primarily on individual and voluntary decisions. From the worker's point of view, the price of labor is important in determining income—and hence purchasing power.

NOMINAL AND REAL WAGES   The *wage rate* is the price of labor per working hour.[6] The *nominal wage* is what workers get paid per hour in current dollars; nominal wages are most useful in comparing the pay of various workers at a given time. *Real wages*, nominal wages divided by some measure of prices, suggest how much can be purchased with workers' nominal wages. For example, if a worker earns $64 a day and a pair of shoes cost $32, one could say the worker earns the equivalent of two pairs of shoes a day (real wage = $64/$32 = 2).

Calculations of real wages are especially useful in comparing the purchasing power of workers' earnings over a period of time when both nominal wages and product prices are changing. For example, suppose we were interested in trying to determine what happened to the real wages of American nonsupervisory workers over the 20-year period from 1974 to 1994. We can note from Table 2.2 that the average hourly earnings of these workers in the private sector were $4.24 in 1974, $8.32 in 1984, and $11.12 in 1994; thus, nominal wage rates were clearly rising over this period. However, the prices such workers had to pay for the items they buy were also rising over this period, so a method of accounting for price inflation must be used in calculating real wages.

The most widely used measure for comparing the prices consumers face over several years is the Consumer Price Index. Generally speaking, this index is derived by determining what a fixed "bundle" of consumer goods and services (including food, housing, clothing, transportation, medical care, and entertainment)

---

[5]Howard N. Fullerton Jr., "Another Look at the Labor Force," *Monthly Labor Review* 116, no. 11 (November 1993): 31–40.

[6]In this book we define the hourly wage in the way most workers would if asked to state their "straight-time" wage. It is the money a worker would lose per hour if he or she had an unauthorized absence. When wages are defined in this way, a paid holiday becomes an "employee benefit," as we note below, because leisure time is granted while pay continues. Thus, a worker paid $100 for 25 hours—20 of which are working hours and 5 of which are time off—will be said to earn a wage of $4 per hour and receive time off worth $20.

An alternative is to define the wage in terms of actual hours worked—or as $5 per hour in the above example. We prefer our definition, because if the worker seizes an opportunity to work one less hour in a particular week, his or her earnings would fall by $4, not $5 (as long as the reduction in hours does not affect the hours of paid holiday or vacation time for which the worker is eligible).

TABLE 2.2

Nominal and Real Hourly Earnings, U.S. Nonsupervisory Workers in the Private Sector, 1974–1994

	1974	1984	1994
Average Hourly Earnings	$4.24	$8.32	$11.12
Consumer Price Index (CPI) using 1982–1984 as a base	49.3	103.9	148.2
Average Hourly Earnings, 1982–1984 dollars (using CPI)	$8.60	$8.01	$7.50
Average Hourly Earnings, 1994 dollars (using CPI)	$12.74	$11.86	$11.12
Average Hourly Earnings, 1994 dollars (using CPI inflation less 1 percent per year)	$10.60	$10.15	$11.12

SOURCE: U.S. President, *Economic Report of the President* (Washington, D.C.: U.S. Government Printing Office, 1995), 326,341.

costs each year. The cost of this bundle in the "base" period is then set to equal 100, and the index numbers for all other years are set proportionately to this base period. For example, if the bundle's average cost over the 1982–1984 period is considered the base (the average value of the index over this period is set to 100), and if the bundle costs 48.2 percent more in 1994, then the index for 1994 is equal to 148.2. From the second line in Table 2.2, one can see that with a 1982–1984 base, the Consumer Price Index was 49.3 in 1974 and 148.2 in 1994—implying that prices had tripled (148.2/49.3 = 3) over that period. Put differently, a 1994 dollar appears to buy about one-third the goods and services of a 1974 dollar.

There are several alternative ways to calculate real wages from the information given in the first two rows of Table 2.2. The most straightforward way is to divide the nominal wage by the Consumer Price Index for each year and multiply by 100. Doing this converts the nominal wage for each year into 1982–1984 dollars; thus, workers paid $4.24 in 1974 could have bought $8.60 worth of goods and services in 1984, while those paid $11.12 in 1994 could have bought $7.50 worth. Alternatively, we could use the table's information to put average hourly earnings into 1994 dollars by multiplying each year's nominal wage rate by the percentage price increase between that year and 1994. Because prices roughly tripled between 1974 and 1994, then, $4.24 in 1974 was equivalent to $12.74 in 1994.

Our calculations in Table 2.2 suggest that real wages for American nonsupervisory workers fell over the period from 1974 to 1994, and we will see later in this chapter and throughout the text that the downward pressure on wages was especially great for less-skilled workers. A lively debate exists, however, on whether real-wage calculations based on the Consumer Price Index are accurate indicators of changes in the purchasing power of an hour of work for the ordinary American. The issues are technical and beyond the scope of this text, but they center on two problems associated with using a fixed bundle of goods and services to compare prices from year to year.

One problem is that consumers *change* the bundle of goods and services they actually buy over time, partly in response to changes in prices. If the price of beef rises, for example, consumers may eat more chicken; pricing a fixed bundle may thus understate the purchasing power of current dollars, because it assumes that consumers still purchase the former quantities of beef. For this reason, the bundles used for pricing purposes are updated periodically.

The more difficult issue has to do with the *quality* of goods and services. Suppose that hospital costs rise by 50 percent over a five-year period, but that at the same time new diagnostic equipment and surgical techniques are perfected. Some of the increased price of hospitalization, then, reflects the availability of new services—or quality improvements in previously provided ones—rather than reductions in the purchasing power of a dollar. The problem is that we have not yet found a satisfactory method for feasibly separating the effects of changes in quality.

After considering these problems, some economists believe that the Consumer Price Index overstates inflation by as much as one percentage-point per year.[7] While not everyone agrees that inflation is overstated by this magnitude, it is instructive to recalculate real-wage changes by supposing that it is. Inflation, as judged by the Consumer Price Index, averaged 5.6 percent per year from 1974 to 1994. If the true decline in the purchasing power of a dollar were instead only 4.6 percent per year during this period, then inflation would have increased prices by two and one-half times, not three times, from 1974 to 1994. Multiplying $4.24 by 2.5 yields $10.60 as the estimated 1974 wage expressed in 1994 dollars. Applying similar adjustments to Consumer Price Index changes over the 1984–1994 period suggests that a dollar in 1984 bought 22 percent more than in 1994; thus, the 1984 wage in 1994 dollars was $10.15. Using these adjustments, then, it appears that average real wages fell from 1974 to 1984, but may have risen after that.

WAGES, EARNINGS, COMPENSATION, AND INCOME   We often apply the term *wages* to payments received by workers who are paid on a salaried basis (monthly, for example) rather than an hourly basis. The term is used this way merely for convenience and is of no consequence for most purposes. It is important, however, to distinguish among wages, earnings, and income, as we do schematically in Figure 2.4. The term *wages* refers to the payment for a *unit* of time, while *earnings* refers to wages multiplied by the number of time units (typically hours) worked. Thus, earnings depend on both wages and the length of time the employee works. *Income*—the total command over resources of a person or family during some time period (usually a year)—includes both earnings and *unearned income*, which includes dividends or interest received on investments

[7]For fuller discussions, see U.S. President, *Economic Report of the President* (Washington, D.C.: U.S. Government Printing Office, 1992): 253–256; M. F. Bryan and S. G. Cecchetti, "The Consumer Price Index as a Measure of Inflation," *Economic Review of the Cleveland Federal Reserve Bank* 29, no. 4 (Quarter 4, 1993): 15–24; and Matthew Shapiro and David Wilcox, "Mismeasurement in the Consumer Price Index: An Evaluation," working paper no. 5590, National Bureau of Economic Research, Cambridge, Mass., 1996.

FIGURE 2.4
Relationship Between Wages, Earnings, Compensation, and Income

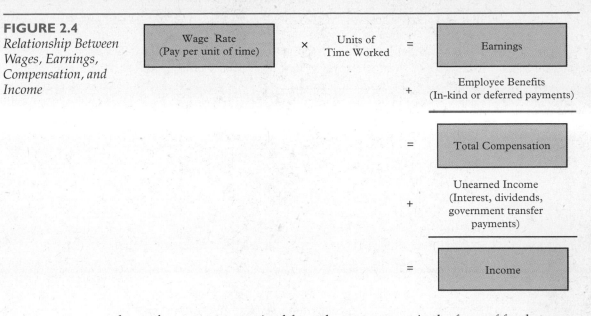

and transfer payments received from the government in the form of food stamps, welfare payments, unemployment compensation, and the like.

Both wages and earnings are normally defined and measured in terms of direct monetary payments to employees (before taxes for which the employee is liable). *Total compensation*, on the other hand, consists of earnings plus *employee benefits*—benefits that are either payments in kind or deferred. Examples of *payments in kind* are employer-provided health care and health insurance, where the employee receives a service or an insurance policy rather than money. Paid vacation time is also in this category, since employees are given days off instead of cash. *Deferred* payments can take the form of employer-financed retirement benefits, including Social Security taxes, for which employers set aside money now that enables their employees to receive pensions later. As we will see in Chapter 5, earnings as conventionally defined constitute only around 70 percent of the total compensation for many workers. Vacations, pensions, and insurance are the largest categories of employee benefits.

The next section will shift from labor market *outcomes* over time to an analysis of how the market *operates* to generate these outcomes. This analysis of labor market functioning is the central focus of labor economics.

How the Labor Market Works

As shown diagrammatically in Figure 2.5, the labor market is one of three markets in which firms must successfully operate if they are to survive; the other two are the capital market and the product market. The labor and capital markets are the major ones in which firms' inputs are purchased, and the product market is the one in which output is sold. In reality, of course, a firm may deal in many different labor, capital, or product markets simultaneously.

FIGURE 2.5
*The Markets in
Which Firms
Must Operate*

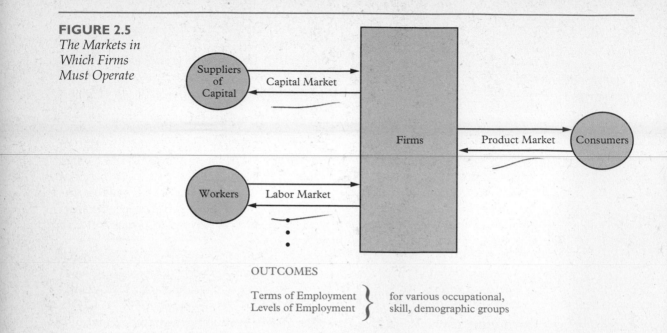

OUTCOMES

Terms of Employment   } for various occupational,
Levels of Employment } skill, demographic groups

Study of the labor market begins and ends with an analysis of the demand for and supply of labor. On the demand side of the labor market are employers, whose decisions about the hiring of labor are influenced by conditions in all three markets. On the supply side of the labor market are workers and potential workers, whose decisions about where (and whether) to work must take into account their other options for how to spend time.

It is useful to remember that the major labor market outcomes are related to (a) the *terms of employment* (wages, compensation levels, working conditions) and (b) the *levels of employment*. In analyzing both these outcomes, one must usually differentiate among the various occupational, skill, or demographic groups that make up the overall labor market. It is also important to remember that any labor market outcome is always affected, to one degree or another, by the forces of both demand and supply. To paraphrase economist Alfred Marshall, it takes both demand and supply to determine economic outcomes, just as it takes both blades of a scissors to cut cloth.

In this chapter we present the basic outlines and broadest implications of the simplest economic model of the labor market. In later chapters we shall add some complexities to this basic model and explain assumptions and implications more fully. However, the simple model of demand and supply presented here offers some insights into labor market behavior that can be very useful in the formulation of social policy. Every piece of analysis in this text is an extension or modification of the basic model presented in this chapter.

THE DEMAND FOR LABOR

Firms combine various factors of production—mainly capital and labor—to produce goods or services that are sold in a product market. Their total output and the way in which they combine labor and capital depend on three forces—

product demand, the amount of labor and capital they can acquire at given prices, and the choice of technologies available to them. When we study the demand for labor, we are interested in finding out how the number of workers employed by a firm or set of firms is affected by changes in one or more of these three forces. To simplify the discussion, we shall study one change at a time and hold all other forces constant.

WAGE CHANGES　Of primary interest for most purposes is the question of how the number of employees (or total labor hours) demanded varies when wages change. Suppose, for example, that we could vary the wages facing a certain industry over a long period of time but keep the technology available, the conditions under which capital is supplied, and the relationship between product price and product demand unchanged. What would happen to the quantity of labor demanded if the wage rate were *increased?*

First, higher wages imply higher costs and, usually, higher product prices. Because consumers respond to higher prices by buying less, employers would tend to reduce their level of output. Lower output levels, of course, imply lower employment levels (other things being equal). This decline in employment is called a *scale effect,* the effect on desired employment of a smaller scale of production.

Second, as wages increase (assuming the price of capital does not change, at least initially), employers have incentives to cut costs by adopting a technology that relies more on capital and less on labor. Thus, if wages were to rise, desired employment would fall because of a shift toward a more "capital-intensive" mode of production. This second effect might be termed a *substitution effect,* because as wages rise, capital is *substituted* for labor in the production process.

The effects of various wages on employment levels might be summarized in a table showing the labor demanded at each wage level. Table 2.3 illustrates such a *demand schedule.* The relationship between wages and employment tabulated in Table 2.3 could be graphed as a *demand curve.* Figure 2.6 shows the demand curve generated by the data in Table 2.3. Note that the curve has a negative slope, indicating that as wages rise, less labor is demanded. (Note also that we follow convention in economics by placing the wage rate on the *vertical* axis despite its being an *independent* variable in the context of labor demand by a firm.)

A demand curve for labor tells us how the desired level of employment, measured in either labor hours or number of employees, varies with changes in the price of labor when the other forces affecting demand are held constant. These other forces, to repeat, are the product demand schedule, the conditions under which capital can be obtained, and the set of technologies available. If wages change and these other factors do not, one can determine the change in the quantity of labor demanded by moving up or down along the demand curve.

CHANGES IN OTHER FORCES AFFECTING DEMAND　What happens when one of the other forces affecting labor demand changes?

First, suppose that *demand for the product* of a particular industry were to increase, so that at any output price, more of the goods or services in question could be sold. Suppose in this case that technology and the conditions under

TABLE 2.3
Labor Demand Schedule for a Hypothetical Industry

Wage Rate	Desired Employment Level
$3.00	250
4.00	190
5.00	160
6.00	130
7.00	100
8.00	70

NOTE: Employment levels can be measured in number of employees or number of labor hours demanded. We have chosen here to use number of employees.

which capital and labor are made available to the industry do not change. Output levels would clearly rise as firms in the industry sought to maximize profits, and this *scale* (or *output*) *effect* would increase the demand for labor at any given wage rate. (As long as the relative prices of capital and labor remain unchanged, there is no *substitution effect*.)

How would this change in the demand for labor be illustrated using a demand curve? Since the technology available and the conditions under which capital and labor are supplied have remained constant, this change in product demand would increase the labor desired at any wage level that might prevail. In other words, the entire labor demand curve *shifts* to the right. This rightward shift, shown as a movement from *D* to *D'* in Figure 2.7, indicates that at every possible wage rate the number of workers demanded has increased.

Second, consider what would happen if the product demand schedule, technology, and labor supply conditions were to remain unchanged, but *the supply of capital* changed so that capital prices fell to 50 percent of their prior level. How would this change affect the demand for labor?

FIGURE 2.6
Labor Demand Curve (based on data in Table 2.3)

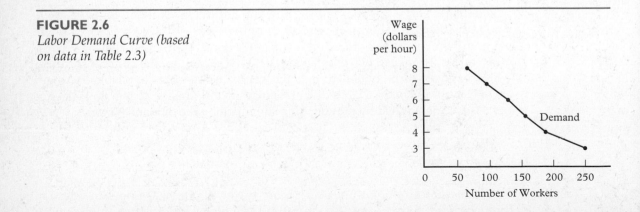

FIGURE 2.7
*Shift in Demand for Labor Due to Increase in
Product Demand*

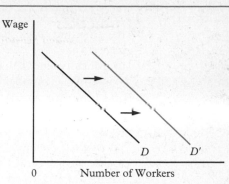

Our method of analyzing the effects on labor demand of a change in the price of *another* productive input is familiar: we must consider the scale and substitution effects. First, when capital prices decline, the costs of producing tend to decline. Reduced costs stimulate increases in production, and these increases tend to raise the level of desired employment at any given wage. The scale effect of a fall in capital prices thus tends to increase the demand for labor at each wage level.

The second effect of a fall in capital prices would be a substitution effect, whereby firms adopt more-capital-intensive technologies in response to cheaper capital. Such firms would substitute capital for labor and would use less labor to produce a given amount of output than before. With less labor being desired at each wage rate, the labor demand curve tends to shift to the left.

A fall in capital prices, then, generates *two opposite* effects on the demand for labor. The scale effect will push the labor demand curve rightward, while the substitution effect will push it to the left. As emphasized by Figure 2.8, either effect could dominate. Thus, economic theory does not yield a clear-cut prediction about how a fall in capital prices will affect the demand for labor. (A *rise* in capital prices would generate the same overall ambiguity of effect on the demand for labor, with the scale effect pushing the labor demand curve left and the substitution effect pushing it to the right.)

FIGURE 2.8
Possible Shifts in Demand for Labor Due to Fall in Capital Prices

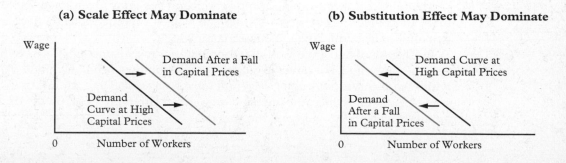

The hypothesized changes in product demand and capital supply just discussed have tended to *shift* the demand curve for labor. It is important to distinguish between a *shift* in a demand curve and *movement along* a curve. A labor demand curve graphically shows the *labor desired* as a function of the *wage rate* (the wage is on one axis and the number of workers desired is on the other). When the *wage* changes and other forces are held unchanged, one *moves along* the curve. However, when one of the *other forces* changes, the labor demand curve *shifts*. Unlike wages, these forces are not directly shown when the demand curve for labor is drawn. Thus, when they change, a different relationship between wages and desired employment prevails, and this shows up as a shift of the demand curve. If more labor is desired at any given wage rate, then the curve has shifted to the right. If less labor is demanded at each wage rate that might prevail, then the demand curve has shifted left.

MARKET, INDUSTRY, AND FIRM DEMAND   The demand for labor can be analyzed on three levels:

1. To analyze the demand for labor *by a particular firm*, we would examine how an increase in the wage of machinists, say, would affect their employment by a particular aircraft manufacturer.
2. To analyze the effects of this wage increase on the employment of machinists *in the entire aircraft industry*, we would utilize an industry demand curve.
3. Finally, to see how the wage increase would affect the *entire labor market* for machinists, in all industries in which they are used, we would use a market demand curve.

We shall see in Chapters 3 and 4 that firm, industry, and market labor demand curves vary in *shape* to some extent because *scale* and *substitution effects* have different strengths at each level. However, it is important to remember that the scale and substitution effects of a wage change work in the same direction at each level, so that firm, industry, and market demand curves *all slope downward*.

LONG RUN VS. SHORT RUN   One can also distinguish between *long-run* and *short-run* labor demand curves. Over very short periods of time, employers find it difficult to substitute capital for labor (or vice versa), and customers may not change their product demand very much in response to a price increase. It takes *time* to fully adjust consumption and production behavior. Over longer periods of time, of course, responses to changes in wages or other forces affecting the demand for labor are larger and more complete.

In Chapters 3 and 4 we shall draw some important distinctions between short-run and long-run labor demand curves. At this point we need only point out that while these curves will differ, *they both slope downward*. Thus, an increase in the wage rate will reduce the demand for labor, although perhaps by different amounts, in both the short and the long run.

THE SUPPLY OF LABOR

Having looked at a simple model of behavior on the buyer (or demand) side of the labor market, we now turn to the seller (or supply) side of the market. For the purposes of this chapter, we shall assume that workers have already decided to work and that the question facing them is what occupation and what employer to choose.

MARKET SUPPLY To first consider the supply of labor to the entire market (as opposed to the supply to a particular firm), suppose that the market we are considering is the one for secretaries. How will supply respond to changes in the wages secretaries might receive? In other words, what does the supply schedule of secretaries look like?

If the salaries and wages in *other* occupations are *held constant* and the wages of secretaries rise, we would expect to find more people wanting to become secretaries. For example, suppose that each of 100 people in a high school graduating class has the option of becoming an insurance agent or a secretary. Some of these 100 people will prefer to be insurance agents even if secretaries are better paid, because they like the challenge and sociability of selling. Some would want to be secretaries even if the pay were comparatively poor, because they hate the pressures of selling. Many, however, could see themselves doing either job; for them the compensation in each occupation would be a major factor in their decision. If secretaries were higher paid than insurance agents, more would want to become secretaries. If the pay of insurance agents were higher, the number of people choosing the insurance occupation would increase and the supply of secretaries would decrease. Of course, at some ridiculously low wage for secretaries, *no one* would want to become one.

Thus, the supply of labor to a particular market is positively related to the wage rate prevailing in that market, holding other wages constant. That is, if the wages of insurance agents are held constant and the secretary wage rises, more people will want to become secretaries because of the relative improvement in compensation (as shown graphically in Figure 2.9).

As with demand curves, each supply curve is drawn holding other prices and wages constant. If one or more of these other prices or wages were to change, it

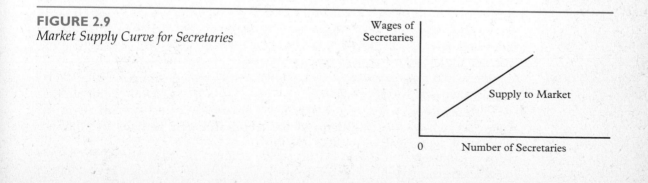

FIGURE 2.9
Market Supply Curve for Secretaries

FIGURE 2.10

Shift in Market Supply Curve for Secretaries As Salaries of Insurance Agents Rise

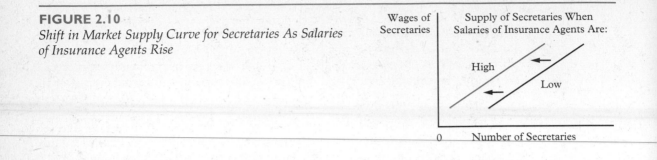

would cause the supply curve to *shift*. As the salaries of insurance agents *rise*, some people will change their minds about becoming secretaries and choose to become insurance agents. Fewer people would want to be secretaries at each level of secretarial wages as salaries of insurance agents rise. In graphic terms (see Figure 2.10), increases in the salaries of insurance agents would cause the supply curve of secretaries to shift to the left.

SUPPLY TO FIRMS   Having decided to become a secretary, the individual would then have to decide which offer of employment to accept. If all employers were offering secretarial jobs that were more or less alike, the choice would be based on compensation. Any firm unwise enough to attempt paying a wage below what others were paying would find it could not attract any employees (or at least none of the caliber it wanted). Conversely, no firm would be foolish enough to pay more than the going wage, because it would be paying more than it would have to pay to attract a suitable number and quality of employees. Supply curves to a firm, then, are horizontal, as shown in Figure 2.11. If the secretarial wage paid by others in the market is W_0 then the firm's labor supply curve is S_0; if the wage falls to W_1, the firm's labor supply curve becomes S_1. The horizontal supply curve to a firm indicates that at the going wage, a firm could get all the secretaries it needs. If it paid less, however, supply would shrink to zero.

The difference in slope between the market supply curve and the supply curve to a firm is directly related to the type of choice facing workers. In deciding whether to enter the secretarial labor market, workers must weigh both the compensation *and* the job requirements of alternative options (such as being an insurance agent). If wages of secretaries were to fall, fewer people would want to enter the secretarial market. However, not everyone would withdraw from the market, because the jobs of insurance agent and secretary are not perfect substitutes. Some people would remain secretaries after a wage decline because they dislike the job requirements of insurance agents.

Once the decision to become a secretary had been made, the choice of which employer to work for would be a choice among alternatives in which the job requirements were nearly the *same*. Thus, the choice would have to be made on the basis of compensation alone. If a firm were to lower its wage offers below those of other firms, it would lose all its applicants. The horizontal supply curve is,

FIGURE 2.11

Supply of Secretaries to a Firm at Alternative Market Wages

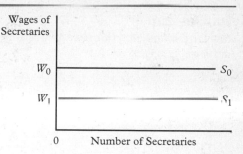

therefore, a reflection of supply decisions made among alternatives that are perfect substitutes for each other.

We have argued that firms wishing to hire secretaries must pay the going wage or lose all applicants. While this may seem unrealistic, it is not. If a firm offers jobs *comparable* to those offered by other firms but at a lower level of total compensation, it might be able to attract a few applicants of the quality it desires because a few people will be unaware of compensation elsewhere. Over time, however, knowledge of the firm's poor relative pay would become more widespread, and the firm would find it had to rely solely on less-qualified people to fill its jobs. It could secure quality employees at below-average pay only if it offered *noncomparable* jobs (more pleasant working conditions, longer paid vacations, and so forth). This factor in labor supply will be discussed in Chapter 8. For now, we will assume that individual firms, like individual workers, are usually *wage takers;* that is, the wages they pay to their workers must be pretty close to the going wage if they face competition in the labor market. Neither individual workers nor firms can set a wage much different from the going wage and still hope to transact. (Exceptions to this general proposition will be developed in later chapters.)

THE DETERMINATION OF THE WAGE

The wage that prevails in a particular labor market is heavily influenced by the forces of demand and supply, regardless of whether the market involves a labor union. However, because unions are labor market institutions designed to alter the market outcome, we shall first discuss wage determination in nonunionized labor markets.

THE MARKET-CLEARING WAGE Recall that the market demand curve indicates how many workers employers would want at each wage rate, holding capital prices and the product demand schedule constant. The market supply curve indicates how many workers would enter the market at each wage level, holding the wages in other occupations constant. These curves can be placed on the same graph to reveal some interesting information, as shown in Figure 2.12.

For example, suppose the market wage were set at W_1. At this low wage, demand is large but supply is small. More important, Figure 2.12 indicates that at W_1 demand *exceeds* supply. At this point, employers will be competing for the few

FIGURE 2.12
Market Demand and Supply

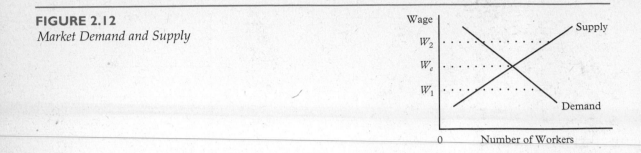

workers in the market and a shortage of workers would exist. The desire of firms to attract more employees would lead them to increase their wage offers, thus driving up the overall level of wage offers in the market.

As wages rose, two things would happen. First, more workers would choose to enter the market and look for jobs (a movement along the supply curve); second, increasing wages would induce employers to seek fewer workers (a movement along the demand curve). If wages were to rise to W_2, supply would exceed demand. Employers would desire fewer workers than the number available, and not all those desiring employment would be able to find jobs, resulting in a surplus of workers. Employers would have long lines of eager applicants for any opening. These employers would soon reason that they could fill their openings with qualified applicants even if they offered lower wages. Further, if they could pay lower wages, they would want to hire more employees. Some employees would be more than happy to accept the lower wages if they could just find a job. Others would leave the market and look for work elsewhere as wages fell. Thus, demand and supply would become more equal as wages fell from the level of W_2.

The wage rate at which demand equals supply is the *market-clearing* or *market equilibrium* wage. At W_e in Figure 2.12, employers can fill the number of openings they have, and all employees who want jobs in this market can find them. At W_e there is no surplus and no shortage. All parties are satisfied, and no forces exist that would alter the wage. The market is in equilibrium in the sense that the wage will remain at W_e.

The market-clearing wage is the wage that eventually prevails in a freely operating market. Wages below W_e will not prevail, because the shortage of workers leads employers to drive up wage offers. Wages above W_e likewise cannot prevail, because the surplus leads to downward pressure on wage rates. The market-clearing wage, W_e, thus becomes the *going wage* that individual employers and employees must face. In other words, wage rates are determined by the market and "announced" to individual market participants. Figure 2.13 graphically depicts market demand and supply in panel (a), along with the demand and supply curves for a typical firm (Firm A) in that market in panel (b). All firms in the market pay a wage of W_e, and total employment of L equals the sum of employment in each firm.

DISTURBING THE EQUILIBRIUM   What could happen to change the market equilibrium wage once it has been reached? Once equilibrium has been achieved,

FIGURE 2.13
Demand and Supply at the "Market" and "Firm" Level

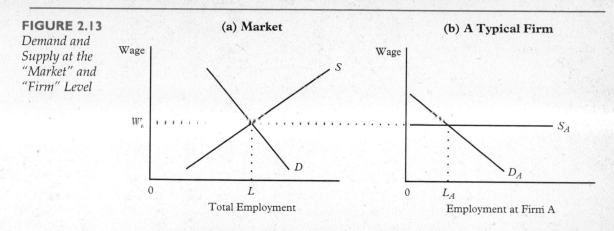

(a) Market

(b) A Typical Firm

changes could arise from shifts in either the demand or the supply curve. Suppose, for example, that the increase in paperwork accompanying greater government regulation of industry caused firms to demand more secretarial help than before. Graphically, as in Figure 2.14, this greater demand would be represented as a rightward shift of the demand curve. This rightward shift would depict a situation in which, for any given wage rate, the number of secretaries desired had risen. The old market equilibrium wage (W_e) would no longer equate demand and supply. If W_e were to persist, there would be a labor shortage in the secretarial market (because demand would exceed supply). This shortage would induce employers, in their efforts to attract employees, to improve their wage offers. Eventually, the secretarial wage would be driven up to W_e^*. Notice that in this case, the equilibrium level of *employment* will also rise.

The market wage can also increase if the labor supply curve shifts to the left. As shown in Figure 2.15, such a shift creates a labor shortage at the old equilibrium wage of W_e, and as employers scramble to fill their job openings, the market wage is bid up to W_e'. In the case of a leftward-shifting labor supply curve, however, the increased market wage is accompanied by a decrease in the equilibrium level of employment. (See Example 2.1 for an analysis of the labor market effects of the leftward shift in labor supply accompanying the Black Death in 1348–1351.)

If a leftward shift in labor supply is accompanied by a rightward shift in labor demand, the market wage can rise dramatically. Such a condition occurred in

FIGURE 2.14
New Labor Market Equilibrium After Demand Shifts Right

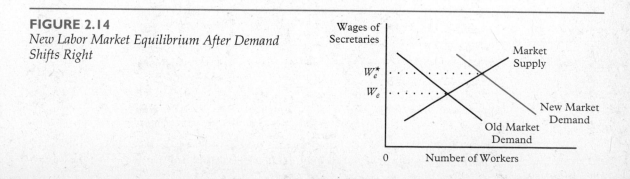

FIGURE 2.15
New Labor Market Equilibrium After Supply Shifts Left

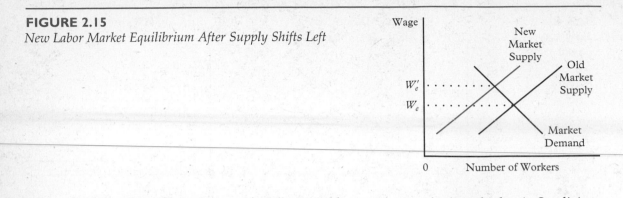

Egypt during the early 1970s. Lured by wages over six times higher in Saudi Arabia and other oil-rich Arab countries, roughly half of Egypt's construction workers left the country just as a residential building boom in Egypt got under way. The combination of a leftward-shifting labor supply curve and a rightward-shifting labor demand curve drove the real wages of Egyptian construction workers up by 53 percent in just five years![8] (This notable wage increase was accompanied by a net employment *increase* in Egypt's construction industry. The student will be asked, in the first review question on page 58, to analyze these events graphically.)

Market-clearing wages can also fall, of course. Although *money* wages are rarely cut, in a period of rising prices *real* wages can fall quite readily. In Table 2.2, it can be seen that the average money wage rose from $4.24 per hour in 1974 to $8.32 per hour in 1984, but because of increased prices, real wages fell. Money wages in an occupation can also fall relative to wages in other occupations. Thus, when we speak of a declining wage rate, it can imply a decline *relative to product prices or to other wages,* as well as a fall in the money wage rate.

A fall in the market equilibrium wage rate would occur if there were increased supply or reduced demand. An increase in supply would be represented by a rightward shift of the supply curve, as more people entered the market at each wage (see Figure 2.16). This rightward shift would cause a surplus to exist at the old equilibrium wage (W_e) and lead to behavior that reduced the wage to W_e'' in Figure 2.16. Note that the equilibrium employment level has increased. What could cause this rightward shift of the supply curve? The early 1970s, when the baby-boom generation first joined the labor force, provide us with an example. Over the six years from 1968 to 1974, the ratio of inexperienced to experienced workers rose by 36 percent. This relatively sudden rightward shift in supply caused the wages of inexperienced workers to fall 13 percent relative to those of experienced workers.[9]

---

[8]Bent Hansen and Samir Radwan, *Employment Opportunities and Equity in Egypt* (Geneva: International Labour Office, 1982).

[9]From Finis Welch, "Effects of Cohort Size on Earnings: The Baby Boom Babies' Financial Bust," *Journal of Political Economy* 87, no. 5 (October 1979): S65–S98. Similar effects were seen in Great Britain; see Stephen Nickell, "Cohort Size Effects on the Wages of Young Men in Britain: 1961–1989," *British Journal of Industrial Relations* 31 (September 1993): 459–469.

FIGURE 2.16
New Labor Market Equilibrium After Supply Shifts Right

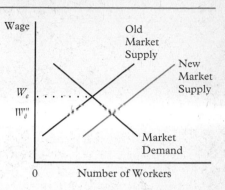

A decrease (leftward shift) in labor demand would also cause a decrease in the market equilibrium wage, although such a shift would be accompanied by a fall in employment. The leftward shift of the demand curve would cause a surplus at the original market wage. When firms found the ratio of applicants to openings was greater than usual, and when workers found that jobs were harder to come by, downward pressure on the wage would exist and the market-clearing wage would fall. Inflation might cause money wages to go up, but any increases would be smaller than those received in other occupations.

It is possible, as we saw earlier with Egyptian construction workers, for both labor demand and labor supply curves to shift at the same time. In the Egyptian case, both shifts tended to increase the market wage. Shifts of both curves in the *other* direction would have put *downward* pressure on wages.

As illustrated by Figure 2.17, however, some simultaneous shifts have ambiguous effects on the market-clearing wage. In both panels of Figure 2.17, a leftward shift in demand is accompanied by a leftward shift in supply, but in panel (a) the market wage falls from its original level (W_{1-1}), while in panel (b) the market wage rises. Note that while a leftward shift of both curves has a theoretically ambiguous effect on the market *wage*, equilibrium *employment* clearly falls.

DISEQUILIBRIUM AND NONMARKET INFLUENCES That a market-clearing wage exists in theory does not imply that it is reached—or reached

FIGURE 2.17
New Labor Market Equilibrium After Supply and Demand Shift Left

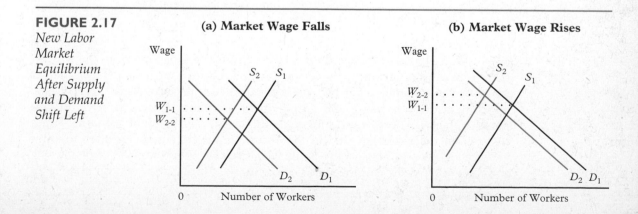

EXAMPLE 2.1

The Black Death and the Wages of Labor

An example of what happens to wages when the supply of labor suddenly shifts occurred when plague—the Black Death—struck England (among other European countries) in 1348–1351. Estimates vary, but it is generally agreed that plague killed between 17 and 40 percent of the English population in that short period of time. This shocking loss of life had the immediate effect of raising the wages of laborers. As the supply curve shifted to the left, a *shortage* of workers was created at the old wage levels, and competition among employers for the surviving workers drove the wage level dramatically upward.

Reliable figures are hard to come by, but many believe wages rose by 50–100 percent over the three-year period. A thresher, for example, earning two and one-half pence per day in 1348 earned four and one-half pence in 1350, while mowers receiving 5 pence per acre in 1348 were receiving 9 pence in 1350. Whether the overall rise in wages was this large or not, there was clearly a labor shortage and an unprecedented increase in wages. A royal proclamation commanding landlords to share their scarce workers with neighbors and threatening workers with imprisonment if they refused work at the pre-plague wage was issued to deal with this shortage, but it was ignored. The shortage was too severe and market forces were simply too strong for the rise in wages to be thwarted.

The discerning student might wonder at this point about the *demand* curve for labor. Did it not also shift to the left as the population—and the number of consumers—declined? The answer is that it did, but this leftward shift was not as pronounced as the leftward shift in supply. While there were fewer customers for labor's output, the customers who remained consumed greater amounts of goods and services per capita than before. The money, gold and silver, and durable goods that had existed prior to 1348 were divided among many fewer people by 1350, and this rise in per capita wealth was associated with a widespread and dramatic increase in the level of consumption, especially of luxury goods. Thus, the leftward shift in labor demand was dominated by the leftward shift in supply, and the predictable result was a large increase in wages.

Sources: Harry A. Miskimin, *The Economy of Early Renaissance Europe, 1300–1460* (Englewood Cliffs, N.J.: Prentice-Hall, 1969); George M. Modlin and Frank T. deVyver, *Development of Economic Society* (Boston: D.C. Heath, 1946); Douglass C. North and Robert Paul Thomas, *The Rise of the Western World* (Cambridge: Cambridge University Press, 1973); Philip Ziegler, *The Black Death* (New York: Harper & Row, 1969).

quickly—in practice. Because labor services cannot be separated from the worker, and because labor income is by far the most important source of spending power for ordinary people, the labor market is subject to forces that impede the adjustment of both wages and employment to changes in demand or supply. Some of these barriers to adjustment are themselves the result of economic forces that will be discussed later in the text. For example, changing jobs often requires an employee to invest in new skills (see Chapter 9) or bear costs of moving (Chapter 10). On the employer side of the market, hiring workers can involve an initial investment in search and training (Chapter 5), while firing them or cutting their wages can be perceived as unfair and therefore have consequences for the productivity of those who remain (Chapter 11).

Other barriers to adjustment are rooted in *nonmarket* forces: laws, customs, or institutions constraining the choices of individuals and firms (choices that underlie the demand and supply curves introduced earlier). Although forces keeping wages *below* their equilibrium levels are not unknown, nonmarket forces usually serve to keep wages *above* market levels. Minimum wage laws (discussed in Chapter 4) and unions (Chapter 13) are examples of influences explicitly designed to raise wages beyond those dictated by "the market" (that is, by the unconstrained choices of workers and employers). Likewise, if there is a widespread belief that cutting wages is "unfair," laws or customs may arise that prevent wages from falling in markets experiencing leftward shifts in demand or rightward shifts in supply.

It is commonly believed that labor markets adjust more quickly to market forces when those forces are calling for wages to rise rather than for them to fall. If wages are quicker to rise than to fall, then those markets observed to be in disequilibrium for long periods will tend to be ones with above-market wages. The existence of above-market wages implies that the supply of labor exceeds the number of jobs being offered (refer to the relative demand and supply at wage W_2 in Figure 2.12); therefore, if enough markets are experiencing this kind of disequilibrium the result will be widespread *unemployment*. In fact, as we will see in the section on international differences in unemployment that closes this chapter, these differences can sometimes be used to identify where market forces are most constrained by nonmarket influences.

Some behavioral and normative consequences of wages "stuck" above or below their market-clearing levels will be discussed in the upcoming section on applications. Before turning to these applications, however, it is useful to illustrate how the demand and supply curves developed in this chapter can be used to analyze nonmarket forces. The examples we present involve the presence of a union.

UNIONS IN THE LABOR MARKET Unions represent workers and thus primarily affect the *supply* curves to labor markets. They do so in two ways. First, most unions operate under labor-management agreements—called *contracts* or *collective bargaining agreements*—that permit employer discretion in the selection of workers. These contracts cover wages, other forms of compensation, working conditions, procedures for employee complaints, and rules governing promotions and layoffs. The provisions of the contracts are the result of a bargain struck between management and all workers collectively. All are bound by the final provisions of the contract, which means that all must receive the agreed-upon wage.

Many of the most prominent collective bargaining agreements, in effect, are industrywide. These agreements affect the supply curves in the relevant labor markets by making them horizontal. No one can get paid more or less than the wage agreed upon in the contract (see Figure 2.18).

In Figure 2.18 the supply curve without a union is S and the market-clearing wage is W_e. However, the union raises the wage above W_e to W_u, the wage specified

FIGURE 2.18
Effects on Labor Market Equilibrium of Industrywide Unions

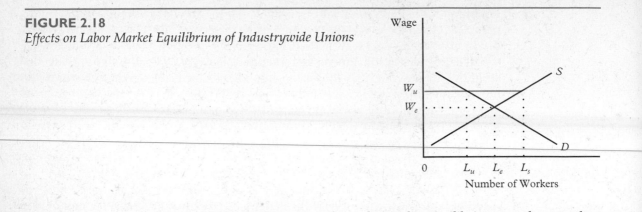

in the contract. The result is a wage above the market equilibrium, employment levels below those that would prevail if the wage were lower, and a "surplus" of labor (at W_u, L_s workers want work in these jobs but only L_u can find work). Because the wage cannot fall, the surplus remains and will manifest itself in long lines of workers applying for job openings with union employers.

The second way in which some unions affect the labor market is by *directly* limiting supply. Some unions operate under agreements in which employers hire all labor from the union and in which the union controls which and how many members it lets in. The dual power of being able to restrict its membership and to require employers to hire only union members permits the union to set the level of labor supply to the market (see Figure 2.19).

In Figure 2.19, S_u represents the level of supply determined by union policy and W_u the resulting wage. S_u is drawn as a vertical line because wage increases or decreases do not affect supply. Supply is set at L_u by union policy. The wage and employment levels under the union—W_u and L_u—can be compared to the lower wages (W_e) and higher employment levels (L_e) that would prevail in the absence of a union.

The major difference between this second case, in which unions control supply, and the more common situation, in which employers choose workers but make contracts with all workers collectively, is that there is no surplus of workers standing at the employer's hiring gate. The long line of disappointed people is at the

FIGURE 2.19
How Unions That Control Supply of Labor to a Market Affect Labor Market Equilibrium

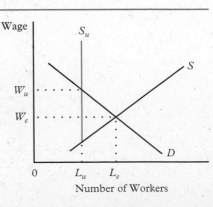

union's office. Examples of labor unions that control supply are those representing skilled construction workers, longshoring workers, and theater lighting technicians.

The above analyses were based on the assumption that unions raised the wage above market-clearing levels. This is probably a useful assumption, given that unions certainly intend to do this. Not all unions have the power to affect wages much, for reasons we shall discuss in Chapters 4 and 13. If these unions agree to wages equal to W_c, the market equilibrium wage, then clearly they do not affect wage or employment outcomes in the labor market.

Applications of the Theory

Although this simple model of how a labor market functions will be refined and elaborated upon in the following chapters, it can explain many important phenomena, including the issues of when workers are overpaid or underpaid and what explains international differences in unemployment.

WHO IS UNDERPAID AND WHO IS OVERPAID?

In casual conversation one often hears a worker say that he or she is "underpaid." Just as often one hears employers claiming workers are "overpaid." Clearly, each is using a different standard for judging wages. People tend to judge the wages paid or received against some notion of what they "need," but there is no universally accepted standard of need. A worker may "need" more income to buy a larger home or finance a recreational vehicle. An employer may "need" greater profits to pay for sending a child to college. In general, almost all of us feel we "need" more income!

Despite the difficulties of assessing needs, there are still important reasons for defining "overpaid" and "underpaid." For example, the public utilities commissions in every state must consider and approve rate increases requested by the gas and electric companies. These companies desire increases partly to keep up with production costs, which the companies obviously want to pass on to consumers. Suppose, however, that a public utilities commission observed that the *level* of wages paid by these companies or the *increases* in such wages were "excessive." In the interests of holding down consumer prices, it might want to consider adopting a policy whereby excessive labor costs could not be passed on to consumers in the form of rate increases. Instead, it might decide that such costs should be borne by the company or its shareholders. Obviously, such a policy would require a definition of what constitutes overpayment.

We pointed out in Chapter 1 that a fundamental value of normative economics is that, as a society, we should strive to complete all those transactions that are mutually beneficial. Another way of stating this value is to say that we must strive to use our scarce resources as effectively as possible, which implies that output should be produced in the least-costly manner so that the most can be obtained from such resources. This goal, combined with the labor market model outlined in this chapter, suggests a useful definition of what it means to be overpaid.

FIGURE 2.20

Effects of an Above-Equilibrium Wage

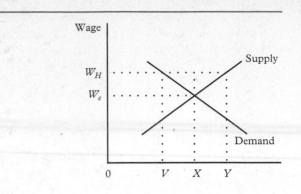

ABOVE-EQUILIBRIUM WAGES   We shall define workers as *overpaid* if their wages are higher than the market equilibrium wage for their job. Because a labor surplus exists for jobs that are overpaid, a wage above equilibrium has two implications (see Figure 2.20). First, employers are paying more than they have to in order to produce (they pay W_H instead of W_e); they could cut wages and still find enough qualified workers for their job openings. In fact, if they did cut wages, they could expand output and make their product cheaper and more accessible to consumers. Second, more workers want jobs than can find them (Y workers want jobs, and only V openings are available). If wages were reduced a bit, more of these disappointed workers could find work. A wage above equilibrium thus causes consumer prices to be higher and output to be smaller than is possible, and it creates a situation in which not all workers who want the jobs in question can get them.

With this definition of overpayment, the public utilities commission in question would want to look for evidence that wages were above equilibrium. The commission might be able to compare wages paid by utilities to those of comparable workers in the general labor market. Doing so would require measures of worker quality, of course—data that are hard to quantify in some cases. Alternatively, the commission could look to employee behavior for signs of above-market wages. If wages were above those for comparable jobs, current employees would be *very* reluctant to quit because they would know their chances of doing better were small. Likewise, the number of applicants would be unusually large.

An interesting example of above-equilibrium wages was seen in Houston's labor market in 1988. Bus cleaners working for the Houston Metropolitan Transit Authority received $10.08 per hour, or 83 percent more than the $5.94 received by cleaners working for private bus companies in Houston. One (predictable) result of this overpayment is that the quit rate among Houston's Transit Authority cleaners was only *one-seventh* as great as the average for cleaners nationwide.[10]

———————————

[10]William J. Moore and Robert J. Newman, "Government Wage Differentials in a Municipal Labor Market: The Case of Houston Metropolitan Transit Workers," *Industrial and Labor Relations Review* 45, no. 1 (October 1991): 145–153.

FIGURE 2.21
Effects of a Below-Equilibrium Wage

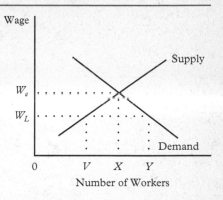

To better understand the social losses attendant on overpayment, let us return to the principles of normative economics. Can it be shown that reducing overpayment will create a situation in which the gainers gain more than the losers lose? Suppose in the case of Houston's Transit Authority cleaners that *only* the wage of *newly hired* cleaners was reduced—to $6.40, say. Current cleaners thus would not lose, but many others who were working elsewhere at $5.94 would jump at the chance to earn a higher wage. Taxpayers, realizing that transit services could now be expanded at lower cost than before, would increase their demand for such services, thus creating jobs for these additional workers. Some workers would gain while no one lost—and social well-being would clearly be enhanced.[11] The wage reduction, in short, would be *Pareto-improving* (see Chapter 1).

BELOW-EQUILIBRIUM WAGES   Employees can be defined as *underpaid* if their wage is below equilibrium. At below-equilibrium wages, employers have difficulty finding workers to meet the demands of consumers, and a labor shortage thus exists (firms want more workers than they can find at the prevailing wage). They also have trouble keeping the workers they do find. If wages were increased, output would rise and more workers would be attracted to the market. Thus, an increase would benefit the people in society in *both* their consumer and their worker roles. Figure 2.21 shows how a wage increase from W_L to W_e would increase employment from V to X (at the same time wages were rising).

Wages in the U.S. Army illustrate how the market adjusts to below-equilibrium wages. Prior to 1973, when the military draft was eliminated, the government could pursue a policy of paying below-market wages to military recruits, because the resultant gap between supply and demand could be filled by conscription (see Example 2.2). Not surprisingly, when comparing wages in the late 1970s with those in the last decade of the military draft, we find that the average military cash wages paid to enlisted personnel rose 19 percent more than those of comparable civilian workers.

---

[11]If the workers who switched jobs were getting paid approximately what they were worth to their former employers, these employers would lose $5.94 in output but save $5.94 in costs—and their welfare would thus not be affected. The presumption that employees are paid what they are worth to the employer is discussed at length in Chapter 3.

EXAMPLE 2.2

Ending the Conscription of Young American Men: The Role of Economists

Before 1973, American men in their late teens and early 20s were liable to be drafted into the Army for a period of two years. The U.S. Navy, Marine Corps, and Air Force all relied solely on voluntary enlistments, but it was widely believed that the draft was necessary to supplement voluntary enlistments in the Army. The decision to end the draft, which had been in place since World War II, was both momentous and controversial—and it was one in which economists played a central role.

Normative economics provided the philosophical underpinnings of the push for an all-volunteer military. The 1970 report of the President's Commission on an All-Volunteer Armed Force, which contained the policy "blueprint" for ending conscription, had an introductory chapter entitled "Conscription Is a Tax." This chapter reflected the normative standard of Pareto efficiency, which rests on the proposition that we can be assured a transaction is mutually beneficial only if it is voluntary:

> Under the present system, first-term servicemen must bear a disproportionately large share of the defense

burden. Draftees and draft-induced volunteers are paid less than they would require to volunteer. The loss they suffer is a tax-in-kind. . . .

Conscription also imposes social and human costs by distorting the personal life and career plans of the young.

Positive economics also provided crucial input to the policy debate. Questions naturally arose concerning whether the Army could attract enough high-quality volunteers and how high pay would have to rise to do so. The answers were provided by a careful estimate of the military labor supply curve, which suggested that to maintain the size and quality of the military in 1970 would require the basic pay of first-term enlisted personnel to rise by 50 percent, the pay of first-term officers to rise by 28 percent, and the pay of second-term enlistees to rise by an average of 9 percent.

Source: President's Commission on an All-Volunteer Armed Force, *Report of the President's Commission on an All-Volunteer Armed Force* (Washington, D.C.: U.S. Government Printing Office, February 1970).

ECONOMIC RENTS   The concepts of underpayment and overpayment have to do with the *social* issue of producing desired goods and services in the least-costly way; therefore, wages paid were compared to the *market-clearing wage*. At the level of *individuals*, however, it is often useful to compare the wage received in a job to one's *reservation wage*, the wage below which the worker would refuse (or quit) the job in question. The amount by which one's wage exceeds one's reservation wage in a particular job is the amount of his or her *economic rent*.

Rents clearly exist when wages are above the market-clearing level. (We will see later in this text that above-market wages can be created by government policy, through employer design, as a result of collective bargaining agreements, or because the equilibrium wage has fallen and wages are inflexible in a downward direction.) However, rents are present even when the market wage prevails. The existence of rents in this latter case is the result of differences in worker preferences, as we explain below.

FIGURE 2.22

Labor Supply to the Military: Different Preferences Imply Different "Rents"

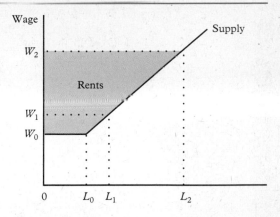

Consider the labor supply curve to, say, the military. As shown in Figure 2.22, if the military is to hire L_1 people, it must pay W_1 in wages. These relatively low wages will attract to the military those who most enjoy the military culture and are least averse to the risks of combat. If the military is to be somewhat larger and to employ L_2 people, then it must pay a wage of W_2. This higher wage is required to attract those who would have found a military career unattractive at the lower wage. If W_2 turns out to be the wage that equates demand and supply, and if the military pays that wage, everyone who would have joined up for less would be receiving an economic rent!

Put differently, the supply curve to an occupation or industry is a schedule of reservation wages that indicates the labor forthcoming at each wage level. The difference between the wage actually paid and workers' reservation wages—the shaded area in Figure 2.22—is the amount of the rent. Since each worker potentially has a different reservation wage, rents may well differ for each worker in the market. In Figure 2.22, the greatest rents are received by those L_0 individuals who would have joined the military even if the wage were only W_0.

Why don't employers reduce the wage of each employee down to his or her reservation level? While capturing employee rents would seem to be lucrative, since by definition it could be done without the workers' quitting, attempting to do so would create resentment and would be extremely costly, if not impossible, to implement. Employers do not know the true reservation wages of each employee or applicant, and finding it would involve experiments in which the wage offers to each worker either started high and were cut or started low and were raised. This would be costly, and if workers realized the firm was *experimenting*, they would attempt to disguise their true reservation wages and adopt the "strategic behavior" associated with bargaining (bluffing, for example). Therefore, firms usually pay according to the job, one's level of experience or longevity with the employer, and considerations of merit—but not according to preferences. An exception to this general rule is the two-tier wage schedule that has arisen in a few cases in which the market is calling for a wage decrease and the firm does not want to cut wages for its current workers; in these cases, discussed later in Example 13.1, lower wages are paid to the firm's new entrants than were paid to its current workers when they were new. Thus, rents are extracted from new workers but no attempt is made to extract them from current employees.

INTERNATIONAL DIFFERENCES IN UNEMPLOYMENT

We noted earlier that labor markets are often influenced by nonmarket forces that keep wages above market-clearing levels. Because these nonmarket forces generally take the form of laws, government programs, customs, or institutions (labor unions, for example), their strength can be expected to vary across countries. Can we form some conclusions about the countries in which they are most pronounced?

Theory presented in this chapter suggests that if wages are above market-clearing levels, unemployment will result (the number of people seeking work will exceed the number of available jobs). Further, if wages are held above market-clearing levels and the labor demand curve *shifts to the left*, unemployment will rise to even higher levels (the student should be able to show this by drawing a graph with an unchanging supply curve, a fixed wage rate, and a leftward-shifting demand curve). Moreover, above-market wages deter the growth of *new* jobs, so wages "stuck" above market-clearing levels also can cause those who suffer a spell of unemployment to remain in that status for a long time. Thus, measures of the incidence and duration of unemployment—which, fortunately, are comparably defined and estimated in several advanced economies—can sometimes be used to infer the relative strength of nonmarket forces across countries. Consider, for example, what happened to unemployment rates in Europe and North America in the 1980s.

One phenomenon characterizing the 1980s was an acceleration of technological change, associated primarily with computerization, in the advanced economies of the world. As we will discuss and document later in Chapter 14, these changes led to a fall in the demand for less-skilled, less-educated, lower-paid workers. In Canada and the United States, the decline in demand for low-skilled workers led to a fall in their real wages throughout the 1980s; despite that, the unemployment rate for less-educated workers rose over the decade—from 7.2 percent to 8.5 percent in the United States, and from 6.3 percent to 9.3 percent in Canada. In the two European countries for which we have data on wages and unemployment by skill level, however, the real wages of low-paid workers *rose* over the decade, with the consequence that increases in unemployment for the less-educated were much more pronounced. In France, real wages among the lowest-paid workers rose 1 percent per year, and their unemployment rate increased from 4.6 percent to 10.7 percent over the decade. In Germany, where the pay of low-wage workers rose an average of 5 percent per year, unemployment rates among these workers went from 4.4 percent to 13.5 percent.[12]

---

[12]Earnings data for all four countries are for workers in the lowest decile (lowest 10%) of their country's earnings distribution. These data are found in Organisation for Economic Co-Operation and Development (OECD), *Employment Outlook: July 1993* (Paris: OECD, 1993), Table 5.3. Data on unemployment rates are from Federal Reserve Bank of Kansas City, *Reducing Unemployment: Current Issues and Policy Options* (Kansas City: Federal Reserve Bank of Kansas City, 1994), 25.

TABLE 2.4

Total and Long-Term Unemployment Rates, Selected European and North American Countries, 1979 and 1990

	Overall Unemployment Rate		Long-Term Unemployment Rate	
	1979	1990	1979	1990
Belgium	7.5%	8.7%	4.6%	6.1%
Canada	7.4	8.1	0.2	0.5
Denmark	6.2	9.5	2.2	3.2
France	6.0	8.9	1.8	3.4
Germany	2.9	4.9	0.8	2.3
Ireland	7.1	13.7	2.7	9.2
Italy	7.8	11.1	4.0	7.9
Netherlands	3.5	6.4	1.3	3.1
Norway	1.9	5.2	0.1	1.0
Spain	8.6	16.3	2.6	8.8
Sweden	1.7	1.5	0.1	0.1
United Kingdom	4.5	5.9	1.3	2.1
United States	5.8	5.5	0.2	0.3

SOURCE: OECD, *Employment Outlook: July 1993* (Paris: OECD, 1993), Tables 3.1, 3.2.

More general evidence that nonmarket forces are probably stronger in Europe than in North America can be seen in Table 2.4, from which three generalizations can be made. First, it can be observed that the *overall* unemployment rates both right before and right after the 1980s were not systematically different in Europe and North America; as of 1990, however, the rates of *long-term* unemployment (spells lasting a year or more) in Europe were higher than in North America. (The European exception is Sweden, which had its historically low rate of unemployment in 1990 but suffered a large increase thereafter.) Second, during the 1980s, overall unemployment rates generally *rose* much more in Europe than in Canada or the United States (the latter being the only country listed in the table besides Sweden in which overall unemployment fell). Third, long-term unemployment rates rose over the decade of the 1980s in every country listed except Sweden, but the increases were greater in Europe than in North America. Clearly, then, changes in the demand or supply of labor during the 1980s were accommodated more quickly—that is, with less unemployment, especially long-term—in North America than in Europe.

Can we conclude from the above analysis that nonmarket forces are generally stronger in Europe than in North America? Probably, and as we proceed with our exploration of the labor market in this text we will identify what some of the different nonmarket forces might be. A relatively low unemployment rate, however, is not an infallible indicator of weak nonmarket forces, especially when government is either directly hiring workers or subsidizing their hire by private employers. The former Soviet Union, for example, had almost no measured unemployment because the government owned virtually all productive resources and hired labor with little regard for market forces.[13] Indeed, Sweden's low rates of unemployment may at least partly have resulted from the fact that it devoted a higher percentage of its national income to the creation of public sector jobs than any country listed in Table 2.4: 0.76 percent of gross domestic product in Sweden as compared to 0.01 percent in the United States and 0.02 percent in Canada.[14] (By 1993, however, Sweden's overall unemployment rate had risen to 8.2 percent, which was still below the European average but in excess of the United States' rate of 6.8 percent. This rise has caused some to question the efficacy of Swedish labor market programs.[15])

REVIEW QUESTIONS

1. On page 46 it was mentioned that in the early 1970s Egypt experienced a dramatic outflow of construction workers, seeking higher wages in Saudi Arabia, at the same time that the demand for their services rose within Egypt. Graphically represent these two shifts of supply and demand, and then use the graph to predict the direction of change in wages and employment within Egypt's construction sector during that period.

2. Analyze the impact of the following changes on wages and employment in a given occupation:
   a. A decrease in the danger of the occupation.
   b. An increase in product demand.
   c. Increased wages in alternative occupations.

3. What would happen to the wages and employment levels of engineers if government expenditures on research and development programs were to fall? Show the effect graphically.

4. Suppose a particular labor market were in equilibrium. What could happen to cause the equilibrium wage to fall? If all money wages rose with inflation each year, how would this market adjust?

5. Assume that you have been hired by a company to do a salary survey of its arc welders, who the company suspects are overpaid. Given the company's expressed desire to maximize profits, what definition of "overpaid" would you apply in this situation and how would you identify whether arc welders were, in fact, overpaid?

6. How will a fall in the civilian unemployment rate affect the supply of recruits for the volunteer army? What will be the effect on military wages?

7. In the past few years, U.S. policymakers have been concerned with the quality of education at the high school level and

---

[13]The hiring of workers to perform tasks that are not in demand is said to create "hidden" (as opposed to "open") unemployment.

[14]OECD, *Employment Outlook: July 1993* (Paris: OECD, 1993), Table 2.B.1.

[15]Anders Forslund, "An Evaluation of the Swedish Active Labor Market Policy: New and Received Wisdom," Princeton University Industrial Relations Section, working paper no. 332, July 1994.

below. It is generally believed that both the *number* and the *quality* of teachers needs to increase. Various proposals for accomplishing this objective have been made, and two are outlined below:

a. In March 1990, a "college professor of the year" from Rice University proposed drafting recent college graduates to teach in the public schools for two years as a means of providing "really qualified inexpensive labor" to schools.

b. In 1990 the New York State Board of Regents proposed tougher licensing examinations for teachers, including examinations after licensure to ensure that teachers remain current. It is argued that tougher licensing "would improve significantly the quality of teachers and make it possible to attract and retain large numbers of able people."

Using the relevant concepts from positive and normative theory, comment on each proposal. Make sure your comments include an analysis of the labor market effects of each.

8. Suppose that the Consumer Product Safety Commission passes a regulation requiring an expensive safety device to be attached to all power lawnmowers. This device does not increase the efficiency with which the lawnmower operates. What, if anything, does this regulation do to the demand for labor of firms manufacturing power lawnmowers? Explain.

9. Suppose the Occupational Safety and Health Administration were to mandate that all punch presses be fitted with a very expensive device to prevent injuries to workers. This device does not improve the efficiency with which punch presses operate. What does this requirement do to the demand curve for labor? Explain.

10. Suppose we observe that employment levels in a certain region suddenly decline as a result of (*a*) a fall in the region's demand for labor, and (*b*) wages that are fixed in the short run. If the *new* labor demand curve remains unchanged for a long period and the region's labor supply curve does not shift, is it likely that employment in the region will recover? Explain.

SELECTED READINGS

Organisation for Economic Co-Operation and Development. *Employment Outlook*. Chapter 1, "Labour Market Trends and Prospects in the OECD Area," 1–31. Paris: OECD, July 1990.

President's Commission on an All-Volunteer Armed Force. *Report of the President's Commission on an All-Volunteer Armed Force*. Chapter 3, "Conscription Is a Tax," 23–33. Washington, D.C.: U.S. Government Printing Office, February 1970.

Rottenberg, Simon, "On Choice in Labor Markets." *Industrial and Labor Relations Review* 9, no. 2 (January 1956): 183–199. Robert J. Lampman. "On Choice in Labor Markets: Comment." *Industrial and Labor Relations Review* 9, no. 4 (July 1956): 636–641.

3

The Demand for Labor

The demand for labor is a derived demand, in that workers are hired for the contribution they can make towards producing some good or service for sale. However, the wages workers receive, the employee benefits they qualify for, and even their working conditions are all influenced, to one degree or another, by the government. There are minimum wage laws, pension regulations, restrictions on firing workers, safety requirements, immigration controls, and government-provided pension and unemployment benefits that are financed through employer payroll taxes. All these requirements and regulations have one thing in common: they increase employers' costs of hiring workers.

We explained in Chapter 2 that both the scale and the substitution effects accompanying a wage change suggest the demand curve for labor is a *downward-sloping function of the wage rate.* If this rather simple proposition is true, then policies that mandate increases in the costs of employing workers will have the undesirable side effect of reducing their employment opportunities. If the reduction is large enough, lost job opportunities actually could undo any help provided to workers by the regulations. Understanding the characteristics of labor demand curves, then, is absolutely crucial to anyone interested in public policy. To a great extent, how one feels about many labor market regulatory programs is a function of one's beliefs about labor demand curves!

This chapter and the next will address economic theory as it relates to the essential nature of labor demand curves. The current chapter will identify *assumptions* underlying the proposition that labor demand is a downward-sloping function of the wage rate. As we proceed, we will also analyze how changes in these assumptions affect the basic characteristics of the labor demand curve.

Chapter 4 will take the downward-sloping nature of labor demand curves as given, addressing instead just what it is that determines the *responsiveness* of employment to changes in wages. That is, Chapter 4 seeks to explain why, in the face of a given wage increase, declines in demand might be large in some cases and barely perceptible in others. We apply the concepts in both chapters to a variety of policy issues, including payroll taxes, payroll subsidies, and minimum wage laws.

Profit Maximization   ← Quiz

The fundamental assumption of labor demand theory is that firms—the employers of labor—seek to maximize profits (or, in the case of not-for-profit employers, some measure of services rendered, net of costs). In doing so, firms are assumed to continually ask, "Can we make changes that will improve profits?" Two things should be noted about this constant search for enhanced profits. First, a firm can make changes only in variables that are within its control. Because the price a firm can charge for its product and the prices it must pay for its inputs are largely determined by others (the "market"), profit-maximizing decisions by a firm mainly involve the question of *whether, and how, to increase or decrease output*.

Second, because the firm is assumed to constantly search for profit-improving possibilities, our theory must address considerations underlying the decisions about *small* ("marginal") changes that must be made almost daily. Really major decisions of whether to open a new plant or introduce a new product line, for example, are relatively rare; once having made them the employer must approach profit maximization incrementally through the trial-and-error process of small changes. We therefore need to understand the basis for these incremental decisions, paying particular attention to when an employer *stops* making changes in output levels or in its mix of inputs.

(With respect to the employment of inputs, it is important to recognize that analyzing marginal changes implies considering a small change in one input *while holding employment of other inputs constant*. Thus, when analyzing the effects of adjusting the labor input by one unit, for example, we will do so on the assumption that capital is held constant. Likewise, marginal changes in capital will be considered assuming the labor input is held constant.)

The criterion used by a profit-maximizing firm in incrementally deciding on its level of *output* is familiar to any student who has had introductory economics: the firm will want to expand its output by one unit if the added revenue from selling that unit is greater than the added cost of producing it. As long as the marginal revenue from an added unit of output exceeds its marginal cost, the profit-maximizing firm will continue to expand output. Likewise, the firm will want to contract output whenever the marginal cost of production exceeds marginal revenue. Profits are maximized (and the firm stops making changes) when the output level is such that marginal revenue equals marginal cost.

A firm can expand or contract output, of course, only by altering its use of *inputs*. In the most general sense, we will assume that a firm produces its output by combining two types of inputs, or *factors of production: labor and capital*. Thus, the rules stated above for deciding whether to marginally increase or reduce output have important corollaries with respect to the employment of labor and capital:

a. If the income generated by one more unit of an input exceeds the additional expense, then add a unit of that input;
b. If the income generated by one more unit of input is less than the additional expense, reduce employment of that input;
c. If the income generated by one more unit of input is equal to the additional expense, no further changes in that input are desirable.

Decision rules (a) through (c) state the profit-maximizing criterion in terms of *inputs* rather than output; as we will see, these rules are useful guides to deciding *how*—as well as *whether*—to marginally increase or decrease output. Let us define and examine the components of these decision rules more closely.

MARGINAL INCOME FROM AN ADDITIONAL UNIT OF INPUT

Employing one more unit of either labor or capital generates additional income for the firm because of the added output that is produced and sold. Similarly, reducing the employment of labor or capital reduces a firm's income flow because the output available for sale is reduced. Thus, the marginal income associated with a unit of input is the multiplication of two quantities: the change in physical output produced (called the input's *marginal product*) and the *marginal revenue* generated per unit of physical output. We will therefore call the marginal income produced by a unit of input the input's *marginal revenue product*. For example, if the presence of a tennis star increases attendance at a tournament by 20,000 spectators, and the organizers net $25 from each additional fan, the marginal income produced by this star is equal to her "marginal product" (20,000 fans) times the "marginal revenue" of $25 per fan. Thus, her "marginal revenue product" equals $500,000. (For an actual calculation of marginal revenue product in professional hockey, see Example 3.1 on page 70.)

MARGINAL PRODUCT   Formally, we will define the *marginal product of labor*, or MP_L, as the change in physical output (ΔQ) produced by a change in the units of labor (ΔL), holding capital constant:[1]

$$MP_L = \Delta Q / \Delta L \text{ (holding capital constant)} \tag{3.1}$$

Likewise, the marginal product of capital (MP_K) will be defined as the change in output associated with a one-unit change in the stock of capital (ΔK), holding labor constant:

$$MP_K = \Delta Q / \Delta K \text{ (holding labor constant)} \tag{3.2}$$

---

[1]The symbol Δ (the Greek letter delta) is used to signify "a change in."

MARGINAL REVENUE   The definitions in (3.1) and (3.2) reflect the fact that a firm can expand or contract its output only by increasing or decreasing its use of either labor or capital. The marginal revenue (*MR*) that is generated by an extra unit of output depends on the characteristics of the product market in which that output is sold. If the firm operates in a purely competitive product market, and therefore has many competitors and no control over product price, the marginal revenue per unit of output sold is equal to product price (*P*). If the firm has a differentiated product, and thus has some degree of monopoly power in its product market, extra units of output can be sold only if product price is reduced (because the firm faces the *market* demand curve for its particular product); students will recall from introductory economics that in this case marginal revenue is less than price (*MR* < *P*).[2]

MARGINAL REVENUE PRODUCT   Combining the definitions presented in this subsection, the firm's marginal revenue product of labor, or MRP_L, can be represented as

$$MRP_L = MP_L \cdot MR \text{ (in the general case), or as} \qquad (3.3a)$$

$$MRP_L = MP_L \cdot P \text{ (if the product market is competitive)} \qquad (3.3b)$$

Likewise, the firm's marginal revenue product of capital (MRP_K) can be represented as $MP_K \cdot MR$ in the general case, or as $MP_K \cdot P$ if the product market is competitive.

MARGINAL EXPENSE OF AN ADDED INPUT

Employing added units of either labor or capital, of course, will add to the firm's total costs. Likewise, reducing the units of labor or capital employed will reduce the firm's costs. If the firm competes with many other firms to hire its inputs, it has no control over the prices of these inputs and must therefore pay the market price. In this case, the marginal expense of an input is simply equal to its unit price. To avoid unnecessary complications at this point, we will regard the wage rate (*W*) as the unit cost of labor; that is, *W* will be assumed to be the expense of hiring one unit of labor for one time period (an hour, for example). The price of capital will be represented in our analyses as *C*, which we will define as the expense of renting a unit of capital for one time period. (The specific calculation of *C* need not concern us here, but clearly it depends on the purchase price of the capital asset, its expected useful life, the rate of interest on borrowed funds, and even special tax provisions regarding capital.)

---

[2]A competitive firm can sell added units of output at the market price because it is so small relative to the entire market that its output does not affect price. A monopolist, however, *is* the supply side of the product market, so to sell extra output it must lower price. Because it must lower price on *all* units of output, and not just on the extra units to be sold, the marginal revenue associated with an additional unit is below price.

If firms have some control over the wages they pay to their workers, they are said to hire labor under *monopsonistic* conditions. Later in this chapter we will discuss what can cause these conditions to exist and how monopsony power changes the labor market behavior of the firm. All that needs to be understood now is that the monopsonistic employer of labor does not simply pay the wage presented to it by the market (as in Chapter 2, Figure 2.13). Because it is the only employer in its labor market, if it wants to increase employment it must attract workers from other markets, not just from similar employers in the same labor market. We will thoroughly explain and explore the implications of monopsony later in this chapter; as we will see, when conditions in a firm's labor market are monopsonistic, the marginal expense associated with an added unit of labor (ME_L) is greater than W.

The Short-Run Demand for Labor When Both Product and Labor Markets Are Competitive

The simplest way to understand how the profit-maximizing behavior of firms generates a labor demand curve is to analyze the firm's behavior over a period of time so short that the firm cannot vary its stock of capital. This period is what we will call the "short run," and of course the time period involved will vary from firm to firm (an accounting service might be able to order and install a new computing system for the preparation of tax returns within three months, while it may take an oil refinery five years to install a new production process). What is simplifying about the short run is that, with capital fixed, a firm's choice of output level and its choice of employment level are two aspects of the very same decision. Put differently, in the short run the firm needs only to decide *whether* to alter its output level; *how* to increase or decrease output is not an issue, because only the employment of labor can be adjusted. (The implications for labor demand when capital can vary, and therefore when the firm's production technology can change, will be analyzed later when we discuss the demand for labor in the long run.)

A CRITICAL ASSUMPTION: DECLINING MP_L ← Quiz

We defined the marginal product of labor (MP_L) as the change in the (physical) output of a firm when it changes its employment of labor by one unit, holding capital constant. Since the firm can vary its employment of labor, we must consider how increasing or reducing labor will affect labor's marginal product. Consider Table 3.1, which illustrates a hypothetical car dealership whose sales personnel are all equally hardworking and persuasive. With no sales staff the dealership is assumed to sell zero cars, but with one salesperson it will sell 10 cars per month. Thus, the marginal product of the first salesperson hired is 10. If a second person is hired, total output is assumed to rise from 10 to 21, implying that the marginal product of a second salesperson is 11. If a third equally persuasive salesperson is hired, sales rise from 21 to 26 ($MP_L = 5$), while if a fourth is hired sales rise from 26 to 29 ($MP_L = 3$).

TABLE 3.1
The Marginal Product of Labor in a Hypothetical Car Dealership (capital held constant)

Number of Salespersons	Total Cars Sold	Marginal Product of Labor
0	0	
		10
1	10	
		11
2	21	
		5
3	26	
		3
4	29	

Table 3.1 assumes that adding an extra salesperson increases output (cars sold) in each case. As long as output *increases* as labor is added, labor's marginal product is *positive*. In our example, however, the marginal product of labor increased at first (from 10 to 11), but then fell (to 5 and eventually to 3). Why?

The initial rise in marginal product is *not* because the second salesperson is better than the first; we ruled out this possibility by our assumption that the salespeople were equally capable. Rather, the rise could be the result of cooperation between the two in generating promotional ideas or helping each other out in some way. Eventually, however, as more salespeople are hired, the marginal product of labor must fall. A fixed building (remember that capital is held constant) can contain only so many customers, and thus each additional increment of labor must eventually produce progressively smaller increments of output. This law of *diminishing marginal returns* is an empirical proposition that derives from the fact that as employment expands, each additional worker has a progressively smaller share of the capital stock to work with. For expository convenience, we shall assume that the marginal product of labor is always decreasing.[3]

FROM PROFIT MAXIMIZATION TO LABOR DEMAND

From the profit-maximizing decision rules discussed earlier, it is clear that the firm should keep increasing its employment of labor as long as labor's marginal revenue product exceeds its marginal expense. Conversely, it should keep reducing its employment of labor as long as the expense saved is greater than the income lost. *Profits are maximized, then, only when employment is such that any further one-unit change in labor would have a marginal revenue product equal to marginal expense:*

$$MRP_L = ME_L \qquad (3.4)$$

---

[3]We lose nothing by this assumption, because we show later in this section that a firm will never be operated at a point where its marginal product of labor is increasing.

Under our current assumptions of competitive product and labor markets, we can symbolically represent the profit-maximizing level of labor input as that level at which

$$MP_L \cdot P = W \tag{3.5}$$

Clearly, equation (3.5) is stated in terms of some *monetary* unit (dollars, for example).

Alternatively, however, we can divide both sides of equation (3.5) by product price, *P*, and state the profit-maximizing condition for hiring labor in terms of *physical quantities*:

$$MP_L = W/P \tag{3.6}$$

We defined MP_L as the change in physical output associated with a one-unit change in labor, so it is obvious that the left-hand side of equation (3.6) is in physical quantities. To understand that the right-hand side is also in physical quantities, note that the numerator (*W*) is the dollars per unit of labor and the denominator (*P*) is the dollars per unit of output. Thus, the ratio W/P has the dimension of physical units. For example, if a woman is paid $10 per hour and the output she produces sells for $2 per unit, from the firm's viewpoint she is paid five units of output per hour ($10 \div 2$). From the perspective of the firm these five units represent her "real wage."[4]

LABOR DEMAND IN TERMS OF REAL WAGES   The demand for labor can be analyzed in terms of either "real" or "money" wages. Which version of demand analysis is used is a matter of convenience only. In this and the following subsection we give examples of both.

Figure 3.1 shows a marginal product of labor schedule (MP_L) for a representative firm. In this figure the marginal product of labor is tabulated on the vertical axis and the number of units of labor employed on the horizontal axis. The negative slope of the schedule indicates that each additional unit of labor employed produces a progressively smaller (but still positive) increment in output. Because the real wage and the marginal product of labor are both measured in the same dimension (units of output), we can also plot the real wage on the vertical axis of Figure 3.1.

Given any real wage (by the market), the firm should thus employ labor to the point at which the marginal product of labor just equals the real wage (equation 3.6). In other words, *the firm's demand for labor in the short run is equivalent to the downward-sloping segment of its marginal product of labor schedule.*[5]

---

[4]Real wages from an employer's perspective represent its costs of hiring labor. Real wages can also be viewed from the *employee's* perspective, and of course employees are concerned about the purchasing power of their earnings. Thus, the term "real wages" is often used to indicate the purchasing power of an hour of work, in which case it is calculated as the nominal wage divided by some measure of product prices (usually the Consumer Price Index, as was done in Chapter 2, Table 2.2).

[5]One should add here, "provided that the firm's revenue exceeds its labor costs." Above some real wage level this may fail to occur, and the firm will go out of business (employment will drop to zero).

FIGURE 3.1

Demand for Labor in the Short Run (Real Wage)

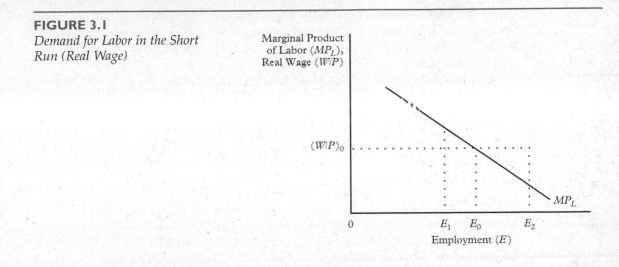

To see that this is true, pick any real wage—for example, the real wage denoted by $(W/P)_0$ in Figure 3.1. We have asserted that the firm's demand for labor is equal to its marginal product of labor schedule and consequently that the firm would employ E_0 employees. Now suppose that a firm initially employed E_2 workers as indicated in Figure 3.1, where E_2 is *any* employment level greater than E_0. At the employment level E_2, the marginal product of labor is less than the real wage rate; the marginal real cost of the last unit of labor hired is therefore greater than its marginal product. As a result, profit could be increased by reducing the level of employment. Similarly, suppose instead that a firm initially employed E_1 employees, where E_1 is *any* employment level less than E_0. Given the specified real wage $(W/P)_0$, the marginal product of labor is greater than the real wage rate at E_1—and consequently the marginal additions to output of an extra unit of labor exceed its marginal real cost. As a result, a firm could increase its profit level by expanding its level of employment.

Hence, to maximize profits, given any real wage rate, a firm should stop employing labor at the point at which any additional labor would cost more than it would produce. This profit-maximization rule implies two things. First, the firm should employ labor up to the point at which its real wage equals the marginal product of labor—but not beyond that point. Second, its profit-maximizing level of employment lies in the range where its marginal product of labor is *declining*. (If $W/P = MP_L$ but MP_L is *increasing*, then adding another unit of labor will create a situation in which marginal product *exceeds* W/P. As long as adding labor causes MP_L to exceed W/P, the profit-maximizing firm will continue to hire labor. It will stop hiring only when an extra unit of labor would reduce MP_L below W/P, which will happen only when MP_L is declining. Thus, the only employment levels that could possibly be consistent with profit maximization are those in the range where MP_L is decreasing.)

LABOR DEMAND IN TERMS OF MONEY WAGES   As shown above, one can conceptualize the demand for labor as a downward-sloping function of the real wage. In some circumstances, however, labor demand curves are more readily conceptualized as downward-sloping functions of money wages. To make the analysis as concrete as possible, in this subsection we analyze the demand for department store detectives.

At a business conference one day, a department store executive boasted that his store had reduced theft to 1 percent of total sales. A colleague shook her head and said, "I think that's too low. I figure it should be about 2 percent of sales." How can more shoplifting be better than less? The answer is based on the fact that reducing theft is costly in itself. A profit-maximizing firm will not want to take steps to reduce shoplifting if the added costs it must bear in so doing exceed the value of the savings it generates.

Table 3.2 shows a hypothetical marginal revenue product of labor (MRP_L) schedule for department store detectives. Hiring one detective would, in this example, save $50 worth of thefts per hour. Two detectives could save $90 worth of thefts each hour, or $40 more than hiring just one. The MRP_L of hiring a second detective is thus $40. A third detective would add $20 more to thefts prevented, and thus add $20 more to revenues.

The MRP_L does *not* decline from $40 to $20 because the added detectives are incompetent; in fact, we shall assume that all are equally alert and well trained. MRP_L declines, in part, because surveillance equipment (capital) is fixed; with each added detective, there is less equipment per person. However, the MRP_L also declines because it becomes progressively harder to generate savings. With just a few detectives, the only thieves caught will be the more obvious, less experienced shoplifters. As more detectives are hired, it becomes possible to prevent theft by the more expert shoplifters, but they are harder to detect and fewer in number. Thus, MRP_L falls because theft prevention becomes more difficult once all those who are easy to catch are apprehended.

To draw the demand curve for labor, we need to determine how many detectives the store will want to employ at a given wage. For example, at a wage of $50

TABLE 3.2

Hypothetical Schedule of Marginal Revenue Productivity of Labor for Store Detectives

Number of Detectives on Duty During Each Hour Store Is Open	Total Value of Thefts Prevented per Hour	Marginal Value of Thefts Prevented per Hour (MRP_L)
0	$ 0	$—
1	50	50
2	90	40
3	110	20
4	115	5
5	117	2

FIGURE 3.2

Demand for Labor in the Short Run (Money Wage)

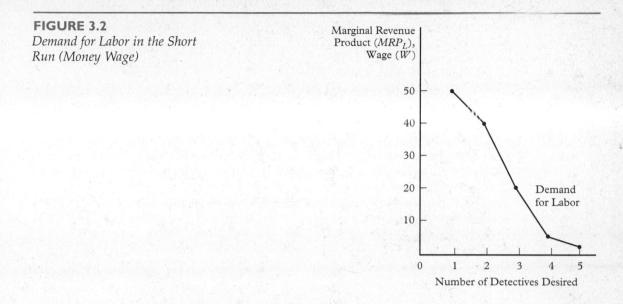

per hour, how many detectives will the store want? Using the $MRP_L = W$ criterion (equation 3.5), it is easy to see that the answer is "one." At $40 per hour, the store would want to hire two, and at $20 per hour the number demanded would be three. The labor demand curve that summarizes the store's profit-maximizing employment of detectives is shown in Figure 3.2.

Figure 3.2 illustrates a fundamental point: the labor demand curve in the short run slopes downward because it *is* the MRP_L curve—and the MRP_L curve slopes downward because of labor's diminishing marginal product. The demand curve and the MRP_L curve coincide, as demonstrated by the fact that if one were to graph the MRP_L schedule in Table 3.2, one would arrive at exactly the same curve as in our graph. When one detective is hired, MRP_L is $50; when two are hired, MRP_L is $40; and so forth. Since <u>MRP_L always equals W for a profit maximizer who takes wages as given</u>, the MRP_L and labor demand curve (expressed as a function of the money wage) must be the same.

(Another point to be made in this example is that there is some level of shoplifting that the store finds more profitable to tolerate than to eliminate. At high wages for store detectives, this level will be higher than at lower wages. To say the theft rate is too low thus implies that the marginal costs of crime reduction exceed the marginal savings generated, and the firm is therefore failing to maximize profits.)

Finally, it is important to emphasize that the marginal product of an individual is *not* a function solely of his or her personal characteristics. As emphasized above, the marginal product of a worker depends upon the number of similar employees the firm has already hired. An individual's marginal product also depends upon the size of the firm's capital stock; increases in the firm's capital stock shift the entire marginal product of labor schedule up. It is therefore incorrect to speak of an individual's productivity as an immutable factor that is associated

EXAMPLE 3.1

Professional Hockey: One Player's Marginal Revenue Productivity

The conditions for hiring labor summarized in the text as equations (3.4) and (3.5) presume that employers are aware of the marginal revenue product (MRP_L) of workers they hire. This awareness is most often implicit, in the sense that employers indirectly find out about the wisdom of their hiring decisions by observing profit levels. Sometimes, however, it is possible to calculate a worker's MRP_L with reasonable precision, as illustrated by an example from professional hockey.

In August 1988, the Los Angeles Kings of the National Hockey League purchased the contract of Wayne Gretzky, then widely thought to be professional hockey's biggest star, from the Edmonton Oilers. The purchase was possible because the Kings, among hockey's worst teams at the time, anticipated that Gretzky's MRP_L would be higher with them than with the Oilers, which had been hockey's best team over the preceding five years.

The Kings paid the Oilers $15 million (plus first-round draft picks in 1989, 1991, and 1993) to obtain Gretzky's contract. The contract was then renegotiated to pay him about $2 million per year for an undisclosed period of time (probably six years).

What was the annual cost of this transaction to the Kings? Amortizing the $15-million payment over six years yields an annual cost of $2.5 million. To this must be added the interest income that could be earned on the $15 million had it not been invested in Gretzky's contract; at 10 percent, this came to $1.5 million for the first year. Adding in Gretzky's yearly pay of $2 million, it is clear that for the Kings to profit from this transaction, Gretzky's yearly MRP_L with them had to exceed $6 million. Did it?

According to the Kings' owner, "We tried to do dozens of case projections before the deal happened, but it was so impossible to predict."* Given the uncertainties and the money at stake, Gretzky's first year with the Kings was a gratifying one for them. Immediately after Gretzky signed, a Los Angeles cable television company announced it would carry 60 of the Kings' 80 games instead of the 37 it had carried the season before. Into the season, the team found that home attendance and average ticket prices had increased by enough to double its "gate" revenues (which are kept entirely by the home team). In addition, advertising and merchandising income increased, with the overall result that Gretzky's financial effect on the team was estimated to be about $200,000 per game. Over the 40 home games, this effect implied that his marginal revenue productivity for the year was around $8 million!

(In early 1996, Gretzky and his by-then $6.5-million salary were traded by the Kings to St. Louis, who hoped that his presence would improve disappointing attendance levels.)

*Larry Wigge, "Shaking Out Gretzky Deal," *The Sporting News*, February 6, 1989, 4. The information for this example was taken from this article, from one in the *New York Times* of September 2, 1988, sec. I, p. 24, and from Paul D. Staudohar, *The Sports Industry and Collective Bargaining*, 2d ed. (Ithaca, N.Y.: ILR Press, 1989), 142.

only with his or her characteristics, independent of the characteristics of the other inputs he or she has to work with. For an illustration of how the MRP_L of the same person can vary with circumstances, and of how one employer approached hiring in the context of profit maximization, see Example 3.1.

MARKET DEMAND CURVES The demand curve (or schedule) for an individual firm indicates how much labor that firm will want to employ at each wage level. A *market demand curve* (or schedule) is just the *summation* of the labor demanded by all firms in a particular labor market at each level of the *real* wage.[6] If there are three firms in a certain labor market, and if at a *given* real wage firm A wants 12 workers, firm B wants 6, and firm C wants 20, then the market demand at that real wage is 38 employees. More important, because market demand curves are so closely derived from firm demand curves, they too will *slope downward* as a function of the real wage. When the real wage falls, the number of workers that existing firms want to employ increases. In addition, the lower real wage may make it profitable for new firms to enter the market. Conversely, when the real wage increases, the number of workers that existing firms want to employ decreases, and some firms may be forced to cease operations completely.

OBJECTIONS TO THE MARGINAL PRODUCTIVITY THEORY OF DEMAND Two kinds of objections are sometimes raised to the theory of labor demand introduced in this section. The first is that almost no employer can ever be heard uttering the words "marginal revenue product of labor," and that the theory assumes a degree of sophistication on the part of employers that is just not there. Employers, it is argued, are both unfamiliar with the textbook "rules" of profit maximization (as stated in equation 3.4, for example) and unable in many situations to accurately measure or value the output of individual units of labor. This objection can be answered as follows: Whether employers can verbalize the profit-maximizing conditions, or whether they can explicitly measure the marginal revenue product of labor, they must at least *intuit* them to survive in a competitive environment. Competition will "weed out" employers who are not good at generating profits, just as competition will weed out pool players who do not understand the intricacies of how speed, angles, and spin affect the motion of bodies through space. Yet one could canvass the pool halls of America and probably not find one player who could verbalize Newton's laws of motion! The point is that employers can *know* concepts without being able to verbalize them. Those that are not good at maximizing profits will not last very long in competitive markets. Conversely, those that survive, whether they can verbalize the general concepts or not, *do* know how to maximize profits.

The second objection to the marginal productivity theory of demand is that in many cases it seems that adding labor while holding capital constant would not add to output at all. For example, one secretary and one word-processing machine

---

[6]If firms' demand curves are drawn as a function of the money wage, they represent (as we noted) the downward-sloping portion of the firms' marginal revenue product of labor curves. In a competitive industry, the price of the product is "given" to the firm, and thus at the firm level the marginal revenue product of labor has imbedded in it a given product price. When aggregating labor demand to the *market* level, product price can no longer be taken as given, and the aggregation is no longer a simple summation. However, the market demand curves drawn against money wages, like those drawn as a function of real wages, slope downward—which at this point is all that is important.

can produce output, but it might seem that adding a second secretary while holding the number of word processors constant could produce nothing extra, since that secretary would have no machine on which to work. The answer to this objection is that the second secretary could address envelopes by hand—a slower process, but one that would free the secretary at the word-processing machine to type more letters per day. The two secretaries could trade off using the word-processing machine, so that neither became fatigued to the extent that mistakes increased and typing speeds slowed down. The second secretary could also answer the telephone and in other ways expedite work. Thus, even with technologies that seem to require one machine per person, labor will generally have a marginal product greater than zero if capital is held constant.

The Demand for Labor in Competitive Markets When Other Inputs Can Be Varied

An implication of our theory of labor demand is that, because labor can be varied in the short run, the profit-maximizing firm will always operate so that labor's marginal revenue product equals the wage rate (which is labor's marginal expense in a competitive labor market). Put differently, a firm seeking to maximize profits will *always* be able to satisfy the equalities in equations (3.5) and (3.6); being able to satisfy them in the short run clearly implies being able to satisfy them in the long run! We defined the short run, however, as a period during which *only* the labor input could be adjusted. What we must now consider is how the firm's ability to adjust *other* inputs affects the demand for labor. We first analyze the implications of being able to adjust capital in the long run, and we then turn our attention to the case of more than two inputs.

LABOR DEMAND IN THE LONG RUN

To maximize profits in the long run, the firm must adjust both labor and capital so that the marginal revenue product of each equals its marginal expense. Using the definitions discussed earlier in this chapter, profit maximization requires that the following two equalities be satisfied:

$$MP_L \cdot P = W \text{ (a restatement of equation 3.5)} \tag{3.7a}$$

$$MP_K \cdot P = C \text{ (the profit-maximizing condition for capital)} \tag{3.7b}$$

Both (3.7a) and (3.7b) can be rearranged to isolate P, so these two profit-maximizing conditions also can be expressed as

$$P = W/MP_L \text{ (a rearrangement of equation 3.7a)} \tag{3.8a}$$

$$P = C/MP_K \text{ (a rearrangement of equation 3.7b)} \qquad (3.8b)$$

Further, because the right-hand sides of both (3.8a) and (3.8b) equal the same quantity, P, profit maximization therefore requires that

$$W/MP_L = C/MP_K \qquad (3.8c)$$

The economic meaning of equation (3.8c) is key to understanding how the ability to adjust capital affects the firm's demand for labor. Consider the left-hand side of (3.8c): the numerator is the cost of a unit of labor, while the denominator is the extra output produced by an added unit of labor. Therefore, the ratio W/MP_L turns out to be the added cost of producing an added unit of output using labor.[7] Analogously, the right-hand side is the marginal cost of producing an extra unit of output using capital. What equation (3.8c) suggests is that, to maximize profits, *the firm must adjust its labor and capital inputs so that the marginal cost of producing an added unit of output using labor is equal to the marginal cost of producing an added unit of output using capital.* Why is this italicized condition a requirement for maximizing profits?

It is self-evident that to maximize profits a firm must be producing its chosen level of output in the least-cost manner. Logic suggests that as long as the firm can expand output more cheaply using one input than the other, it cannot be producing in the least-cost way. For example, if the marginal cost of expanding output by one unit using labor were $10, and the marginal cost using capital were $12, the firm could keep output constant and lower its costs of production! How? It could reduce its capital by enough to cut output by one unit (saving $12), and then add enough labor to restore the one-unit cut (costing $10). Output would be the same, but costs would have fallen by $2. Thus, for the firm to be maximizing profits, it must be operating at the point such that further marginal changes in both labor and capital would neither lower costs nor otherwise add to profits.

With equations (3.8a) to (3.8c) in mind, what would happen to the demand for labor in the long run if the wage rate (W) facing a profit-maximizing firm were to rise? First, as we discussed in the section on the short-run demand for labor, the rise in W disturbs the equality in (3.8a), and the firm will want to cut back on its use of labor even before it can adjust capital. Because the marginal product of labor is assumed to rise as employment is reduced, any cuts in labor will raise MP_L. Second, because each unit of capital now has less labor working with it, the marginal product of capital (MP_K) falls, disturbing the equality in (3.8b). By itself, this latter inequality will cause the firm to want to reduce its stock of capital.

Third, the rise in W will initially end the equality in (3.8c), meaning that the marginal cost of producing using labor now exceeds the marginal cost using

---

[7]Because $MP_L = \Delta Q/\Delta L$, the expression W/MP_L can be rewritten as $W \cdot \Delta L/\Delta Q$. Since $W\Delta L$ represents the added cost from employing one more unit of labor, the expression $W\Delta L/\Delta Q$ equals the cost of an added unit of output when that unit is produced by added labor.

capital. If the above cuts in labor are made in the short run, the associated increase in MP_L and decrease in MP_K will work toward restoring equality in (3.8c); however, if it remains more costly to produce an extra unit of output using labor than using capital, the firm will want to substitute capital for labor in the long run. Substituting capital for labor means that the firm will produce its profit-maximizing level of output (which is clearly reduced by the rise in W) in a more capital-intensive way. The act of substituting capital for labor also will serve to increase MP_L and reduce MP_K, thereby reinforcing the return to equality in (3.8c).

In the end, the increase in W will cause the firm to reduce its desired employment level for two reasons. The firm's profit-maximizing level of output will fall, and the associated reduction in required inputs (both capital and labor) is an example of the "scale effect." The rise in W also causes the firm to substitute capital for labor, so that it can again produce in the least-cost manner; changing the mix of capital and labor in the production process is an example of the "substitution effect." The scale and substitution effects of a wage increase will have an ambiguous effect on the firm's desired stock of *capital*, but both effects serve to reduce the demand for *labor*. (See Example 3.2 on page 82 for evidence that even those pushing for wage increases recognize the existence of both scale and substitution effects on the demand for labor.) Thus, the long-run ability to adjust capital lends further theoretical support to the proposition that the labor demand curve is a downward-sloping function of the wage rate.

MORE THAN TWO INPUTS

Thus far we have assumed that there are only two inputs in the production process: capital and labor. In fact, labor can be subdivided into many categories; for example, labor can be categorized by age, ethnicity, gender, race, educational level, and occupation. Other inputs that are used in the production process include materials and energy. If a firm is seeking to minimize costs, in the long run it should employ all inputs up until the point that the marginal cost of producing an added unit of output is the same regardless of which input is used. This generalization of equation (3.8c) leads to the somewhat obvious result that the demand for *any* category of labor will be a function of its own wage rate *and* (through the scale and substitution effects) the wage or prices of all other categories of labor, capital, and supplies.

The demand curve for each category of labor will be a downward-sloping function of the wage rate paid to workers in that category, for the reasons discussed earlier. If two inputs are *substitutes in production* (that is, if the greater use of one in producing output can compensate for reduced use of the other), then increases in the price of the *other* input may shift the entire demand curve for a *given* category of labor either to the right or to the left, depending on the relative strength of the substitution and scale effects. If an increase in the price of one input shifts the demand for *another* input to the left, as in panel (a) of Figure 3.3, the scale effect has dominated the substitution effect and the two inputs are *gross complements*; if it shifts the demand for the other input to the right, as in panel (b) of Figure 3.3, the substitution effect has dominated and the two inputs are *gross substitutes*.

FIGURE 3.3
Effect of Increase in the Price of One Input (k) on Demand for Another Input (j), Where Inputs Are Substitutes in Production

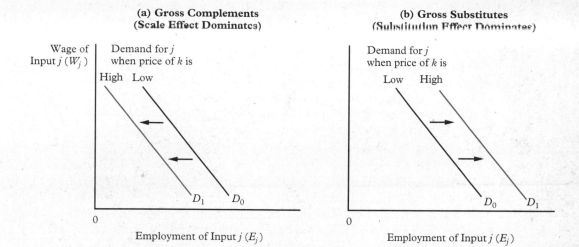

If, instead, the two inputs are *complements in production*, which means they must be used together, then reduced use of one implies reduced use of the other. In this case, there is no substitution effect, only a scale effect, and the two inputs must be gross complements.

Consider an example of a snow-removal firm in which skilled and unskilled workers are substitutes in production—snow can be removed using either unskilled workers (with shovels) or skilled workers driving snowplows. Let us focus on demand for the skilled workers. Other things equal, an increase in the wage of skilled workers would cause the firm to employ fewer of them; their demand curve would be a downward-sloping function of their wage. If only the wage of *unskilled* workers increased, however, the employer would want fewer unskilled workers than before, and more of the now relatively cheaper skilled workers, to remove any given amount of snow. To the extent that this substitution effect dominated over the scale effect (the higher unskilled wage leads to reduced output), the demand for skilled workers would shift to the right. In this case, skilled and unskilled workers would be gross substitutes. In contrast, if the reduction in the scale of output caused employment of skilled workers to be reduced, on balance, even though skilled workers were being substituted for unskilled workers in the production process, skilled and unskilled workers would be considered gross complements.[8]

In the above firm, snowplows and skilled workers are complements in production. If the price of snowplows went up, the employer would want to cut back on

---

[8]This example highlights that *both* the production process *and* product demand conditions determine whether two inputs are gross substitutes or gross complements. We return to this issue in Chapter 4.

their usage, which would result in a reduced demand at each wage for the skilled workers who drove the snowplows. As noted above, inputs that are complements in production are always gross complements.[9]

Labor Demand When the Product Market Is Not Competitive

Our analysis of the demand for labor, in both the short and the long run, has so far taken place under the assumption that the firm operates in competitive product and labor markets. This is equivalent to assuming that the firm is both a price taker and a wage taker; that is, that it takes both P and W as given and makes decisions only about the levels of output and inputs. We complete our theoretical analysis of labor demand by exploring the effects of noncompetitive markets. In this section we assume that the product market is monopolistic; in the next, we assume that the labor market is monopsonistic.

We have assumed so far that firms take product prices as given. If a firm faced a downward-sloping demand curve for its output—so that as it expanded employment and output, its product price fell—then the marginal revenue (MR) it received from the last unit of output it produced would not be the product price (P). Rather, as noted in footnote 2, the marginal revenue would be less than the product price because the lower price is applied to all units it sold, not just the marginal unit.

A monopoly trying to maximize profits and facing a competitive *labor* market will hire workers until its marginal revenue product of labor (MRP_L) equals the wage rate:

$$MRP_L = (MR) \cdot (MP_L) = W \tag{3.9}$$

Now one can express the demand for labor in the short run in terms of the real wage by dividing equation (3.9) by the firm's product price, P, to obtain

$$\frac{MR}{P} \cdot MP_L = \frac{W}{P} \tag{3.10}$$

Since marginal revenue is always less than a monopoly's product price, the ratio (MR/P) in equation (3.10) is less than 1. Therefore the labor demand curve for a firm that has monopoly power in the output market will lie below and to the left of the labor demand curve for an *otherwise identical* firm that takes product price as given. Put another way, just as output is lower under monopoly than it is under competition, other things equal, so is the level of employment.

---

[9]This statement assumes that all inputs are *noninferior* inputs—i.e., that an increase in output does not reduce the usage of any input. We maintain this assumption throughout.

The *wage* rates that monopolies pay, however, are not necessarily different from competitive levels even though *employment* levels are. An employer with a product market monopoly may still be a very small part of the market for a particular kind of employee, and thus be a *price taker* in the labor market. For example, a local utility company might have a product market monopoly, but it would have to compete with all other firms to hire secretaries and thus would have to pay the going wage.

There are circumstances, however, in which economists suspect that product market monopolies might pay wages that are *higher* than competitive firms would pay.[10] The monopolies that are legally permitted to exist in the United States are regulated by governmental bodies in an effort to prevent them from exploiting their favored status and earning monopoly profits. This regulation of profits, it can be argued, gives monopolies incentives to pay higher wages than they would otherwise pay for two reasons.

First, regulatory bodies allow monopolies to pass the costs of doing business on to consumers. Thus, while unable to maximize profits, the managers of a monopoly can enhance their *utility* by paying high wages and passing the costs along to consumers in the form of higher prices. The ability to pay high wages makes a manager's life more pleasant by making it possible to hire people who might be more attractive or personable or have other characteristics managers find desirable.

Second, monopolies that are as yet unregulated may not want to attract attention to themselves by earning the very high profits usually associated with monopoly. Therefore they, too, may be induced to pay high wages in a partial effort to "hide" their profits. The excess profits of monopolies, in other words, may be partly taken in the form of highly preferred workers—paid a relatively high wage rate—rather than in the usual monetary form.

The evidence on monopoly wages, however, is not very clear as yet. Some studies suggest that firms in industries with relatively few sellers *do* pay higher wages than competitive firms for workers with the same education and experience. Other studies of regulated monopolies, however, have obtained mixed results on whether wages tend to be higher for comparable workers in these industries.[11]

---

[10]For a full statement of this argument, see Armen Alchian and Reuben Kessel, "Competition, Monopoly, and the Pursuit of Money," in *Aspects of Labor Economics,* ed. H. G. Lewis (Princeton, N.J.: Princeton University Press, 1962).

[11]James Long and Albert Link, "The Impact of Market Structure on Wages, Fringe Benefits and Turnover," *Industrial and Labor Relations Review* 36 (January 1983): 239–250; John S. Heywood, "Labor Quality and the Concentration-Earnings Hypothesis," *Review of Economics and Statistics* 68 (May 1986): 342–346; Ronald Ehrenberg, *The Regulatory Process and Labor Earnings* (New York: Academic Press, 1979); Barry Hirsch, "Trucking Regulation, Unionization, and Labor Earnings," *Journal of Human Resources* 23 (Summer 1988): 296–319; Jari Vainiomaki and Sushil Wadhwani, "The Effects of Changes in a Firm's Product Market Power on Wages," discussion paper no. 18, Centre for Economic Performance, London School of Economics and Political Science, February 1991; and S. Nickell, J. Vainiomaki, and S. Wadhwani, "Wages, Unions, Insiders, and Product Market Power," discussion paper no. 77, Centre for Economic Performance, London School of Economics and Political Science, May 1992.

Monopsony in the Labor Market

When only one firm is the buyer of labor in a particular labor market, such a firm is called a *monopsonist*. Because the firm is the only demander of labor in this market, it can influence the wage rate. Rather than being a *wage taker* and facing the horizontal labor supply curve that competitive firms are confronted with, monopsonists face an upward-sloping labor supply curve. The supply curve confronting them, in other words, is the *market* supply curve. To expand its workforce, a monopsonist must increase its wage rate to attract workers from other labor markets. (In contrast, a competitive firm can expand its workforce while paying the prevailing market wage, because there are many employers with similar jobs from which workers can be attracted.)

PROFIT MAXIMIZATION

The unusual aspect of a firm's being confronted with an upward-sloping labor supply curve is that the *marginal expense of hiring labor exceeds the wage*. If a competitive firm wants to hire 10 workers instead of 9, the hourly cost of the additional worker is equal to the wage rate. If a monopsonist hires 10 instead of 9, it must pay a higher wage to all workers *in addition to* paying the bill for the added worker. For example, suppose that a monopsonist could get 9 workers if it paid $7 per hour but that if it wished to hire 10 workers it would have to pay a wage of $7.50. The labor cost associated with 9 workers would be $63 per hour (9 times $7), but the labor cost associated with 10 workers would be $75 per hour (10 times $7.50). Hiring the additional worker would cost $12 per hour—far more than the $7.50 wage rate![12]

The fact that the marginal expense of hiring labor is above the wage rate affects the labor market behavior of monopsonists. To maximize profits, we know that any firm should hire labor until the point at which the marginal revenue product of labor (MRP_L) equals labor's marginal expense. Hence, the monopsonist should hire workers up to the point at which MRP_L equals the marginal expense of hiring additional workers (ME_L):

$$MRP_L = ME_L \qquad (3.11)$$

The profit-maximizing level of employment for a monopsonist is shown in Figure 3.4. The firm has a conventional MRP_L curve, but its labor supply curve is upward-sloping. As usual, this supply curve depicts that amount of labor available to the firm at each wage rate. What is different about monopsony is that the *marginal expense of hiring labor exceeds the wage*; hence, the (dashed) ME_L curve lies

---

[12]We assume here that the monopsonist does not know which workers it can hire for $7 per hour and which workers could only be hired at $7.50. All it knows is that if it wants to hire 10 workers it must pay $7.50, while if it wants to hire 9 it can pay only $7. Therefore, all workers get paid the same wage.

FIGURE 3.4

The Effects of Monopsony

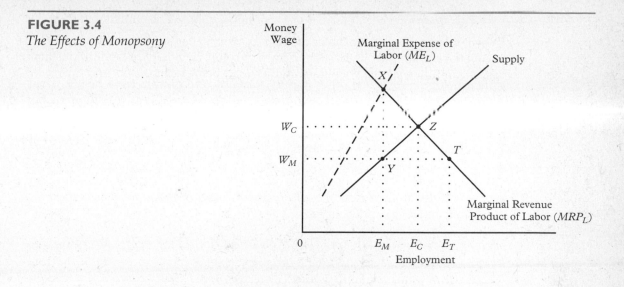

above the labor supply curve. With the marginal expense of hiring labor along the dashed curve, the firm's profit-maximizing level of employment is found at the point where the ME_L and MRP_L curves intersect (at point X). Thus, the monopsonist will want to hire E_M workers. The wage rate necessary to attract E_M workers to the firm—which can be read off the supply curve—is W_M (see point Y). Thus for a profit-maximizing monopsonist, MRP_L is *above*, not equal to, the wage rate.

If the market depicted in Figure 3.4 were competitive, each firm in the market would hire labor until labor's marginal revenue product equaled the wage, and the marginal revenue product schedule would be the demand curve for labor. Thus, the wage rate would be W_C and the employment level would be E_C. Note that in a labor market that is monopsonized, wages and employment levels are *below* W_C and E_C.

Examples of pure monopsony in the labor market are difficult to cite. Isolated coal-mining towns or sugar plantations, where the mines or sugar companies are literally the only employers, are increasingly rare. Some economists argue that the market for registered nurses, particularly in small towns, is partially monopsonized. Hospitals employ the majority of registered nurses, and in many small towns there is only one hospital. These hospitals, it is argued, behave like monopsonists and pay lower wages than they otherwise would.[13] Another market that

---

[13]For a recent study of monopsony in coal mining, see William M. Boal, "Testing for Employer Monopsony in Turn-of-the-Century Coal Mining," *RAND Journal of Economics* 26, no. 3 (August 1995): 519–536. For studies of monopsony in the market for nurses, see James Robinson, "Market Structure, Employment and Skill Mix in the Hospital Industry," *Southern Economic Journal* 52, no. 2 (April 1988): 315–325, and Daniel Sullivan, "Monopsony Power in the Market for Nurses," *Journal of Law and Economics* 32, no. 2, pt. 2 (October 1989): S135–S178.

may be monopsonized is the market for public school teachers outside metropolitan areas.[14]

While examples of a single buyer of labor services may be difficult to cite, the monopsony model still offers useful insights if the labor supply curves to firms are upward-sloping for some other reason. Recently, economists have begun to explore a variety of labor market conditions that would yield upward-sloping labor supply curves to individual firms even when there are many employers competing for workers in the same labor market. We will examine these conditions and the economic models based on them when analyzing mobility (Chapter 10) and issues of hiring and motivating employees (Chapter 11). For now, we simply note that monopsonistic behavior can arise in competitive labor markets; therefore, we must carefully analyze how the employment levels of monopsonists respond to shifts in their labor supply curves.

HOW DO MONOPSONISTS RESPOND TO SUPPLY SHIFTS AND MANDATED WAGE INCREASES?

The central theme of this chapter is that, with competitive labor markets (that is, each firm is a wage taker) the demand curve for labor is downward-sloping. Thus, if market labor supply curves shift to the left, or if wages are mandated to rise above their market-clearing levels, employment will decline as wages rise. We now inquire whether, under monopsonistic conditions (that is, with upward-sloping labor supply curves to firms), similar employment declines will accompany leftward shifts in labor supply curves or the imposition of above-market wages.

We must begin our inquiry by emphasizing that, with monopsony, the firm does not have a labor demand curve! Labor demand curves for a firm are essentially derived from sequentially asking (as we pointed out in Chapter 2), "If the market wage were at some level ($5, say), what would be the firm's profit-maximizing level of employment? If, instead, the wage were $6, what would be the firm's desired level of employment? What if the wage were $7 or $8?" With monopsony, the firm is not a wage taker, so asking hypothetical questions about the level of wages facing the firm is meaningless. Given the firm's labor supply curve and its schedule of marginal revenue product (MRP_L at various levels of employment), there is only one profit-maximizing level of employment and only one associated wage rate, both of which are chosen by the firm.

SHIFTS IN LABOR SUPPLY THAT INCREASE ME_L   First let us consider the short-run and long-run effects on a monopsonistic firm's desired level of employment if the supply curve facing the firm shifts (but remains upward-sloping). Suppose, for example, that the labor supply curve were to shift to the left, reflecting a situation in which fewer people are willing to work at any given wage

---

[14]Ronald Ehrenberg and Joshua Schwarz, "Public Sector Labor Markets," in *Handbook of Labor Economics,* ed. Orley Ashenfelter and Richard Layard (Amsterdam: North-Holland, 1987), summarize the evidence on this point.

FIGURE 3.5

The Monopsonist's Short-Run Response to a Leftward Shift in Labor Supply: Employment Falls and Wage Increases

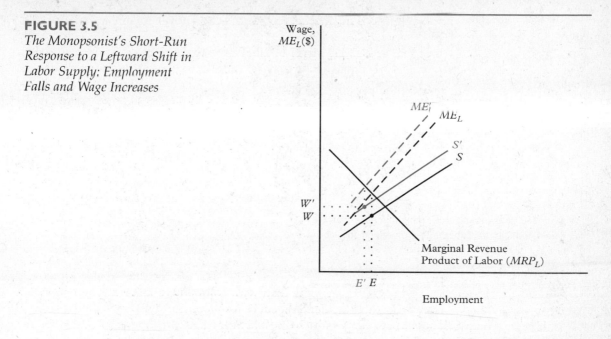

level. With the competitive model of labor demand, a leftward shift of a market supply curve would cause the market wage to increase and the level of employment to fall, as employers moved to the left along their labor demand curves (refer back to Chapter 2, Figure 2.15). Will these changes in wages and employment occur with monopsony?

Consider Figure 3.5, in which the MRP_L curve is fixed (we are in the short run) and the leftward shift of the labor supply curve is represented by a movement to curve S' from the original curve, S. With a supply curve of S, the firm's marginal expense of labor curve was ME_L, and it chose to hire E workers and pay them a wage of W. When the supply curve shifts to S', the firm's marginal labor costs shift to a higher curve, ME'_L. Therefore, its new profit-maximizing level of employment falls to E', and its new wage rate increases to W'. Thus, with monopsony just as with the competitive model, a leftward shift in labor supply increases ME_L, raises wages, and reduces firms' desired levels of employment in the short run.

In the long run, labor's increased marginal expense will induce the substitution of capital for labor as firms seek to find the cost-minimizing mix of capital and labor. The student will recall that the cost-minimizing conditions for capital and labor under *competitive* conditions were given in equation (3.8c), in which the wage rate was treated as the marginal expense of labor. In a noncompetitive labor market, ME_L exceeds W, so the left-hand side of equation (3.8c) must be written in its general form:

$$ME_L/MP_L = C/MP_K \qquad (3.12)$$

EXAMPLE 3.2

Coal Mining

That wage increases have both a *scale effect* and a *factor substitution effect*, both of which tend to reduce employment, is widely known—even by many of those pushing for higher wages. John L. Lewis was president of the United Mine Workers during the 1920s, 1930s, and 1940s, when wages for miners were increased considerably with full knowledge that this would induce the substitution of capital for labor. Lewis explained:

> Primarily the United Mine Workers of America insists upon the maintenance of wage standards guaranteed by the existing contractual relations in the industry, in the interests of its own membership. . . . But in insisting on the maintenance of an American wage standard in the coal fields the United Mine Workers is also doing its part, probably more than its part, to force a

reorganization of the basic industry of the country upon scientific and efficient lines. The maintenance of these rates will accelerate the operation of natural economic laws, which will in time eliminate uneconomic mines, obsolete equipment, and incompetent management. . . .

The policy of the United Mine Workers of America will inevitably bring about the utmost employment of machinery of which coal mining is physically capable. . . . Fair wages and American standards of living are inextricably bound up with the progressive substitution of mechanical for human power. It is no accident that fair wages and machinery will walk hand-in-hand.

SOURCE: John L. Lewis, *The Miners' Fight for American Standards* (Indianapolis: Bell Publishing Co., 1925), 40, 41, 108.

Clearly, if a monopsonist is minimizing its costs of production and its ME_L is increased, it will want to restore equality to condition (3.12) by substituting capital for labor. Thus, employment decreases even more in the long run than in the short run.

EFFECTS OF A MANDATED WAGE   Let us next consider what would happen if some nonmarket force were to compel the firm to pay a particular wage rate that was higher than the one it was paying. Would the firm's desired level of employment decline? For the monopsonist's short-run response, refer to Figure 3.6, where a monopsonistic firm initially equates MRP_L and ME_L at point A and chooses to hire E_0 workers, which requires it to pay a wage of W_0.

Suppose now that a mandated wage of W_m is set in Figure 3.6. This mandate prevents the firm from paying a wage less than W_m and effectively creates a horizontal portion (BD) in the labor supply curve facing the firm (which is now BDS). The firm's marginal expense of labor curve is now $BDEM$, because up to employment level E_1 the marginal costs of labor are equal to W_m. The firm, which maximizes profits by equating marginal revenues with marginal costs (which equality is now at point C), will hire E_m workers. Even though wages have risen from W_0 to W_m, employment rises from E_0 to E_m.

For a monopsonist, then, a mandated wage can simultaneously increase the *average* cost of labor (that is, the wages paid to workers) and reduce labor's *marginal*

FIGURE 3.6

Minimum Wage Effects under Monopsony: Both Wages and Employment Can Increase in the Short Run

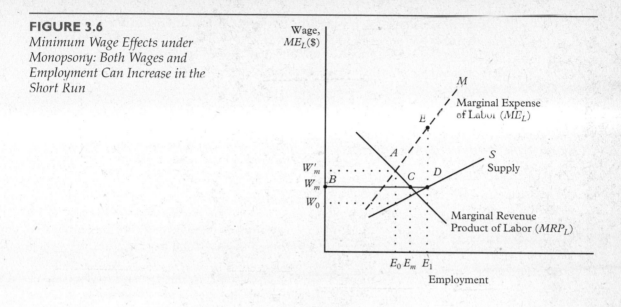

expense. It is the decrease in *marginal* expense that induces the firm to expand output and employment in the short run. Thus, because an upward-sloping supply curve is converted to one that is horizontal, at least for employment near the current level, it is possible that both wages and employment can increase with the imposition of a mandated wage on a monopsonist. This possibility is subject to two qualifications, however.

First, in the context of Figure 3.6, employment will increase only if the mandated wage is set between W_0 and W'_m. A mandated wage above W'_m would increase ME_L and cause the profit-maximizing level of employment to fall below E_0. (The student can verify this by drawing a horizontal line from any point above W'_m on the vertical axis and noting that it will intersect the MRP_L curve to the left of E_0.)

Second, Figure 3.6, with its fixed MRP_L curve, depicts only the short-run response to a mandated wage. In the long run, two (opposing) effects on employment are possible. With a mandated wage that is *not too high*, a monopsonist's ME_L is reduced, causing a substitution of labor for capital in the long run. While the monopsonist's marginal cost of labor may have fallen, however, labor's average cost has increased. It is now more expensive to produce even the same level of output as before; thus, profits will decline. A firm may have monopsony power in the labor market, but it also may have many competitors in its product market. If it is in a competitive product market, its initial profit level will be "normal," so the decline will push its profits below normal. Some owners will get out of the market, putting downward pressure on employment. If this latter (scale) effect is large enough, employment in monopsonistic sectors could fall in the long run if a mandated wage were imposed.

In summary, then, the presence of monopsony introduces uncertainty into how employment will respond to the imposition of a mandated wage *if* the new wage reduces the firm's marginal expense of labor. Any shift in the supply of labor curve that *increases* the marginal expense of labor, of course, will unambiguously reduce employment.

Policy Application: The Labor Market Effects of Employer Payroll Taxes and Wage Subsidies

Having carefully examined the theory of labor demand, we turn now to an application of this theory to the phenomena of *employer* payroll taxes and wage subsidies. Governments widely finance certain social programs through taxes that require employers to remit payments based on their total payroll costs. As we will see, new or increased payroll taxes levied on the employer raise the cost of hiring labor, and they might therefore be expected to reduce the demand for labor. Conversely, it can be argued that if the government were to subsidize the wages paid by employers, the demand for labor would increase; indeed, wage subsidies for particular disadvantaged groups in society are sometimes proposed as a way to increase their employment. In this section we will analyze the effects of payroll taxes and subsidies.

WHO BEARS THE BURDEN OF A PAYROLL TAX?

In the United States several social insurance programs are financed by payroll taxes. Employers, and in some cases employees, make mandatory contributions of a fraction of the employees' salaries, up to a maximum level (or taxable wage base), to the social insurance trust funds. For example, the Social Security retirement, disability, and Medicare programs (OASDHI) are financed by a payroll tax paid by both employers and employees, while in most states unemployment insurance and workers' compensation insurance programs are financed solely by payroll-tax payments made by employers. It is not clear just why payroll taxes on *employers* are so heavily used in the social insurance area. There seems to be a prevailing notion that such taxes result in employers' "footing the bill" for the relevant programs, but this is not necessarily the case.

With our simple labor market model, we can show that the party making the social insurance payment is not necessarily the one that bears the burden of the tax. Suppose for expository convenience that only the employer is required to make payments and that the tax is a fixed amount (X) per labor hour, rather than a percentage of payroll. Now consider the market demand curve D_0 in Figure 3.7, which is drawn in such a way that desired employment is plotted against the wage *employees receive*. Prior to the imposition of the tax, the wage employees receive is the same as the wage employers pay. Thus, if D_0 were the demand curve before the tax was imposed, it would have the conventional interpretation of indicating how much labor firms would be willing to hire at any given wage. How-

FIGURE 3.7

The Market Demand Curve and Effects of an Employer-financed Payroll Tax

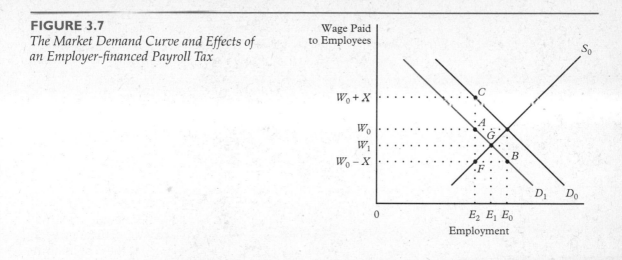

ever, *after* imposition of the tax, employer wage costs would be X above what employees received.

Thus, if employees received W_0, employers would face costs of $W_0 + X$. They would no longer demand E_0 workers; rather, because their costs were $W_0 + X$, they would demand E_2 workers. Point A (where W_0 and E_2 intersect) would become a point on a new market demand curve, formed when demand shifted down because of the tax (remember, the wage on the vertical axis of Figure 3.7 is the wage *employees receive*, not the wage employers pay). Only if employee wages fell to $W_0 - X$ would firms want to continue hiring E_0 workers, for then *employer* costs would be the same as before the tax. Thus, point B would also be on the new, shifted demand curve. Note that, with a tax of X, the new demand curve (D_1) is parallel to the old one and the vertical distance between the two is X.

Now, the tax-related shift in the market demand curve to D_1 implies that there would be an excess supply of labor at the previous equilibrium wage of W_0. This surplus of labor would create downward pressure on the *employee* wage, and this downward pressure would continue to be exerted until the employee wage fell to W_1, the point at which the quantity of labor supplied just equaled the quantity demanded. At this point, employment would also have fallen to E_1. Thus, *employees* bear part of the burden of an employer payroll tax in the form of *lower wage rates and lower employment levels*. The lesson is clear: The party legally liable for the contribution (the employer) is not necessarily the one that bears the full burden of the actual cost.

Figure 3.7 does suggest, however, that employers may bear at least *some* of the tax, because the wages received by employees do not fall by the full amount of the tax ($W_0 - W_1$ is smaller than X, which is the vertical distance between the two demand curves). The reason for this is that, with an upward-sloping labor market supply curve, employees withdraw labor as their wages fall, and it becomes more difficult for firms to find workers. If wages fell to $W_0 - X$, the withdrawal of workers would create a labor shortage that would serve to drive wages to some point (W_1 in our example) between W_0 and $W_0 - X$. Only if the labor market supply

FIGURE 3.8
Payroll Tax with a Vertical Supply Curve

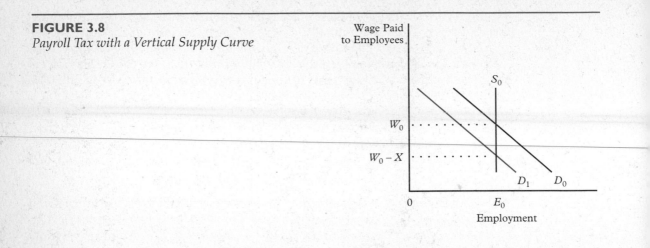

curve were *vertical*—meaning that lower wages have no effect on labor supply—would the *entire amount of the tax* be shifted to workers in the form of a decrease in their wages by the amount of X, as shown by supply curve S_0 in Figure 3.8.

In general, the extent to which the labor market *supply* curve is sensitive to wages determines the proportion of the employer payroll tax that gets shifted to employees' wages. The less responsive labor supply is to changes in wages, the fewer the employees who withdraw from the market and the higher the proportion of the tax that gets shifted to workers in the form of a wage decrease (compare the outcomes in Figure 3.7 and 3.8). It must also be pointed out, however, that to the degree employee wages do *not* fall, employment levels *will;* when employee wages do not fall much in the face of an employer payroll-tax increase, employer labor costs are increased—and this increase reduces the quantity of labor employers demand.[15]

A number of empirical studies have sought to ascertain what fraction of employers' payroll-tax costs are actually passed on to employees in the form of lower wages (or lower wage increases). Although the evidence is somewhat ambiguous,

---

[15]Another major influence on the extent to which payroll taxes are shifted to employees is the shape of the demand curve. If the demand curve were very sensitive to changes in labor costs, there would be relatively large employment losses and strong downward pressures on employee wages. On the other hand, if employer demand were not very responsive to labor costs, both employment losses and employee wage changes would be small.

The analyses presented in this section so far have examined just the effects of employer payroll taxes on labor demand. A complete analysis of such taxes must take account of supply-curve shifts associated with benefits paid by the programs for which the taxes are collected. As we shall see in Chapters 6 and 7, the benefits made available by the Social Security, unemployment compensation, and workers' compensation systems all provide incentives for individuals to alter their labor supply behavior. To the extent that these benefits cause the labor supply curve to shift, conclusions about the wage and employment effects of programs financed by payroll taxes must be modified. For example, if the labor supply curve shifts to the left (because the benefits financed by the tax make working less attractive), wages will fall to an extent smaller than that caused by shifts in the demand curve alone. However, with the smaller wage decrease, the decline in employment will be larger.

a comprehensive review of these studies led to at least a tentative conclusion that most of a payroll tax is eventually shifted to wages, with little long-run effect on employment.[16] Government policies, however, are frequently judged by their near-term results, and there is also research indicating that imposing a payroll tax could cause employer wage costs to rise, and employment therefore to fall, for a period of five to ten years before the tax is fully shifted to employee wages.[17] It is not surprising, therefore, that payroll taxes have been suspected as a possible cause of the rise in European, relative to North American, unemployment during the 1980s (a rise documented in Chapter 2, Table 2.4).

ARE PAYROLL TAXES RESPONSIBLE FOR EUROPEAN UNEMPLOYMENT?

Most developed countries, and many developing nations, have a variety of social programs designed to compensate workers who have retired or who are sick, injured, permanently disabled, or unemployed. In addition, such countries typically provide their citizens with general health insurance in some form or other. As noted earlier, a common characteristic of these various social insurance programs is that most often they are financed by employer payroll taxes or by employer payments to private insurers that are based on payroll. Table 3.3 displays these employer taxes and payments as a percentage of payrolls (for manufacturing industries) in the United States, Canada, and several European countries.

Two facts are immediately apparent from Table 3.3. First, payroll-based taxes and payments required of employers in the countries shown are a substantial percentage of employee earnings: 15 percent in Canada, 22.6 percent in the United States, and over 25 percent in Belgium, France, Italy, and Sweden. Second, the rates displayed in the table are generally higher in Europe than in North America. In commenting on the growth in European unemployment relative to that in North America during the 1980s, one economist called European payroll taxes "mass job-killers."[18] Another report on the unemployment problems facing Europe stated the issue in this way:

> One particular policy concern is that taxes imposed on the wage bill may reduce employment, either through making production unprofitable, or through encouraging the use of more capital-intensive methods of production.[19]

[16]Daniel S. Hamermesh, *Labor Demand* (Princeton, N.J.: Princeton University Press, 1993), 169–173); Jonathan Gruber, "The Incidence of Payroll Taxation: Evidence from Chile," working paper no. 5053, National Bureau of Economic Research, Cambridge, Mass., March 1995.

[17]Organisation for Economic Co-Operation and Development, *Employment Outlook* (Paris: OECD, July 1990), 157–158.

[18]Edmund S. Phelps, "Commentary: Past and Prospective Causes of High Unemployment," in *Reducing Unemployment: Current Issues and Policy Options* (Kansas City: Federal Reserve Bank of Kansas City, 1994), 85.

[19]Organisation for Economic Co-Operation and Development, *Employment Outlook* (Paris: OECD, July 1990), 153.

TABLE 3.3

Payroll-related Taxes and Other Mandated Expenses as a Percent of Hourly Compensation, Manufacturing Production Workers, 1980 and 1992

Country	1980	1992
Belgium	23.2%	27.0%
Canada	10.6	15.0
Denmark	4.4	3.0
France	27.3	28.5
Germany	21.0	22.8
Ireland	12.2	15.6
Italy	29.3	30.6
Netherlands	24.0	22.6
Norway	19.6	18.6
Spain	25.8	24.6
Sweden	27.4	31.3
United Kingdom	18.0	16.5
United States	19.1	22.6

SOURCE: U.S. Bureau of Labor Statistics, "International Comparisons of Hourly Compensation Costs for Production Workers in Manufacturing, 1992," report no. 844, April 1993, Table 11.

It is difficult to argue that payroll-tax rates were responsible for increasing unemployment in Europe during the 1980s because, as also can be seen from Table 3.3, these tax rates were generally higher in Europe than in North America even before the big relative rise in European unemployment. Moreover, of the countries listed in Table 3.3, Canada had the largest increase from 1980 to 1992, and only two European countries had payroll-tax increases larger than those experienced in the United States. Five European countries listed actually reduced their employer payroll-tax rates over this period! Thus, a recent survey of research on increased European unemployment rejects payroll-tax increases as a major cause.[20]

EMPLOYMENT SUBSIDIES AS A DEVICE TO HELP THE POOR

The opposite of a payroll tax on employers is a government subsidy of employers' payrolls. In Figure 3.7, for example, if instead of *taxing* each hour of labor by $X the government *paid* the employer $X, the market labor demand curve would shift *up-*

---

[20]Charles R. Bean, "European Unemployment: A Survey," *Journal of Economic Literature* 32 (June 1994): 573–619.

ward by a vertical distance of *X*. This upward movement of the demand curve would create pressures to increase employment and the wages received by employees; as with a payroll tax, whether the eventual effects would be felt more on employment or on wage rates depends on the shape of the labor market supply curve. (Students should test their understanding in this area by drawing labor demand curves that reflect a new payroll subsidy of $X per hour, and then analyzing the effects on employment and employee wages with market supply curves that are, alternatively, upward-sloping and vertical. *Hint:* The outcomes should be those that would be obtained if demand curve D_1 in Figures 3.7 and 3.8 were shifted to curve D_0.)

Payroll subsidies to employers can take many forms. They can be in the form of cash payments, as implied by the above hypothetical example, or they can be in the form of tax credits. These credits might directly reduce a firm's payroll-tax rate, or they might reduce some other tax by an amount proportional to the number of labor hours hired; in either case, the credit has the effect of reducing the cost of hiring labor. Further, wage subsidies can apply to a firm's employment *level*, to any *new* employees hired after a certain date (even if they just replace workers who have left), or only to new hires that serve to *increase* the firm's level of employment. Finally, subsidies can be either *general* or *selective*. A general subsidy is not conditional on the characteristics of the people hired, while a selective, or *targeted*, plan makes the subsidy conditional on hiring people from certain target groups (such as the disadvantaged).

The beneficial effects on wages and employment that are expected to derive from payroll-tax subsidies have led to their proposed use as a policy to help alleviate poverty. One economist concerned about unemployment and earnings levels among low-wage workers recently wrote,

> What to do? The solution for which I have pleaded the past five years: a low-wage employment subsidy. It would best take the form of a tax credit that employers could use to offset the payroll taxes they owe from their employment of low-wage workers. Lower unemployment and better pay would result at the low end of the labor market—the less of the one, the more of the other.[21]

Experience in the United States with targeted wage subsidies, such as the one proposed above, has not been encouraging, however. The Targeted Jobs Tax Credit Program, which began in 1979 and was changed slightly over the years until it was finally discontinued in 1995, targeted unemployed youth (up to age 22), the handicapped, and welfare recipients, providing their employers with a tax credit that lasted for one year. Evaluations of this program found that it had little effect, for three reasons.

First, as with an earlier, short-lived payroll subsidy program, few employers seemed to be aware of the payroll-tax credit. Second, the characteristics required for workers to be eligible were stigmatizing (see Example 3.3); that is, eligible job

---

[21]Phelps, "Commentary: Past and Prospective Causes of High Unemployment," 89.

EXAMPLE 3.3

Are Targeted Wage Subsidies Harmful?

In 1980–1981 the U.S. Department of Labor conducted an experiment in the Dayton, Ohio, area to try to estimate the effectiveness of two targeted wage subsidy plans. A number of economically disadvantaged welfare recipients, all of whom were eligible for the Targeted Jobs Tax Credit Program, were randomly assigned to three groups. The first group received vouchers that could be presented to prospective employers. These vouchers informed employers that if the disadvantaged workers were hired, the government would grant the employers tax credits equal to 50 percent of the employees' first-year salaries and 25 percent of their second-year salaries, with a maximum credit per worker of $3,000 and $1,500 per year, respectively. The second group received vouchers informing prospective employers that they would receive direct cash payments of the above amounts, rather than tax credits, for hiring workers. The third served as a control group and received no vouchers.

The experiment's purpose was to see if having disadvantaged welfare recipients inform prospective employers of their eligibility for wage subsidies would increase their labor market success; as discussed in the text, employers often failed to realize that the tax credit program existed. Moreover, since employers with zero tax liabilities (because their profits were low or they were suffering losses) would have no economic incentive to hire disadvantaged workers under a tax credit plan, it was felt that the vouchers calling for direct cash payments to employers might prove more beneficial to disadvantaged workers.

For political reasons the experiment was ended after only six months. By that time, 13.0 percent of

the tax credit group and 12.7 percent of the direct cash treatment group had found employment; in this experiment direct cash payments *did not* work better than tax credits. Quite strikingly, however, 15.3 percent of the control group had found employment; this group did *better* than the two groups who advertised their eligibility for subsidies. Although the "vouchered" groups were able to offer themselves to employers at a discount, apparently employers were also made aware that they were "welfare recipients." This may have led them to conclude that people with vouchers were probably not very productive, thus reducing their willingness to hire them. That is, the voucher system may well have had a *stigmatizing* effect on members of the first two groups.

This example illustrates that the effects of targeted wage-subsidy or tax-credit programs will often depend upon more than the relative cost advantages they provide for the targeted groups. The example also illustrates that individuals are often at least partly judged by the characteristics of the group to which they belong rather than by their own personal characteristics. (Targeted social programs should be designed in ways that minimize their stigmatizing effects. The implications of such judgments, often called *statistical discrimination*, will be more fully discussed in Chapter 12.)

Source: Gary Burtless, "Are Targeted Wage Subsidies Harmful? Evidence from a Wage Voucher Experiment," *Industrial and Labor Relations Review* 39 (October 1985): 105–114.

applicants had to prove they were on welfare, for example, which most employers took as a negative indicator of productivity. Third, some of the required characteristics—welfare recipiency and disabling conditions, for example—could be established only by interview questions, creating an uncomfortable situation for both employer and applicant. Thus, many employers waited until applicants were already hired before investigating their eligibility for the tax credit. One study concluded that 92 percent of the employees for whom tax credits were received would have been hired even if the credit were not available.[22]

That the ineffectiveness of the Targeted Jobs Tax Credit Program was in part a function of its eligibility characteristics suggests that a payroll subsidy with an improved method of targeting might still create the desirable results predicted by economic theory. Ways to target the poor that might not be stigmatizing could include basing eligibility on residential neighborhood or simply subsidizing any job that paid less than a certain wage ($7 per hour, say). The latter targeting method has the drawback that it would apply to a *job*, not a *personal* characteristic, so the program could not focus exclusively on the disadvantaged (members of nonpoor households could qualify if they were willing to work at the low-wage job). An added advantage of targeting *all* low-wage jobs, however, is that the pool of eligible applicants would be large enough that employers might have incentives to at least find out about the program!

REVIEW QUESTIONS

1. "It is generally agreed that the volunteer army is a dismal failure—the quality of volunteers is down and the number is not sufficient to meet desired force levels. The only alternatives are to raise the pay of volunteers or to reinstitute a draft system. Since the cost to society is clearly higher in the former than in the latter case, from an economist's perspective a draft system would be preferable." Evaluate this position.

2. Suppose the government were to subsidize the wages of all women in the population by paying their *employers* 50 cents for every hour they work. What would be the effect on the wage rate women received? What would be the effect on the net wage employers paid? (The net wage would be the wage women received less 50 cents.)

3. The Occupational Safety and Health Administration promulgates safety and health standards. These standards typically apply to machinery (capital), which is required to be equipped with guards, shields, etc. An alternative to these standards is to require the employer to furnish personal protective devices to employees (labor)—such as earplugs, hard hats, and safety shoes. *Disregarding* the issue of

---

[22]U.S. Department of Labor, Office of the Inspector General, "Targeted Jobs Tax Credit Program: Employment Inducement or Employer Windfall?" report no. 04–94–021–03–320, August 18, 1994; John Bishop and Mark Montgomery, "Does the Targeted Jobs Tax Credit Create Jobs at Subsidized Firms?" *Industrial Relations* 32, no. 3 (Fall 1993): 289–306.

which alternative approach offers greater protection from injury, what aspects of each alternative must be taken into account when analyzing the possible *employment* effects of the two approaches to safety?

4. Assume that there are two grades of professional football players. There are a limited number of "stars," whom the fans most want to watch, and an unlimited number of "nonstars." There are too few stars to fully staff each team, but there are enough for a few to be on each team if an owner decided to hire them.

   a. Assume that football teams keep all the "gate" and TV revenues they generate and that players are free to choose their teams at the end of any season. Do stars earn more than nonstars? How are the wages of each group determined?

   b. Continue to assume that players are free to choose their teams, but assume now that teams agree to share *all* their gate and TV revenues equally (they put them into a "pool" and divide it equally among the team owners). What happens now to salaries of stars and nonstars?

5. Several years ago Great Britain adopted a program that placed a tax—to be collected from employers—on wages in *service* industries. Wages in manufacturing industries were not taxed. Discuss the wage and employment effects of this tax policy.

6. Suppose the government is considering imposing a payroll tax of $1 per person-hour worked to finance a massive training program for the unemployed. Will the new equilibrium wage and employment level depend upon whether it is *employers* or *employees* who are legally liable for the tax? Explain.

7. In the last decade or two the United States has been subject to huge increases in the illegal immigration of workers from Mexico, most of them unskilled, and the government has recently considered ways to reduce the flow. One policy that has been considered is to impose financial penalties on employers who are discovered to have hired illegal immigrants.

   What effect would this policy have on the employment of unskilled illegal immigrants? What effect would it have on the demand for skilled "native" labor?

8. The city of Rochester, New York, was declared a "foreign-trade zone" by the U.S. Department of Commerce. A foreign-trade zone is designated as "international ground," and companies in that zone are exempt from paying customs duties on component parts they import to manufacture their products. Analyze the effects of designating Rochester a foreign-trade zone on the demand for labor in the area.

9. In its proposals for both the Democratic and Republican parties to consider during the 1992 presidential election, one organization, commenting on the low wages paid by U.S. firms to workers in their Mexican plants, stated, "It is clear that current levels of compensation for these workers have no relationship with their productivity." Comment on the logic or assumptions of this statement.

SELECTED READINGS

Blank, Rebecca M., ed. *Social Protection Versus Economic Flexibility: Is There a Trade-Off?* Chicago: University of Chicago Press, 1994.

Hamermesh, Daniel. *Labor Demand*. Princeton, N.J.: Princeton University Press, 1993.

Graphic Derivation of a Firm's Labor Demand Curve

Chapter 3 described verbally the derivation of a firm's labor demand curve. This appendix will present the *same* derivation graphically. This graphic representation permits a more rigorous derivation, although our conclusion that demand curves slope downward in both the short and the long run remains unchanged.

The Production Function

Output can generally be viewed as being produced by combining capital and labor. Figure 3A.1 illustrates this production function graphically and depicts several aspects of the production process.

Consider the convex curve labeled $Q = 100$. Along this line, every combination of labor (L) and capital (K) produces 100 units of output (Q). That is, the combination of labor and capital at point A (L_a, K_a) generates the same 100 units of output as the combinations at points B and C. Because each point along the $Q = 100$ curve generates the same output, that curve is called an *isoquant* (iso = "equal"; quant = "quantity").

Two other isoquants are shown in Figure 3A.1 ($Q = 150$, $Q = 200$). These isoquants represent higher levels of output than the $Q = 100$ curve. The fact that these isoquants indicate higher output levels can be seen by holding labor constant at L_b (say) and then observing the different levels of capital. If L_b is combined with K_b in capital, 100 units of Q are produced. If L_b is combined with K_b', 150 units are produced (K_b' is greater than K_b). If L_b is combined with even more capital (K_b'', say), 200 units of Q could be produced.

Note that the isoquants in Figure 3A.1 have *negative* slopes, reflecting an assumption that labor and capital are substitutes. If, for example, we cut capital from K_a to K_b, we could keep output constant (at 100) by increasing labor from L_a to L_b. Labor, in other words, could be substituted for capital to maintain a given production level.

Finally, note the *convexity* of the isoquants. At point A, the $Q = 100$ isoquant has a steep slope, suggesting that to keep Q constant at 100, a given decrease in capital could be accompanied by a *modest* increase in labor. At point C, however, the slope of the isoquant is relatively flat. This flatter slope means that the same given decrease in capital would require a much *larger* increase in labor for output to be held constant. The decrease in capital permitted by a given increase in labor in order for output to be held constant is called the *marginal rate of technical substitution* (MRTS) between capital and labor. Symbolically, the MRTS can be written as

$$MRTS = \frac{\Delta K}{\Delta L} \mid \overline{Q} \tag{3A.1}$$

where Δ means "change in" and $\mid \overline{Q}$ means "holding output constant." The MRTS is *negative*, because if L is increased, K must be reduced to keep Q constant.

Why does the absolute value of the marginal rate of technical substitution diminish as labor increases? When labor is highly used in the production process and capital is not very prevalent (point C in Figure 3A.1), there are many jobs that capital can do. Labor is easy to replace; if capital is increased, it will be used as a substitute for labor in parts of the production process where it will have the highest payoff. As capital becomes progressively more utilized and labor less so, the few remaining workers will be doing jobs that are hardest for a machine to do, at which point it will take a lot of capital to substitute for a worker.[1]

Demand for Labor in the Short Run

Chapter 3 argued that firms will maximize profits in the short run (K fixed) by hiring labor until labor's marginal product (MP_L) is equal to the real wage (W/P). The reason for this decision rule is that the real wage represents the *cost* of an added unit of labor (in terms of output), while the marginal product is the *output* added by the extra unit of labor. As long as the firm, by increasing labor (K fixed), gains

---

[1]Only a decade or two ago, most long-distance telephone calls were made through operators. Over time, operators have been increasingly replaced by a very capital-intensive direct-dialing system. Those operators who remain employed, however, perform tasks that are the most difficult for a machine to perform—handling collect calls, dispensing directory assistance, and acting as troubleshooters when problems arise.

FIGURE 3A.1
A Production Function

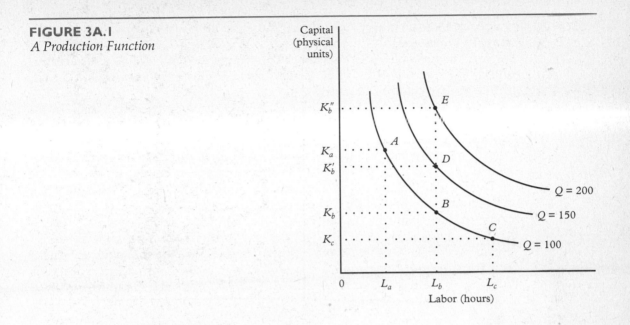

more in output than it loses in costs, it will continue to hire employees. The firm will stop hiring when the marginal cost of added labor exceeds MP_L.

The requirement that $MP_L = W/P$ in order for profits to be maximized means that the firm's labor demand curve in the short run (in terms of the *real* wage) is identical to its marginal product of labor schedule (refer to Figure 3.1). Remembering that the marginal product of labor is the extra output produced by one-unit increases in the amount of labor employed, holding capital constant, consider the production function displayed in Figure 3A.2. Holding capital constant at K_a, the firm can produce 100 units of Q if it employs labor equal to L_a. If labor is increased to L_a', the firm can produce 50 more units of Q; if labor is increased from L_a' to L_a'', the firm can produce an additional 50 units. Notice, however, that the required increase in labor to get the latter 50 units of added output, $L_a'' - L_a'$, is larger than the extra labor required to produce the first 50-unit increment $(L_a' - L_a)$. This difference can only mean that as labor is increased when K is held constant, each successive labor hour hired generates progressively smaller increments in output. Put differently, Figure 3A.2 graphically illustrates the diminishing marginal productivity of labor.

Why does labor's marginal productivity decline? Chapter 3 explained that labor's marginal productivity declines because, with K fixed, each added worker has less capital (per capita) with which to work. Is this explanation proven in Figure 3A.2? The answer is, regrettably, no. Figure 3A.2 is drawn *assuming* diminishing marginal productivity. Renumbering the isoquants could produce a different set of marginal productivities. (To see this, change $Q = 150$ to $Q = 200$, and change $Q = 200$ to $Q = 500$. Labor's marginal productivity would then rise.) However, the logic that labor's marginal product must eventually fall as labor is increased,

FIGURE 3A.2

The Declining Marginal Productivity
of Labor

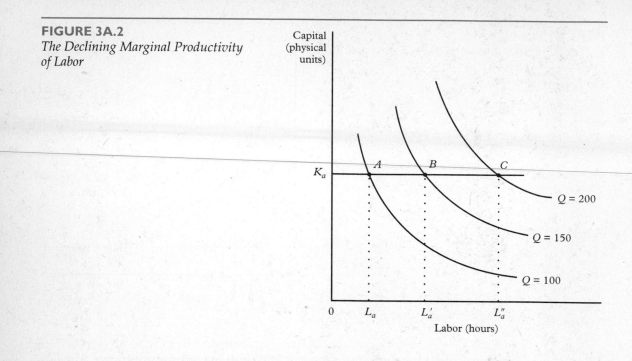

holding buildings, machines, and tools constant, is very compelling. Further, as Chapter 3 pointed out, even if MP_L rises initially, the firm will stop hiring labor only in the range where MP_L is declining; as long as MP_L is above W/P and *rising*, it will pay to continue hiring.

The assumptions that MP_L declines eventually and that firms hire until $MP_L = W/P$ are the bases for the assertion that a firm's short-run demand curve for labor slopes downward. The graphic, more rigorous derivation of the demand curve in this appendix confirms and supports the verbal analysis in the chapter. However, it also emphasizes more clearly than a verbal analysis can that the downward-sloping nature of the short-run labor demand curve is based on an *assumption*—however reasonable—that MP_L declines as employment is increased.

Demand for Labor in the Long Run

Recall that a firm maximizes its profits by producing at a level of output (Q^*) where marginal cost equals marginal revenue. That is, the firm will keep increasing output until the addition to its revenues generated by an extra unit of output just equals the marginal cost of producing that extra unit of output. Because marginal revenue, which is equal to output *price* for a competitive firm, is not shown in our graph of the production function, the profit-maximizing level of output cannot be determined. However, continuing our analysis of the production function can illustrate some important aspects of the demand for labor in the long run.

FIGURE 3A.3

Cost Minimization in the Production of
Q* (Wage =$10 per Hour; Price of a
Unit of Capital=$20)

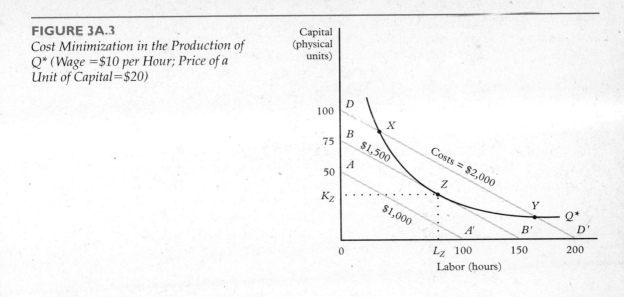

CONDITIONS FOR COST MINIMIZATION

In Figure 3A.3, profit-maximizing output is assumed to be Q^*. How will the firm combine labor and capital to produce Q^*? It can maximize profits only if it produces Q^* in the least expensive way; that is, it must minimize the costs of producing Q^*. To better understand the characteristics of cost minimization, refer to the three *isoexpenditure* lines—AA', BB', DD'—in Figure 3A.3. Along any one of these lines the costs of employing labor and capital are equal.

For example, line AA' represents total costs of $1,000. Given an hourly wage (W) of $10 per hour, the firm could hire 100 hours of labor and incur total costs of $1,000 if it used no capital (point A'). In contrast, if the price of a unit of capital (C) is $20, the firm could produce at a total cost of $1,000 by using 50 units of capital and no labor (point A). All the points between A and A' represent combinations of L and K that, at $W = $10 and $C = $20, cost $1,000 as well.

The problem with the isoexpenditure line of AA' is that it does not intersect the isoquant Q^*, implying that Q^* cannot be produced for $1,000. At prices of $W = $10 and $C = $20, the firm cannot buy enough resources to produce output level Q^* and hold total costs to $1,000. The firm can, however, produce Q^* for a total cost of $2,000. Line DD', representing expenditures of $2,000, intersects the Q^* isoquant at points X and Y. The problem with these points, however, is that they are not cost-minimizing; Q^* can be produced for less than $2,000.

Since isoquant Q^* is convex, the cost-minimizing combination of L and K in producing Q^* will come at a point where an isoexpenditure line is *tangent* to the isoquant (that is, just barely touches isoquant Q^* at only one place). Point Z, where labor equals L_Z and capital equals K_Z, is where Q^* can be produced at minimal cost, *given* that $W= $10 and $C = $20. No lower isoexpenditure curve touches the isoquant, meaning that Q^* cannot be produced for less than $1,500.

An important characteristic of point Z is that the slope of the isoquant at point Z and the slope of the isoexpenditure line are the same (the slope of a curve at a given point is the slope of a line tangent to the curve at that point). The slope of the isoquant at any given point is the *marginal rate of technical substitution* as defined in equation (3A.1). Another way of expressing equation (3A.1) is:

$$MRTS = \frac{-\Delta K/\Delta Q}{\Delta L/\Delta Q} \tag{3A.2}$$

Equation (3A.2) directly indicates that the $MRTS$ is a ratio reflecting the reduction of capital required to *decrease* output by one unit if enough extra labor is hired so that output is tending to *increase* by one unit. (The ΔQs in equation 3A.2 cancel each other and keep output constant.) Pursuing equation (3A.2) one step further, the numerator and denominator can be rearranged to obtain the following:[2]

$$MRTS = \frac{-\Delta K/\Delta Q}{\Delta L/\Delta Q} = -\frac{\Delta Q/\Delta L}{\Delta Q/\Delta K} = -\frac{MP_L}{MP_K} \tag{3A.3}$$

where MP_L and MP_K are the marginal productivities of labor and capital, respectively.

The slope of the *isoexpenditure line* is equal to the negative of the ratio W/C (in Figure 3A.3, W/C equals 10/20, or 0.5).[3] Thus, at point Z, where Q^* is produced in the minimum-cost fashion, the following equality holds:

$$MRTS = -\frac{MP_L}{MP_K} = -\frac{W}{C} \tag{3A.4}$$

Equation (3A.4) is simply a rearranged version of equation (3.8c) in the text.[4]

The economic meaning, or logic, behind the characteristics of cost minimization can most easily be seen by stating the $MRTS$ as $-\dfrac{\Delta K/\Delta Q}{\Delta L/\Delta Q}$ (see equation 3A.2) and equating this version of the $MRTS$ to $-\dfrac{W}{C}$:

$$-\frac{\Delta K/\Delta Q}{\Delta L/\Delta Q} = -\frac{W}{C} \tag{3A.5}$$

or

$$\frac{\Delta K}{\Delta Q} \cdot C = \frac{\Delta L}{\Delta Q} \cdot W \tag{3A.6}$$

Equation (3A.6) makes it very plain that to be minimizing costs, the cost of producing an extra unit of output by adding only labor must equal the cost of producing that extra unit by employing only additional capital. If these costs differed, the company could reduce total costs by expanding its use of the factor with which

---

[2]This is done by making use of the fact that dividing one number by a second one is equivalent to *multiplying* the first by the *inverse* of the second.

[3]Note that $10/20 = 75/150$, or $0B/0B'$.

[4]The negative signs on each side of equation (3A.4) cancel each other and can therefore be ignored.

output can be increased more cheaply and cutting back on its use of the other factor. Any point where costs can still be reduced while Q is held constant is obviously not a point of cost minimization.

THE SUBSTITUTION EFFECT

If the wage rate, which was assumed to be $10 per hour in Figure 3A.3, goes up to $20 per hour (holding C constant), what will happen to the cost-minimizing way of producing output of Q^*? Figure 3A.4 illustrates the answer that common sense would suggest: total costs rise, and more capital and less labor are used to produce Q^*. At $W = 20, 150 units of labor can no longer be purchased if total costs are to be held to $1,500; in fact, if costs are to equal $1,500, only 75 units of labor can be hired. Thus, the isoexpenditure curve for $1,500 in costs shifts from BB' to BB'' and no longer is tangent to isoquant Q^*. Q^* can no longer be produced for $1,500, and the minimum-cost way of producing Q^* will rise. In Figure 3A.4 we assume that it rises to $2,250 (isoexpenditure line EE' is the one tangent to isoquant Q^*).

Moreover, the increase in the cost of labor relative to capital induces the firm to use more capital and less labor. Graphically, the old tangency point of Z is replaced by a new one (Z'), where the marginal productivity of labor is higher relative to MP_K, as our discussions of equations (3.8c) and (3A.4) explained. Point Z' is reached (from Z) by adding more capital and reducing employment of labor. The movement from L_Z to L'_Z is the *substitution effect* generated by the wage increase.

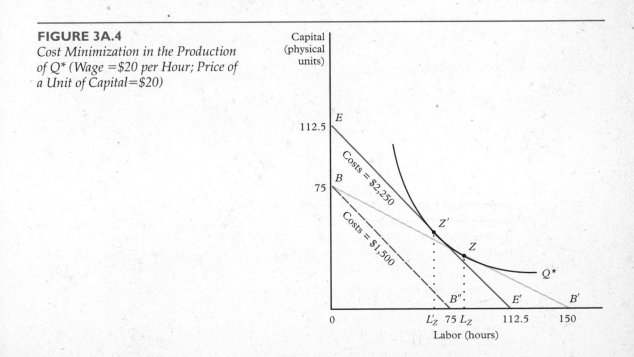

FIGURE 3A.4

Cost Minimization in the Production of Q^* (Wage =$20 per Hour; Price of a Unit of Capital=$20)

THE SCALE EFFECT

The fact that Q^* can no longer be produced for \$1,500, but instead involves at least \$2,250 in costs, will generally mean that it is no longer the profit-maximizing level of production. The new profit-maximizing level of production will be less than Q^* (how much less cannot be determined unless we know something about the product demand curve).

Suppose that the profit-maximizing level of output falls from Q^* to Q^{**}, as shown in Figure 3A.5. Since all isoexpenditure lines have the new slope of -1 when $W = \$20$ and $C = \$20$, the cost-minimizing way to produce Q^{**} will lie on an isoexpenditure line parallel to EE'. We find this cost-minimizing way to produce Q^{**} at point Z'', where an isoexpenditure line (FF') is tangent to the Q^{**} isoquant.

The *overall* response in the employment of labor to an increase in the wage rate has been a fall in labor usage from L_Z to L''_Z. The decline from L_Z to L'_Z is called the substitution effect, as we have noted. It results because the *proportions* of K and L used in production change when the ratio of wages to capital prices (W/C) changes. The *scale effect* can be seen as the reduction in employment from L'_Z to L''_Z wherein the usage of both K and L is cut back solely because of the reduced *scale* of production. Both effects are simultaneously present when wages increase and capital prices remain constant, but as Figure 3A.5 emphasizes, the effects are conceptually distinct and occur for different reasons. Together, these effects lead us to assert that the long-run labor demand curve slopes downward.

FIGURE 3A.5

The Substitution and Scale Effects of a Wage Increase

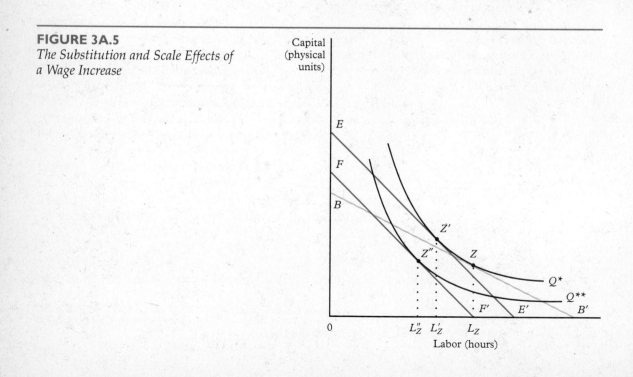

4

Labor Demand Elasticities

In 1995 a heated debate broke out among economists and policymakers about the employment effects of minimum wage laws. Clearly, the standard theory developed in Chapter 3 predicts that if wages are raised above their market level by a minimum wage law, employment opportunities will be reduced as firms move up (and to the left) along their labor demand curves. Two prominent labor economists, however, after reviewing previous work on the subject and doing new studies of their own, published a 1995 book in which they concluded that the predicted job losses associated with increases in the minimum wage simply could not be observed to occur, at least with any regularity.[1] On one level, the findings in this book raised a controversy about the usefulness of standard labor demand theory. Those who found the book and related research persuasive called for the use of new labor demand models (especially ones that are monopsony-like in character), while others argued that the new studies in this book were flawed and confidently asserted that appropriately executed studies would yield the results predicted by standard theory.[2]

On another level, however, the 1995 book simply triggered a highly charged discussion of a long-standing question: just how responsive is employment demand to given changes in wages? Hardly anyone doubts that jobs would be lost if mandated wage increases were huge, but how many are lost with modest increases? One economist framed the issue in this way:

---

[1]David Card and Alan B. Krueger, *Myth and Measurement: The New Economics of the Minimum Wage* (Princeton: Princeton University Press, 1995).

[2]Six reviews of Card and Krueger, *Myth and Measurement*, appear in the book review section of the July 1995 issue of *Industrial and Labor Relations Review* 48, no. 4. These reviews give an excellent overview of the range of responses to the Card and Krueger book.

Economists . . . are divided into two basic groups. On one side are those who believe that responses to price incentives are usually large—the Big Responders (BRs). On the other side are those who believe that responses to price incentives are generally small—Small Responders (SRs). . . . Logic tells us that massive changes in prices . . . will have large effects on quantities. . . . But *whether the BR or SR perspective applies to minimum wages in the range observed in the United States is a purely empirical question.*[3]

The focus of this chapter is on the degree to which employment responds to changes in wages. Chapter 3 examined theory underlying the general nature of labor demand curves. In the context of minimum wages, for example, its major contribution was in helping us understand why we expect at least some job loss if wages are increased above market levels. In contrast, Chapter 4 will examine issues concerning the magnitude of the job loss. Put in the context of the above quotation, this chapter will analyze both theory and evidence in the Big Responder–Small Responder debate.

The responsiveness of labor demand to a change in wage rates is normally measured as an "elasticity," which is the percentage change in employment brought about by a 1 percent change in wages. We begin our analysis by defining, analyzing, and measuring "own-wage" and "cross-wage" elasticities. We then apply these concepts to analyses of minimum wage laws and the employment effects of technological innovations. (Because the effects of free trade on the demand for labor are qualitatively similar to those of technological change, we analyze the employment effects of free trade in the appendix to this chapter.)

The Own-Wage Elasticity Of Demand

The *own-wage elasticity of demand* for a category of labor is defined as the percentage change in its employment (E) induced by a 1 percent increase in its wage rate (W):

$$\eta_{ii} = \frac{\%\Delta E_i}{\%\Delta W_i} \tag{4.1}$$

In equation (4.1), we have used the subscript i to denote category of labor i, the Greek letter η (eta) to represent elasticity, and the notation $\%\Delta$ to represent "percentage change in." Since the previous chapter showed that labor demand curves slope downward, an increase in the wage rate will cause employment to decrease; the own-wage elasticity of demand is therefore a negative number. What is at issue is its magnitude. The larger its *absolute* value (its magnitude, ignoring its sign), the larger will be the percentage decline in employment associated with any given percentage increase in wages.

Labor economists often focus on whether the absolute value of the elasticity of demand for labor is greater than or less than 1. If it is greater than 1, a 1 percent in-

---

[3]Richard Freeman, "Comment," *Industrial and Labor Relations Review* 48, no. 4 (July 1995): 830–831.

FIGURE 4.1
Relative Demand Elasticities

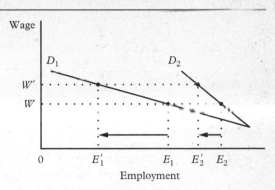

crease in wages will lead to an employment decline of greater than 1 percent; this situation is referred to as an *elastic* demand curve. In contrast, if the absolute value is less than 1, the demand curve is said to be *inelastic:* a 1 percent increase in wages will lead to a proportionately smaller decline in employment. If demand is elastic, aggregate earnings (defined here as the wage rate times the employment level) of individuals in the category will decline when the wage rate increases, because employment falls at a faster rate than wages rise. Conversely, if demand is inelastic, aggregate earnings will increase when the wage rate is increased. If the elasticity just equals −1, the demand curve is said to be *unitary elastic,* and aggregate earnings will remain unchanged if wages increase.

Figure 4.1 shows that the flatter of the two demand curves graphed (D_1) has greater elasticity than the steeper (D_2). Beginning with any wage (W, for example), a given wage change (to W', say) will yield greater responses in employment with demand curve D_1 than with D_2. To judge the different elasticities of response brought about by the same percentage wage increase, compare $(E_1 − E'_1)/E_1$ with $(E_2 − E'_2)/E_2$. Clearly, the more elastic response occurs along D_1.

To speak of a demand curve as having "an" elasticity, however, is technically incorrect. Given demand curves will generally have elastic and inelastic ranges—and while we are usually just interested in the elasticity of demand in the range around the current wage rate in any market, one cannot fully understand elasticity without understanding that it can vary along a given demand curve.

To illustrate, suppose we examine the typical straight-line demand curve that we have used so often in Chapters 2 and 3 (see Figure 4.2). One feature of a straight-line demand curve is that, at *each* point along the curve, a unit change in wages induces the *same* response in terms of units of employment. For example, at any point along the demand curve shown in Figure 4.2, a $2 decrease in wages will increase employment by 10 workers.

However, the same responses in terms of *unit* changes along the demand curve do *not* imply equal *percentage* changes. To see this point, look first at the upper end of the demand curve in Figure 4.2 (the end where wages are high and employment is low). A $2 decrease in wages when the base is $12 represents a 17 percent reduction in wages, while an addition of 10 workers when the starting point is also 10 represents a 100 percent increase in demand. Demand at this point is clearly *elastic*.

However, if one looks at the same unit changes in the lower region of the demand curve (low wages, high employment), demand there is inelastic. A $2 reduction in wages from a $4 base is a 50 percent reduction, while an increase of 10 workers from a base of 50 is only a 20 percent increase. Since the percentage increase in employment is smaller than the percentage decrease in wages, demand is seen to be inelastic at this end of the curve.

Thus, the upper end of a straight-line demand curve will exhibit greater elasticity than the lower end. Moreover, a straight-line demand curve will actually be elastic in some ranges and inelastic in others (as shown in Figure 4.2).

THE HICKS-MARSHALL LAWS OF DERIVED DEMAND

Knowledge of own-wage elasticities of demand is very important for making policy decisions. The factors that influence own-wage elasticity can be summarized by the Hicks-Marshall laws of derived demand—four "laws" named after the two distinguished British economists, Alfred Marshall and John Hicks, who are closely associated with their development.[4] These laws assert that, other things equal, the own-wage elasticity of demand for a category of labor is high under the following conditions:

1. When the price elasticity of demand for the product being produced is high;
2. When other factors of production can be easily substituted for the category of labor;
3. When the supply of other factors of production is highly elastic (that is, usage of other factors of production can be increased without substantially increasing their prices); and
4. When the cost of employing the category of labor is a large share of the total costs of production.

Not only are these laws generally valid as an empirical proposition, but the first three can be shown to always hold. There are conditions, however, under which the final law does not hold.

In seeking to explain why these laws hold, it is useful to act as if we could divide the process by which an increase in the wage rate affects the demand for labor into two steps: First, an increase in the wage rate increases the relative cost of the category of labor in question and induces employers to use less of it and more of other inputs (the *substitution effect*). Second, when the wage increase causes the marginal costs of production to rise, there are pressures to increase product prices and reduce output, causing a fall in employment (the *scale effect*). The four laws of derived demand each deal with substitution or scale effects.

---

[4]John R. Hicks, *The Theory of Wages*, 2d ed. (New York: St. Martin's Press, 1966), 241–247, and Alfred Marshall, *Principles of Economics*, 8th ed. (London: Macmillan, 1923), 518–538.

FIGURE 4.2
Different Elasticities Along a Demand Curve

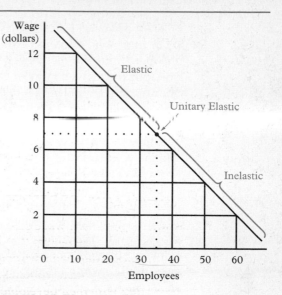

DEMAND FOR THE FINAL PRODUCT   We noted above that wage increases cause production costs to rise and tend to result in product price increases. The greater the price elasticity of demand for the final product, the larger will be the decline in output associated with a given increase in price—and the greater the decrease in output, the greater the loss in employment (other things equal) Thus, *the greater the elasticity of demand for the product, the greater the elasticity of demand for labor will be.* One implication of this result is that, other things equal, the demand for labor at the *firm* level will be more elastic than the demand for labor at the *industry,* or market, level. For example, the product demand curves facing *individual* carpet-manufacturing companies are highly elastic because the carpet of company X is a very close substitute for the carpet of company Y. Compared to price increases at the *firm* level, however, price increases at the *industry* level will not have as large an effect on demand because the closest substitutes for carpeting are hardwood, ceramic, or some kind of vinyl floor covering—none a very close substitute for carpeting. The demand for labor is thus much more elastic for an individual carpet-manufacturing firm than for the carpet-manufacturing industry as a whole. (For the same reasons, the labor demand curve for a monopolist is less elastic than for an individual *firm* in a competitive industry. Monopolists, after all, face *market* demand curves for their product because they are the only seller in the particular market.)

Another implication of this first law is that *wage elasticities will be higher in the long run than in the short run.* The reason for this is that price elasticities of demand in product markets are higher in the long run. In the short run there may be no good substitutes for a product, or consumers may be locked into their current stock of consumer durables. After a period of time, however, new products that are substitutes may be introduced and consumers will begin to replace durables that have worn out.

SUBSTITUTABILITY OF OTHER FACTORS   As the wage rate of a category of labor increases, firms have an incentive to try to substitute other, now relatively cheaper, inputs for the category. Suppose, however, that there were no substitution possibilities; a given number of units of the type of labor *must* be used to produce one unit of output. In this case, there is no reduction in employment due to the substitution effect. In contrast, when substitution possibilities do present themselves, a reduction in employment owing to the substitution effect will accompany whatever reductions are caused by the scale effect. Hence, other things equal, *the easier it is to substitute other factors of production, the higher the wage elasticity of labor demand will be.*

Limitations on substitution possibilities need not be solely technical ones. For example, as we shall see in Chapter 13, unions often try to limit substitution possibilities by including specific work rules in their contracts (e.g., minimum crew size for railroad locomotives). Alternatively, the government may legislate limitations by specifying minimum employment levels for safety reasons (for example, each public swimming pool in New York State must always have a lifeguard present). Such collectively bargained or legislated restrictions make the demand for labor less elastic. Note, however, that substitution possibilities that are not feasible in the short run may well become feasible over longer periods of time, when employers are free to vary their capital stock. For example, if the wages of railroad workers went up, companies could buy more powerful locomotives and operate with larger trains and fewer locomotives. Likewise, if the wages of lifeguards rose, cities might build larger, but fewer, swimming pools. Both adjustments would occur only in the long run, which is another reason why the demand for labor is more elastic in the long run than in the short run.

THE SUPPLY OF OTHER FACTORS   Suppose that, as the wage rate increased and employers attempted to substitute other factors of production for labor, the prices of these inputs were bid up substantially. This situation might occur, for example, if one were trying to substitute capital equipment for labor. If producers of capital equipment were already operating their plants near capacity, so that taking on new orders would cause them substantial increases in costs because they would have to work their employees overtime and pay them a wage premium, they would accept new orders only if they could charge a higher price for their equipment. Such a price increase would dampen firms' "appetites" for capital and thus limit the substitution of capital for labor.

For another example, suppose an increase in the wages of unskilled workers caused employers to attempt to substitute skilled employees for unskilled employees. If there were only a fixed number of skilled workers in an area, their wages would be bid up by employers. As in the prior example, the incentive to substitute alternative factors would be reduced, and the reduction in unskilled employment due to the substitution effect would be smaller. In contrast, if the prices of other inputs did not increase when employers attempted to increase their usage, other things equal, the substitution effect—and thus the wage elasticity of demand—would be larger.

Note again that prices of other inputs are less likely to be bid up in the long run than in the short run. In the long run, existing producers of capital equipment can expand their capacity and new producers can enter the market. Similarly, in the long run more skilled workers can be trained. This observation is an additional reason why the demand for labor will be more elastic in the long run.

THE SHARE OF LABOR IN TOTAL COSTS   Finally, the share of the category of labor in total costs is crucial to the size of the elasticity of labor demand. If the category's initial share were 20 percent, a 10 percent increase in the wage rate, other things equal, would raise total costs by 2 percent. In contrast, if its initial share were 80 percent, a 10 percent increase in the wage rate would increase total costs by 8 percent. Since employers would have to increase their product prices by more in the latter case, output, and hence employment, would fall more in that case. *Thus, the greater the category's share in total costs, the higher the wage elasticity of demand will tend to be.*

The discussion of this law, however, has ignored the ease of substituting other factors when the category's cost increases. *An exception to the law occurs when it is easier for employers to substitute other factors of production for the category of labor than it is for customers to substitute other products for the product being produced*; in this case the law is reversed. An example illustrates this exception.[5]

Suppose we classify the carpenters who build houses by their race/ethnicity. For example, we might divide carpenters into African-, Asian-, German-, Hispanic-, Irish-, Italian-, and Polish-American carpenters. Suppose further that carpenters from each group are equally productive and thus that they are perfect substitutes for each other. Finally, suppose that a fixed number of carpenters is required to build each house.

Since the wages of any one subgroup of carpenters would be a small fraction of the aggregate wages paid to *all* carpenters, if the last law always held it would lead one to believe that the wage elasticity of any one group of carpenters would be less than that of all carpenters as a group. This conclusion would be incorrect, however, because if any one group's wages rose, construction contractors could easily substitute employment of other carpenters for the group's members. Thus, the demand for any one group of carpenters would be highly elastic despite its small share in total cost. In contrast, the demand for all carpenters would be less elastic, as long as the price elasticity of the demand for houses was not high. Put another way, even a relatively small share in total cost cannot "protect" inputs with very good substitutes; their wage elasticities of demand will tend to be elastic.

---

[5]This example was called to our attention by Mark Killingsworth and is adapted from George J. Stigler, *The Theory of Price*, 4th ed. (New York: Macmillan, 1987), 254. For a formal derivation of the conditions under which this last law holds, see Hicks, *The Theory of Wages*.

ESTIMATES OF OWN-WAGE LABOR DEMAND ELASTICITIES

We started this chapter by pointing out that, to a large extent, the issue of labor demand elasticities is an empirical one. We now turn to the results of studies that estimate own-wage demand elasticities for labor as a generic input (that is, labor undifferentiated by skill level). The estimates we discuss are based on studies that utilize wage, output, and employment data from firms or narrowly defined industries (as opposed to a large aggregation of industries, such as the entire manufacturing sector). Thus, the employment responses being estimated approximate those that would be expected to occur in a firm that had to raise wages to remain competitive in the labor market.

As our analysis has indicated, employers' labor demand responses to a wage change can be broken down into two components: a scale and a substitution effect. These two effects can themselves be expressed as elasticities, and their sum is the own-wage labor demand elasticity. In Table 4.1 we display the results of recent estimates of (*a*) the short-run scale effect, (*b*) the substitution effect, and (*c*) the overall elasticity of demand for labor in the long run.

The scale effect (expressed as an elasticity) is defined as the percentage change in employment associated with a given percentage change in the wage, *holding capital constant*; that is, it is the employment response that occurs without a substitution effect. By definition, the *short-run* labor demand elasticity includes *only* the scale effect, although we noted earlier that the scale effect is likely to be greater in the long run than it is in the short run (owing to greater possibilities for *product market* substitutions in the long run). Therefore, estimates of short-run labor demand elasticities will be synonymous with the short-run scale effect, which may approximate the long-run scale effect if product market substitutions are relatively swift. A study using data from British manufacturing plants estimated that the short-run, own-wage labor demand elasticity is −0.53 (see Table 4.1). The short-run labor demand curve for a typical firm or narrowly defined sector, therefore, would appear to be inelastic.

The substitution effect, when expressed as an elasticity, is the percentage change in employment associated with a given percentage change in the wage rate, *holding output constant*. That is, it is a measure of how employers change their production techniques in response to wage changes, even if output does not change (that is, even if the scale effect is absent). It happens that substitution effects are easier to credibly estimate, so there are many more studies of these effects. One careful summary of 32 studies estimating substitution-effect elasticities placed the average estimated elasticity at −0.45 (which is what is displayed in Table 4.1), with most estimates falling into the range of −0.15 to −0.75.[6]

With the short-run scale elasticity and the substitution elasticity each very close to −0.5, it is not surprising that estimates of the long-run overall elasticity of demand for labor are close to unitary in magnitude. Table 4.1 indicates that a study of plants across several British industries estimated an own-wage elasticity of −0.93, while

---

[6]Daniel Hamermesh, *Labor Demand* (Princeton: Princeton University Press, 1993), 103.

TABLE 4.1

Components of the Own-Wage Elasticity of Demand for Labor: Empirical Estimates Using Plant-Level Data

	Estimated Elasticity
Short-Run Scale Effect	
British manufacturing firms, 1974–1982	−0.53
Substitution Effect	
32 studies using plant or narrowly	Average: −0.45
defined industry data	(Typical range: −0.15 to −0.75)
Overall Labor Demand Elasticity	
British plants, 1984	−0.93
British coal mines, 1950–1980	−1.0 to −1.4

Source: Daniel S. Hamermesh, *Labor Demand* (Princeton: Princeton University Press, 1993), 94–104.

another of British coal mines placed the elasticity of demand for labor in the range of −1.0 to −1.4.[7] Thus, these estimates suggest that if the wages a firm must pay rise by 10 percent, the firm's employment will shrink by close to 10 percent in the long run, other things being equal (that is, unless something else occurs that also affects the demand for labor).

Many more studies estimating the short-run and long-run own-wage elasticities of labor demand must be completed before we can have much confidence in predicting employment responses to changes in labor costs. For now, many policy decisions affecting these costs must be made without definitive predictions concerning their employment effects. The next section illustrates that, fortunately, theory can provide at least some rough guidance about expected magnitudes when precise knowledge is lacking.

APPLYING THE LAWS OF DERIVED DEMAND: INFERENTIAL ANALYSIS

Because empirical estimates of demand elasticities that may be required for making decisions are often lacking, it is frequently necessary to try to guess what these elasticities are likely to be. In making these guesses, we can apply the laws of derived demand to predict at least relative magnitudes for various types of labor. Consider first the demand for unionized New York City garment workers. As we shall discuss in Chapter 13, because unions are complex organizations, it is not always possible to specify what their goals are. Nevertheless, it is clear that most

---

[7]These estimates are very close to those from an earlier study of coal mines in the United States; see Morris Goldstein and Robert Smith, "The Predicted Impact of the Black Lung Benefits Program on the Coal Industry," in *Evaluating the Labor-Market Effects of Social Programs*, ed. Orley Ashenfelter and James Blum (Princeton: Princeton University Press, 1976).

unions value both wage *and* employment opportunities for their members. This observation leads to the simple prediction that, other things equal, the more elastic the demand for labor, the smaller will be the wage gain that a union will succeed in winning for its members. The reason for this prediction is that the more elastic the demand curve, the greater will be the percentage employment decline associated with any given percentage increase in wages. As a result, we can expect the following:

1. Unions would win larger wage gains for their members in markets with inelastic labor demand curves;
2. Unions would strive to take actions that reduce the wage elasticity of demand for their members' services; and
3. Unions might first seek to organize workers in markets in which labor demand curves are inelastic (because the potential gains to unionization are higher in these markets).

As we shall see in Chapter 13, many of these predictions are borne out by empirical evidence.

Because of foreign competition, the price elasticity of demand for the clothing produced by New York City garment workers is extremely high. Furthermore, employers can easily find other inputs to substitute for these workers—namely, lower-paid nonunion garment workers in the South (this substitution would require moving the plant to the South, a strategy that many manufacturers have followed). These facts lead one to predict that the wage elasticity of demand for New York City unionized garment workers should be very elastic, a prediction that seems to be borne out by union policies in the industry. That is, because the garment workers' union faces a highly elastic demand curve, its wage demands historically have been moderate. However, the union has also aggressively sought to reduce the elasticity of product demand by supporting policies that reduce foreign competition; in addition, it has pushed for higher federal minimum wages in order to reduce employers' incentives to move their plants to the South. (For another illustration of how an elastic *product* demand inhibits union wage increases, see Example 4.1.)

Next, consider the wage elasticity of demand for unionized airplane pilots on commercial scheduled airlines in the United States. Only a small share of the costs of operating large airplanes goes to pay pilots' salaries; such salaries are dwarfed by fuel and capital costs. Furthermore, substitution possibilities are limited; there is little room to substitute unskilled labor for skilled labor (although airlines can contemplate substituting capital for labor by reducing the number of flights they offer while increasing the size of airplanes). In addition, before the deregulation of airline industry in 1978, many airlines faced no competition on many of their routes or were prohibited from reducing their prices to compete with other airlines that flew the same routes. These factors all suggest that the wage elasticity of demand for airline pilots was quite inelastic. As one might expect, pilots' wages were also quite high because their union could push for large wage increases without fear that these increases would substantially reduce pilots' employment levels.

EXAMPLE 4.1

Why Are Union Wages So Different in Two Parts of the Trucking Industry?

The trucking industry's "general freight" sector, made up of motor carriers that handle nonspecialized freight requiring no special handling or equipment, is split into two distinct segments. One type of general freight carrier exclusively handles full truckloads, taking them directly from a shipper to a destination. The other type of carrier handles less-than-truckload shipments, which involve multiple shipments on each truck and an intricate coordination of pickups and deliveries. These two segments of the general freight industry have vastly different *elasticities of product demand,* and thus the union that represents truck drivers has a very different ability to raise wages (without suffering unacceptable losses of employment) in each segment.

The full truckload (TL) part of the industry has a product market that is very competitive, because it is relatively easy for firms or individuals to enter the market; one needs only a truck, the proper driver's license, and access to a telephone (to call a freight broker, who matches available drivers with shipments needing delivery). Because this part of the industry has many competing firms, with the threat of even more if prices rise, each firm faces a relatively elastic product demand curve.

Firms specializing in less-than-truckload (LTL) shipments must have a complex system of coordinated routes running between and within cities, and they must therefore be sufficiently large to support their own terminals for storing and transferring shipments from one route to another. The LTL segment of the industry is not easily entered and thus is partially monopolized. From 1980 to 1995—a time period over which the number of TL carriers tripled—virtually the only new entrants into the LTL market were regional subsidiaries of preexisting national carriers! To contrast competition in the two product markets somewhat differently, in 1987 the four largest LTL carriers accounted for 37 percent of total LTL revenues, while the four largest TL carriers accounted for only 11 percent of TL revenues.

The greater extent of competition in the TL part of the industry implies that, at the firm level, *product* demand is more elastic there than in the LTL sector; other things being equal, then, we would expect the *labor* demand curve also to be more elastic in the TL sector. Because unions worry about potential job losses when negotiating with carriers about wages, we would expect to find that union wages are lower in the TL than in the LTL part of the industry. In fact, a 1991 survey revealed that the union mileage rates (drivers are typically compensated on a cents-per-mile basis) were dramatically different in the two sectors:

TL sector
Average union rate: 28.4 cents per mile
Ratio, union to nonunion rate: 1.23

LTL sector
Average union rate: 35.8 cents per mile
Ratio, union to nonunion rate: 1.34

The above data support the theoretical implication that a union's power to raise wages is greater when product (and therefore labor) demand is relatively inelastic. In the less competitive LTL segment of the trucking industry, union drivers' wages are higher, both absolutely and relative to nonunion wages, than they are in the more competitive TL sector.

SOURCES: Michael H. Belzer, "Collective Bargaining After Deregulation: Do the Teamsters Still Count?" *Industrial and Labor Relations Review* 48, no. 4 (July 1995): 636–655; and Michael H. Belzer, *Paying the Toll: Economic Deregulation of the Trucking Industry* (Washington, D.C.: Economic Policy Institute, 1994).

However, after airline deregulation, competition among airline carriers increased substantially, leading to a more elastic labor demand for pilots. As a result, many airlines "requested," and won, reduced wages from their pilots (see Example 13.1).

Finally, consider the wage elasticity of demand for *domestic* farmworkers. This elasticity will depend heavily on the supply of immigrants, either legal or illegal, who are willing to work as farmworkers at wages less than the wages paid to domestic farmworkers. The successful unionization of farmworkers, coupled with union or government rules that prevent illegal immigrants from accepting such employment, obviously will make the demand curve for domestic farmworkers less elastic. Similarly, government regulations that either limit the quantity of foreign farm products that can be imported into the United States (quotas), place tariffs on such products, or limit foreign producers from *dumping* (selling their farm products in the United States at prices less than they charge in their own countries) will reduce the price elasticity of demand for U.S. farm products (and hence the wage elasticity of demand for domestic farmworkers). This example indicates how government policies on international trade, to be more completely analyzed in the appendix to this chapter, can influence wage elasticities of demand in particular labor markets.

The Cross-Wage Elasticity of Demand

Because firms may employ several categories of labor and capital, the demand for any one category can be affected by price changes in the others. For example, if the wages of carpenters rose, more people might build brick homes and the demand for *masons* might increase. On the other hand, an increase in carpenters' wages might decrease the overall level of home building in the economy, which would decrease the demand for *plumbers*. Finally, changes in the price of *capital* could increase or decrease the demand for workers in all three trades.

The direction and magnitude of the above effects can be summarized by examining the elasticities of demand for inputs with respect to the prices of *other* inputs. The *elasticity of demand for input j with respect to the price of input k* is the percentage change in the demand for input j induced by a 1 percent change in the price of input k. If the two inputs are both categories of labor, these *cross-wage elasticities of demand* are given by

$$\eta_{jk} = \frac{\%\Delta E_j}{\%\Delta W_k} \tag{4.2}$$

and

$$\eta_{kj} = \frac{\%\Delta E_k}{\%\Delta W_j}$$

where, again, the Greek letter η is used to represent the elasticity. If the cross-elasticities are positive (with an increase in the price of one increasing the demand for the other), the two are said to be *gross substitutes*. If these cross-elasticities are negative (and an increase in the price of one reduces the demand for the other), the two are said to be *gross complements* (refer back to Figure 3.3).

It is worth restressing that whether two inputs are gross substitutes or gross complements depends on the relative sizes of the scale and substitution effects. To see this, suppose we assume that adults and teenagers are substitutes in production. A decrease in the teenage wage will thus have opposing effects on adult employment. On the one hand, there is a substitution effect: for a given level of output, employers will now have an incentive to substitute teens for adults in the production process and reduce adult employment. On the other hand, there is a scale effect: a lower teenage wage provides employers with an incentive to increase employment of all inputs, including adults.

If the scale effect proves to be smaller than the substitution effect, adult employment will move in the same direction as teenage wages and the two groups will be gross substitutes. In contrast, if the scale effect is larger than the substitution effect, adult employment and teenage wages will move in opposite directions and the two groups will be gross complements. Knowing that two groups are substitutes in production, then, is not sufficient to tell us whether they are gross substitutes or gross complements.[8]

Because economic theory cannot indicate in advance whether two given inputs will be gross substitutes or gross complements, the major policy questions about cross-wage elasticities of demand relate to the issue of their *sign*; that is, we often want most to know whether a particular cross-elasticity is positive (the inputs are gross substitutes) or negative (they are gross complements). Before turning to a review of actual findings, we analyze underlying forces that determine the signs of cross-elasticities.

CAN THE LAWS OF DERIVED DEMAND BE APPLIED TO CROSS-ELASTICITIES?

The four laws of derived demand developed in the last section *cannot* be applied directly to cross-elasticities; however, *the technological or market considerations that underlie the laws* are still useful in understanding cross-wage elasticities. Stated more fully, the Hicks-Marshall laws of derived demand are based on four technological or market conditions that determine the size of *own-wage* elasticities. Each of the four conditions influences the substitution or the scale effect and, as noted above, the relative strengths of these two effects are also what determine the sign of *cross-elasticities*. The laws that apply to own-wage elasticities cannot be applied directly to cross-elasticities, because with cross-elasticities the substitution effect (if there is one) and the scale effect work in opposite directions. The same (or at least very similar) underlying considerations, however, are basic to an analysis of cross-elasticities.

---

[8]As noted in Chapter 3, if two groups are complements in production, a decrease in the price of one should lead to increased employment of the other. Complements in production are always gross complements.

As we discuss these four considerations in the context of cross-elasticities, it will be helpful to have a hypothetical referent in mind. Let us return, therefore, to the question of what might happen to the demand for adult workers if the wages of teenage workers were to fall. As noted above, the answer depends on the relative strengths of the scale and substitution effects. What determines the strength of each?

THE SCALE EFFECT The most immediate effect of a fall in the wages of teenagers would be reduced production costs for those firms that employ them. Competition in the product market would ensure that lower costs are followed by price reductions, which should stimulate increases in both product demand and the level of output. Increased levels of output will tend to cause increases in employment of all kinds of workers, including adults. This chain of events obviously describes behavior underlying the scale effect, and we now investigate what conditions are likely to make for a strong (or weak) scale effect.

The initial cost (and price) reductions would be greater among those employers for whom teenage wages constituted a higher proportion of total costs. Other things equal, greater price reductions would result in greater increases in both product demand and overall employment. Thus, *the share of total costs devoted to the productive factor whose price is changing* will influence the size of the scale effect. The larger this share is, other things equal, the greater will be the scale effect (and the more likely it is that gross complementarity will exist). This tendency is analogous to the fourth Hicks-Marshall law discussed earlier; the difference is that with cross-elasticities, the factor whose *price* is changing is not the same as the one for which *employment* changes are being analyzed.

The other condition that greatly influences the size of the scale effect is product demand elasticity. In the above case of teenage wage reductions, the greater the increase in product demand when firms reduce their prices, the greater will be the tendency for employment of all workers, including adults, to increase. More generally, *the greater the price elasticity of product demand, other things equal, the greater will be the scale effect (and thus the greater the likelihood of gross complementarity).* The effects of product demand elasticity are thus similar with both own-wage and cross-wage elasticities.

THE SUBSTITUTION EFFECT After teenage wages fall, firms will also have incentives to alter their production techniques so that teenagers are more heavily used. Whether the greater use of teenagers causes an increase or some loss of adult jobs partially depends on a technological question: Are teenagers and adults substitutes or complements in production? If they are complements in production, the effect on adults of changing productive techniques will reinforce the scale effect and serve to unambiguously increase adult employment (meaning, of course, that adults and teenagers would be gross complements). If they are substitutes in production, however, then changing productive techniques involves using a higher ratio of teenagers to adults, and the question then becomes whether this substitution effect is large or small relative to the scale effect.

A technological condition affecting the size of the substitution effect is a direct carryover from the second Hicks-Marshall law discussed previously: *the substitution effect will be greater when the category of labor whose price has changed is easily substituted for other factors of production.* When analyzing the effects on adult employment of a decline in the teenage wage, it is evident that when teenagers are more easily substituted for adults, the substitution effect (and therefore the chances of gross substitutability between the two categories of labor) will be greater.

Another condition influencing the size of the substitution effect associated with a reduction in the teenage wage relates to the labor supply curve of adults. If the adult labor supply curve were upward-sloping and rather steep, then adult wages would tend to fall as teenagers were substituted for adults and the demand curve for adults shifted left. This fall would blunt the substitution effect, because adults would also become cheaper to hire. Conversely, if the adult labor supply curve were relatively flat, adult wages would be less affected by reduced demand and the substitution effect would be less blunted. As with the case of own-wage elasticities (the third Hicks-Marshall law discussed above), *more-elastic factor supply curves thus also lead to a greater substitution effect, other things equal, in the case of cross-wage elasticities.*

Finally, holding other things constant, the share of the teenage wage bill in total costs influences the substitution as well as the scale effect in the example we are analyzing. For example, if teenage labor costs were a very large fraction of total costs, the possibilities for further substitution of teenagers for adults would be rather limited (this can be easily seen by considering an example in which teenagers constituted 100 percent of all production costs). Thus, while a larger share of teenagers in total cost would make for a relatively large scale effect, it also could reflect a situation in which the possibilities of substituting teenagers for adults are smaller than they would otherwise be (smaller, that is, holding other influences constant).

ESTIMATES RELATING TO CROSS-ELASTICITIES

Estimating at least the sign of cross-wage labor demand elasticities is useful for purposes of evaluating public policies, because a policy aimed at one group can have unintended consequences for other groups. For example, as implied above, a policy to subsidize the wages of teenagers could reduce employers' demand for adult workers. Likewise, a policy that reduces the costs of capital investments could create substitution effects that ultimately reduce firms' demand for labor. Thus, it is important to know which categories of labor and capital are substitutes for or complements with each other in the production process. Also, we would like to know whether particular categories of labor exhibit *gross* substitutability or complementarity with each other or with capital.

Most of the cross-wage empirical studies to date have focused on the issue of whether two factors are substitutes or complements in production. These studies estimate the employment response for one category of labor to a wage or price change elsewhere, *holding output constant* (which in effect allows us to focus just on changes in the *mix* of factors used in production). The factors of production paired together for analysis in these studies are numerous and the results are not always clear-cut; nevertheless, the findings taken as a whole offer at least a few generalizations:[9]

1. Labor and energy are clearly substitutes in production, although their degree of substitutability is small.
2. Labor and materials are probably substitutes in production, with the degree of substitutability again being small.
3. We are not certain whether either skilled or unskilled labor is a substitute for or a complement with capital in the production process. What does appear to be true is that skilled (or well-educated) labor is more likely to be complementary with capital than is unskilled labor—and that if they are both substitutes for capital, the degree of substitutability is smaller for skilled labor.[10]
4. The finding summarized in 3 above suggests that skilled labor is more likely than unskilled labor to be a *gross* complement with capital. This finding is important to our understanding of recent trends in the earnings of skilled and unskilled workers (see Chapter 14), because the prices of computers and other high-tech capital goods have fallen dramatically in the past decade or so.
5. The finding in 3 above also implies that if the wages of both skilled and unskilled labor were to rise by the same percentage, the magnitude of any employment loss associated with the substitution effect (as capital is substituted for labor) will be greater for the unskilled. Thus, we expect that, other things equal, *own-wage* labor demand elasticities will be larger in magnitude for unskilled than skilled workers.
6. The extent of complementarity or substitutability in production between immigrant and native workers, or between new immigrants and older groups of immigrants, is very small. This may help explain the findings, discussed later in Chapter 10, that changing flows of immigrants have had relatively minor effects on the wages of native workers.[11]

---

[9] Hamermesh, *Labor Demand,* 105–127.

[10] Evidence has been offered that the degree of substitutability depends on the age of capital equipment. Specifically, Ann Bartel and Frank Lichtenberg, "Technology: Some Empirical Evidence," *Review of Economics and Statistics* 69 (February 1987): 1–11, present evidence that the relative demand for highly educated workers vis-à-vis less-educated workers declines as the capital stock ages. They attribute this to the comparative advantage that highly educated workers have with respect to learning and implementing new technologies; thus as the capital stock ages, the complementarity of these workers with capital declines.

[11] See George J. Borjas, "The Economics of Immigration," *Journal of Economic Literature* 32, no. 4 (December 1994): 1667–1717, for a review of the literature on this point, especially on pages 1695–1700.

Policy Application: Effects of Minimum Wage Laws

HISTORY AND DESCRIPTION

The Fair Labor Standards Act of 1938 was the first major piece of protective labor legislation adopted at the national level in the United States. Among its provisions were a minimum wage rate, or floor, below which hourly wages could not be reduced, an overtime-pay premium for workers who worked long workweeks, and restrictions on the use of child labor. The minimum wage provisions were designed to guarantee each worker a reasonable wage for his or her work effort and thus to reduce the incidence of poverty.

When initially adopted, the minimum wage was set at $0.25 an hour and covered roughly 43 percent of all nonsupervisory wage and salary workers—primarily those employed in larger firms involved in interstate commerce (manufacturing, mining, and construction). As Table 4.2 indicates, both the basic minimum wage and coverage under the minimum wage have expanded over time. Indeed, after April of 1991, the minimum wage was set at $4.25 an hour, and over 88 percent of all nonsupervisory workers were covered by its provisions.

It is important to emphasize that the minimum wage rate is specified in *nominal* terms and not in terms *relative* to some other wage or price index. Historically, this specification of the minimum wage has led to a pattern of changes that can be represented by Figure 4.3, where time is plotted on the horizontal axis and the value of the minimum wage relative to average hourly earnings in manufacturing is plotted on the vertical axis. Congress initially specifies the nominal level of the minimum wage (MW_0), which, given the level of average hourly earnings that prevails in the economy (AHE_0), leads to an initial value of the minimum wage relative to average hourly earnings (MW_0/AHE_0). Over time this relative value declines as average hourly earnings increase with inflation or productivity growth. The reduced relative value of the minimum wage creates pressure on Congress to legislate an increase in the nominal minimum wage, and after the passage of time (point t_1 in Figure 4.3) Congress returns the relative value of the minimum wage approximately to its initial level. Over time the process is repeated, and the saw-toothed time profile of relative minimum wage values portrayed in Figure 4.3 emerges. Although it varies from peak to peak, the value of the minimum wage relative to average hourly earnings in manufacturing after each legislated change was typically in the range of 0.45 to 0.50 until the 1990 change (see Table 4.2).

EMPLOYMENT EFFECTS: THEORETICAL ANALYSIS

Since the minimum wage was first legislated, a concern has been that it will reduce employment, especially among the groups it is intended to benefit. Specifically, in the face of downward-sloping labor demand curves, a policy that compels firms to raise the wages paid to all low-wage workers can be expected to *reduce employment opportunities* for the least-skilled or least-experienced. Thus, while those low-wage workers who remained employed would be helped by an increase in the minimum

TABLE 4.2
Federal Minimum Wage Legislation in the United States, 1938–1995

Effective Date of Minimum Wage Change	Nominal Minimum Wage	Percent of Nonsupervisory Employees Covered[a]	Minimum Wage Relative to Average Hourly Wage in Manufacturing[c]	
			Before	After
10/24/38	$0.25	43.4	—	0.403
10/24/39	0.30	47.1	0.398	0.478
10/24/45	0.40	55.4	0.295	0.394
1/25/50	0.75	53.4	0.278	0.521
3/1/56	1.00	53.1	0.385	0.512
9/3/61	1.15	62.1	0.431	0.495
9/3/63	1.25	62.1	0.467	0.508
9/3/64	1.25	62.6		
2/1/67	1.40	75.3	0.441	0.494
2/1/68	1.60	72.6	0.465	0.531
2/1/69	1.60	78.2		
2/1/70	1.60	78.5		
2/1/71	1.60	78.4		
5/1/74	2.00	83.7	0.363	0.454
1/1/75	2.10	83.3	0.423	0.445
1/1/76	2.30		0.410	0.449
1/1/78	2.65		0.430	0.480
1/1/79	2.90		0.402	0.440
1/1/80	3.10		0.417	0.445
1/1/81	3.35		0.403	0.435
4/1/90	3.80	88.6[b]	0.329	0.373
4/1/91	4.25		0.342	0.382

[a]Excludes executive, administrative, and professional personnel (including teachers in elementary and secondary schools) from the base.

[b]As of September 1987.

[c]Ideally, one would like to contrast the value of the minimum wage to average hourly earnings in the economy as a whole. However, prior to 1964 such data were not collected, and hence we express the minimum wage relative to average hourly earnings in manufacturing here to maintain historical comparability. In both 1964 and 1991, average hourly earnings in the private nonfarm sector of the economy were a little over 90 percent of average hourly earnings in manufacturing.

FIGURE 4.3

*Time Profile of the Minimum Wage
Relative to Average Hourly Earnings*

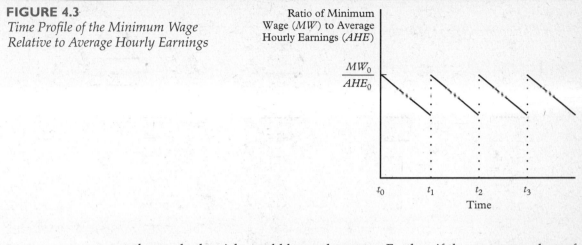

wage, those who lost jobs could be made poorer. Further, if the percentage loss of employment among low-wage workers is greater than the percentage increase in their wages—that is, if the demand curve for low-wage workers is *elastic*—then the *aggregate* earnings of low-wage workers could be made smaller by an increase in the minimum wage.

Much research effort has been devoted over the years to understanding the employment effects of increases in the minimum wage. In evaluating the findings of this research, we must keep in mind that good research has to be guided by good theory. Theory gives us insight into the effects we expect to see from certain causes, thus providing us with a road map that directs our explorations into the real world. With the minimum wage and its effects on employment, we will see that a sophisticated grasp of labor demand theory is necessary in directing us how and where to look for these effects. In particular, theory suggests several issues that must be addressed by any research study of the minimum wage.

NOMINAL VS. REAL WAGES   We have already indicated that minimum wage levels in the United States have been set in nominal terms and adjusted by Congress only sporadically. The result is that general price inflation gradually lowers the real minimum wage during the years between congressional action; thus, what appears to be a fixed minimum wage during periods between congressional action turns out to have constantly changing incentives for employment. One will recall that the demand for labor is a downward-sloping function of real wages, so as the real minimum wage falls from the point when it is newly enacted to just before it is raised again, its adverse effects on employment can be expected to decline.

Researchers generally take account of changes in the real minimum wage in one of two ways. First, if looking at employment effects over several years, one can divide the nominal minimum wage by average hourly earnings or some other measure that reflects general price movements.

FIGURE 4.4
*Minimum Wage Effects: Growing
Demand Obscures Job Loss*

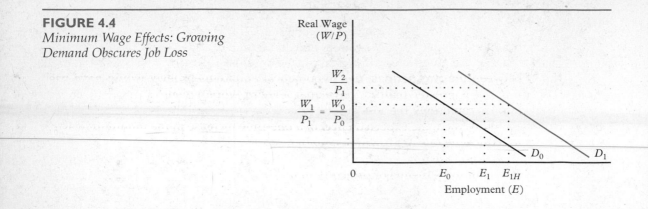

Second, the federal minimum wage in the United States is uniformly applied to a large country characterized by regional differences in prices. Taking account of regional differences in prices or wages, we find that the real minimum wage in Alaska (where wages and prices are very high) is lower than it is in Mississippi. Recognizing that there are regional differences in the real minimum wage leads to the prediction that employment effects of a uniformly applied minimum wage law generally will be most adverse in regions with the lowest costs of living. (Researchers must also take into account the fact that many states have their own minimum wage laws, some having minimums that exceed the federal minimum.)

HOLDING OTHER THINGS CONSTANT   It is important to remember that predictions of job loss associated with higher minimum wages are made *holding other things constant*. In particular, the prediction grows out of what is expected to happen to employment as one moves up and to the left along a *fixed* labor demand curve. If the labor demand curve were to shift at the same time that a new minimum becomes effective, the employment effects of the shift could be confounded with those of the new minimum.

Consider, for example Figure 4.4, where for simplicity we have omitted the labor supply curve and focused on only the demand side of the market. Suppose that D_0 is the demand curve for low-skilled labor in year 0, in which year the real wage is W_0/P_0 and the employment level is E_0. Further assume that in the absence of any change in the minimum wage, the money wage and the price level would both increase by the same percentage over the next year, so that the real wage in year 1 (W_1/P_1) would be the same as that in year 0.

Now suppose that in year 1, two things happen. First, the minimum wage rate is raised to W_2, which is greater than W_1, so that the real wage increases to W_2/P_1. Second, because the economy is expanding, the demand for low-skilled labor shifts out to D_1. The result of these two changes is that employment increases from E_0 to E_1.

Comparisons of observed employment levels at two points of time have led some investigators to conclude that minimum wage increases had no adverse employment effects. However, this simple before/after comparison is *not* the correct one if labor demand has shifted, as in Figure 4.4. Rather, one should ask, "How did the actual employment level in period 1 compare to the level that *would have prevailed* in the absence of the increase in the minimum wage?" Since demand grew between the two periods, this hypothetical employment level would have been E_{1H}. E_{1H} is greater than E_1, the actual level of employment in period 1, so that $E_{1H} - E_1$ represents the loss of jobs caused by the minimum wage. In a growing economy, then, the expected effect of a one-time increase in the minimum wage is to reduce the rate of growth of employment.

Controlling for all the "other things" besides wages that affect labor demand turns out to be the major difficulty in measuring employment changes caused by the minimum wage. A partial way to control for these influences is to examine the effects of a legislated increase in the minimum over a time period so short that changes in consumer preferences or the availability of new products cannot be consequential. Unfortunately, before-and-after studies over a short period of time still must take account of new trends or temporary deviations from old ones, and in any event they capture only the short-run elasticity of demand for labor.

EFFECTS OF UNCOVERED SECTORS   The federal minimum wage law, like many government regulations, has an "uncovered" sector. As can be seen from Table 4.2, coverage has steadily increased over the years, but the law still does not apply to about 10 percent of nonsupervisory workers (the major exemptions are for very small firms in the retail trade and service industries). Also, with millions of employers and limited resources for governmental enforcement, *noncompliance* with the law may be widespread, creating another kind of noncoverage.[12] The existence of uncovered sectors significantly affects how the overall employment of low-wage workers will respond to increases in the minimum wage.

Consider the labor market for unskilled, low-wage workers that is depicted in Figure 4.5. The market has two sectors. In one, employers must pay wages equal to at least the minimum wage of W_1 ; wages in the uncovered sector are free to vary with market conditions. While the total labor supply to both markets taken as a whole is fixed at E_T (that is, the total labor supply curve is vertical), workers can freely move from one sector to the other seeking better job offers. Free movement between sectors suggests that, in the absence of minimum wage regulations, the wage in each sector will be the same. Referring to Figure 4.5, let us assume that this "pre-minimum" wage is W_0 and that total employment of E_T is broken down into E_0^C in the covered sector plus E_0^U in the uncovered sector.

If a minimum wage of W_1 is imposed on the covered sector, all unskilled workers will prefer to work there. However, the increase in wages in that sector, from W_0 to W_1, reduces demand, and covered-sector employment will fall from E_0^C to E_1^C. Some workers who previously had, or would have found, jobs in the covered

---

[12]Orley Ashenfelter and Robert Smith, "Compliance with the Minimum Wage Law," *Journal of Political Economy* 87 (April 1979): 335–350.

sector must now seek work in the uncovered sector. Thus, to the E_0^U workers formerly working in the uncovered sector are added $E_0^C - E_1^C$ other workers seeking jobs there. Thus, all unskilled workers in the market who are not lucky enough to find "covered jobs" at W_1 must now look for work in the uncovered sector,[13] and the (vertical) supply curve to that sector becomes E_1^U [$= E_0^U + (E_0^C - E_1^C) = E_T - E_1^C$]. The increased supply of workers to that sector drives down the wage there from W_0 to W_2.

The presence of an uncovered sector thus suggests the possibility that employment among unskilled workers will be rearranged, but not reduced, by an increase in the minimum wage. In the above example, all E_T workers remained employed after the minimum was imposed. Rather than reducing overall employment of the unskilled, then, a partially covering minimum wage law might serve to shift employment out of the covered to the uncovered sector, with the further result that wages in the uncovered sector would be driven down.

The magnitude of any employment shift from the covered to the uncovered sector, of course, depends on the *size* of the latter; the smaller it is, the lower are the chances that job losers from the covered sector will find employment there. Whatever the size of the uncovered sector, however, its very presence means that the *overall* loss of employment is likely to be less than the loss of employment in the *covered sector*.

INTERSECTORAL SHIFTS IN PRODUCT DEMAND It is important to remember that the employment effects of a wage change are the result of scale and substitution effects. Substitution effects stem from changes in the way in which firms choose to produce, while scale effects are rooted in consumer adjustments to changes in product prices. The student will recall that, faced with a given increase (say) in the minimum wage, firms' increases in costs will generally be greater when the share of low-wage labor in total costs is greater; thus, the same increase in the minimum wage can lead to rather different effects on product prices among different parts of the covered sector. Further, if these subsectors compete with each other for customers, it is possible that scale effects of the increased wage will serve to *increase* employment among some firms in the covered sector.

To illustrate how mandated increases in wages can cause intersectoral shifts in product demand, we briefly turn from minimum wages to an analysis of a proposed law (later modified) that would have required coal mine operators to buy

---

[13]Under some circumstances it may be rational for these unemployed workers to remain unemployed for a while and to search for jobs in the covered sector. We shall explore this possibility—which is discussed by Jacob Mincer in "Unemployment Effects of Minimum Wage Changes," *Journal of Political Economy* 84 (August 1976): S87–S104—in Chapter 13. At this point we simply note that if it occurs, unemployment will result.

FIGURE 4.5

Minimum Wage Effects: Incomplete Coverage Causes Employment Shifts

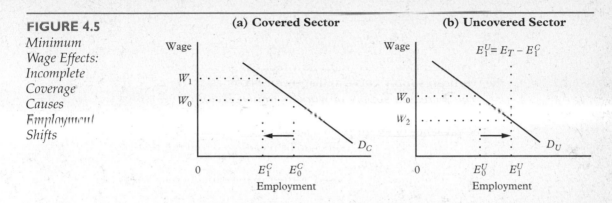

(a) Covered Sector   (b) Uncovered Sector

insurance for their workers against the risk of dust-related lung disease. The costs of this insurance would have been directly proportional to payroll costs, and the effect would have been to mandate an increase of about 10 percent in the hourly labor costs of miners.[14] Understandably, the government wanted to know what the employment effects of this law might be.

Estimates of the likely employment effects started with the fact that coal mining had two sectors that produced the same product in two very different ways. Underground mines were very labor-intensive, with roughly half of their total costs associated with labor. Surface mines (also called strip mines) dug coal with huge earthmoving equipment, and labor in this sector constituted only 25 percent of total costs. The mandated insurance, therefore, would have raised costs (and prices) in the underground sector more than in the surface sector, with the result that surface-mined coal would have become *relatively* cheaper. To be sure, increased prices across both sectors would have reduced the *overall* use of coal to some extent, but those who still bought coal would now be more likely to buy it from surface mines than before. The government estimated, in fact, that the demand for surface-mined coal would have increased by about 4 percent if coal mines had been forced to buy this insurance.

In summary, an increased minimum wage may apply equally to all firms in the covered sector, but the employment effects may not be negative in all parts of this sector. An increased minimum will have different effects on product prices in different subsectors, with the result that certain firms may be relatively advantaged even if their total costs go up to some extent! Their costs may rise, but if they rise by less than the costs of their competitors, the new minimum wage actually could serve to stimulate the demand for their products. Measuring the employment effects of minimum wages, then, is best done by looking at an *entire* sector rather than individual firms or narrowly defined subsectors.

---

[14]The details of this example are reported in Morris Goldstein and Robert Smith, "The Predicted Impact of the Black Lung Benefits Program on the Coal Industry."

EMPLOYMENT EFFECTS: EMPIRICAL ESTIMATES

Currently there is no consensus among economists about the effects of minimum wages on employment. After some three hundred studies over the past two decades, what at first seemed like a straightforward way to test the prediction that labor demand curves are negatively sloped has proven to yield results that are frustratingly ambiguous. As a consequence, labor economists are now engaged in a spirited inquiry into whether the problem lies with the use of a theory of labor demand that is too simple or with the research methods used to test that theory.

This textbook is not the place to discuss the intricacies of research design and statistical methodology, but one general feature of the results to date is that reasonable, defensible changes in design or methodology drastically alter estimates of the effects of minimum wages on employment.[15] After our discussion of the theoretical complexities posed by regional differences in living costs, the existence of an uncovered sector, intersectoral shifts within the covered sector, and difficulties in accounting for the "other things" that can affect employment, it is not surprising that research design is critical. What is surprising is that seemingly minor changes in design can have such substantial effects on the results.

One example of the minor changes that cause estimates to vary significantly is found in *time-series* analyses of employment effects among teenagers (a notoriously low-paid group whose wages are likely to be affected by the minimum wage). These analyses involve estimating how some measure of teenage employment varies over time with the level of the real minimum wage, after controlling for other variables in each year, such as the adult unemployment rate, that could also affect teenage employment. Studies that have applied exactly the same estimating procedures to data from different time periods often obtain dramatically different estimates. For example, an analysis using data from the 1949 to 1994 period estimated that increases in the minimum wage would have no effect on the employment rate (employment divided by population) of 16- and 17-year-olds; applying the same procedures to the 1954 to 1993 period, however, resulted in estimated employment effects that were significantly negative. Another study estimated qualitatively different effects of minimum wages on teenage employment rates over the 1954–1979 and 1954–1986 periods.[16]

A second example of a seemingly minor design change that has caused a major difference in results comes from a comparison of two recent studies of how the employment of teenagers was affected by the 1990 and 1991 increases in the federal minimum wage.[17] Both used data from the same basic source, both analyzed the teenage employment rate in each state for years before and after the increases, and

---

[15]Card and Krueger, *Myth and Measurement*, Chapters 6–8.

[16]See John Kennan, "The Elusive Effects of Minimum Wages," *Journal of Economic Literature* 33, no. 4 (December 1995): 1950–1965, and Card and Krueger, *Myth and Measurement*, 197.

[17]The first study discussed is Donald Deere, Kevin M. Murphy, and Finis Welch, "Employment and the 1990–1991 Minimum Wage Hike," *American Economic Review* 85, no 2 (May 1995): 232–237; the second is found in Card and Krueger, *Myth and Measurement*, Chapter 4.

both used each state's yearly *overall* employment rate to partially control for the "other things" that can affect teenage employment. Both also tested, although in different ways, the hypothesis that employment effects will be larger when mandated wage increases are larger.

One study estimated the average relationship, across all states, between the *teenage* and the *overall* employment rates in 1990 and 1991–1992, as compared to the same relationship in the late 1980s. It found that, as expected, the 1990 teenage employment rate was lower, compared to the overall rate, than before; it was lower yet in 1991 and 1992, when the minimum wage was even higher. Further, the declines were greatest for minorities and females, whose wages were most affected by the minimum wage increases. These findings are consistent with the predictions that, other things equal, higher minimum wages will reduce teenage employment opportunities, and that they will reduce them most where mandated wage increases are greatest.

The other study compared 1989 to 1992 changes in states' teenage employment rates with the fraction of teenagers whose wages were affected by the legislated increases in 1990 and 1991, after controlling for changes in each state's overall employment rate over that period. The hypothesis of the study was that employment reductions would be greater in "high-impact" states (states in which the legislation caused the greatest wage increases among teenagers). This study found, contrary to expectations, no evidence that higher minimum wages in 1990 and 1991 reduced teenage employment rates.

The two studies both searched for greater employment effects among the very groups of teenagers whose wages were more likely to be raised by the mandated increases. The former study tested for employment responses associated with two different mandated wage changes on three different demographic groups, while the latter study tested for different responses of the mandated increases in high- and low-impact states. Because both studies employed defensible research designs, one must wonder why such a strong prediction of standard labor demand theory (that the demand curve slopes downward) does not have more robust empirical support.[18]

One is tempted to conclude that even if the employment effects of minimum wages are negative, they are probably relatively small and thus hard to detect. The estimates of own-wage elasticities cited earlier in this chapter, which derived from very different kinds of studies, suggested that a typical long-run elasticity of demand for labor (as a generic input) was roughly unitary, and we expect the elasticity

---

[18]Empirical support for a downward-sloping labor demand curve has also been rather difficult to find in studies of minimum-wage laws in other countries. See, for example, Stephen Machin and Alan Manning, "The Effects of Minimum Wages on Wage Dispersion and Employment: Evidence from U.K. Wage Councils," *Industrial and Labor Relations Review* 47, no. 2 (January 1994): 319–329; and John Abowd, Francis Kramarz, Thomas Lemieux, and David Margolis, "Minimum Wages and Youth Employment in France and the United States," Cornell University School of Industrial and Labor Relations, July 1995.

to be even greater for less-skilled workers and teenagers. After reviewing the estimated labor demand elasticities of teenagers based on changes in the minimum wage, even those who believe that teenage employment declines when the minimum is raised concede that observed labor demand elasticities are far smaller than unitary (an elasticity of −0.1 or −0.2 is typical).[19]

Is it possible that the actual job losses among teenagers are small because uncovered sectors—legal or illegal—absorb those workers displaced from covered employment? If this occurs, we would have found that the 1990–1991 legislated increases, for example, did not widely increase the wages of teenagers. Both studies of the 1990–1991 mandates compared above, however, carefully documented the widespread increase in teenage wages that took place in response to the legislated increases; thus, this possibility is not the most likely explanation. It is somewhat more likely, as we found with our analysis of payroll taxes in Chapter 3, that the demand for labor fully adjusts to relatively modest increases in wage costs only with a long lag. If so, before-and-after studies may not be measuring changes in employment over a long enough period to capture the full effects of legislated increases.[20]

As noted earlier, however, the rather fragile results of minimum wage studies have also spurred some economists to wonder if the monopsony model of labor demand might have relevance to a wide variety of labor markets. As we saw in Chapter 3, one feature of the monopsony model is that it generates ambiguous predictions about how employment might be expected to respond to modest increases in the minimum wage, especially in the short run. The student will remember that the ambiguity concerns only the response of employment to *mandated* wage increases, which flatten the labor supply curve, not to those wage changes generated by shifts in labor supply curves that still leave them upward-sloping. Thus, the monopsony model might help account for the differences in labor demand elasticities based on minimum wage changes and the larger elasticities cited earlier, which were estimated using wage changes generated under different conditions. We will inquire later in this text, especially in Chapters 10, 11, and 12, into labor-market characteristics, employment conditions, and issues of supervision and compensation that could create the upward-sloping labor supply curves to firms that are so central to the monopsony model.

---

[19]For studies on this topic, see Hamermesh, *Labor Demand*, 187; David Neumark and William Wascher, "Employment Effects of Minimum and Subminimum Wages: Panel Data on State Minimum Wage Laws," *Industrial and Labor Relations Review* 46, no. 1 (October 1992): 55–81; and Alison J. Wellington, "Effects of the Minimum Wage on the Employment Status of Youths," *Journal of Human Resources* 26, no. 1 (Winter 1991): 27–46.

[20]A related problem of before-and-after studies (including time-series analyses) of minimum wages is that employers know well in advance the effective date of a new minimum. If some adjust to the new minimum *in advance* of the date selected by the researcher as the "before" period, these adjustments will not be associated by the researcher with the new minimum. For a nice discussion of this problem, see Daniel Hamermesh's comments on Card and Krueger, *Myth and Measurement*, in the volume cited in footnote 2 above.

DOES THE MINIMUM WAGE FIGHT POVERTY?

As noted above, the short-run response of low-wage employment to changes in the minimum wage is widely believed to be inelastic; that is, the percentage decline in employment is smaller than the percentage increase in the wage rate. Given an inelastic response of employment, we expect that an increase in the minimum would serve to increase the total earnings going to low-wage workers as a whole. Can it be said, then, that minimum wage laws are effective weapons in the struggle to reduce poverty?

Identifying those who are considered to be living in poverty is done by comparing the income of each family with the poverty line set for families of its particular size; thus, *family* income and family size are the critical variables for defining poverty. Teenagers earning below the minimum, for example, may be benefited if their wages are raised by a legislated increase, but if these teenagers mostly live in nonpoor families, then the increased overall income among teenagers may do very little to reduce poverty.

One study of the 1990–1991 increases in the minimum wage found that, of those who earned between the old and new minimums (that is, between $3.35 and $4.24), only 22 percent lived in poor families. Conversely, of those workers in 1990 who lived in poverty, only 26 percent earned between the old and new minimums. All told, assuming no employment effects, only 19 percent of the estimated earnings increases associated with the 1990 and 1991 minimum wage increases went to poor families.[21] Thus, the minimum wage is a relatively blunt instrument with which to reduce poverty; most of its benefits go to workers in nonpoor families. In Chapter 6 we will analyze the strengths and weaknesses of other programs that provide income support to poor families, and in Chapter 14 we will raise the question of whether the minimum wage plays a significant role in reducing *earnings* inequality.

Applying Concepts of Labor Demand Elasticity To the Issue of Technological Change

Technological change, which can encompass the introduction of new products and production techniques as well as changes in technology that serve to reduce the cost of capital (for example, increases in the speed of computers), is frequently viewed as a blessing by some and a curse by others. Those who view it positively point to the enormous gains in the standard of living made possible by new technology, while

---

[21]In 1990, the poverty line for a single individual under age 65 was $6,800, while for a family of three it was $10,419 and for a family of four it was $13,359 (see U.S. Bureau of the Census, *Poverty in the United States: 1990*, Series P-60, no. 175, August 1991). The percentages in this paragraph are based on Richard V. Burkhauser, Kenneth A. Couch, and David C. Wittenburg, "'Who Gets What' from Minimum Wage Hikes: A Replication and Re-Estimation of Card and Krueger," *Industrial and Labor Relations Review* (forthcoming). Also see Card and Krueger, *Myth and Measurement*, Chapter 9.

those who see technological change as a threat often stress its adverse consequences for workers. Are the concepts underlying the elasticity of demand for labor useful in making judgments about the effects of technological change?

There are two aspects of technological change that affect the demand for labor. One is product demand. *Shifts* in product demand curves will tend to shift labor demand curves in the same direction, and changes in the *elasticity* of product demand with respect to product price will tend to cause qualitatively similar changes in the own-wage elasticity of labor demand. The invention of new products (word processors, for example) that serve as substitutes for old ones (typewriters) will tend to shift the labor demand curve in the older sector to the left, causing loss of employment in that sector. If greater product substitution possibilities are also created by these new inventions, it is possible that the introduction of new products can increase the *elasticity* of product—and hence, labor—demand. Increasing the own-wage elasticity of labor demand increases the amount of job loss associated with collectively bargained wage increases, for example, and it therefore reduces the power of unions to secure large wage increases in the older sector. While benefiting people as consumers, and while providing jobs in the new sectors, the introduction of new products does necessitate some painful changes in established sectors of the economy as workers, unions, and employers must all adjust to a new environment.

A second aspect of technological change is often associated with automation, or the substitution of capital for labor. For purposes of analyzing its effects on labor demand, this second aspect of technological change should be thought of as reducing the cost of capital. In some cases—the mass production of personal computers is one example—a fall in capital prices is what literally occurs. In other cases of technological change—the miniaturization of computer components, for example, which has made possible new production techniques—an invention makes completely new technologies available. When something is unavailable, it can be thought of as having an infinite price (it is not available at any price); therefore, the availability of a new technique is equivalent to observing a decline in its price to some finite number. In either case, with a decline in its cost, capital tends to be substituted for labor in the production process.

Earlier in this chapter, we introduced the concept that the demand for a given category of labor is responsive to changes in the prices of other factors of production; in general, we refer to this responsiveness as a "cross-elasticity" (if the other factor is another category of labor, it is "cross-wage elasticity"). The *sign* of the cross-elasticity of demand for a given category of labor with respect to a fall in the price of capital depends on whether capital and the category of labor are gross substitutes or gross complements. If a particular category of labor is a substitute in production for capital, *and* if the scale effect of the reduced capital price is relatively weak, then capital and the category of labor are gross substitutes and automation reduces demand for workers in this category. For categories of labor that are not close substitutes for the new technology, however, the scale effect may dominate and the two can be gross complements. Thus, the effect of automation on the demand for *particular* categories of labor can be either positive or negative.

Under what conditions are capital and labor most likely to be gross substitutes? Referring back to our earlier discussion, the substitution effect will be stronger to the extent that capital is a substitute for labor in the production process, that it is relatively easy for firms to make the substitution, and that the current share of capital in overall costs is relatively small. The scale effect will be relatively weak if there is an inelastic product demand and if capital constitutes a small share of total cost in the industry experiencing automation.

Clearly, whether capital and a given type of labor are gross substitutes depends on several factors, all of which are highly specific to particular industries and production processes. Perhaps the most that can be said generally is that, as pointed out in a prior section, unskilled labor and capital are more likely to be substitutes in production than are skilled labor and capital, which some studies have identified as complements in production. Because factors of production that are complementary must be gross complements, technological change is more likely to increase the demand for skilled than for unskilled labor.[22]

Before concluding that technological change is a threat to the unskilled, however, three things must be kept in mind. First, even factors that are substitutes in production can be gross complements (if scale effects are large enough). Second, as illustrated in Example 4.2, substitution of capital for labor can destroy some unskilled jobs, but accompanying scale effects can create others, sometimes in the same industry.

Finally, although the fraction of all workers who are unskilled laborers has declined over the course of this century, this decline is not in itself convincing evidence of gross substitutability between capital and unskilled labor. The concepts of elasticity and cross-elasticity refer to changes in labor demand caused by changes in wages or capital prices, *holding all else constant.* That is, labor demand elasticities focus on the labor demand curve at a particular point in time. Actual employment outcomes over time are also influenced by labor *supply* behavior of workers. Thus, from simple observations of employment levels over time it is impossible to tell anything about own-wage demand elasticities or about the signs or magnitudes of cross-elasticities of labor demand.

The effects of technological change on *total* employment and on society in general are less ambiguous. Technological change permits society to achieve greater and often more varied consumption possibilities, and it leads to scale effects that both enlarge and change the mix of output. As the productive mix changes, some firms, occupations, and industries decline or are eliminated (see, for example, the data inside the front cover, which show declining employment

---

[22]Alan B. Krueger, "How Computers Have Changed the Wage Structure: Evidence from Microdata, 1984–1989," *Quarterly Journal of Economics* 108 (February 1993): 33–60, concluded that workers who use computers on their jobs earn 10 to 15 percent more than otherwise comparable workers and that the expansion of computer usage in the 1980s accounted for a substantial part of the increased earnings of highly educated workers vis-à-vis less-educated workers that took place during the decade (see Chapter 14 for a discussion of this and other earnings changes).

EXAMPLE 4.2

Gross Complementarity and Substitutability: The Rise and Fall of the Handloom Weavers, 1780–1850

In the 1770s a new technique for spinning cotton yarn was developed, making it possible to produce a much stronger, higher-quality yarn than was previously available. This new spinning technology offered substantial cost reductions to producers, and the increased availability of cheaper and better yarn induced a substantial scale effect on the demand for cotton fabrics. One result of this increased demand was that the employment of handloom weavers in England's Lancashire region (where almost all of England's cotton manufacturing took place) grew from something like 40,000 in 1780 to 200,000 in 1820. These weavers, who were often women and children, worked primarily at home as self-employed subcontractors. In terms of our discussion of the cross-elasticity of demand for labor, it is clear that there was gross complementarity between handloom weaving and the new spinning technology.

By 1820, however, another technological change was taking place that would adversely affect the employment of weavers. The powerloom, which had been invented several years earlier, had been improved to the point that it began to substitute for the handloom. Powerloom weaving, which had to be done in factories, gradually replaced home-centered handloom weaving (the two were substitutes in production), and by 1851 there were only 50,000 handloom weavers left in Lancashire.

We normally think of the cross-elasticity of the demand for labor in terms of changes in the number of jobs within a particular *occupation,* and it is in this sense that handloom weaving and the powerloom were gross substitutes. However, it may also be useful to think of cross-elasticities in terms of changes in employment opportunities for workers within a particular *industry.* In this context the invention of the powerloom apparently increased the number of jobs for low-skilled workers in the cotton textile industry. The improvements in powerloom weaving had a scale effect on employment in the textile industry, and while there was a fall of 150,000 jobs in handloom weaving, the number of those employed in Lancashire's cotton mills rose from roughly 85,000 in 1820 to 275,000 in 1850. Thus, although powerloom and handloom weavers were clearly gross substitutes, the improvements in the powerloom did increase the market for cotton goods sufficiently to create other (factory) jobs in the cotton textile industry.

SOURCES: Duncan Bythell, *The Handloom Weavers* (Cambridge: Cambridge University Press, 1969); John S. Lyons, "Family Response to Economic Decline: English Cotton Handloom Weavers in Early-Nineteenth-Century Lancashire," *Research in Economic History* 12 (1989): 45–91.

shares in agriculture and goods-producing industries, where technological changes have reduced the labor required per unit of output). Other sectors of the economy—the services, for example—expand. While these dislocations can create pockets of unemployment as some workers must seek new jobs or acquire new skills, there is no evidence that technological change (over the course of this century, say) has led to permanent problems of unemployment. In fact, real wages have risen rather dramatically from their levels earlier this century, a rise that has been at least partly fueled by technological change.

REVIEW QUESTIONS

1. One organization representing labor argued that interest rates in 1992 were too high and that the government must seek to lower them so that productive, job-creating investments could take place. Do lower interest rates unambiguously increase the demand for labor?

2. A national study concludes that the hourly pay received by part-time workers is always less than the hourly pay received by full-time workers in comparable jobs. It also concludes that part-time workers are disproportionately women, teenagers, the elderly, and the hard-to-employ. Thus, the study suggests that Congress pass a law compelling employers offering part-time jobs to pay the *full-time* wage rate prevailing in their area for the relevant jobs. Analyze as completely as you can the effects on both part-time and full-time workers.

3. Many employers provide health insurance for their employees, but others—primarily small employers—do not. Suppose that the government wants to ensure that all employees are provided with health insurance coverage that meets or exceeds some standard. Suppose also that the government wants employers to pay for this coverage and is considering three options:

   Option A: An employer not voluntarily offering its employees acceptable coverage would be required to pay a tax of X cents per hour for each labor hour employed. The funds collected would support government-provided health coverage.

   Option B: Same as option A, except that the government-provided coverage would be financed by a tax collected as a fraction of the employer's total revenues.

   Option C: Same as option A, except that government-provided coverage would be financed by a property tax on the buildings, land, and machines owned by the employer.

   Compare and contrast the labor market effects of each of the three options.

4. Union A faces a demand curve in which a wage of $4 per hour leads to demand for 20,000 person-hours and a wage of $5 per hour leads to demand for 10,000 person-hours. Union B faces a demand curve in which a wage of $6 per hour leads to demand for 30,000 person-hours, while a wage of $5 per hour leads to demand for 33,000 person-hours.
   a. Which union faces the *more* elastic demand curve?
   b. Which union will be more successful in increasing the total income (wages times person-hours) of its membership?

5. A government intends to pursue policies that will encourage investment in infrastructure (roads, especially), capital goods, and technology. These policies, for example, might involve subsidies of firms' research and development activities, tax credits (tax reductions) for companies that invest in new machinery, or public funding of road building or road repair. Ignoring the issue of how these programs affect tax rates, analyze how each of these policies will affect the labor market.

6. Clerical workers represent a substantial share of the U.S. work force—over 15 percent in recent years. Concern has been expressed that computerization and office automation will lead to a substantial decline in white-collar employment and increased unemployment of clerical workers. Is this concern well founded?

7. Briefly explain how the following programs would affect the elasticity of demand for labor in the steel industry:
   a. an increased tariff on steel imports;
   b. a law making it illegal to lay off workers for economic reasons;

c. a "boom" in the machinery industry (which uses steel as an input)—causing production in that industry to rise;

d. a decision by the owners of steel mills to operate each mill longer than has been the practice in the past;

e. an increase in the wages paid by employers in the steel industry;

f. a tax on each ton of steel produced.

8. In 1942 the government promulgated regulations that prohibited the manufacture of many types of garments by workers who did the sewing, stitching, and knitting in their homes. If these prohibitions are repealed, so that clothing items may now be made either by workers in factories or by independent contractors doing work in their homes, what effect will this have on the labor demand curve for *factory workers* in the garment industry?

SELECTED READINGS

Card, David, and Alan B. Krueger. *Myth and Measurement: The New Economics of the Minimum Wage*. Princeton: N.J.: Princeton University Press, 1995.

Hamermesh, Daniel. *Labor Demand*. Princeton, N.J.: Princeton University Press, 1993.

Kennan, John. "The Elusive Effects of Minimum Wages." *Journal of Economics Literature* 33, no. 4 (December 1995).

"Review Symposium: *Myth and Measurement: The New Economics of the Minimum Wage*, by David Card and Alan B. Krueger." *Industrial and Labor Relations Review* 48, no. 4 (July 1995).

International Trade and The Demand for Labor: Can High-Wage Countries Compete?

The question of how international trade affects labor demand in the long run has been highlighted recently by the increasing importance of exports and imports in the U.S. economy. As late as 1970, imports represented only slightly less than 6 percent of gross domestic purchases, while exports were less than 6 percent of gross national product. By 1993, however, imports had doubled, to over 11 percent of purchases, and exports had grown to over 10 percent of gross national product.[1]

The public is often inclined to support laws restricting free trade on the grounds that lower wages and living standards in other countries inevitably cause employment losses among American workers—losses that could be mitigated only by a large decline in American living standards. This section will show that the effects of international trade on the demand for labor are analogous to the effects of technological change, that they do not depend on relative living standards, and that two countries will generally find trade mutually beneficial regardless of their respective wage rates. To keep things simple, we assume in what follows that goods and services can be traded across countries but that capital and labor are immobile (international mobility of labor is discussed in Chapter 10).[2]

---

[1]U.S. President, *Economic Report of the President* (Washington, D.C.: U.S. Government Printing Office, 1995), Table B-1.

[2]The model presented here is necessarily simplified. More-complex models and a discussion of the conditions under which free trade may not be in a country's best interests are found in Robert E. Baldwin, "Are Economists' Traditional Trade Policy Views Still Valid?" *Journal of Economic Literature* 30 (June 1992): 804–829.

Production in the United States Without International Trade

Suppose that the available supplies of labor and capital in the United States can be combined to produce two goods, food and clothing.[3] If all inputs were devoted to food production, 200 million units of food could be produced; similarly, if all available resources were devoted to the production of clothing, 100 million units of clothing could be produced. If 15 percent (say) of the resources were devoted to food and 85 percent to clothing, 30 million units of food and 85 million units of clothing could be produced. All the possible combinations of food and clothing that could be produced in the United States are summarized graphically by line XY in Figure 4A.1, which is called a "production possibilities curve."

Two things should be noted about the production possibilities curve in Figure 4A.1. It is negative in slope, indicating that if more of one good is produced, less of the other can be produced. It has a slope of −0.50, symbolizing the real cost

FIGURE 4A.1

Hypothetical Production Possibilities Curves, United States

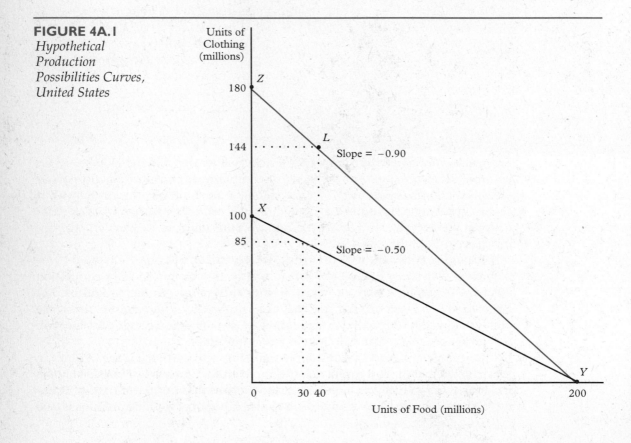

---

[3]To allow a graphic presentation, the analysis will be in the context of just two goods; however, the results are applicable to more.

of producing food: if the country chooses to produce one more unit of food, it must forgo 0.50 units of clothing. (Conversely, if it wants to produce one more unit of clothing it must give up two units of food.)[4]

The ultimate mix of food and clothing produced depends on consumer preferences. If the United States is assumed to have 100 million workers and chooses to allocate 15 percent to the production of food, incomes would average 0.30 units of food and 0.85 units of clothing per worker.

Suppose an inventor were to come along with a device that could increase the efficiency of inputs in the production of clothing, so that if all inputs were devoted to clothing, 180 million units could be produced. The production possibilities curve would shift out to the colored line (YZ) in Figure 4A.1, and per capita real incomes in the United States would rise (it is possible to produce more of both food and clothing with the resources available, as can be seen at point L). After this innovation, only 1.11 (200/180) units of food would have to be given up to obtain one unit of clothing.

(Note that when the real cost of clothing falls from 2 to 1.11 units of food, the *real cost* of food is *automatically* increased from 0.50 to 0.90 units (180/200) of clothing. The reason for this food cost increase is straightforward: if a given set of inputs can now produce more clothing but the same amount of food, diverting enough from the production of clothing to produce one more unit of food will now result in a larger decline in clothing output than before. It is this decline in clothing output that is the real cost, or "opportunity cost," of producing a unit of food.)

Production in a Foreign Country Without International Trade

It would be an amazing coincidence if the rates at which food and clothing could be traded off were equal in all countries. Land quality differs, as do the quality and quantity of capital and labor. Therefore, let us assume that a country—call it China—can produce either 300 million units of food, or 500 million units of clothing, or any other combination of food and clothing along the production possibilities curve, *AB*, in Figure 4A.2.

If 40 percent of its productive inputs were devoted to farming, China could produce 120 million units of food and 300 million units of clothing. With a population of, say, 500 million workers, China's average income per worker would be 0.24 units of food and 0.60 units of clothing. Clearly, then, living standards (real wage rates) are lower in China than in the United States (since the average consumption per worker of *both* food and clothing is lower in China).

After analyzing China's production possibilities curve (*AB* in Figure 4A.2) it can be calculated that the real cost of a unit of food within China is 1.67 (500/300) units of clothing; to produce one more unit of food means that 1.67 fewer units of clothing can be produced. Conversely, the real price of a unit of clothing in China is 0.60 (300/500) units of food.

---

[4]The production possibilities "curve" in Figure 4A.1 is a straight line, which reflects the simplifying assumption that the ratio at which food can be "transformed" into clothing, and vice versa, never changes. This assumption is not necessary to the argument but does make it a bit easier to grasp initially.

FIGURE 4A.2
Hypothetical Pro-
duction Possibilities
Curves, China

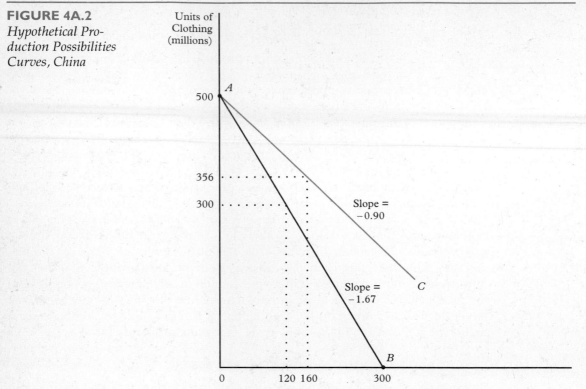

The Mutual Benefits of International Trade

In the absence of innovation in the clothing industry, discussed earlier, the price of food within the United States is 0.50 units of clothing and the price of clothing is 2 units of food. In contrast, the price of food in China is 1.67 units of clothing and the price of clothing is 0.60 units of food. These prices are summarized in columns (a) and (b) of Table 4A.1. Because the real internal cost of food is lower in the United States than in China, while the real internal cost of clothing is higher, economists therefore say that the United States has a *comparative advantage* in producing food and China has a *comparative advantage* in producing clothing.

It is important to note that the real costs of each good in the two countries depend *only* on the *internal trade-offs* between food and clothing output. Despite the assumed fact, for example, that real wages in China are lower than in the United States, food is much more costly in the former country than in the latter! Further, despite the generally more productive inputs in the United States, the real cost of clothing is lower in China.

The costs listed in columns (a) and (b) of Table 4A.1 make it plain that both countries could benefit from trade. China would be willing to buy food from the United States as long as it had to give up something less than 1.67 units of clothing per unit of food (its internal real cost of production). The United States would be willing to trade away food as long as it could obtain something more than 0.50 units of clothing

TABLE 4A.1

Hypothetical Costs and Quantities of Food and Clothing in the United States and China, before and after Trade

Good	Before Trade		After Trade	
	(a) U.S.	**(b) China**	**(c) U.S.**	**(d) China**
Food costs	0.50 units of clothing	1.67 units of clothing	0.90 units of clothing	0.90 units of clothing
Clothing costs	2 units of food	0.60 units of food	1.11 units of food	1.11 units of food
Assumed Food consumption:				
Total	30 million	120 million	40 million	160 million
Per capita	0.30	0.24	0.40	0.32
Assumed Clothing consumption:				
Total	85 million	300 million	144 million	356 million
Per capita	0.85	0.60	1.44	0.71
World production of food	150 million		200 million	
World production of clothing	385 million		500 million	

in return (0.50 units represents what the United States can now obtain internally if it gives up one unit of food). The divergent internal values placed on food and clothing make it possible for mutually beneficial trades to take place.

With a lower-bound price of 0.50 units of clothing per unit of food, and an upper-bound price of 1.67, the ultimate price at which the two countries would trade is not predictable. Trade at any price in between these two bounds would benefit both countries and be preferable to each over no trade at all; however, the closer the price of food is to 0.50 units of clothing the less the United States gains and the more China benefits.

Let us assume that the bargaining strengths of the two countries are such that units of food are traded by the United States to China in return for 0.90 units of clothing. From the perspective of the United States, one unit of food can now be transformed into 0.90 units of clothing instead of just 0.50 units. In this example, trade will therefore accomplish exactly what the previously discussed technological innovation in clothing production did: it will move the production possibilities curve out and give the country a greater command over resources. In terms of Figure 4A.1, trade by itself could move the production possibilities curve from *XY* to *YZ*. This outward shift allows the United States to consume more food *and* more clothing.

From the Chinese perspective, trading 0.90 units of clothing for one unit of food is equivalent to allowing the transformation of one unit of clothing into 1.11 units of food (up from 0.60 units of food). This increase represents an outward shift in the Chinese production possibilities curve (see curve AC in Figure 4A.2), and the output that can be consumed by each Chinese worker clearly increases.

To obtain a sense of how trade could affect per capita consumption in our example, let us suppose that the United States specialized in food production and that China specialized in the production of clothing.[5] The United States would produce 200 million units of food, and if it consumed 40 million units the remaining 160 million units could be traded to China for 144 million units of clothing (0.9 × 160). China would produce 500 million units of clothing, exporting 144 million so that its total internal consumption of clothing would equal 356 million units. China, of course, would consume 160 million units of food under these assumptions. As can be seen from Table 4A.1, where the pre- and post-trade units of production and consumption are compared, per capita real incomes rise in both countries as a result of trade. Conversely, when trade is restricted, consumers in both countries can lose.[6]

Labor Market Implications

International trade is driven by the relative internal (real) costs of producing various goods. Conclusions from our two-good analysis of trade between the United States and China are not at all affected by the assumptions about living standards (real wages) in the two countries. If the production possibilities curves remained the same but the assumed populations of the two countries had been reversed—and living standards were posited to be higher in China—trade would still have taken place, and the United States would still have traded food for Chinese-made clothing.

The general conclusion one can reach from this simple model of trade is that the advent of free trade between two countries will tend to cause each to specialize in producing goods for which it has a comparative advantage and to reduce its production of goods for which its real internal costs are relatively high. Trade, just like an important technological improvement in a given industry, will tend to *shift* employment from one industry to another.[7] However, there is no reason to believe

---

[5]Complete specialization in production will occur in one or both countries if the production possibilities curves are straight lines; in these cases the internal rate of transformation between the two goods is unchanging. Specialization may not be total when the production possibilities curves are concave from below. A concave curve implies that the real costs of food production, say, rise with food output so that at some point the United States could lose its comparative advantage.

[6]For a review of empirical studies on this issue, see Sebastian Edwards, "Openness, Trade Liberalization, and Growth in Developing Countries," *Journal of Economic Literature* 31 (September 1993): 1358–1393.

[7]The available evidence for U.S. and Canadian manufacturing firms suggests that increased foreign competition, in the form of an increase in the share of imports in domestic markets, does lead to lower employment levels in these firms but has no major effect on the wages they pay. See, for example, John Abowd and Thomas Lemieux, "The Effects of International Trade on Collective Bargaining Outcomes: A Comparison of the United States and Canada," in *Immigration, Trade, and the Labor Market*, ed. John Abowd and Richard Freeman (Chicago: University of Chicago Press, 1991): 343–369, and Ana L. Revenga, "Exporting Jobs: The Impact of Import Competition on Employment and Wages in U.S. Manufacturing," *Quarterly Journal of Economics* 107 (February 1992): 255–284. For a description of the number of workers displaced by international trade, and their subsequent experiences with reemployment, see U.S. Congressional Budget Office, *Displaced Workers: Trends in the 1980s and Implications for the Future* (Washington, D.C.: Congressional Budget Office, 1993).

that the advent of free trade will create a permanent loss of employment in the country with higher real wages. To repeat, it is the production possibilities curves, not real-wage rates, that drive international trade.

If, within a country, individual *firms* paying very high wages are "punished" by the market and forced out of business, what prevents a high-wage *country* from being similarly punished by international trade? Put differently, if the average wages for production workers in, say, Haiti are 20 percent of the average wages in the United States, why can't Haiti undersell American producers in every product line? How can American workers hope to remain employed at high wages when faced with such low-wage competitors?

It is important to realize that Haiti has labor and capital resources that are fixed at any moment. It cannot produce *everything!* If, for example, several thousand Haitian workers are employed sewing garments for export to the United States, they are thus not available for (say) the growing and harvesting of agricultural produce. Thus, while there may be a benefit to Haiti when jobs in the garment trades open up, there is also a cost in terms of forgone output that must now be purchased from the United States (the place where dollars received from the export of clothes to the United States must ultimately be spent). Haiti will benefit from increasing the labor it devotes to garment exports *only* if it can replace its forgone production of food more cheaply.

To make the above concepts more concrete, suppose that shirts costing $10 to sew in the United States can be produced in Haiti for $2. Will American garment workers lose their jobs to foreign exports? If the food production forgone in Haiti when one additional shirt is made cannot be purchased from the United States for $2 or less, neither Haitian workers nor their country as a whole will be better off by taking the new jobs. In this case, American workers—despite their higher wages— would not lose jobs to Haitians.

If, however, the food production forgone when a shirt is produced can be purchased from the United States for $2 or less, American jobs in the garment trades will tend to be lost to Haitians. However, it is equally true that Haitian agricultural jobs are thereby lost to the much higher paying agricultural sector in the United States!

To repeat, international trade can cause employment to shift across industries, and these shifts may well be accompanied by unemployment if workers, employers, or market wages are slow in adapting to change. However, there is no reason to believe that the transitional unemployment associated with international trade will become permanent; trade does not condemn jobs in high-wage countries to extinction.[8]

---

[8]For evidence on the extent to which displaced workers earn less, or are unemployed more, than their nondisplaced colleagues after an adjustment period, see Christopher J. Ruhm, "Are Workers Permanently Scarred by Job Displacement?" *American Economic Review* 81 (March 1991): 319–324.

5

Quasi-Fixed Labor Costs and Their Effects on Demand

To this point in our detailed discussion of the demand for labor, we have treated all labor costs as *variable*—that is, as being strictly proportional to the length of time the employee works. Variable labor costs, such as the hourly wage rate, recur every period and, of course, can be reduced if the hours of work are reduced. Many labor costs, however, are *quasi-fixed*, in that they are not strictly proportional to hours of work. Such costs are borne by the firm on a *per-worker* basis that is largely independent of the hours each employee works. This chapter traces the effects these quasi-fixed costs have on the demand for labor.

Because quasi-fixed labor costs are generally *nonwage*, the first section discusses the nature and magnitude of nonwage labor costs. Included in our discussion are the costs to firms of hiring and training new employees, the costs of legally required social insurance programs (such as Social Security and unemployment compensation), and the costs of privately negotiated employee benefits (such as health insurance, vacation and sick-leave pay, and private pensions).

One important effect that quasi-fixed costs have on the demand for labor concerns the choice firms have between hiring more (or fewer) workers and employing those already on the payroll for longer (or shorter) hours. As discussed in the second section of this chapter, the fact that many nonwage labor costs do *not* vary with weekly hours of work explains why some employers decide to regularly work their employees overtime at legally required premium wage rates rather than increasing the level of employment.

The third section looks in detail at the nature and consequences of one important type of quasi-fixed labor cost: *investments* by firms in the hiring and training of their employees. Investments generally involve a current outlay of funds with a future payback, so that investments in workers cause firms' employment decisions to extend over multiple periods. Thus, this section discusses two critical issues: the ways current costs and future returns can be meaningfully compared, and the multiperiod criterion for profit maximization in the hiring of labor. The application of these concepts to the issue of *training* investments is made in the section that follows, in which we discuss the conditions under which these investments by a firm will meet the profit-maximizing criterion.

Turning from training to *hiring* investments, the final section briefly discusses the choices firms face in the often costly process of selecting employees. The underlying rationale for the existence of *internal labor markets* and the use of credentials in screening employees is discussed here.

Nonwage Labor Costs

Although simple textbook models of the labor market often refer to the hourly wage rate paid to workers as the cost of labor, substantial *nonwage* labor costs have important implications for labor market behavior. In general, they fall into two categories: hiring and training costs and employee benefits.

HIRING AND TRAINING COSTS

Firms incur substantial costs in hiring and training new employees. *Hiring costs* include all costs involved in advertising positions, screening applicants to evaluate their qualifications, and processing successful applicants who have been offered jobs. One might also include in this category of costs the overhead costs of maintaining employees on the payroll once they have been employed; these costs would include recordkeeping costs, the costs of computing and issuing paychecks, and the costs of providing forms to the government (such as W–2 forms to the Internal Revenue Service) giving information on employees' earnings.

New employees typically undergo formal or informal training and orientation programs. These programs may teach new skills, such as how to use a machine, that directly increase the employees' productive abilities. Alternatively, orientation programs may simply provide newcomers with background information on how the firm is structured, such as who to call if a machine breaks down or how to requisition supplies. Such information, while not changing skill levels, does increase productivity by enabling workers to make more efficient use of time.

Firms incur at least three types of *training costs:*

1. The *explicit* monetary costs of employing individuals to serve as trainers and the costs of materials used up during the training process;

2. The *implicit* or opportunity costs of using capital equipment and experienced employees to do the training in less formal training situations (for example, an experienced employee demonstrating to a new recruit how he or she does a job may work at a slower pace than normal); and

3. The *implicit* or opportunity costs of the trainee's time (individuals undergoing training are not producing as much output as they would if all of their time were devoted to production activities).

Since a large share of employers' hiring and training costs are implicit, quantifying their dollar magnitudes is difficult. However, two surveys of employers that asked about the hours spent recruiting and training a new employee yield at least some idea of hourly magnitudes. A 1982 survey, weighted toward employers hiring less-skilled workers, found that almost 22 hours were spent screening and interviewing applicants for a vacancy if these applicants were recruited through newspaper ads. If an employment agency was used to find applicants, the hours spent by the employer on these hiring activities were reduced to around 15.[1]

The most recent information on hours spent training new workers comes from a 1992 survey that asked employers about training activities in a worker's first three months on the job. These data, summarized in Table 5.1, indicate that, of the roughly 520 hours each employee was at work during the three months, 153 hours (almost 30 percent) were spent in some form of training. Very little of this training was formal, classroom instruction; most took place informally at the workstation.[2]

Because of the cost of recruiting and training workers, employers must decide on an overall hiring strategy. Firms choosing a *high-wage* strategy generate many applicants for each opening and can be selective, taking only trained, experienced workers. By paying high wages they avoid the explicit and implicit costs of hiring the inexperienced. Firms choosing a *low-wage* strategy can attract only inexperienced applicants, and they must be prepared not only to undertake a period of training but to sustain the risks later on of losing to higher-wage employers the workers they have trained. Thus, low-wage employers save on hourly costs but must incur higher training and recruiting expenses.

EMPLOYEE BENEFITS

Employee benefits include *legally required* social insurance contributions and *privately provided* benefits. Examples of legally required benefits are payroll-based payments employers must make to fund programs that compensate workers for

---

[1]John Bishop, "Improving Job Matches in the U.S. Labor Market," *Brookings Papers on Economic Activity: Microeconomics* (1993), 379.

[2]Corroborating evidence is found in Jonathan R. Veum, "Sources of Training and Their Impact on Wages," *Industrial and Labor Relations Review* 48, no. 4 (July 1995): 812–826, which cites a survey of workers in their twenties. This survey indicates that only 18 percent received some kind of *formal* employer training during the period 1986 to 1990. For those receiving it, 134 hours were spent on formal training over these five years. We do not know how much of this training took place after the first three months on the job.

TABLE 5.1

Hours Devoted by Firms to Training a New Worker During First Three Months on Job, 1992

Activity	Average Hours
Hours of formal instruction by training personnel	19
Hours spent by management in orientation, informal training, extra supervision	59
Hours spent by co-workers in informal training	34
Hours spent by new worker watching others do work	41
Total	153

SOURCE: John Bishop, "The Incidence of and Payoff to Employer Training," Cornell University Center for Advanced Human Resource Studies Working Paper 94–17, July 1994, 11.

unemployment (unemployment insurance), injury (workers' compensation), and retirement (old-age, survivors', disability, and health insurance—Social Security). Examples of privately provided benefits are holiday pay, vacation and sick leave, private pensions, and private health and life insurance.

Table 5.2 gives some idea of employee benefits as a percentage of total compensation, at least among the large firms responding to a recent U.S. Chamber of Commerce survey. The data indicate that nonwage benefits constitute over one-quarter of total compensation, with the largest categories being pay for time not worked (9.0%), insurance (8.3%), legally required payments (6.1%), and retirement (4.7%). These nonwage benefits have been growing over time, although in the last decade their growth has slowed. Thirty years ago, however, nonwage benefits were 19 percent of total compensation in large firms, and in the late 1940s they constituted just 13 percent of compensation.

THE QUASI-FIXED NATURE OF MANY NONWAGE COSTS

The distinction between wage and nonwage costs of employment is important because many nonwage costs are *costs per worker* rather than *costs per hour worked*. That is, many nonwage costs do not vary at the margin with the number of hours an employee works. Economists thus refer to them as *quasi-fixed,* in the sense that once an employee is hired the firm is committed to a cost that does not vary with his or her hours of work.

It should be obvious that hiring and training costs are quasi-fixed; they are associated with each new employee, not with the hours he or she works after the training period. Many benefit costs, however, are also quasi-fixed. For example, most life and medical insurance policies are paid on a per-worker basis, as is pay for time not worked (breaks, holidays, vacation, and sick leave). Some pension costs are proportional to hours worked, because some employers (those with "defined contribution" plans) agree to contribute a certain percentage of employee pay to a pension fund. However, most private sector pension plans promise benefits that are a function of years of service rather than hours of work; the costs of these "defined benefit" plans are quasi-fixed in most cases.

In the category of legally required benefits, workers' compensation costs are strictly proportional to hours worked, because they are levied as a percentage of payroll, and Social Security taxes are proportional for most employees.[3] However, the unemployment insurance payroll-tax liability is specified to be a percentage (the tax rate) of each employee's earnings up to a maximum earnings level (the taxable wage base), which in 1995 was between $7,000 and $12,000 in over two-thirds of all states.[4] Since most employees earn more than $12,000 per year, having an employee work an additional hour per week will *not* cause any increase in the employer's payroll-tax liability. Therefore, unemployment insurance costs are a quasi-fixed cost to most employers.

In Table 5.2 we have indicated (by an asterisk) which nonwage costs are usually of a quasi-fixed nature. The data suggest that, at least for large employers, around 22 percent of total compensation (three-quarters of nonwage costs) is quasi-fixed. These quasi-fixed costs averaged roughly $11,000 per employee in 1993. The quasi-fixed nature of many nonwage labor costs has important effects on employer hiring and overtime decisions. These effects are discussed below.

The Employment/Hours Trade-Off

The simple model of the demand for labor presented in the preceding chapters spoke to the quantity of labor demanded, making no distinction between the number of individuals employed by a firm and the average length of its employees' workweek. Holding all other inputs constant, however, a firm can produce a given level of output with various combinations of the number of employees hired and the number of hours worked per week. Presumably increases in the number of employees hired will allow for shorter workweeks, while longer workweeks will allow for fewer employees, other things equal.

In Chapter 3 we defined the marginal product of labor (MP_L) as the change in output generated by an added unit of labor, holding capital constant. Once we distinguish between the *number* of workers hired (which we will denote by M) and the *hours* each works on average (H), we must think of two marginal products of

---

[3]The Social Security payroll-tax liability of employers is specified as a percentage of each employer's earnings up to a maximum taxable wage base. In 1996, this tax was 6.20 percent of earnings up to $62,700 for retirement and disability insurance, and 1.45 percent on all earnings for Medicare. Because the maximum earnings base exceeded the annual earnings of most workers, the employer's payroll-tax liability *is* increased when a typical employee works an additional hour per week.

[4]National Foundation for Unemployment Compensation and Workers' Compensation, *Highlights of State Unemployment Compensation Laws: January 1996* (Washington, D.C., 1996), Table 3.

TABLE 5.2
Employee Benefits as a Percent of Total Compensation Among Large Employers, 1993

(Average Yearly Cost in Parentheses)

Legally required payments	**6.1**	**($3,130)**
Social Security	4.9	($2,471)
Workers' compensation	0.8	($417)
* Unemployment insurance and other	0.4	($242)
Retirement	**4.7**	**($2,372)**
* Employer costs based on benefit formulas (defined benefit plans)	2.2	($1,108)
Employer costs proportional to earnings (defined contribution plans)	1.8	($897)
* Other (including insurance, annuities, and administrative costs)	0.7	($367)
* **Insurance** (medical, life)	**8.3**	**($4,193)**
* **Paid rest** (coffee breaks, meal periods, set-up and wash-up time)	**1.6**	**($829)**
* **Paid vacations, holidays, sick leave**	**7.4**	**($3,725)**
* **Miscellaneous** (discounts on products bought, employee meals, child care)	**1.1**	**($559)**
Total	**29.2**	**($14,808)**

*Category of costs believed by authors to be largely *quasi-fixed* (see discussion in the text).

SOURCE: U.S. Chamber of Commerce, *Employee Benefits 1993* (Washington, D.C.: U.S. Chamber of Commerce, 1994), Table 4a, 8.

labor. MP_M is the added output associated with an added worker, holding both capital and average hours per worker constant. MP_H is the added output generated by increasing average hours per worker, holding capital and the number of employees constant. As with MP_L, we assume that both MP_M and MP_H are positive, but that they decline as M and H (respectively) increase.[5]

How does a firm determine its optimal employment/hours combination? Is it ever rational for a firm to work its existing employees overtime on a regularly scheduled basis, even though it must pay them a wage premium, rather than hiring additional employees?

---

[5]When the number of employees is increased, the decline in MP_M may be due to the reduced quantity of capital now available to each individual employee. When the hours each employee works per week are increased, the decline in MP_H may occur because after some point fatigue sets in.

DETERMINING THE MIX OF WORKERS AND HOURS

The fact that certain labor costs are *not* hours-related and others are makes it important to examine the marginal expense an employer faces when employing an additional *worker* for whatever length workweek its other employees are working (ME_M). This marginal expense will be a function of the quasi-fixed labor costs plus the weekly wage and variable (with hours) employee-benefit costs for the specified length of workweek. Similarly, it is important to examine the marginal expense a firm faces when it seeks to increase the *average workweek* of its existing work force by one hour (ME_H). This marginal expense will equal the hourly wage and variable employee-benefit costs multiplied by the number of employees in the workforce. Of course, if the employer is in a situation in which an overtime premium (such as time and a half or double time) must be paid for additional hours, that higher rate is the relevant wage rate to use in the latter calculation.

Viewed in this way, a firm's decision about its optimal employment/hours combination is no different from its decision about the usage of any two factors of production, which was discussed in Chapter 3 (see equation 3.8c). Specifically, to minimize the cost of producing any given level of output, a firm should adjust both its employment level and its average workweek so that the costs of producing an added unit of output are equal for each:

$$\frac{ME_M}{MP_M} = \frac{ME_H}{MP_H} \tag{5.1}$$

Thus, if ME_M rises relative to ME_H, for example, a profit-maximizing firm will want to substitute *hours* for *workers* by hiring fewer employees but having each work more hours per week. Conversely, if ME_H rises relative to ME_M, the employer will want to produce its profit-maximizing level of output with a higher ratio of workers to average hours per worker.

The Fair Labor Standards Act (FLSA) requires that all employees covered by the legislation receive an overtime-pay premium of at least 50 percent of their regular hourly wage (time and a half) for each hour per week they work in excess of 40 hours.[6] A large proportion of overtime hours are worked because of disequilibrium phenomena—rush orders, seasonal demand, mechanical failures, and absenteeism, for example—and Example 5.1 discusses how the presence of quasi-fixed costs affects the hiring strategies employers adopt in response to these phenomena. A substantial amount of overtime, however, appears to be regularly sched-

---

[6]Approximately two-thirds of all workers are subject to the overtime-pay provisions of the FLSA [see U.S. Department of Labor, *Minimum Wage and Maximum Hours Standards under the Fair Labor Standards Act* (Washington, D.C.: U.S. Government Printing Office, 1993, Table 10)]. The major categories of excluded employees are executive, administrative, and professional personnel, outside salespersons, and agricultural workers.

EXAMPLE 5.1

"Renting" Workers as a Way of Coping with Fluctuations in Product Demand

The demand for a firm's product fluctuates from week to week and month to month. If a firm finds it feasible to hold inventories of its finished goods, these fluctuations can be absorbed by changes in *product inventories,* thus permitting the firm to keep its employment and production levels constant during the period. Many firms, however, find that the costs of maintaining inventories are very high, and other firms produce services, which by their very nature are impossible to produce ahead of demand. How can such firms cope with fluctuating demand?

The firms might use overtime to meet fluctuations in product demand, but this option requires paying a substantial wage premium. Overtime can also lead to problems associated with fatigue, and it causes production coordination problems in some industries.

Another way to cope with fluctuating demand is to hire workers on a temporary basis when demand is unusually high. As indicated in the text, however, the one-time costs of recruiting can be quite high. If the tenure of a job is relatively short, the firm may have insufficient time to recoup these costs. In this case the firm might consider "renting" workers from a temporary-help agency.

Temporary-help agencies specialize in recruiting workers who are then put to work in client firms that need temporary workers. The temporary-help agency bills its clients, and its hourly charges are gen-erally above the wage the client would pay if it hired workers directly—a premium the client is willing to pay because it is spared the investment costs associated with hiring. Because obtaining jobs through the temporary-help agency also saves employees repeated investment costs associated with searching and applying for available temporary openings, its employees are willing to take a wage less than they otherwise would receive. The difference between what its clients are charged and what its employees are paid permits the successful temporary-help agency to cover its recruiting costs. A survey of U.S. employers found that, by 1990, over three-quarters hired workers from temporary-help agencies in the course of a year and that firms with highly seasonal or cyclical product demand patterns were more likely to make use of temporary workers.

SOURCE: Katharine Abraham, "Flexible Staffing Arrangements and Employers' Short-Term Adjustment Strategies," in *Employment, Unemployment, and Labor Utilization,* ed. Robert Hart (Boston: Unwin Hyman, 1988), 288–311, and Katharine Abraham, "Restructuring the Employment Relationship: The Growth of Market Mediated Work Arrangements," in *New Developments in the Labor Market,* ed. Katharine Abraham and Robert McKersie (Cambridge, Mass.: MIT Press, 1990): 85–118.

uled; equation (5.1) indicates why this scheduling of overtime may occur. Although overtime hours require premium pay, they also enable an employer to avoid the quasi-fixed employment costs associated with employing an additional worker. This point can be illustrated by considering what would happen if the overtime-pay premium were to be increased.

POLICY ANALYSIS: THE OVERTIME-PAY PREMIUM

Periodically proposals have been introduced in Congress to raise the overtime premium to double time.[7] The argument made to support such an increase is that even though unemployment remains a pressing national problem, the use of overtime hours has not diminished. Moreover, the argument continues, the deterrent effect of the overtime premium on the use of overtime has been weakened since the FLSA was enacted because of the growing share in total compensation of hiring and training costs, employee benefits, and government-mandated insurance premiums. As already noted, many of these costs are *quasi-fixed,* or employee-related rather than hours-related, and thus do not vary with overtime hours of work. An increase in these costs increases employers' marginal expense of hiring new employees relative to the expense of working their existing workforces overtime. It is claimed, therefore, that the growth of quasi-fixed costs has been at least partly responsible for the greater usage of overtime hours and that an increase in the overtime premium is required to better "spread the work" and increase employment.

Would an increase in the overtime premium prove to be an effective way of increasing employment and reducing unemployment? A number of economists have sought to answer this question. Although the overtime premium is, for the most part, legislatively fixed at a point in time, ME_M and ME_H vary across employers, depending on their quasi-fixed and hourly-wage costs. Thus, the first step in estimating the effects on employment of increasing the overtime premium is to find out whether, as predicted, the use of overtime actually increases as ME_M rises relative to ME_H. Indeed, several studies do indicate that the predicted relationship, summarized in Figure 5.1, holds; that is, in firms whose quasi-fixed costs are high relative to their hourly labor costs, more overtime is scheduled.[8]

If the number of overtime hours scheduled per week is sensitive to the ratio ME_M/ME_H, then an increase in the overtime premium to double time should lower the ratio and induce employers to cut back on the use of overtime (from H_0 to H_1 in Figure 5.1). Will all these overtime hours be converted to added employment, thereby reducing unemployment? Our theory suggests that the answer is no, and it also suggests that employment itself could fall—for several reasons.

First, an increase in the overtime premium raises the average cost of labor even if all overtime is eliminated! The reason for this increase is that firms eliminating overtime and increasing employment must bear the quasi-fixed costs of employment discussed earlier. Firms using overtime *before* the imposition of the double-time premium *could* have hired more workers and reduced overtime usage earlier; the fact that they did not make this choice suggests it was a more costly one. If the

---

[7]For example, Congressman John Conyers of Michigan introduced HR 1784 into Congress in 1979 and HR2933 in 1985. To quote a supporter of the proposal, "The AFL-CIO endorses the double-time provision as a means of generating additional jobs. The evidence is persuasive that the overtime-pay requirements of the Fair Labor Standards Act have lost their effectiveness as a deterrent to regularly scheduled overtime work." (See the statement by Rudolph Oswald, Director of Research, AFL-CIO, in the minutes of the Hearings before the Subcommittee on Labor Standards on HR 1784, October 23, 1979.)

[8]For a summary of these studies, see Hamermesh, *Labor Demand,* 127–134.

FIGURE 5.1

The Predicted Relationship Between ME_M/ME_H and Overtime Hours

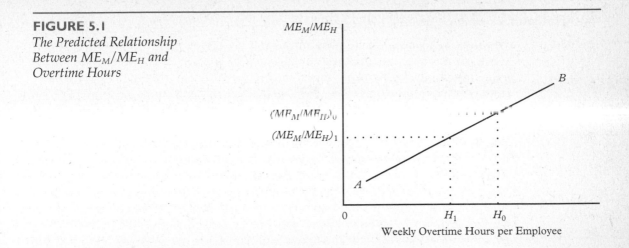

double-time premium now induces this more costly choice, their labor costs will clearly rise. This increase may cause the total hours of labor hired to decrease as firms shift to more-capital-intensive modes of production.

Second, even if the firms that used overtime prior to the double-time premium were to shift to more-capital-intensive modes of production, their unit costs of output would tend to increase (they could have chosen to substitute capital for labor *before* but decided not to—presumably because of the higher cost). If this cost increase were passed on to consumers in the form of higher prices, a reduction in the quantity of output would occur. This *scale effect* should also lead to a decline in the number of labor hours purchased by employers.

Third, the degree of substitutability between those who work overtime and those who are unemployed may be low. If, for example, those working overtime are skilled while those who are unemployed are unskilled, it might be difficult to convert overtime hours to added jobs for the unemployed.

Finally, it is possible that employers and employees mutually agree on a "package" of weekly hours and total compensation. If so, firms that schedule overtime hours might respond to a legislated increase in the overtime premium by reducing the straight-time hourly wage by a sufficient amount to leave total compensation per worker unchanged. Because the original package of weekly hours and total compensation that both employers and employees had agreed upon would be unchanged, neither party would have any incentive to alter weekly hours. Empirical evidence suggests that straight-time hourly wages do adjust partially to changes in the overtime premium.[9] These adjustments further moderate the "job creation" effects of any increase in the overtime premium.

---

[9]Stephen J. Trejo, "The Effects of Overtime Pay Regulation on Worker Compensation," *American Economic Review* 81 (September 1991): 719–739. Noncompliance with the FLSA is also a phenomenon that could reduce employment growth; see Ronald G. Ehrenberg and Paul L. Schumann, "Compliance with the Overtime Pay Provisions of the Fair Labor Standards Act," *Journal of Law and Economics* 25 (April 1982): 159–181; and Brigitte Sellekaerts and Stephen Welch, "Noncompliance with the Fair Labor Standards Act: Evidence and Policy Implications," *Labor Studies Journal* 8 (Fall 1983): 124–136.

POLICY ANALYSIS: PART-TIME EMPLOYMENT AND MANDATED EMPLOYEE BENEFITS

Overtime is one example of how employers can adjust their mix of workers and hours per worker; part-time employment is another. Just as the usage of overtime hours has increased, part-time employment has grown as a share of total employment in most European countries and in the United States in recent years. For example, between 1955 and 1995 the percentage of employees in U.S. nonagricultural industries who were employed part-time (defined as less than 35 hours per week) rose from 10.5 to 17.9.[10] Explanations for this growth have focused mainly on the supply side of the labor market and on the changing industrial composition of employment. The growing shares of married women with children in the labor force (see Chapter 6), of older workers phasing into retirement, and of students who need to work to finance their educations are all thought to have increased the number of workers willing to work part-time. On the demand side of the market, growth in the share of service-sector employment (Figure 2.3) has increased the number of jobs in which part-time workers can be easily employed.

Recently, however, attention has shifted to the role that relative costs play in the growth of part-time employment. Assuming that part-time workers and full-time workers are substitutes in production, if the hourly labor costs or the quasi-fixed costs of part-time workers fall relative to those of full-time workers, part-time employment should expand relative to full-time employment.

One study showed that employment of part-time workers in Great Britain expanded most rapidly during periods when they were covered by relatively few social insurance programs and protective regulations. Specifically, Britain's passage of the Employment Protection Act of 1975, which increased the eligibility of part-time employees for job separation payments and maternity benefits (both of which increase quasi-fixed costs), seemed to be associated with a slowdown in its part-time employment growth.[11] Studies that used U.S. data at a point in time have also documented that across industries in the United States, the part-time/full-time employment ratio is negatively related to the part-time/full-time wage ratio. Thus, holding other factors constant, in industries in which part-time workers' wages are lowest relative to full-time workers' wages, usage of part-time employees is highest relative to that of full-time employees.[12]

A recurrent policy proposal aimed at expanding health insurance coverage of American citizens is to require employers to provide medical insurance to *all* employees. Health insurance costs are quasi-fixed, and mandating employer-provided health insurance for all employees is predicted to disproportionately reduce the demand for part-time workers, on two accounts. First, relatively few part-time workers are currently provided with health insurance by their employ-

---

[10]U.S. Department of Labor, *Monthly Labor Review* 118 (July 1995), Table 5.

[11]R. Disney and E. M. Szyszczak, "Protective Labor Legislation and Part-Time Employment in Great Britain," *British Journal of Industrial Relations* 22 (March 1984): 78–100.

[12]Ronald G. Ehrenberg, Pamela Rosenberg, and Jeanne Li, "Part-Time Employment in the United States," in *Employment, Unemployment, and Labor Utilization*, ed. Robert A. Hart (Boston: Unwin Hyman, 1988): 256–281.

ers, so firms that heavily use part-time workers would face the greatest cost increases, other things equal. Second, mandated health insurance would raise the quasi-fixed costs of hiring workers relative to employing fewer workers for longer hours, thus increasing the costs of hiring part-time workers relative to full-time employees. Indeed, a recent study estimated that requiring firms to provide health insurance to their employees would cause a sizable reduction in the demand for part-time workers.[13] (Similarly, reductions in employment relative to hours can be expected to result when *firing* workers becomes more costly; see Example 5.2.)

Firms' Labor Investments and the Demand for Labor

The models of the demand for labor given in Chapters 3 and 4 were static in the sense that they considered only *current* marginal productivities and *current* labor costs. If all of a firm's labor costs are variable each year, then it will employ labor *each period* to the point at which labor's marginal revenue product equals the wage. Once we begin to consider hiring and training costs, however, the analysis changes somewhat.

Hiring and training costs are usually heavily concentrated in the initial periods of employment and do not recur. Later on, however, these early investments in hiring and training raise the productivity of employees. Once the investments are made, it is cheaper for the firm to *continue* using its current workers than to hire, at the same wage rate, new ones (who would have to be trained). Likewise, with an investment required for all *new* workers, employers have to consider not only *current* marginal productivity and labor cost but also *future* marginal productivity and labor costs in deciding whether (and how many) to hire. In short, the presence of investment costs—hiring and training expenses—means that hiring decisions must take into account past, present, and future factors.

To illustrate the hiring decision in the face of labor-investment costs, let us consider a firm that is seeking to determine its employment level over a two-period horizon. To keep the discussion simple, we shall ignore employee-benefit costs and the decision about how many hours employees will work; all workers employed in a period will be assumed to work for the entire period. We shall also assume that the firm is in a competitive product market and therefore takes its product price as given. Finally, firms that invest in their workers do so in the initial period (period 0) and reap their returns in the final period (period 1).

We will assume, with reference to Figure 5.2, that in the absence of training the firm's marginal product of labor schedule is MP^*. If the firm decides to invest in training during period 0, however, the marginal product of labor schedule during this period is reduced to MP_0. After training (that is, in period 1), the schedule of labor's marginal product rises to MP_1, where MP_1 exceeds both MP_0 and MP^*.[14]

---

[13]Mark Montgomery and James Cosgrove, "The Effect of Employee Benefits on the Demand for Part-Time Workers," *Industrial and Labor Relations Review* 47, no. 1 (October 1993): 87–98.

[14]In the remainder of this chapter, the subscript L is omitted from the algebraic representation of labor's marginal product. The subscripts used designate time period; the L is omitted to avoid clutter.

EXAMPLE 5.2

Unjust Dismissal Policies

In most European nations, workers have some protection against "unjust dismissals." Typically the legislation mandates the use of labor courts or industrial tribunals to resolve disputes, and while reinstatement of unjustly dismissed workers is rare, often severance pay is required. In contrast, the doctrine of *employment-at-will,* under which employers (and employees) have the right to terminate the employment relationship at any time, for any reason, has historically prevailed in the United States. Those not subject to this doctrine in the United States have included unionized workers with contract provisions governing discharges, tenured teachers, and workers under some civil service systems.

Recently, however, a number of state courts have adopted exceptions to this doctrine based on public policy or the existence of implicit contracts. The former exceptions prevent an employee from being discharged for an action that is consistent with public policy (e.g., reporting an employer for failing to pay the minimum wage), while the latter prevent discharges "without cause" if an employer's oral statements, established past practices, or statements in a personnel manual implicitly promise such protection. In one state, Montana, legislation has been passed requiring employers to have a "just reason" to fire a worker.

Relaxation of the employment-at-will doctrine effectively increases the costs of both terminating and hiring workers (the latter occurs because employers are likely to respond by expending more resources to screen out undesirable job applicants). Economic theory suggests that these increased hiring and firing costs provide firms with an incentive to reduce employment and substitute additional hours per worker; firms will also respond to fluctuations in demand by varying hours more than employment.

Do such predicted adjustments actually occur? One study of European countries found that, holding other factors constant, more stringent severance pay requirements were associated with lower employment levels. A U.S. study found that states that had adopted exceptions to the employment-at-will doctrine had lower levels of employment, other factors held constant, than other states. Finally, a third study found that fluctuations in demand were met more through hours adjustments and less through employment adjustments after the relaxation of the employment-at-will doctrine in the United States. These unintended side effects of unjust dismissal policies must be weighed against the protection they provide for workers.

SOURCES: Ronald Ehrenberg, "Workers' Rights: Rethinking Protective Labor Legislation," in *Rethinking Employment Policy,* ed. Lee Bawden and Felicity Skidmore (Washington, D.C.: Urban Institute, 1989); Edward Lazear, "Job Security Provisions and Employment," *Quarterly Journal of Economics* (August 1990): 696–726; James M. Dertouzos and Lynn A. Karoly, "Employment Effects of Worker Protection: Evidence from the United States," in *Employment Security and Labor Market Behavior,* ed. Christoph F. Buechtermann (Ithaca, N.Y.: ILR Press, 1993); Alan B. Krueger, "The Evolution of Unjust Dismissal Legislation in the United States," *Industrial and Labor Relations Review* 44 (July 1991): 644–660; Daniel Hamermesh, "Employment Protection: Theoretical Implications and Some U.S. Evidence," in *Employment Security and Labor Market Behavior,* ed. Christoph F. Buechtermann.

We will also assume that the direct outlays on training the firm would have to make during period 0 are Z per worker in real terms (dollar costs divided by product price). Further, it will be assumed that the real wage it pays during the training period is W_0 and that the posttraining wage is W_1; for now, we take these wages as given, although we shall shortly examine how they are determined.

FIGURE 5.2

Effects of Training on Marginal Product Schedules

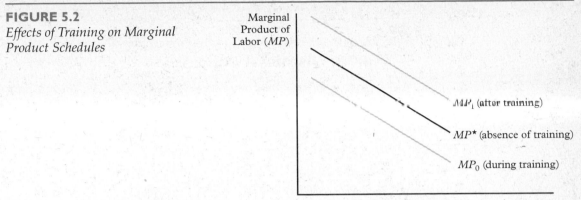

THE CONCEPT OF PRESENT VALUE

In determining its optimal employment level over the two periods, the firm clearly must consider the costs of employing workers in both periods and their marginal products in both periods. A *naive* approach would be to simply add up the costs ($W_0 + W_1 + Z$), add up the marginal products ($MP_0 + MP_1$), and then stop hiring when the sum of the marginal products that the last worker produces over the two periods is just equal to the sum of his or her real wages and training costs. This approach is naive because it ignores the fact that revenues accruing in the future are worth less to the firm than an equal level of revenues that accrue now. Similarly, costs that occur in the future are less burdensome to the firm than equal dollar costs that occur in the present.

Why should this be the case? The answer hinges on the role of interest rates. A dollar of revenue earned by a firm today can be invested at some market rate of interest so that by the next period it will be worth more than a dollar. Hence, faced with a choice of employing a worker whose marginal product is 5 in period 0 and 2 in period 1, or a worker whose marginal product is 2 in period 0 and 5 in period 1, the firm would prefer the former (if wages for the two workers were equal in each period). The sooner the product is produced and sold, the more quickly the firm can gain access to the funds, invest them, and earn interest.[15] Similarly, faced with the option of paying $100 today or $100 next period, the firm should prefer the second option. It could invest and earn interest on the $100 now, make the payment in the next period, and have the interest left over. If the firm makes the payment now, it cannot earn interest income on the $100.

These examples illustrate why firms prefer benefit streams in which the benefits occur as early as possible and cost streams in which the costs occur as late as possible. But how do we compare different benefit and cost streams when benefits and costs occur in more than one period? Economists rely on the concept of

---

[15]We are assuming here, of course, that the price the firm receives for its product is constant and that the rate of interest is positive.

present value, which we define to be the value *now* of an entire stream of future benefits or costs.

Suppose a firm receives the sum of $\$B_0$ in the current period and will receive nothing in the next period. How much money could it have in the next period if it invested $\$B_0$ at a rate of interest that equals r? It would have its original sum, B_0, plus the interest it earned, rB_0:

$$B_1 = B_0 + rB_0 = B_0(1 + r) \qquad (5.2)$$

Since assets of B_1 can be automatically acquired by investing B_0 at the market rate of interest, *B_0 now and B_1 next period are equivalent values.* That is, a person who is offered B_0 now or B_1 in one year would regard the offers as exactly the same as long as $B_1 = B_0(1 + r)$.

Following this line of reasoning, suppose that the firm knows it will receive B_1 in the next period. What is the *current* value of that sum? Receiving B_1 in one year is equivalent to receiving a smaller amount (call it X) now and investing it so that it equals B_1 in a year. That is, the firm would need to have amount X now in order to invest it and wind up with principal plus interest equal to B_1 in the next period:

$$X(1 + r) = B_1 \qquad (5.3)$$

Dividing both sides by $(1 + r)$:

$$X = \frac{B_1}{1 + r} \qquad (5.4)$$

The quantity X in equation (5.4) is called the *discounted value* of B_1 earned one period in the future.

The *present value* of the firm's earnings over two periods is equal to its earnings in the initial period plus the discounted value of its earnings in the next period.[16] Returning to our two-period hiring decision example given at the start of this section, the *present value* of marginal productivity (*PVP*) can now be seen as

$$PVP = MP_0 + \frac{MP_1}{1 + r} \qquad (5.5)$$

That is, the value *now* of a worker's marginal productivity over two periods is the marginal productivity in the current period (MP_0) plus the marginal productivity in the next period *discounted* by $(1 + r)$. Likewise, the present value of the real marginal expense of labor (*PVE*) is equal to

$$PVE = W_0 + Z + \frac{W_1}{1 + r} \qquad (5.6)$$

where r is the market rate of interest. W_0 and Z are not discounted because they are incurred in the current period. However, W_1 is discounted by $(1 + r)$ because it is incurred one year in the future.

---

[16]Earnings in the initial period are not discounted because they are received *now*, not in the future.

The present value calculation reduces a stream of benefits or costs to a single number that summarizes a firm's entire stream of revenues or liabilities over different time periods. For example, the *PVE* can be thought of as the answer to the question, "Given that a firm incurs costs per worker of $W_0 + Z$ this period and W_1 next period, how much does it have to set aside today to be able to cover both periods' costs?" The *PVE* is *less* than $W_0 + Z + W_1$ because W_1 is not owed until the latter period and any funds set aside to cover W_1 can be invested now. If the firm sets aside $W_1/(1 + r)$ to cover its labor cost in the next period and invests this amount earning a rate of return r, the interest, $r[W_1/(1 + r)]$, plus principal, $W_1/(1 + r)$, available in the next period will just equal W_1.

Similarly, the *PVP* can be thought of as the answer to the question, "Given that a worker's marginal product will be MP_0 in this period and MP_1 next period, what is the value of that output stream to the employer today?" The *PVP* is less than $MP_0 + MP_1$ because if the firm were to attempt to borrow against the employee's future marginal product, it could borrow at most $MP_1/(1 + r)$ today and still afford to repay this principal plus the interest, $r[MP_1/(1 + r)]$, out of earnings in the next period.[17]

THE MULTIPERIOD DEMAND FOR LABOR

The concept of present value can help clarify what determines the labor demand function in our two-period model. Rather than focusing on the marginal product of labor schedule for each period separately, the firm must consider them jointly by summarizing their present values. Thus, the present value of schedules MP_0 and MP_1 in Figure 5.3 is shown as curve *PVP*. Similarly, rather than focusing on the hiring and training costs and the wage rates in each period separately, an employer must consider the *present value* of the marginal cost of labor (*PVE*). To maximize its present value of profits, a firm should employ labor up until the point that adding an *additional* employee yields as much as it costs (when both yields and costs are stated as present values). That is, the profit-maximizing condition in our two-period example is

$$PVP = PVE, \text{ or} \qquad\qquad (5.7a)$$

---

[17] More generally, if the firm expects to receive benefits of $B_0, B_1, B_2, \ldots, B_n$ dollars over the current and next n periods, and if it faces the same interest rate, r, in each period, its present value of benefits (*PVB*) is given by

$$PVB = B_0 + \frac{B_1}{1 + r} + \frac{B_2}{(1 + r)^2} + \frac{B_3}{(1 + r)^3} + \cdots + \frac{B_n}{(1 + r)^n}$$

An analogous expression exists for the present value of costs. The reader should make sure that he or she understands why the denominator of B_2 is $(1 + r)^2$, the denominator of B_3 is $(1 + r)^3$, etc. If one thinks in terms of a series of one-period loans or investments, it should become obvious. For example, X_0 invested for one period yields $X_0(1 + r)$ at the end of the period. Let us call $X_0(1 + r) = X_1$. Now X_0 invested for two periods is equal to its value after one period (X_1) multiplied by $(1 + r)$— or $X_2 = X_1(1 + r)$. But $X_1 = X_0(1 + r)$, so $X_2 = X_0(1 + r)^2$. To find the present value of X_2 we divide by $(1 + r)^2$, so $X_0 = X_2/(1 + r)^2$.

$$MP_0 + \frac{MP_1}{1 + r} = W_0 + Z + \frac{W_1}{1 + r} \tag{5.7b}$$

Given the particular values of W_0, W_1, Z, and r that are specified in Figure 5.3, profits are maximized at employment level E^*.

Now, equation (5.7b) merely states the familiar profit-maximizing condition, that marginal returns should equal marginal costs, in a multiperiod context. If Z were zero, for example, equation (5.7b) implies that profits could be maximized when labor is hired so that $MP_0 = W_0$ and $MP_1/(1 + r) = W_1/(1 + r)$, or, since $1 + r$ is the denominator on both sides of the equation, $MP_1 = W_1$. Thus, when there are no hiring or training costs ($Z = 0$), the conditions demonstrated in Chapter 3 are sufficient to guarantee profit maximization in the multiperiod context. However, when Z is positive, which means that firms make initial investments in their workers, the conditions for maximizing profits change.

To understand the change in profit-maximizing conditions suggested by equation (5.7b), suppose that in the initial period the real wage an additional worker receives (W_0) plus the firm's direct investment outlays (Z) exceed the worker's output (MP_0). We can call this difference the *net expense* to the firm of hiring an additional worker in the initial period (NE_0):

$$NE_0 = W_0 + Z - MP_0 > 0 \tag{5.8}$$

In order for the firm to maximize the present value of its profit stream, it must thus get a net *surplus* in the subsequent period. If it does not, the firm will not have any incentive to hire the additional worker.

The discounted value of the subsequent period's surplus (G) is defined as:

$$G = \frac{MP_1}{1 + r} - \frac{W_1}{1 + r} = \frac{MP_1 - W_1}{1 + r} \tag{5.9}$$

From equations (5.7b), (5.8), and (5.9), we see that, if the firm is to maximize profits, labor must be hired until the discounted value of the subsequent-period surplus equals the net expense (NE_0) in the initial period:

$$W_0 + Z - MP_0 = \frac{MP_1 - W_1}{1 + r} \tag{5.10}$$

A subsequent-period surplus can exist *only* if real wages in that period (W_1) lie *below* marginal product (MP_1). This surplus makes up for the fact that the employer's labor costs in the initial period ($W_0 + Z$) were above the worker's marginal product (MP_0).

To this point we have established two things. First, equation (5.7b) has shown that in a multiperiod model of labor demand, the firm's demand curve is the same as the curve representing the *present value* of labor's marginal product over the periods of hire. Thus, the firm maximizes profits when the present value of its marginal labor expense equals the present value of labor's marginal product. Second, we

FIGURE 5.3
Multiperiod Demand for Labor

Marginal Product of Labor (*MP*)
Present Value of Marginal Product of Labor (*PVP*)
Present Value of Real Marginal Expense of Labor (*PVE*)

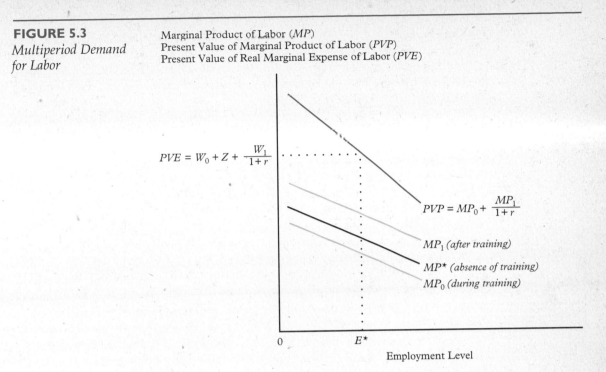

$$PVE = W_0 + Z + \frac{W_1}{1+r}$$

$$PVP = MP_0 + \frac{MP_1}{1+r}$$

MP_1 *(after training)*

MP^* *(absence of training)*

MP_0 *(during training)*

0   E^*

Employment Level

demonstrated in equation (5.10) that maximizing profits when the firm's labor costs in the initial period exceed the worker's initial-period marginal product requires real wages in the subsequent period to be below marginal product in the subsequent period (so that a surplus is generated). The only times when a subsequent-period surplus is not necessary to induce the hiring of an additional employee are when investment costs (Z) are zero in the initial period or when investment costs of Z exist but the initial-period real wage is decreased to such an extent that it equals $MP_0 - Z$. (In the latter case, employees pay for their own training by accepting a wage in the initial period that is decreased by the direct costs of training.)

CONSTRAINTS ON MULTIPERIOD WAGE OFFERS

In the single-period model of labor demand introduced in Chapter 3, a firm in a competitive labor market takes the market wage as given and adjusts its hiring of labor so that labor's marginal product is equal to it. Our discussion above, however, implies that a profit-maximizing firm employing its workers for more than one period has some choice about its wage stream over these periods; it can pay more than marginal product in some periods and less in others. While such choice potentially does exist, it is constrained by the need to make a multiperiod "package" of wage offers that is competitive with the offers being made by other employers in the market. Just as the concept of present value was useful in expressing the profit-maximizing conditions in a multiperiod context, the concept is also useful in summarizing the constraints on a firm's stream of wage offers.

To take a very simple example, suppose that the market wage for firms offering single-period jobs is W^*; that is, assume that workers can always find a job paying W^*. Suppose, further, that firm X wants to offer its job applicants a written, two-period employment contract, guaranteeing a wage of W_0 in the first period and W_1 in the second. It would *not* have to pay its workers W^* in both periods! It could pay wages in one period that were below W^* as long as its wages in the other period were enough above W^* that the following condition was met:

$$W_0 + \frac{W_1}{1 + r} \geq W^* + \frac{W^*}{1 + r} \tag{5.11}$$

Condition (5.11) states that, with a market wage of W^* in each period, firm X could select a W_0 and a W_1 that varied from W^* as long as the *present value of its wages over the two periods were at least as large as the present value of wages the workers could obtain elsewhere*. If, for example, $W^* = \$100$ and we continue our two-period assumption, firm X could make several offers of W_0 and W_1 that yielded present values equivalent to receiving $100 in both periods. A few of these alternative wage streams are shown in Table 5.3, which assumes a discount rate of 6 percent. We can see from the table that, given our assumption, if firm X wished to pay its workers $81 in the first period, for instance, it must pay them at least $120 in the second period to be competitive in the labor market.

Does the fact that all five alternative wage streams in Table 5.3 have equal present values mean that all are equally attractive to firm X and its potential workers? *If a two-period employment contract were legally binding on both the firm and its employees,* and if both used the same 6 percent discount rate, then all five wage streams would indeed be equally attractive to both parties. Generally speaking, however, written employment contracts are legally binding only on the *employer*, which means that employees are free to quit at any time.[18] Alternative A is therefore unattractive to the employer, because employees could take the $128 offered in the first period and then, when wages are cut to $70, quit to take an always-available $100 job elsewhere in the second period.

If instead of offering its workers a written ("formal") contract of employment, firm X were offering a set of promises about employment and wages over two periods that were not legally enforceable (often called an "informal" or "implicit" contract), it would face further constraints. Specifically, with implicit contracts, alternatives C, D, and E are unattractive to employees. With these alternatives, workers would fear that the firm might profit from paying a wage less than $100 in the first period and then fire them in the second period, when their wages were due to rise above what they could obtain elsewhere.

If firm X always rules out alternative A and, in the absence of a formal contract, its employees rule out alternatives C, D, and E, is there any practical choice other

---

[18]An obvious exception to this general rule in the United States is the contract military recruits sign with the armed forces. (While professional athletes are bound to a particular team during their contract period, even they cannot be sued for quitting their sport altogether and pursuing another line of work!)

TABLE 5.3
Alternative Two-Period Wage Streams That Have Equal Present Values Using a 6 Percent Discount Rate

Alternative	W_0	W_1	Present Value
A	$128	$ 70	$194
B	100	100	194
C	81	120	194
D	62	140	194
E	43	160	194

than paying the market wage in each period? If the firm wants to offer a wage stream that departs from paying W^* in both periods, it must offer a stream whose present value is *above* that of a stream paying W^* in each period. In terms of Table 5.3, if firm X, in the absence of a formal contract, wants to pay wages below $100 in the first period, it must alter alternatives C, D, or E by increasing either W_0 or W_1 so that the present value of its offer rises above $194. Only by so doing can firm X induce at least some workers to take the risk that the firm will renege on its promises and fire them in the second period.

How, then, can a firm offering multiperiod employment afford to pay its workers a wage stream whose present value is above the market? One way is to train its workers so that their marginal product is increased beyond that of untrained workers. The other, which is useful when workers differ in their abilities, is to carefully select applicants so that only the best are hired. We therefore turn our attention to training and hiring investments to see just how it is that firms can profit from them.

General and Specific Training

It is useful to conceptually distinguish between two types of training: *general training* that increases an individual's productivity *to many employers* equally, and *specific training* that increases an individual's productivity *only at the firm* in which he or she is currently employed.[19] Pure general training might include teaching an applicant basic reading skills or teaching a would-be secretary how to type and use a word-processing program. Pure specific training might include teaching a worker how to use a machine that is unique to a single employer or showing him

---

[19]Gary Becker, *Human Capital*, 2d ed. (New York: National Bureau of Economic Research, 1975), was first to formalize this distinction. A recent refinement can be found in Margaret Stevens, "A Theoretical Model of On-the-Job Training with Imperfect Competition," *Oxford Economic Papers* 46, no. 4 (October 1994): 537–562.

or her the organization of the production process in the plant. The distinction is primarily a conceptual one because most training contains aspects of both types; however, the distinction does yield some interesting insights.

Suppose, continuing our two-period model, that a firm offers *general* training to its employees, who have a marginal product of MP^* (and can obtain wage offers of $W^* = MP^*$ elsewhere). Suppose, too, that the firm incurs an initial-period net cost of training equal to NE_0 of equation (5.8). This training increases employee marginal product to MP_1 $(>MP^*)$ in the subsequent period, and the firm scales its wages (W_1) in the subsequent period so that there is a surplus in that period whose present value (G) equals NE_0. What will happen?

The trained employee is worth MP_1 to several other firms, but is getting paid less than MP_1 by the firm doing the training (so that it can obtain the required surplus). The employee can thus get *more* from some other employer, who did not incur training costs and thus will not demand a surplus, than he or she can get from the employer offering the training. This situation is likely to induce the employee to quit after training and seek work elsewhere. Assuming all other conditions of employment are the same, the firm would have to pay its employees MP_1 after general training to keep them from quitting.

If firms must pay a wage equal to MP_1 after training, they will not be willing to pay for general training of their employees. Either they will not offer it, or they will force trainees to bear the full cost of their training by paying wages that are less than marginal product in the period of training by an amount equal to the direct training costs (that is, NE_0 must equal zero).

In contrast, consider an individual who receives *specific training* that increases marginal productivity with the *current* employer to MP_1 in the subsequent period. Since the training is firm-specific, the trainee's marginal product in *other* firms remains at its pretraining level of MP^*; therefore, the most the employee can obtain elsewhere is still W^*. The firm that trains the worker in firm-specific skills *will* have an incentive to offer (and at least partially pay for) the job training because it can pay a wage above W^* but below MP_1 in the subsequent period. We explain below.

SPECIFIC TRAINING AND THE WAGE PROFILE

With regard to specific training investments, firms have two related decisions to make: how much to invest in training their employees and, if they offer training, how to structure wages during and after training so that they can recoup their investment. How much training to offer any group of employees is affected by how much their productivity can be enhanced and by how likely they are to remain with the firm after being trained; clearly, firms are more likely to offer training to workers who learn efficiently and are less inclined to job-hop or to quit for some other reason (to leave the labor force or to retire, for example). While some workers are more likely to quit than others in any given situation, firms can also adopt pay policies that reduce their workers' quit rates, as we will see in a moment.

FIGURE 5.4

A Two-Period Wage Stream Associated with Specific Training

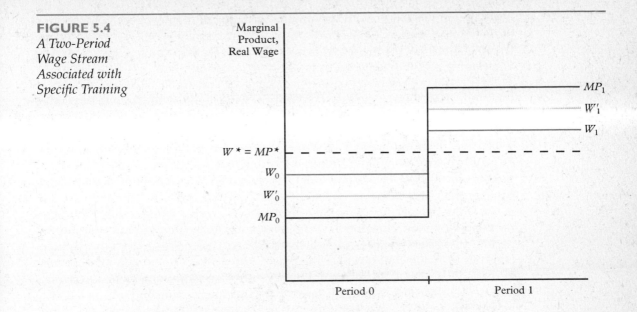

To help understand how a firm offering specific training decides on the wage stream it will offer, refer to the two-period example summarized in Figure 5.4. The firm's workers come to it with a marginal product of MP^*, and they can obtain a wage of W^* ($= MP^*$) elsewhere. If they receive specific training in the first period of employment, their marginal product with the firm is reduced to MP_0 during the training period but rises to MP_1 ($>MP^*$) in the posttraining period. How will the firm set wages in the training and posttraining periods?

In selecting its stream of wage offers, the firm must meet three conditions. First, it must not incur wage and training expenses whose present value is larger than that of its workers' marginal products; that is, in maximizing profits, it must satisfy equation (5.7b). Second, it must offer a wage stream whose present value is at least as large as that of alternative employers, as indicated by equation (5.11). Third, it must offer a posttraining wage that is high enough to discourage its trained workers from quitting right after training, for if they do, the firm's training investments will be lost. Clearly, these conditions imply that the posttraining wage will lie above W^* (to discourage quits) but below MP_1 (to allow the firm to recoup investment costs).

As we will learn in Chapter 10, quitting one job and taking another often involves some costs for the employee, especially if a change of residence is involved or if the job search process is costly in some way. If the firm believes that its workers will find it relatively costly to quit after training, then it could offer a wage stream similar to (W_0, W_1) in Figure 5.4, in which W_1 is only slightly more than W^* and W_0 is only slightly less. Put differently, if workers are not very mobile, the firm can offer a wage profile that rises only modestly after training. W_1 need not be much above W^* to induce those workers to stay with the firm in the posttraining period, which means that the firm can (and must) pay a wage closer to W^* during training. Note that the higher W_0 is relative to MP_0 during training, the greater are the training costs borne by the firm.

If its workers have lower costs of job changing and are therefore more likely to quit in the posttraining period, then the firm will want to force them to bear more of any training costs by paying a relatively low wage during the training period. This will allow (and require) them to pay a relatively high posttraining wage, which will have the benefit of reducing their workers' likelihood of quitting. Firms, then, are less willing to invest in groups of workers who are more "quit-prone," and if offered, specific training is associated with a more steeply rising wage profile, such as the one labeled (W_0', W_1') in Figure 5.4.[20]

From the perspective of employees, if they are paid a wage below W^* during the training period, they too have an investment to "protect" in the posttraining period. Just as employers can reduce employees' incentives to quit by paying a posttraining wage that is higher relative to W^*, workers can obtain more protection from being fired after training by accepting a posttraining wage lower relative to MP_1. If *employees* bore all the costs of specific training and received all the returns (by receiving a posttraining wage equal to MP_1), then employers would have no investment of their own to protect, would receive no posttraining surplus from their employees, and would not be inhibited from firing employees after training. If *employers* bore all the costs, they might not be able to pay their employees enough in the subsequent period to guard against their quitting. It is in the *mutual* interest of both employers and employees, then, to share the costs of specific training and thereby foster a long-term employment relationship. As emphasized by Example 5.3, we expect that the presence of more job training will be associated with employees who are more permanently attached to their employers.

Empirical studies measuring the wage profiles associated with on-the-job training in the United States suggest that employers bear much of the costs and reap most of the returns. There is evidence that wages are not depressed enough initially to offset employers' direct costs of training,[21] and there is corresponding evidence that subsequent wage increases are much smaller than productivity increases. A recent survey of employers, summarized in Figure 5.5, estimates that productivity increases, which generally rise with the hours of initial on-the-job training, are far larger than wage increases over a worker's first two years with an employer. Other studies that directly link the wage profiles of American workers

---

[20]For more theory and evidence on this issue, see Elizabeth Becker and Cotton Lindsay, "Sex Differences in Tenure Profiles: Effects of Shared Firm-Specific Investment," *Journal of Labor Economics* 12, no. 1 (January 1994): 98–118.

[21]John Bishop, "The Incidence of and Payoff to Employer Training," 41, and Margaret Stevens, "An Investment Model for the Supply of General Training by Employers," *Economic Journal* 104 (May 1994): 556–570.

EXAMPLE 5.3

Training and Job Tenure Levels in the United States and Japan

We emphasized in the text that the presence of employer training and a low employee quit rate should go hand in hand. A lower propensity to quit among its employees will induce firms to offer them more training, and once having offered training, firms will adopt compensation policies designed to reduce quits. Thus, a lower quit rate is both a cause and an effect of more employer training.

Among the developed nations of the world, Japan stands out as offering relatively high levels of employer training while the United States offers relatively little. In 1991, for example, 79 percent of Japanese workers went through a formal employer training program during their first year of employment with a firm, as compared to only 8 percent for American workers. (In the Netherlands, to take a European example, the comparable percentage was 19.) It should not be surprising to learn, then, that the average length of time Japanese workers remain with their employers is much longer than in the United States. For example, among workers between the ages of 25 and 34, the following comparisons can be made:

	Years with Current Employer	
	Japan	United States
Men, large firms	8.2	4.8
Women, large firms	7.5	4.3
Men, small firms	5.9	4.0
Women, small firms	5.1	3.1

Clearly, Japanese workers, who are more likely to receive on-the-job training, are more "attached" to their employers than are American workers.

SOURCE: Organisation for Economic Co-Operation and Development, *Employment Outlook 1993* (Paris: OECD, 1993), Tables 4.8 and 4.9. Job tenure data for Japan are for 1989, while tenure data for the United States are for 1991. For a study that questions the link between job training and turnover in the two countries, see David I. Levine, "Worth Waiting For? Delayed Compensation, Training, and Turnover in the United States and Japan," *Journal of Labor Economics* 11, no. 4 (October 1993): 724–752.

with the amount of training they have received find that posttraining wage increases are relatively modest.[22]

---

[22]Lisa Lynch, "Private-Sector Training and the Earnings of Young Workers," *American Economic Review* 82, no. 1 (March 1992): 299–312; David Blanchflower and Lisa Lynch, "Training at Work: A Comparison of U.S. and British Youths," in *Training and the Private Sector: International Comparisons*, ed. Lisa Lynch (Chicago: University of Chicago Press for the National Bureau of Economic Research, 1994), 233–260; Jonathan Veum, "Sources of Training and Their Impact on Wages"; Alan Krueger and Cecilia Rouse, "New Evidence on Workplace Education," working paper no. 329, Industrial Relations Section, Princeton University, May 1994; Harry Holzer, Richard N. Block, Marcus Cheatham, and Jack H. Knott, "Are Training Subsidies for Firms Effective? The Michigan Experience," *Industrial and Labor Relations Review* 46, no. 4 (July 1993): 625–636; Lauri Bassi, "Workplace Education for Hourly Workers," *Journal of Policy Analysis and Management* 13, no.1 (Winter 1994): 55–74; and Judith K. Hellerstein and David Neumark, "Are Earnings Profiles Steeper Than Productivity Profiles? Evidence from Israeli Firm-Level Data," *Journal of Human Resources* 30, no.1 (Winter 1995): 89–112.

FIGURE 5.5

Productivity and Wage Growth, First Two Years on Job, by Occupation and Initial Hours of Employer Training

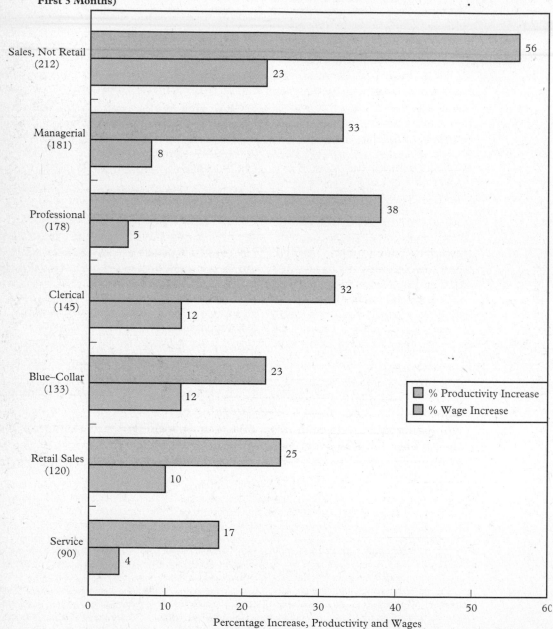

Occupation (Hours of Training in First 3 Months)

- Sales, Not Retail (212): 56 / 23
- Managerial (181): 33 / 8
- Professional (178): 38 / 5
- Clerical (145): 32 / 12
- Blue–Collar (133): 23 / 12
- Retail Sales (120): 25 / 10
- Service (90): 17 / 4

Legend:
- % Productivity Increase
- % Wage Increase

X-axis: Percentage Increase, Productivity and Wages (0, 10, 20, 30, 40, 50, 60)

Source: John Bishop, "The Incidence of and Payoff to Employer Training," Cornell University Center for Advanced Human Resource Studies Working Paper 94-17, July 1994, Table 1.

IMPLICATIONS OF THE THEORY

LAYOFFS One major implication of the provision of specific training is the above-mentioned reluctance of firms to lay off workers in whom they have invested. We have seen that in the posttraining period, wages must be less than marginal productivity if the firm is to have any incentive at all to bear some initial training costs. This gap between MP_1 and W_1 provides protection against employee layoffs, even in a recession.

Suppose a recession were to occur and cause product demand to fall. The marginal productivity associated with each employment level would fall (from MP' to MP'' in Figure 5.6). For workers whose wage was equal to marginal productivity before the recession, this fall would reduce their marginal productivity to *below* their wage—and profit-maximizing employers would reduce employment, as shown in panel (a) of Figure 5.6, in order to maximize profits under the changed market conditions. In terms of Figure 5.6(a), employment would fall from E' to E''.

For a worker whose wage was *less* than marginal productivity, owing to past specific training, the decline in marginal productivity might *still* leave such productivity *above* the wage. Firms would not be making enough surplus in the posttraining period to earn back the net labor costs they incurred during the training period. However, these costs have already been spent and the firms cannot get them back. They will not hire and train *new* workers, but neither will they fire the ones they have trained. After all, these trained workers are still generating more than the company is paying them, and to lay them off would only reduce profits further. Thus, as panel (b) of Figure 5.6 shows, workers in whom their employers have invested are shielded to some extent from being laid off in business downturns. Of course, if marginal productivity fell to the point where it was below the wage, even trained workers might be laid off.[23]

Thus, this model suggests that during an economic downturn firms have an incentive to lay off workers with either no training or general training, but that it may prove profitable for firms to retain workers who have specific training. Although it is difficult to estimate the extent to which workers have specific training "imbedded" in them, there is some evidence that layoffs are lower for workers with higher skill levels, holding all other things, including their wage rates, constant.[24] Since the divergence between skill (productivity) and wages during the posttraining period can be taken as a measure of the extent of specific training, this finding provides some support for the theory.

---

[23]If the downturn is expected to be short and if marginal productivity is not too much below the wage, firms might not lay off workers and chance losing them. Why any adjustment would come in the form of layoff, rather than by temporarily reducing wages or hours of work, is discussed in Chapter 15.

[24]For a summary of the evidence, see Donald O. Parsons, "The Employment Relationship: Job Attachment, Work Effort and the Nature of Contracts," in *Handbook of Labor Economics,* vol. 2, ed. Orley Ashenfelter and Richard Layard (New York: North-Holland, 1986): 789–848. Jacob Mincer, "Education and Unemployment," working paper no. 3838, National Bureau of Economic Research, Cambridge, Mass., September 1991, similarly shows that workers who are more highly educated are less likely to lose their jobs than are their less educated counterparts.

LABOR PRODUCTIVITY   A second phenomenon our revised theory of demand can help explain is the fall in average productivity—output per labor hour—that occurs in the early stages of a recession. As demand and output start to fall, firms that have invested in specific training respond by maintaining their specifically trained workers on their payrolls. Such *labor hoarding* causes measured productivity to fall. Of course, the converse of this is that when demand picks up, firms can increase their output levels without proportionately increasing their employment levels because, in effect, they have maintained an *inventory* of skilled labor. Labor hoarding due to specific investments in human capital thus causes average productivity to increase in the early stages of a cyclical expansion and decrease in the early stages of a recession.

MINIMUM WAGE EFFECTS AGAIN   A third implication of our theory has to do with training effects of the minimum wage. If the minimum wage prevented the training-period wage from going low enough, firms offering specific training might *not* be able to offer posttraining wages that are very much higher than workers' alternative offers. If this is the case, trained workers will always be on the verge of quitting in the posttraining period, which places the firm's initial-period investment at risk. Under these conditions, firms will have little incentive to offer specific training. Minimum wage legislation may thus reduce the number of jobs offering training options that are available to low-skilled youths and therefore lower their rates of wage growth. In fact, there is some evidence that this has occurred. [25]

DO EMPLOYERS EVER PAY FOR GENERAL TRAINING?

Our theory suggests that the costs of general training must be borne by employees, because any attempts by employers to obtain a posttraining surplus will be met with an exodus of already-trained workers seeking higher wages elsewhere. Despite this clear implication of theory, and despite the just-cited evidence that firms with training programs bear much of their costs and are able to collect much of their returns, a national survey of American firms found that managers believed most skills taught in their on-the-job training programs were transferable to other employers.[26] While not all economists are persuaded that general training is widely provided and paid for by employers,[27] some have hypothesized that per-

[25]Masanori Hashimoto, "Minimum Wage Effects and Training on the Job," *American Economic Review* 72 (December 1982): 1070–1087, and Linda Leighton and Jacob Mincer, "Effects of Minimum Wages on Human Capital Formation," in *The Economics of Legal Minimum Wages,* ed. Simon Rottenberg (Washington, D.C.: American Enterprise Institute, 1981), 155–173. A different method of testing for the training effects of the minimum wage found no training effects; see Card and Krueger, *Myth and Measurement,* 172.

[26]John Bishop, "The Incidence of and Payoff to Employer Training," 44. For other evidence that firms at least sometimes pay for general training, see Margaret Stevens, "An Investment Model for the Supply of General Training by Employers"; Alan Krueger, "How Computers Have Changed the Wage Structure: Evidence from Micro Data, 1984–1989," *Quarterly Journal of Economics* (February 1994): 33–60; Lauri Bassi, "Workplace Education for Hourly Workers."

[27]See Lisa Lynch, "Private-Sector Training and the Earnings of Young Workers."

FIGURE 5.6

The Effect of a Decline in Demand on Employment with General and Specific Training

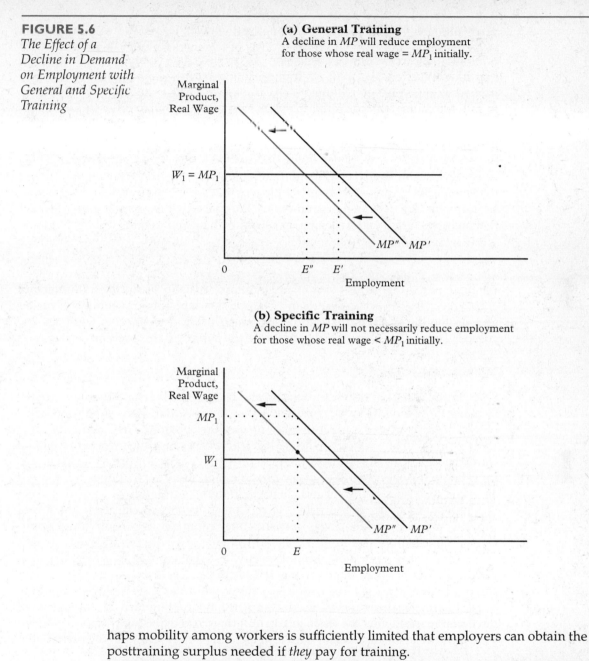

(a) General Training
A decline in *MP* will reduce employment for those whose real wage = MP_1 initially.

(b) Specific Training
A decline in *MP* will not necessarily reduce employment for those whose real wage < MP_1 initially.

haps mobility among workers is sufficiently limited that employers can obtain the posttraining surplus needed if *they* pay for training.

Sometimes employees who receive general training can be "tied" to their employer by a contract requiring them to pay back the costs of educational programs if they quit within, say, two years of completing them. Such legal barriers to quitting, however, are rare (although see Example 5.4 for examples from professional sports). More often, mobility is inhibited only by various costs employees naturally must bear in finding other offers and switching employers: time must be spent filling out applications and being interviewed, travel and relocation costs must be borne, and there are psychic costs of leaving a familiar environment for the unknown. These mobility costs, which we will analyze more fully in Chapter 10, may generate monopsonistic conditions in many labor markets and thereby enable firms to pay a real wage less than marginal product.[28]

In addition to training employees, firms must also evaluate them when making hiring, placement, and promotion decisions. They may therefore find that training programs—even ones with a "general" component—can be used to help discover the learning abilities, work habits, and motivation levels of new employees.[29] Thus, some of what appears to be general training may actually represent an investment in firm-specific information about employees that will be useful later on in making assignments and deciding on promotions. We conclude this chapter with a section that analyzes hiring and screening investments in greater detail.

Hiring Investments

We have noted that firms often incur significant costs in recruiting and selecting employees. These costs cause them to adopt standards or conventions in hiring and promoting workers that can be explained using the concepts we have discussed. The implications of hiring costs are the subject of this section.

THE USE OF CREDENTIALS

Since firms often bear the costs of hiring and training workers, it is in their interest to make these costs as low as possible. Other things equal, firms should prefer to obtain a workforce of a given quality at the least possible cost. Similarly, they should prefer to hire workers who are fast learners because such workers could be trained at less cost. Unfortunately, it may prove expensive for firms to extensively investigate the background of every possible individual who applies for a job to ascertain his or her skill level and ability to undertake training.

One way to reduce these costs is to rely on *credentials, or signals*, in the hiring process, rather than intensively investigating the qualities of individual applicants.[30] For example, if *on average* college graduates are more productive than high school graduates, an employer might specify that a college degree is a requirement for the job. Rather than interviewing and testing all applicants to try to ascertain the productivity of each, the firm may simply select its new employees from the pool of applicants who meet this educational standard. Similarly, if employers believe that married men are less likely to quit their jobs than single men, or that 25-year-olds are less likely to quit than teenagers, they may want to give preferential

---

[28]Margaret Stevens, "A Theoretical Model of On-the-Job Training with Imperfect Competition."

[29]Margaret Stevens, "An Investment Model for the Supply of General Training by Employers."

[30]See Michael Spence, "Job Market Signaling," *Quarterly Journal of Economics* 87 (August 1973): 355–374. Refer to Chapter 9 for a more detailed discussion of signaling.

EXAMPLE 5.4

Paying for America's Minor Leagues and Spain's "Stone Quarries"

The lack of employer incentives to pay for employees' general training is a problem that must be addressed by professional sports leagues. Teams often invest huge sums of money in selecting and training players, but the resulting skills can be used with *other* teams as well. If trained players can be bid away by teams with no investment costs to recoup, and if the teams making the investments are not provided with a mechanism for recovering their costs, then such training will clearly be curtailed. How can professional sports leagues be structured to provide the incentives necessary for the major league teams to scout and train players?

A major league baseball team in the United States spends about 4 million dollars each year to scout and train players, over 90 percent of whom never make it to the major leagues. Those who do typically spend four or five years in the minor leagues, with the result that the team's minor league system will "graduate" only two or three players a year to the major league club. Because the major league teams receive none of the minor league revenues, but must pay the salaries of minor league players and instructors, their yearly investment costs must be recouped by paying the few players who make it less than their marginal revenue productivity.

The recovery of scouting and training investments in baseball is facilitated by the "reserve clause," under which a player with less than six years of major league experience is not free to choose the team for which he plays. Only after six years can he become a "free agent" and obtain offers from other teams. Presumably, the competitive bidding process for free agents results in their salaries being roughly equal to their marginal revenue productivity. However, since players

with more than three years of major league experience are eligible for salary arbitration, and since these awards often establish pay similar to that received by free agents, players' salaries are probably close to marginal revenue productivity from their fourth year on. Thus, each team really has only three years in which it can pay its players much less than their marginal revenue productivity and thereby recover minor league costs.

In Spain, each professional soccer team also has a network of minor league teams—called its "stone quarry"—in which player development takes place. Unlike American baseball players, Spanish soccer players are free from the very start to change teams once their contracts have expired; in other words, there is no reserve clause in Spanish soccer. To preserve incentives for "major league" soccer teams to develop players, however, Spanish labor law requires that teams acquiring free agents must compensate the team from which the player came for its training and development investments ("*indemnización de preparación y formación*"). This compensation is the subject of negotiation between the two teams, and if agreement cannot be reached, it is then decided by arbitration. This system clearly tries to balance the rights all workers (including professional athletes) have under Spanish labor law to freely choose their employer against the need for teams to recover general training costs if the "stone quarry" system is to survive.*

*Information on the Spanish system was provided to us by a former Cornell graduate student, Miguel Rodriguez-Piñero Royo, from Madrid.

treatment to married men and 25-year-olds over single men and teenagers in their hiring decisions.

Such forms of *statistical discrimination*, judging individuals by *group* characteristics, have obvious costs. On the one hand, for example, some high school graduates may be fully qualified to work for a firm that insists on college graduates. Excluding them from the pool of potential applicants imposes costs on them (they do not get the job); however, it also imposes costs on the employer *if* other qualified applicants cannot be readily found. On the other hand, there may be some unproductive workers among the group of college graduates, and an employer who hires them may well suffer losses while they are employed. However, if the reduction in hiring costs that arises when *signals* (such as educational credentials, marital status, or age) are used is large, it may prove profitable for an employer to use them even if an occasional unsatisfactory worker sneaks through. Put another way, the total costs of hiring, training, and employing workers may well be lower for some firms when hiring standards are used than when such firms rely upon more intensive investigations of applicant characteristics. (Chapter 12 will return to the issue of statistical discrimination.)

INTERNAL LABOR MARKETS

A major problem with the use of credentials to predict which applicants will become good employees is that these credentials may only be loosely related to actual productivity on the job. Such personal attributes as dependability, motivation, honesty, and flexibility are difficult to observe using credentials, yet for many jobs such attributes may be crucial. This difficulty with credentials has induced some firms to adopt a policy of hiring workers at low-level jobs, observing their behavior in training programs and on the job, and filling all upper-level jobs from within the firm. Thus, all upper-level vacancies are filled with people whose characteristics have been carefully observed in other jobs the firm has given them to do.

This second approach to the problem of minimizing hiring costs while maximizing the productivity of employees creates an *internal labor market*, because most jobs in the firm are filled from within the ranks of current employees.[31] The hiring done from outside the firm tends to be heavily concentrated at certain low-level "ports of entry." These jobs—such as "general laborer," "machine cleaner," and "packer" for blue-collar applicants or "management trainee" for white-collar applicants—are at sufficiently low responsibility levels that a bad employee cannot do too much damage to the firm or its equipment. However, these jobs do give the firm a chance to observe *actual* productive characteristics of the employees hired, and this information is then used to determine who stays with the firm and how fast and how high employees are promoted.

---

[31]For a detailed discussion of internal labor markets, see Oliver Williamson et al., "Understanding the Employment Relation: The Analysis of Idiosyncratic Exchange," *Bell Journal of Economics* 16 (Spring 1975): 250–280; and Paul Osterman, ed., *Internal Labor Markets* (Cambridge, Mass.: MIT Press, 1984).

The *benefits* of using an internal labor market to fill vacancies are that the firm knows a lot about the people working for it. Hiring decisions for upper-level jobs in either the blue-collar or the white-collar workforces will thus offer few surprises to the firm. The *costs* of using the internal labor market are associated with the restriction of competition for the upper-level jobs to those in the firm. Those in the firm may not be the best employees available, but they are the only ones the firm considers for those jobs. Firms most likely to decide that the benefits of using an internal labor market outweigh the costs are those whose upper-level workers must have a lot of firm-specific knowledge and training that can best be attained by on-the-job learning over the years. For those firms, the number of qualified *outside* applicants for upper-level jobs is relatively small. Firms in the steel, petroleum, and chemical industries tend to rely on internal labor markets to fill vacancies, while those in the garment and shoe industries do not. The former group of industries has highly automated, complicated, and interdependent production technologies that can be mastered only through years on the job. The garment- and shoe-manufacturing industries employ workers who perform certain discrete crafts, skills that are not specific to one firm.

As noted earlier, firms that pay for *training* will want to ensure that they obtain employees who can learn quickly and will remain with them long enough that training costs can be recouped through the posttraining "surplus." For these firms, the internal labor market offers two attractions. First, it allows the firm to observe workers on the job, where it can see firsthand who learns quickly, who is easily motivated, who is dependable, and so forth, and thus make better decisions about which workers will be the recipients of later, perhaps very expensive, training. Second, the internal labor market tends to foster an attachment to the firm by its employees. They know that they have an inside track on upper-level vacancies because outsiders will not be considered. If they quit the firm, they would lose this privileged position. They are thus motivated to become long-term employees of the firm. The full implications of internal labor markets for wage policies within the firm will be discussed in Chapter 11.

HOW CAN THE EMPLOYER RECOUP ITS HIRING INVESTMENTS?

Whether a firm invests in training its workers or in selecting them, it will do so only if it believes it can generate an acceptable rate of return on its investment. For a labor investment to be worthwhile, an employer must be able to benefit from a situation in which workers are paid less than their marginal value to the firm in the postinvestment period. We have seen that training adds to a worker's productivity and can therefore generate the required postinvestment surplus *if* the worker is discouraged from putting his or her new skills to work for another employer at higher pay. How can employers generate a postinvestment surplus for their *hiring* investments?

Suppose that applicants for a job vacancy have either average, below-average, or above-average productivity, but that the employer cannot tell which without making some kind of investment in acquiring that information. If the firm does not make this investment, it must assume that any particular applicant is of average ability and pay accordingly. If the firm makes an investment in acquiring information about its applicants, however, it could then hire *only* those whose productivity is above average. The surplus required to pay back its investment costs would then be created by paying these above-average workers a wage less than their true productivity.

Would the firm pay its new workers the average wage even though they are above average in productivity, thereby obtaining the full surplus? As with the case of training, the firm would probably decide to pay a wage greater than the average, but still below workers' actual productivity, to increase the likelihood that the workers in whom it has invested will remain. If its workers quit, the firm would have to invest in acquiring information about their replacements. Interestingly enough, though, the firm can recoup its hiring and screening investments *only* if its workers find job changing costly or if other employers cannot costlessly find out what it knows about its workers' true productivities.

Firms' problems of recouping their hiring and screening costs are therefore similar to those of recouping training costs. If employees are very mobile and can easily change jobs, and if other employers can observe what the firm learns from its careful screening and selection process, then the knowledge produced by the firm's investment is "general" and the firm cannot obtain the surplus needed to justify its investment.

REVIEW QUESTIONS

1. Both low-skilled workers and high-paid college professors have high rates of voluntary quits. What do they have in common that leads to a high quit rate?

2. Wages in the U.S. Postal Service have been attacked for being higher than wages elsewhere for people of the same age and education. The Postal Service answers that it *must* pay higher wages than workers could get elsewhere in order to keep the quit rate below the quit rate in other jobs. Are there circumstances under which this argument has any merit?

3. Compared to American firms, large Japanese firms invest more resources in training their workers, and the training they provide is broader in scope (instead of training for just one job, Japanese workers are trained to do a variety of different jobs within the firm). Based on this fact, make

reasonable predictions about the relative levels of both temporary and permanent layoffs in the two countries.

4. As noted in the text, unemployment insurance is financed in most states through a payroll tax levied on the employer. Rather than applying to all earnings, in most states the tax applies only to the first $7,000 to $12,000 per year an employee earns. How would you expect the existence of this low taxable wage base to affect employers' relative demands for skilled and unskilled workers?

5. For decades, most large employers bought group health insurance from insurers who charged them premiums on a *per-worker* basis. In 1993, a proposal for a national health insurance plan contained a provision requiring group health insurers to charge premiums based on *payroll* (in ef-

fect, financing health insurance by a payroll "tax"). Assuming the *total* premiums paid by employers remain the same, what are the labor market implications of this proposed change in the way in which health insurance is financed?

6. Suppose that the United States adopts a policy requiring employers to offer four months of *paid leave* for mothers of newly born babies. Analyze the labor demand effects of mandated paid child-care leave on women of childbearing age and on women past childbearing age.

7. In recent years there has been discussion of taxing employees for the nonwage benefits they receive. (At present, most benefits—medical and life insurance, for example—are not subject to the personal income tax.) If benefits such as insurance are taxed, they will become less attractive to employees, who may prefer to obtain increases in compensation in the form of wage increases rather than increases in nonwage benefits. Should this happen, what would be the likely effect on hours of work per employee per week?

8. Major league baseball teams scout and hire younger players whom they then train in the minor leagues for a period of three to five years. Very few of their trainees (perhaps 5 percent) actually make it to the major leagues, but if they do they are bound to the team that owns their contract for a period of six years. After six years, the player can become a "free agent" and choose any major league team on which to play. Keeping in mind that the major league teams pay the costs of, but derive no revenues from, their minor league teams, what would be the most important predictable effects of allowing players to become free agents immediately upon their entry into the major leagues?

9. The government of South Africa has attempted to attract businesses to the resettlement area of Botshabelo by offering various subsidies for firms located in that area. The most notable substantial subsidy is the government's payment of 95 percent of workers' wages up to a wage of $12 a week. Analyze the labor market implications of this wage subsidy for employment and wages, assuming that wages of full-time workers in Botshabelo average $20 per week.

SELECTED READINGS

Becker, Gary. *Human Capital*. 2d ed. New York: National Bureau of Economic Research, 1975.

Ehrenberg, Ronald G., and Paul L. Schumann. *Longer Hours or More Jobs? An Investigation of Amending Hours Legislation to Create Employment*. Ithaca, N.Y.: ILR Press, 1982.

Hart, Robert. *Working Time and Employment*. London: Allen and Unwin, 1986.

Lynch, Lisa, ed. *Training and the Private Sector: International Comparisons*. Chicago: University of Chicago Press, 1994.

Osterman, Paul, ed. *Internal Labor Markets*. Cambridge, Mass.: MIT Press, 1984.

Parsons, Donald. "The Firm's Decision to Train," in *Research in Labor Economics* 11, ed. Lauri J. Bassi and David L. Crawford (Greenwich, Conn.: JAI Press, 1990): 53–75.

Williamson, Oliver, et al. "Understanding the Employment Relation: The Analysis of Idiosyncratic Exchange." *Bell Journal of Economics* 16 (Spring 1975): 250–280.

6

Supply of Labor to the Economy: The Decision to Work

This and the next four chapters will focus on issues of *worker* behavior. That is, Chapters 6–10 will discuss and analyze various aspects of *labor supply* behavior. Labor supply decisions can be roughly divided into two categories. The first, which is addressed in this chapter and the next, includes decisions about whether to work at all and, if so, how long to work. Questions that must be answered include whether to participate in the labor force, whether to seek part-time or full-time work, and how long to work both at home and for pay. The second category of decisions, which is addressed in Chapters 8–10, deals with the questions that must be faced by a person who has decided to seek work for pay: the occupation or general class of occupations in which to seek offers (Chapters 8–9) and the geographical area in which offers should be sought (Chapter 10).

This chapter begins with some basic facts concerning labor force participation rates and hours of work. We then develop a theoretical framework that can be used in the analysis of decisions to work for pay. This framework is also useful for analyzing the structure of various income maintenance programs.

Trends in Labor Force Participation and Hours of Work

When a person actively seeks work, he or she is, by definition, in the *labor force*. As pointed out in Chapter 2, the *labor force participation rate* is the percentage of a given population that either has a job or is looking for one. Thus, one clear-cut statistic important in measuring people's willingness to work outside the home is the labor force participation rate.

Perhaps the most revolutionary change taking place in the labor market today is the tremendous increase in the proportion of women, particularly married women, working outside the home. Table 6.1 shows the dimensions of this change in the United States. As recently as 1950 only 21.6 percent of married women were in the labor force. By 1960 this percentage had risen to 31.9 percent, and recently it has reached roughly 60 percent—over two and a half times what it was in 1950.

We need not dwell here on the social changes that have been associated with this increasing tendency for women to seek work outside the home. Changes in family income, child-rearing practices, and the family itself are obvious. Less obvious are the effects on the demand for education by females and on the unemployment rate, which will be discussed in Chapters 9 and 15. Our interest in this chapter is in understanding the factors that have influenced this fundamental change in the propensity of women to seek work outside the home.

A second major trend in labor force participation is the decrease in length of careers for males, as can be seen in Table 6.2. The overall labor force participation

TABLE 6.1

Labor Force Participation Rates of Females in the U.S. over 16 Years of Age, by Marital Status, 1990–1994 (percent)

Year	All Females	Single	Widowed, Divorced	Married
1900	20.6	45.9	32.5	5.6
1910	25.5	54.0	34.1	10.7
1920	24.0			9.0
1930	25.3	55.2	34.4	11.7
1940	26.7	53.1	33.7	13.8
1950	29.7	53.6	35.5	21.6
1960	37.7	58.6	41.6	31.9
1970	43.3	56.8	40.3	40.5
1980	51.5	64.4	43.6	49.8
1988	56.6	67.7	46.2	56.7
1994	58.8			59.6

SOURCES: 1900–1950: Clarence D. Long, *The Labor Force Under Changing Income and Employment* (Princeton: Princeton University Press, 1958), Table A–6.

1960–1994: U.S. Department of Labor, Bureau of Labor Statistics, *Handbook of Labor Statistics*, Bulletin 2340 (Washington, D.C.: U.S. Government Printing Office, 1989), Table 6; and U.S. Department of Labor, Bureau of Labor Statistics, *Employment and Earnings* 42 (January 1995), Table 3. The last figure in the "Married" column is for 1993.

TABLE 6.2

Labor Force Participation Rates for Males in the U.S., by Age, 1900–1994 (percent)

Year	Age Groups					
	14–19	16–19	20–24	25–44	45–64	Over 65
1900	61.1		91.7	96.3	93.3	68.3
1910	56.2		91.1	96.6	93.6	58.1
1920	52.6		90.9	97.1	93.8	60.1
1930	41.1		89.9	97.5	94.1	58.3
1940	34.4		88.0	95.0	88.7	41.5
1950	39.9	63.2	82.8	92.8	87.9	41.6
1960	38.1	56.1	86.1	95.2	89.0	30.6
1970	35.8	56.1	80.9	94.4	87.3	25.0
1980		60.5	85.9	95.4	82.2	19.1
1994		57.7	85.5	93.9	80.6	17.2

SOURCES: 1900–1950: Clarence D. Long, *The Labor Force Under Changing Income and Employment* (Princeton: Princeton University Press, 1958), Table A–2.

1960: U.S. Department of Commerce, Bureau of the Census, *Census of Population, 1960: Employment Status,* Subject Reports PC(2)–6A, Table 1.

1970: U.S. Department of Commerce, Bureau of the Census, *Census of Population, 1970: Employment Status and Work Experience,* Subject Reports PC(2)–6A, Table 1.

1980: U.S. President, *Employment and Training Report of the President, 1981* (Washington, D.C.: U.S. Government Printing Office, 1981), Table A2, and U.S. Bureau of Labor Statistics, *Handbook of Labor Statistics,* Bulletin 2175 (Washington, D.C.: U.S. Government Printing Office, 1983), Table 4 (this source was used for the rates for 16–19-year olds for 1950–80).

1994: U.S. Bureau of Labor Statistics, *Employment and Earnings* 42 (January 1995), Table 3. (The data for 1980 and 1994 are not strictly comparable to those for earlier years because they are derived from a monthly survey, not the decennial census.)

rate of men has been falling, as was noted in Chapter 2, especially among the young and the old. The most substantial decreases in the United States have been among those 65 and over—from 68.3 percent in 1900 down to 17.2 percent by 1994. Participation rates for men of "prime age" have declined only slightly, although among 45- to 64-year-olds there were sharp decreases in the 1930s and 1970s. Clearly, men are starting their careers later and ending them earlier than they were at the beginning of this century.

The trends in American labor force participation rates have been observed in other industrialized countries as well. In Table 6.3 we display, for countries with comparable data, the trends in participation rates for women in the 25–54 age group and for men near the age of "early retirement" (55 to 64 years old). Typically, the fraction of women in the labor force rose from half or less in 1965 to roughly two-thirds or more some thirty years later. Among men between the ages

TABLE 6.3
Labor Force Participation Rates of Women and Older Men, Selected Countries,
1965 to 1993

Country	Women, aged 25 to 54			
	1965	1973	1983	1993
Canada	33.9	44.0	65.1	75.6
France	42.8	54.1	67.0	76.0
Germany	46.1	50.5	58.3	64.1[a]
Japan	—	53.0[b]	59.5	65.2
Sweden	56.0	68.9	87.0	87.6
United States	45.1	52.0	67.1	74.7
	Men, aged 55 to 64			
Canada	86.4	81.3	72.3	60.9
France	76.0	72.1	53.6	43.5
Germany	84.6	73.4	63.1	57.9[a]
Japan	—	86.3[b]	84.7	85.4
Sweden	88.3	82.7	77.0	70.5
United States	82.9	76.9	69.4	66.5

[a]Data are for 1990.

[b]Data are for 1974 (earlier data not comparable).

SOURCE: Organisation for Economic Co-Operation and Development, *Labor Force Statistics* (Paris: OECD, various dates).

of 55 and 64, participation fell markedly in each country except Japan, although the declines were much larger in some countries (France, for example) than others (Sweden). Thus, while there are some differences in trends across the countries, it is likely that common forces are influencing labor supply trends in the industrialized world.

Because data on labor force participation include both the employed and those who want a job but do not have one, they are a relatively pure measure of labor supply. To be sure, as we will see in Chapter 7, participation rates are influenced to some extent by forces on the demand side of the market; nevertheless, it is clear that they are predominantly a labor supply phenomenon. In contrast, the weekly or yearly hours of work put in by the typical employee are often thought to be determined only by the demand side of the market. After all, don't employers, in responding to the factors discussed in Chapter 5, set the hours of work expected of their employees? They do, of course, but hours worked are also influenced by *employee* preferences on the supply side of the market, especially in the long run.

Even though employers set work schedules, employees can exercise their preferences regarding hours of work through their selection of occupations and employers. A major dimension of occupational choice relates to hours of work. In 1994, for example, women managers working full-time averaged three and a half more hours of work per week than did full-time clerical workers, and male sales workers worked over four more hours per week than did their full-time counterparts in skilled craft jobs.[1] Moreover, different employers can (and do) offer different mixes of full- and part-time work, different weekly work schedules, and have different policies regarding vacations and paid holidays. Employer offers regarding both hours and pay are intended to enhance their profits, but in doing so they must also satisfy the preferences of current and prospective employees. For example, if employees receiving an hourly wage of $X for 40 hours per week really wanted to work only 30 hours at $X per hour, some enterprising employer (presumably one with relatively lower quasi-fixed costs) would eventually seize on their dissatisfaction and offer jobs with a 30-hour workweek, ending up with a more satisfied, productive workforce in the process.

While the labor supply preferences of employees must be satisfied in the long run, most of the short-run changes in hours of work seem to emanate from the *demand* side of the market.[2] Workweeks typically vary over the course of a business cycle, with longer hours worked in periods of robust demand. In years of sluggish demand, some workers cannot find as many hours of employment as they want; these workers experience involuntary reductions in work hours through unemployment, acceptance of part-time work when they want to work full-time, or elimination of overtime hours. Demand-side forces can also constrain workers' choice of hours worked over longer periods if there are major shifts in labor demand or supply taking place that have not been fully accommodated by the market. If the demand for unskilled labor falls, for example, and its wage remains above equilibrium, the resulting gap between demand and supply can be thought of as constraining the hours of unskilled workers (they want more hours of work than they are offered by employers). Thus, in analyzing trends in hours of work, one must carefully distinguish between the forces of demand and supply.

Over the course of this century, the hours of work have clearly and dramatically fallen. In the first decade of this century, for example, production workers in American manufacturing industries were working 55-hour weeks during years in which economic activity was strong; recently they have averaged 38 hours of ac-

---

[1] U.S. Bureau of Labor Statistics, *Employment and Earnings* 42, no. 1 (January 1995): 195.

[2] See, for example, Joseph G. Altonji and Christina H. Paxon, "Job Characteristics and Hours of Work," in *Research in Labor Economics*, vol. 8, ed. Ronald Ehrenberg (Greenwich, Conn.: JAI Press, 1986); Orley Ashenfelter, "Macroeconomic Analyses and Microeconomic Analyses of Labor Supply," *Carnegie-Rochester Conference Series on Public Policy* 21 (1984): 117–156; and John C. Ham, "On the Interpretation of Unemployment in Empirical Labour Supply Analysis," in *Unemployment, Search, and Labour Supply,* ed. Richard Blundell and Ian Walker (Cambridge, Eng.: Cambridge University Press, 1986), 121–142. Altonji and Paxon show, for example, that hours of work fluctuate much more over time for individuals who change employers than they do for individuals who remain with the same employer.

tual work per week in years of peak demand.[3] All of the drop in the manufacturing workweek, however, came before World War II; since 1948 there has been no trend at all.

Looking beyond manufacturing, Table 6.4 compares the average workweek in 1950 and 1988 for American workers in four race/sex groups. Both 1950 and 1988 were years in which the level and the direction of the national unemployment rate were comparable, and the data in Table 6.4 suggest that some interesting changes in work hours have taken place over the past four decades. For workers with a high school education or less, weekly hours of work fell by approximately 10 percent or more for each of the race/sex groups. For those with at least a college degree, average hours of work rose slightly for all groups shown except white women. The result of these movements is that the workweeks of skilled and less-skilled workers, which in 1950 were similar within each demographic group, are now different by about three hours (or about 9 percent) per week.

Can labor supply theory help us to understand the long-run trends in labor force participation and hours of work noted above? Because labor is the most abundant factor of production, it is fair to say that any country's well-being in the long run is heavily dependent on the willingness of its people to work. As we shall demonstrate, leisure and other ways of spending time that do not involve

TABLE 6.4
Average Weekly Hours of Work in the United States, by Education, Race, and Sex, 1950 and 1988

	Year	
Group	1950	1988
College graduates		
White women	40.4	38.0
White men	43.7	44.9
Black women	40.3	40.6
Black men	42.1	42.5
High School or less		
White women	41.1	34.8
White men	43.3	41.3
Black women	40.3	36.5
Black men	42.8	39.0

SOURCES: Mary T. Coleman and John Pencavel, "Changes in Work Hours of Male Employees, 1940–1988," *Industrial and Labor Relations Review* 46, no. 2 (January 1993): 262–283; Mary T. Coleman and John Pencavel, "Trends in Market Work Behavior of Women Since 1940," *Industrial and Labor Relations Review* 46, no. 4 (July 1993): 653–676.

[3]Actual hours of work are to be distinguished from the more commonly cited "hours paid for"; the latter includes paid time off for vacations, holidays, sick days, and so forth.

work for pay are also important in generating well-being; however, any economy relies heavily on goods and services produced for market transactions. Therefore, it is important to understand the *work-incentive* effects of higher wages and incomes, different kinds of taxes, and various forms of income maintenance programs.

A Theory of the Decision to Work

The decision to work is ultimately a decision about how to spend time. One way to use one's available time is to spend it in pleasurable leisure activities. The other major way in which people use time is to work.[4] One can work around the home, performing such *household production* as raising children, sewing, building, or even growing food. Alternatively, one can work for pay and use one's earnings to purchase food, shelter, clothing, and child care.

Because working for pay and engaging in household production are two ways of getting the same jobs done, we shall initially ignore the distinction between them and treat work activities as working for pay. We shall therefore be characterizing the decision to work as a choice between leisure and working for pay. Most of the crucial factors affecting work incentives can be understood in this context, but insight into labor supply behavior can be enriched by a consideration of household production as well; this we do in Chapter 7.

If we regard the time spent eating, sleeping, and otherwise maintaining ourselves as more or less fixed by natural laws, then the discretionary time we have (16 hours a day, say) can be allocated to either work or leisure. Since the amount of discretionary time spent on leisure is time not spent on working, and vice versa, the *demand for leisure* can be considered the reverse side of the coin labeled *supply of labor*. It is actually more convenient to analyze work incentives in the context of the demand for leisure, because one can apply the standard analysis of the demand for any good to the demand for leisure, and then simply subtract leisure hours from total discretionary hours available to obtain the *labor supply* effects.

SOME BASIC CONCEPTS

Having chosen to analyze work incentives in the context of the demand for leisure, it is instructive to briefly review the factors that affect the demand for any good. Basically, the demand for a good is a function of three factors:

1. The *opportunity cost* of the good (which is often equal to *market price*),
2. One's level of *wealth*, and
3. One's set of *preferences*.

---

[4]Another category of activity is to spend time acquiring skills or doing other things that enhance one's future earning capacity. These activities will be discussed in Chapters 9 and 10.

For example, consumption of heating oil will vary with the *cost* of such oil; as that cost rises, consumption tends to fall unless one of the other two factors intervenes. As *wealth* rises, people generally want larger and warmer houses that obviously require more oil to heat.[5] Even if the price of energy and the level of personal wealth were to remain constant, the demand for energy could rise if a falling birthrate and lengthened life span resulted in a higher proportion of the population being aged and therefore wanting warmer houses. This change in the composition of the population amounts to a shift in the overall *preferences* for warmer houses and thus leads to a change in the demand for heating oil. (Economists usually assume that preferences are given and not subject to immediate change. For policy purposes, changes in prices and wealth are of paramount importance in explaining changes in demand because these variables are more susceptible to change by government or market forces.)

To apply this general analysis of demand to the demand for leisure, we must first ask, "What is the opportunity cost of leisure?" The cost of spending an hour watching television is basically what one could earn if one had spent that hour working. Thus, the opportunity cost of an hour of leisure is equal to one's *wage rate*—the *extra earnings* a worker can take home from an *extra hour of work*.[6] This measure of leisure's opportunity cost is clearly affected by the tax rate on earned income, and it emphasizes the *marginal* cost of leisure because labor supply decisions are incremental (that is, they represent adjustments to current behavior).

Next, we must understand and be able to measure wealth. Naturally, wealth includes a family's holdings of bank accounts, financial investments, and physical property. Workers' skills can also be considered assets, since these skills can be, in effect, rented out to employers for a price. The more one can get in wages, the larger is the value of one's human assets. Unfortunately, it is not usually possible to directly measure people's wealth. It is much easier to measure the *returns* from that wealth, because data on total *income* are readily available from government surveys. Economists thus often use total income as an indicator of total wealth, since the two are conceptually so closely related.[7]

Theory suggests that if income increases while wages and preferences are held constant, the number of leisure hours demanded will rise. Put differently, *if income increases, holding wages constant, desired hours of work will go down.* (Conversely, if income is reduced while the wage rate is held constant, desired hours

---

[5]When the demand for a good rises with wealth, economists say the good is a *normal good.* If demand falls as wealth rises, the good is said to be an *inferior good* (traveling or commuting by bus is sometimes cited as an example of an inferior good).

[6]This assumes that individuals can work as many hours as they want at a fixed wage rate. While this assumption may seem overly simplistic, it will not lead to wrong conclusions with respect to the issues analyzed in this chapter. More rigorously, it should be said that leisure's *marginal* opportunity cost is the *marginal* wage rate (the wage one could receive for an extra hour of work).

[7]The best indicator of wealth is one's *permanent,* or long-run potential, *income.* One's current income may differ from one's permanent income for a variety of reasons (unemployment, illness, unusually large amounts of overtime work, etc.). For our purposes here, however, the distinction between current and permanent income is not too important.

of work will go up.) Economists call the response of desired hours of leisure to changes in income, with wages held constant, the *income effect*. The income effect is based on the simple notion that as incomes rise, holding leisure's opportunity cost constant, people will want to consume more leisure (which means working less).

Because we have assumed that time is spent either in leisure or in working for pay, the income effect can be expressed in terms of the *supply of working hours* as well as the demand for leisure hours. Because the ultimate focus of this chapter is labor supply, we choose to express this effect in the context of supply.

Using algebraic notation, we define the income effect as the change in hours of work (ΔH) produced by a change in income (ΔY), holding wages constant ($\overline{W}$):

$$\text{Income Effect} = \frac{\Delta H}{\Delta Y}\bigg|_{\overline{W}} < 0 \tag{6.1}$$

We say the income effect is *negative* because the *sign* of the *fraction* in equation (6.1) is *negative*. If income goes up (wages held constant), hours of work fall. If income goes down, hours of work increase. The numerator (ΔH) and denominator (ΔY) in equation (6.1) move in opposite directions, giving a negative sign to the income effect.

Theory also suggests that *if income is held constant, an increase in the wage rate will raise the price and reduce the demand for leisure, thereby increasing work incentives.* (Likewise, a decrease in the wage rate will reduce leisure's opportunity cost and the incentives to work, holding income constant.) This *substitution effect* occurs because as the cost of leisure changes, income held constant, leisure and work hours are substituted for each other.

In contrast to the income effect, the substitution effect is *positive*. Because this effect is the change in hours of work (ΔH) induced by a change in the wage (ΔW), holding income constant ($\overline{Y}$), the substitution effect can be written as:

$$\text{Substitution Effect} = \frac{\Delta H}{\Delta W}\bigg|_{\overline{Y}} > 0 \tag{6.2}$$

Because numerator (ΔH) and denominator (ΔW) always move in the same direction, at least in theory, the substitution effect has a positive sign.

At times it is possible to observe situations or programs that create pure income or pure substitution effects. Usually, however, both effects are simultaneously present, often working against each other.

A "PURE" INCOME EFFECT   Receiving an inheritance is an example of the income effect by itself. The bequest enhances one's wealth (income) *independent* of the hours of work. Thus, income is increased *without* a change in the compensation received from an hour of work. In this case, the income effect induces the person to consume more leisure, thereby reducing the willingness to work. (Some support for this theoretical prediction can be seen later in Example 6.1.) It is important to note that if the change in nonlabor income were *negative*, the income effect suggests that people would work *more*.

A "PURE" SUBSTITUTION EFFECT   In the 1980 presidential campaign, candidate John Anderson proposed a program aimed at conserving gasoline. His plan consisted of raising the gasoline tax but offsetting this increase by a reduced Social Security tax payable by individuals on their earnings. The idea was to raise the price of gasoline without reducing people's overall spendable income.

For our purposes, this plan is interesting because it creates a pure substitution effect on labor supply. Social Security revenues are collected by a tax on earnings, so reductions in the tax are, in effect, increases in the wage rate for most workers.[8] For the average person, however, the increased wealth associated with this wage increase is exactly offset by increases in the gasoline tax.[9] Hence, wages are increased while income is held more or less constant. This program would thus create a substitution effect that induces people to work more hours.

BOTH EFFECTS OCCUR WHEN WAGES RISE   While the above examples illustrate situations in which the income or the substitution effect is present by itself, normally both effects are present, often working in opposite directions. The presence of both effects working in opposite directions creates ambiguity in predicting the overall labor supply response in many cases. Consider the case of a person who receives a wage increase.

The labor supply response to a simple wage increase will involve *both* an income effect and a substitution effect. The *income effect* is the result of the worker's enhanced wealth (or potential income) after the increase. For a given level of work effort, he or she now has a greater command over resources than before (because more income is received for any given number of hours of work). The *substitution effect* results from the fact that the wage increase raises the opportunity costs of leisure. Because the actual labor supply response is the *sum* of the income and substitution effects, we cannot predict the response in advance; theory simply does not tell us which effect is stronger.

If the *income* effect is dominant, the person will respond to a wage increase by decreasing his or her labor supply. This decrease will be *smaller* than if the same change in wealth were due to an increase in *nonlabor* wealth, because the substitution effect is present and acts as a moderating influence. However, when the *income* effect dominates, the substitution effect is not large enough to prevent labor supply from *declining*. It is entirely plausible, of course, that the *substitution* effect will dominate. If so, the actual response to wage increases will be to *increase* labor supply.

Should the substitution effect dominate, the person's labor supply curve—relating, say, desired hours of work to wages—will be *positively sloped*. That is, labor supplied will increase with the wage rate. If, on the other hand, the income effect dominates, the labor supply curve will be *negatively sloped*. Economic theory cannot say which

---

[8] See footnote 3 in Chapter 5 for more details on Social Security taxes.

[9] An increase in the price of gasoline will reduce the income people have left for expenditures on non-gasoline consumption only if the demand for gasoline is inelastic. In this case, the percentage reduction in gasoline consumption is smaller than the percentage increase in price: total expenditures on gasoline would thus rise. Our analysis assumes this to be the case.

effect will dominate, and in fact individual labor supply curves could be positively sloped in some ranges of the wage and negatively sloped in others. In Figure 6.1, for example, the person's desired hours of work increase (substitution effect dominates) when wages go up as long as wages are low (below W^*). At higher wages, however, further increases result in reduced hours of work (the income effect dominates); economists refer to such a curve as "backward-bending."

ANALYSIS OF THE LABOR/LEISURE CHOICE

This section introduces indifference curves and budget constraints—graphic material that may already be familiar to students with a background in these fundamentals. Graphic analysis incorporates visual aids that make the analysis easier to understand and to apply to complex policy issues. These graphic aids visually depict the basic factors underlying the demand for leisure (supply of labor) discussed above.

PREFERENCES   Let us assume that there are two major categories of goods that make people happy—leisure time and the goods people can buy with money. If, for simplicity, we take the prices of the latter goods as fixed, then they can be compressed into one index that is measured by money income. (Put differently, with prices fixed, more money income always means that it is possible to consume more of these goods.) Collapsing all goods into two categories, leisure and money income, allows our graphs to be drawn in two-dimensional space.

Since both leisure and money can be used to generate satisfaction (or *utility*), these two goods are to some extent substitutes for each other. If one were forced to give up some money income—by cutting back one's hours of work, for example—there would be some increase in leisure time that could be substituted for this lost income to keep the person as happy as before. A very thoughtful consumer/worker, in fact, could reveal a whole *variety* of combinations of money income and leisure hours that would yield him or her this same level of satisfaction.

To understand how preferences can be graphed, suppose a thoughtful consumer/worker were asked to decide how happy he or she would be with a daily income of $64 combined with 8 hours of leisure (point *a* in Figure 6.2). This level of happiness could be called utility level *A*. Our consumer/worker could name *other combinations* of money income and leisure hours that would *also* yield utility level

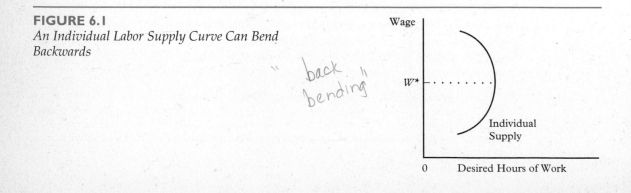

FIGURE 6.1
An Individual Labor Supply Curve Can Bend Backwards

" back bending"

A. Assume that our respondent named five other combinations. All six combinations of money income and leisure hours that yield utility level *A* are represented by heavy dots in Figure 6.2. The curve connecting these dots is called an *indifference curve*, a curve connecting the various combinations of money income and leisure that yield equal utility. (The term *indifference curve* is derived from the fact that, since each point on the curve yields equal utility, a person is truly indifferent about where on the curve he or she will be.)

Our worker/consumer could no doubt achieve a higher level of happiness if he or she could combine the 8 hours of leisure with an income of $100 per day, instead of just $64 a day. This higher satisfaction level could be called utility level *B*. The consumer could name other combinations of money income and leisure that would also yield *this* higher level of utility. These combinations are denoted by the ×'s in Figure 6.2 that are connected by a second indifference curve.

Indifference curves have certain specific characteristics that are reflected in the way they are drawn:

1. Utility level *B* represents more happiness than level *A*. Every level of leisure consumption is combined with a higher income on *B* than on *A*. Hence our respondent prefers all points on indifference curve *B* to any point on curve *A*. A whole *set* of indifference curves could be drawn for this one person, each representing a different utility level. Any such curve that lies to the northeast of another one is preferred to any curve to the southwest because the northeastern curve represents a higher level of utility.

2. Indifference curves *do not intersect*. If they did, the point of intersection would represent *one* combination of money income and leisure that yielded

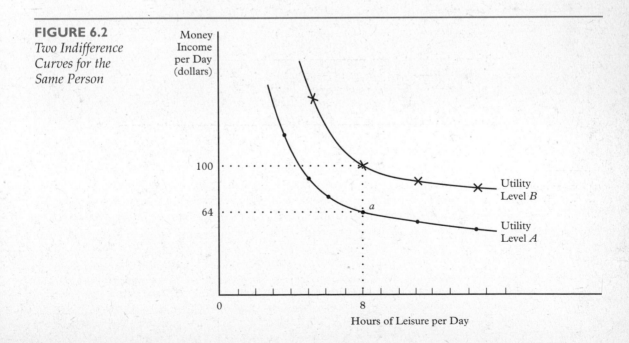

FIGURE 6.2

Two Indifference Curves for the Same Person

FIGURE 6.3
An Indifference Curve

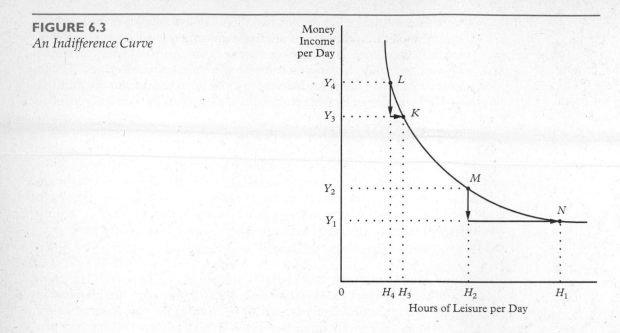

two different levels of satisfaction. We assume our worker/consumer is *not* so inconsistent in stating his or her preferences that this could happen.

3. Indifference curves are *negatively sloped,* because if either income or leisure hours are increased, the other is reduced in order to preserve the same level of utility. If the slope is steep, as at segment *LK* in Figure 6.3, a given loss of income need not be accompanied by a large increase in leisure hours to keep utility constant.[10] When the curve is relatively flat, however, as at segment *MN* in Figure 6.3, a given decrease in income must be accompanied by a large increase in the consumption of leisure to hold utility constant. Thus, when indifference curves are relatively steep, people do not value money income as highly as when such curves are relatively flat; when they are flat, a loss of income can only be compensated for by a large increase in leisure if utility is to be kept constant.

4. Indifference curves are *convex*—steeper at the left than at the right. This shape reflects the assumption that when money income is relatively high and leisure hours are relatively few, leisure is more highly valued than when leisure is abundant and income relatively scarce. At segment *LK* in Figure 6.3, a great loss of income (from Y_4 to Y_3, for example) can be compensated for by

---

[10]Economists call the change in money income needed to hold utility constant when leisure hours are changed by one unit the *marginal rate of substitution* between leisure and money income. This marginal rate of substitution can be graphically understood as the slope of the indifference curve at any point. At point *L*, for example, the slope is relatively steep, so economists would say that the marginal rate of substitution at point *L* is relatively high.

just a little increase in leisure, whereas a little loss of leisure time (from H_3 to H_4, for example) would require a relatively large increase in income to maintain equal utility. What is relatively scarce is more highly valued.

Conversely, when income is low and leisure is abundant (segment MN in Figure 6.3), income is more highly valued. Losing income (by moving from Y_2 to Y_1, for example) would require a huge increase in leisure for utility to remain constant. To repeat, what is relatively scarce is assumed to be more highly valued.

5. Finally, different people have different sets of indifference curves. The curves drawn in Figures 6.2 and 6.3 were for *one person*. Another person would have a completely different set of curves. People who value leisure more highly, for example, would have had indifference curves that were generally steeper (see Figure 6.4a). People who do not value leisure highly would have relatively flat curves (see Figure 6.4b). Thus, individual preferences can be portrayed graphically.

INCOME AND WAGE CONSTRAINTS Now, everyone would like to maximize his or her utility, which would be ideally done by consuming every available hour of leisure combined with the highest conceivable income. Unfortunately, the resources anyone can command are limited. Thus, all that is possible is to do the best one can, given limited resources. To see these resource limitations graphically requires superimposing constraints on one's set of indifference curves to see which combinations of income and leisure are available and which are not.

Suppose the person whose indifference curves are graphed in Figure 6.2 had no source of income other than labor earnings. Suppose, further, that he or she could earn $8 per hour. Figure 6.5 includes the two indifference curves shown in Figure 6.2 as well as a straight line (DE) connecting combinations of leisure and income that are

FIGURE 6.4
Indifference Curves for Two Different People

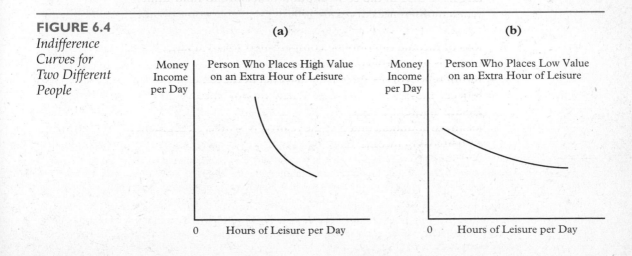

possible for a person with an $8 wage and no outside income. If 16 hours per day are available for work and leisure[11] and if this person consumes all 16 in leisure, then money income will be zero (point *D* in Figure 6.5). If 5 hours a day are devoted to work, income will be $40 per day (point *M*), and if 16 hours a day are worked, income will be $128 per day (point *E*). Other points on this line—for example, the point of 15 hours of leisure (1 hour of work) and $8 of income—are also possible. This line, which reflects the combinations of leisure and income that are possible for the individual, is called the *budget constraint*. Any combination to the right of the budget constraint is not achievable; the person's command over resources simply is not sufficient to attain these combinations of leisure and money income.

The *slope* of the budget constraint is a graphic representation of the wage rate. One's wage rate is properly defined as the increment in income (ΔY) derived from an increment in hours of work (ΔH):

$$\text{Wage Rate} = \frac{\Delta Y}{\Delta H} \tag{6.3}$$

Now, $\Delta Y/\Delta H$ is exactly the slope of the budget constraint (in absolute value).[12] Figure 6.5 shows how the constraint rises $8 for every one-hour increase in work: if the person works zero hours, income per day is zero; if the person works one hour, $8 in income is possible; if he or she works 5 hours, $40 in income is achieved. The constraint rises $8 for every unit increase in hours of work because the wage rate is $8 per hour. If the person could earn $16 per hour, the constraint would rise twice as fast and therefore be twice as steep.

It is clear from Figure 6.5 that our consumer/worker cannot achieve utility level *B*. He or she can achieve *some* points on the indifference curve representing utility level *A*—specifically, those points between *L* and *M* in Figure 6.5. However, if our consumer/worker is a utility maximizer, he or she will realize that a utility level *above A* is possible. Remembering that an infinite number of indifference curves can be drawn between curves *A* and *B* in Figure 6.5, one representing each possible level of satisfaction between *A* and *B*, we can draw a curve (*A'*) that is northeast of curve *A* and just *tangent* to the budget constraint at point *N*. Any movement

---

[11]Our assumption that 8 hours per day are required for sleeping and other "maintenance" activities is purely for ease of exposition. These activities themselves are a matter of economic choice, at least to some extent; see for example, Jeff E. Biddle and Daniel Hamermesh, "Sleep and the Allocation of Time," *Journal of Political Economy* 98, no. 5, pt. 1 (October 1990): 922–943. Modeling a three-way choice between work, leisure and maintenance activities would complicate our analysis without changing the essential insights theory can offer about the labor/leisure choice workers must make.

[12]The vertical change for a one-unit change in horizontal distance is the definition of *slope*. *Absolute value* refers to the magnitude of the slope, disregarding whether it is positive or negative. The budget constraint drawn in Figure 6.5 is a straight line (and thus has a constant slope). In economic terms, a straight-line budget constraint reflects the assumption that the wage rate at which one can work is fixed, and that it does not change with the hours of work. However, the major theoretical implications derived from using a straight-line constraint would be unchanged by employing a convex one, so we are using the fixed-wage assumption for ease of exposition.

FIGURE 6.5
Indifference Curves and Budget Constraint

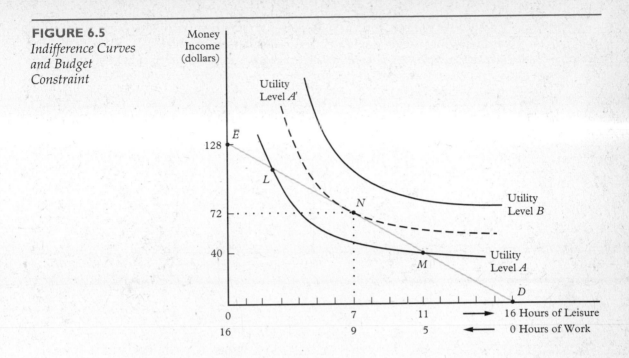

along the budget constraint *away* from the tangency point places the person on an indifference curve lying *below A'.*

An indifference curve that is just tangent to the constraint represents the highest level of utility that the person can obtain given his or her constraint. It is the most northeast curve with an achievable point on it, and no curve superior to it can be reached. If this highest possible curve is denoted as utility level A' in Figure 6.5, then point N represents the utility-maximizing combination of leisure and income. Thus, our consumer/worker is best off, given his or her preferences and constraints, working 9 hours a day, consuming 7 hours of leisure, and having a daily income of $72. All other possible combinations, such as 5 hours of work and $40 of income, yield lower utility.

Workers who face the same budget constraint, but who have different preferences for leisure, will make different choices about hours of work. If the person whose preferences were depicted in Figure 6.5 had placed lower values on leisure time—and therefore had indifference curves that were comparatively flatter, such as the one shown in Figure 6.4b—then the point of tangency with constraint ED would have been to the left of point N (indicating more hours of work). Conversely, if he or she had steeper indifference curves, signifying that leisure time was more valuable (see Figure 6.4a), then the point of tangency in Figure 6.5 would have been to the right of point N, and fewer hours of work would have been desired. Indeed, some people will have indifference curves so steep (that is, preferences for leisure so strong) that there is no point of tangency with ED. For

FIGURE 6.6

The Decision Not to Work Is a "Corner Solution"

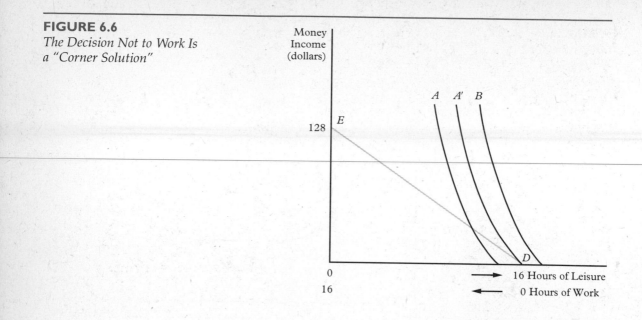

these people, as is illustrated by Figure 6.6, utility is maximized at the "corner" (point *D*); these people desire no work at all and therefore are not in the labor force.

THE INCOME EFFECT   Suppose now that the person depicted in Figure 6.5 receives a source of income independent of work. Suppose, further, that this *nonlabor* income amounts to about $36 per day. Thus, even if this person worked zero hours per day, his or her daily income would be $36. Naturally, if the person worked more than zero hours, his or her daily income would be equal to $36 plus earnings (the wage multiplied by the hours of work).

Our person's command over resources has clearly increased, as can be shown by drawing a new budget constraint to reflect the nonlabor income. As shown by the darker blue line in Figure 6.7, the endpoints of the new constraint are point *d* (zero hours of work and $36 of money income) and point *e* (16 hours of work and $164 of income—$36 in nonlabor income plus $128 in earnings). Note that the new constraint is *parallel* to the old one. Parallel lines have the same slope; since the slope of each constraint reflects the wage rate, we can infer that the increase in nonlabor income has not changed the person's wage rate.

We have just described a situation in which a pure *income effect* should be observed. Income (wealth) has been increased, but the wage rate has remained unchanged. The previous section noted that if wealth increased and the opportunity cost of leisure remained constant, the person would consume more leisure and work less. We thus concluded that the income effect was negative; as income went up (holding wages constant) hours of work went down, or as income went down

FIGURE 6.7

Indifference Curves and Budget Constraint (with an increase in nonlabor income)

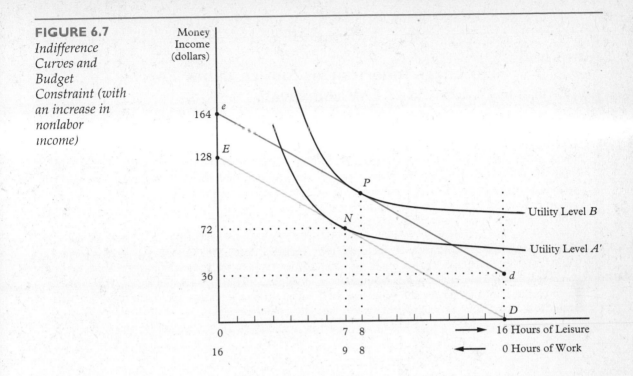

(holding wages constant) hours of work went up. This negative relationship is illustrated graphically in Figure 6.7.

When the old budget constraint (*DE*) was in effect, the person's highest level of utility was reached at point *N*, where he or she worked 9 hours a day. With the new constraint (*de*), the optimum hours of work are 8 per day (point *P*). The new source of income, because it does not alter the wage, has caused an income effect that results in one less hour of work per day. (For an illustration of the income effect, see Example 6.1.)

INCOME AND SUBSTITUTION EFFECTS WITH A WAGE INCREASE Suppose that, instead of increasing one's command over resources by receiving a source of nonlabor income, the wage rate were to be increased from $8 to $12 per hour. This increase, as noted earlier, would cause *both* an income and a substitution effect; workers would be wealthier *and* face a higher opportunity cost of leisure. Theory tells us in this case that the substitution effect pushes them toward more hours of work and the income effect toward fewer, but it cannot tell us which effect will dominate.

Figures 6. 8 and 6. 9 illustrate the possible effects of the above wage change on a person's labor supply, which we now assume is initially 8 hours per day. Figure 6.8 illustrates the case in which the observed response by a worker is to increase

---

EXAMPLE 6.1

Do Large Inheritances Induce Labor Force Withdrawal?

Do large bequests of unearned income reduce people's incentives to work? A recent study allows us to divide people who received inheritances in 1982–1983 into two groups: those who received small bequests (averaging $7,700) and those who received bequests averaging $346,200. The study then analyzed changes in the labor force participation behavior of the two groups between 1982 and 1985. Not surprisingly, those who received the larger inheritances were more likely to drop out of the labor force. Specifically, during a period in which the labor force participation rate among the "small-bequest" group rose from 76 to 81 percent, the rate in the

"large-bequest" group fell from 70 to 65 percent. Somewhat more surprising was the fact that, perhaps in anticipation of the large bequest, the labor force participation rate among the people in that group was lower to begin with!

SOURCE: Douglas Holtz-Eakin, David Joulfaian, and Harvey S. Rosen, "The Carnegie Conjecture: Some Empirical Evidence," *Quarterly Journal of Economics* 108, no. 2 (1993): 413–435. The findings reported above hold up even after controlling for such factors as age and earnings.

---

the hours of work; in this case the substitution effect is stronger than the income effect. Figure 6.9 illustrates the case in which the income effect is stronger and the response to a wage increase is to reduce the hours of work. The difference between the two figures lies *solely* in the shape of the indifference curves that might describe a person's preferences; the budget constraints, which reflect wealth and the wage rate, are exactly the same.

Figures 6.8 and 6.9 both show the old constraint, *AB*, the slope of which reflects the wage of $8 per hour. They also show the new one, *AC*, which reflects the $12 wage. Because we assume workers have no source of nonlabor income, both constraints are anchored at point *A*, where income is zero if a person does not work. Point *C* on the new constraint is now at $192 (16 hours of work times $12 per hour), whereas point *B* on the old constraint was at $128 (16 hours times $8).

With the preferences depicted by the indifference curves in Figure 6.8, the wage increase makes utility level U_2 the highest that can be reached. The tangency point at N_2 suggests that 11 hours of work is optimum. When the old constraint was in effect, the utility-maximizing hours of work were 8 per day (point N_1). Thus, given the set of preferences in Figure 6.8, the wage increase would cause the person's desired hours of work to increase by 3 per day.

With the preferences depicted in Figure 6.9, the wage increase would make utility level U_2' the highest one possible (the "prime" emphasizes that preferences differ, and that utility *levels* in Figures 6.8 and 6.9 cannot be compared). Utility is maximized at N_2', at 6 hours of work per day. Thus, with preferences like those in Figure 6.9, working hours fall from 8 to 6 as the wage rate increases.

FIGURE 6.8
Wage Increase with
Substitution Effect
Dominating

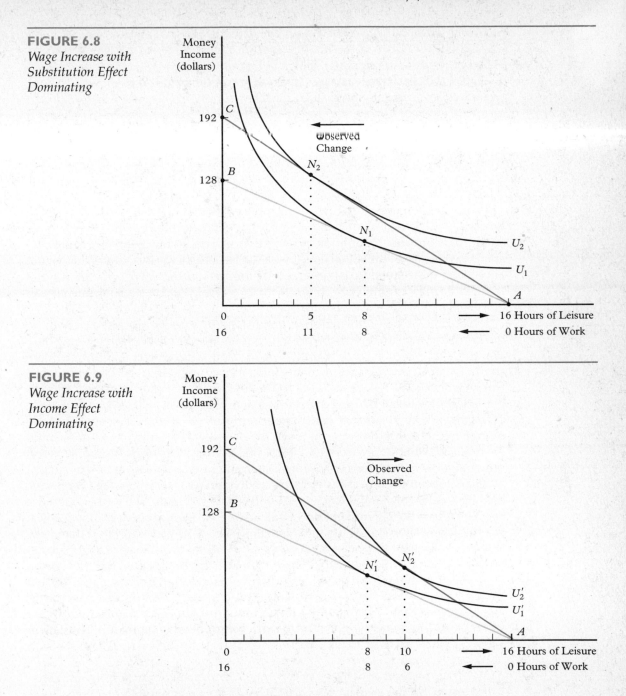

FIGURE 6.9
Wage Increase with
Income Effect
Dominating

ISOLATING INCOME AND SUBSTITUTION EFFECTS.   We have graphically depicted the income effect by itself (Figure 6.7) and the two possible outcomes of an increase in wages (Figure 6.8 and 6.9), which combines the income and substitution effects. Is it possible to graphically isolate the substitution effect? The answer is yes, and the most meaningful way to do this is to return to the context of a wage change, such as the one depicted in Figures 6.8 and 6.9. We arbitrarily choose to analyze the response shown in Figure 6.8.

Figure 6.10 has three panels. Panel (a) repeats Figure 6.8; it shows the final, overall effect of a wage increase on the labor supply of the person whose preferences are depicted. As we saw earlier, the effect of the wage increase in this case is to raise the person's utility from U_1 to U_2 and to induce this worker to increase desired hours of work from 8 to 11 per day. Imbedded in this overall effect of the wage increase, however, is an income effect pushing toward less work and a substitution effect pushing toward more. These effects are graphically separated in panels (b) and (c).

Panel (b) of Figure 6.10 shows the income effect that is imbedded in the overall response to the wage change. By definition, the income effect is the change in desired hours of work brought on by increased wealth, holding the wage rate constant. To reveal this imbedded effect, we ask a hypothetical question: "What would have been the change in labor supply if the person depicted in panel (a) had reached the new indifference curve (U_2) with a change in *nonlabor* income instead of a change in his or her wage rate?"

We begin to answer this question graphically by moving the old constraint to the northeast, which depicts the greater command over leisure time and goods—and hence the higher level of utility—associated with greater wealth. The constraint is shifted outward while maintaining its original slope (reflecting the old $8 wage), which holds the wage constant. The broken line in panel (b) depicts this hypothetical movement of the old constraint, and it results in a tangency point at N_3. This tangency suggests that had the person received nonlabor income, with no change in the wage, sufficient to reach the new level of utility, he or she would have *reduced* work hours from 8 (N_1) to 7 (N_3) per day. This shift is graphic verification that the income effect is negative, assuming that leisure is a normal good.

The substitution effect is the effect on labor supply of a change in the wage rate, holding wealth constant. It can be seen in panel (c) of Figure 6.10 as the difference between where the person actually ended up on indifference curve U_2 (tangency at N_2) and where he or she would have ended up with a pure income effect (tangency at N_3). Comparing tangency points on the *same* indifference curve is a graphic approximation to holding wealth constant.[13] Thus, *with* the wage change, the person represented in Figure 6.10 ended up at point N_2, working 11 hours a day. *Without* the wage change, the person would have chosen to work 7 hours a day (point N_3). The wage change *by itself*, holding utility (or real wealth) constant, caused work hours to increase by 4 per day. This increase demonstrates that the substitution effect is positive.

---

[13]The reader may have noted that in our initial definition of the substitution effect we held *money income* constant, while in the graphic analysis we held *utility* constant. These slightly different approaches were followed for explanatory convenience, and they represent (respectively) the theoretical analyses suggested by Evgeny Slutsky and John Hicks. For an easily followed explanation of the two approaches, see Heinz Kohler, *Intermediate Microeconomics* (Glenview, Ill.: Scott, Foresman & Co., 1986), 76–81.

FIGURE 6.10

Wage Increase with Substitution Effect Dominating: Isolating Income and Substitution Effects

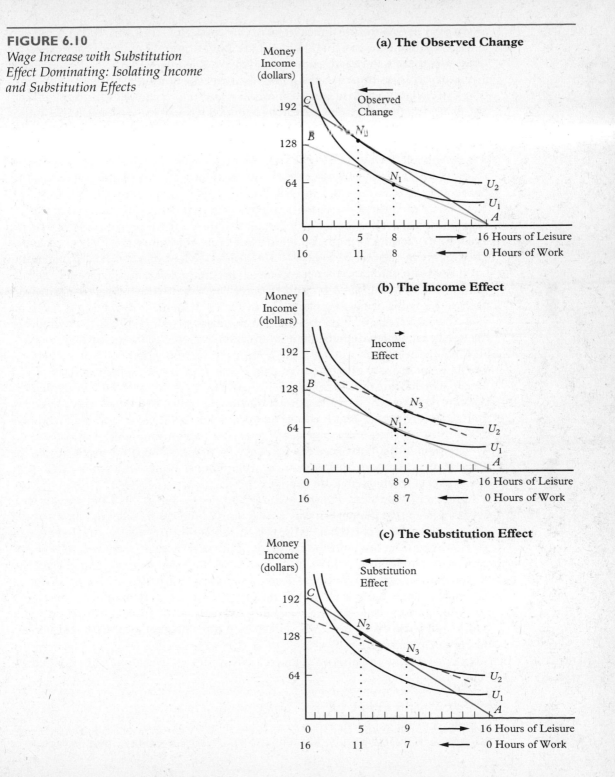

To summarize, the observed effect of raising wages from $8 to $12 per hour increased the hours of work in Figure 6.10 from 8 to 11 per day. This observed effect, however, is the *sum* of two component effects. The income effect, which operates because a higher wage increases one's real wealth, tended to *reduce* the hours of work from 8 to 7 per day. The substitution effect, which captures the pure effect of the change in leisure's opportunity cost, tended to push the person toward 4 more hours of work per day. The end result was an increase of 3 in the hours worked each day.

WHICH EFFECT DOMINATES?   In discussing the different responses to a wage change in Figures 6.8 and 6.9, both of which had exactly the same old and new budget constraints, it was pointed out that whether the income or the substitution effect dominates is dependent on the person's preferences. We discuss one easily identified effect of preferences at this point; another will be discussed thoroughly in Chapter 7.

Suppose that a wage increase changes the budget constraint facing a worker from *CD* to *CE* in Figure 6.11. If the worker had a relatively flat set of indifference curves, the initial tangency along *CD* might be at point *A*, implying a relatively heavy work schedule. If the person had more steeply sloped indifference curves, the initial tangency might be at point *B*, where hours at work are fewer.

One important influence on the size of the income effect is the extent of the northeast movement of the new constraint: the more the constraint shifts outward, the greater the income effect will tend to be. For a person with an initial tangency at point *A*, for example, the northeast movement is larger than for a person whose initial tangency is at point *B*. Put in words, the increased command over resources made possible by a wage increase is only attainable if one works, and the more work-oriented the person is, the greater will be his or her increase in resources. Other things equal, people who are working longer hours will exhibit greater income effects when wage rates change.

To take this reasoning to the extreme, suppose a person's indifference curves were so steep that the person was initially out of the labor force (that is, when the budget constraint was *CD* in Figure 6.11, his or her utility was maximized at point *C*). The wage increase and the resultant new constraint, *CE*, can induce only two outcomes: the person will either begin to work for pay or remain out of the labor force. *Reducing* the hours of paid employment is not possible. Therefore, if the wage increase induces a change in the hours of work, that change must be positive, which means the substitution effect dominates. Graphically, if one starts at point *C* and actually responds to a wage increase, the income effect is *zero*. Put differently, *the substitution effect tends to be dominant in labor force participation decisions*. We turn now to a more detailed analysis of the decision whether to join the labor force.

THE RESERVATION WAGE   An implication of labor supply theory is that if people who are not in the labor force place a value of $X on the marginal hour of leisure, then they would be unwilling to take a job unless the offered wage were

FIGURE 6.11

The Size of the Income Effect is Affected by the Initial Hours of Work

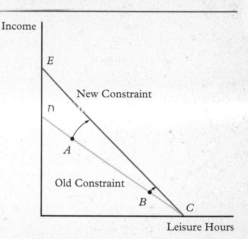

greater than $X. Because they will "reserve" their labor unless the wage is $X or more, economists say that they have a *reservation wage* of $X. The reservation wage, then, is the wage below which a person will not work, and in the labor/leisure context it represents the value placed on an hour of lost leisure time.[14]

Looking back at Figure 6.6, which graphically depicted a person choosing not to work, the reason there was no tangency between an indifference curve and the budget constraint—and the reason why the person remained out of the labor force—was that the person's wage (represented by the slope of *DE*) was everywhere lower than his or her marginal value of leisure time (represented by the slope of the indifference curves at positive hours of work). Put in different terms, the person depicted could not obtain an offered wage equal to or greater than his or her reservation wage and therefore chose not to take a job.

Often, people are thought to behave as if they have both a reservation wage *and a certain number of work hours* that must be offered before they will consider taking a job. The reasons are not difficult to understand and are illustrated by Figure 6.12. Suppose that taking a job entails two hours of commuting time (round-trip) per day. These hours, of course, are unpaid, so the worker's budget constraint must reflect that, if a job is accepted, two hours of leisure are given up with no increase in income. These "fixed costs" of working are reflected in Figure 6.12 by segment *AB*. Segment *BC*, of course, reflects the earnings that are possible (once one gets to work), and the slope of *BC* represents the person's wage rate.

---

[14]In Chapter 7 we will expand this definition to include the value of lost "time at home," whether this time would have been spent in leisure or in some form of household work. See Richard A. Hoffler and Kevin J. Murphy, "Estimating Reservation Wages of Employed Workers Using a Stochastic Frontier," *Southern Economic Journal* 60, no. 4 (April 1994): 961–976, for a recent study of reservation wages.

Is the wage underlying *BC* great enough to induce the person to work? Consider indifference curve U_1, which represents the highest level of utility this person can achieve, given budget constraint *ABC*. Utility is maximized at point *A*, and the person chooses not to work. It is clear from this choice that the offered wage (given the two-hour commute) is below the person's reservation wage, but can we show the latter wage graphically?

To take work with a two-hour commute, the person depicted in Figure 6.12 must find a job able to generate a combination of earnings and leisure time that yields a utility level equal to, or greater than, U_1. This is possible only if the person's budget constraint is equal to (or to the right of) *ABD*, which is tangent to U_1 at point *X*. The person's reservation wage, then, is equal to the slope of *BD*, and the student can readily note that in this case the slope of *BD* exceeds the slope of *BC*, which represents the offered wage. Moreover, to bring utility up to the level of U_1 (the utility associated with not working), the person shown in Figure 6.12 must be able to find a job at the reservation wage that offers 4 hours of work per day. Put differently, at this person's reservation wage, he or she wants to consume 10 hours of leisure daily, and with a two-hour commute this implies 4 hours of work. (A more detailed analysis of reservation wages and the fixed costs of working can be found in the appendix to this chapter.)

EMPIRICAL FINDINGS ON THE INCOME AND SUBSTITUTION EFFECTS

Labor supply theory suggests that the choices workers make concerning their desired hours of work depend on their wealth and the wage rate they can command, in addition to their preferences. In particular, this theory suggests the existence of a negative income effect and a positive substitution effect. Empirical tests of labor supply theory generally attempt to determine if these two effects can be observed, if they operate in the expected directions, and what their relative magnitudes are. Data used for these tests are generally of two kinds:

1. *Cross-sectional* data can be used to analyze the patterns of labor supply across individuals at a given point in time.
2. *Time-series* data can be used to look at *trends* in labor force participation and hours of work over a period of several years. (Cross-sectional and time-related data can also be combined, as illustrated in Example 6.2.)

CROSS-SECTIONAL DATA   Numerous studies of labor supply behavior have relied on cross-sectional data. These studies basically analyze labor force participation or annual hours of work as they are affected by wage rates and income, holding other influences (age, for example) constant. The most reliable and informative studies are those done on large samples of men, primarily because the labor supply behavior of women has been complicated by child-rearing and household work arrangements for which data are sketchy at best.

The cross-sectional studies of male labor supply behavior, especially for men between the ages of 25 and 55, generally conclude that both income and substitution effects are small—perhaps even zero. Probably because responses to wage

FIGURE 6.12
*Reservation Wage with Fixed
Time Costs of Working*

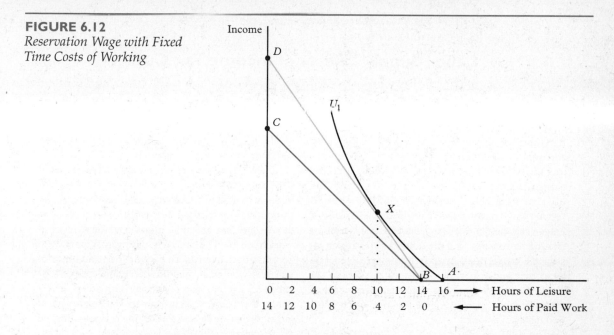

changes are so small, the results of studies that attempt to isolate income and sub-stitution effects are highly dependent on the statistical methods used.[15]

Cross-sectional estimates of the labor supply behavior among married women generally find a greater responsiveness to wage changes than is found among men. The studies also commonly find that the substitution effect dominates the income effect. Recent work, however, suggests that the response of working women's *hours* of work to wage changes are about like those of men (that is, very small); it may be the labor force *participation* decision that is most distinctive for married women.[16] As noted in our discussion of Figure 6.11, participation decisions tend to have a dominant substitution effect.

---

[15]See Thomas MaCurdy, David Green, and Harry Paarsch, "Assessing Empirical Approaches for Analyzing Taxes and Labor Supply," *Journal of Human Resources* 25 (Summer 1990): 415–490, for a reference to prior work and an explanation of some methodological issues. This entire issue of the *Journal of Human Resources* is devoted to estimates of the effects, in five countries, of income taxation on labor supply (increasing or reducing income tax rates is equivalent, respectively, to reducing or raising one's wage rate). For a recent study of labor supply in Canada, see Lars Osberg and Shelley Phipps, "Labour Supply with Quantity Constraints: Estimates from a Large Sample of Canadian Workers," *Oxford Economic Papers* 45 (1993): 269–291.

[16]See Thomas A. Mroz, "The Sensitivity of an Empirical Model of Married Women's Hours of Work to Economic and Statistical Assumptions," *Econometrica* 55, no. 4 (July 1987): 765–800. Articles on women's labor supply in the United States and 11 other countries appear in the *Journal of Labor Economics*, January 1985 supplement. Mark Killingsworth, *Labor Supply*, Cambridge Surveys of Economic Literature (Cambridge, Eng.: Cambridge University Press, 1983), offers a very comprehensive review of what the author calls "first- and second-generation" estimates of income and substitution effects. For more recent contributions, see Robert K. Triest, "The Effect of Income Taxation on Labor Supply in the United States," *Journal of Human Resources* 25 (Summer 1990): 491–516; Lars Osberg and Shelley Phipps, "Labour Supply with Quantity Constraints"; and Nada Eissa, "Taxation and Labor Supply of Married Women: The Tax Reform Act of 1986 as a Natural Experiment," working paper no. 5023, National Bureau of Economic Research, Cambridge, Mass., February 1995.

EXAMPLE 6.2

Labor Supply Effects of Income Tax Cuts

In 1986, Congress changed the personal income tax system in the United States by drastically reducing tax rates on upper levels of income. Before this change, for example, families paid a 50 percent tax rate on taxable incomes over $170,000; after the change, this tax rate was reduced to 28 percent. The tax rate on taxable incomes over $50,000 was also set at 28 percent, down from about 40 percent. Lower income tax rates have the effect of increasing take-home earnings, and they therefore act as an increase in wage rates. Because lower rates generate an income and a substitution effect that work in opposite directions, they have an ambiguous anticipated effect on labor supply. Can we find out which effect dominates in practice?

The 1986 changes served as a "natural experiment," because the changes were sudden, large, and very different for families of different incomes. For married women in families that, without their earnings, had incomes at the 99th percentile of the income distribution (that is, the upper 1 percent), the tax rate cuts meant a 29 percent increase in their take-home wage rates. For women in families with incomes at the 90th percentile, the smaller tax rate cuts meant a 12 percent increase in take-home wages. It turns out that married women at the 99th and 90th percentiles of family income are similar in age, education, and occupation—and increases in their labor supply had been similar prior to 1986.

Therefore, comparing their responses to very different changes in their after-tax wage rates should yield insight into how the labor supply of married women responds to tax rate changes.

One study compared labor supply increases, from 1984 to 1990, for married women in the 99th and 90th percentiles. It found that the labor force participation rate for women in the 99th percentile rose by 19.4 percent and that, if working, their hours of work rose by 12.7 percent during that period. In contrast, both labor force participation and hours of work for women at the 90th percentile rose only by about 6.5 percent. The data from this natural experiment, then, suggest that women who experienced larger increases in their take-home wages desired greater increases in their labor supply—which implies that the substitution effect dominated the income effect for these women. Also, consistent with both theory and the results from other studies (discussed in the text), the dominance of the substitution effect was more pronounced for labor force participation decisions than it was hours-of-work decisions.

SOURCE: Nada Eissa, "Taxation and Labor Supply of Married Women: The Tax Reform Act of 1986 as a Natural Experiment," working paper no. 5023, National Bureau of Economic Research, Cambridge, Mass., February 1995.

TIME-SERIES DATA This chapter began with tables that indicated some significant trends in labor force participation and hours of work in the United States and elsewhere. Economists have attempted to explain these trends over time through the use of labor supply theory, thereby using time-series data to estimate the size of both income and substitution effects. The use of time-series data to test labor supply theory presents some problems that the researcher must take into account. One problem was mentioned earlier in our discussion of trends in work hours: over a period of any given length, there will be years in which labor market disequilibrium causes many workers to work fewer hours than they really want to.

Another cluster of problems in trying to relate labor supply trends to changes in income (or wealth) and wage rates is that, over long periods of time, *other* factors that affect desired participation and hours of work can also change. For example, the growth of pensions and the greater availability of disability payments have directly affected the incentives for older workers to withdraw from the labor force.[17] Inventions such as washing machines, dishwashers, microwave ovens, and prepared foods have reduced the time needed to perform household work; as we will see in Chapter 7, these changes have undoubtedly affected the incentives of married women, especially, to work outside the home. Finally, it is difficult to dismiss the possibility that changes in the labor force behavior of married women were affected by changes in attitudes toward work outside the home or changes in the legal environment affecting the employment of women (prior to World War II, for example, almost no U.S. school districts would hire a woman who was married).

If the other factors that affect labor supply change at the same time that incomes and real wages change, it is difficult to isolate the separate effects of each. Nevertheless, studies that have made serious efforts to control for these other factors have found evidence that the income and substitution effects are indeed important in explaining labor supply behavior. A recent and comprehensive analysis of the labor supply trends of married women concluded that income and substitution effects have worked in their expected directions throughout this century, with the substitution effect clearly dominant after 1950. There is evidence, however, that the *magnitudes* of both effects have become smaller over the past forty years, with the result that the substitution effect for married women is now less dominant and their labor supply behavior is thus becoming less responsive to changes in wages.[18]

A recent analysis of the labor force participation behavior of older men concludes that their trend toward earlier retirement also suggests a dominant substitution effect.[19] This study finds that the sharp rise in early retirement (mostly at age 62) is primarily among men with lower levels of education, for whom demand has fallen in recent years. As demand has fallen for men of less education (we will document and analyze this decline in Chapter 14), wages for many workers have been pushed below the level of their reservation wage. Appar-

---

[17]For a recent paper on retirement and public pensions, see Donald O. Parsons, "Male Retirement Behavior in the United States, 1930–1950," *Journal of Economic History* 51, no. 3 (September 1991): 657–674. On the topic of disability and labor force participation, see John Bound, "The Health and Earnings of Rejected Disability Insurance Applicants," *American Economic Review* 79, no. 3 (June 1989): 482–503, and Jonathan Gruber and Jeffrey Kubik, "Disability Insurance Rejection Rates and the Labor Supply of Older Workers," working paper no. 4941, National Bureau of Economic Research, Cambridge, Mass., November 1994.

[18]Claudia Goldin, *Understanding the Gender Gap* (New York: Oxford University Press, 1990), Chapter 5.

[19]Franco Peracchi and Finis Welch, "Trends in the Labor Force Transitions of Older Men and Women," *Journal of Labor Economics* 12, no. 2 (April 1994): 210–242. For a companion study, see Chinhui Juhn, Kevin M. Murphy, and Finis Welch, "Why Has the Natural Rate of Unemployment Increased over Time?" *Brookings Papers on Economic Activity* (2: 1991): 75–126.

ently, then, a dominant substitution effect has been responsible for the declining participation rates of older men (a subject we will return to in Chapter 7).

Policy Applications

Many income maintenance programs create budget constraints that either encourage corner solutions (that is, encourage people to drop out of the labor force) or simultaneously increase income while reducing the take-home wage rate (thus causing the income and substitution effects to work in the same direction). Therefore, using labor supply theory to analyze the work-incentive effects of various social programs is both instructive and important. We characterize these programs by the budget constraints they create for their recipients.

BUDGET CONSTRAINTS WITH "SPIKES"

Some social insurance programs compensate workers who are unable to work because of a temporary work injury, a permanent disability, or a layoff. Workers' compensation insurance replaces most of the earnings lost when workers are hurt on the job, and private or public disability programs do the same for workers who become physically or emotionally unable to work for other reasons. Unemployment compensation is paid to those who have lost a job and have not been able to find another. While exceptions can be found in the occasional jurisdiction,[20] it is generally true that these "income replacement" programs share a common characteristic: they pay benefits only to those who are not working.

To understand the consequences of paying benefits only to those who are not working, let us suppose that a workers' compensation program is structured so that, after injury, workers receive their preinjury earnings for as long as they are off work. Once they work even one hour, however, they are no longer considered disabled and cannot receive further benefits. The effects of this program on work incentives are analyzed in Figure 6.13, in which it is assumed that the preinjury budget constraint was AB and preinjury earnings were E_0. Further, we assume that the worker's "market" budget constraint (that is, the constraint in the absence of a workers' compensation program) is unchanged, so that after recovery the preinjury wage can again be earned. Under these conditions, the postinjury budget constraint is BAC, and the person maximizes utility at point C— a point of no work.

The student will note that constraint BAC contains the segment AC, which looks like a spike. It is this spike that creates severe work-incentive problems, for two reasons. First, the returns associated with the first hour of work are *negative*. That is, a person at point C (a point of no work) who returns to work for one hour would find his or her income to be considerably reduced by working. Earnings from this hour of work would be more than offset by the reduction in benefits,

---

[20]Unemployment insurance and workers' compensation programs in the United States are run at the state level and thus vary in their characteristics to some extent. Benefits in both programs are bounded by minimums and maximums.

FIGURE 6.13
*Budget Constraint
with a "Spike"*

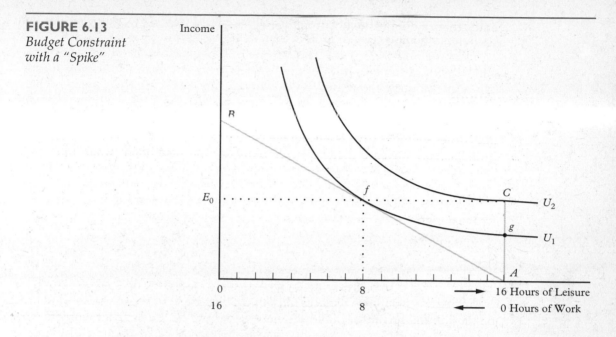

which creates a negative "net wage."[21] The substitution effect associated with this program characteristic clearly discourages work.

Second, our assumed no-work benefit of AC is equal to E_0, the preinjury level of earnings. If the worker values leisure at all (as is assumed by the standard downward slope of indifference curves U_1 and U_2), being able to receive the old level of earnings while also enjoying more leisure clearly enhances utility. The worker is better off at point C than at point f, the preinjury combination of earnings and leisure hours, because he or she is on indifference curve U_2 rather than U_1. Allowing workers to reach a higher utility level without working generates a strong income effect that discourages, or at least slows, the return to work.[22]

Given that the work-incentive aspects of income replacement programs often quite justifiably take a backseat to the goal of making unfortunate workers "whole" in some economic sense, creating programs that avoid work disincentives is not easy. With the preferences of the worker depicted in Figure 6.13, for example, a benefit of slightly less than Ag would ensure minimal loss of utility while still providing incentives to return to work as soon as physically possible (work would allow indifference curve U_1 to be attained—see point f — while receiving a benefit of less than Ag would not). Unfortunately, workers differ in their

---

[21]In graphic terms, the budget constraint contains a vertical "spike," and the slope of this vertical segment is infinitely negative. In economic terms, the implied infinitely negative (net) wage arises from the fact that even one minute of work causes one to lose his or her entire benefit.

[22]We are assuming here that the psychic costs of injury or layoff are small. It could be argued that complete income replacement is justified on the grounds that it compensates for large psychic losses, but our analysis of work-incentive effects would be unchanged.

preferences, so the optimal benefit—one that would provide work incentives yet ensure only minimal loss of utility—differs for each individual.

With programs that create "spikes," the best policymakers can do is set a no-work benefit as some fraction of previous earnings and then use administrative means to encourage the return to work among any whose utility is greater when not working. Unemployment insurance, for example, replaces something like half of lost earnings for the typical worker, but puts an upper limit on the weeks each unemployed worker can receive benefits. Workers' compensation replaces two-thirds of lost earnings for the average worker, but must rely on doctors—and sometimes judicial hearings—to determine whether a worker continues to be eligible for benefits. (For evidence that more-generous workers' compensation benefits do indeed induce longer absences from work, see Example 6.3.)

PROGRAMS WITH NET WAGE RATES OF ZERO

The programs just discussed were intended to confer benefits on those who are unable to work, and the "spike" was created by the eligibility requirement that to receive benefits, one must not be working. Other programs, such as "welfare," have different eligibility criteria and calculate benefits differently. These programs fac-

---

EXAMPLE 6.3

Staying Around One's Kentucky Home: Workers' Compensation Benefits and the Return to Work

Workers injured on the job receive workers' compensation insurance benefits while away from work. These benefits differ across states, but they are calculated for most workers as some fraction (normally two-thirds) of weekly, pretax earnings. For high-wage workers, however, weekly benefits are typically "capped" at a maximum, which again varies by state.

On July 15, 1980, Kentucky raised its maximum weekly benefit by 66 percent. It did not alter benefits in any other way, so this change effectively granted large benefit increases to high-wage workers without awarding them to anyone else. Because those injured before July 15 were ineligible for the increased benefits, even if they remained off work *after* July 15, this policy change created a nice "natural experiment": one group of injured workers was able to obtain

higher benefits, while another group was not. Did the group receiving higher benefits show evidence of reduced labor supply, as suggested by theory?

The effects of increased benefits on labor supply were unmistakable. High-wage workers ineligible for the new benefits typically stayed off the job for 4 weeks, but those injured after July 15 stayed away for 5 weeks—25 percent longer! No increases in the typical time away from work were recorded among lower-paid injured workers, who were unaffected by the changes in benefits.

SOURCE: Bruce D. Meyer, W. Kip Viscusi, and David L. Durbin, "Workers' Compensation and Injury Duration: Evidence from a Natural Experiment," *American Economic Review* 85, no. 3 (June 1995): 322–340.

tor income "needs" into their eligibility criteria and then pay benefits based on the difference between one's actual earnings and one's needs. We will see that paying people the difference between their earnings and their needs creates a net wage rate of zero; thus, the work-incentive problems associated with these welfare programs result from the fact that they increase the income of program recipients while also drastically reducing the price of leisure.

Welfare programs have generally taken the form of a guaranteed annual income.[23] A welfare worker determines the income needed by an eligible person (Y_n in Figure 6.14) based on family size, area living costs, and local welfare regulations. Actual earnings are then subtracted from this needed level, and a check is issued to the person each month for the difference. If the person does not work, he or she receives a subsidy of Y_n. If the person works, and if any earnings cause dollar-for-dollar reductions in welfare benefits, then a budget constraint like $ABCD$ in Figure 6.14 is created. The person's income remains Y_n as long as he or she is subsidized. If one is receiving the subsidy, then, an extra hour of work yields *no* net increase in income, because the extra earnings result in an equal reduction in welfare benefits. The net wage of a person on the program—and therefore his or her price of leisure—is zero, which is graphically shown by the segment of the constraint having a slope of zero (BC).

FIGURE 6.14
Income and Substitution Effects for the Basic Welfare System

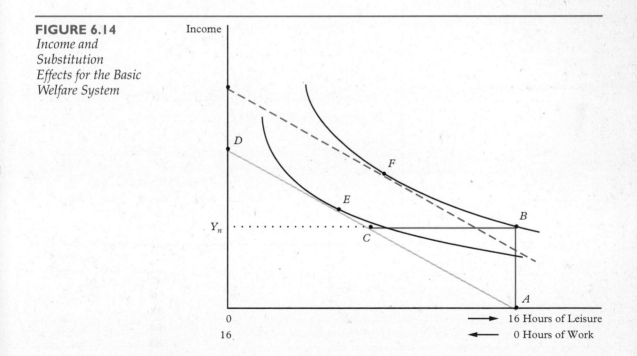

[23]Recent legislation has allowed states more latitude in setting their own eligibility criteria and benefit levels. Despite this, however, the general approach historically characterizing welfare programs is likely to remain much as described in the text.

Thus, a welfare program like the one summarized in Figure 6.14 increases the income of the poor by moving the lower end of the budget constraint out from *AC* to *ABC*; as indicated by the dashed hypothetical constraint in Figure 6.14, this shift creates an *income effect* tending to reduce labor supply from the hours associated with point *E* to those associated with point *F*. However, it *also* causes the wage to effectively drop to zero: every dollar earned is matched by a dollar reduction in welfare benefits.[24] This dollar-for-dollar reduction in benefits induces a huge *substitution effect*, causing those accepting welfare to reduce their hours of work to zero (point *B*). Of course, if a person's indifference curves were sufficiently flat so that the curve tangent to segment *CD* passed *above* point *B* (see Figure 6. 15), then that person's utility would be maximized by choosing work instead of welfare.[25]

One "solution" to the work-incentive problems of guaranteed-income programs is a work requirement. Suppose, for example, that the government were to require people to work three hours a day to qualify for welfare. This requirement is equivalent to saying that if they work less than that they face their "market" constraint. That is, at less than three hours of work per day they are not eligible for welfare and must rely solely on labor market earnings for their income. In terms of Figure 6.16, they face segment *AB* in the region in which hours of work total less than three.

FIGURE 6.15
The Basic Welfare System: A Person Not Choosing Welfare

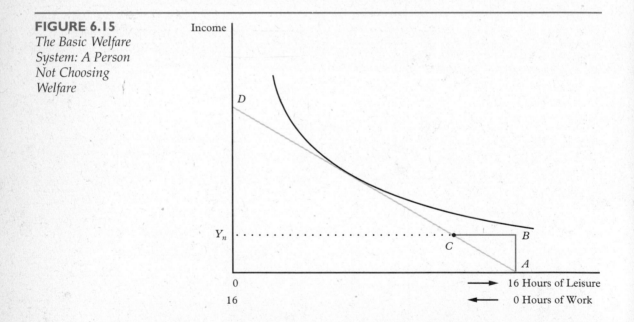

[24]Gary Burtless, "The Economist's Lament: Public Assistance in America," *Journal of Economic Perspectives* 4 (Winter 1990): 57–78, summarizes a variety of public assistance programs in the United States prior to 1990. This article suggests that, in actual practice, benefits usually have been reduced by something less than dollar for dollar (perhaps by 80 or 90 cents per dollar of earnings).

[25]See Robert Moffitt, "Incentive Effects of the U.S. Welfare System: A Review," *Journal of Economic Literature* 30, no. 1 (March 1992): 1–61, for a summary of the literature on labor supply effects of the welfare system.

At the point at which they work three hours per day, they become eligible for welfare if they are poor enough to otherwise qualify. Thus, after three hours of work they qualify for welfare payments that bring their total income up to Y_n; however, if they work more than three hours a day their welfare check is reduced one dollar for each dollar of earnings. These facts are reflected in segment *BCD* of the constraint in Figure 6.16. Of course, if their earnings rise above Y_n they no longer qualify for welfare and are on segment *DE* of their "market" constraint.

The work-incentive effects of the "work requirement" modification just described can be inferred from studying Figure 6.16. If indifference curves are steep enough so that utility is maximized at point *C*, those on welfare will desire to work three hours a day, but no more than that. If indifference curves are flat enough so that the curve tangent to segment *DE* passes *above* point *C*, then, analogous to the result in Figure 6.15 for the basic welfare system, the person would choose not to receive welfare. Thus, the effect of the work requirement is to induce welfare recipients to work, but as long as they are on welfare they will have incentives to work only the minimum hours needed to qualify. Above the required hours of work, a program recipient's effective wage is still zero.

With respect to the above conclusion, two points need to be made. First, working the minimum number of hours needed to qualify does not imply that welfare recipients are "lazy"; they are *induced* to choose that level of work by the budget constraint implicit in the program. Second, we must stress that *actual* hours of work might differ from *desired* hours if there are limitations that employers place

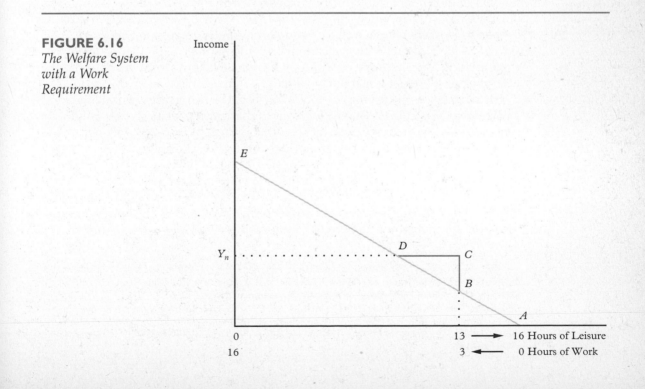

FIGURE 6.16
The Welfare System with a Work Requirement

on the hours of jobs for which they hire. (For labor supply responses to different forms of a work requirement—requisitions of food from farmers during wartime—see Example 6.4.)

SUBSIDY PROGRAMS WITH POSITIVE EFFECTIVE WAGE RATES

So far we have analyzed the work-incentive effects of income maintenance programs that create net wage rates for program recipients that are either negative or zero (that is, they create constraints that have either a spike or a horizontal segment). Programs can be devised, however, that create positive net wages for those who are eligible. Do these programs offer a solution to the problem of work incentives? We will answer this question by analyzing a relatively recent and rapidly growing program, the Earned Income Tax Credit (EITC).

The EITC program makes income tax credits available to low-income families with at least one worker. A tax credit of one dollar reduces a person's income taxes by one dollar, and in the case of the EITC, if the tax credit for which workers qualify exceeds their total income tax liability, the government will mail them a check for the difference. Thus, the EITC functions as an earnings subsidy, and because the subsidy goes only to those who work, the EITC is seen by many as an income maintenance program that preserves work incentives. This view led Congress to vastly expand the EITC under President Clinton, and it is now the largest cash subsidy program directed at low-income households.[26]

The tax credits offered by the EITC program vary with one's earnings and the number of dependent children. For purposes of our analysis, which is intended to illustrate the work-incentive effects of the EITC, we will focus on the 1994 credits offered to workers with one child. Figure 6.17 graphs the relevant program characteristics for a worker with one child who could earn a "market" (unsubsidized) wage reflected by the slope of *AC*. As we will see below, for such a worker, the EITC created a budget constraint of *ABDEC*.

For workers with earnings of $7,750 or less, the tax credit was calculated at 26.3 percent of earnings. That is, for every dollar earned, a tax credit of about 26 cents was also earned; thus, for those with earnings of under $7,750, net wages ($W_n$) were 26 percent higher than market wages (W). The student will note that this tax credit is represented by segment *AB* on the EITC constraint in Figure 6.17, and that the slope of *AB exceeds the slope of the market constraint, AC*.

The maximum tax credit allowed for a worker with one child was $2,038 ($7,750 × 0.263). Workers who earned between $7,750 and $11,000 per year qualified for this maximum tax credit. Because these workers experienced no in-

---

[26]John Karl Scholz, "The Earned Income Tax Credit: Participation, Compliance, and Antipoverty Effectiveness," discussion paper no. 1020–93, University of Wisconsin Institute for Research on Poverty, September 1993; Saul D. Hoffman and Laurence S. Seidman, *The Earned Income Tax Credit: Antipoverty Effectiveness and Labor Market Effects* (Kalamazoo, Mich.: W. E. Upjohn Institute for Employment Research, 1990); and Robert L. Moore, "Recent Proposals to Redesign the EITC: An Economist's Response," *Tax Notes* (July 5, 1993): 105–108, offer accessible analyses of the EITC.

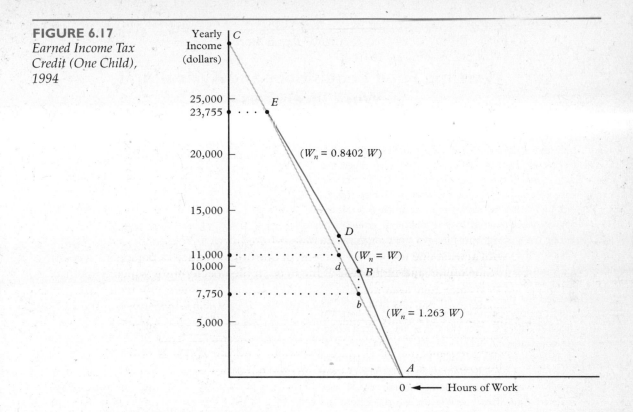

FIGURE 6.17
Earned Income Tax Credit (One Child), 1994

creases or reductions in tax credits per added dollar of earnings, for them the net wage was equal to the market wage. The constraint facing workers with $7,750 to $11,000 of earnings is represented by segment *BD* in Figure 6.17, and it should be noted that the slope of *BD*, which represents the net wage rate, is equal to the slope of *AC* (*bB* = *dD* = 2,038).

For earnings above $11,000, the tax credit was gradually phased out, so that when earnings reached $23,755 the tax credit was zero (in other words, workers with one child who had earnings above $23,755 did not qualify for the EITC program). Because after $11,000 in earnings, each dollar earned *reduced* the tax credit for which one qualified, the net wage of anyone earning between $11,000 and $23,755 was *below* one's market wage by about 16 percent;[27] this segment of the constraint is shown by *DE* in Figure 6.17, which has a flatter slope than *AC*.

Inspection of Figure 6.17 will disclose that, among workers eligible for the EITC, work-incentive effects are different in three earnings "zones." The *incomes* of workers in all three zones are enhanced, which means that all EITC recipients experience an income effect that pushes them in the direction of less work. However,

---

[27]The formula used to calculate tax credits when earnings were above $11,000 was as follows: credit = 2,038 − .1598(earnings−11,000).

EXAMPLE 6.4

Wartime Food Requisitions and Agricultural Work Incentives

Countries at war often adopt "work requirement" policies to obtain needed food supplies involuntarily from their farming populations. Not surprisingly, the way in which these requisitions are carried out can have enormous effects on the work incentives of farmers. Two alternative methods are contrasted in this example: one was used by the Bolshevik government during the civil war that followed the Russian revolution, and the other by Japan during World War II.

From 1917 to 1921, the Bolsheviks requisitioned from farmers all food in excess of the amounts needed for the farmers' own subsistence; in effect, the surplus was confiscated and given to soldiers and urban dwellers. Graphically, this policy created a budget constraint for farmers like ACY_s, in diagram (a) at right. Because farmers could keep their output until they reached the subsistence level of income (Y_s), the market wage prevailed until income of Y_s was reached. After that, their effective wage was zero (on segment CY_s), because any extra output went to the government. Thus, a prewar "market" constraint of AB was converted to ACY_s with the consequence that most farmers maximized utility near point C. Acreage planted dropped by 27 percent from 1917 to 1921, while harvested output fell by 50 percent!

Japan, during World War II, handled its food requisitioning policy completely differently. It required a quota to be delivered by each farmer to the government at very low prices, but it allowed farmers to sell any produce *above* the quota at higher (market) prices. This policy converted the prewar constraint of AB to one much like EFG in diagram (b). In effect, farmers had to work AE hours for the government at lower than market pay (EF), but were allowed to earn the market wage after that. This preserved farmers' work incentives and apparently created an income effect that *increased* the total hours of work by Japanese farmers, for despite war-induced shortages of capital and labor, rice production was greater in 1944 than in 1941!

(a) Farmers' Budget Constraint During Russian Civil War

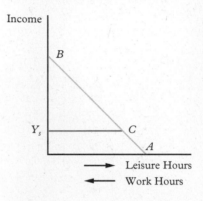

(b) Farmers' Budget Constraint in Japan During World War II

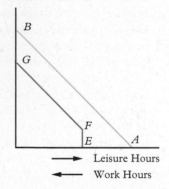

SOURCE: Jack Hirshleifer, *Economic Behavior in Adversity* (Chicago: University of Chicago Press, 1987), 16–21, 39–41.

the program creates quite different net wage rates in the zones, and therefore the substitution effect differs across zones.

For workers with earnings below $7,750, the net wage is greater than the market wage (by 26.3 percent), so along segment *AB* workers experience an increase in the price of leisure. Workers with earnings below $7,750, then, experience a substitution effect that pushes them in the direction of more work. With an income effect and a substitution effect that push in opposite directions, it is uncertain which effect will dominate, and it is thus unclear whether workers in this zone will increase or decrease their labor supply. What we can predict, though, is that some of those who would have been out of the labor force in the absence of the EITC program will now decide to seek work (earlier we discussed the fact that, for nonparticipants in the labor force, the substitution effect dominates).

Segments *BD* and *DE* represent two other zones in which theory predicts that labor supply will *fall*. Along *BD* the net wage is equal to the market wage, so the price of leisure in this zone is unchanged while income is enhanced. Workers in this zone experience a pure income effect. Along segment *DE* the net wage is actually below the market wage, so in this zone *both* the income and the substitution effects push in the direction of reduced labor supply.

Labor supply theory, then, suggests that workers in two of the three earnings zones will reduce their labor supply in response to the EITC; the responses of those in the other zone are not predictable, except we can anticipate that some who were previously out of the labor force will now seek work. For policy purposes, of course, it is important to estimate *how large* these labor supply responses are likely to be. One study, which used labor supply responses found in experimental income maintenance programs to simulate those of an earlier (less generous) version of the EITC, estimated very modest effects on labor supply. Those in the lowest earnings zone, where the predicted response is ambiguous, were estimated to *increase* their supply of labor by 18 hours per year, while those in the middle and upper zones were estimated to reduce theirs by 35 and 51 hours per year, respectively.[28]

Given the rather modest labor supply reductions that can be expected in response to the EITC, and given that labor supply probably will increase among the lowest-income group, many now believe the EITC to be the most effective way to subsidize the working poor. Its benefits are much more concentrated on the poor than are the benefits of the minimum wage, and because the subsidy is issued to workers through the income tax system, it avoids the stigmatizing effects associated with

---

[28]Saul Hoffman and Laurence Seidman, *The Earned Income Tax Credit,* 45. For studies that summarize the labor supply findings of the experimental welfare programs, see Philip K. Robins, "A Comparison of the Labor Supply Findings from the Four Negative Income Tax Experiments," *Journal of Human Resources* 20, no. 4 (Fall 1985): 567–582. For other reviews of these experimental findings, see Pencavel, "Labor Supply of Men: A Review"; Michael C. Keeley, *Labor Supply and Public Policy: A Critical Review* (New York: Academic Press, 1981); Killingsworth, *Labor Supply*; Robert Moffitt and Kenneth Kehrer, "The Effect of Tax and Transfer Programs on Labor Supply: The Evidence from the Income-Maintenance Experiments," in *Research in Labor Economics,* vol. 4, ed. R. Ehrenberg (Greenwich, Conn.: JAI Press, 1981); and Gary Burtless, "The Economist's Lament."

wage subsidies to the employer.[29] It is clearly not an income maintenance program suited to the needs of those who cannot work, but for those who can, it at least preserves incentives to *participate* in the labor force.

REVIEW QUESTIONS

1. Referring to the definitions in footnote 5, is the following statement true, false, or uncertain: "Leisure must be an inferior good for an individual's labor supply curve to be backward-bending." Explain your answer.

2. The way the workers' compensation system works now, employees permanently injured on the job receive a payment of $X each year whether they work or not. Suppose the government were to implement a new program in which those who did not work at all got $0.5X but those who did work got $0.5X plus workers' compensation of 50 cents *for every hour worked* (of course, this subsidy would be in addition to the wages paid by their employers). What would be the change in work incentives associated with this change in the way workers' compensation payments were calculated?

3. Suppose a government is considering several options to ensure that legal services are provided to the poor:

   Option A: All lawyers would be required to devote 5 percent of their work time to the poor, free of charge.
   Option B: Lawyers would be required to provide 100 hours of work, free of charge, to the poor.
   Option C: Lawyers who earn over $50,000 in a given year would have to donate $5,000 to a fund that the government would use to help the poor.

Discuss the likely effects of each option on the hours of work among lawyers. (It would help to *draw* the constraints created by each option.)

4. Suppose the Social Security disability insurance (DI) program was structured so that otherwise eligible recipients lost their *entire* disability benefit if they had any labor market earnings at all. Suppose, too, that Congress was concerned about the *work disincentives* inherent in this program, and that the relevant committee was studying two alternatives for increasing work incentives among those disabled enough to qualify for it. One alternative was to *reduce* the benefits paid to all DI recipients but make no other changes in the program. The other was to maintain the old benefit levels (for those who received them) but allow workers to earn $300 per month and still keep their benefits; those who earned over $300 per month would lose all DI benefits.

   Analyze the work-incentive effects of both alternatives. (The use of graphic analyses will be of great help to you.)

5. A firm wants to offer paid sick leave to its workers, but it wants to encourage them not to abuse it by being unnecessarily absent. The firm is considering two options:
   a. Ten days of paid sick leave per year; any unused leave days at end of year are

---

[29]See Richard V. Burkhauser and Andrew J. Glenn, "Public Policies for the Working Poor: The Earned Income Tax Credit Versus Minimum Wage Legislation," paper no. 8, Income Security Policy Series, Maxwell School of Citizenship and Public Affairs, Syracuse University, February 1994. Scholz, "The Earned Income Tax Credit," found that in stark contrast to the underutilization of employer wage subsidies, 85 percent of those eligible for the EITC program participated.

converted to cash at the worker's daily wage rate.

b. Ten days of paid sick leave per year; if no sick days are used for two consecutive years, the company agrees to buy the worker a $100,000 life insurance policy.

Compare the work-incentive effects of the two options, both immediately and in the long run.

6. When the late François Mitterand was the president of France, he instituted a number of programs designed to appeal to his "blue-collar" constituency. He raised the income tax rate applicable to the rich and expanded the free, government-provided social service programs to all (medical services and education being prominent among these). Analyze the work-incentive effects of Mitterrand's programs.

7. Suppose there is a proposal to provide poor people with housing subsidies that are tied to their income levels. These subsidies will be in the form of vouchers the poor can turn over to their landlords in full or partial payment of their housing expenses. The yearly subsidy will equal $2,400 as long as earnings do not exceed $8,000 per year. The subsidy is to be reduced 60 cents for every dollar earned in excess of $8,000; that is, when earnings reach $12,000, the person is no longer eligible for rent subsidies.

Draw an arbitrary budget constraint for a person assuming that he or she receives no government subsidies. Then draw in the budget constraint that arises from the above housing subsidy proposal. After drawing in the budget constraint associated with the proposal, analyze the effects of this proposed housing subsidy program on the labor supply behavior of various groups in the population.

8. The Tax Reform Act of 1986 was designed to reduce the marginal tax rate (the tax rate on the last dollars earned) while eliminating enough deductions and loopholes so that total revenues collected by the government could remain constant. Analyze the work-incentive effects of tax reforms that lower marginal tax rates while keeping total tax revenues constant.

SELECTED READINGS

Ellwood, David T. *Poor Support: Poverty in the American Family.* New York: Basic Books, 1988.

Keeley, Michael C. *Labor Supply and Public Policy: A Critical Review.* New York: Academic Press, 1981.

Killingsworth, Mark R. *Labor Supply.* Cambridge, Eng.: Cambridge University Press, 1983.

Linder, Staffan B. *The Harriet Leisure Class.* New York: Columbia University Press, 1970.

Moffitt, Robert. "Incentive Effects of the U.S. Welfare System: A Review," *Journal of Economic Literature* 30 (March 1992): 1–62.

Pencavel, John. "Labor Supply of Men: A Review." In *Handbook of Labor Economics,* ed. Orley Ashenfelter and Richard Layard. Amsterdam: North-Holland, 1986.

APPENDIX 6A

Child Care, Commuting, and the Fixed Costs of Working

This appendix generalizes the static model of labor supply discussed in Chapter 6 to include *costs of working*.[1] These costs typically include both monetary *and* time components. For example, the commute to work involves both time and such monetary outlays as fares on public transportation or the costs of operating an automobile. Similarly, in addition to paying for child care, a working parent often must spend time transporting a child back and forth to the place where the care is provided.

For expository convenience, we will analyze the effects of monetary and time costs of work separately. We will also treat these costs as being fixed, in the sense that they will be assumed not to vary with the number of hours an individual actually works. At first glance this latter assumption may seem overly restrictive, as child-care costs often do depend on the number of hours that care is given. However, the astute student will realize that introducing hours-related costs of work is analytically equivalent to reducing the wage rate. Since we have already stressed how wage changes affect hours of work in the text, we lose little by focusing on the fixed costs of work here.[2]

---

[1]Our discussion draws heavily on Mark Killingsworth, *Labor Supply* (Cambridge: Cambridge Universtiy Press, 1983), 23–27.

[2]It is straightforward to introduce into the model money costs of work that vary directly with hours of work. An increase in hourly child-care costs, for example, would be equivalent to a decrease in the hourly wage and have both income and substitution effects on hours decisions, but only a substitution effect on the labor force participation decision. A number of recent studies have found, in fact, that higher costs of child care lead to lower labor force participation rates among mothers with small children, with single women exhibiting greater responsiveness than married women. See Rachel Connelly, "The Effect of Child Care Costs on Married Women's Labor Force Participation," *Review of Economics and Statistics* 74 (February 1992): 83–90, and three articles in the *Journal of Human Resources* 27 (Winter 1992): David C. Ribar, "Child Care and the Labor Supply of Married Women," 134–165; Charles Michalopoulos, et. al., "A Structural Model of Labor Supply and Child Care Demand," 166–203; and Siv Gustafsson and Frank Stafford, "Child Care Subsidies and Labor Supply in Sweden," 204–230.

FIGURE 6A.1

*Work/Leisure Choice
with Fixed Money
Costs of Working*

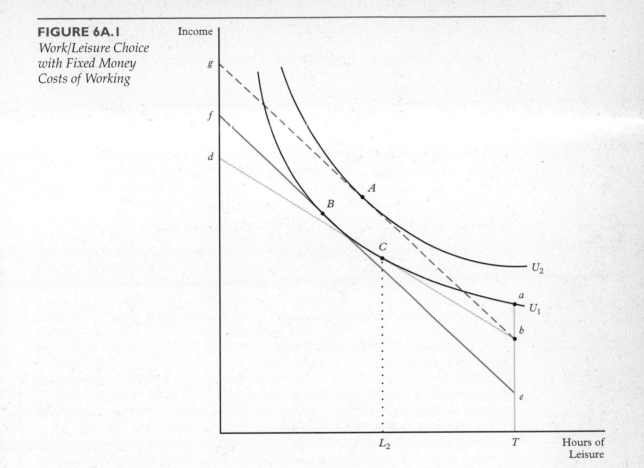

Fixed Monetary Costs of Working

Consider first the case of fixed *monetary* costs of work. Figure 6A.1 shows several indifference curves for an individual who has nonlabor income in the amount aT. If this individual chooses not to work at all, he or she will locate at point a and have a utility level of U_1. If the individual does choose to work, we assume that a fixed per-period cost of ab is incurred. Hence, if the individual works, the budget line starts from point b, not from a.

How large does the wage rate need to be to induce the person depicted in Figure 6A.1 to work for pay—and for how many hours will he or she work at this wage? The absolute value of the slope of the budget line represents the wage rate. Rotating hypothetical budget lines around point b, we eventually reach tangency (at point C) with the indifference curve that represents the individual's utility level, U_1, if he or she doesn't work at all. At point C the individual is receiving a wage equal to the absolute value of the slope of budget line bd, is working $T - L_2$ hours, and is just indifferent to not working. Any decrease in this wage will cause the individual to drop out of the labor force, because utility level U_1 will no longer be attainable if he or she works any hours. Thus, the wage represented by the slope of *bd* is the person's *reservation wage,* the lowest wage for which he or she will work.

This fixed-cost model thus provides an explanation for why we tend to observe that even part-time workers do not work a very small number of hours a week.[3] Given the fixed costs of work, individuals who receive a wage close to the minimum they require and who work only a small number of hours would not do as well in terms of utility as they would if they didn't work at all.

What would happen to the minimum hours of work and to reservation wages if the fixed costs were to increase to, say, *ae* in Figure 6A.1? As is graphically illustrated by the fact that the budget line starting at point *e* and tangent to U_1—line *ef*—has a steeper slope than does *bd*, an increase in the fixed costs of work will tend to raise the reservation wage of potential workers. It can also be noted that the tangency point of budget line *ef* with indifference curve U_1 is at point *B*, which because it lies to the left of point *C* implies that those who work will work longer and consume fewer leisure hours than was the case with fixed costs of *ab*.

How will an increase in these fixed costs of working affect workers who, when fixed costs were *ab*, could earn enough by working that they were not close to choosing the option of dropping out of the labor force? Suppose, for example, workers facing fixed working costs of *ab* could earn the wage implied by budget line *bg* in Figure 6A.1. These workers would locate at point *A* and could thereby achieve utility level U_2. Since points on curve U_2 are superior to points on curve U_1, these workers clearly prefer working to being out of the labor force.

However, if the fixed costs of work were to increase from *ab* to *ae*, and wages were to remain constant, the relevant budget line for these workers becomes *ef*. Now they can achieve only utility level U_1, the same utility they can get by not working. If they continue to work they will desire to work more hours (the increase in fixed cost causes an income effect in this case). These workers, however, may decide *not* to work and to drop out of the labor force, because the rise in the fixed monetary costs of work has increased their reservation wage to the point at which it equals their actual wage.

Increasing fixed costs of work, then, will tend to increase the hours of work for some workers but cause others to drop out of the labor force. Conversely, decreasing fixed costs (for example, by subsidizing commuting or child-care costs) would decrease hours of work for some workers but induce others to enter the labor force.[4] On balance, the net effect on labor supply of such policy changes is ambiguous a priori; empirical estimates are required to pin down the direction of the net effect.

---

[3]Average weekly hours of part-time employees in nonagricultural establishments in the United States were about 22 in the mid-1990s.

[4]Research results reported in Jean Kimmel, "Child Care Costs as a Barrier to Employment for Single and Married Mothers," working paper no. 92–14, W. E. Upjohn Institute for Employment Research, Kalamazoo, Mich., October 1994, and Susan L. Averett, H. Elizabeth Peters, and Donald M. Waldman, "Tax Credits, Labor Supply, and Child Care" (Department of Economics, University of Colorado, March 1994), suggest that subsidized child care *increases* the labor force participation of mothers.

FIGURE 6A.2
*Work/Leisure Choice
with Fixed Time
Costs of Working*

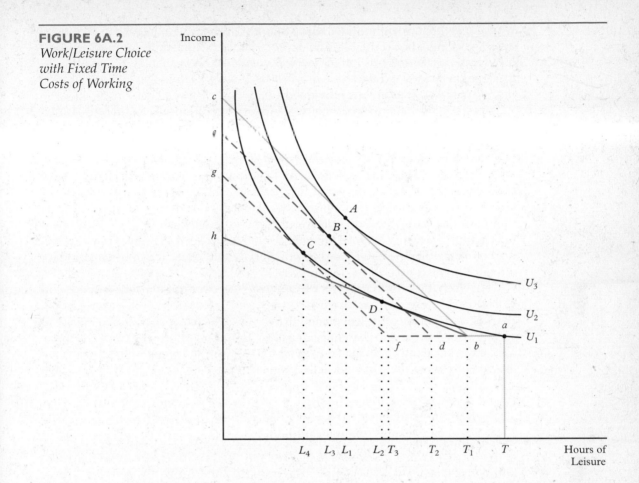

Fixed Time Costs of Working

Consider next the case of a fixed *time* cost of working, associated perhaps with commuting or transporting children to day care. In Figure 6A.2 an individual again has nonlabor income in the amount aT and, if this individual does not work at all, will have a utility level of U_1. Now suppose that if the individual does work, he or she incurs fixed time costs in the amount ab. In this case, the maximum number of hours a day available for work or leisure is no longer T but rather T_1. The individual's budget line thus starts at point b if he or she works, and its slope is minus the wage rate. If this budget line is bc the individual will locate at point A and work $T_1 - L_1$ hours.

If the individual's wage rate were lower, the budget line would rotate around point b and become flatter than the slope of bc. If the budget line were bh, the individual *could* maximize utility by locating at point D and by working $T_1 - L_2$ hours. At this point, however, the individual's utility is equal to U_1, the utility level he or she would attain from *not* working, so he or she would be indifferent between working and not working. Any lower wage would clearly induce the individual to drop out of the labor force, as utility level U_1 could no longer be attained by working. Thus, if working, this individual will never work less than $T_1 - L_2$ hours, and it can be seen that fixed *time* costs of work also help explain why we rarely observe individuals working only small numbers of hours per week.

Suppose now that the fixed time costs of work increase from ab to ad, perhaps because of increased traffic congestion faced by commuters. A worker originally facing budget line bc now faces budget line de, will locate at point B, and will work $T_2 - L_3$ hours while consuming L_3 hours of leisure. As long as leisure and income are both assumed to be normal goods, hours of *both* work and leisure time will be reduced by the increase in time costs of work.[5] Further increases in the time cost of work will lead to further reduction in hours of work. Indeed, as drawn in Figure 6A.2, if the time costs reached af, the individual would locate at point C, work $T_3 - L_4$ hours, and have a utility level of U_1. Since this is just equal to the level of utility at point a, any further increase in the fixed time costs of work would cause the individual to drop out of the labor force.

Conversely, this model suggests that anything that decreases the time costs of work will lead to increases in hours of work, *ceteris paribus*. So, for example, if a firm agreed to provide day care of equivalent quality to that which its employees' children were receiving elsewhere, and to charge an equivalent price, it would reduce employees' time cost of work (getting children to day care is now easier) and would increase the hours its employees are willing to work at the wages they are paid.

Policies Affecting Both Monetary And Time Costs

Combining the insights we have obtained from the fixed *money* and *time* cost models outlined above, it is possible to analyze the effects of policy changes that affect both simultaneously. For example, the introduction of a costly new high-speed mass transit system that is financed by high fares may simultaneously reduce the time costs and increase the monetary costs of commuting to work. The former change should increase the desired hours of work for existing labor force participants and tend to increase the labor force participation rate. The latter change should also increase hours of work for those workers who remain in the labor force, but it would tend to reduce the labor force participation rate. Thus, while average hours of work for workers previously in the labor force would tend to rise, the effect of these changes on the labor force participation rate is indeterminate a priori.

---

[5]Note that leisure falls from L_1 to L_3 while hours of work fall from $T_1 - L_1$ to $T_2 - L_3$ or by $(T_1 - T_2) - (L_1 - L_3)$ hours. The increase in fixed time costs of work has an income effect that reduces the worker's demand for both leisure and the goods that income will buy (if leisure and these goods are normal goods). Given a constant wage rate, a fall in income implies that hours of work have been reduced.

7

Labor Supply: Household Production, the Family, and the Life Cycle

In Chapter 6 the theory of labor supply focused on the simple case in which individuals deciding how to allocate their time were choosing between labor and leisure. This chapter elaborates on this simple labor supply model by taking account of three issues. First, much of the time spent at home is on work activities (cooking and child care, for example), not leisure. Second, for those who live with partners, decisions about work for pay, household work, and leisure are usually made in a way that takes account of the activities and income of other household members. Third, just as time at paid work is substitutable with time at home, time spent working for pay in one part of the life cycle is substitutable with time later on; in theory, therefore, one must allocate work and leisure time over the entire life cycle. These refinements of our simple model, it will be seen, do not alter the fundamental considerations or predictions of labor supply theory, but they do add useful richness to it.

The Theory of Household Production

The labor supply model in Chapter 6 conceived of household time as leisure, and it was assumed that utility was generated by directly consuming leisure time and purchased goods. Much of household time, however, is actually closer in nature to work than to leisure. We will see in this section that a labor supply model built on the assumption that household work, not leisure, is the alternative to working for pay, yields labor supply implications that are virtually identical to those of the labor/leisure model in Chapter 6.

A model based on choice between household work and paid work assumes that household time and purchased goods (made possible by paid work and any non-labor income) are combined to produce commodities that are then consumed. Food and energy are combined with preparation time to produce meals, for example, while books, toys, and supervision time contribute to the development of children. Thus, household time is viewed as an *input* to the production of household commodities, not as an item that is directly consumed. It is the *commodities* that are ultimately consumed and that generate utility for household members.

In this section, we initially derive a model of the labor supply decision based on the simplifying assumption that an individual must choose only between working for pay and working at home.[1] A model of choice between just two alternatives is conveniently summarized graphically, and it will be seen that the graphic depiction of the model looks like—and has the same implications as—the model derived in Chapter 6. Later, we discuss the more realistic, tripartite choice between work for pay, work at home, and leisure.

To obtain a sense of how we can model the production of household commodities, let us consider a household with just one decision maker: a single mother who derives satisfaction (utility) from raising her children.[2] Her objective is to maximize utility for herself and her children, and this she will do by allocating available time to both working for pay and working at home in a way that best satisfies her preferences. In making this allocation, as we will see, she will be deciding simultaneously on how much to work for pay *and* how to accomplish her child-rearing duties.

Equal satisfaction from child-rearing can be generated in a number of different ways. One can minimize the use of goods and services purchased outside the household by staying home to supervise the children, prepare their meals, and even make some of their clothing. A very different approach would rely heavily on purchased goods or services, and less on one's input of household time, by working for pay and then, for example, purchasing the services of a babysitter, serving prepared foods, and buying all clothing. Because various combinations of household time and purchased goods or services potentially generate equally satisfactory results, we could plot a curve that represents all the time/goods combinations that produce equal utility for the single mother in our example. Such a curve can be called a utility *isoquant*, where *iso* means "equal" and *quant* means "quantity" (of utility). Two utility isoquants are depicted in Figure 7.1 as M_0 and M_1.

---

[1]Models of household production are based on the pioneering work of Gary Becker, "A Theory of the Allocation of Time," *Economic Journal* 75 (September 1965): 493–517. Another early study in this area is by Reuben Gronau, "The Measurement of Output of the Nonmarket Sector: The Evaluation of Housewives' Time," in *The Measurement of Economic and Social Performance*, ed. Milton Moss (New York: National Bureau of Economic Research, 1973), 163–189.

[2]She would also derive utility from other things, of course, but to keep things simple we focus just on one activity for now.

FIGURE 7.1

The Production of Child Care

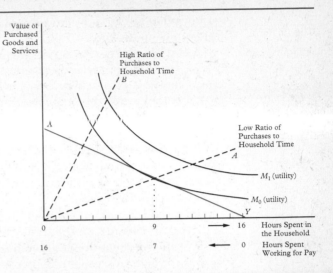

Several things should be noted about the isoquants in Figure 7.1. First, along M_0 the utility provided by child-rearing is constant. The utility produced by the time/goods combinations along M_1 is also constant, but it is greater than the utility represented by M_0 because more can be done for the children (that is, the child-rearing process involves more parental time and more, or higher-quality, purchased goods or services).

Second, the isoquants M_0 and M_1 are both negative in slope and convex (as viewed from below) in shape. The negative slope reflects an assumption that household time and purchased goods or services are substitutes in the "production" of child-rearing. If household time is reduced, child-rearing affording equal satisfaction can be produced by increasing the purchases of goods or services outside the home.

The convexity of the isoquants reflects an assumption that as household time devoted to child-rearing progressively falls, it becomes increasingly difficult to make up for it with purchased goods or services and still hold utility constant. If the parent spends a lot of time at home (making clothes, for example), it is relatively easy to replace some of that time with just a few purchased goods (store-bought clothing) and maintain equal levels of satisfaction. However, when parental household time is very short to begin with, a further cut in such time may be very difficult to absorb and still keep utility constant (it may take a large increase in the quality of child-care services to replace an hour of parental time if a parent is already out of the home for, say, 10 hours a day).

The slope of the utility isoquants, therefore, reflects the trade-offs a person is willing to make between household time and purchased goods or services in the production of household commodities. When isoquants are steeply sloped, it is relatively difficult to satisfactorily substitute purchased goods or services for the loss of an hour of household time; as a result, the marginal hour of such time is highly valued. A flatter slope depicts a situation in which it is easier to substitute for household time, and in this case it can be said that an extra hour of household time is less highly valued.

Finally, along any ray (*A* or *B*, for example) emanating from the origin of Figure 7.1, the ratio of purchased goods and services to household time in the production of child-rearing is constant. When household time and purchased goods or services are used in the combinations along ray *A*, child-rearing is accomplished using a relatively low ratio of purchases to household time. Along ray *B*, the child-rearing process uses a higher ratio of purchases goods and services to household time.

Because we have assumed that the only two uses of time are paid (or "market") work and household work, deciding on the utility-maximizing mode of child-rearing is the same as deciding on the utility-maximizing supply of hours to the labor market. This decision is influenced by the utility isoquants, discussed above, and one's budget constraint. Just as in Chapter 6, a budget constraint—like *XY* in Figure 7.1—reflects the combinations of purchases and household time that are possible for the individual. Also as before, the slope of the budget constraint reflects the person's wage rate, because it indicates the increased value of purchases made possible by an additional hour of paid work.

Given the isoquants and the constraint *XY* in Figure 7.1, this person's utility is maximized by spending 7 hours working for pay and 9 hours working at home each day. It should be noted that if the person depicted in Figure 7.1 faced the same budget constraint but had isoquants with a generally flatter slope—indicating that in her view purchased goods or services could more easily substitute for an hour of her own parental time—then the utility-maximizing point of tangency would have been further to the left along *XY* and she would have decided to work more hours outside the home.

The student will note that the utility-maximization process depicted in Figure 7.1 looks just like the graphic depictions in Chapter 6, even though the models assume different uses of household time. In both models the budget constraints reflect the combinations of purchased goods or services and household time (whether for leisure or for household work) that can be attained by the person. In both models the slope of the budget constraint indicates the person's wage rate (the dollar value of purchases made available by giving up one more hour of household time). In both models, convex isoquants reflect the trade-offs between purchased goods or services and household time in the generation of utility. In both models, steeply sloped isoquants represent a person who highly values an added hour at home (whether that hour is spent in leisure or whether it is spent performing household work). And in both models, a person with steeply sloped isoquants will have a tangency point toward the lower end of the budget constraint, therefore spending relatively few hours in paid work.

Thus, whether household time is conceived of as work or as leisure time, the resulting theory of labor supply is unchanged. One's supply of hours to paid work is a function of income, the wage rate, and the trade-offs a person is willing to make between household time and money income (which can be used to purchase goods and services) in the generation of utility. If, for example, the woman depicted in Figure 7.1 were to receive unearned income in a way that did not alter her wage rate, her new budget constraint would lie to the northeast of XY (and be parallel to it). Because the added income would allow a greater command over resources, she would now be able to increase her utility by doing more for (or with) her children. She would tend to purchase more, or higher-quality, goods and services, and she would also spend more time at home. Thus, there is an *income effect* that operates just as it did in Chapter 6; in this case, the *added* income would tend to *reduce* labor supply to the market.

Likewise, if the woman's *wage* were to rise, there would be an income *and* a substitution effect. The income effect would serve to reduce labor supply, but it would be offset to some extent by the fact that the higher wage increases the cost of spending an extra hour at home. In short, there would be a *substitution effect* associated with the wage increase that would push her in the direction of more paid work (and, at the same time, would push her toward a mode of child-rearing that relies more on purchased goods or services). As we also found in Chapter 6, theory cannot tell us whether, if wages increase, it is the income or the substitution effect that will dominate; that will depend on the shape of the utility isoquants.

The Tripartite Choice: Market Work, Household Work, and Leisure

While the household production model of labor supply does not change the conclusions in Chapter 6 about the influence of income and substitution effects, consideration of household production does introduce the notion that there is really a *tripartite* choice of how to spend time. That is, people can choose to spend time in market work (for pay), in household work, or in leisure activities. Explicit recognition of this tripartite choice enriches our understanding of how people allocate their time.

Consider data from time-use diaries in Table 7.1, which summarizes how men and women in the United States and Norway allocated their weekly hours in 1980–81.[3] From the table we learn that American men averaged 44 hours of market work, almost 14 hours of household work, and roughly 42 hours of leisure per week; sleep, rest, and personal care amounted to 68 hours per week. In contrast, American women averaged 24 hours of market work, over 30 hours of household work, and the same 42 hours of leisure. Norwegian men and women spent far fewer hours in market work, somewhat more hours in household work, and more hours consuming leisure than their American counterparts. Hours differentials in each activity between men and women, however, were similar in the two countries.

---

[3]It is worth noting that diary-based estimates of market work hours included commuting time, hours of job search, hours at a second job, and unpaid time spent at the workplace before and after work; thus, these data are not fully comparable to the hours data discussed at the beginning of Chapter 6. F. Thomas Juster and Frank P. Stafford, "The Allocation of Time: Empirical Findings, Behavioral Models, and Problems of Measurement," *Journal of Economic Literature* 29 (June 1991): 471–522, argue that the diary-based measures are superior to conventional interview data. The most recent year for which published diary-based data are available is 1981.

TABLE 7.1

The Allocation of Weekly Hours to Work and Leisure, United States and Norway, 1980–1981

Hours at Each Activity	United States		Norway	
	Men	Women	Men	Women
Market work, including commuting, moonlighting, job search	44.0	23.9	34.2	17.6
Household work	13.8	30.5	16.8	33.0
Total work	57.8	54.4	51.0	50.6
Total leisure	41.8	41.9	45.5	45.2
Personal care, including sleep and rest	68.2	71.6	71.4	72.1

SOURCE: F. Thomas Juster and Frank P. Stafford, "The Allocation of Time: Empirical Findings, Behavioral Models, and Problems of Measurement," *Journal of Economic Literature* 29 (June 1991): 477.

In Chapter 6 we noted that the substitution effect has tended to dominate the income effect in the labor supply of women. We also noted that, as time has passed and as women's labor force participation has increased, the dominance of the substitution effect for women has appeared to fade, and the relative size of the two effects for men and women has begun to converge. The historical differences in the substitution effects of men and women, and their apparently growing convergence, can be at least partly understood by the presence of *two* substitution effects attendant upon a market wage increase: one between market and household work and the other between market work and leisure. We argue below that the magnitudes of these two effects differ and that the weight of the former in one's overall response to a wage change is related to one's role in household production. Therefore, historical differences in the substitution effects for women and men (and any convergence over time) may be the result of the roles each plays in the household.

Recall from Figure 6.10 of Chapter 6 that the substitution effect is graphically depicted by changing the slope of the budget constraint, keeping it tangent to the same indifference curve. One can see from comparing the two panels in Figure 7.2 that the substitution effect is larger if the isoquant is gently bent (panel a), as opposed to abruptly bent (panel b). What can cause these isoquants to bend differently?

Both panels of Figure 7.2 place the value of goods (and services) used in producing utility on the vertical axis; thus, the vertical axis depicts the goods that can be purchased with the money derived from market work. Panel (a), however, shows the trade-offs between these goods and household *work* time that keep utility constant, while panel (b) shows the goods/*leisure* trade-off. The gradual bend in panel (a) implies that reductions in hours of household work can be easily compensated by purchasing more goods; that is, reduced time devoted to such house-

FIGURE 7.2

Large vs. Small Substitution Effects Attendant to a Wage Increase

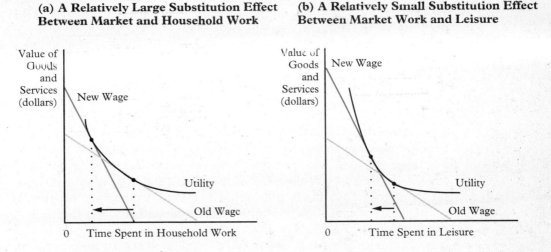

(a) A Relatively Large Substitution Effect Between Market and Household Work

(b) A Relatively Small Substitution Effect Between Market Work and Leisure

hold chores as cooking, cleaning, and child care can be easily replaced through the purchase of a microwave oven, prepared foods, an electric dishwasher, or the services of a babysitter.

The steeper bend in the goods/leisure indifference curve (panel b) reflects the greater difficulty in substituting goods for *leisure* time without loss of utility.[4] Leisure activities normally include time as an essential input, and the possibilities for economizing on time are thus limited. A television show can be taped and watched more quickly later by fast-forwarding through commercials, and one can listen to a Beethoven symphony while doing other things, such as driving or jogging. These examples, however, highlight how difficult it is to substitute satisfactorily for time in leisure activities.

Married women have traditionally been—and remain today, judging by Table 7.1—the primary household producers in most families. Therefore, as wages have risen, the (stronger) market/household-work substitution effect shown in panel (a) of Figure 7.2 probably has been of greater importance for women than for men. Moreover, as women have increased their hours of paid work markedly over recent decades, they have undoubtedly substituted many

---

[4] To prove this to yourself, ask, "If an hour of time at home is given up, what amount of goods will have to be added to keep utility constant?" When it is difficult to substitute goods for time, it will take many goods to keep utility constant, and the indifference curve will rise steeply. Students should be able to convince themselves that the limiting case in which no substitution is possible involves an indifference curve that is L-shaped; in this case no change in the wage rate will change the optimum mix of inputs. Another limiting case involves an indifference curve that is a negatively sloped straight line; in this case a change in the wage rate could cause the family to flip-flop from the use of only one input to using only the other.

purchased goods for household-work time—with the result that further substitutions now may be more difficult. In short, many households now may be at a more steeply sloped point on the trade-off curve in panel (a) than they were several years ago. The historical dominance of the substitution effect for women, and the apparent fall in this dominance, thus may at least partially reflect the prominent role of women in household production and the adjustments in household production made over the years as their labor force participation has increased.

Joint Labor Supply Decisions Within the Household

The models depicted in Chapter 6 and so far in this chapter have been for a single decision maker, who was assumed to be trying to maximize his or her own utility. For those who live with partners, however, some kind of *joint* decision-making process must be used to allocate the time of each and to agree on who does what in the household. There can be little doubt that usefully modeling this process is complicated by emotional relationships between the partners, and that their decisions about market and household work are heavily influenced by custom.[5] Nevertheless, economic theory may help provide insight into at least some of the forces that shape the decisions all households must make, and it is the purpose of this section to highlight those forces that most affect the labor supplied to market work.

Just how to model the different decision-making processes that can be used by households, and what influences the outcomes of each process, are questions economists have only begun to study. The formal models of decision making among married couples that have been developed to date, all of which are based on principles of utility maximization, fall into three general categories.[6] The simplest models extend the assumption of a single decision maker to marriage partners, either by assuming they both have exactly the same preferences or by assuming one makes all the decisions (but maximizes the utility of the other in the process). A second type of model assumes that the partners engage in a bargaining process (a "cooperative game") in making household decisions; each is assumed to have resources and "threat points" that affect their bargaining power. Finally, some models assume that the partners act independently to maximize their own utility, but each does so by considering the likely actions, and reactions, of the other (a "noncooperative game").

However, whatever process partners use to decide on the allocation of their time, and it may be different in different households, there are certain issues and

---

[5]See Julie A. Nelson, "I, Thou, and Them: Capabilities, Altruism, and Norms in the Economics of Marriage," *American Economic Review* 84, no. 2 (May 1994): 126–131; and Claire Brown, "An Institutional Model of Wives' Work Decisions," *Industrial Relations* 24, no. 2 (Spring 1985): 182–204.

[6]See Shelly Lundberg and Robert A. Pollak, "Noncooperative Bargaining Models of Marriage," *American Economic Review* 84, no. 2 (May 1994): 132–137; and Robert A. Pollak, "For Better or Worse: The Roles of Power in Models of Distribution Within Marriage," *American Economic Review* 84, no. 2 (May 1994): 148–152.

considerations that nearly all households must face. We turn now to a brief analysis of some joint decisions that affect labor supply.

SPECIALIZATION OF FUNCTION

Partners often find it beneficial to specialize to some extent in the work that needs to be done, both in the market and in the household. Often, but not always, one or the other partner will bear primary responsibilities for meal planning, shopping, home maintenance, child-rearing, and so forth. It may also be the case that, when both work for pay, one or the other of the partners will be more available for overtime, for job-related travel, or for cutting short a workday if an emergency arises at home. What factors are weighed in deciding who specializes in what?

Consider a couple trying to decide which spouse, if either, will take primary responsibility for child-rearing by staying at home (say) or by taking a job that has a less demanding schedule or a shorter commute. Because the person with primary child-care duties will probably end up spending more hours in the household, the couple need to answer two questions: Who is relatively more productive at home? Who is relatively more productive in market work? The answer to the first question depends upon who can produce more commodities (more utility) for a given amount of goods and home production time. The answer to the second question depends upon who can generate the greater increase in command over goods by working an extra hour for pay.

For example, a couple deciding whether one partner should stay home more and perform most of the child-rearing would want to consider what gains and losses are attendant on either the husband or the wife assuming this responsibility. The losses from staying home are related to the market wage of each, while the gains depend on their enjoyment of, and skill at, child-rearing. (Since enjoyment of the parenting process increases utility, we can designate both higher levels of enjoyment *and* higher levels of skill as indicative of greater "productivity" in child-rearing.) Wage rates for women, for whatever reasons, typically have been below those for men. (Discrimination will be treated in Chapter 12; other reasons for male/female wage differences are dealt with in Chapter 9.) It is also likely that, because of socialization, wives have been historically more productive than husbands in child-rearing. If a given woman's wage rate is lower than her husband's and the woman is more productive in child-rearing, the family gives up less in market goods and gains more in child-rearing if the wife takes primary responsibility in this area.

Modeling the choice of who handles most of some household duty as influenced by relative household and market productivities is not meant to imply that customs are not important in shaping preferences or in limiting choices concerning household production; clearly they are. What the theory of household production emphasizes is that the distribution of household work may well change as wages, incomes, and home productivities change (a point made historically by Example 7.1). Interestingly, a recent study found that, when both spouses work outside the home, the weekly hours that each spends in household work are affected by their relative wage rates, although not to the same extent. That is, as wives' wages

EXAMPLE 7.1

Differences in Swiss Child-Rearing Practices Around 1800

Household production theory views choices concerning both household and labor market activities as functions of household productivity, market wages, and wealth. An example of the theory "in action" was seen in child-rearing practices that developed around 1800 in rural Switzerland. A vigorous cottage industry had developed in the highlands near Zurich, with households performing spinning and weaving operations at home. In the households that owned their own land and had relatively spacious accommodations, equipment was brought into the home and the spinning and weaving activities provided a remunerative activity for all household members, including children. In these households it became common for parents to set a quota for spinning or weaving that was required before children were free to play; the quota became known as the *Rast* (rest).

Among the poorer, landless families, this system of *Rast* became very different. Because of rapid population growth and prohibitions against increasing the housing supply, these families could not secure accommodations large enough to house spinning and

weaving equipment for the entire family. In these households children were a "burden" in two senses. They were a net drain on family wealth, and the time required for their upbringing became more costly as the parents' earning power increased. As a result of their low level of wealth, their growing cost of child-rearing, and their children's low productivity at home, these families tended to board their children in the homes of wealthier families. In effect, these children were placed in "market" instead of household work, and they were expected to pay (by spinning and weaving) for their own upkeep. The money required by the boarding family to maintain the child was called the *Rast*. Thus, child-rearing practices—and the meaning of *Rast*—varied with differences in household productivity.

Source: Rudolf Braun, "Early Industrialization and Demographic Change in the Canton of Zurich," in *Historical Studies of Changing Fertility*, ed. Charles Tilly (Princeton: Princeton University Press, 1978), 289–334.

---

rise relative to those of their husbands, the household work done by husbands appears to increase, while the work done by wives decreases.[7]

DO BOTH PARTNERS WORK FOR PAY?

It is clearly not necessary, of course, that either partner stay at home full-time. Many household chores, from cooking and cleaning to child care, can be hired out or otherwise performed in a goods-intensive manner. The considerations underlying the decision about whether both should work can be best understood by looking at Figure 7.3. The utility isoquants there (U_1 and U_2) represent the various combinations of household time and goods that can be used to generate family (or individual) utility of two levels (level 1 and level 2).

---

[7]Joni Hersch and Leslie S. Stratton, "Housework, Wages, and the Division of Household Time for Employed Spouses," *American Economic Review* 84, no. 2 (May 1994): 120–125. (The effects of relative wages in this study can be inferred from the effects of "husband's share of labor income," holding the combined income and the hours of work of both husbands and wives constant.)

FIGURE 7.3
Home vs. Market Productivities

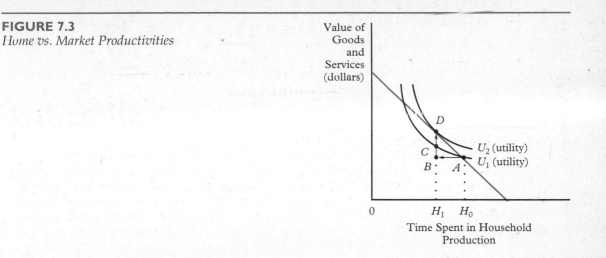

As long as an extra hour of market work by both partners creates the ability to buy more goods than are required to make up for the hour of lost home production time, both can enhance household resources if they work for pay that extra hour. In terms of Figure 7.3, if a person spending H_0 hours at home decides to work an extra hour for pay, so that H_1 hours are now spent at home, he or she will gain *BD* in goods.[8] Since an increase of only *BC* in goods is required to compensate for the lost hour of home production to keep utility constant, household resources are clearly increased if the person works for pay. In other words, at point *A* the person is relatively more productive in the marketplace than at home. Thus, decisions about household labor supply must be made in full consideration of the market and household productivities of both partners.

As we saw earlier in this chapter, the level of household income can also be expected to affect the labor supply of each partner (with lower income levels inducing more market work, other things equal). This income effect apparently plays a prominent role in affecting the labor supply of married women who face relatively high probabilities of marital dissolution. Namely, the *prospect* of reduced income associated with separation and divorce induces them to gradually increase their labor force participation rates and hours of work *prior to* separation, and the separation itself is associated with a relatively large jump in participation rates and hours worked.[9]

---

[8]We are talking here of *after*-tax spending power. The value of what one produces at home is not taxed, but earnings in the marketplace are—a difference that forces us to focus here on wages and earnings *net* of taxes.

[9]William R. Johnson and Jonathan Skinner, "Labor Supply and Marital Separation," *American Economic Review* 76, no. 3 (June 1986): 455–469. The more general issue of the forces that influence marital dissolution rates has been a subject of some interest to economists; a pioneering theoretical and empirical study that uses a generalization of the framework developed in this chapter is Gary S. Becker, Elisabeth M. Landes, and Robert T. Michael, "An Economic Analysis of Marital Instability," *Journal of Political Economy* 85, no. 6 (December 1977): 1141–1188.

THE JOINT DECISION AND CROSS-EFFECTS

We have seen that family labor supply decisions are enhanced by jointly considering the household and market productivities of each partner. However, one partner's productivity in both production and consumption at home is affected by the *other* partner's labor supply to the market, so that modeling the joint decision is quite complex. On the one hand, if a married woman decides to increase her hours worked outside the home, her husband's marginal productivity for a given number of hours at home may rise as he takes over chores she once performed. Thus, if both wife and husband are *substitutes* in the household production of commodities, one spouse's increased labor supply to the market may tend to decrease the labor supply of the other.

On the other hand, both spouses may be *complementary* in the *consumption* of household commodities. That is, if the woman above takes a job that involves working until 8:00 P.M. each night, her husband may decide that dinners at 6:00 P.M. have less utility than before, and as a result, he might decide that the benefits of working later outweigh the utility lost by so doing. In this case, one spouse's decision to increase hours worked for pay may induce the other spouse to likewise increase labor supply.

Theory cannot predict whether the spouses are substitutes or complements in household production and consumption; similarly, it is impossible to say which cross-effect will dominate if their signs conflict. Thus, the question of how one spouse's labor supply will respond to changes in the labor supply of the other is essentially an empirical one. There is as yet no real consensus on the sizes and signs of these cross-effects for husbands and wives.[10]

LABOR SUPPLY IN RECESSIONS: THE "DISCOURAGED" VS. THE "ADDITIONAL" WORKER

Changes in one partner's productivity, either at home or in market work, can alter the family's basic labor supply decision. Consider, for example, a "traditional" family in which market work is performed by the husband and in which the wife

---

[10]For reviews of these issues, see Mark Killingsworth, *Labor Supply* (Cambridge, Eng.: Cambridge University Press, 1983); Marjorie B. McElroy, "Appendix: Empirical Results from Estimates of Joint Labor Supply Functions of Husbands and Wives," in *Research in Labor Economics*, vol. 4, ed. Ronald Ehrenberg (Greenwich, Conn.: JAI Press, 1981), 53–64; Shelly Lundberg, "Labor Supply of Husbands and Wives: A Simultaneous Equations Approach," *Review of Economics and Statistics* 70 (May 1988): 224–234; and Joni Hersch and Leslie S. Stratton, "Housework, Wages, and the Division of Household Time for Employed Spouses." For a recent study using Dutch data, see Arthur van Soest, "Structural Models of Family Labor Supply: A Discrete Choice Approach," *Journal of Human Resources* 30, no. 1 (Winter 1995): 63–88.

We mentioned earlier that there are different approaches economists have taken to modeling the family's decision-making process. One implication of the model that assumes the spouses have identical preferences is that the effect of increases in the wife's wage (income held constant) on the husband's labor supply would be the same as the effects on the wife's labor supply of increases in the husband's wage. The empirical studies cited above tend to reject this built-in assumption about the symmetry of the two cross-effects, thus casting doubt on the relevance of this model. See Marjorie B. McElroy, "The Empirical Content of Nash-Bargained Household Behavior," *Journal of Human Resources* 25 (Fall 1990): 559–583.

is employed full-time in the home. What will happen if a recession causes the husband to become unemployed?

The husband's market productivity declines, at least temporarily. He may be a highly specialized worker and unable to find similar work at the moment. The drop in his market productivity relative to his household productivity (which is unaffected by the recession) makes it more likely that the family will find it beneficial for him to engage in household production. If the wage his wife can earn in paid work is not affected, the family *may* decide that, to try to maintain the family's prior level of utility (which might be affected by both consumption and *savings* levels), *she* should seek market work and *he* should substitute for her in home production for as long as the recession lasts. He may remain a member of the labor force as an unemployed worker awaiting recall, and as she begins to look for work, she becomes an "added" member of the labor force. Thus, in the face of falling family income, the number of family members seeking market work may increase. This potential response is akin to the income effect in that, as family income falls, fewer commodities are consumed—and less time spent in consumption tends to be matched by more desired hours of work for pay.

At the same time, however, we must look at the *wage rate* someone without a job can *expect* to receive if he or she looks for work. This expected wage, denoted by $E(W)$, can actually be written as a precise statistical concept:

$$E(W) = \pi W \qquad (7.1)$$

where W is the wage rate of people who have the job and π is the probability of obtaining the job if out of work. For someone without a job, the price of an hour at home—the opportunity cost of staying home—is $E(W)$. The reduced availability of jobs that occurs when the unemployment rate rises causes the *expected wage of those without jobs to fall* sharply for two reasons. First, an excess of labor supply over demand tends to push down real wages (for those with jobs) during recessionary periods. Second, the chances of getting a job fall in a recession. Thus, both W and π fall in a recession, causing $E(W)$ to decline. Noting the *substitution effect* that accompanies a falling expected wage, some have argued that people who would otherwise have been looking for work become "discouraged" in a recession and tend to remain out of the labor market. Looking for work has such a low expected payoff for them that such people decide that spending time at home is more productive than spending time in job search. The reduction of the labor force associated with discouraged workers in a recession is a force working against the "added-worker" effect—just as the substitution effect works against the income effect.

It is possible, of course, for both the added-worker and the discouraged-worker effects to coexist, because "added" and "discouraged" workers will be different groups of people. Which group predominates, however, is the important question. If the labor force is swollen by "added workers" during a recession, the published unemployment rate will likewise become swollen (the added workers will increase the number of people looking for work). If workers become "discouraged" and drop out of the labor market after having been unemployed, the decline in people seeking jobs will depress the unemployment rate. Knowledge of which effect predominates is needed in order to make accurate inferences about the actual state of the labor market from the published unemployment rate.

We know that the added-worker effect does exist, although it tends to be rather small.[11] The added-worker effect is confined to the relatively few families whose sole breadwinner loses a job (the overall unemployment rate rarely goes above 10 percent), and as more and more women become regularly employed for pay, the added-worker effect will tend to both decline and become increasingly confined to teenagers. In contrast, the fall in expected real wages occurs in nearly *every* household, and since the substitution effect is relatively strong for married women, it is not surprising that studies have consistently found the discouraged-worker effect to be large and dominant.[12] Other things equal, *the labor force tends to shrink during recessions and grow during periods of economic recovery.*

The dominance of the discouraged-worker effect creates what some call the "hidden" unemployed—people who would like to work but believe jobs are so scarce that looking for work is of no use. Because they are not looking for work, they are not counted as unemployed in government statistics. Focusing on the period from the beginning of 1990 to the end of 1991, when the overall official unemployment rate rose from 5.2 percent to 6.9 percent, can give some indication of the size of hidden unemployment.

In the first quarter of 1990 an average of 6.5 million people (5.2 percent of the labor force) were counted as unemployed at any given time. In addition, 776,000 people indicated that they wanted work but were not seeking it because they felt jobs were unavailable to them; this group constituted 1.2 percent of those adults not in the labor force. By the fourth quarter of 1991, some 8.7 million people (6.9 percent of the labor force) were officially counted as unemployed, but there were 1.1 million others among the group not seeking work because they felt jobs were unavailable. Coincident with reduced job opportunities, the number of "discouraged workers" had grown to 1.7 percent of those adults not in the labor force. If "discouraged workers" were counted as unemployed members of the labor force, the unemployment rate would have been 5.8 percent at the beginning of 1990 and 7.7 percent by the end of 1991;[13] thus, while the official unemployment

---

[11]Shelly Lundberg, "The Added Worker Effect," *Journal of Labor Economics* 3, no. 1 (January 1985): 11–37.

[12]The landmark study on this topic is Jacob Mincer, "Labor Force Participation and Unemployment: A Review of Recent Evidence," in *Prosperity and Unemployment*, ed. R. A. Gordon and M. S. Gordon (New York: John Wiley & Sons, 1966).

[13]To say that including "discouraged workers" in unemployment statistics would change the published unemployment rate does not imply that it *should* be done. For a summary of the arguments for and against counting discouraged workers as unemployed, see the final report of the National Commission on Employment and Unemployment Statistics, *Counting the Labor Force* (Washington, D.C., 1979), 44–49. In 1994, the government changed its definition of discouraged workers to require that they be persons who want a job and are available for work, have searched for work in the past year, but have not looked for work in the past four weeks because they believed search would be futile.

rate went up 1.7 percentage points, the rate that includes "discouraged workers" went up 1.9 percentage points.

Life-Cycle Aspects of Labor Supply

Because market productivity (wages) and household productivity vary over the life cycle, people vary the hours they supply to the labor market over their lives. In the early adult years relatively fewer hours are devoted to work than in later years, and more time is devoted to schooling. In the very late years people fully or partially retire, though at varying ages. In the middle years (say, 25 to 50) most males are in the labor force continuously but, for married women, labor force participation rates rise with age. While the issue of schooling is dealt with in Chapter 9, expanding the model of household production discussed in this chapter to include life-cycle considerations can enrich our understanding of labor supply behavior in several areas, three of which are discussed below.

THE LABOR FORCE PARTICIPATION PATTERNS OF MARRIED WOMEN

When one examines married women's labor force participation rates using cross-sectional data—data on women of different ages at a point in time—it appears that married women have falling labor force participation during their twenties and rising participation rates from ages 30 to 50. However, a study that followed separate birth cohorts of women (women born in the same years) found that cross-sectional data may be misleading if one wants to describe the participation patterns of the "typical" married woman over her life cycle. Following cohorts of married women throughout each decade of the life cycle suggests that labor force participation rates rise in each decade of life, with the increases after age 30 typically being much greater than those from ages 20 to 30.[14] Can household production theory help to explain these more steeply rising participation rates after age 30?

The basic premise of the household production model is that people are productive in two places: in the home and in a "market" job. Their decisions about whether to seek market work and for how many hours are a function of their *relative* productivities in both places. As long as an extra hour of market work allows

---

[14]Claudia Goldin, *Understanding the Gender Gap* (New York: Oxford University Press, 1990), 21–26. The reason for the discrepancy between cross-sectional and cohort studies is that labor force participation of each successive cohort has exceeded that of its predecessors. Hence, while the participation rates within a cohort increase with age, the increased rates of successive cohorts has caused labor force participation among 20-year-olds to exceed that of 30-year-olds (an older cohort) at a given point in time.

A recent study by David Shapiro and Frank L. Mott, "Long-Term Employment and Earnings of Women in Relation to Employment Behavior Surrounding First Birth," *Journal of Human Resources* 29, no. 2 (Spring 1994): 248–275, found that women most "attached" to the labor force returned to work almost immediately after childbirth. It is among those less attached that we observe the rising labor force participation rates as children age.

FIGURE 7.4
*Household Productivity Can
Change over the Life Cycle*

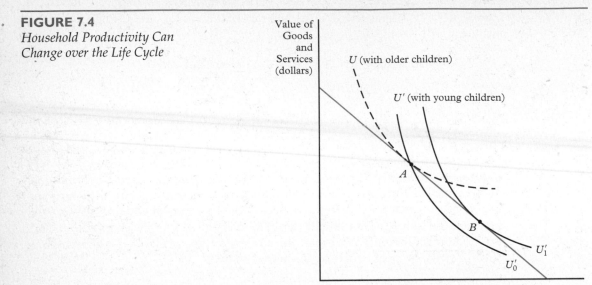

the person to buy more goods than are required to make up for the hour of lost production time at home, the person will work for pay that extra hour.

Home productivity of at least one parent is relatively higher at the margin when young children are present, and it probably falls as children become older (see Example 7.2). Higher household productivity can be represented by a steeper tilt to the utility isoquants, as shown by the U' curves in Figure 7.4. The U' "family" of isoquants implies that the parent who is the primary caregiver (historically the mother) will have a tangency point near B with relatively less time in market work and more time at home. As children grow older, the isoquants take on a flatter slope, as shown by the dashed curve U in Figure 7.4 (to see the flatter slope, compare the slopes of U and U' at a common point, A). The flatter slope of the dashed isoquant results in a tangency point to the left of point B, implying reduced time at home by the primary caregiver and more time in market work.

THE SUBSTITUTION EFFECT AND WHEN TO WORK OVER A LIFETIME

Just as joint decisions about market and household work involve comparing market and home productivities of the two partners, deciding *when* to work over the course of one's life involves comparing market and home productivities *over time*. The basic idea here is that a person will tend to perform the most market work when his or her earning capacity is high relative to home productivity. Conversely, people will engage in household production when their earning capacity is relatively low.

EXAMPLE 7.2

The Value of a Homemaker's Time

The services performed by homemakers are not sold in the marketplace, but this does not imply they are not valuable. For purposes of settling claims involving the permanent injury or wrongful death of a homemaker, and often in cases in which property must be divided upon divorce, it is important to place a value on homemakers' services. There are three approaches that can be taken.

Market-Price Approach. One method is to measure how much a homemaker's services (cooking, child care, recordkeeping, etc.) would cost if they were to be individually purchased in the marketplace. The problem with this approach is that in cases in which the services are available but not purchased, the family must believe such services are not worth their cost; for these households, the value assigned by the market-price approach overstates the value of the homemaker's services.

Opportunity-Cost Approach. A second method is to estimate what the homemaker would have been able to earn, after taxes, if she (or he) had worked for pay. Of course, some homemakers do not work at all, which implies they value the services they provide at home at more than their potential market earnings. Using the forgone wage to place a value on each hour of household work thus results in an underestimate of the value of a homemaker's services.

Self-Employment Approach. A third method is to treat homemakers as self-employed individuals who can either increase hours at home if their marginal household productivity (MHP) exceeds their market wage (W) or reduce hours at home if W exceeds MHP. If MHP exceeds W even when hours of paid work are zero, the homemaker works full-time at home; if W exceeds MHP even when working full-time for pay, the person works full-time outside the home. If a person is at home part of the time and also works part-time for pay, we can infer that MHP and W must be equal. It is from part-time workers, then, that we obtain estimates of marginal household productivities, and from these estimates it is possible to derive a relationship between hours at home and the total value of household services.

Estimated Values. The first two approaches above, while less theoretically satisfactory, are computationally more feasible. Studies that estimate time spent on various household services from diary data have estimated the value of household services under both the market-price and opportunity-cost approaches. The estimated yearly values for full-time homemakers are as follows (1994 dollars):

	Market Price	**Opportunity Cost**
With children ages 2–5	$22,455	$19,943
Youngest child aged 6–14	20,209	17,211
No children	16,330	16,190

SOURCES: William H. Gauger and Kathryn E. Walker, *The Dollar Value of Household Work* (Ithaca, N.Y.: College of Human Ecology, 1979); W. Keith Bryant, Cathleen D. Zick, and Hyoshin Kim, *Household Work: What's It Worth and Why?* (Ithaca, N.Y.: Cornell Cooperative Extension, 1992); Carmel Ullman Chiswick, "The Value of a Housewife's Time," *Journal of Human Resources* 16 (Summer 1982): 412-425.

Suppose a sales representative working on a commission basis knows that his potential income is around $30,000 in a certain year, but that July's income potential will be twice that of November's. Would it be rational for him to schedule his vacation (a time-intensive activity) in November? The answer depends on his market productivity relative to his "household productivity" for the two months. Obviously his market productivity, his wage rate, is higher in July than November, which means that the opportunity costs of a vacation are greater in July. However, if he has children who are free to vacation only in July, he may decide that his household productivity (in terms of utility) is so much greater in July than November that the benefits of vacationing in July outweigh the costs. If he does not have children of school age, the utility generated by a November vacation may be sufficiently close to that of a July vacation that the smaller opportunity costs make a November vacation preferable.

Similar decisions can be made over longer periods of time, even one's entire life. As Chapter 9 will show, market productivity (which is reflected in one's wage) starts low in the young adult years, rises rapidly with age, then levels off and even falls in the later years, as shown in panel (a) of Figure 7.5. This general pattern occurs within each of the broad educational groupings of workers, although the details of the wage "trajectories" differ. With an *expected* path of wages over their lives, workers can generate predictions of two variables critical to labor supply decisions: lifetime wealth and the costs of leisure or household time they will face at various ages. Thus, if home productivity is more or less constant as they age, workers who make labor supply decisions by taking expected lifetime wealth into account will react to *expected* (life-cycle) wage increases by unambiguously increasing their labor supply. Such wage increases raise the cost of leisure and household time but do not increase expected lifetime wealth; these wage increases, then, are accompanied only by a substitution effect.

Introducing life-cycle considerations into labor supply theory yields a prediction that the profiles of time spent at, and away from, market work will resemble those shown in panel (b) of Figure 7.5; that is, workers will spend more time at paid work activities in their (relatively high-wage) middle years. Similarly, life-cycle considerations suggest that the consumption of very time-intensive leisure activities will occur primarily in one's early and late years. (That travelers to Europe are predominantly young adults and the elderly is clearly related to the fact that, for these groups, opportunity costs of time are lower. They make the time to go because, at these stages in their lives, time is relatively inexpensive.)

Life-cycle considerations, therefore, add yet another dimension to the basic theory of labor supply discussed so far. If workers make labor supply decisions with the life cycle in mind, they will react differently to expected and unexpected wage changes. Expected wage changes will generate only a substitution effect, because estimates of lifetime wealth will remain unchanged. *Unexpected* wage changes, however, will cause them to revise their estimates of lifetime wealth, and these changes will be accompanied by both substitution and income effects. Empirical tests of the life-cycle model of labor supply are relatively recent; to date, they

FIGURE 7.5
Life-Cycle Allocation of Time

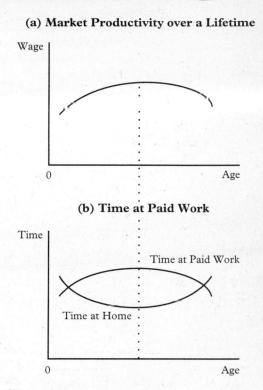

(a) Market Productivity over a Lifetime

Wage

0   Age

(b) Time at Paid Work

Time

Time at Paid Work

Time at Home

0   Age

suggest that life-cycle considerations are at best of modest importance in the labor supply decisions of most workers.[15]

THE CHOICE OF RETIREMENT AGE

A life-cycle, or at least a multiyear, perspective is also required to more fully model workers' retirement decisions, because *yearly* retirement benefits, expected *lifetime* benefits, and lifetime earnings are all influenced by the date of retirement. The purpose of this section is to explore some of the economic factors that affect the age

---

[15]For recent studies that refer to earlier work, see Jean Kimmel and Thomas J. Kniesner, "The Intertemporal-Substitution Hypothesis is Alive and Well (but Hiding in the Data)," staff working paper no. 93–19, W. E. Upjohn Institute for Employment Research, May 1993; and Kevin T. Reilly, "Annual Hours and Weeks in a Life-Cycle Labor Supply Model: Canadian Evidence on Male Behavior," *Journal of Labor Economics* 12, no. 3 (July 1994): 460–477. Intertemporal changes in wage rates, and the labor supply responses they generate through the substitution effect, are emphasized by some economists in explaining employment changes across the business cycle. This view regards employment reductions in recessions as labor *supply* withdrawals in response to wages made lower by a negative "shock" to productivity. The controversies surrounding this theory of the business cycle are summarized in Charles I. Plosser, "Understanding Real Business Cycles," and N. Gregory Mankiw, "Real Business Cycles: A New Keynesian Perspective," both in the *Journal of Economic Perspectives* 3 (Summer 1989): 51–90.

TABLE 7.2
Social Security Benefits and Earnings for a Hypothetical Male, Aged 62 (Yearly wage = $30,600; discount rate = 2%; life expectancy = 17 years)

Age of Retirement	Yearly Soc. Sec. Benefit*	Present Value† of Remaining Lifetime:		
		Earnings	Soc. Sec. Benefits	Total
62	$9,816	$ 0	$140,290	$140,290
63	10,728	30,000	142,810	172,810
64	11,544	59,410	142,570	201,980
65	12,372	88,250	141,140	229,390
66	13,056	116,520	136,880	253,400
67	13,728	144,230	131,490	275,720
68	14,412	171,400	125,250	296,650
69	15,096	198,040	118,050	316,090
70	15,768	224,160	109,850	334,010

*Source: Hay/Huggins Company, *1995 Social Security Summary* (Philadelphia: Hay/Huggins Company, Inc., 1995), Tables IV, XVII.
†Present values calculated as of age 62. All dollar values are as of 1995.

of retirement. For the sake of illustration, we discuss the retirement incentives facing a 62-year-old male who has earned, and can continue to earn, $30,600 per year (in 1995 dollars), as shown in Table 7.2. To further simplify our discussion, we assume this man has no pension other than that provided by Social Security and that, for him, retirement means the cessation of all paid work.

The retirement incentives facing this worker are related to three basic factors: (a) the present value of income available to him over his remaining life expectancy if he retires at age 62; (b) the *change* in this sum if retirement is delayed; and (c) preferences regarding household time and the goods one can buy with money. As we will show below, in terms of the labor supply analyses in this chapter and Chapter 6, factor (a) is analogous to nonlabor income, and factor (b) is analogous to the wage rate.

Table 7.2 summarizes the present value (at age 62) of pension and earned income available to our hypothetical worker at each possible retirement age, up to age 70. If he retires at age 62, the present value of income over his remaining life expectancy is $140,290. If he delays retirement until age 63, the present value of his remaining lifetime income rises by $32,520, to $172,810. Note from the second and third columns that delaying retirement from age 62 to 63 increases the present value of both lifetime earnings *and* Social Security benefits. Delays after age 63, however, are implicitly "penalized" by reductions in lifetime Social Security benefits; yearly pension benefits rise, but not by enough to offset the reduced number

FIGURE 7.6

Choice of Optimum Retirement Age for Hypothetical Male Worker (based on data in Table 7.2)

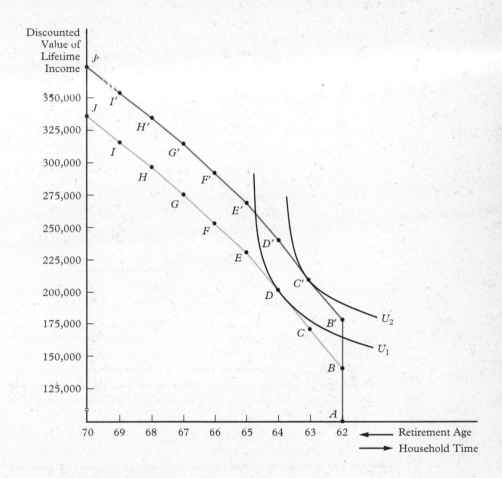

of years such benefits will be received. For example, despite causing a $684 increase in yearly pension benefits, the present value of Social Security benefits falls by $4,260 if one delays retirement from age 65 to 66.

The data in the last column of Table 7.2 are presented graphically in Figure 7.6 as budget constraint *ABJ*. Segment *AB* represents the present value of lifetime income if our worker retires at age 62 and, as such, represents "nonlabor" income. The slope of segment *BC* represents the $32,520 increase in lifetime income (to $172,810) if retirement is delayed to age 63, and the slopes of the other segments running from points *B* to *J* similarly reflect the increases in discounted lifetime income associated with delaying retirement by a year. These slopes, therefore, represent the yearly "effective wage." The slight concavity of *BJ* reflects the successively smaller increments to lifetime income from delaying retirement after age 63.

Given preferences summarized by curve U_1, the optimum age of retirement for our hypothetical worker is age 64. How would his optimum age of retirement change if Social Security benefits were increased?[16] The answer depends on how the increases are structured. If the benefit increases were such that a fixed amount was unexpectedly added to lifetime benefits at each retirement age, the constraint facing our 62-year-old male would shift up (and out) to *AB'J'*.[17] The slopes along the segments between *B'* and *J'* would remain parallel to those along *BJ*; thus, there would be an income effect with no substitution effect (that is, no change in the yearly effective wage). The optimum age of retirement would be unambiguously reduced, as shown in Figure 7.6.[18]

Alternatively, if Social Security benefits were to be increased by removing the implicit penalties for delaying retirement, so that the segments between *B* and the vertical axis became more steeply sloped, both an income and a substitution effect would be present. Greater lifetime wealth would move our hypothetical worker in the direction of earlier retirement, but a higher effective wage from working an extra year would push toward delay. While the effects on retirement age could not be predicted by theory alone, there is some empirical evidence that the substitution effect would dominate.[19]

Our graphic model of the retirement decision emphasizes that this decision is a function of both preferences for household time and the budget constraint facing an individual over his or her remaining lifetime. Changes in Social Security benefits, of course, alter the budget constraint, but they are only one of the factors that do so. There are two other factors that have had important effects on older (especially male) workers' lifetime budget constraints in recent years. First, as we will

[16]The analysis in this section borrows heavily from Olivia S. Mitchell and Gary S. Fields, "The Effects of Pensions and Earnings on Retirement: A Review Essay," *Research in Labor Economics*, vol. 5, ed. Ronald Ehrenberg (Greenwich, Conn.: JAI Press, 1982), 115–155.

[17]Our example is of an *unanticipated* benefit increase, because as noted in the prior section, *expected* benefit increases might not change our worker's projection of his lifetime wealth and thus might not alter his retirement decision. As a practical matter, however, two studies of retirement behavior raise doubts about the extent to which expected changes in future benefits affect current decisions; see David W. Wilcox, "Social Security Benefits, Consumption Expenditures, and the Life Cycle Hypothesis," *Journal of Political Economy* 97, no. 2 (April 1989): 288–304, and Cordelia Reimers and Marjorie Honig, "The Perceived Budget Constraint Under Social Security: Evidence from Reentry Behavior," *Journal of Labor Economics* 11, no. 1, pt. 1 (1993): 184–204.

[18]For recent discussions of Social Security wealth effects, see Richard Ippolito, "Toward Explaining Earlier Retirement After 1970," *Industrial and Labor Relations Review* 43 (July 1990): 556–569; Alan B. Krueger and Jorn-Steffen Pischke, "The Effect of Social Security on Labor Supply: A Cohort Analysis of the Notch Generation," *Journal of Labor Economics* 10 (October 1992): 412–437; David M. Blau, "Labor Force Dynamics of Older Men," *Econometrica* 62, no. 1 (January 1994): 117–156; and Christopher J. Ruhm, "Secular Changes in the Work and Retirement Patterns of Older Men," *Journal of Human Resources* 30, no. 2 (Spring 1995): 362–385.

[19]Edward P. Lazear, "Retirement from the Labor Force," in *Handbook of Labor Economics*, ed. Orley Ashenfelter and Richard Layard (Amsterdam: North-Holland, 1986); Alan L. Gustman, Olivia S. Mitchell, and Thomas L. Steinmeier, "The Role of Pensions in the Labor Market," *Industrial and Labor Relations Review* 47 (April 1994): 417–438; and Krueger and Pischke, "The Effect of Social Security on Labor Supply."

discuss in Chapter 14, the labor demand for men with modest educational backgrounds has fallen in the past decade or so, with the result that the real wages of such workers have been reduced. This development, by itself, tends to flatten the budget constraint—and while in theory the effects on retirement age are ambiguous, in practice the substitution effect has tended to dominate (driving men to retire earlier).[20]

Second, perhaps because of the fall in labor demand noted above and employers' related desire to induce older workers to leave, the present value of *private* pension benefits associated with early retirement changed after 1975.[21] In particular, the present value of benefits typically associated with *early* retirement was raised relative to that of retiring at the normal age of (usually) 65, which, in terms of Figure 7.6, lengthened segment *AB* while it flattened the slope of *BJ*. The combination of these effects can be confidently predicted to lower the age of retirement.

Finally, unless one lives alone, the retirement decision must be made in the context of how one's partner is allocating time. If, for example, the leisure time of each partner is complementary with that of the other, then when one partner retires the utility isoquants of the other will tend to steepen. Steeper isoquants, of course, reflect a rising marginal value of time at home, which would push toward earlier retirement of the other spouse as well.[22]

Policy Application: Child Care and Labor Supply

For many families, a critical element of what we have called "household production" is the supervision and nurture of children. Most parents are concerned about providing their children with quality care, whether this care is produced mostly in the household or is purchased to a great extent outside the home. Society at large also has a stake in the quality of care parents provide for their children. There are many forms such programs take, from tax credits for child-care services purchased by working parents to governmental subsidies for day care, school lunches, and health care. The purpose of this section is to consider the labor market implications of one type of program that is of recent origin: "child support assurance."

---

[20]Franco Peracchi and Finis Welch, "Trends in the Labor Force Transitions of Older Men and Women," *Journal of Labor Economics* 12, no. 2 (April 1994): 210–242.

[21]Edward P. Lazear, "Pensions as Severance Pay," in *Financial Aspects of the United States Pension System,* ed. Zvi Bodie and John B. Shoven, National Bureau of Economic Research Project Report (Chicago: University of Chicago Press, 1983), 57–90; Laurence J. Kotlikoff and David A. Wise, "The Incentive Effects of Private Pensions," in *Issues in Pension Economics,* ed. Zvi Bodie, John Shoven, and David Wise (Chicago: University of Chicago Press, 1987), 283–336; and Ippolito, "Toward Explaining Earlier Retirement After 1970."

[22]Alan L. Gustman and Thomas L. Steinmeier, "Retirement in a Family Context: A Structural Model for Husbands and Wives," working paper no. 4629, National Bureau of Economic Research, Cambridge, Mass., January 1994, discusses this issue and provides some early evidence on joint retirement decision making.

The vast majority of children who live in poor, single-parent households have an absent parent. The federal government has taken several steps to ensure, for families receiving welfare, that absent parents contribute adequately to their children's upbringing. Greater efforts to collect child support payments are restricted in their effectiveness by the lack of resources among some absent parents, deliberate noncompliance by others, and the lack of court-awarded child support obligations in many more cases of divorce. To enhance the resources of single-parent families, some have proposed the creation of child support assurance programs. The essential feature of these programs is a guaranteed child support benefit that would be paid by the government to the custodial parent in the event the absent parent does not make payments. If the absent parent makes only a portion of the required support payment, the government would make up the remainder.[23]

A critical question to ask about such a program is how it would affect child-rearing by the custodial parent. Remembering that decisions about household and market work are closely intertwined, it is natural to ask how child support assurance can be expected to affect the allocation of work between the market and the household. The answer provided by economic theory is not completely straightforward.

Consider a single mother who has two options for supporting herself and her children. One option is to work outside the home with no support from the absent father or from the welfare system. In Figure 7.7, we assume that the budget constraint provided by this option can be graphed as *AB*, which has a slope that represents her wage rate. The mother's other option is to apply for welfare benefits, which we assume would guarantee her an income of *AC*. The student will recall from Chapter 6 that welfare payments typically are calculated by subtracting from a family's "needed" level of income (*AC*) its actual income from other sources, including earnings. Thus, the "welfare" constraint is *ACDB*, and it can be seen that segment *CD* is reflective of a take-home wage rate equal to zero.

If the mother's utility isoquants are steeply sloped (meaning, of course, that she is less able or less willing to substitute for her time at home), her utility is maximized at point *C*; she applies for welfare and does not work for pay. If her utility isoquants are relatively flat, her utility will be maximized along segment *DB*, and in this case she works for pay and does not rely on welfare benefits to supplement her income.

Suppose, now, that a child support assurance program is adopted that guarantees support payments of *AE* to the mother, regardless of her income. If she works, the effect of the new program would be to add the amount *AE* (=*BF)* to her earnings. If she does not work and remains on welfare, her *welfare* benefits are reduced by *AE*; thus, her child support benefits *plus* her welfare benefits continue to equal

[23]Irwin Garfinkel, Philip K. Robins, Pat Wong, and Daniel R. Meyer, "The Wisconsin Child Support Assurance System: Estimated Effects on Poverty, Labor Supply, Caseloads, and Costs," *Journal of Human Resources* 25, no. 1 (Winter 1990): 1–31.

FIGURE 7.7

Budget Constraints Facing u Single Parent Before and After Child Support Assurance Program Adopted

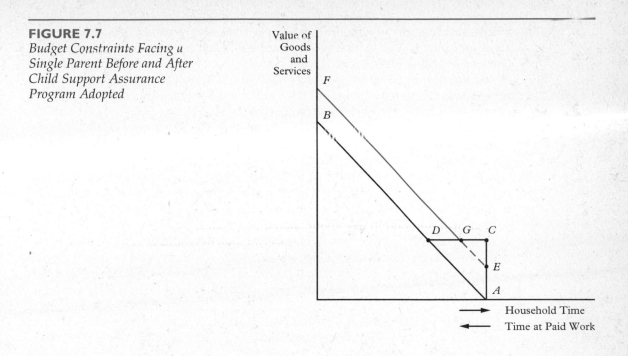

AC. After the child support assurance program is implemented, then, her budget constraint is *ACGF*.

How will the new child support programs affect the mother's time in the household and her hours of paid work? There are three possibilities. First, some mothers will have isoquants so steeply sloped that they will remain out of the labor force and spend their time in the household (they will remain at point *C* in Figure 7.7). These mothers would receive child support payments of *AE* and welfare benefits equal to *EC*.

Second, for those who worked for pay before, and were therefore along segment *DB*, the new program produces a pure income effect. These mothers will continue to work for pay, but their utility is now maximized along *GF* and they can be expected to reduce their desired hours of work outside the home.

Third, some women, like the one whose isoquants (U_1 and U_2) are shown in Figure 7.8, will move from being on welfare to seeking paid work; for these women, the supply of labor to market work increases. These women formerly maximized utility at point *C*, but the new possibility of working *and* still being able to receive an income subsidy now places their utility-maximizing hours of paid work along segment *GF*.

On balance, then, the hypothetical child support assurance program discussed above can be expected to *increase the labor force participation rate* among single mothers (and thus reduce the numbers on welfare), while *reducing the desired hours of paid work* among those who take jobs. Studies of child support assurance programs have yet to be published, but one study that analyzed the labor market

FIGURE 7.8
A Single Parent Who Joins the Labor Force After Child Support Assurance Program Adopted

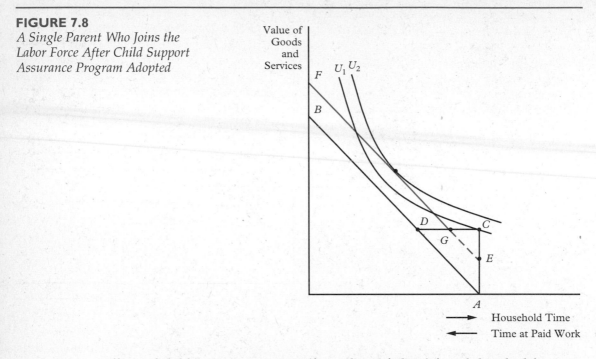

effects of child support payments (from absent fathers) found that the labor supply responses among single mothers were consistent with theoretical expectations. These responses were very small, however, which may have reflected the uncertainty many single mothers attach to the future receipt of such payments (that is, they hesitate to change their hours of paid work in most cases because they are uncertain about the continuation of support payments).[24]

REVIEW QUESTIONS

1. Suppose that 5 percent unemployment is defined as "full employment" and currently unemployment is 7 percent. Suppose further that we have the following information:

Unemployment Rate	Labor Force	Unemployment	Employment
5 percent	6,000	300	5,700
7 percent	5,600	392	5,208

   a. What is the amount of "hidden" unemployment when the unemployment rate is 7 percent?
   b. If the population is 10,000, what change occurs in the participation rate as a result of the marginal change in the unemployment rate?
   c. What is the economic significance of hidden unemployment? Should mea-

---

[24]John W. Graham and Andrea H. Beller, "The Effect of Child Support Payments on the Labor Supply of Female Family Heads," *Journal of Human Resources* 24, no. 4 (Fall 1989): 664–688. An entire issue of the *Journal of Human Resources* (vol. 27, no. 1, Winter 1992) is devoted to issues of child care.

sured and hidden unemployment be added to obtain a "total unemployment" figure?

2. Several studies have indicated that for prime-age males, the income effect of a wage increase tends to dominate the substitution effect. Other recent studies point out that hourly wages tend to rise over the early stages of the life cycle (the young receive lower wages than the middle-aged) *and* that young males tend to work fewer hours than middle-aged males, *ceteris paribus*. Employing a theory of life-cycle allocation of time, explain the apparent discrepancy.

3. In the first debate of the 1976 Presidential campaign, candidate Jimmy Carter argued, "While it is true that much of the recent rise in employment is due to the entrance of married women and teenagers into the labor force, this influx of people into the labor force is itself a sign of economic decay. The reason these people are now seeking work is because the primary breadwinner in the family is out of work and extra workers are needed to maintain the family income." Comment.

4. A recent study of the labor force participation rates of women in the post–World War II period notes:

> Over the long run women have joined the paid labor force because of a series of changes affecting the nature of work. Primary among these was the rise of the clerical and professional sectors, the increased education of women, labor-saving advances in households, declining fertility rates, and increased urbanization.

Relate each of these factors to the household production model of labor supply outlined in Chapter 7.

5. Suppose day-care centers charge working parents for each hour their children spend at the centers. Suppose, too, that the federal government passes legislation that subsidizes half of the hourly cost per child (so that the hourly cost per child now borne by the parents is cut in half). Would this policy cause an increase in the labor supply of parents with small children? Would it induce an *overall increase in labor supply?*

6. Is the following statement true, false, or uncertain? Why? "If a married woman's husband gets a raise, she tends to work less, but if *she* gets a raise, she tends to work more."

7. Suppose that, as the ratio of the working population to the retired population continues to fall, the voters approve a change in the way Social Security benefits are calculated—a way that effectively reduces every retired person's benefits by half. This change affects everyone in the population, no matter what their age or current retirement status, and it is accompanied by a 50 percent reduction in payroll taxes. What would be the labor supply effects on those workers who are very close to the typical age of retirement (62 to 65)? What would be the labor supply effects on those workers just beginning their careers (workers in their twenties, for example)?

8. Suppose that, under state law, the financial settlement in a divorce case that does not involve dependent children depends upon the economic contribution each marriage partner made up to the date of divorce. Thus, if the wife contributed half of the couple's initial assets and earned an income equal to her husband's throughout the years, she would be determined to qualify for half of the assets at the date of divorce. Based on what you have learned in Chapter 7, how could an equitable settlement be determined in the case of a woman who stayed home, raised the family's children, and never worked for pay?

9. Teenagers under age 18 in New York State are prohibited from working more than 8 hours a day, except if they work as golf caddies, babysitters, or farmworkers. Consider a 16-year-old whose primary household work in the summer is studying for college entrance exams and practicing a musical instrument, but who also has two options for paid work. She can work for $6 per hour with a catering service (limited to 8 hours per day), or work for $5 per hour as a babysitter (with no limitations on hours worked).

    a. First, draw the daily budget constraints for each of her paid-work options (assume she can work either for the catering service or as a babysitter, but cannot do both).

    b. Next, analyze the possible labor supply decisions this 16-year-old can make, making special reference to the effects of the state law restricting most paid work to 8 hours a day.

SELECTED READINGS

Becker, Gary. "A Theory of the Allocation of Time." *Economic Journal* 75 (September 1965): 493–517.

Fields, Gary S., and Mitchell, Olivia S. *Retirement, Pensions, and Social Security.* Cambridge, Mass.: MIT Press, 1984.

Ghez, G. R., and G. S. Becker. *The Allocation of Time and Goods over the Life Cycle.* New York: Columbia University Press, 1975. Chapter 3.

Gronau, Reuben. "The Measurement of Output of the Nonmarket Sector: The Evaluation of Housewives' Time." In *The Measurement of Economic and Social Performance,* ed. Milton Moss. New York: National Bureau of Economic Research, 1973. 163–189.

Layard, Richard, and Jacob Mincer, eds. *Journal of Labor Economics* 3 (January 1985, pt. 2).

Lazear, Edward P. "Retirement from the Labor Force." In *Handbook of Labor Economics,* ed. Orley Ashenfelter and Richard Layard. Amsterdam: North-Holland, 1986.

"Special Issue on Child Care." *Journal of Human Resources* 27, no. 1 (Winter 1992).

8

Compensating Wage Differentials and Labor Markets

Chapters 6 and 7 analyzed workers' decisions about *whether to seek employment* and *how long to work.* Chapters 8 and 9 will analyze workers' decisions about the industry, occupation, or firm in which they will work. This chapter will emphasize the influence on job choice of such daily, *recurring* job characteristics as the work environment, the risk of injury, and the generosity of employee benefits. The following chapter will analyze the effects of required educational *investments* on occupational choice.

This chapter contains elements of both positive and normative analysis. It begins with the (positive) theory of how worker preferences regarding the nonwage aspects of their jobs affect the allocation of labor generally and individual wages more particularly. Later, a graphical analysis of this theory is used to normatively analyze governmental regulation of both job safety and employer-provided pensions. An appendix considers the relationship between wages and the probability of being laid off from one's job.

Job Matching: The Role of Worker Preferences and Information

One of the major functions of the labor market is to provide the signals and the mechanisms by which workers seeking to maximize their utility can be matched to employers trying to maximize profits. Matching is a formidable task, because workers have varying skills and preferences and because employers offer jobs that differ in requirements and working environment. The process of finding the worker–employer pairings that are best for each is truly one of trial and error, and whether the process is woefully deficient or reasonably satisfactory is a question implicitly underlying this and the succeeding two chapters.

The assumption that workers are attempting to maximize utility implies that they are interested in both the pecuniary and the nonpecuniary aspects of their jobs. On the one hand, we expect that higher compensation levels in a job (holding job tasks constant) would attract more workers to it. The reason for this was discussed in Chapter 2. Different jobs have different tasks, and workers have different preferences concerning these duties. At a given level of pay only certain numbers of workers will be interested in a particular job, but if the level of pay were to rise, others would become attracted to it. On the other hand, it is clear from the factors just discussed that pay is not all that matters; occupational tasks and how workers' preferences mesh with those tasks are critical elements in the matching process. The focus of this chapter is on how the labor market accommodates worker preferences.

If all jobs were *exactly alike* and located in the *same place*, an individual's decision about where to seek work would be relatively simple. He or she would attempt to obtain a job in which the expected compensation was highest. Any differences in compensation would cause workers to seek work with the highest-paying employers and avoid applying for work with the low-paying ones. The high-paying employers, having an abundance of applicants, might decide they were paying more than they had to in order to staff their vacancies. The low-paying employers would have to raise their wage offers in order to compete for workers. Ultimately, if the market worked without hindrance, the compensation paid by all employers would equalize.

All jobs are not the same, however. Some jobs are in clean, modern spaces, and others are in noisy, dusty, or dangerous environments. Some permit the employee discretion over the hours or the pace of work, while others allow less flexibility. Some employers offer more generous employee-benefit packages than others, and different *places* of employment involve different commuting distances and neighborhood characteristics. We discuss below the ways that differences in job characteristics influence individual choice and observable market outcomes.

INDIVIDUAL CHOICE AND ITS OUTCOMES

Suppose several unskilled workers have received offers from two employers. Employer X pays $8 per hour and offers clean, safe working conditions. Employer Y also pays $8 per hour, but offers employment in a dirty, noisy factory. Which employer would the workers choose? Most would undoubtedly choose employer X, because the pay is the same while the job is performed under more agreeable conditions.

Clearly, however, $8 is not an equilibrium wage in both firms.[1] Because firm X finds it easy to attract applicants at $8, it will "hold the line" on any future wage increases. Firm Y, however, must clean up the plant, pay higher wages, or do both if it wants to fill its vacancies. Assuming it decides not to alter working conditions, it must pay a wage *above* $8 to be competitive in the labor market. The *extra* wage it must pay to attract workers is called a *compensating wage differential* because the higher wage is paid to compensate workers for the undesirable working conditions. If such a differential did not exist, firm Y could not attract the unskilled workers that firm X can obtain.

Suppose that firm Y raises its wage offer to $8.50 while the offer from X remains at $8.00. Will this 50-cent-per-hour differential—an extra $1,000 per year—attract *all* the workers in our group to firm Y? If it did attract them all, firm X would have an incentive to raise its wages and firm Y might want to lower its offers a bit; the 50-cent differential in this case would *not* be an equilibrium differential.

More than likely, however, the higher wage in firm Y would attract only *some* of the group to firm Y. Some people are not bothered by dirt and noise as much as others are, and these people may decide to take the extra pay and put up with the poorer working conditions. Others, however, are very sensitive to noise or allergic to dust, and they may decide that they would rather be paid less than expose themselves to such working conditions. If both firms could obtain the quantity and quality of workers they wanted, the 50-cent differential *would* be an equilibrium differential, in the sense that there would be no forces causing the differential to change.

The desire of workers to avoid unpleasantness or risk, then, should force employers offering unpleasant or risky jobs to pay higher wages than they would otherwise have to pay. Put another way, in order to attract a workforce, these employers will have to pay higher wages to their workers than firms that offer pleasant, safe jobs to comparable workers. As we discuss below, this wage differential serves two related, socially desirable ends. First, it serves a *social* need by giving people an incentive to voluntarily do dirty, dangerous, or unpleasant work. Likewise, the existence of a compensating wage differential imposes a financial penalty on employers who have unfavorable working conditions. Second, at an *individual* level, it serves as a reward to workers who accept unpleasant jobs by paying them more than comparable workers in more pleasant jobs.

THE ALLOCATION OF LABOR   Society has a number of jobs that are unavoidably nasty or that it would be very costly to make safe and pleasant (coal mining, deep-sea diving, and police work are examples). There are essentially two ways to recruit the necessary labor for such jobs. One is to compel people to do these jobs (the military draft is the most obvious contemporary example of forced labor). The second way is to induce people to do the jobs voluntarily.

---

[1]There may be a few people who really are indifferent to noise and dirt in the workplace. We assume here that these people are so rare, or firm Y's demand for workers is so large, that Y cannot fill all its vacancies with just those who are totally insensitive to dirt and noise.

Most modern societies rely mainly on incentives, compensating wage differentials, to recruit labor to unpleasant jobs voluntarily. Workers will mine coal, bolt steel beams together fifty stories off the ground, or agree to work at night because, compared to alternative jobs for which they could qualify, these jobs pay well. Night work, for example, can be stressful because it disrupts normal patterns of sleep and family interactions; however, employers often find it efficient to keep their plants and machines in operation around the clock. The result is that manufacturing production employees working night shifts are paid about 3 percent more than they would receive if they worked during the day.[2]

COMPENSATION FOR WORKERS   Compensating wage differentials also serve as *individual* rewards by paying those who accept bad or arduous working conditions more than they would otherwise receive. In a parallel fashion, those who opt for more pleasant conditions have to "buy" them by accepting lower pay (see Example 8.1). For example, if a person takes the $8.00-per-hour job with firm X, he or she is giving up the $8.50-per-hour job with less pleasant conditions in firm Y. The better conditions are being bought, in a very real sense, for 50 cents per hour.

Thus, compensating wage differentials become the prices at which good working conditions can be purchased by, or bad ones sold to, workers. Contrary to what is commonly asserted, a monetary value *can* often be attached to events or conditions whose effects are primarily psychological in nature. Compensating wage differentials provide the key to the valuation of these nonpecuniary aspects of employment.

For example, how much do workers value a work schedule that permits them to enjoy leisure activities and sleep at the usual times? If we know that night-shift workers earn 3 percent—or about $725 per year for a typical worker—more than they otherwise would earn, the reasoning needed to answer this question is straightforward. Those who have difficulty sleeping during the day, or whose favorite leisure activities require the companionship of family or friends, are not likely to be attracted to night work for only $725 extra per year; they are quite willing to forgo a $725 earnings premium to obtain a normal work schedule. Others, however, are less bothered by the unusual sleep and leisure patterns, and they are willing to work at night for the $725 premium. While some of these latter workers would be willing to give up a normal work schedule for *less* than $725, others find the decision to work at night a "close call" at the going wage differential. If the differential were to marginally fall, a few working at night would change their minds and refuse to continue, while if the differential rose a bit above $725 a few more could be recruited to night work. Thus, the $725 yearly premium represents what those "at the margin" (the ones closest to changing their minds) are willing to pay for a normal work schedule.

---

[2]Sandra L. King and Harry B. Williams, "Shift Work Pay Differentials and Practices in Manufacturing," *Monthly Labor Review* 108, no. 12 (December 1985): 26–33.

EXAMPLE 8.1

What Price Status?

The quest for status in one's job, like the consumption of other amenities, conceivably can lead to the creation of compensating wage differentials If workers are concerned about status, firms that are prestigious should find it easier to attract workers than their less prestigious counterparts. The ease with which internationally acclaimed universities, for example, can attract and retain professors suggests that they can recruit them at lower salaries than their less prestigious counterparts would have to pay.

The status conferred by one's job, then, becomes part of one's compensation package. When status is lacking, a higher wage must be paid to compensate for its absence. When high status is present, theory raises the intriguing possibility that status-seekers pay a price in the form of a lower salary than they otherwise would receive.

The trade-off between pay and status helps to explain why bureaucracies pay such keen attention to job titles and office trappings. While the title "vice president" perhaps once implied being second in command of an organization, one New York City bank is now reported to have several hundred vice presidents, fifty senior vice presidents, and ten executive vice presidents Is it cheaper for a firm to compensate valued employees if they are awarded high-sounding job titles?

Many government bureaucracies have pay ceilings that effectively eliminate monetary differentials between workers, so the most dedicated government employees must be rewarded (and retained) through other means. Government employers therefore give careful attention to status, offering a bewildering array of job titles and regulations concerning office furnishings. A "deputy undersecretary," for example, occupies a more important position in the U.S. federal hierarchy than a "deputy assistant secretary," and regulations determine both the size of office for which each qualifies and what the offices of each shall contain in terms of wooden or steel desks, types of chairs, carpeting, wastebaskets, water carafes, and plumbing.

SOURCE: For an economic analysis of status-seeking, see Robert H. Frank, *Choosing the Right Pond: Human Behavior and the Quest for Status* (New York: Oxford University Press, 1985).

ASSUMPTIONS AND PREDICTIONS

We have seen how a simple theory of job choice by individuals leads to the *prediction* that compensating wage differentials will be associated with various job characteristics. Positive differentials (higher wages) will accompany "bad" characteristics, while negative differentials (lower wages) will be associated with "good" ones. However, it is very important to understand that this prediction can *only* be made *holding other things equal.*

Our prediction about the existence of compensating wage differentials grows out of the reasonable assumption that if an informed worker has a choice between a job with "good" working conditions and a job of equal pay with "bad" working conditions, he or she will choose the "good" job. If the employee is an unskilled laborer, he or she may be choosing between an unpleasant job spreading hot asphalt or a more comfortable job in an air-conditioned warehouse. In either case, he or she is going to receive something close to the wage rate unskilled workers typically receive. However, our theory would predict that this worker would receive *more* from the asphalt-spreading job than from the warehouse job.

Thus, the predicted outcome of our theory of job choice is *not* that employees working under "bad" conditions receive more than those working under "good" conditions. The prediction is that, *holding worker characteristics constant*, employees in bad jobs receive higher wages than those working under more pleasant conditions. The characteristics that must be held constant include all the other things that influence wages: skill level, age, experience, race, gender, union status, region of the country, and so forth. Three assumptions have been used to arrive at this prediction.

ASSUMPTION 1: UTILITY MAXIMIZATION Our first assumption is that workers seek to maximize their *utility*, not their income. If workers sought to maximize income, they would always choose the highest-paying job available to them. As stated earlier, this behavior would eventually cause wages to be equalized across the jobs open to any set of workers.

In contrast, compensating wage differentials will arise only if some people do *not* choose the highest-paying job offered, preferring instead a lower-paying but more pleasant job. This behavior allows the employers offering the lower-paying, pleasant jobs to be competitive. Wages do not equalize in this case. Rather, the *net advantages*—the overall utility from the pay and the psychic aspects of the job— tend to equalize for the marginal worker.

ASSUMPTION 2: WORKER INFORMATION The second assumption implicit in our analysis is that workers are aware of the job characteristics of potential importance to them. Whether they know about them before they take the job or find out about them soon after taking it is not too important. In either case, a company offering a "bad" job with no compensating wage differential would have trouble recruiting or retaining workers, trouble that would eventually force it to raise its wage.

It is quite likely, of course, that workers would quickly learn of danger, noise, rigid work discipline, job insecurity, and other obvious bad working conditions. It is equally likely that they would *not* know the *precise* probability of being laid off, say, or of being injured on the job. However, even with respect to these probabilities, their own direct observations or word-of-mouth reports from other employees could give them enough information to evaluate the situation with some accuracy. For example, the proportions of employees considering their work dangerous have been shown to be closely related to the actual injury rates published by the government for the industries in which they work.[3] This finding illustrates that, while

---

[3] W. Kip Viscusi, "Labor Market Valuations of Life and Limb: Empirical Evidence and Policy Implications," *Public Policy* 26 (Summer 1978): 359–386. W. Kip Viscusi and Michael J. Moore, "Worker Learning and Compensating Differentials," *Industrial and Labor Relations Review* 45 (October 1991): 80–96, suggest that the accuracy of risk perceptions rises with job tenure.

workers probably cannot state the precise probability of being injured, they do form accurate judgments about the relative risks of several jobs.

Where predictions may disappoint us, however, is with respect to *very* obscure characteristics. For example, while we now know that asbestos dust is highly damaging to worker health, this fact was not widely known forty years ago. One reason information on asbestos dangers in plants was so long in being generated is that it takes more than twenty years for asbestos-related disease to develop. Cause and effect were thus obscured from workers and researchers alike, creating a situation in which job choices were made in ignorance of this risk. Compensating wage differentials for this danger thus could not possibly have arisen at that time. Our predictions about compensating wage differentials, then, hold only for job characteristics that workers know about.

ASSUMPTION 3: WORKER MOBILITY   The final assumption implicit in our theory is that workers have a range of job offers from which to choose. Without a range of offers, workers would not be able to select the combination of job characteristics they desired or avoid the ones to which they did not wish exposure. A compensating wage differential for risk of injury, for example, simply could not arise if workers were able to obtain only dangerous jobs. It is the act of choosing safe jobs over dangerous ones that forces employers offering dangerous work to raise wages.

One manner in which this choice can occur is for each job applicant to receive several job offers from which to choose. However, another way in which choice could be exercised is for workers to be (at least potentially) highly mobile. In other words, workers with few concurrent offers could take jobs and continue their search for work if they thought an improvement could be made. Thus, even with few offers at any *one* time, workers could conceivably have relatively wide choice over a *period* of time, which would eventually allow them to select jobs that maximized their utility.

While there are no general data on the number of concurrent offers a typical job applicant receives, job mobility among American workers is relatively high. One recent study, for example, found that in 1993 over 25 percent of men and women in the 25 to 34 age group had just taken a job with their employers (that is, they had been with their current employers for less than one year). Among those 35 to 44 years of age, the comparable percentages were 21 percent for women and 16 percent for men, while among 45- to 54-year-olds roughly 13 percent of both men and women had been with their employers for less than one year.[4] While some of this mobility is voluntary and some is initiated by employers, what is of significance is that a large fraction of the labor force is "in the market" at any given time.

---

[4]Henry S. Farber, "Are Lifetime Jobs Disappearing? Job Duration in the United States: 1973–1993," working paper no. 341, Industrial Relations Section, Princeton University, January 1995.

EMPIRICAL TESTS FOR COMPENSATING WAGE DIFFERENTIALS

The prediction that there are compensating wage differentials for undesirable job characteristics is over two hundred years old. Adam Smith, in his *Wealth of Nations*, published in 1776, proposed five "principal circumstances which . . . make up for a small pecuniary gain in some employments, and counterbalance a great one in others." One of these, the *constancy of employment*, is discussed in the appendix to this chapter. Another two will be discussed in other chapters: the *difficulty of learning the job* (Chapter 9) and the *probability of success* (Chapter 11). Our discussion in this chapter, while it could draw upon any of Smith's "principal circumstances" to illustrate the concept of compensating wage differentials, will focus on his assertion that *"the wages of labour vary with the ease or hardship, the cleanliness or dirtiness, the honourableness or dishonourableness of the employment."*[5]

One would think that two hundred years is a sufficient period of time over which to have accumulated substantial evidence concerning an important prediction. Unfortunately, the prediction has been seriously tested only in the past twenty years, and only in a limited way. The reasons for this lack of evidence are twofold. First, the prediction is that, *other things equal,* wages will be higher in unpleasant jobs. The prediction can be tested validly only if the researcher is able to control for the effects of age, education, gender, region, race, union status, and all the other factors that typically influence wages. Only when the effects of these factors on wages are known can the researcher filter out the *separate* influence on wages of the unpleasant or risky characteristic. Statistical procedures can control for these other factors, but these procedures require large data samples and the use of computers, and only in the past two decades have the necessary data and computers been widely available to researchers.[6]

The second problem that has hindered the empirical testing for compensating wage differentials is the problem of specifying, in advance of these tests, job characteristics that are generally regarded as disagreeable. For example, while some people dislike outdoor work and would have to be paid a premium in order to accept it, others prefer such work and dislike desk jobs. Similar observations can be made about such job characteristics as repetitiveness, chances to make decisions,

---

[5]See Adam Smith, *Wealth of Nations* (New York: Modern Library, 1937), Book I, Chapter 10. The fifth "principal circumstance" is "the small or great trust which be reposed in the workmen"; on this, see Joel Waldfogel, "The Effect of Criminal Conviction on Income and the 'Trust Reposed in the Workmen,'" *Journal of Human Resources* 29, no. 1 (Winter 1994): 62–81.

[6]The adequacy of studies in which the wage/risk relationship is inferred from a simple *cross section* of workers has been challenged by several authors on the grounds that there are many unmeasured characteristics whose omission from the data set could bias the results. Recent examples are Hae-shin Hwang, W. Robert Reed, and Carlton Hubbard, "Compensating Wage Differentials and Unobserved Productivity," *Journal of Political Economy* 100 (August 1992): 835–858, and W. S. Siebert and X. Wei, "Compensating Wage Differentials for Workplace Accidents: Evidence for Union and Nonunion Workers," *Journal of Risk and Uncertainty* 9, no. 1 (July 1994): 61–76. Some authors propose the use of longitudinal data in which two or more observations on each worker are recorded, permitting unmeasured, person-specific characteristics to be controlled for. See, for example, Greg Duncan and Bertil Holmlund, "Was Adam Smith Right After All? Another Test of the Theory of Compensating Wage Differentials," *Journal of Labor Economics* 1 (October 1983): 366–379.

and amount of physical exertion. Tests of the theory require selecting job characteristics on which there is widespread agreement about what is "good" or "bad" at
the margin.

Some of the earliest tests for the existence of compensating wage differentials
were done with respect to the risks of injury or death on the job, primarily because
higher levels of such risks are unambiguously "bad." These studies are generally,
but not completely, supportive of the theory. Studies using comparative data on
the risks of fatal injury in various *industries* tend to find that, other things equal,
wages are higher in more-risky environments. These studies generally find, for example, that wages are one-half to 2 percent higher for workers in industries having the average risk of job fatalities (about 1 in 10,000 per year) than for
comparable workers in industries with half that level of risk.[7] If the death risk data
are collected and correlated with wages by *occupation* instead of industry, however,
the theory finds less support.[8]

Many other studies of compensating wage differentials have been done, but because they are spread thinly across a variety of job characteristics, judging the
strength of their support for the theory is problematic. Nonetheless, positive wage
premiums have been related, holding other influences constant, to such disagreeable characteristics as longer work hours, intense and inflexible work schedules,
and jobs located in places that are unpleasant, dangerous, expensive, or necessitate
a long commute from home (see Example 8.2).[9] Similarly, wage rates appear
higher, other thing equal, when job security is lower; however, as discussed in the
appendix to this chapter, the relationship between wages and the probability of
layoff is complex.

Hedonic Wage Theory and the Risk of Injury

Having presented the general concepts and assumptions behind the theory of
compensating wage differentials, and having briefly reviewed empirical evidence
relating to unfavorable job characteristics, we now turn to a graphic presentation

---

[7]For a recent review that summarizes previous studies, see W. Kip Viscusi, "The Value of Risks to Life
and Health," *Journal of Economic Literature* 31, no. 4 (December 1993): 1912–1946.

[8]J. Paul Leigh, "No Evidence of Compensating Wages for Occupational Fatalities," *Industrial Relations*
30 (Fall 1991): 382–395; however, for different results see Jean-Michel Cousineau, Robert Lacroix, and
Anne-Marie Girard, "Occupational Hazard and Wage Compensating Differentials," *Review of Economics
and Statistics* 73 (February 1992): 166–169, and Siebert and Wei, "Compensating Wage Differentials for
Workplace Accidents."

[9]Jeff E. Biddle and Gary A. Zarkin, "Choice Among Wage-Hours Packages: An Empirical Investigation of Male Labor Supply," *Journal of Labor Economics* 7 (October 1989): 415–437; Joseph Gyourko and
Joseph Tracy, "The Importance of Local Fiscal Conditions in Analyzing Local Labor Markets," *Journal
of Political Economy* 97 (October 1989): 1208–1231; Sherwin Rosen, "The Theory of Equalizing Differences," in *Handbook of Labor Economics*, ed. Orley C. Ashenfelter and Richard Layard (New York: North-
Holland, 1986): 641–692; Mahmood Arai, "Compensating Wage Differentials Versus Efficiency Wages:
An Empirical Study of Job Autonomy and Wages," *Industrial Relations* 33, no. 2 (April 1994): 249–262;
and Timothy J. Gronberg and W. Robert Reed, "Estimating Workers' Willingness to Pay for Job Attributes
Using Duration Data," *Journal of Human Resources* 29, no. 3 (Summer 1994): 911–931.

EXAMPLE 8.2

Working on the Railroad: Making a Bad Job Good

While compensating wage differentials are difficult to measure with precision, the theory in this chapter can often find general support in "everyday" discussions of job choice. This example is based on a newspaper article about the exclusive use of Navajos by the Santa Fe Railway to repair and replace its 9,000 miles of track between Los Angeles and Chicago.

The 220 Navajos are organized into two "steel gangs." Workers do what machines cannot: pull and sort old spikes, weld the rails together, and check the safety of the new rails. The grueling work is intrinsically unappealing: jobs last for only five to eight months per year; much of the work is done in sweltering desert heat; workers must live away from their families and are housed in bunk cars with up to 16 other workers; and the remote locations can render the off-hours boring and lonely.

Two hypotheses about jobs such as these can be derived from the theory in this chapter. These hypotheses are listed below, along with supporting quotations or facts from the newspaper article.

Hypothesis 1. Companies offering unappealing jobs find it difficult to recruit and retain employees. Workers who take these jobs are the ones for whom the conditions are least disagreeable.

They had tried everyone. The Navajos were the only ones willing to be away from home, to do the work, and to do a good job.

[A Santa Fe recruiter]

Lonely? No, I never get lonely. There is nothing but Navajo here. . . . We speak the same language and understand one another. . . . It's a good job.

[A steel gang worker with 16 years' experience]

Hypothesis 2. The jobs are made appealing to the target group of workers by raising wages well above those of their alternatives.

I wish I could stay home all the time and be with my family. It's just not possible. Where am I going to find a job that pays $900 every two weeks?

[A steel gang veteran of 11 years]

(Steel gang wages in the early 1990s ranged between $12 and $17 per hour, well above the national average of about $10 per hour for "handlers and laborers.")

SOURCE: Paula Moñarez, "Navajos Keep Rail Lines Safe," *Long Beach Independent Press-Telegram,* May 14, 1992, DI.

of the theory, which has become known as "hedonic" wage theory.[10] The graphic tools used permit additional insights into the theory and greatly clarify the normative analysis of important regulatory issues. In this section we analyze the theory of compensating wage differentials for a *negative* job characteristic, the risk of injury, and apply the concepts to a normative analysis of governmental safety regulations. The same concepts are then applied in the following section to the provi-

---

[10]The philosophy of hedonism is usually associated with Jeremy Bentham, a philosopher of the late eighteenth century who believed people always behaved in ways that they thought would maximize their happiness. The analysis that follows is adapted primarily from Sherwin Rosen, "Hedonic Prices and Implicit Markets," *Journal of Political Economy* 82 (January/February 1974): 34–55.

sion and regulation of a *desirable* job characteristic, the availability of employee benefits.

Job injuries are an unfortunate characteristic of the workplace, and injury rates vary considerably across occupations and industries. For example, while we noted that the average yearly rate of fatal injury in the American workplace is about 1 in 10,000, the rates for construction workers and truck drivers are twice and four times higher, respectively. Roughly 3 percent of American workers are injured seriously enough each year that they lose at least a day of work, but even in just the manufacturing sector these rates vary from less than 1.5 percent in petroleum plants, for example, to over 5.5 percent in the lumber industry.[11]

To simplify our analysis of compensating wage differentials for the risk of injury, we shall assume that compensating differentials for every *other* job characteristic have already been established. This assumption allows us to see more clearly the outcomes of the job selection process, and since the same analysis could be repeated for every other dimension, our conclusions are not obscured by it. To obtain a complete understanding of the job selection process and the outcomes of that process, it is necessary, as always, to consider both the employer and the employee sides of the market.

EMPLOYEE CONSIDERATIONS

Employees, it may safely be assumed, dislike the risk of being injured on the job. A worker who is offered a job for $8 per hour in a firm in which 3 percent of the workforce is injured each year would achieve a certain level of utility from that job. If the risk of injury were increased to 4 percent, holding other job characteristics constant, the job would have to pay a higher wage to produce the same level of utility (except in the unlikely event that the costs of wage loss, medical treatment, and suffering caused by the added injuries were completely covered by the firm or its insurance company after that fact).[12]

Other combinations of wage rates and risk levels could be devised that would yield the same utility as the $8/hour–3 percent risk offer. These combinations can be connected on a graph to form an indifference curve (for example, the curve U_2 in Figure 8.1). Unlike the indifference curves drawn in Chapters 6 and 7, those in Figure 8.1 slope upward because risk of injury is a "bad" job characteristic, not a

---

[11]Bureau of Labor Statistics, "National Census of Fatal Occupational Injuries, 1994," USDL-95-288, August 3, 1995, Table 3; and U.S. Bureau of Labor Statistics, "Workplace Injuries and Illnesses in 1993," USDL-94-600, December 21, 1994, Table 6.

[12]Compensating wage differentials provide for *ex ante*—"before the fact"—compensation related to injury risk. Workers can also be compensated (to keep utility constant) by *ex post*—or after-injury—payments for damages. Workers' compensation insurance provides for *ex post* payments, but these payments are typically incomplete. There is no way to compensate a worker for his or her own death, and workers' compensation does not cover the psychic costs of disfigurement due to permanent impairment. Moreover, the lost income associated with temporary impairments is not *completely* replaced by workers' compensation. Because not all injury-related losses are completely compensated *ex post*, compensating wage differentials must exist *ex ante* for worker utility to be held constant in the face of increased risk.

FIGURE 8.1

A Family of Indifference Curves Between Wages and Risk of Injury

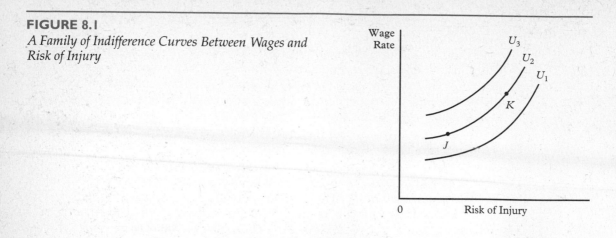

"good" (such as leisure, for example). In other words, if risk increases, wages must rise if utility is to be held constant.

As in the previous chapters, there is one indifference curve for each possible level of utility. Because a higher wage at a given risk level will generate more utility, indifference curves lying to the northwest represent higher utility.[13] Thus, all points on curve U_3 in Figure 8.1 are preferred to those on U_2, and those on U_2 are preferred to U_1. The fact that each indifference curve is convex (when viewed from below) reflects the normal assumption of diminishing marginal rates of substitution. At point K of curve U_2, the person receives a relatively high wage and faces a high level of risk. He or she will be willing to give up a lot in wages to achieve a given reduction in risk because risk levels are high enough to place one in imminent danger, and the consumption level of the goods that are bought with wages is already high. However, as risk levels and wage rates fall (to point J, say), the person becomes less willing to give up wages in return for the given reduction in risk; the danger is no longer imminent, and consumption of other goods is not as high.

People differ, of course, in their aversion to the risk of being injured. Those who are very sensitive to this risk will require large wage increases for any increase in risk, while those who are less sensitive will require smaller wage increases to hold utility constant. The sensitive workers will have indifference curves that are steeper at any level of risk than those of workers who are less sensitive, as illustrated in Figure 8.2. At risk level R_1, the slope at point C is steeper than at point D. Point C lies on the indifference curve of worker A, who is highly sensitive to risk, while point D lies on an indifference curve of a worker (B) who is less sensitive. Of

---

[13]When two "goods" were on the axes of our graphs, as in Chapters 6 and 7, indifference curves lying to the northeast represented higher levels of utility (people wanted more of each). When a "bad" is on the horizontal axis (as in Figure 8.1) and a "good" on the vertical axis, people with more of the "good" and less of the "bad" are unambiguously better off, and this combination is achieved by moving in a northwest direction on the graph.

FIGURE 8.2

Representative Indifference Curves for Two Workers Who Differ in Their Aversion to Risk of Injury

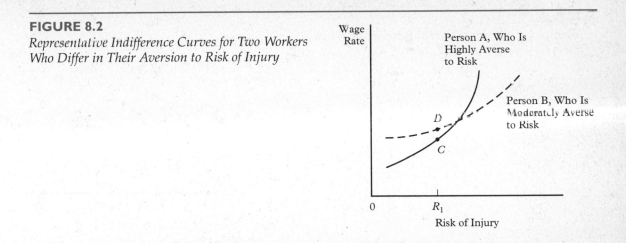

course, each person has a whole family of indifference curves that are not shown in Figure 8.2, and each will attempt to achieve the highest level of utility possible.

EMPLOYER CONSIDERATIONS

Employers are faced with a wage/risk trade-off of their own that derives from three assumptions. First, it is presumably costly to reduce the risk of injury facing employees. Safety equipment must be placed on machines, production time must be sacrificed for safety training sessions, protective clothing must be furnished to workers, and so forth. Second, competitive pressures will presumably force many firms to operate at *zero profits* (that is, at a point at which all costs are covered and the rate of return on capital is about what it is for similar investments).[14] Third, all *other* job characteristics are presumably given or already determined. The consequence of these three assumptions is that, if a firm undertakes a program to reduce the risk of injury, it must reduce wages to remain competitive.

Thus, forces on the employer side of the market tend to cause low risk to be associated with low wages and high risk to be associated with high wages, *holding other things constant*. These "other things" may be employee benefits or other job characteristics; assuming they are given will not affect the validity of our analysis (even though it may seem at first unrealistic). The major point is that if a firm spends *more on safety*, it must spend *less on other things* if it is to remain competitive.[15] The term *wages* can thus be thought of as shorthand for "terms of employment" in our theoretical analyses.

---

[14]If returns are permanently below normal, it would benefit the owners to close down the plant and invest their funds elsewhere. If returns are above normal, investors will be attracted to the industry and profits will eventually be driven down by increased competition.

[15]We *could* focus on the trade-off between safety and employee benefits or safety and other working conditions, because certainly our theory would predict that such trade-offs exist. However, we choose to focus on the *wage* trade-off because wages are easy to measure and form the largest component of compensation.

FIGURE 8.3

A Family of Isoprofit Curves for an Employer

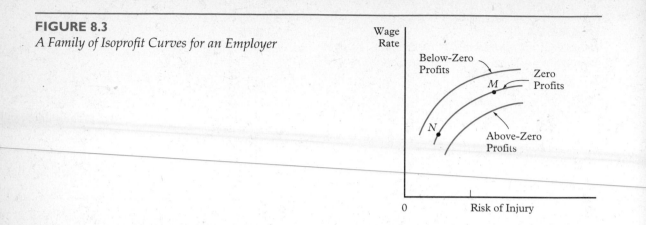

The employer trade-offs between wages and levels of injury risk can be graphed through the use of *isoprofit curves,* which show the various combinations of risk and wage levels that yield a given level of profits (*iso-* means "equal"). Thus, all the points along a given curve, such as those depicted in Figure 8.3, are wage/risk combinations that yield the *same* level of profits. Curves to the southeast represent higher profit levels because with all other items in the employment contract given, each risk level is associated with a *lower* wage level. Curves to the northwest represent, conversely, lower profit levels.

Note that the isoprofit curves in Figure 8.3 are concave (from below). This concavity is a graphic representation of our assumption that there are diminishing marginal returns to safety expenditures. Suppose, for example, that the firm is operating at point *M* in Figure 8.3, a point where the risk of injury is high. The first expenditures by the firm to reduce risk will have a relatively high return, because the firm will clearly choose to attack the safety problem by eliminating the most obvious and cheaply eliminated hazards. Because the risk (and accompanying cost) reductions are relatively large, the firm need not reduce wages by very much to keep profits constant. Thus, the isoprofit curve at point *M* is relatively flat. At point *N*, however, the curve is steeply sloped, indicating that wages will have to be reduced by quite a bit if the firm is to maintain its profits in the presence of a program to reduce risk. This large wage reduction is required because, at this point, further increases in safety are very costly; all the easy-to-solve safety problems have been dealt with.

We also assume that employers differ in the ease (cost) with which they can eliminate hazards. We have just indicated that the cost of reducing risk levels is reflected in the *slope* of the isoprofit curve. In firms where injuries are costly to reduce, large wage reductions will be required to keep profits constant in the face of a safety program; the isoprofit curve in this case will be steeply sloped. The isoprofit curve of one such firm is shown as the dashed curve *YY′* in Figure 8.4. The isoprofit curves of firms where injuries are easier to eliminate are flatter. Note that the solid curve *XX′* in Figure 8.4 is flatter at each level of risk than *YY′*; this indicates that firm X can reduce risk more cheaply than firm Y.

FIGURE 8.4
The Zero-Profit Curves of Two Firms

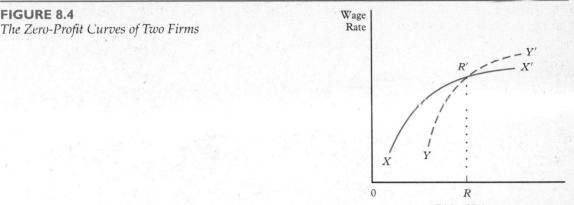

THE MATCHING OF EMPLOYERS AND EMPLOYEES

The aim of employees is to achieve the highest possible utility from their choice of a job. If they receive two offers at the same wage rate, they will choose the lower-risk job. If they receive two offers in which the risk levels are equal, they will accept the offer with the higher wage rate. More generally, they will choose the offer that falls on the highest, or most northwest, indifference curve.

In obtaining jobs, employees are constrained by the offers they receive from employers. Employers, for their part, are constrained by two forces. On the one hand, they cannot make outrageously lucrative offers because they will be driven out of business by firms whose costs are lower. On the other hand, if their offered terms of employment are very low, they will be unable to attract employees (who will choose to work for other firms). These two forces compel firms in competitive markets to operate on their zero-profit isoprofit curves.

To better understand the offers firms make, refer to Figure 8.4, where two different firms are depicted. Firm X, the firm that can cheaply reduce injuries, can make higher wage offers at low levels of risk (left of point R') than can firm Y. Because it can produce safety (reduce risk) more cheaply, it can pay higher wages at low levels of risk and still remain competitive. Any point along segment XR' will be preferred by employees to any point along YR' because, for given levels of risk, higher wages are paid.

At higher levels of risk, however, firm Y can outbid firm X for employees. Firm X does not save much money if it permits the risk level to rise above R, because risk reduction is so cheap. Because firm Y *does* save itself a lot by operating at levels of risk beyond R (it may be a sawmill where risk reduction is prohibitively costly), it is willing to pay relatively high wages at high risk levels. Since offers along $R'Y'$ will be preferable to those along $R'X'$—again, because higher wages at any level of risk are paid by firm Y—employees working at high-risk jobs will work for Y.

Graphing worker indifference curves and employer isoprofit curves together can show which workers choose which offers. Figure 8.5 contains the zero-profit curves of two employers (X and Y) and the indifference curves of two employees

FIGURE 8.5
Matching Employers and Employees

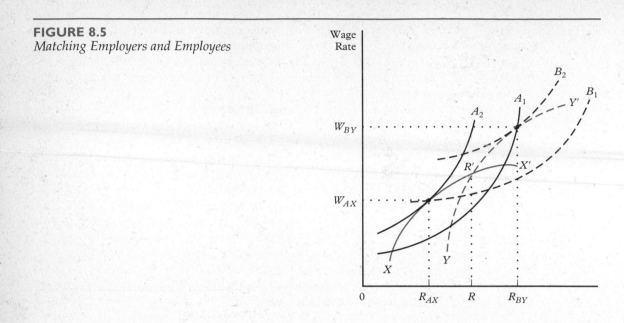

(A and B). Employee A maximizes utility (along A_2) by working for employer X at wage W_{AX} and risk level R_{AX}, while person B maximizes utility by working for employer Y at wage W_{BY} and risk level R_{BY}.

Looking at A's choice more closely, we see that if he or she took the offer B accepted—W_{BY} and R_{BY}—the level of utility achieved would be A_1, which is less than A_2. Person A values safety very highly, and wage W_{BY} is just not high enough to compensate for the high level of risk. Person B, whose indifference curves are flatter (signifying he or she is less averse to risk), finds the offer of W_{BY} and R_{BY} on curve B_2 superior to the offer A accepts. Person B is simply not willing to take a cut in pay to W_{AX} in order to reduce risk from R_{BY} to R_{AX}, because that would place B on curve B_1.

The matching of A with firm X and B with firm Y is thus not accidental or random. Firm X can generate safety relatively cheaply and does not reduce cost much by operating at high risk levels. Since X can "produce" safety more cheaply than Y, it is logical that X will be a low-risk producer who attracts employees, like A, who value safety highly. Likewise, employer Y generates a lot of cost savings by operating at high risk levels and can thus afford to pay high wages and still be competitive. Y attracts people like B, who have a relatively strong preference for money wages and a relatively weak preference for safety. Firm Y, then, has a comparative advantage (over X) in offering high-risk, high-paying jobs.

THE OFFER CURVE   The above job-matching process, of course, can be generalized beyond the case of two employees and two employers. To do this it is helpful to note that in Figures 8.4 and 8.5, the only offers of jobs to workers with a chance of being accepted lie along $XR'Y'$. The curve $XR'Y'$ can be called an "offer curve," because only along *XR'Y'* will offers employers can afford to make be potentially acceptable to employees. The concept of an offer curve is useful in generalizing our discussion beyond two firms, because a single offer curve can summarize the potentially acceptable offers any number of firms in a particular labor market can make.

Consider, for example, Figure 8.6, which contains the zero-profit isoprofit curves of firms L through Q. We know from our discussions of Figures 8.4 and 8.5 that employers will accept offers along only the most northwest segments of this set of curves; to do otherwise would be to accept a lower wage at each level of risk. Thus, the potentially acceptable offers will be found along the darkened curve of Figure 8.6, which we shall call the offer curve. The more types of firms there are in a market, the smoother this offer curve will be; however, it will always slope upward because of our twin assumptions that risk is costly to reduce and that employees must be paid higher wages to keep their utility constant if risk is increased. In some of the examples that follow, the offer curve is used to summarize the feasible, potentially acceptable offers employers are making in a labor market, because using an offer curve saves our diagrams from becoming cluttered with the isoprofit curves of many employers.

MAJOR BEHAVIORAL INSIGHTS From the perspective of "positive economics," our hedonic model generates two major insights. The first is that wages rise with risk, other things equal. According to this prediction, there will be compensating wage differentials for job characteristics that are viewed as undesirable by workers whom employers must attract (see Example 8.3). Second, workers with strong preferences for safety will tend to take jobs in firms where safety can be

---

FIGURE 8.6
An Offer Curve

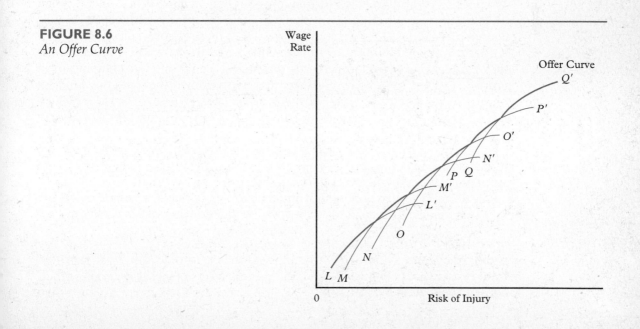

generated most cheaply. They thus tend to seek out and accept safer, lower-paying jobs. Workers who are not as averse to accepting risk will seek out and accept the higher-paying, higher-risk jobs offered by firms that find safety costly to "produce." The second insight, then, is that the job-matching process—if it takes place under the conditions of knowledge and choice—is one in which firms and workers offer and accept jobs in a fashion that makes the most of their strengths and preferences.

NORMATIVE ANALYSIS: OCCUPATIONAL SAFETY AND HEALTH REGULATION

The hedonic analysis of wages in the context of job safety can be normatively applied to government regulation of workplace safety. In particular, we now have the conceptual tools to analyze such questions as the *need* for regulation and, if needed, what the *goals* of the regulation should be.

ARE WORKERS BENEFITED BY THE REDUCTION OF RISK?   In 1970 Congress passed the Occupational Safety and Health Act, which directed the U.S. Department of Labor to issue and enforce safety and health standards for all private employers. Safety standards are intended to reduce the risk of traumatic injury, while health standards address worker exposure to substances thought to cause disease. The stated goal of the act was to ensure the "highest degree of health and safety protection for the employee."[16]

Despite the *ideal* that employees should face the minimum possible risk in the workplace, implementing this ideal as social *policy* is not necessarily in the best interests of workers. Our hedonic model can show that reducing risk in some circumstances will lower the workers' utility levels. Consider Figure 8.7.

Suppose a labor market is functioning about like our textbook models, in that workers are well-informed about dangers inherent in any job and are mobile enough to avoid risks they do not wish to take. In these circumstances, wages will be positively related to risk (other things equal), and workers will sort themselves into jobs according to their preferences. This market can be modeled graphically in Figure 8.7, where, for simplicity's sake, we have assumed there are two kinds of workers and two kinds of firms. Person A, who is very averse to the risk of injury, works at wage W_{AX} and risk R_{AX} for employer X. Person B works for employer Y at wage W_{BY} and risk R_{BY}.

Now suppose the Occupational Safety and Health Administration (OSHA), the Department of Labor agency responsible for implementing the federal safety and health program, promulgates a standard that, in effect, says that risk levels above R_{AX} are illegal. The effects, although unintended and perhaps not immediately obvious, would be detrimental to employees like B. Reducing risk is costly, and the

---

[16]For an assessment of the extent to which the act's goals have actually been met, see Robert S. Smith, "Have OSHA and Workers' Compensation Made the Workplace Safer?" in *Research Frontiers in Industrial Relations,* ed. David Lewin, Olivia Mitchell, and Peter Sherer (Madison, Wis.: Industrial Relations Research Association, 1992).

FIGURE 8.7

The Effects of Government Regulation in a Perfectly Functioning Labor Market

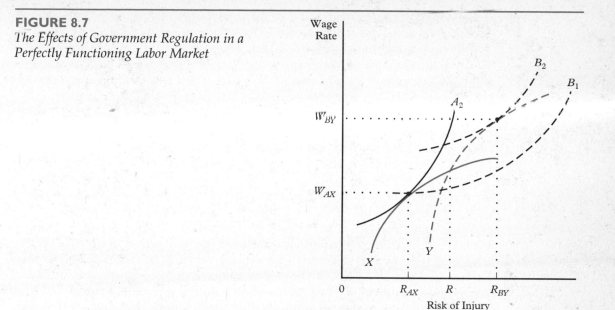

best wage offer a worker can obtain at risk R_{AX} is W_{AX}. For B, however, wage W_{AX} and risk R_{AX} generate *less utility* than did Y's offer of W_{BY} and R_{BY}. Figure 8.7 shows that X's offer of W_{AX} and R_{AX} lies on indifference curve B_1, whereas Y's old (now illegal) offer was on the higher curve B_2.

When the government mandates the reduction of risk in a market where workers are compensated for the risks they take, it penalizes workers like B, who are not terribly sensitive to risk and appreciate the higher wages associated with higher risk. The critical issue, of course, is whether workers have the knowledge and choice necessary to generate compensating wage differentials. Many people believe that workers are uninformed, unable to comprehend different risk levels, or immobile, and thus that most do not choose risky jobs voluntarily. If this belief were true, government regulation *could* make workers better off. Indeed, while the evidence of a positive relationship between wages and risk of fatal injury should challenge the notion that information and mobility are *generally* insufficient to create compensating differentials, there are specific areas in which problems obviously exist. For example, the introduction each year of new workplace chemicals whose health effects on humans may be unknown for two or more decades (owing to the long gestation periods for most cancers and lung diseases) clearly presents substantial informational problems to affected labor market participants.

To say that worker utility *can* be reduced by government regulation does not, then, imply that it *will* be reduced. The outcome depends on how well the unregulated market functions and how careful the government is in setting its standards for risk reduction. The following section will analyze a government program implemented in a market that has *not* generated enough information about risk for employees to make informed job choices.

HOW STRICT SHOULD OSHA STANDARDS BE?   Consider a labor market, like that mentioned previously for asbestos workers, in which ignorance or worker immobility hinders labor market operation. Let us suppose also that the government becomes aware of the health hazard involved and wishes to set a standard regulating worker exposure to this hazard. How stringent should this standard be?

The crux of the problem in standard-setting is that reducing hazards is costly; the greater the reduction, the more it costs. While businesses bear these costs initially, they ultimately respond to them by cutting costs elsewhere and raising prices (to the extent that cutting costs is not possible). Since labor costs constitute the largest cost category for most businesses, it is natural for firms facing large government-mandated hazard reduction costs to hold the line on wage increases or to adopt policies that are the equivalent of reducing wages: speeding up production, being less lenient with absenteeism, reducing employee benefits, and so forth. It is also likely, particularly in view of any price increases (which, of course, tend to reduce product demand), that employment will be cut back. Some of the job loss will be in the form of permanent layoffs that force workers to find other jobs—jobs they presumably could have had before the layoff but chose not to accept. Some of the loss will be in the form of cutting down on hiring new employees who would have regarded the jobs as their best employment option.

Thus, whether in the form of smaller wage increases, more difficult working conditions, or inability to obtain or retain one's first choice in a job, the costs of compliance with health standards will fall on employees. Employees will bear these costs in ways that reduce their earnings below what they *would have been in the absence of OSHA.* These losses may not be immediate or very obvious, since it is hard to know what wages would have been without the OSHA standard. However, the fact that this outcome of government regulation is masked does not justify ignoring it. A graphic example can be used to make an educated guess about whether worker utility will be enhanced or not as a result of the increased protection from risk mandated by an OSHA health standard.

Figure 8.8 depicts a worker who believes she has taken a low-risk job, when in fact she is exposing herself to a hazard that has a relatively high probability of damaging her health in twenty years. She receives a wage of W_1 and *believes* she is at point J, where the risk level is R_1 and the utility level is U_1. Instead, she is in fact at point K, receiving W_1 for accepting (unknowingly) risk level R_2; she would thus experience lower utility (indifference curve U_0) if she knew the extent of the risk she was taking.

Suppose now that the government discovers that her job is highly hazardous. The government could simply inform the affected workers and let them move to other work. However, if it has little confidence in the ability of workers to understand the information or to find other work, the government could pass a standard that limits employee exposure to this hazard. But what level of protection should this standard offer?

If the government forces the risk level down to R', the best wage offer the woman in our example could obtain is W' (at point D on the offer curve). Given the market, no employer would or could pay her more at risk level R', other things equal. Point

FIGURE 8.8
A Worker Accepting Unknown Risk

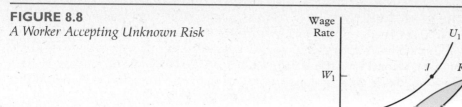

D, however, lies on indifference curve U', which represents a lower level of utility than she is in fact getting now (U_0). She would be worse off under the government-imposed standard. On the other hand, if the government forced risk levels down to a level between R_0 and R_2, she would be better off because she would be able to reach an indifference curve above U_0 (see shaded area of Figure 8.8).

How can one estimate, in a practical way, how much wage loss workers would be willing to bear in exchange for a reduction in risk and still feel at least as well off as they are currently? The answer lies in estimating compensating wage differentials in markets that appear to work. Suppose, in a properly functioning market, that workers facing risk level R_1—the one our hypothetical worker *thought* she was facing in Figure 8.8—accept wage cuts of $925 per year for reductions in the yearly death rate of 1 in 10,000.[17] These workers appear to feel that, other things equal, $925 is a price they are willing to pay for this reduction in risk. Thus, as noted earlier in the case of night-shift work, compensating wage differentials can be used to estimate the value workers place on seemingly intangible aspects of their jobs. The use of such differentials should not be oversold, because the difficulties of establishing which markets are properly functioning are considerable. However, estimating compensating wage differentials is probably the best way of finding out what value workers attach to various job characteristics.[18]

Since one cannot rule out the possibility—indeed, the likelihood—that one way or another workers will ultimately pay for the costs of their reduced workplace

---

[17]On page 255 it was noted that workers facing the average risk of being killed at work received up to 2 percent more than workers facing half that risk level. Since the average risk of a job fatality is about 1 in 10,000, the compensating wage differential for a complete elimination of risk can be extrapolated to 4 percent. In 1994, average yearly earnings were $23,150, and 4 percent of this sum is roughly $925.

[18]See E. J. Mishan, "Evaluation of Life and Limb: A Theoretical Approach," *Journal of Political Economy* 79, no. 4 (July/August 1971): 687–705.

EXAMPLE 8.3

Compensating Wage Differentials in 19th-Century Britain

English mill towns in the mid–1800s were often beset by violence and unhealthy living conditions. Infant deaths, a common indicator of health conditions, averaged over 200 per 1,000 live births in English towns, a rate well above those that typically prevail today in the poorest countries. Violence was also a common part of life, and corporal punishment was often used by factory supervisors against child laborers.

It is interesting, however, that the conditions varied from town to town and factory to factory. Infant mortality rates ranged from 110 to 344 per 1,000 live births in English towns in 1834, and not all factories used corporal punishment as a means of industrial discipline. These differences in conditions have led economic historians to wonder whether workers' *information* and *choices* back then were sufficient to generate compensating wage differentials for the more unpleasant or unhealthy sectors of employment.

More specifically, workers were leaving rural areas to work in towns during this era, and the towns and factories in which conditions were unhealthy would be less attractive to potential migrants. If workers had reasonably good information on health conditions and could obtain work in several places, they would tend to gravitate toward the more pleasant places. Factories in the more squalid towns, and those

that used corporal punishment, would have had to offer higher wages to compete for migrants.

While data from the 1800s are such that research results are probably only suggestive, two intriguing findings have emerged. First, it appears that once the cost of living and regional wage differences are accounted for, in areas where infant mortality rates were 10 percent greater than average, the unskilled wage was 2–3 percent higher than average. It also appears that boys who worked in factories where corporal punishment was used received wages some 16–18 percent higher than boys of the same age, experience, and literacy who worked in plants where violence was not used. (Because workers receive compensating wage differentials only if employers are willing to pay them, one must entertain the notion that the threat, and use, of corporal punishment raised productivity by 16–18 percent.)

Sources: Jeffrey G. Williamson, "Was the Industrial Revolution Worth It? Disamenities and Death in 19th-Century British Towns," *Explorations in Economic History* 19 (1982): 221–245; Clark Nardinelli, "Corporal Punishment and Children's Wages in Nineteenth Century Britain," *Explorations in Economic History* 19 (1982): 283–295. We are indebted to Professor Ronald Warren, University of Virginia, for suggesting this general topic as an example.

---

risks, economists argue strongly that the government should conduct studies to estimate whether the value workers place on risk reduction is commensurate with the costs of the program. These studies are called *benefit/cost* studies, and they weigh the costs of a program against the value workers (or other beneficiaries) attach to the benefits of reduced risk. Estimates of compensating wage differentials can be very useful in estimating these benefits.

Consider, for example, two alternative standards limiting the exposure of chemical workers to acrylonitrile, a substance used in making acrylic fibers and a certain type of resin. Exposure to acrylonitrile is believed to increase one's chances of contracting cancer; reducing worker exposure from 20 parts per million (ppm) of air to 2 ppm would reduce the yearly risk of cancer-related deaths by 8.4 per 10,000 exposed workers. We know from our estimates of compensating differentials that the *most* we can assume workers would be willing to give up to obtain this reduction in risk is about $7,770 per year.[19] Since obtaining this new level of risk would cost $6,640 per worker (per year), it is conceivable that the standard would improve worker utility if workers bore the costs.[20]

Alternatively, reducing acrylonitrile exposure to 1 ppm (from 20 ppm) would reduce death risk by 9 per 10,000 exposed workers at a yearly cost of $58,650 per worker. Given that the most workers seem willing to pay for a 9-in-10,000 reduction in risk is $8,325 per year, there is no chance that a 1-ppm standard could improve their utility if they bore the costs. Thus, while a 2-ppm standard may be worth promulgating, a 1-ppm standard would not be. Perhaps because of the high costs and small benefits, OSHA chose to set the acrylonitrile standard at 2 ppm.

JUDGING OSHA UNDER ALTERNATIVE NORMS   In our analysis of OSHA above, we argued that a safety or health standard is socially desirable only if the value workers place on risk reduction is commensurate with the costs of complying with the standard. As was shown above, the value workers place on risk reduction can be estimated, in theory at least, from knowledge of compensating wage differentials. However, even if compensating wage differentials were accurately calculated from observations in a market characterized by both widespread information and choice, there are still objections to their use in assessing the benefits of OSHA standards.

First, compensating wage differentials reflect the preferences of only those directly involved in the employer–employee contract. It is frequently argued that members of society who are not directly affected by the risk reduction program might be willing to pay *something* for the benefits that accrue to those who *are* directly affected. Presumably, this "willingness to pay" is strongest for family members, relatives, and close friends and weakest for strangers. However, even strangers would have some interest in reducing injury and disease if they were taxed to subsidize the medical treatment of those who are injured or become ill. Thus, it is argued, the benefits of OSHA standards extend beyond the direct beneficiaries to other external parties whose willingness to pay should also be counted.

The major issue for policymaking is not whether these external benefits exist, but how large they are and whether they are already included in the willingness to pay of those directly benefited by an OSHA standard. For example, one could plausibly argue that a worker's *family* might be heavily involved in his or her choice of jobs so that compensating wage differentials *already* reflect family

---

[19]This figure is obtained by multiplying the upper estimate of $925 for a 1-in-10,000 reduction by 8.4.

[20]This analysis is based on data reported in James Miller, "Occupational Exposure to Acrylonitrile," statement before the Occupational Safety and Health Administration on behalf of Vistron Corporation, Washington, D.C., 1978. Cost estimates were converted to current dollars using the Consumer Price Index.

preferences. Put differently, the opinions and preferences of family members and close relatives *could* affect the indifference curves of the workers directly at risk and thus play a role in determining what jobs such workers choose at what wages. To date, no research has addressed this issue.

Also unclear at present is the degree to which medical care for job-related injuries and illnesses is subsidized by parties who are not direct beneficiaries of an OSHA standard. Workers' compensation insurance premiums, for example, are established at the *industry* level and are subject to some modification based on the experience of the individual firm in that industry; it seems unlikely that one industry's workers subsidize the medical treatment of injured workers in other industries. Since OSHA standards apply to *entire industries,* it does not appear probable that subsidies by external parties through workers' compensation are very large. However, because most occupational *illnesses* are not effectively covered by workers' compensation, treatment of those who contract a disease from their work is paid for by them, their insurance, or public subsidies (Medicare and Medicaid).[21] The likelihood that external parties subsidize the treatment of those directly at risk of occupational disease is thus very high; what is unknown at present is the magnitude of the subsidy.[22]

A second argument against using only the apparent willingness of workers to pay for risk reduction as a measure of its benefit is that workers really may not know what is best for themselves in the long run. Society frequently prohibits (or at least tries to prohibit) people from indulging in activities that are dangerous to their welfare; laws against the use of narcotics and gambling are two examples. Some argue that OSHA standards limiting exposure to dangerous substances or situations fall into the category of preventing workers from doing harm to themselves by being lured into dangerous work; therefore, it is argued that to ask how much they value risk reduction is irrelevant. The conflict between those who claim that workers know what is best for themselves and those who claim they do not can only be resolved on philosophical grounds.

However, one offshoot of the argument that workers do not know what is best for themselves deserves special mention. Some argue that worker preferences are molded by the environment in which they were raised and that there is no reason to take that environment as "given" or unchangeable. Once all workers at risk are required to wear protective clothing and equipment, and once they are prevented from taking certain risks on the job (in return for higher pay, perhaps), their attitudes and preferences will change. Not too many years ago, for example, wearing hard hats was considered "sissified," but today it is commonly accepted. Thus,

---

[21]When a worker contracts lung cancer, it is usually very difficult to tell whether the cause was job related, due to personal habits, related to residential location, or a combination of all three. Because it cannot usually be proven to be job related, workers' compensation does not apply.

[22]This lack of knowledge need not prevent us from making benefit estimates, however. We could, for example, calculate benefits in two ways: We could first assume no subsidy and use compensating wage differentials as discussed in the text. Alternatively, we could assume a 100 percent subsidy of medical costs and add to the willingness to pay implied by the compensating differentials the medical cost savings associated with the OSHA standard. These calculations would at least indicate the range into which benefits are likely to fall.

OSHA standards are regarded as an engine for changing worker, as well as employer, attitudes and behavior.

How far one wants to go in imposing present costs on workers to induce a change of attitude is a philosophical issue. We should add, however, that the value judgment underlying normative economics—that of mutual benefit, or making some better off and no one else worse off—is usually interpreted as applying to *current* (observed) preferences. Thus, the policy analyses of this text, by taking indifference curves and the current set of prices (compensating wage differentials, for example) as given, have implicitly assumed that workers know what is best for themselves.

Hedonic Wage Theory and Employee Benefits

In Table 5.2 we saw that employee benefits are now roughly 29 percent of total compensation for workers in larger firms. Over half of such benefits relate to pensions and medical insurance, both of which have grown in importance over the past thirty years and have attracted the attention of policymakers. In this section we first use hedonic theory in a *positive* mode to analyze the labor market effects of employee benefits, and then we use it in a *normative* mode to assess one aspect of an important government program that regulates privately provided pensions. As before, we begin with a consideration of both the employee and the employer sides of the market.

EMPLOYEE PREFERENCES

The distinguishing feature of most employee benefits is that they compensate workers in a form *other* than currently spendable cash. In general, there are two broad categories of such benefits. First are *payments in kind*—that is, compensation in the form of some commodity. As we have seen, it is very common for employers to partly or completely pay for insurance policies of one kind or another on behalf of their employees. Slightly less obvious as payments in kind are paid vacations and holidays. A woman earning $15,000 per year for 2,000 hours of work can have her hourly wage increased from $7.50 to $8.00 by either a straightforward increase in current money payments or a reduction in her working hours to 1,875 with no reduction in yearly earnings. If she receives her raise in the form of paid vacation time, she is in fact being paid in the form of a commodity: leisure time.

The second general type of employee benefit is *deferred compensation*, compensation that is earned now but will be paid in the form of money later on. Employer contributions to employee pension plans make up the largest proportion of these benefits.

PAYMENTS IN KIND   It is a well-established tenet of economic theory that, *other things equal*, people would rather receive $X in cash than a commodity that costs $X. The reason is simple. With $X in cash the person can choose to buy the particular commodity or choose instead to buy a variety of other things. Cash is thus the form of payment that gives the recipient the most discretion and the most options in maximizing utility. In-kind payments are inherently more restrictive, and while they generate utility, they do not ordinarily generate as much as cash payments of equal monetary value.

As might be suspected, however, "other things" are not equal. Specifically, such in-kind payments as employer-provided health insurance offer employees a sizable tax advantage because, for the most part, they are not taxable under current income tax regulations. The absence of a tax on important in-kind payments is a factor that tends to offset their restrictive nature. A worker may prefer $1,000 in cash to $1,000 in some in-kind payment, but if his or her income tax and payroll-tax rates total 25 percent, the comparison is really between $750 in cash and $1,000 in the in-kind benefit.

DEFERRED COMPENSATION   Like payments in kind, deferred compensation schemes enjoy a tax advantage over current cash payments. In the case of pensions, for example, employers contribute currently to a pension fund, but employees do not obtain access to this fund until they retire. Neither the pension fund *contributions* made on behalf of employees by employers nor the *interest* that compounds when these funds are invested is subject to the personal income tax. Only when the retirement benefits are received does the ex-worker pay taxes. A pension fund thus defers the taxation of part of one's compensation (the pension fund contributions) until old age and permits funds for retirement to accumulate on a tax-free basis. What one *loses* with saving for retirement through a pension fund is the ability to currently control one's assets: by putting money into a pension fund, one is forgoing the ability to use that money now for routine or emergency needs.

INDIFFERENCE CURVES   Two opposing forces are therefore at work in shaping workers' preferences for employee benefits. On the one hand, these benefits are accorded special tax treatment, a feature of no small significance when one considers that income and Social Security taxes come to well over 20 percent for most workers. On the other hand, benefits involve a loss of discretionary control over one's total compensation. The result is that if we graph worker preferences regarding cash compensation (the wage rate) and employee benefits, we would come up with indifference curves shaped generally like the one shown in Figure 8.9. When cash earnings are relatively high and employee benefits are small (point J), workers are willing to give up a lot in terms of cash earnings to obtain the tax advantages of employee benefits. However, once one's compensation is heavily weighted toward such benefits (point K), further increases in benefits reduce discretionary earnings so much that the tax advantages seem small; at point K, then, the indifference curve is flatter. Hence,

FIGURE 8.9

An Indifference Curve Between Wages and Employee Benefits

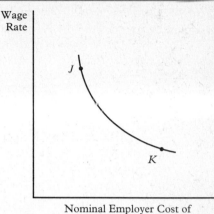

Wage Rate

J

K

Nominal Employer Cost of Employee Benefits

indifference curves depicting preferences between cash earnings and employee benefits are shaped like those in Chapters 6 and 7.[23]

EMPLOYER PREFERENCES

Suppose employers are totally indifferent about whether to spend $X on wages or $X on benefits. Both expenditures are of equal sums of money and are equally deductible as a business expense. If this is the case, the *composition* of total compensation is of no concern to them; only the *level* of compensation matters.

The easiest way to depict the willingness of a firm to offer employee benefits is through the use of isoprofit curves. Suppose a firm offers a certain type of job for which it must pay at least $X in total compensation to attract workers. Suppose also that if it paid more than $X, its profits would fall below zero. Thus, it must compensate its workers $X per year to remain competitive in both the labor and the product markets. However, if the composition of total compensation is a matter of indifference to the firm, it will be willing to offer any combination of wages and benefits that totals $X in value. The various compensation packages a firm is willing to offer fall along the zero-profit isoprofit curve drawn between wages and benefits (see Figure 8.10).

---

[23]As noted in footnote 13, the indifference curves in the prior section were *upward*-sloping because a "bad," not a "good," was on the horizontal axis. For detailed analyses of employee demand for benefits, see Stephen Woodbury and Wei-Jang Huang, *The Tax Treatment of Fringe Benefits* (Kalamazoo, Mich.: W. E. Upjohn Institute for Employment Research, 1991); Stephen Woodbury and Daniel Hamermesh, "Taxes, Fringe Benefits, and Faculty," *Review of Economics and Statistics* 74 (May 1992): 287–296; and William Gentry and Eric Peress, "Taxes and Fringe Benefits Offered by Employers," working paper no. 4764, National Bureau of Economic Research, Cambridge, Mass., 1994.

FIGURE 8.10

An Isoprofit Curve Showing the Wage/Benefit Offers a Firm Might Be Willing to Make to Its Employees: A Unitary Trade-off

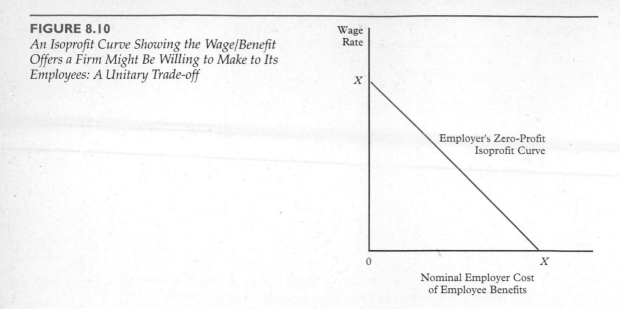

Any combination of wages and benefits along the isoprofit curve shown in Figure 8.10 would yield the firm equal profits (assuming it could recruit workers). Thus, it is willing to offer $X in wages and no employee benefits, benefits that cost (say) $300 and wages that equal $(X − 300), or any other combination totaling $X in cost. The slope of the isoprofit curve is *negative,* reflecting the fact that the firm can increase benefits only if it reduces wages (again, because of competitive pressures). Further, in this case the isoprofit curve has a slope of −1, which reflects employer indifference about the composition of compensation. If employees want a health insurance policy costing $300, it will cost them $300 in wages.

There are some reasons to expect that firms might offer benefits to their employees on something other than the dollar-for-dollar basis assumed above. For one, by increasing compensation in the form of benefits rather than wages, employers can often avoid taxes and required insurance payments that are levied *on them* as a fraction of payroll. Social Security taxes and workers' compensation premiums are examples of employer costs that generally increase with salaries and wages but not with employee benefits, thus making it more costly for an employer to increase compensation by increasing salaries than by increasing benefits. Illustrated by line *A* in Figure 8.11, payroll taxes tend to flatten the isoprofit curve (a $300 increase in benefits could be accompanied by a reduction in wages of perhaps only $280, and the firm would be equally profitable).

There are also more subtle factors that might cause firms to offer benefits to their employees on something other than the dollar-for-dollar basis in Figure 8.10. Some benefits allow firms to attract a certain kind of worker in situations in which the use of wage rates would be of questionable legal validity. For example, suppose a firm prefers to hire mature adults, preferably those with children, in the hopes of acquiring a stable, dependable workforce. Attempting to attract these

FIGURE 8.11

Alternative Isoprofit Curves Showing the
Wage/Benefit Offers a Firm Might Be Willing to
Make to Its Employees: Nonunitary Trade-offs

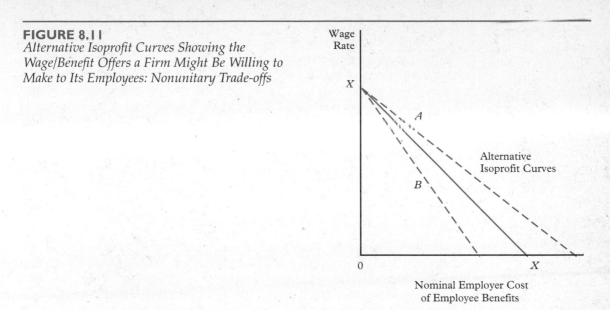

people by offering them higher wages than it offers to single, younger, or much older adults would risk charges of discrimination. Instead, the firm can accomplish the same effect by offering its employees benefits that are of much more value to the group it is trying to attract than to others. For example, offering *family coverage* under a health insurance plan has the effect of compensating those with families more than others because single or childless people cannot really take advantage of the full benefit. Offering dental insurance covering orthodontia or tuition assistance for children who attend college accomplishes similar purposes. Because offering these benefits allows firms to hire the workers it wants more effectively, a $300 increase in benefits could be accompanied by a less than $300 reduction in wages to keep profits constant.

While some benefits tend to flatten the isoprofit curve, others steepen it (line *B* in Figure 8.11 suggests that a $300 increase in these other benefits would have to be accompanied by a decrease in wages of more than $300). For example, some benefits could conceivably increase absenteeism, thus reducing the firm's profitability. Life insurance, health insurance, and pensions, for instance, are all awarded to current employees regardless of their actual hours of work during the year (assuming they work enough to keep their jobs). If an increase in compensation comes in the form of increasing one of these benefits, workers' *incomes* are increased in the sense that they need to save less for "rainy days" and are thus freer to spend their cash income. However, this enhancement of income is accomplished without an increase in the price of leisure because the hourly wage has not risen. Recall from Chapter 6 that increased income with no change in the price of leisure causes people to want to work less. In this case workers will not quit their jobs, but they may be absent from work more often. The connection between absenteeism and an employee benefit is even more obvious in the case of paid sick leave. Thus, the payment of certain types of employee benefits may indirectly impose *other* costs on the employer, which steepens the slope of the relevant isoprofit curve.

The major point of our analysis of benefits from the employer's perspective is that a dollar spent on benefits could cost employers more or less than a dollar nominally spent on wages or salaries. When benefits enhance productivity more or increase costs less than a similar expenditure on wages would, the isoprofit curve (*XX*) in Figure 8.10 will flatten. Figure 8.11 showed this as isoprofit curve *A*. When benefits increase other costs or reduce productivity, the isoprofit curve will steepen. In this case (curve *B* in Figure 8.11) a $300 benefit would have to be accompanied by a $320 fall in wages, say, to keep profits constant.[24]

THE JOINT DETERMINATION OF WAGES AND BENEFITS

The offer curve in a particular labor market can be obtained by connecting the relevant portions of each firm's zero-profit isoprofit curve. When all firms have isoprofit curves with a slope of −1, the offer curve is a straight line with a negative and unitary slope. One such offer curve is illustrated in Figure 8.12, and the only difference between this curve and the zero-profit isoprofit curve in Figure 8.10 is that the latter traced out *hypothetical* offers *one* firm could make, while this one traces out the *actual* offers made by *all* firms in this labor market. Of course, if firms have isoprofit curves whose slopes are different from −1, the offer curve will not look exactly like that depicted in Figure 8.12. Whatever its shape or the absolute value of its slope at any point, however, it will slope downward.

Employees, then, face a set of wage/benefit offers that imply the necessity for making trade-offs. Those employees (like worker Y in Figure 8.12) who attach relatively great importance to the availability of currently spendable cash will choose to accept offers in which total compensation is largely in the form of wages. Employees who may be less worried about current cash income but more interested in the tax advantages of benefits will accept offers in which employee benefits form a higher proportion of total compensation (see the curve for worker Z in Figure 8.12). Thus, employers will tailor their compensation packages to suit the preferences of the workers they are trying to attract. If their employees tend to be young or poor, for example, their compensation packages may be heavily weighted toward wages and include relatively little in the way of pensions and insurance. Alternatively, if they are trying to attract people in an area where family incomes are high and hence employee benefits offer relatively large tax savings, firms may offer packages in which benefits constitute a large proportion of the total.

---

[24]See Steven G. Allen, "Compensation, Safety, and Absenteeism: Evidence from the Paper Industry," *Industrial and Labor Relations Review* 34 (January 1981): 207–218, and also his "An Empirical Model of Work Attendance," *Review of Economics and Statistics* 63 (February 1981): 77–87. For evidence on teacher absenteeism, see Ronald G. Ehrenberg, et al., "School District Leave Policies, Teacher Absenteeism, and Student Achievement," *Journal of Human Resources* 26 (Winter 1991): 72–105.

FIGURE 8.12

Market Determination of the
Mix of Wages and Benefits

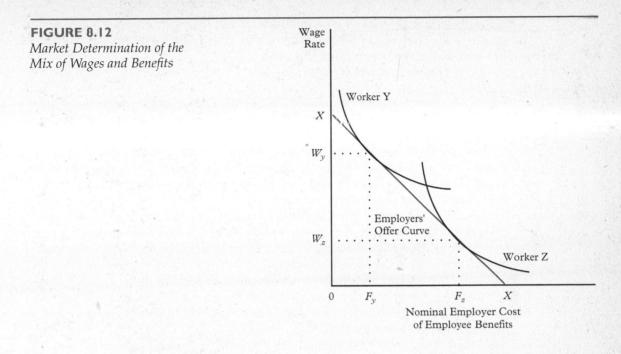

Figure 8.12 shows that workers receiving more generous benefits pay for them by receiving lower wages, other things being equal. Further, if employer isoprofit curves have a unitary slope, a benefit that costs the employer $1 to provide will cost workers $1 in wages. In other words, economic theory suggests that workers pay for their own benefits.

Actually observing the trade-off between wages and employee benefits is not easy. Because firms that pay high wages usually also offer very good benefits packages, it often appears to the casual observer that wages and employee benefits are *positively* related. Casual observation in this case is misleading, however, because it does not allow for the influences of *other factors,* such as the demands of the job and the quality of workers involved, that influence total compensation. The other factors are most conveniently controlled for statistically, and the few statistical studies on this subject tend to support the prediction of a negative relationship between wages and benefits.[25]

The policy consequences of a negative wage/benefits trade-off are enormously important, because government legislation designed to improve employee benefits

---

[25]For papers on pensions and wages, which have references to earlier studies, see Edward Montgomery, Kathryn Shaw, and Mary Ellen Benedict, "Pensions and Wages: An Hedonic Price Theory Approach," *International Economic Review* 33 (February 1992): 111–128, and Morley Gunderson, Douglas Hyatt, and James E. Pesando, "Wage–Pension Trade-offs in Collective Agreements," *Industrial and Labor Relations Review* 46, no. 1 (October 1992): 146–160. For a recent paper on wages and mandated insurance coverage, see Jonathan Gruber, "The Incidence of Mandated Maternity Benefits," *American Economic Review* 84, no. 3 (June 1994): 622–641.

might well be paid for by workers in the form of lower future wage increases. We thus turn now to a policy application.

POLICY APPLICATION: PENSION REFORM LEGISLATION

Pension plans provided by employers are of two general types: *defined contribution* plans and *defined benefit* plans. *Defined contribution* plans are ones in which the employer promises to contribute a certain amount each year to a fund to which the employee has access upon retirement. The fund is increased each year by employer, and perhaps also employee, contributions and by returns from investments made by the fund's managers. One's retirement benefits depend solely on the size of the fund at the age of retirement.

Defined benefit pension plans are those in which the employer promises employees a certain benefit upon retirement. This benefit may be a fixed sum per month or a fixed fraction of one's earnings prior to retirement. In either case employers guarantee the size of the pension benefit, and it is up to them to make sure that the funds are there when the promised benefits need to be paid.

The *vesting* provisions of any pension plan are the rules about who becomes eligible to receive a pension. If a plan is unvested, any worker who quits the company before retirement age loses all rights to a pension benefit. Once workers are vested, they can receive a pension from company X even if they quit X before retirement age and work elsewhere. How much they receive from X at retirement, of course, depends on their length of service with X and their preretirement earnings; however, the point is that they receive *something* from X upon retirement if they are vested.

In 1974 Congress passed the Employee Retirement Income Security Act (ERISA), which, among other things, required private sector employers to adopt liberalized vesting rules. The Tax Reform Act of 1986 required even more liberalized (earlier) vesting beginning in 1989. The intent of these mandated changes was to help employees by making it more likely that they would receive pensions in their old age. However, as we have seen with other programs designed to help workers, good intentions can sometimes be undone by unintended side effects. What are the side effects of liberalized vesting provisions?

From the employees' perspective, rules that entitle them to become vested, or vested sooner, enhance their welfare if nothing else in the compensation package is changed. They are not penalized as much for voluntarily leaving an employer, nor are they as economically vulnerable to being fired. However, the value different workers attach to liberalized vesting may vary widely. The Tax Reform Act of 1986, for example, requires full vesting after five years of service, as compared to the ten-year vesting required under ERISA.[26] Employees who plan on working for a given employer less than five years do not benefit at all from the liberalized vesting; nei-

---

[26]The vesting referred to here is known as "cliff vesting," in which a worker suddenly goes from being unvested to being fully vested. Both ERISA and the Tax Reform Act allowed for *partial* vesting plans, under which a fractional right to a pension upon retirement is granted earlier than ten or five years, respectively, but full vesting occurs somewhat later.

ther do workers who have more than ten years of service with the company. However, workers who might want to change employers after five to ten years of service, or who might be fired during that period, stand to gain from liberalized vesting.

From the employers' perspective, the new vesting rules impose added costs because they make it possible for more workers to qualify for pensions. Will firms simply absorb these added costs, or will they force workers to pay for their more liberal pension benefits in the form of lower wages? Our theory suggests that employers probably will not—and in a competitive market cannot—absorb the added pension costs. Those firms for which pension costs are increased will have to hold the line on future wage increases to remain competitive in the product market, and over time the wages they pay will fall below the level that would have held had it not been for the pension reform legislation. Alternatively, firms whose expected pension costs rise because of vesting may choose to offset this rise with a reduction in promised pension benefits.[27] In either case, theory suggests that workers bear the added costs, as well as reap the benefits, of the mandated change in vesting.

REVIEW QUESTIONS

1. Is the following true, false, or uncertain: "Certain occupations, such as coal mining, are inherently dangerous to workers' health and safety. Therefore, unambiguously, the most appropriate government policy is the establishment and enforcement of rigid safety and health standards." Explain your answer.

2. Statement 1: "Business executives are greedy profit maximizers, caring only for themselves." Statement 2: "It has been established that workers doing filthy, dangerous work receive higher wages, other things equal." Can both of these statements be generally true? Why?

3. Building the oil pipeline across Alaska required the use of many construction workers recruited from the continental United States, who lived in dormitories and worked in an inhospitable climate. Discuss the creation of a compensating wage differ-

ential for these jobs using ordinary supply and demand concepts.

4. "The concept of compensating wage premiums for dangerous work does not apply to industries like the coal industry, where the union has forced all wages and other compensation items to be the same. Since all mines must pay the same wage, owners of dangerous mines will have to pay the same wage as owners of safe mines. Therefore, compensating differentials cannot exist." Is this statement correct? (Assume wages and other forms of pay must be equal for dangerous and nondangerous work and consider the implications for individual labor supply behavior.)

5. "There are three methods of allocating labor across a spectrum of jobs that may differ substantially in working conditions. One is the use of force, one is the use of trickery, and one is the use of compensating wage differentials." Comment.

---

[27]David E. Bloom and Richard B. Freeman, "The Fall in Private Pension Coverage in the U.S.," *American Economic Review* 82 (May 1992): 539–545, document a fall in pension coverage during the 1980s but doubt that liberalized vesting rules contributed much to this decline.

6. Some employers offer jobs for which overtime is mandatory. Others offer jobs for which overtime hours are usually available to workers if they wish to work them, and still others offer jobs for which overtime hours are not commonly worked. Suppose a careful study of wages finds that jobs for which overtime hours are commonly available pay lower wages than jobs for which overtime is not usually worked (after controlling for all other factors affecting the wage rate). Moreover, jobs for which overtime is required are found to pay wages comparable to those in jobs for which overtime is unusual, again controlling for all other factors affecting wages. What would the results of this study tell us about worker attitudes regarding overtime? Why?

7. In 1986 the federal government was considering the removal of prohibitions on the production of various garments and apparel items by independent contractors working out of their homes. These prohibitions had been in effect since 1942, at which time the government decided that many homeworkers were being exploited by garment manufacturers who paid them extremely low wages. Those who, in 1986, favored retaining the prohibitions argued that homeworkers (primarily women) would end up getting considerably less than factory workers. These supporters of the 1942 prohibitions asserted that the earnings differential between factory and homeworkers is a measure of the degree to which the latter are exploited. Evaluate this assertion.

8. Suppose we observe a city in which highway workers are required to give the Supervisor of Highways an under-the-table payment of X dollars per year. Suppose we were to compare the wages paid by this city with the market-clearing wage paid to comparable workers in the area. Would we expect wages paid to highway workers by this city to be higher or lower than the market wage? Would we expect the salary paid by the city to its Supervisor of Highways to be above or below market? Explain.

9. In 1991 Germany proposed that the European Community countries collectively agree that no one be allowed to work on Sundays (exceptions could be made for Muslims, Jews, and other religious groups celebrating the Sabbath on a day other than Sunday). Use economic theory both *positively* and *normatively* to assess, as completely as you can, the effects of prohibiting work on Sundays.

SELECTED READINGS

Duncan, Greg, and Bertil Holmlund. "Was Adam Smith Right After All? Another Test of the Theory of Compensating Wage Differentials." *Journal of Labor Economics* 1 (October 1983): 366–379.

Gustman, Alan L., Olivia S. Mitchell, and Thomas L. Steinmeier. "The Role of Pensions in the Labor Market: A Survey of the Literature." *Industrial and Labor Relations Review* 47, no. 3 (April 1994): 417–438.

Rosen, Sherwin. "Hedonic Prices and Implicit Markets." *Journal of Political Economy* 82 (January–February 1974): 34–55.

———. "The Theory of Equalizing Differences." In *Handbook of Labor Economics*, ed. Orley Ashenfelter and Richard Layard (New York: North-Holland, 1986): 641–692.

Smith, Robert S. "Compensating Wage Differentials and Public Policy: A Review." *Industrial and Labor Relations Review* 32 (April 1979): 339–352.

Viscusi, W. Kip. "The Value of Risks to Life and Health." *Journal of Economic Literature* 31, no. 4 (December 1993): 1912–1946.

APPENDIX $8A$

Compensating Wage Differentials and Layoffs

As mentioned in the chapter text, one of the circumstances identified by Adam Smith under which compensating wage differentials would arise relates to the "constancy or inconstancy of employment." While there is evidence, as we shall see, to support this prediction, the relationship of wages to layoff probabilities is by no means as simple as Smith thought. In particular, there are three issues relevant to the analysis, all of which we shall discuss briefly.[1]

Unconstrained Choice Of Work Hours

Suppose that, in the spirit of Chapters 6 and 7, employees are free to choose their hours of work in a labor market that offers an infinite choice of work hours. Given the wage a particular worker can command and his or her nonwage income, the utility-maximizing choice of working hours would be selected. For the person depicted in Figure 8A.1, the utility-maximizing choice of work hours is H^*, given his or her offered wage rate (W^*) and level of nonwage income (assumed here to be zero).

If H^* is thought of in terms of yearly work hours, it is easy to understand that a worker may *prefer* a job involving layoff! Suppose H^* is 1,500 hours per year, or essentially three-quarters of the typical "full-time" job of 2,000 hours. One could work 6 hours a day, 5 days a week, for 50 weeks a year, or one could work 8 hours

---

[1]The analysis in this appendix draws heavily upon John M. Abowd and Orley Ashenfelter, "Anticipated Unemployment, Temporary Layoffs, and Compensating Wage Differentials," in *Studies in Labor Markets*, ed. Sherwin Rosen (Chicago: University of Chicago Press, 1981), 141–170.

a day, 5 days a week, for 9 months and agree to be laid off for 3 months. Which alternative holds more appeal to any given individual depends on his or her preferences with respect to large blocks of leisure or household time, but it is clear that many people value such large blocks. Teachers, for example, typically work full-time during a 9-month school year, and then some of them vacation during the summer. Many other jobs, from the construction trades to work in canning factories, involve predictable seasonal layoffs, and workers in these jobs may have chosen them because they value the leisure or household production time accompanying the layoffs.

Putting the point differently, the theory of compensating wage differentials suggests they will be positive only when a job characteristic is regarded as bad by the marginal worker. Predictable blocks of leisure or household time accompanying seasonal layoffs may not be regarded as bad by the marginal worker. In fact, workers in some markets may see layoffs as a mechanism through which they can best achieve their desired yearly hours of work.

Constrained Hours of Work

Suppose that the worker depicted in Figure 8A.1 is offered a choice between a job offering wage W^* and hours H^*, and one offering fewer hours than desired because of a predictable layoff each year that reduces hours of work to H'. Clearly, if the wage for the latter job remains at W^*, the worker's utility will be reduced by taking the job offering H' hours because he or she will be on an indifference curve passing through point A. The job offering W^* and H^* is thus clearly preferred.

However, suppose that H' is offered at a wage of W', where W' exceeds W^* by enough so that point B can be reached. Point B, where the wage is W' and hours of work are H', is on the *same* indifference curve as point C (the utility-maximizing point when W^* is the offered wage). Point B is not a point of utility maximization[2] at a wage offer of W', but if the worker is offered an unconstrained choice of hours at wage rate W^*, or a wage of W' where working hours are *constrained* to equal H', he or she would be indifferent between the two job offers.

In the above example, $(W' - W^*)$ is the compensating wage differential that would have to arise for the worker to consider a job where hours of work were constrained to lie below those otherwise desired. Many people view layoffs as an event that prevents workers from working the number of hours they would otherwise desire to work. If this is the case, and if these layoffs are predictable and known with certainty, such as layoffs accompanying model changeovers in the auto industry, then compensating wage differentials associated with the pre-

---

[2]It is not a point of tangency; that is, at a wage of W' the worker depicted in Figure 8A.1 would prefer to work more than H' hours if he or she were free to choose work hours. We have assumed in the discussion that the choice is constrained so that hours cannot exceed H'.

FIGURE 8A.1

Choice of Hours of Work

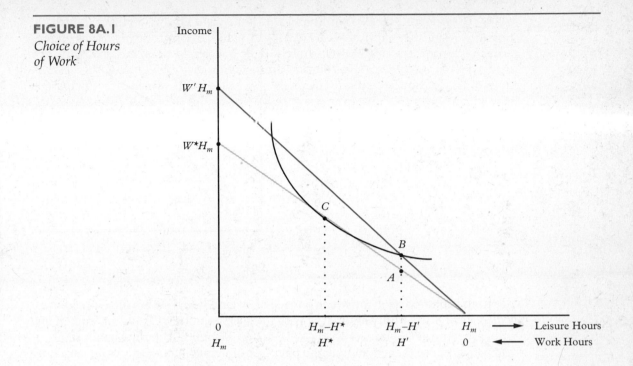

dictable, certain layoff rate would arise in a well-functioning labor market (that is, one where workers are informed and mobile).[3]

THE EFFECTS OF UNCERTAIN LAYOFFS

In the above section, we assumed that layoffs were predictable and known with certainty. In most cases, however, they are not. While one might expect layoff rates to be higher in some industries than in others, they are in fact often subject to considerable random fluctuation *within* industries over the years. This *uncertainty* of layoffs is itself another aspect of affected jobs that is usually thought to be a negative feature and for which a compensating wage differential might arise.

Suppose that utility is measurable and is a function only of income, so that it can be graphed against income (Y), as in Figure 8A.2.[4] Suppose also that the person

---

[3]A similar argument can be used to predict that workers will receive compensating wage differentials if they are forced to work longer hours than they would otherwise prefer. For the argument and evidence in support of it, see Ronald G. Ehrenberg and Paul L. Schumann, "Compensating Wage Differentials for Mandatory Overtime," *Economic Inquiry* 22 (December 1984).

[4]Although economists typically work with *ordinal* utility functions, which specify the relative ranking of alternatives without assigning each alternative a numerical value of utility, the analysis of choice under uncertainty requires the use of *cardinal* utility functions (ones in which each alternative is assigned a specific numerical value of utility).

FIGURE 8A.2

*The Choice Between H' Hours
with Certainty and H' Hours on
Average*

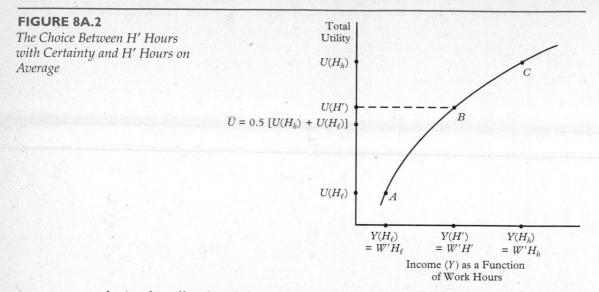

depicted is offered a job for which a wage of W' and yearly hours of H' are known *with certainty*. The utility associated with these H', hours $U(H')$, is a function of his or her income at H' hours of work: $W'H'$ (again assuming no nonwage income).

Now suppose there is another job paying W' in which the *average* hours of work per year are H' but half the time H_h is worked and half the time H_ℓ $U(H')$ is worked. Although we have assumed that $0.5\,H_h + 0.5\,H_\ell = H'$, so that over the years the person averages H' hours of work, it turns out that with the convex utility function we have drawn, the person's average utility is *below* $U(H')$. To understand this we must look closely at Figure 8A.2.

When the person's working hours are H_h, which is half the time, he or she earns $W'H_h$, and this income yields a utility of $U(H_h)$. Thus, half the time the worker will be at point C enjoying utility level $U(H_h)$. The other half of the time, however, the person will be working H_ℓ hours, earning $W'H_\ell$ in income, and be at point A enjoying utility of $U(H_\ell)$. His or her average utility is thus $\overline{U}$, which is $\overline{U} = 0.5\,U(H_h) + 0.5\,U(H_\ell)$. Note that $\overline{U}$, which is midway between $U(H_h)$ and $U(H_\ell)$ in our example, lies *below* $U(H')$—the utility derived from a job paying W' and employing the person for H' hours *with certainty* every year.

Why is $\overline{U} < U(H')$ even though H' hours are worked on *average* in both cases? The answer lies in the convexity of the utility function, which economists define as exhibiting *risk aversion*. Moving from $Y(H')$ to $Y(H_h)$ covers the same absolute distance on the horizontal axis as moving from $Y(H')$ to $Y(H_\ell)$, but the changes in *utility* are not the same in magnitude. In particular, moving from $Y(H')$ to $Y(H_h)$ (points B to C) in the good years adds *less* to utility than moving from $Y(H')$ to $Y(H_\ell)$ (points B to A) in the bad years takes away. Put differently, the convexity of the total utility curve in Figure 8A.2 implies diminishing marginal utility of income. Thus, in the unlucky years, when hours are below H', there is a relatively big drop in utility (as compared to the utility associated with H' hours), while in the lucky years the added income increases utility by a relatively small amount.

The upshot of this discussion is that when workers are averse to risk—that is, when their utility functions are convex so that they in essence place a larger value on negative changes from a given level of income than they do on positive changes of equal dollar magnitude—they would prefer a job paying W' and offering H' hours with certainty to one paying W' and offering only H' hours on average. Thus, to compensate them for the loss in utility associated with *risk aversion*, they would require a wage above W' for the job offering H' hours only on average.

The Observed Wage/Layoff Relationship

The discussion above centered on worker preferences regarding layoffs. For compensating wage differentials to arise, of course, employers must be willing to pay them. That is, employers must profit from being able to lay off workers, and if we are to observe firms pursuing a high-wage/high-layoff strategy, their gains from layoff must exceed their costs of higher wages.

The discussion above also neglected unemployment insurance (UI) payments to laid-off workers. This topic is discussed in some detail in Chapter 15. Here we need note only that if UI payments fully compensate laid-off workers for their lost utility, compensating wage differentials will not arise. Compensating wage differentials will arise only if UI payments do not fully compensate laid-off workers.

One study that looked very carefully at the relationship between wages and layoffs suggests that the compensating wage differential for an average probability of layoff is around 4 percent of wages, with over 80 percent of this differential related to the aversion to risk associated with the variability (uncertainty) in layoff rates facing workers over time. Workers in the high-layoff industries of automobile manufacturing and construction received estimated compensating wage differentials ranging over the early 1970s from 6 to 14 percent and 6 to 11 percent, respectively.[5]

---

[5]These estimates are from the Abowd and Ashenfelter article in footnote 1 of this appendix. Similar evidence for the late 1970s can be found in Robert H. Topel, "Equilibrium Earnings, Turnover, and Unemployment: New Evidence," *Journal of Labor Economics* 2, no. 4 (October 1984): 500–522. For those interested in how UI benefits affect wages, see David A. Anderson, "Compensating Wage Differentials and the Optimal Provision of Unemployment Insurance," *Southern Economic Journal* 60, no. 3 (January 1994): 644–656.

9

Investments in Human Capital: Education and Training

Chapters 6, 7, and 8—on the decision to work and job choice—emphasized the effects of *current* wages, employee benefits, and psychic income on worker decisions. Many labor supply choices, however, require a substantial initial *investment* on the part of the worker. Recall that investments, by definition, entail an initial cost that one hopes to recoup over some period of time. Thus, for many labor supply decisions, *current* wages and working conditions are not the only deciding factors. Modeling these decisions requires developing a framework that incorporates investment behavior and a *lifetime* perspective.

Workers undertake three major kinds of labor market investments: education and training, migration, and search for new jobs. All three investments involve an initial cost, and all three are made in the hope and expectation that the investment will pay off well into the future. To emphasize the essential similarity of these investments to other kinds of investments, economists refer to them as investments in *human capital,* a term that conceptualizes workers as embodying a set of skills that can be "rented out" to employers. The knowledge and skills a worker has—which come from education and training, including the learning that experience yields—generate a certain *stock* of productive capital. However, the *value* of this amount of productive capital is derived from how much these skills can earn in the labor market. Job search and migration are activities that increase the value of one's human capital by increasing the price (wage) received for a given stock of skills.

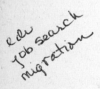

Society's total wealth should therefore be thought of as a combination of both human and nonhuman capital. Human capital includes accumulated investments in such activities as education, job training, and migration, whereas nonhuman capital includes society's stock of natural resources, buildings, and machinery. Total wealth in the United States was around $421,000 per person in 1990, 59 percent of which ($248,000 per person) was in the form of human capital.[1] Estimates of human capital per person in Canada, Germany, and Japan were $155,000, $315,000, and $458,000, respectively. Thus, investments in human capital are an enormously important component of the overall wealth in any society, averaging 64 percent of per capita wealth worldwide (see Example 9.1 for a further indication of the relative importance of human capital).

Investment in the knowledge and skills of a particular worker can be thought of as having taken place in three stages. First, in early childhood, the acquisition of human capital was largely determined by the decisions of others. Parental resources and guidance, plus one's cultural environment and early schooling experiences, help to influence basic language and mathematical skills, attitudes toward learning, and one's general health and life expectancy (which themselves affect the ability to work). Second, teenagers and young adults go through a stage in which their acquisition of knowledge and skills is as full-time students in a high school, college, or vocational training program. Finally, after entering the labor market, workers' additions to their human capital generally take place on a part-time basis, through on-the-job training, night school, or participation in relatively short formal training programs.

In this chapter we analyze the choices made by teenagers and adults about investing in their own *education and training* over a lifetime; in Chapter 10 we analyze their investments in *job search* and *migration*. In both chapters we focus on the latter two stages above, when people are old enough to make considered choices about occupations and the related human capital investments. This focus arises from our central concern with *labor market* behavior, but the influence of early childhood (or "premarket") experiences on later human capital decisions and economic outcomes is worthy of at least brief comment.

One of the challenges of any behavioral theory is to explain why people faced with what appears to be the same environment make different choices. In Chapter 6, for example, we saw that an important factor in decisions about the hours of work an individual supplies to the market is his or her preferences regarding income and leisure. Similarly, the compensating wage differentials for job injury risk in Chapter 8 were generated by workers' varying degrees of aversion to the risk of injury. We will see in this chapter that individuals' decisions about investing in human capital are affected by the ease and speed with which they learn, their aspirations and expectations about the future, and their access to financial resources.

Parental wealth and educational attainment are thought to play an important role in developing children's basic cognitive skills and their attitudes toward learning

---

[1] Peter Passel, "The Wealth of Nations: A "Greener" Approach Turns List Upside Down," *New York Times*, September 19, 1995, C1, C12.

EXAMPLE 9.1

Hiroshima, Hamburg, and Human Capital

An insight into the relative magnitudes and importance of physical and human capital is obtained by noting some interesting facts concerning severely war-damaged cities. The atomic attack on Hiroshima destroyed 70 percent of its buildings and killed about 30 percent of the population. Survivors fled the city in the aftermath of the bombing, but people began returning within 24 hours; within three months two-thirds of city's surviving population had returned. Because the air-burst bomb left the city's underground utility networks intact, power was restored to surviving areas one day after the bombing. Through railway service began again in two days, and telephone service was restarted in a week. The U.S. Strategic Bombing Survey estimated that plants responsible for three-quarters of the city's industrial production (many of these were located on the outskirts of the city and were undamaged) could have begun normal operations within 30 days.

In Hamburg, Germany, a city of around 1.5 million in the summer of 1943, Allied bombing raids over a ten-day period in July and August destroyed about half of the buildings in the city and killed about 3 percent of the city's population. Although there was considerable damage to the water supply system,

electricity and gas service were adequate within a few days after the last attack, and within four days the telegraph system was again operating. The central bank was reopened and business had begun to function normally after one week, and postal service was resumed within 12 days of the attack. The Strategic Bombing Survey reported that within five months Hamburg had recovered up to 80 percent of its former productivity.

The speed and success of recovery from these disasters has prompted one economist to offer the following two observations:

> (1) the fraction of the community's real wealth represented by visible material capital is small relative to the fraction represented by the accumulated knowledge and talents of the population, and (2) there are enormous reserves of energy and effort in the population not drawn upon in ordinary times but which can be utilized under special circumstances such as those prevailing in the aftermath of disaster.

SOURCE: Jack Hirshleifer, *Economic Behavior in Adversity* (Chicago: University of Chicago Press, 1987), 12–14, 78–79.

and work.[2] Neighborhoods, and even preschool experiences, can also be hypothesized to affect one's aspirations and learning skills.[3] Thus, as we begin our analysis of the human capital choices made by workers, it is important to keep in mind that these "market" decisions about human capital are being made by workers who differ in their attitudes toward, and abilities for, learning. These "premarket"

---

[2]For seminal work in this vein, see Gary S. Becker and Nigel Tomes, "An Equilibrium Theory of the Distribution of Income and Intergenerational Mobility," *Journal of Political Economy* 87, no. 6 (December 1979): 1153–1189, and Gary S. Becker and Nigel Tomes, "Human Capital and the Rise and Fall of Families," *Journal of Labor Economics* 4, no. 3, pt. 2 (July 1986): S1–S39. For a recent empirical article, see Mark R. Rosenzweig and Kenneth I. Wolpin, "Are There Increasing Returns to the Intergenerational Production of Human Capital?" *Journal of Human Resources* 29, no. 2 (Spring 1994): 670–693.

[3]For recent empirical studies on these topics, see George J. Borjas, "Ethnicity, Neighborhoods, and Human-Capital Externalities," *American Economic Review* 85, no. 3 (June 1995): 365–390, and Janet Currie and Duncan Thomas, "Does Head Start Make a Difference?" *American Economic Review* 85, no. 3 (June 1995): 341–364.

differences are, at least in part, influenced by the decisions, values, and resources of others during each worker's childhood.[4]

Human Capital Investments: The Basic Model

As with any other investment, an investment in human capital entails costs that are borne in the near term with the expectation that benefits will accrue in the future. Generally speaking, the *costs* of adding to one's human capital can be divided into three categories:

1. *Out-of-pocket* or *direct* expenses include tuition costs and expenditures on books and other supplies.
2. *Forgone earnings* are another source of cost, because during the investment period it is usually impossible to work, at least not full-time.
3. *Psychic losses* are a third kind of cost incurred, because learning is often difficult and tedious.

In the case of educational and training investments by workers, the expected *returns* are in the form of higher future earnings, increased job satisfaction over one's lifetime, and a greater appreciation of nonmarket activities and interests. Calculating the benefits of an investment over time requires the progressive discounting of benefits lying further into the future (see Chapter 5). Benefits that are received in the future are worth less to us now than an equal amount of benefits received today for two reasons. First, if people plan to consume their benefits, they prefer to consume earlier. (One is relatively sure of being able to enjoy such consumption now, for example, but the uncertainties of life make future enjoyment problematic.) Second, if people plan to invest the monetary benefits rather than use them for consumption, they can earn interest on the investment and enlarge their funds in the future. Thus, no matter how people intend to use their benefits, they will discount future receipts to some extent.

As Chapter 5 explained, the present value of a stream of yearly benefits (B_1, B_2 . . .) over time (T) can be calculated as follows:

$$\text{Present Value} = \frac{B_1}{1 + r} + \frac{B_2}{(1 + r)^2} + \frac{B_3}{(1 + r)^3} + \cdots + \frac{B_T}{(1 + r)^T} \tag{9.1}$$

where the interest rate (or discount rate) is r. As long as r is positive, benefits into the future will be progressively discounted. For example, if $r = 0.06$, benefits payable in 30 years would receive a weight that is only 17 percent of the weight

---

[4]A recent book that considers the role of genetic factors in determining cognitive abilities is Richard J. Herrnstein and Charles Murray, *The Bell Curve: Intelligence and Class Structure in American Life* (New York: Free Press, 1994). For a critical review of this book by two prominent economists, see Arthur S. Goldberger and Charles F. Manski, "Review Article: 'The Bell Curve' by Herrnstein and Murray," *Journal of Economic Literature* 33, no. 2 (June 1995): 762–776.

placed on benefits payable immediately ($1.06^{30} = 5.74$; $1/5.74 = 0.17$). The smaller r is, the greater the weight placed on future benefits; for example, if $r = 0.02$, a benefit payable in 30 years would receive a weight that is 55 percent of the weight given to an immediate benefit.

Our model of human capital investment assumes that people are utility maximizers and take a lifetime perspective when making choices about education and training. They are therefore assumed to compare the near-term investment costs (C) with the present value of expected future benefits when making a decision, say, about additional schooling. Investment in additional schooling is attractive if the present value of future benefits exceeds costs:

$$\frac{B_1}{1 + r} + \frac{B_2}{(1 + r)^2} + \cdots + \frac{B_T}{(1 + r)^T} > C \qquad (9.2)$$

Utility maximization, of course, requires that people continue to make additional human capital investments as long as condition (9.2) is met, and that they stop only when the benefits of additional investment are equal to or less than the additional costs.

There are two ways one can measure whether the criterion in (9.2) is met. Using the *present-value method,* one can specify a value for the discount rate, r, and then determine how the present value of benefits compares to costs. Alternatively, one can adopt the *internal rate of return method,* which asks, "How large could the discount rate be and still render the investment profitable?" Clearly, if the benefits are so large that even a very high discount rate would render investment profitable, then the project is worthwhile. In practice, one calculates this internal rate of return by setting the present value of benefits equal to costs and solving for r. The internal rate of return is then compared to the rate of return on other investments. If the internal rate of return exceeds the alternative rates of return, the investment project is considered profitable.

Some basic implications of the model embedded in expression (9.2) are illustrated graphically in Figure 9.1a, which depicts human capital decisions in terms of marginal costs and marginal benefits (focus for now on the black lines in the figure). The marginal costs, *MC*, of each additional unit of human capital (the tuition, supplies, forgone earnings, and psychic costs of an additional year of schooling, say) are assumed to be constant. The present value of the marginal benefits, *MB*, is shown as declining, because each added year of schooling means fewer years over which benefits can be "collected." The utility-maximizing amount of human capital (*HC**) for any individual is shown as that amount for which $MC = MB$.

Earlier, we noted that as people arrive at the point in their lives when human capital decisions must be made, they do so with different resources, learning abilities, and expectations about the future. Those who find learning to be especially arduous, for example, will implicitly attach a higher marginal psychic cost to acquiring human capital. As shown by the blue line, *MC'*, in Figure 9.1a, individuals, with higher marginal costs will acquire lower levels of human capital (compare *HC'* with *HC**). Similarly, those who expect smaller future benefits from additional

FIGURE 9.1

The Optimum Acquisition of Human Capital

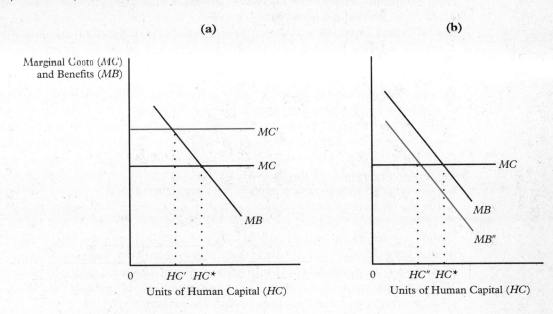

human capital investments (the blue line, *MB''*, in Figure 9.1b) will acquire less human capital.

This straightforward theory yields some interesting insights about the behavior and earnings of workers. Many of these insights can be discovered by analyzing the decision confronting young adults about whether to invest full-time in educational or training programs after leaving high school. We illustrate how our theory can be used by looking in some detail at the decision to attend college full-time; however, analyzing the demand for full-time vocational training programs would utilize the same principles and generate the same insights.

The Demand for a College Education

The demand for a college education, as measured by the percentage of graduating high school seniors who enroll in college, is surprisingly variable.[5] For males, enrollment rates went from 55.2 percent in 1970, down to 46.7 percent in 1980, and

---

[5]Strictly speaking, enrollments equal demand only if all students who want to invest in a college education are able to do so. The barriers of failing to meet admissions criteria or failing to have the necessary financial resources may prevent some from investing, so the *level* of enrollments may understate the level of demand. Unless the importance of these barriers changes significantly over time, however, the *direction* of enrollment changes—which is our major interest—should reflect the direction of changes in demand.

back up to 59.7 percent by 1993. The comparable enrollment rates for women started lower, at 48.5 percent in 1970, and rose continuously throughout this period to a high of 65.4 percent by 1993; however, while the yearly increase in enrollment rates averaged 0.3 percentage points in the 1970s, it averaged 1.0 points in the 1980s and early 1990s. Why have enrollment rates followed these patterns?

WEIGHING THE COSTS AND BENEFITS OF COLLEGE

Clearly, people attend college when they believe they will be better off by so doing. For some, at least part of the benefits may be short-term—they like the courses or the lifestyle of a student—and to this extent college is at least partially a *consumption* good. The consumption benefits of college, however, are unlikely to change much over the course of a decade, so changes in college attendance rates over relatively short periods of time probably reflect changes in marginal costs or benefits associated with the *investment* aspects of college attendance.

Earlier we noted that the costs of college attendance are both monetary and psychic. The monetary costs alone (that is, the direct costs of tuition and books plus forgone earnings) are in the range of $17,000 to $32,000 per year.[6] The investment-related benefits of a college education are associated with increased future earnings and any nonmonetary rewards from having access to occupations requiring a college education. Because only the monetary benefits are measurable, our analysis of the marginal benefits of college focuses on them.

A person considering college has, in some broad sense, a choice between two streams of earnings over his or her lifetime. Stream A begins immediately but does not rise very high; it is the earnings stream of a high school graduate. Stream B (the college graduate) has a negative income for the first four years (owing to college tuition costs), followed by a period when the salary may be less than the high school graduate makes, but then it takes off and rises above stream A. Both streams are illustrated in Figure 9.2. (Why these streams are differentially *curved* will be discussed later in this chapter.) The streams shown in the figure are stylized so that we can emphasize some basic points. Actual earnings streams will be shown in Figures 9.3 and 9.4.

Obviously, the earnings of the college graduate would have to rise above those of the high school graduate to induce someone to invest in a college education (unless, of course, the consumption-related returns were large). The gross benefits, the difference in earnings between the two streams, must total much more than the costs because such returns are in the future and are therefore discounted. For example, suppose it costs $25,000 per year to obtain a four-year college education and the real interest rate (the nominal rate less the rate of inflation) is 2 percent. The after-tax returns—if they were the same each year—must be $3,652 in constant-dollar terms (that is, after taking away the effects of

---

[6]Cost estimates are from Charles T. Clotfelter, Ronald G. Ehrenberg, Malcolm Getz, and John Siegfried, *Economic Challenges in Higher Education* (Chicago: University of Chicago Press, 1991), 72, expressed in 1995 dollars.

FIGURE 9.2
Alternative Earnings Streams

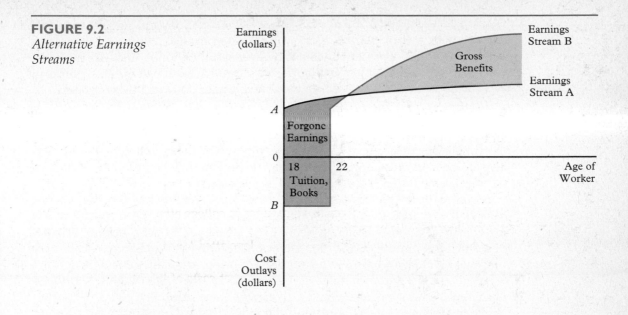

inflation) each year for 40 years in order to justify the investment on purely monetary grounds. These returns must be $3,652 because $100,000 invested at a 2 percent interest rate can provide a payment (of interest and principal) totaling $3,652 a year for 40 years.[7]

PREDICTIONS OF THE THEORY

In deciding whether to attend college, no doubt few students make the very precise calculations suggested in expression (9.2). Nevertheless, if they make less formal estimates that take into account the same factors, <u>four predictions concerning the demand for college education can be made:</u>

1. <u>Present-oriented people are less likely to go to college</u> than forward-looking people (other things equal).
2. Most college students will be young.

---

[7]This calculation is made using the *annuity formula:*

$$Y = X \ \frac{1 - [1/(1 + r)^n]}{r}$$

where Y equals the total investment ($100,000 in our example), X = the yearly payment ($3,652), r = the rate of interest (0.02), and n = the number of years (40). In this example, we treat the costs of a college education as being incurred all in one year rather than being spread out over four, a simplification that does not alter the magnitude of required returns much at all.

3. College attendance will decrease if the costs of college rise (other things equal).

4. College attendance will increase if the gap between the earnings of college graduates and high school graduates widens (again, other things equal).

PRESENT-ORIENTEDNESS   Psychologists use the term *present-oriented* to describe people who do not weight future events or outcomes very heavily. While all people discount the future with respect to the present, those who discount it more than average—or, at the extreme, ignore the future altogether—could be considered present-oriented. In terms of expressions (9.1) and (9.2), a present-oriented person is one who uses a very high discount rate (r).

Suppose one were to calculate investment returns using the *present-value method*. If r is large, the present value of benefits associated with college will be lower than if the discount rate being used is smaller. Thus, a present-oriented person would impute smaller benefits to college attendance than one who is less present-oriented, and those who are present-oriented would be less likely to attend college. Using the *internal rate of return method* for evaluating the soundness of a college education, one would arrive at the same result. If a college education earns an 8 percent rate of return but the individuals in question are so present-oriented that they would insist on a 25 percent rate of return before investing, they would likewise decide not to attend.

The prediction that present-oriented people are less likely to attend college than forward-looking ones is difficult either to substantiate or to disprove. The rates of discount that people use in making investment decisions are rarely available, because such decisions are not made as formally as expression (9.2) implies. However, the model does suggest that people who have a high propensity to invest in education will also engage in other forward-looking behavior. Certain medical statistics tend to support this prediction.

In the United States there is a strong statistical correlation between education and health status.[8] People with more years of schooling have lower mortality rates, fewer symptoms of disease (such as high blood pressure, high cholesterol levels, abnormal X-rays), and a greater tendency to report themselves to be in good health. This effect of education on health is independent of income, which appears to have no effect of its own on health status except at the lowest poverty levels. Is this correlation between education and health a result of better use of medical resources by the well-educated? It appears not. Better-educated people undergoing surgery choose the same doctors, enter the hospital at the same stage of disease, and have the same length of stay as less-educated people of equal income.

What *may* cause this correlation is a more forward-looking attitude among those who have obtained more education. People with lower discount rates will be more likely to attend college, and they will *also* be more likely to adopt forward-looking habits of health. They may choose healthier diets, be more aware of health risks,

---

[8]The analysis of the correlation between education and health status is taken from Victor Fuchs, "The Economics of Health in a Post-Industrial Society," *The Public Interest* (Summer 1979): 3–20.

and make more use of preventive medicine. This explanation for the correlation between education and health is not the only plausible one, but it receives some direct support from American data on cigarette smoking.[9] From 1966 to 1987, the proportion of male college graduates who smoked fell by 50 percent. During the same time period, the proportion of smokers among male high school dropouts was essentially unchanged. It is unlikely that the less-educated group was uninformed of the smoking dangers revealed during that period. It is more likely that they were less willing to give up a present source of pleasure for a distant benefit. Thus, we have at least some evidence that people who invest in education also engage in *other* forward-looking behavior.

AGE Given similar *yearly* benefits of going to college, young people have a larger present value of *total* benefits than older workers simply because they have a longer remaining work life ahead of them. In terms of expression (9.2), T for younger people is greater than for older ones. We would therefore expect younger people to have a greater propensity than older people to obtain a college education or engage in other forms of training activity. This prediction is parallel to the predictions in Chapter 5 about which workers employers will decide to invest in when they make decisions about hiring or specific training.

COSTS A third prediction of our model is that human capital investments are more likely when costs are lower. The major monetary costs of college attendance are forgone earnings and the direct costs of tuition, books, and fees. (Food and lodging are not always opportunity costs of going to college because some of these costs would have to be incurred in any event.) Thus, if forgone earnings or tuition costs rise, other things equal, we would expect a decrease in college enrollments. Similarly, if offers of financial aid to college applicants fall, other things equal, we would expect fewer enrollments. Are college enrollments responsive to cost?

Financial aid packages, including loans, rarely cover all the out-of-pocket expenses of college, and so the financial resources of students' families must be tapped for at least some of their costs. Given this fact, it is not surprising that, other things equal, students from relatively wealthy families are more likely to attend college. For example, 44 percent of high-ability students from low-income families enroll in four-year colleges, while the comparable figure for high-ability students from relatively wealthy backgrounds is 74 percent. Moreover, from 1974 to 1984, when financial aid to students from lower-income families rose more slowly than tuition and more slowly than financial aid to upper-income students, the proportion of college students from lower-income backgrounds fell.[10]

---

[9]It could be, for example, that healthy people, with longer life spans, are more likely to invest in human capital because they expect to experience a longer payback period. Alternatively, one could argue that the higher incomes of college graduates later in life mean they have more to lose from illness than do non-college graduates. Data on smoking are from U.S. Department of Health and Human Services, Public Health Service, *Smoking Tobacco and Health*, DHHS publication no. (CDC)87–8397, October 1989, 5.

[10]Charles Clotfelter, et al., *Economic Challenges in Higher Education*, 43, 72, 103, 105, and 110.

The costs of college attendance offer an additional reason why we observe older people attending less often than younger people. As workers age, they acquire levels of experience and maturity that employers are willing to reward with higher wages. Because older workers thus command higher wages (on average), their opportunity costs of college attendance are higher than those for younger students. Older people are thus doubly discouraged from attending college: their forgone earnings are relatively high and the period over which they can capture benefits is comparatively short. Interestingly, however, college attendance by military veterans (who are older than the typical college student) has been quite responsive to the educational subsidies for which they are eligible.[11]

The subject of cost raises an interesting question: just who is most *responsive* to cost considerations? Economic theory postulates that, in any set of market transactions, some people are *at the margin*—meaning that they are close to the point of not transacting. Those closer to the margin, then, are the ones most likely to change their decisions in response to relatively small changes in the monetary costs of college. Who are those for whom the decision to attend is a "close call"? Our theoretical considerations have suggested several possibilities: those with lower cognitive achievement levels, lower levels of parental wealth, or higher personal discount rates (a greater degree of present-orientation). Interestingly, studies that have analyzed how the cost advantages of having a college in one's hometown affect an individual's enrollment decision find that these effects are largest for students who would otherwise be least likely to attend (that is, students with lower cognitive achievement and parents with lower levels of educational attainment themselves).[12]

EARNINGS DIFFERENTIALS   The fourth prediction of human capital theory is that the demand for education is positively related to the increases in lifetime earnings that a college education allows. Strictly speaking, it is the benefits one *expects* to receive that are critical to this decision, and the expected benefits for any individual are rather uncertain. Future earnings can never be perfectly foretold, and in addition, many students are uncertain about their later occupational choice.[13] As a first approximation, however, it is reasonable to conjecture that the *average* returns received by recent college graduates have an-

---

[11]See Joshua D. Angrist, "The Effect of Veterans Benefits on Education and Earnings," *Industrial and Labor Relations Review* 46, no. 4 (July 1993): 637–652.

[12]C. A. Anderson, M. J. Bowman, and B. Tinto, *Where Colleges Are and Who Attends* (New York: McGraw-Hill, 1972); and David Card, "Using Geographic Variation in College Proximity to Estimate the Return to Schooling," in *Aspects of Labour Market Behavior: Essays in Honour of John Vanderkamp*, ed. L. N. Christofides, E. K. Grant, and R. Swindinsky (Toronto: University of Toronto Press, 1995).

[13]For studies that incorporate uncertainty into the formal model of choice, see Joseph G. Altonji, "The Demand for and Return to Education When Education Outcomes Are Uncertain," *Journal of Labor Economics* 10 (January 1993): 48–83; and Peter F. Orazem and J. Peter Mattila, "Human Capital, Uncertain Wage Distributions, and Occupational and Educational Choices," *International Economic Review* 32 (February 1991): 103–122. For a paper on the accuracy of students' knowledge about the salaries in various fields, see Julian R. Betts, "What Do Students Know About Wages? Survey Evidence on Mechanisms of Occupational Choice," working paper no. 93–45, University of California–San Diego, Department of Economics, October 1993.

TABLE 9.1

Changes in College Enrollments and the College/High School Earnings Differential, by Gender, 1970–1993

Year	College Enrollment Rates of New High School Graduates		Ratios of Mean Earnings of College to High School Graduates, Ages 25-34, Prior Year[a]	
	Male	Female	Male	Female
1970	55.2%	48.5%	1.38	1.42
1975	52.6	49.0	1.16	1.29
1980	46.7	51.8	1.19	1.29
1985	58.6	56.9	1.27	1.35
1990	57.8	62.0	1.48	1.59
1993	59.7	65.4	1.54	1.53

[a]For year-round, full-time workers. Data for the first two years are for personal income, not earnings; however, in the years for which both income and earnings are available, the ratios are essentially equal.

SOURCES: U.S. Department of Education, *Digest of Education Statistics* 1994 (October 1994), Table 180; U.S. Bureau of the Census, *Money Income of Families and Persons in the United States*, Current Population Reports P–60, no. 66 (Table 41), no. 101 (Table 58), no. 129 (Table 53), no. 151 (Table 34), no. 174 (Table 29), no. 184 (Table 30).

important influence on students' decisions. Thus, if the average earnings differential between recent college graduates and recent high school graduates of similar age were to narrow, we should expect to find that college enrollment rates subsequently decline. In contrast, if this differential were to widen, enrollment rates should increase.[14]

Dramatic changes in the average monetary returns to a college education over the past two decades are at least partially, if not largely, responsible for the changes in college enrollment rates noted earlier. It can be seen from the first and third columns of Table 9.1, for example, that the decline in male enrollment rates during the 1970s was correlated with declines in the college/high school earnings differential, while the higher enrollment rates in the 1980s and early 1990s were associated with larger earnings differentials. (Interestingly, as discussed in Example 9.2, recent increases in the earnings differential between male college and high school graduates have not been created by a robust market for college graduates, but rather by a dramatic decline in the prospects of male high school graduates.)

The second and fourth columns of Table 9.1 document changes in enrollment rates and earnings differentials for women. Unlike enrollment rates for men, those for women rose throughout the two decades; however, it is notable that they rose much more slowly in the 1970s, when the college/high school earnings differential fell. Why did enrollment rates among women increase even when the

---

[14]Mary T. Coleman, "Movements in the Earnings-Schooling Relationship, 1940–88," *Journal of Human Resources* 28, no. 3 (Summer 1993): 660–680, provides a careful documentation of the college/high school earnings differential since 1940.

earnings differential fell? Because women's labor force participation rates and their hours of work outside the home have increased over time, the period over which their human capital investment returns can be received has lengthened. It is quite plausible that, for women during the 1970s, increases in the expected number of years over which returns will be received more than offset declines in the returns expected for any given year—with the result that expected rates of return to a college education still grew.[15]

While changes in average earnings differentials are a useful indicator of relative labor market conditions, individuals must assess their *own* probabilities of success in specific fields or occupations. Recent studies have pointed to the importance of friends, ethnic affiliation, and neighborhoods in the human capital decisions of individuals, even after controlling for the effects of parental income or education.[16] The educational and occupational choices of friends and acquaintances appear to have a significant effect on an individual's human capital decisions, perhaps because the presence of role models helps to reduce the uncertainty that inevitably surrounds estimates of future success in specific areas.

MARKET RESPONSES TO CHANGES IN COLLEGE ATTENDANCE

It is clear from Table 9.1 that the returns to college attendance have varied considerably over the past two decades, but the root causes of these changes are not immediately obvious. While we will inquire more deeply into these causes in Chapter 14, the student should be reminded at this point that, like other market prices, the returns to college attendance are determined by the forces of both employer demand and employee supply. Thus, if more high school students decide to attend college when presented with higher returns to such an investment, market forces are put into play that will tend to lower these returns in the future. Increased numbers of college graduates put downward pressure on the wages observed in labor markets for these graduates, other things equal, while a smaller number of high school graduates will tend to raise wages in markets for less-educated workers.[17]

---

[15]For evidence that women with "traditional" views of their economic roles receive lower rates of return on, and invest less in, human capital, see Francis Vella, "Gender Roles and Human Capital Investment: The Relationship Between Traditional Attitudes and Female Labour Market Performance," *Economica* 61, no. 242 (May 1994): 191–211. For an interesting analysis of historical trends in female college attendance, see Claudia Goldin, "Career and Family: College Women Look to the Past," working paper no. 5188, National Bureau of Economic Research, Cambridge, Mass., 1995.

[16]George J. Borjas, "Ethnic Capital and Intergenerational Mobility," *Quarterly Journal of Economics* 107 (February 1992): 123–150; Borjas, "Ethnicity, Neighborhoods, and Human Capital Externalities"; and James D. Montgomery, "Social Networks and Labor-Market Outcomes: Toward an Economic Analysis," *American Economic Review* 81 (December 1991): 1408–1418.

[17]One recent study estimated that, if the demand for college graduates remains steady, the increased supply of college graduates in response to the currently high returns to college would, by the year 2000, reduce the college/high school earnings differential by 25 percent. See Jacob Mincer, "Investment in U.S. Education and Training," working paper no. 4844, National Bureau of Economic Research, Cambridge, Mass., 1994.

EXAMPLE 9.2

Is the Market for College Graduates That Good, or Is the One for High School Graduates That Bad?

The rising returns to a college education evident in Table 9.1 may have seemed illusory to a college graduate who, in the early 1990s, was in the labor market. Compared to graduates in the late 1980s, college graduates in the early 1990s were increasingly likely to be unemployed, to start their careers in lower-paying sectors of the economy, and to be paid by the hour. How do these facts square with the claim that the returns to an investment in college were rising?

Human capital theory emphasizes that the monetary benefits of an educational investment are a function of the differential between one's expected earnings with and without the investment. Because it is the earnings *differential* that matters to a prospective student, one can observe an increase in the returns to college even in a market in which college graduates face the prospect of falling earnings; what is required is that the earnings of high school graduates be falling even faster!

In 1992, male college graduates between the ages of 25 and 29 earned an average of $32,225 per year if they worked full-time, whereas in 1985 they made an average of $35,032 if the Consumer Price Index is used to adjust for inflation. (As noted in Chapter 2, especially Table 2.2, the Consumer Price Index may overstate inflation to an unknown extent, but we use it here because it is readily available.) This 8 percent decline in real earnings reflect the labor market difficulties, noted above, that faced college graduates immediately after graduation in the early 1990s. During

this period, however, the average earnings of male high school graduates of similar age fell by 15 percent. Thus, however bad was the market for male college graduates, the market for male high school graduates was even worse, so that the wage differential between the two grew. Investing in a college education thus became more attractive, mainly as a way to escape the market's harsh treatment of male high school graduates during this period.

(The changing market conditions for women were not as adverse for either educational group. The real earnings of 25- to 29-year-old women who graduated from college and who worked full-time rose by 1 percent over this period, while comparable earnings for female high school graduates fell by 3 percent. We will analyze, in Chapter 14, why these earnings patterns developed for men and women of different educational groups.)

SOURCES: U.S. Bureau of the Census, *Money Income of Households, Families, and Persons in the United States,* Current Population Reports P–60, no. 156 (Table 36) and no. 184 (Table 30); Paul Ryscavage, "Recent Data on Job Prospects of College-Educated Youth," *Monthly Labor Review* 116, no. 8 (August 1993): 16–26. On this same subject, see John Tyler, Richard Murnane, and Frank Levy, "Are More College Graduates Really Taking High School Jobs? *Monthly Labor Review* 118, no. 12 (December 1995): 18–28.

The fact that the *future* salaries commanded by college graduates are affected by the number of people who *currently* decide to attend may seem obvious, but it adds another element of uncertainty to an individual's estimation of the expected returns to a college investment. An individual may observe that the returns to college attendance have recently increased, but *others* will observe this increase as well. If the improved returns cause a large rise in the percentage of high school graduates who attend college, the influx of workers four years from now into the labor markets for college graduates will put downward pressure on their wages at that time. Thus, current returns may be an unreliable estimate of future returns. (For an analysis of how the labor market might respond when workers behave as if the returns observed currently will persist into the future, see Appendix 9A.)

Education, Earnings, and Postschooling Investments in Human Capital

The preceding section used human capital theory to analyze the decision to undertake a formal educational program (college) on a full-time basis. We now turn to an analysis of workers' decisions to acquire training after they leave school and start working. Frequently, the human capital investments made after one has started to work arise from training received at the workplace. The presence of this type of training is difficult for the economist to directly observe; much of it is informal and not publicly recorded. We can, however, use human capital theory and certain patterns in workers' lifetime earnings to draw inferences about their demand for this type of training.

Figures 9.3 and 9.4 graph the 1992 earnings of men and women of various ages with different levels of education. An examination of these figures reveals four notable characteristics:

1. Average earnings of full-time workers rise with the level of education;
2. The most rapid increase in earnings occurs early in one's working life, thus giving a convex shape to the age/earnings profiles of both men and women;
3. Age/earnings profiles tend to fan out, so that education-related earnings differences later in workers' lives are greater than those early on;
4. The age/earnings profiles of men tend to be more convex and to fan out more than those for women.

In the sections that follow, we use human capital theory to help explain the above empirical regularities, with special attention given to the last three.

AVERAGE EARNINGS AND EDUCATIONAL LEVEL

It is an implication of our *investment* model of educational choice that earnings rise with the level of education, for if they did not, the incentives for students to invest in more education would disappear. It is thus not too surprising to see in Figures 9.3 and 9.4 that the average earnings of more-educated workers exceed those of less-educated workers.

It is worthwhile to remember, however, that *earnings* are influenced by both wage rates and hours of work. Data on *wage rates* are probably most relevant when looking at the returns to an educational investment, because they indicate

FIGURE 9.3
Money Earnings (Mean), for Full-Time, Year-Round Male Workers, 1992

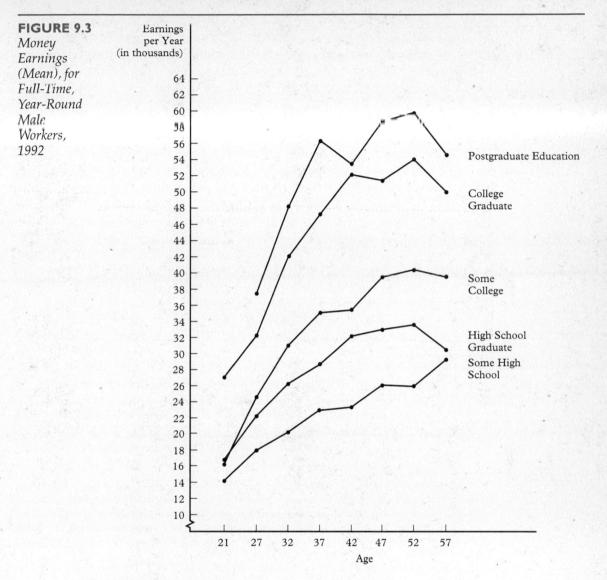

Earnings per Year (in thousands)

Postgraduate Education

College Graduate

Some College

High School Graduate

Some High School

Age

SOURCE: See footnote 18.

one's pay per unit of time at work. Wage data, however, are less widely available than earnings data. A crude, but readily available, way to control for working hours when using earnings data is to focus on full-time, year-round workers—which we do in Figures 9.3 and 9.4. More careful statistical analyses, however, which control for hours of work and factors other than education that can increase wage rates, come to the same conclusion suggested by Figures 9.3

and 9.4: namely, that more education is associated with higher pay. (A more rigorous theoretical analysis of the association between education and pay can be found in Appendix 9B, which presents the analysis in the context of hedonic wage theory.)

ON-THE-JOB TRAINING AND THE CONVEXITY OF AGE/EARNINGS PROFILES

The age/earnings profiles in Figures 9.3 and 9.4 typically rise steeply early on, then tend to flatten, and may eventually fall.[18] In fact, the early increases are so steep relative to those later on that a study of men's wage rates found that two-thirds of their *career* wage growth occurred in their first ten years of work![19] While in the next two chapters we will encounter other potential explanations for why earnings rise in this way with age, human capital theory explains the convexity of these profiles in terms of *on-the-job training*.[20]

Some on-the-job training is *learning by doing* (as one hammers nails month after month, one's skills naturally improve), but much of it takes place either in formal training programs run by employers or informally, in which case a trainee works under the close supervision of a more experienced worker. All forms of training are costly, in the sense that the productivity of learners is low, and all represent a conscious *choice* on the part of the employer to accept lower current productivity in exchange for higher output later. Both formal and informal training also involve the commitment of time by trainers or supervisors to the teaching process.[21]

Who bears the cost of on-the-job training? You will recall from Chapter 5 that the cost of *specific training*, training of use *only* to one's employer, is shared by the

---

[18]The data reflected in Figures 9.3 and 9.4 do not "follow" specific individuals through time; rather, they match earnings with age and education in a given year. Thus, the generally declining profiles for men in their fifties could reflect reduced job opportunities for older men, changes in the composition of men still working full-time at age 57, or some factor that depressed the earnings of men born in the middle 1930s. Data in these figures are from U.S. Bureau of the Census, *Money Income of Households, Families and Persons in the United States,* Current Population Reports P-60, no.184, Table 30.

[19]Kevin M. Murphy and Finis Welch, "Empirical Age-Earnings Profiles," *Journal of Labor Economics* 8 (April 1990): 202–229.

[20]For recent discussions of the relative importance of the human capital explanation for rising age/earnings profiles, see Ann P. Bartel, "Training, Wage Growth, and Job Performance: Evidence from a Company Database," *Journal of Labor Economics* 13, no. 3 (July 1995): 401–425, and Charles Brown, "Empirical Evidence on Private Training," in *Research in Labor Economics,* vol. 11, ed. Lauri J. Bassi and David L. Crawford (Greenwich, Conn.: JAI Press, 1990), 97–114.

[21]It has been estimated that employers spend between $18 and $43 billion each year (1995 dollars) on *formal* training programs. The amount spent on informal training is unknown. See Stephen C. Mangum, "Evidence on Private Sector Training," in *Investing in People,* Background Papers, vol. 1, Commission on Workplace Quality and Labor Market Efficiency, U.S. Department of Labor (September 1989): 332–385.

FIGURE 9.4

Money Earnings (Mean), for Full-Time, Year-Round Female Workers, 1992

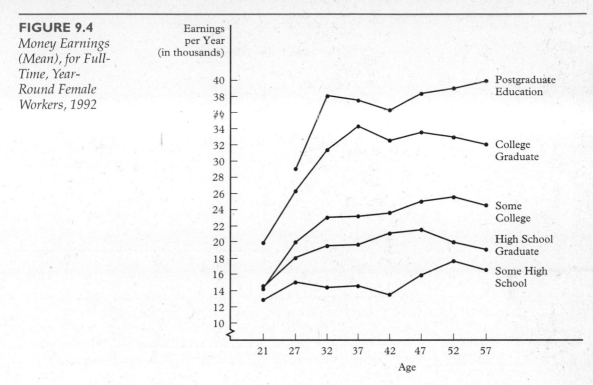

SOURCE: See footnote 18.

worker and the firm. The employee might be paid a wage greater than marginal product during the training period (MP_0), but after training the employee's wage is below his or her posttraining marginal product (MP_1). In the case of *general training*, in which employees acquire skills usable elsewhere, they alone pay the training costs.

How do employees pay the costs of general training provided by their employer? They work for a wage lower than they would get if they were not receiving training. Their wage is always equal to their *MP*, which is, of course, decreased during the training period when trainees require close supervision or time off the job to engage in classroom learning. Why do employees accept this lower wage? They accept it for the same reason that some decide to obtain formal schooling: in the expectation of improving the present value of their lifetime earnings. In other words, employees incur current investment costs (lower wages) to obtain increased earnings later.

Earlier, we argued that if people are going to invest in themselves they will tend to undertake most of the investment at younger ages. Human capital investments made at younger ages have a longer period over which to capture returns, and

FIGURE 9.5

Investment in On-the-Job Training over the Life Cycle

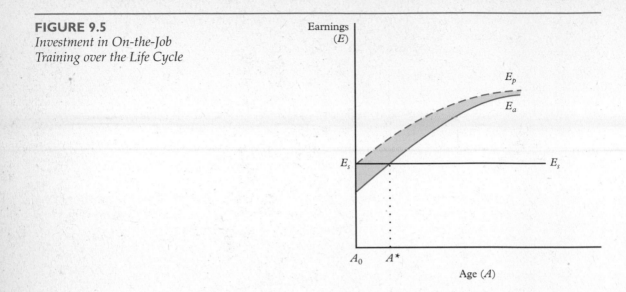

earnings that must be forgone during the period of training are lower when one is younger. Thus, other things equal, investments made earlier have higher rates of return.

Figure 9.5 graphically depicts the life-cycle implications of human capital theory as it applies to on-the-job training. The individual depicted has completed full-time schooling, and with this schooling is able to earn E_s at age A_0. Without further training, if the knowledge and skills the worker possesses from his or her schooling do not depreciate over time, earnings would remain at E_s over the life cycle. If the worker chooses to invest in on-the-job training, his or her future earnings potential can be enhanced, as shown by the (dashed) curve E_p in the figure. Investment in on-the-job training, however, has the near-term consequence that actual earnings are below potential; thus, in terms of Figure 9.5, actual earnings (E_a) lie below E_p as long as the worker is investing. In fact, the gap between E_p and E_a equals the worker's investment costs.

Figure 9.5 is drawn to reflect the theoretical implication, noted above, that human capital investments decline with age. With each succeeding year, actual earnings become closer to potential earnings; further, because workers become less willing to invest in human capital as they age, the yearly *increases* in potential earnings become smaller and smaller. Thus, curve E_p takes on a convex shape, quickly rising above E_s but flattening later in the life cycle.

Curve E_a also takes on a convex shape over the life cycle. Actual earnings start below E_s and do not rise above it until after age A^*. As human capital investments decline with age, however, E_a rises more quickly than E_p, until at some point later in the life cycle actual and potential earnings are virtually identical.

At this point, of course, the worker is no longer making on-the-job investments in human capital. [22]

THE FANNING OUT OF AGE/EARNINGS PROFILES

Earnings differences across workers with different educational backgrounds tend to become more pronounced as they age. This phenomenon is also consistent with what human capital theory would predict.

Investments in human capital tend to be more likely when the expected earnings differentials are greater, when the initial investment costs are lower, and when the investor has either a longer time to recoup the returns or a lower discount rate. Earlier, we argued that both younger people and those most willing to defer current consumption for future gains are more likely to invest in human capital. It should also be obvious that the same can be said of people who have the ability to learn more quickly. The ability to learn rapidly shortens the training period, and fast learners probably also experience lower psychic costs (lower levels of frustration) during training.

Thus, people who have the ability to learn quickly are those most likely to seek out, and be presented by employers with, training opportunities. [23] But who are

---

[22] A^* is sometimes called the "overtaking" age, and it is of great theoretical interest to economists. Because we cannot observe E_p— and can only observe E_a— it is not possible to directly measure workers' investments in on-the-job training. Thus, we cannot directly test the theoretical implication that investments in on-the-job training decline with age. One indirect test of the theory is to see if age/earnings profiles are convex, but another lies with A^*. If human capital theory provides a useful explanation for the shape of age/earnings profiles, then there should be some age (beyond A_0) at which differences in formal schooling do a better job of explaining differences in actual earnings than at either earlier or later ages. The age at which differences in formal schooling and differences in earnings are most closely related is A^*—the age at which actual earnings equal E_s, the potential earnings absent on-the-job training. Before A^*, actual earnings are below E_s and reflect an unknown amount of on-the-job training; after A^*, earnings are also "contaminated" by both the costs and returns to an unknown amount of on-the-job training. Landmark research on this topic estimated that, indeed, schooling has maximum correlation with earnings at about ten years after labor market entry; see Jacob Mincer, *Schooling, Experience, and Earnings* (New York: Columbia University Press for National Bureau of Economic Research, 1974), 57.

For other evidence consistent with the human capital model summarized in Figure 9.5, see David Neumark and Paul Taubman, "Why Do Wage Profiles Slope Upward? Tests of the General Human Capital Model," *Journal of Labor Economics* 13, no. 4 (October 1995): 736–761.

[23] For studies showing that on-the-job training is positively correlated with both educational level and ability, see Joseph G. Altonji and James R. Spletzer, "Worker Characteristics, Job Characteristics, and the Receipt of On-the-Job Training," *Industrial and Labor Relations Review* 45 (October 1991): 58–79; Jonathan R. Veum, "Training Among Young Adults: Who, What Kind, and For How Long?" *Monthly Labor Review* 116, no.8 (August 1993): 27–32; and Jill Constantine and David Neumark, "Training and the Growth in Wage Inequality," working paper no. 4729, National Bureau of Economic Research, Cambridge, Mass., May 1994.

these fast learners? They are most likely the people who, because of their abilities, were best able to reap benefits from formal schooling! Thus, human capital theory leads us to expect that workers who invested more in schooling will also invest more in postschooling job training.

The tendency of the better-educated workers to invest more in job training explains why their age/earnings profiles start low, rise quickly, and keep rising after the profiles of their less educated counterparts have leveled off. Their earnings rise more quickly because they are investing more heavily in job training, and they rise for a longer time for the same reason. In other words, people with the ability to learn quickly select the ultimately high-paying jobs where much learning is required and thus put their abilities to greatest advantage.

WOMEN AND THE ACQUISITION OF HUMAN CAPITAL

A comparison of Figures 9.3 and 9.4 discloses immediately that the earnings of women who work full-time year-round are lower than for men of equivalent age and education, and that women's earnings within each educational group rise less steeply with age. The purpose of this section is to analyze these differences in the context of human capital theory (a more complete analysis of male/female wage differentials is presented in Chapter 12).

As we have seen, human capital theory begins with an analysis of people's incentives to invest in education and training, and the expected monetary returns to such an investment are critical to their decisions. Anything that reduces these expected returns is hypothesized to reduce the incentives for workers (or their employers) to invest in human capital.

A major difference in the incentives of men and women to make human capital investments has historically been in the length of work life over which the costs of a human capital investment can be recouped. Chapters 6 and 7 clearly showed how rapidly working for pay has increased among women in recent decades, and this fact obviously should have made human capital investments more lucrative for women. Nevertheless, Table 9.2 shows that it is still the case that, on average, women can be expected to work (for pay) fewer years than men. In addition, Table 9.2 indicates that within the occupations shown—all of which require the acquisition of skills—women average fewer hours of work per week than do men.

To the extent that there is a shorter expected work life for women than for men, it is caused primarily by the role women have historically played in child-rearing and household production. This traditional role, while undergoing significant change, has caused many women to drop out of the labor market for a period of time in their childbearing years. Thus, female workers often have not had the continuity of experience that their male counterparts accumulate. If this historical experience causes younger women who are making important human capital decisions to expect a discontinuity in their own labor force participation, they might understandably avoid occupations or fields of study in which one's skills

TABLE 9.2

Average Work Life and Hours of Work, by Gender

Remaining Expected Years of Paid Work at Age 25[a]:	Male	Female
High school graduates	34.1 (years)	25.1 (years)
Some college	35.4	27.8
College graduates	37.2	30.3

Average Weekly Hours of Paid Work for Those Working Full-Time in 1994:		
Executive, administrative, managerial workers	47.6 (hours)	43.1 (hours)
Professional specialty workers	45.9	41.6
Technicians and related support workers	43.4	40.4
Sales workers	47.5	42.1
Precision production, craft, and repair workers	43.2	41.5

[a]Data relate to nondisabled individuals in 1988.

SOURCES: Anthony M. Gamboa, "The New Worklife Expectancy Tables for Disabled and Nondisabled Persons by Sex and Level of Educational Attainment," Vocational Econometrics, Louisville, Kentucky (1991); U.S. Bureau of Labor Statistics, *Employment and Earnings* 42 (January 1995): Table 23.

depreciate during the period out of the labor market.[24] Moreover, historical experience could cause employers to avoid hiring women for jobs requiring much on-the-job training—a practice that itself will affect the returns women can expect from a human capital investment. Human capital theory, however, *also* predicts that recent changes in the labor force participation of women, especially married

---

[24]Jacob Mincer and Haim Ofek, "Interrupted Work Careers: Depreciation and Restoration of Human Capital," *Journal of Human Resources* 17 (Winter 1982): 3–24, documented women's loss of earnings associated with withdrawal from the labor force. This study found that, upon reentry, women earn a lower real wage than when they withdrew. While wage growth is relatively rapid after reentry, the earnings of women who withdrew from the labor market never fully recover. Similar losses were suffered by men who involuntarily "withdrew" from their careers by being drafted into military service during the Vietnam War; see Joshua D. Angrist, "Lifetime Earnings and the Vietnam Era Draft Lottery: Evidence from Social Security Administrative Records," *American Economic Review* 80 (June 1990): 313–336. For a recent paper on skill depreciation rates, see Moon-Kak Kim and Solomon W. Polachek, "Panel Estimates of Male-Female Earnings Functions," *Journal of Human Resources* 29, no. 2 (Spring 1994): 406–428.

women of childbearing age, are causing dramatic changes in the acquisition of schooling and training by women. We turn now to a discussion of recent changes in these two areas.

WOMEN AND JOB TRAINING   There is little doubt that women receive less on-the-job training than men. A study of formal company training given to workers in their twenties found that, over the period 1986 to 1991, a lower percentage of women workers received such training and, of those who did, the hours of training were fewer than those for men.[25] To the extent that the presence and patterns of on-the-job training cause age/earnings profiles to be convex, an explanation for the flatter age/earnings profiles of women may well be rooted in their lower levels of on-the-job training. This human capital "explanation" for the flatter age/earnings profiles among women does not directly address whether the lower levels of job training emanate from the employer or the employee side of the market, but both possibilities are theoretically plausible. If employers expect women workers to have shorter work lives, they are less likely to provide training to them. Alternatively, if women themselves expect shorter work lives, they will be less inclined to seek out jobs requiring high levels of training to reach full productivity. Finally, if women expect employers to bar them from occupations requiring substantial amounts of training or experience, their expected returns to investments in these occupations will be diminished, thus reducing their incentives for such investments.[26]

While human capital theory predicts that the "traditional" role of women in child-rearing will lead to reduced incentives for training investments, it also quite strongly suggests that as this role changes, the incentives for women to acquire training will change.[27] We should thus expect to observe a growing convexity in women's age/earnings profiles over the past decades, and Figure 9.6 indicates this expectation is generally supported.

The darker lines in Figure 9.6 are the 1992 profiles for college and high school graduates that appeared in Figure 9.4. The lighter lines indicate the comparable profiles for 1977 (with earnings adjusted to 1992 dollars using the Consumer Price Index). A visual comparison reveals that the age/earnings profile for college-educated women has become much steeper for those in their twenties and early thirties. For example, in 1977 the earnings of a 32-year-old female college graduate were 26 percent greater than those of a 21-year-old college graduate, while in 1992 they were 59 percent greater. For women with high school educations, the profile for those in their twenties is only slightly steeper; 32-year-olds with high school educations earned 25 percent more than 21-year-olds in 1977 and 33 percent more

[25]Veum, "Training Among Young Adults: Who, What Kind, and For How Long?"

[26]Francine D. Blau and Marianne A. Ferber, "Career Plans and Expectations of Young Women and Men," *Journal of Human Resources* 26 (Fall 1991): 581–607, found that female college seniors, who expected starting salaries equal to those expected by men, expected much lower salaries later in their careers.

[27]See Elizabeth T. Hill, "Labor Market Effects of Women's Post-School-Age Training," *Industrial and Labor Relations Review* 49, no. 1 (October 1995): 138–149.

FIGURE 9.6

The Increased Convexity of Women's Age/Earnings Profiles

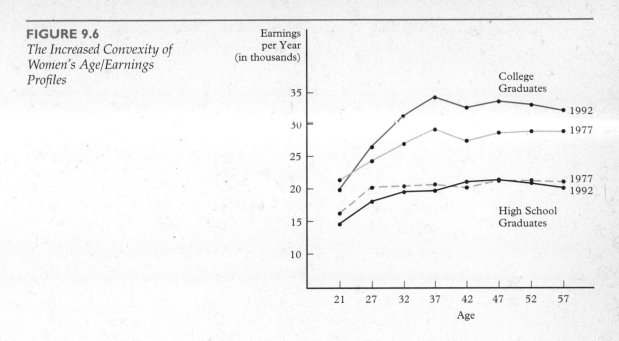

in 1992. The faster earnings growth among younger women in 1992, as compared to 1977, suggests that their receipt of on-the-job training may have increased as their expected work lives have lengthened.

It is interesting to note that in a survey of workers who entered the labor force between 1979 and 1983, women did indeed experience lower average wage growth than did their male counterparts over their first four years of work (22.5 percent growth in four years for women, 27.6 percent for men). Different growth rates, however, were found, *only* among those who *changed employers*; men and women who stayed with the same employer had essentially the same rate of wage growth.[28] While some of the relatively slower wage growth for women who changed jobs was explained by their greater propensity to seek part-time work, most of this differential wage growth remained unexplained. An intriguing possibility raised by this study, however, is that recently hired women who stay with their employers may now be receiving the same levels of on-the-job training as their male colleagues.

WOMEN AND FORMAL SCHOOLING   As Table 9.1 suggested, there have been dramatic changes in the level of formal education received by women in recent years. Their fields of study have also changed markedly. These changes undoubtedly reflect the increased returns to human capital investments arising

---

[28]Pamela J. Loprest, "Gender Differences in Wage Growth and Job Mobility," *American Economic Review* 82 (May 1992): 526–532.

TABLE 9.3

Percentages of Women Among College and University Graduates, by Degree and Field of Study, 1971 and 1991

Percentage of Women Among:	Bachelor's Degree		Master's Degree	
	1971	1991	1971	1991
Total	43.4%	53.9%	40.1%	51.0%
Business majors	9.1	47.2	3.9	34.9
Computer science majors	13.6	29.3	10.3	29.6
Education majors	74.5	78.9	56.2	76.6
Engineering majors	0.8	13.9	1.1	14.1
English majors	66.7	67.8	61.0	66.8
Health professionals	77.1	83.6	55.9	79.0
First professional degree[a]			6.3	39.0

[a]Degrees in this category are largely doctor's degrees in law, medicine, and dentistry.

SOURCE: U.S. National Center for Education Statistics, *Digest of Education Statistics 1993* (1993), Tables 235, 269, 271–273, 275, 278.

from women's increased attachment to the labor force and longer expected work lives. Table 9.3 outlines some of the magnitudes of these changes.

Women, who traditionally were less likely than men to graduate from college, now represent over half of both bachelor's and master's graduates. Increases have been especially great at the master's level, indicating that for many women, expected labor force attachment is now so great than an investment in postgraduate education is considered worthwhile. The most stunning changes, however, have occurred in the fields of study. Bachelor's business graduates, for example, are now almost 50 percent women; in 1971, women were only 9 percent of the total. A sixfold increase can be seen among those receiving law and doctor of medicine degrees, and even greater percentage gains were recorded in the field of engineering and in business programs at the master's level.[29] (The traditionally "female" fields of English, education, and health care have become slightly more heavily female, largely because college campuses themselves are more heavily female.)

---

[29]For a study of how changes in college majors, for both women and men, have affected the rate of return to college in recent years, see Jeff Grogger and Eric Eide, "Changes in College Skills and the Rise in the College Wage Premium," *Journal of Human Resources* 30, no. 2 (Spring 1995): 280–310. For a study of how college major, among other things, affects earnings, see Linda Datcher Loury and David Gorman, "College Selectivity and Earnings," *Journal of Labor Economics* 13, no. 2 (April 1995): 289–308.

Although the data in Table 9.3 indicate a very rapid change in the human capital decisions among women, it is still true that women are "underrepresented" in certain fields: engineering, computer science, business at the master's degree level, and the professions of law and medicine. While interests that develop in the process of socialization may account for some of this underrepresentation, some women's expectations of a discontinuity in labor market experience may also be part of the explanation. The fields in which women are still underrepresented tend to be highly technical, and concerns about the depreciation of human capital during any expected period out of the labor force could reduce the incentives of women to invest heavily in these fields.

Is Education a Good Investment?

It is well established that workers with more education tend to earn higher wages. However, an individual deciding whether to go to college would naturally ask, "Will I increase my monetary and psychic income enough to justify the costs of going to college?" Further, government policymakers trying to decide whether to improve educational programs or subsidize increased enrollments must ask, "Will the benefits of improved productivity outweigh the costs?"

It will be recalled from our discussion earlier in this chapter that there are two methods of assessing the returns to an investment. The *present-value method* involves choosing a discount rate and then summing the present value of expected future benefits so that the total returns can be compared to investment costs. If the present value of returns exceeds such costs, the investment can be considered worthwhile. Example 9.3 presents a situation in which calculating the present value of future investment returns is necessary.

The *internal rate of return method* calculates the discount rate that equates the present value of benefits with the investment cost. If the future returns from a particular investment decision are so large that the discount rate required to equate benefits and costs exceeds the rate of return an individual insists upon before investing, then the decision will be considered worthwhile. The next two subsections deal, respectively, with *individual* and *social* returns from educational investments, primarily using the rate-of-return method of analysis.

IS EDUCATION A GOOD INVESTMENT FOR INDIVIDUALS?

Individuals about to make an investment in a college education are typically committing themselves to costs of at least $17,000 per year. Is there evidence that this investment pays off for the typical student? Several studies have tried to answer this question by calculating the internal rates of return to educational investments. While the methods and data used vary, these studies normally estimate benefits by calculating earnings differentials at each age from age/earnings profiles such as those in Figures 9.3 and 9.4. (*Earnings* are usually used to measure benefits because

EXAMPLE 9.3

Valuing a Human Asset: The Case of the Divorcing Doctor

State divorce laws typically provide for the assets acquired during marriage to be divided in some equitable fashion. Such laws in the state of New York recognize, among the assets to be divided, the asset value of human capital investments made by either spouse during the period of marriage. How these acquired human capital values are estimated can be illustrated by the following example.

Dr. Doe married his wife right after he had acquired a license to practice medicine as a general practitioner. Instead of opening a general (family) practice, however, Dr. Doe undertook specialized training to become a surgeon. During his training (residency) period, the income of Dr. Doe and his wife was much lower than it would have been had he been working as a general practitioner (thus both spouses were investing, albeit to different degrees, in Dr. Doe's human capital). Shortly after his residency was completed and he had acquired board certification as a general surgeon, Dr. Doe and his wife decided to divorce. She sued him for an equitable division of the asset value of his certification as a general surgeon. How can this asset value be estimated?

The asset value of Dr. Doe's certificate as a general surgeon is the present value of his estimated *increase in lifetime earnings* made possible by the investment undertaken during marriage. In the absence of a specific work history as a surgeon, the most reasonable estimate of his increase in yearly earnings is calculated by subtracting from what the typical general surgeon earns in a year the average earnings of general practitioners (which is an estimate of what Dr. Doe could have earned in the absence of his training as a surgeon). In 1988, the median earnings of general surgeons were $135,000, while the median earnings of general practitioners were $79,000, implying a yearly earnings differential of $56,000.* Assuming a remaining worklife of 25 years and a real interest rate (which takes account of what inflation will do to the earnings differential) of 2 percent, the present value of the asset Dr. Doe "acquired" as the result of his surgical training comes to $1,092,560. (It would then be up to the court to divide this asset equitably between the two divorcing spouses.)

---

*The earnings data used are national medians for doctors with office practices in 1988. They were obtained with permission from *Medical Economics* magazine from "Earnings: Are You One of Those Losing Ground?" by Arthur Owens, *Medical Economics* (September 4, 1989): 130. The formula used to calculate present value is the one given in footnote 7 of this chapter, where $X = \$56,000$, $r = 0.02$, and $n = 25$.

---

higher wages and more stable jobs are both payoffs to more education.) It should be stressed that all such studies have analyzed only the monetary, not the psychic, costs of and returns on educational investments.

The rates of return typically estimated for the United States generally fall in the range of 5–15 percent (after adjusting for inflation).[30] These findings are interesting

---

[30]For a review of rate-of-return studies, see George Psacharopoulos, "Returns to Education: A Further International Update and Implications," *Journal of Human Resources* 20, no. 4 (Fall 1985): 583–604; and David Card, "Earnings, Schooling, and Ability Revisited," *Research in Labor Economics*, ed. Solomon Polachek, forthcoming.

because most other investments generate returns in the same range. Thus, it appears, at least at first glance, that an investment in education is about as good as an investment in stocks, bonds, or real estate. This conclusion must be qualified, however, by recognizing that there are systematic biases in the estimated rates of return to education. These biases, which are of unknown size, work in opposite directions.

THE UPWARD BIAS   The typical estimates of the rate of return on further schooling may overstate the gain an individual student could obtain by investing in education because they are unable to separate the contribution that *ability* makes to higher earnings from the contribution made by *schooling*.[31] The problem is that (*a*) people who are smarter, harder-working, and more dynamic are likely to obtain more schooling, and (*b*) such people might be more productive, and hence earn higher-than-average wages, even if they did not complete more years of schooling than others. When measures of ability are not observed or accounted for, the studies attribute *all* the earnings differentials associated with college to college itself and none to ability, even though *some* of the added earnings college graduates typically receive may have been received by an equally able high school graduate who did not attend college.

Recent studies that attempt to control for "ability bias" in estimating rates of return to schooling have utilized several strategies. Some have estimated the separate effects of schooling and aptitude-test scores on earnings. Others have estimated how much the earnings of people are affected when a random event, not ability, affects their level of schooling.[32] Still others analyze differences among family members, who have the same family background, and even among identical twins, who share the same inherited characteristics.[33] These studies generally conclude that the problem of ability bias is small.

---

[31]Another source of upward bias has been pointed out by C. M. Lindsay, "Measuring Human Capital Returns," *Journal of Political Economy* 79 (November/December 1971): 1195–1215. Lindsay reasons that if human capital investments earn a normal rate of return, they do not change the wealth of those who invest; postinvestment returns, in other words, just make up for the costs of investment. Human capital investments, however, do raise wages, and hence the price of leisure. As the principles of labor supply in Chapters 6 and 7 suggested, an increased wage with unchanged wealth would cause hours of leisure consumed to fall. Thus, human capital investments cause an increased price, and reduced consumption, of the important consumer good we call "leisure." Some of the differential in earnings we observe between those with more human capital and those with less is offset by utility lost by the former group when leisure is reduced. To count the entire earnings differential as a return on the investment without correcting for lost leisure overstates the *real gains* (that is, those expressed in terms of *utility*) to human capital investments.

[32]See Card, "Earnings, Schooling, and Ability Revisited," for a summary of many of these studies; see also McKinley Blackburn and David Neumark, "Omitted-Ability Bias and the Increase in the Return to Schooling," *Journal of Labor Economics* 11 (July 1993): 521–544.

[33]Orley Ashenfelter and David J. Zimmerman, "Estimates of the Returns to Schooling from Sibling Data: Fathers, Sons, and Brothers," *Review of Economics and Statistics,* forthcoming; and Orley Ashenfelter and Alan Krueger, "Estimates of the Economic Returns to Schooling from a New Sample of Twins," *American Economic Review* 84, no. 5 (December 1994): 1157–1173.

THE DOWNWARD BIAS   There are three reasons to believe that conventionally estimated rates of return to educational investments may be downward-biased. First, some benefits of college attendance are not necessarily reflected in higher productivity, but rather in an increased ability to understand and appreciate the behavioral, historical, and philosophical foundations of human existence. Second, most rate-of-return studies fail to include employee benefits; they measure money earnings, not total compensation. Because employee benefits as a percentage of total compensation tend to rise as money earnings rise, ignoring benefits tends to create a downward bias in the estimation of rates of return to education.

Third, some of the job-related rewards of college are captured in the form of psychic or nonmonetary benefits. Jobs in the executive or professional occupations are probably more interesting and pleasant than the more routine jobs typically available to people with less education. While executive and professional jobs do pay more than others, the total benefits of these jobs may be understated when only earnings differences are analyzed.[34]

SELECTION BIAS   A third source of bias in the standard estimates of rates of return on education arises from what has become known in recent years as the *selectivity* problem. Briefly put, one who decides to go to college and become a manager, rather than terminate schooling with high school and become a mechanic, may do so in part because he or she has very little mechanical aptitude; thus, becoming a mechanic might yield this person *less* income than would be earned by others who chose to become mechanics rather than go to college. Likewise, those who go to college may have aptitudes that generate more income in managerial jobs than could have been earned in those jobs by terminal high school graduates if they had acquired the college education needed to qualify for the managerial jobs. The significance of the selectivity phenomenon described above is that conventionally calculated rates of return may *understate* the returns to a college education for those who decide to attend college and *overstate* the returns forgone by someone who decides not to go.

To understand the potential selectivity biases in the conventionally calculated returns to a college education, keep in mind that the returns to a college education

---

[34]While not strictly an issue of downward bias, there is reason to believe that the conventionally measured rates of return to educational investments are below the rates of return that would be observed if some intervention (for example, the opening of a college in one's own hometown) were to cause people with lower educational attainment to increase their schooling. Human capital theory suggests that when deciding whether to make an investment, people compare their expected rate of return to their personal discount rate (that is, their "required" rate of return). Only if the expected rate of return exceeds the required return is the investment worth making. Suppose, now, that the yearly monetary costs and returns associated with the same educational investment do not vary much across individuals, but that personal discount rates vary considerably. Suppose too that each person continues to invest in education until the monetary rate of return equals (or is about to fall below) his or her personal discount rate. Under these conditions, those who had previously invested less did so because they had higher rates of discount, and a higher *required* rate of return implies a higher *observed* rate of return. For more on this topic, see Card, "Earnings, Schooling, and Ability Revisited."

are usually based on differences between the actual earnings of college and high school graduates. For people who graduated from college, the rate-of-return calculation thus assumes that, in the absence of a college education, their earnings would have been equal to those of the average high school graduate. If, instead, their earnings would have been *less* than those of the high school graduate, the conventional calculation *understates* their gains from a college investment. Analogously, the conventionally calculated rate of return to a college education may *overstate* the returns that could have been received by those who decided against attending college, because they might have been unable to earn as much with a college education as do those who actually attended college.

Fortunately, the selectivity bias in estimated rates of return to schooling appears to be small.[35] Nevertheless, raising the selectivity issue does serve to remind us that the principle of comparative advantage is potentially important in making choices about schooling and occupations.

IS EDUCATION A GOOD SOCIAL INVESTMENT?

The issue of education as a social investment has been of heightened interest in the United States during the past decade especially because of three related developments. First, product markets have become more global, increasing the elasticity of both product and labor demand. As a result, American workers are now facing more competition from workers in other countries. Second, the growing availability of high-technology capital, especially the desktop computer, has created new products and production systems that require workers to have greater cognitive skills and to be adaptable, efficient learners. Indeed, a recent study has indicated that the returns to a worker's having greater quantitative skills— especially the skills taught in the United States prior to high school—have risen in recent years.[36]

Third, American elementary and secondary school students score poorly relative to students elsewhere in language proficiency, scientific knowledge, and (especially) mathematical skills. For example, Table 9.4 displays the average scores on a mathematical proficiency test given on a comparable basis (that is, to all 13-year-olds) in six different countries. The American score lies below that in every other country shown. The combination of these three developments has caused concern about the productivity of America's future workforce, relative to workers elsewhere, and to a series of questions about our educational system: Are we devoting enough resources to educating our current and future workforce? Should the re-

---

[35]The discussion in this subsection is based on Robert J. Willis and Sherwin Rosen, "Education and Self-Selection," *Journal of Political Economy* 87 (October 1979): S7–S36. Also see Kevin Hollenbeck, "Postsecondary Education as Triage: Returns to Academic and Technical Programs," *Economics of Education Review* 12, no. 3 (September 1993): 213–232.

[36]Richard J. Murnane, John B. Willett, and Frank Levy, "The Growing Importance of Cognitive Skills in Wage Determination," working paper no. 5076, National Bureau of Economic Research, Cambridge, Mass., 1995.

TABLE 9.4

International Comparisons of Proficiency in Mathematics at Age 13, 1991

Country	Test Score
Canada	513
France	519
Spain	495
Switzerland	539
Taiwan	545
United States	494

SOURCE: National Center for Education Statistics, *The Condition of Education 1993* (NCES 93–290, June 1993), Table 15.2.

sources we devote to education be reallocated in some way? Should we demand more of students in elementary and secondary schools?

As Table 9.5 indicates, the United States devotes at least as many resources to elementary and secondary education as do other developed countries. In terms of dollars per student, the United States ranks first among the six countries shown, and in terms of student/teacher ratios or the percentages of the population completing secondary school, it ranks in the middle. Moreover, the percentage of the population completing college is higher than in every comparison country, and double that of the European countries shown. Thus, with almost 8 percent of its gross domestic product devoted to the direct costs of formal education (elementary, secondary, and college), and with forgone earnings (especially of college students) adding another 4 or 5 percent, the United States devotes a substantial fraction of its available resources to formal schooling.[37] Whether this huge social investment pays off, and whether its returns can be enhanced, are important questions. In beginning to answer them, we must try to understand how education and productivity are related.

The view that increased educational investments increase worker productivity is a natural outgrowth of the observation that such investments enhance the earnings of individuals who undertake them. However, this view that the educational investment is what *causes* productivity to rise is not the only possible interpretation for the positive relationship between earnings and schooling. Another interpretation is that the educational system provides society with a screening device that sorts people by their (predetermined) ability. As discussed below, this alternative view, in its extreme form, sees the educational system as a means of *finding out* who is productive, not of enhancing worker productivity.

---

[37]The forgone earnings of high school and college students have been estimated to equal 60 percent of the *direct* cost outlays at those schooling levels. See Theodore Schultz, *The Economic Value of Education* (New York: Columbia University Press, 1963).

TABLE 9.5
International Comparisons of Schooling, 1991

Country	Public Expenditures per Pupil Grades 1–12 (in U.S. $)	Pupils per Teacher, Elementary Schools	% of Those, Ages 25–44, Who Have Completed	
			Secondary School	University
Canada	$3,508	15.3	86.0%	17.5%
France	2,627	15.7	65.9	11.6
Germany	2,750	17.7	89.3	11.5
Japan	2,115	21.2	90.6	22.9
United Kingdom	2,492	19.7	79.2	11.7
United States	3,917	18.0	86.1	23.7

SOURCES: National Center for Education Statistics: *The Condition of Education 1993* (NCES 93–290, June 1993), 64, 140; *Digest of Education Statistics 1993* (NCES 93–292, October 1993), Table 383.

THE SIGNALING MODEL[38] An employer seeking to hire workers is never completely sure of the actual productivity of any applicant, and in many cases the employer may remain unsure long after an employee is hired. What an employer *can* observe are certain indicators that firms believe to be correlated with productivity: age, experience, education, and other personal characteristics. Some indicators, such as age, are immutable. Others, like formal education, can be *acquired* by workers. Indicators that can be acquired by individuals can be called *signals*; our analysis here will focus on the signaling aspect of formal education.

Let us suppose that firms wanting to hire new employees for particular jobs know that there are two groups of applicants that exist in roughly equal proportions. One group has a productivity of 2, let us say, and the other has a productivity of 1. Further, suppose that these productivity levels are *immutable* (they cannot be changed by education or training) and that employers *cannot readily distinguish* which applicants are from which group. If they were unable to make such distinctions, firms would be forced to assume that all applicants are "average"; that is, they would have to assume that each had a productivity of 1.5 (and would offer them wages of up to 1.5).

While workers in this simple example would be receiving what they were worth on *average*, any firm that could devise a way to distinguish between the two groups

---

[38]This analysis is based on Michael Spence, "Job Market Signaling," *Quarterly Journal of Economics* 87 (August 1973): 205–221.

(at little or no cost) could enhance its profits. When wages equal 1.5, workers with productivities equal to 1 are receiving more than they are worth. If these applicants could be discovered, and either rejected or placed into lower-paying jobs, the firm could obviously increase its profits. It turns out that using educational attainment as a hiring standard—even if education does not enhance productivity—is profitable for the employer *if* it so happens that the cost to workers of acquiring the required schooling is a signal of (that is, is related to) on-the-job productivity.

To illustrate the use of educational signaling, suppose that employers come to believe that applicants with at least e^* years of education beyond high school are the ones with productivity 2, and that those with less than e^* are in the lower-productivity group. With this belief, workers with less than e^* years would be rejected for any job paying a wage above 1, while those with at least e^* would find that competition among employers drives their wages up to 2. This simple hypothetical wage structure is illustrated in Figure 9.7. If additional schooling does not enhance productivity, can requiring the signal of e^* really distinguish between the two groups of applicants? The answer is yes *if the costs to the worker of acquiring the added schooling are negatively related to his or her on-the-job productivity.*

If workers with at least e^* years of education beyond high school can obtain a wage of 2, while those with less can earn a wage of only 1, all workers would want to acquire the signal of e^* if it were costless for them to do so; in this case, using educational attainment as a signaling device would fail, because workers in both groups would acquire the same signal. As we argued earlier, however, schooling costs are both large and different for different individuals. In particular, the *psychic* costs of education are probably inversely related to one's ability: those who learn easily can acquire the educational signal (of e^* in this case) more cheaply than others. If—and this is critical—those who have *lower* costs of acquiring education are *also* more productive on the job, then requiring educational signals can be useful for employers.

To understand the role of costs in signaling, refer to Figure 9.8, in which the reward structure from Figure 9.7 is expressed in terms of the present value of life-

FIGURE 9.7
The Benefits to Workers of Educational Signaling

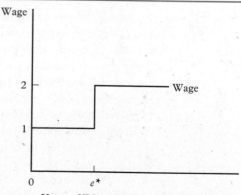

Wage

2

1

0   e^*

Years of Education Beyond High School

Wage

FIGURE 9.8
The Lifetime Benefits and Costs of Educational Signaling

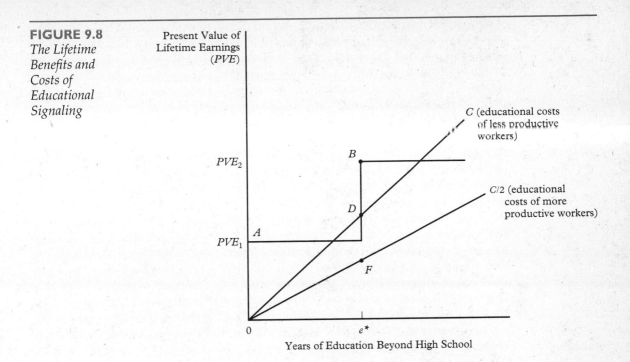

Years of Education Beyond High School

time earnings (at a wage of 1 their discounted lifetime earnings sum to PVE_1, while at a wage of 2 they sum to PVE_2). If we assume that each year of education costs C for those with less productivity, and $C/2$ for those with greater productivity, the fundamental influences on worker choices concerning education are easily seen.

Workers will choose the level of schooling at which the difference between their discounted lifetime earnings and their total educational costs is maximized. For those with yearly educational costs of C, the difference between lifetime earnings and total educational costs is maximized at zero years of education beyond high school. For these workers, the net benefit of e^* years beyond high school (distance BD) is less than the net benefit of zero additional years (distance $A0$), and for them, the benefits of acquiring the signal of e^* years is not worth the added costs. For those whose costs are $C/2$, it can be seen that the net benefits of investing in e^* (distance BF) exceed the net benefits of other schooling choices. Therefore, only those with costs of $C/2$—the workers with productivities of 2—find it advantageous to acquire e^* years of schooling.

Three points should be made about our simple example of signaling above. First, workers may not think of themselves as acquiring a signal if they attend school, even though in our example they are. All most workers will know is that by obtaining more education they can increase their wages, and their decision about how much education to acquire depends on the costs and returns to them.

Second, our simple example demonstrated how education could have signaling value even if it did not directly enhance worker productivity. It is necessary to stress, though, that for education to have signaling value in this case, on-the-job productivity and the costs of education must be *negatively* related. In our example, if the higher costs reflected along line C were associated with lower cognitive ability or a distaste for learning, then it is conceivable that in many jobs these costs could be indicative of lower productivity. If, however, those with costs along C have higher costs only because of lower family wealth (and therefore smaller "contributions" from others toward their schooling costs), then they may be no less productive on the job than those along line C/2. In this latter case, signaling would fail in the sense that it would only indicate those with low family wealth, not lower productivity.

Third, even if educational signaling is a useful way to predict future productivity, there is an *optimum* signal beyond which society would not find it desirable to go. Suppose, for example, that employers now requiring e^* years for entry into jobs paying a wage of 2 were to raise their hiring standards to e' years, as shown in Figure 9.9. Those with educational costs along C would still find it in their best interests to remain at zero years of schooling beyond high school, and those with costs along C/2 would find it profitable to invest in the required signal of e' (because distance $B'F'$ is greater than $A0$). Requiring more schooling of those who are selected for high-wage jobs, however, is more costly for those workers (and thus for society as a whole). While the new required signal would distinguish between the two groups of workers, it would do so at increased social cost. Put differently, using e^* as the required signal would be just as effective as using e', yet would entail lower opportunity costs. Therefore, using e' cannot be socially optimal.[39]

Whether schooling is purely a signaling device or adds to productivity is not a particularly important question for individuals. Whatever role schools play, additional schooling does enhance one's lifetime income. Where the issue of signaling is important is at the social level. If the only purpose of schools is to provide signals, why encourage investments in the expansion or qualitative upgrading of schooling? If forty years ago being a high school graduate signaled above-average intelligence and work discipline, why incur the enormous costs of expanding college attendance only to find out that now these qualities are signaled by having a bachelor's degree? The issue is of even more importance in less-developed countries, where mistakes in allocating extremely scarce capital resources could be disastrous (see Example 9.4).

---

[39]Some critics of the human capital view of education argue that escalation of educational standards has occurred for jobs in which work requirements have remained largely unchanged. These critics can be understood as saying that firms require e' when requiring e^* would be cheaper and work just as well. See, for example, Ivar Berg, *Education and Jobs: The Great Training Robbery* (New York: Praeger Publishers, 1970).

FIGURE 9.9

Requiring a Greater Signal May Have Costs Without Benefits

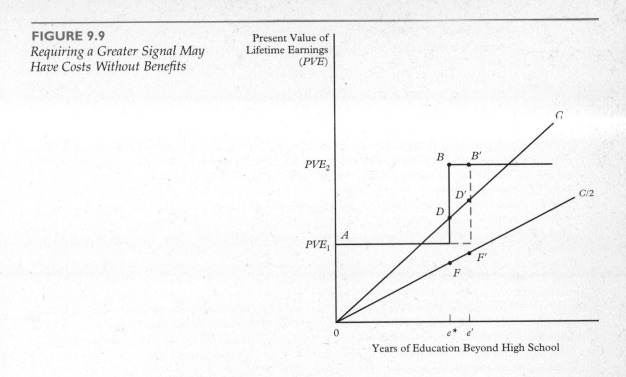

SIGNALING OR HUMAN CAPITAL? Direct evidence on the role schooling plays in society is difficult to obtain. Advocates of the signaling viewpoint, for example, might point to the higher rates of return for college *graduates* than for college *dropouts* as evidence that schooling is a signaling device.[40] They argue that what is learned in school is proportional to the time spent there and that an added bonus (rate of return) just for a diploma is proof of the signaling hypothesis. Advocates of the view that schooling enhances human capital could counter that one who graduates after four years probably has learned more than four times what the freshman dropout has learned. They argue that dropouts are more likely to be poorer students—the ones who overestimated their returns on schooling and quit when they discovered their mistake. Thus, their relatively low rate of return is associated not with their dropping out but with their *reason* for dropping out.

_____

[40]Dropouts naturally have lower earnings than graduates, but because they have also invested less, it is not clear that their *rates of return* should be lower. For further discussion and evidence, see Andrew Weiss, "High School Graduation, Performance, and Wages," *Journal of Political Economy* 96 (August 1988): 785–820; and Jin Heum Park, "Estimation of Sheepskin Effects and Returns to Schooling Using the Old and the New CPS Measures of Educational Attainment," working paper no. 338, Industrial Relations Section, Princeton University, August 1994. Thomas J. Kane and Cecilia Elena Rouse, "Comment on W. Norton Grubb: 'The Varied Economic Returns to Postsecondary Education: New Evidence from the Class of 1972'," *Journal of Human Resources* 30, no. 1 (Winter 1995): 205–221, calls into question the benefits of graduation independent of the number of *credits* taken.

EXAMPLE 9.4

The Socially Optimal Level of Educational Investment

In additional to asking whether schooling is a good social investment, we could also ask, What is the socially optimal *level* of schooling? The general principle guiding our answer to this question is that society should increase or reduce its educational investments until the marginal rate of return (to society) equals the marginal rate of return on other forms of capital investment (investment in physical capital, for example).

The rationale for the above principle is that if society has some funds it wants to invest, it will desire to invest them in projects yielding the highest rates of return. If an investment in physical capital yields a 20 percent rate of return and the same funds invested in schooling yield (all things considered) only a 10 percent return, society will clearly prefer to invest in physical capital. As long as the two rates of return differ, society could be made better off by reducing its investments in low-yield projects and increasing them in those with higher rates of return.

The text has discussed many of the difficulties and biases inherent in estimating rates of return to schooling. However, the general principle of equating the rates of social return on all forms of investments is still a useful one to consider. It suggests, for example, that capital-poor countries should invest in additional schooling only if the returns are very high—higher, in all probability, than the rates of return required for optimality in more-capital-rich countries. Indeed, the rates of return to both secondary schooling and higher education appear to be generally higher in less-developed countries than in developed countries. One review estimated that the rate of return on secondary schooling investment was 10 percent for a developed country (on average), while for a less-developed country it was 13 to 15 percent. Comparable rates of return on investments in higher education were 8 percent and 11 percent, respectively.

SOURCE: George Psacharopoulos, "Returns to Investment in Education: A Global Update," *World Development* 22, no. 9 (1994): 1325–1343.

To take another example, proponents of the human capital view of education could argue that the fact that earnings differentials between college and high school graduates grow with age supports their view. If schooling were just a signaling device, employers would rely on it *initially,* but as they accumulated direct information from experience with their employees, schooling would play a smaller role in determining earnings. Signaling advocates could counter that continued growth in earnings differentials and the continued association of schooling and earnings only illustrate that educational attainment is a *successful* signaling device.

As a final example, proponents of the signaling view of education point to the widespread placement of workers into jobs for which they are "overqualified." Put succinctly, if education is purely a signaling device and if levels of education are increasing over time, then as time goes on employers will be led to hire workers whose educational levels exceed the true requirements for their jobs. One study, however, found that workers who were educationally overqualified tended to be less experienced and to have received less job training than others; thus, their "extra" human capital from schooling appeared to be compensating for deficiencies in other forms of human capital.[41] Here again, the "human capital" and "signaling" views of education are difficult to distinguish with available data.[42]

SCHOOL QUALITY   Given the difficulty of generating predictions of labor market outcomes that can directly distinguish the signaling from the human capital hypothesis, one is led to wonder if there are other ways to resolve the debate. A research strategy with some potential grows out of issues related to school quality.

As mentioned earlier, concerns have been raised about the cognitive achievement of American students.[43] If schooling performs primarily a signaling function, by helping to *discover* people's cognitive abilities, one would not necessarily look to the educational system to remedy the problem of low cognitive achievement. However, if schooling can enhance the kinds of skills that pay off in the labor market, then increased investment in the quality of the nation's schools could be warranted.

There is little doubt that workers of higher cognitive skill have higher earnings, even among those with equal levels of education.[44] Proponents of the signaling and human capital views of education can agree that people of higher ability are likely to be more productive; where they disagree is on whether better schools can enhance worker productivity by improving cognitive skills. Advocates of the signaling viewpoint cite a substantial literature suggesting there is almost no demonstrated relationship between schooling expenditures and student performance on

[41]Nachum Sicherman, "'Overeducation' in the Labor Market," *Journal of Labor Economics* 9 (1991): 101–122.

[42]Attempts to distinguish between the two views of schooling continue, especially in the context of secondary schooling. For example, Joseph Altonji, "The Effects of High School Curriculum on Education and Labor Market Outcomes," *Journal of Human Resources* 30, no. 3 (Summer 1995): 409–438, finds evidence suggesting that *completing* high school, not what is learned in particular courses, is associated with higher wages among less-educated workers in the United States. This finding can be interpreted as support for the view that high school completion is valued by employers as a signal (of good work habits, presumably learned earlier) rather than for what is learned in various high school classes. For more on this, see Andrew Weiss, "Human Capital vs. Signaling Explanations of Wages," *Journal of Economic Perspectives* 9, no. 4 (Fall 1995): 133–154. Somewhat different results are found in a study using data from the Netherlands; see Wim Groot and Hessel Oosterbeek, "Earnings Effects of Different Components of Schooling; Human Capital versus Screening," *Review of Economics and Statistics* 76, no. 2 (May 1994): 317–321.

[43]John Bishop, "Is the Test Score Decline Responsible for the Productivity Growth Decline?" *American Economic Review* 79 (March 1989): 178–197.

[44]M. Bossiere, J. Knight, and R. Sabot, "Earnings, Schooling, Ability, and Cognitive Skills," *American Economic Review* 75 (December 1985): 1016–1031, and Ethel B. Jones and John D. Jackson, "College Grades and Labor Market Rewards," *Journal of Human Resources* 25 (Spring 1990): 253–266.

tests of cognitive skill.[45] Advocates of the human capital view, however, find support in studies of *earnings* and school quality. These studies generally indicate that students attending higher-quality schools (that is, ones with greater resources per student) have higher subsequent earnings, other things equal.[46]

Clearly, assessments of the social returns to schooling that examine the role of school quality have so far yielded somewhat ambiguous results. Better schools may enhance labor market earnings, but evidence that they enhance measured cognitive abilities is relatively weak. One possibility, of course, is that better schools enhance productivity by teaching useful problem-solving skills or better work habits—characteristics that may be valued in the labor market but not captured especially well by standardized tests of cognitive achievement. Another possibility, however, is that better schools give students better information about their own interests and abilities, thus helping them to make more successful career choices. Some important questions, then, remain unanswered.

DOES THE DEBATE MATTER?   In the end, perhaps the debate between advocates of the signaling and human capital views of schooling is not terribly important. The fact is that schooling investments offer *individuals* monetary rates of return that are comparable to those received from other forms of investment. For individuals to recoup their human capital investment costs requires willingness on the part of employers to pay higher wages to people with more schooling; and for employers to be willing to do this, schools must be providing a service that employers could not perform more cheaply themselves.

For example, we argued earlier that to profit from an investment of $100,000 in a college education, college graduates must be paid at least $3,652 more per year than they would have received otherwise. Naturally, this requires that they find employers who are willing to pay them the higher yearly wage. If college directly or indirectly adds to one's labor market productivity, it is obvious why employers should be willing to pay this premium and how society benefits from human capital investments. But what if colleges merely help to *reveal* who is more productive?

---

[45]See Eric A. Hanushek, "The Economics of Schooling: Production and Efficiency in Public Schools," *Journal of Economic Literature* 24 (September 1986): 1141–1177, and more recently, Eric A. Hanushek, "When School Finance 'Reform' May Not Be Good Policy," *Harvard Journal on Legislation* 28 (Summer 1991): 423–456. For contrary evidence, see Susanna Loeb and John Bound, "The Effect of Measured School Inputs on Academic Achievement: Evidence from the 1920s, 1930s, and 1940s Birth Cohorts," working paper no. 5331, National Bureau of Economic Research, Cambridge, Mass., November 1995.

[46]For a review of these studies, see David Card and Alan B. Krueger, "Labor Market Effects of School Quality: Theory and Evidence," working paper no. 357, Industrial Relations Section, Princeton University, January 1996. For a recent study with largely contrary evidence, see James J. Heckman, Anne Layne-Farrar, and Petra Todd, "The Schooling Quality-Earnings Relationship: Using Economic Theory to Interpret Functional Forms Consistent with the Evidence," working paper no. 5288, National Bureau of Economic Research, Cambridge, Mass., October 1995.

If employers believed they could create tests or other devices that reveal productivity characteristics for less than a yearly cost of $3,652 per worker, they would have strong incentives to adopt these alternative modes of screening workers. The fact that employers continue to emphasize (and pay for) educational requirements in the establishment of hiring standards suggests one of two things. Either more education *does* enhance worker productivity, or it is a *less expensive* screening tool than any other that firms could use. In either case, the fact that employers are willing to pay a high price for an educated workforce seems to suggest that education produces social benefits.[47]

IS PUBLIC SECTOR TRAINING A GOOD SOCIAL INVESTMENT?

The same developments leading American policymakers to ask resource-allocation questions about elementary and secondary schooling have also led to similar questions about job-training programs. Much of the job training available to workers is provided formally or informally at the workplace, and as indicated in Chapter 5 (Example 5.3), there is some evidence that American workers receive less employer-provided training than other workers in the developed world. Higher turnover rates among American workers might be a partial explanation, as might the lower cognitive achievement levels among those who end their formal education with high school.[48] If American workers are ill equipped to receive—or are for some other reasons not receiving—job training in the private sector, would increased public sector training programs be a good social investment?

During the past four decades, the federal government has funded a variety of training programs that primarily targeted disadvantaged men, women, and youth. Some of these programs have provided relatively inexpensive help in searching for work, while others have directly provided work experience or (in the case of the Job Corps) comprehensive services associated with living away from home. Over these decades, however, roughly half of those enrolled received classroom training at vocational schools or community colleges, and another 15 percent received in-plant training. The per-student costs of these latter two types of programs have been in the range of $3,000 to $6,000 (in 1994 dollars).[49]

Evaluating these programs requires comparing their costs to an estimate of the present value of their benefits. The programs were intended to increase the

---

[47]Kevin Lang, "Does the Human Capital/Educational Sorting Debate Matter for Development Policy?" *American Economic Review* 84, no. 1 (March 1994): 353–358, comes to a similar conclusion through a more formal argument.

[48]For a summary of major issues and a comparative overview of job training in Europe, North America, and Japan, see Lisa Lynch, "Introduction," in *Training and the Private Sector: International Comparisons*, ed. Lisa Lynch (Chicago: University of Chicago Press, 1994), 1–24.

[49]Robert J. LaLonde, "The Promise of Public Sector–Sponsored Training Programs," *Journal of Economic Perspectives* 9, no. 2 (Spring 1995): 149–168, gives a brief history of federally sponsored training programs and summarizes several issues relevant to evaluating their efficacy.

productivity of trainees, and in the case of this kind of (general) training, enhancements of trainee productivity should be reflected by their increased earnings. Thus, evaluators have set out to estimate by how much the earnings of trainees were increased as a result of their training. Measuring this increase in earnings involves estimating what the trainee would have earned in the absence of the program, and there are several thorny issues the researcher must successfully confront. Nevertheless, a recent summary of two dozen credible studies came to some rather firm conclusions about the benefits of these programs.

First, adult women were the only group among the disadvantaged that clearly experienced earnings gains as a result of training; adult men and youth showed no consistent earnings increases across the various studies. Second, the estimated average increase in earnings for women in the various studies was typically around $1,500 per year.[50] Although one evaluation found enhanced earnings seven years after training, the typical study was unable to follow the trainees' earnings for very long after the program, so little is known about the long-run effects on earnings. Third, most of the earnings increases resulted from higher rates of employment, and there is little evidence that *wage rates* were increased by training.

For disadvantaged men and youth, then, investments in federally sponsored training apparently had a negative return; costs were expended, but no clear-cut increases in productivity resulted. For disadvantaged women, earnings increases did result. Were these latter increases large enough to justify program costs?

The programs had direct costs of $3,000 to $6,000 per trainee, but they also had opportunity costs in the form of forgone output. The typical trainee was in her program for 16 weeks, and while many of the trainees had been on welfare prior to training, the opportunity costs of their time surely were not zero; indeed, the student will recall from Chapter 7 that a person can be productive in the home as well as the workplace. If one were to place a value on time at home equal to $18,000 per year (see Example 7.2 in Chapter 7), spending one-third of a year in training had opportunity costs of roughly $6,000. Thus, the total costs of training were probably in the range of $9,000 to $12,000 per woman.

If benefits of $1,500 per year were received annually for 20 years after training, and if the appropriate discount rate is 2 percent, the present value of benefits comes to $24,500.[51] Benefits of this magnitude are clearly in excess of costs. Indeed, the present value of benefits would still be in excess of $12,000 even if the yearly earnings increases lasted for only 9 years. Therefore, it appears likely that federally sponsored training for disadvantaged women has been a social investment worth making.

---

[50]Robert LaLonde, "The Promise of Public Sector–Sponsored Training Programs," Table 1.

[51]The real rate of interest—that is, the nominal rate less the rate of inflation—on government securities has been in the neighborhood of 2 percent during the postwar period. The real rate of interest is the appropriate discount rate if, as in our example, benefits are not inflation-adjusted.

Chapter 9 - Reading Notes

Worker investments: 3 kinds human capital investments
    education + training   overall wealth in
    migration   economy
    job search

choice to educate depends on
- ease + speed of learning   } different for all
- expectations   } people
- financial resources

Human Capital Costs to Worker
1) out of pocket or direct
2) foregone earnings
3) Psychic losses

Expected returns
1) higher future earnings
2) incr job satisfaction
3) incr appreciation in non mkt activities/interests

Schooling attractive if PV exceeds costs

Demand f/ College: 4 Predictions
1) Future-oriented people Yes - Present oriented No
2) Most students will be young
3) Attendance ↓ if costs ↑
4) Attendance ↑ if gap between earnings } college vs
    widens   } noncollege

Earnings characteristics
1) avg earnings ↑ w/ edu ↑
2) incr rapid early in career
3) age/earnings profiles fan out so that edu-related earnings differences later in workers' lives are greater than early on
4) mens more convex + fanned out than f/ women

upward bias - ability bias
downward bias benefits not considered
selection bias -

Education as social investment
  ↑ productivity?
    screening device
        ↓ signals → education

REVIEW QUESTIONS

1. Women receive lower wages, on average, than men of equal age. What concepts of human capital help to explain this phenomenon? Explain. Why does the discrepancy between earnings for men and women grow with age?

2. Suppose financial aid to college students were financed by income taxes on the general population and the President cut this aid significantly (correspondingly cutting taxes). Analyzing the likely *labor market* effects of these cuts, identify the various groups that would *gain* and *lose* from these cuts over their lifetimes. Discuss your reasoning concerning each in turn. Then analyze the likely effects on the retirement ages of these groups.

3. Many crimes against property (burglary, for example) can be thought of as acts that have immediate gains but entail long-run costs (sooner or later the criminal may be caught and imprisoned). If imprisoned, the criminal loses income from both criminal and noncriminal activities. Using the framework for occupational choice in the long run, analyze what kinds of people are most likely to engage in criminal activities. What can society do to reduce crime?

4. The United States is currently facing an education crisis in its high schools, which are graduating people with insufficient skills in mathematics and communications to perform tasks now required in the workplace. One suggested solution is to increase the level of competency required for high school graduation. The other suggestion stems from the observation that employers seem to care much more about job applicants' possession of a high school *degree* than their high school *grades;* this sugges-

tion is that employers tie wage offers for entry-level jobs to applicants' high school grades (higher grades would mean higher wages). Compare the labor market effects of these two strategies for improving competency levels among high school graduates.

5. Why do those who argue that more education "signals" greater ability believe that the most able people will obtain the most education?

6. Currently, anyone can advertise as an auto mechanic. Some of those who offer their services as mechanics are highly competent, but others are less well trained or otherwise not as good. Suppose that the government, in an effort to upgrade the quality of mechanics, promulgates legislation requiring all new mechanics to take three years of post–high school training and to pass a competency test. Those who are currently mechanics will not be subjected to these requirements. What are the likely labor market effects of this legislation? Which labor and consumer groups would gain and which would lose?

7. In many countries higher education is heavily subsidized by the government (that is, university students do not bear the full cost of their college education). While there may be good reasons for heavily subsidizing university education, there are also some dangers in it. Using human capital theory, explain what these dangers are.

8. "The vigorous pursuit by a society of tax policies that tend to equalize wages across skill groups will frustrate the goal of optimum resource allocation." Comment.

SELECTED READINGS

Becker, Gary. *Human Capital.* New York: National Bureau of Economic Research, 1975.

Borjas, George J. "Earnings Determination: A Survey of the Neoclassical Approach." In *Three Worlds of Labor Economics,* ed. Garth Mangum and Peter Philips. Armonk, N.Y.: M. E. Sharpe, 1988.

Clotfelter, Charles T., Ronald G. Ehrenberg, Malcolm Getz, and John Siegfried. *Economic Challenges in Higher Education.* Chicago: University of Chicago Press, 1991.

Freeman, Richard B. *The Overeducated American.* New York: Academic Press, 1976.

LaLonde, Robert J. "The Promise of Public Sector–Sponsored Training Programs." *Journal of Economic Perspectives* 9, no. 2 (Spring 1995): 149–168.

Mincer, Jacob. *Schooling, Experience, and Earnings.* New York: National Bureau of Economic Research, 1974.

Schultz, Theodore. *The Economic Value of Education.* New York: Columbia University Press, 1963.

Spence, Michael. "Job Market Signaling." *Quarterly Journal of Economics* 87 (August 1973): 355–374.

A "Cobweb Model" of Labor Market Adjustment

The adjustment of college enrollments to changes in the returns to education is not always smooth or rapid, particularly in special fields, like engineering and law, that are highly technical. The problem is that if engineering wages (say) were to go up suddenly in a given year, the supply of graduate engineers would not be affected until three or four years later (owing to the time it takes to learn the field). Likewise, if engineering wages were to fall, those students enrolled in an engineering curriculum would understandably be reluctant to immediately leave the field. They have already invested a lot of time and effort and may prefer to take chances in engineering rather than devote more time and money to learning a new field.

The failure of supply to respond immediately to changed market conditions can cause *boom-and-bust cycles* in the market for highly technical workers. If educational planners in government or the private sector are unaware of these cycles, they may seek to stimulate or reduce enrollments at times when they should be doing exactly the opposite, as illustrated below.

An Example of "Cobweb" Adjustments

Suppose the market for engineers is in equilibrium, where the wage is W_0 and the number of engineers is N_0 (see Figure 9A.1). Let us now assume that the demand curve for engineers shifts from D_0 to D_1. Initially, this increase in the demand for engineers does *not* induce the supply of engineers to increase beyond N_0, because

FIGURE 9A.1

The Labor Market for Engineers

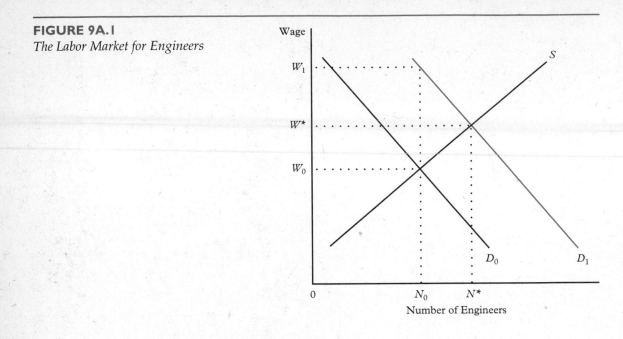

it takes a long time to become an engineer once one has decided to do so. Thus, while the increased demand for engineers causes more people to decide to enter the field, the number available for employment *at the moment* is N_0. These N_0 engineers, therefore, can *currently* obtain a wage of W_1 (in effect, there is a vertical supply curve, at N_0, for a few years until the supply of engineering graduates is increased).

Now W_1, the *current* engineering wage, is above W^*, the new *long-run* equilibrium wage caused by the intersection of D_1 and S. The market, however, is unaware of W^*, observing only W_1. If people are myopic and assume W_1 is the new equilibrium wage, N_1 people will enter the engineering field (see Figure 9A.2). When these N_1 all graduate, there will be a *surplus* of engineers (remember that W_1 is *above* long-run equilibrium).

With the supply of engineers now temporarily fixed at N_1, the wage will fall to W_2. This fall will cause students and workers to shift *out* of engineering, but that effect will not be fully felt for a few years. In the meantime, note that W_2 is below long-run equilibrium (still at W^*). Thus, when supply *does* adjust, it will adjust too much—all the way to N_2. Now there will be another shortage of engineers, because after supply adjusts to N_2, demand exceeds supply at a wage rate of W_2. This causes wages to rise to W_3, and the cycle repeats itself. Over time, the swings become smaller, and eventually equilibrium is reached. Because the adjustment path in Figure 9A.2 looks somewhat like a cobweb, the adjustment process described above is sometimes called a *cobweb model*.

FIGURE 9A.2
The Labor Market for Engineers: A Cobweb Model

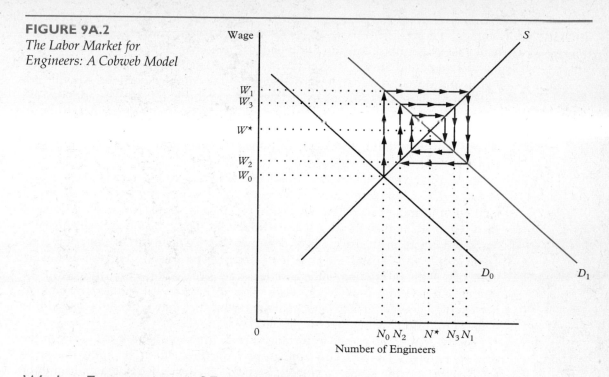

Number of Engineers

Worker Expectations of Future Wages

Critical to cobweb models is the assumption that workers form myopic expectations about the future behavior of wages.[1] In our example, they first assume that W_1 will prevail in the future and ignore the possibility that the occupational choice decisions of others will, in four years, drive the wage below W_1. Just how workers (and other economic actors, such as investors and taxpayers) form expectations about future wage (price) levels is very important to the understanding of many key issues affecting the labor market.

The simplest and most naive way to predict future wage levels is to assume that what is observed today is what will be observed in the future; this naive assumption, as noted above, underlies the cobweb model. A more sophisticated way to form predictions about the future is with an *adaptive expectations* approach. Adaptive expectations are formed by setting future expected wages equal to a weighted

---

[1]Also critical to cobweb models is that the demand curve be flatter than the supply curve; if it is not, the cobweb "explodes" when demand shifts and an equilibrium wage is never reached. An exploding cobweb model is an example from economics of the phenomenon of "chaos," which has attracted much scientific attention recently. For a general introduction to this fascinating topic, see James Gleick, *Chaos* (New York: Penguin Books, 1987). For an article on chaos in the economic literature, see William J. Baumol and Jess Benhabib, "Chaos: Significance, Mechanism, and Economic Applications," *Journal of Economic Perspectives* 3, no. 1 (Winter 1989): 77–106.

average of current and past wages. While more weight may be given to current than past wages in forecasting future wage levels, changes in those levels prior to the current period are not ignored; thus, it is likely that wage expectations formed adaptively do not alternatively "overshoot" and "undershoot" the equilibrium wage as much as those formed using the naive approach. If, however, adaptive expectations also lead workers to first overpredict and then underpredict the equilibrium wage, cobweb-like behavior of wages and labor supply will still be observed (although the fluctuations will be of a smaller magnitude if the predictions are closer to the mark than those made naively).

The most sophisticated way to predict future market outcomes is to use a full-blown model of the labor market. Those who believe in the *rational expectations* method of forming predictions about future wages assume that workers do have such a model in their heads, at least implicitly. Thus, they will realize that a marked increase in the earnings of engineers (say) is likely to be temporary, because supply will expand and eventually bring the returns to an investment in engineering skills in the line with those for other occupations. Put differently, the rational expectations model assumes workers behave as if they have taken (and mastered!) a good course in labor economics and that they will not be fooled into over- or underpredicting future wage levels.

Clearly, how people form expectations is an important empirical issue. In the case of engineers, lawyers, and dentists, periodic fluctuations in supply that characterize the cobweb model have been found.[2] Whether these fluctuations are the result of naive expectations or not, the lesson to be learned from cobweb models should not be lost on government policymakers. If the government chooses to take an active role in dealing with labor shortages and surpluses, it must be aware that, because supply adjustments are slow in highly technical markets, wages in those markets tend to *over*adjust. In other words, to the extent possible, governmental predictions and market interventions should be based on rational expectations. For example, at the initial stages of a shortage, when wages are rising toward W_1 (in our example), the government should be pointing out that W_1 is likely to be *above* the long-run equilibrium. If instead it attempts to meet the current shortage by *subsidizing* study in that field, it will be encouraging an even greater *surplus* later on. The moral of the story is that a complete knowledge of how markets adjust to changes in demand or supply is necessary before one can be sure that government intervention will do more good than harm.

---

[2]See Richard B. Freeman, "A Cobweb Model of the Supply and Starting Salary of New Engineers," *Industrial and Labor Relations Review* 29 (January 1976): 236–246, and Michael G. Finn and Joe G. Baker, "Future Jobs in Natural Science and Engineering: Shortage or Surplus?" *Monthly Labor Review* 116, no. 2 (February 1993): 54–61. Gary Zarkin, "Occupational Choice: An Application to the Market for Public School Teachers," *Quarterly Journal of Economics* 100 (May 1985): 409–446, and Peter Orazem and Peter Mattila, "Human Capital, Uncertain Wage Distributions, and Occupational and Educational Choices," *International Economic Review* 32 (February 1991): 103–122, use rational expectations models of occupational choice.

A Hedonic Model of Earnings and Educational Level

Chapter 9 employed human capital theory to explore the demand for education and the relationship between education and pay. This appendix uses the hedonic theory of wages to more formally explore the factors underlying the positive association between wage and educational levels. Thus, it treats the higher pay associated with a higher education level as a compensating wage differential.

In Chapter 9 we argued that the prospect of improved lifetime earnings served as a major inducement for people to invest in an education or training program. Indeed, unless education is acquired purely for purposes of consumption, people will not undertake an investment in education or training without the expectation that, by so doing, they can improve their stream of lifetime earnings or psychic rewards. In order to obtain these higher benefits, however, *employers* must be willing to pay for them. Therefore, it is necessary to examine both sides of the market to fully understand the prediction made over two hundred years ago by Adam Smith that wages rise with the "difficulty and expense" of learning the job.[1]

Supply (Worker) Side

Consider a group of people who have chosen selling as a desired career. These salespersons-to-be have a choice of how much education or training to invest in,

---

[1] See Adam Smith, *Wealth of Nations*, Book I, Chapter 10. The five "principal circumstances" listed by Smith as affecting wages were first discussed in Chapter 8.

FIGURE 9B.1

Indifference Curves for Two Different Workers

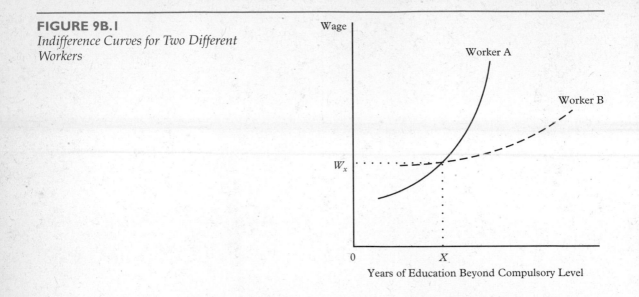

given their career objectives. In making this choice they will have to weigh the returns against the costs. Crucial to this decision is how the *actual* returns compare with the returns each would *require* in order to invest.

Figure 9B.1 shows the indifference curves between yearly earnings and education for two workers, A and B. To induce A or B to acquire X years of education would require the assurance of earning W_x after beginning work. However, to induce A to increase his or her education beyond X years (holding utility constant) would require a larger salary increase than B would require. A's greater aversion to making educational investments could be explained in several ways. Person A could be older than B, thus having higher forgone earnings and fewer years over which to recoup investment costs. Person A could be more present-oriented and thus more inclined to discount future benefits heavily, or could have less ability in classroom learning or a greater dislike of schooling. Finally, A may find it more difficult to finance additional schooling. Whatever the reason, this analysis points up the important fact that people differ in their propensity to invest in schooling.

Demand (Employer) Side

On the demand side of the market, employers must consider whether they are willing to pay higher wages for better-educated workers. If they are, they must also decide how much to pay for each additional year. Figure 9B.2 illustrates employers' choices about the wage/education relationship. Employers Y and Z are *both* willing to pay more for better-educated sales personnel (to continue our example) because they have found that better-educated workers are more

FIGURE 9B.2
*Isoprofit Curves for Two
Different Firms*

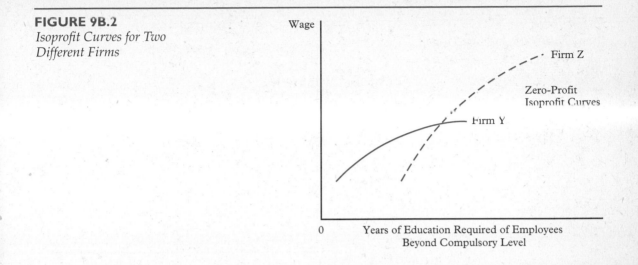

productive.[2] Thus, they can achieve the same profit level by paying either lower wages for less-educated workers or higher wages for more-educated workers. Their isoprofit curves are thus upward-sloping (see Chapter 8 for a description of isoprofit curves).

The isoprofit curves in Figure 9B.2 have three important characteristics:

1. For each firm the curves are concave; that is, they get flatter as education increases. This concavity results from the assumption that, at some point, the added benefits to the employer of an additional year of employee schooling begin to decline. In other words, we assume that schooling is subject to diminishing marginal productivity.
2. The isoprofit curves are the *zero-profit curves*. Neither firm can pay higher wages for each level of education than those indicated on the curves; if they did so, their profits would be negative and they would cease operations.
3. The added benefits from an extra year of schooling are smaller in firm Y than in firm Z, causing Y to have a flatter isoprofit curve. Firm Y, for example, may be a discount department store in which "selling" is largely a matter of working a cash register. While better-educated people may be more productive, they are not *too* much more valuable than less-educated people; hence, firm Y is not willing to pay them much more. Firm Z, on the other hand, may sell technical instruments for which a knowledge of physics and of customer engineering problems is needed. In firm Z, additional education adds a relatively large increment to worker productivity.

---

[2]Whether schooling causes workers to be more productive or simply reflects—or "signals"—higher productivity is not important at this point.

FIGURE 9B.3
The Education/Wage Relationship

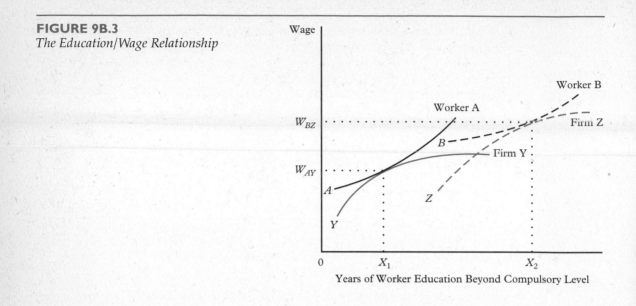

Market Determination of The Education/Wage Relationship

Putting both sides of the market for educated workers together, it is clear that the education/wage relationship will be positive, as indicated in Figure 9B.3. Worker A will work for Y, receiving a wage equal to W_{AY} and obtaining X_1 years of education. The reason for this matching is simple. Firm Z cannot pay higher wages (for each level of education) than those shown on the isoprofit curve in Figure 9B.3, for the reasons noted above. Clearly, then, worker A could never derive as much utility from Z as he or she could from Y; working for firm Z would involve a loss of utility to worker A. For similar reasons, worker B will accept work with firm Z, obtain X_2 years of schooling, and receive higher pay (W_{BZ}).

FIGURE 9B.4
Unwillingness of a Firm to Pay for More Education of Employees

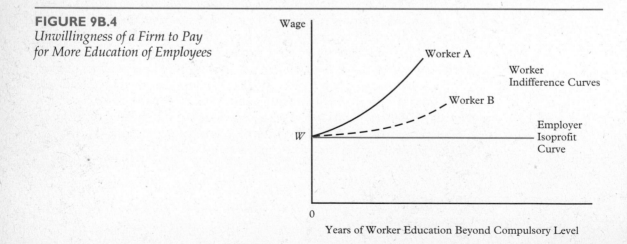

When examined from an overall social perspective, the positive wage/education relationship is the result of a very sensible sorting of workers and employers performed by the labor market. Workers with the greatest aversion to investing in education (A) will work for firms where education adds least to employee productivity (Y). People with the least aversion to educational investment (B) are hired by those firms most willing to pay for an educated workforce (Z).

Given the assertion by the critics of the human capital view of education that education adds nothing to worker productivity, it is interesting to consider the implications of an unwillingness by employers to pay higher wages to workers with more education. If employers were unwilling to pay higher wages for more-educated workers, no education-related differentials would exist and employer iso-profit curves would be horizontal. Without a positive education/wage relationship, employees would have no incentive to invest in an education (see Figure 9B.4). The fact that educational wage differentials exist and that workers respond to them when making schooling decisions suggests that, for some reason or other, employers *are* willing to pay higher wages to more-educated workers.

10

Worker Mobility: Migration, Immigration, and Turnover

Worker mobility plays a critical role in market economies. Because the job of any market is to promote voluntary exchange, society relies on the free movement of workers among employers to allocate labor in a way that achieves maximum satisfaction for both workers and consumers. The flow (either actual or threatened) of workers from lower-paying to higher-paying jobs, for example, is what forces firms that are paying below-equilibrium wages to increase their wage offers. The existence of compensating wage differentials, to take another example, also depends on the ability of informed workers to exercise choice among employment opportunities in the search for enhanced utility.

Mobility, however, is costly. Workers must take time to seek out information on wage offers and conditions of work elsewhere, and for many workers, job search is most efficient if they quit their current job first (this is especially the case if a new job is being sought in another geographic area). Severing ties with the current employer means leaving friends and familiar surroundings and may mean giving up valuable employee benefits, such as pensions and health insurance, or the "inside track" on future promotions. Once a new job is found, workers may well face *monetary,* and will almost certainly face *psychic,* costs of moving to new surroundings. In short, workers who move to new employers bear costs in the near term so that utility can be enhanced later on. Therefore, the human capital model introduced in Chapter 9 can be used to analyze mobility investments by workers.

The basic model that is briefly summarized in the next section is one of "voluntary" mobility undertaken by workers who perceive it to be in their self-interest. The factors underlying employer-initiated mobility—layoffs, for example—are different and discussed elsewhere in this text (Chapters 5 and 15).[1] The implications of human capital theory for geographic migration are then analyzed, followed by an application of economic theory to the important topic of immigration policy. We conclude this chapter with a general analysis of employee turnover and its role in matching individual workers with jobs that make the most of their skills; we also analyze how mobility costs might lead to monopsonistic behavior by employers even in labor markets in which they are not the sole purchasers of labor services. This concluding section provides some linkage between the relatively simple theory of demand and supply that has been emphasized to this point in the text and the more complex models of worker and firm behavior that are analyzed in succeeding chapters.

The Determinants of Worker Mobility

The human capital model presented in Chapter 9 can be used to understand and predict worker-initiated mobility. This model views voluntary mobility as an investment in which costs are borne in some early period in order to obtain returns over a longer period of time. If the present value of the benefits associated with mobility exceeds the costs, both monetary and psychic, we assume that people will decide to change jobs or move, or both. If the discounted stream of benefits is not as large as the costs, then people will decide against such a change.

What determines the present value of the net benefits of mobility—that is, the benefits minus the costs—determines the mobility decision. These factors can be better identified by writing out the formula one would use if one were to precisely calculate these net benefits:

$$\text{Present Value of Net Benefits} = \sum_{t=1}^{T} \frac{B_{jt} - B_{ot}}{(1 + r)^t} - C \tag{10.1}$$

where:

B_{jt} = the utility derived from the new job (j) in the year t;
B_{ot} = the utility derived from the old job (o) in the year t;
T = the length of time (in years) one expects to work at job j;
r = the rate of discount;
C = the utility lost in the move itself (direct and psychic costs); and

[1]The distinction between "employee-initiated" and "employer-initiated" mobility is more apparent than real, as we point out later in this chapter. For a detailed discussion of this point, see Kenneth J. McLaughlin, "A Theory of Quits and Layoffs with Efficient Turnover," *Journal of Political Economy* 99 (February 1991): 1–29.

$\sum$ = a summation—in this case the summation of the yearly discounted net benefits over a period running from year 1 to year T.

Clearly, the present value of the net benefits of mobility will be larger the greater is the utility derived from the new job, the less happy one is in the job of origin, the smaller are the immediate costs associated with the change, and the longer one expects to be in the new job or live in the new area (that is, the greater T is). These observations lead to some clear-cut predictions about which groups in society will be most mobile and about the *patterns* of mobility one would expect to observe. These predictions are analyzed in the following sections on migration and quit behavior.

Geographic Mobility

Mobility of workers among countries, and among regions within a country, is an important fact of economic life. Roughly 100 million people in the world live in a country different from the one in which they were born, and Table 10.1 indicates that for the world's larger economies, immigrants typically constitute from 5 to 20 percent of the labor force. One study indicated that of the 5 million people who migrated to another country from 1975 to 1980, two-thirds went to the United States, Canada, or Australia.[2]

Within the United States during a recent one-year period (1993–1994), over 3 million workers—2.5 percent of all those employed—moved between states, and almost half of those moved to a different *region* (the South experienced the largest net influx, while the Northeast had the largest net outflow).[3] When asked about their reasons for moving, 70 to 85 percent of workers cite economic reasons. Roughly one-third of those moving among states stay with their current employers, but taking account of those whose move is motivated by economic factors *and* who change employers, about half of all interstate moves are precipitated by a change in employment.[4] This emphasis on job change suggests that human capital theory can help us understand which workers are most likely to undertake investments in geographic mobility and the directions in which mobility flows will take place.

In the subsections that follow, we analyze migration in terms of the direction (and distance) of the flows, the characteristics of the migrants, and the returns to investments in migration. Many of the empirical studies of these topics use data

[2]Rachel M. Friedberg and Jennifer Hunt, "The Impact of Immigrants on Host Country Wages, Employment, and Growth," *Journal of Economic Perspectives* 9, no. 2 (Spring 1995): 23–44.

[3]U.S. Bureau of the Census, *Geographic Mobility: March 1993 to March 1994*, Current Population Reports, Series P-20, no. 485 (August 1995).

[4]Ann P. Bartel, "The Migration Decision: What Role Does Job-Mobility Play?" *American Economic Review* 69 (December 1979): 775–786. See also Larry Schroeder, "Interrelatedness of Occupational and Geographical Labor Mobility," *Industrial and Labor Relations Review* 29 (April 1976): 405–411.

TABLE 10.1

Immigrants as a Percentage of the Population and Labor Force, Selected Countries, 1991–1993

Country	Immigrants as a Percentage of	
	Population	Labor Force
Australia	22.7	24.8
Canada	15.6	18.5
France	6.3	6.2
Germany	8.5	8.8
Italy	1.7	na
Japan	1.1	na
Sweden	5.8	5.1
United Kingdom	3.5	3.6
United States	7.9	9.3

na = data not available.

SOURCE: Organisation for Economic Co-Operation and Development, *Trends in International Migration*, Annual Report 1994 (OECD, 1995), Table 1.2.

on internal migration within the United States, but international migration is also analyzed.

THE DIRECTION OF MIGRATORY FLOWS

Human capital theory predicts that migration will flow from areas of relatively poor earnings possibilities to places where opportunities are better. Whether one observes the flow of immigration to the United States from Mexico, for example, or the internal flows from the South to the North in the 1950s—it is clear that migratory flows generally support this prediction. The prediction, however, can also be tested by looking at the characteristics of more specific areas from which and to which people move. In general, the results of such studies suggest that the "pull" of good opportunities in the areas of destination are stronger than the "push" of poor opportunities in the areas of origin. In other words, while people are more attracted to places where earnings are expected to be better, they do not necessarily come from areas where opportunities are poorest.

The most consistent finding in these detailed studies is that people are attracted to areas where the real earnings of full-time workers are highest. One might also expect that the chances for obtaining work in a new area would also affect that area's attractiveness. One way to measure job availability in an area is to use the unemployment rate, but the studies find no consistent relationship between unemployment and in-migration, perhaps because the number of people moving with a job already in hand is three times as large as the number moving *to look* for work.[5] If one already has a job in a particular field, the area's unemployment rate is irrelevant.

Most studies have found that, contrary to what one might expect, the characteristics of the place of origin do not appear to have much net influence on migration. One reason for this finding is that while those in the poorest places have the greatest *incentives* to move, the very poorest areas also tend to have people with lower levels of wealth, education, and skills—the very people who seem least *willing* (or able) to move. To understand this phenomenon, we must turn from the issue of *where* people go to a discussion of *who* is most likely to move.

PERSONAL CHARACTERISTICS OF MOVERS

Migration is highly selective in the sense that it is not an activity in which all people are equally likely to be engaged. To be specific, mobility is much higher among the young and the better-educated, as human capital theory would suggest.

AGE Age is the single most important factor in determining who migrates. The peak years for mobility are the ages 20–24; 12 percent of this age group migrates across county or state lines each year. By age 32 the rate of migration is roughly 8 percent, and by age 47 it is only 4 percent.

There are two explanations for the fact that migration is an activity primarily for the young. First, the younger one is, the greater the potential returns from any human capital investment. As noted earlier, the longer the period over which benefits from an investment can be obtained, the larger the present value of these benefits.

Second, a large part of the costs of migration are psychic, the losses associated with giving up friends, community ties, and the benefits of knowing one's way around. When one is starting out as an adult, these losses are comparatively small because one is not well established in the adult world. However, as one grows older, community ties become stronger and the losses associated with leaving loom larger, thus inhibiting mobility. This line of reasoning is underscored by the fact that, within age groups, unmarried people are more likely to migrate between states than married ones, and married people without children are more mobile than those with children.[6]

---

[5]The level of *new hires* in an area appears to explain migration flows much better than the unemployment rate; see Gary Fields, "Place to Place Migration: Some New Evidence," *Review of Economics and Statistics* 61, no. 1 (February 1979): 21–32. Robert H. Topel, "Local Labor Markets," *Journal of Political Economy* 94, no. 3, pt. 2 (June 1986): S111–S143, contains an analysis of how permanent and transitory shifts in an area's demand affect migration and wages.

[6]See Jacob Mincer, "Family Migration Decisions," *Journal of Political Economy* 86, no. 5 (October 1978): 749–773.

TABLE 10.2
U.S. Migration Rates for People 30–34, by Educational Level, 1993–1994 (in percentages)

Educational Level (in Years)	Moving Between Counties Within States	Moving Between States
9–11	3.9	2.7
12	4.4	2.6
13–15	4.8	3.3
16	4.9	4.4
17 or more	6.7	5.0

SOURCE: U.S. Bureau of the Census, *Geographical Mobility: March 1993 to March 1994,* Current Population Reports, Series P–20, no. 485, Table 4.

EDUCATION   While age is probably the best predictor of who will move, education is the single best indicator of who will move *within* an age group. As can be seen from Table 10.2, which presents U.S. migration rates for people ages 30–34, more education does make one more likely to move.

One cost of migration is that of ascertaining *where* opportunities are and *how good* they are likely to be. If one's occupation has a national labor market, as is the case for many college graduates, it is relatively easy to find out about opportunities in distant places. Jobs are advertised in national newspapers. Recruiters from all over visit college campuses. Employment agencies make nationwide searches. In cases such as these, people usually move with a job already in hand.

However, if the relevant labor market for one's job is localized, it is difficult to find out where opportunities might be better. For a janitor in Beaumont, Texas, finding out about employment opportunities in the north-central region is like looking for the proverbial needle in a haystack. That such moves occur at all, let alone in reasonably large numbers, is testimony to the fact that people are able to acquire information despite the obstacles.

THE ROLE OF DISTANCE

Human capital theory clearly predicts that as migration costs rise, the flow of migrants will fall. The costs of moving increase with distance for two reasons. First, as noted above, for people in local labor markets, acquiring *information* on opportunities elsewhere can be very difficult (costly). Surely it is easier to find out about employment prospects closer to home than farther away; newspapers are easier to obtain, phone calls are cheaper, friends and relatives are more useful contacts, and knowledge of employers is greater. Second, the *money costs* of transportation for the move and for trips back to see friends and relatives, and hence the *psychic costs* of the move, obviously rise with distance. Thus, one would clearly expect to find that people are more likely to move short distances than long distances.

In general, this expectation is borne out by the statistics. Of the 41.6 million Americans who changed their place of residence during the March 1993–March 1994 period, 64 percent moved to a different house in the same county, 20 percent moved to a different county within the same state, 9 percent changed states within the same region, and only 7 percent moved to a state in a different region.[7] Clearly, the propensity to move far away is smaller than the propensity to stay close to home.

Related to the desire to minimize psychic and informational costs is the fact that people tend to migrate to areas where friends or relatives have previously migrated. This *chain migration* is especially evident in the stream of migration from Puerto Rico to the mainland: most Puerto Ricans go to Chicago and to the tristate area of New York–New Jersey–Connecticut.

Interestingly, lack of education appears to be a bigger deterrent to long-distance migration than does age (other influences held constant), a fact that can shed some light on whether information costs or psychic costs are the primary deterrent. As suggested by our arguments in the previous subsection, the age deterrent is closely related to psychic costs, while educational level and ease of access to information are closely linked. The apparently larger deterrent of educational level suggests that information costs have more influence on the relationship between migration and distance.[8]

SKILLS, THE EARNINGS DISTRIBUTION, AND INTERNATIONAL MIGRATION

To this point, our examples of factors that influence geographic mobility have related to domestic migration—movements within the United States. The influences of age, access to information, the potential gains in earnings, and distance are all relevant to international migration as well, although the international migration actually observed is often so highly regulated that not all people who want to change their country of residence can do so. One aspect of the potential gains from migration that is especially important when analyzing international flows of labor is the distribution of earnings in the sending as compared with the receiving country. The relative distribution of earnings can help us predict which skill groups within a sending country are most likely to emigrate.

---

[7]U.S. Bureau of the Census, *Geographical Mobility: March 1993–March 1994*, Current Population Reports, Series P–20, no. 485, Table 1.

[8]Aba Schwartz, "Interpreting the Effect of Distance on Migration," *Journal of Political Economy* 81 (September/October 1973): 1153–1167.

Some countries have a more compressed (equal) earnings distribution than is found in the United States. In these countries, the average earnings differential between skilled and unskilled workers is smaller, implying that the returns to human capital investments are lower than in the United States. Skilled and professional workers from these countries (northern European countries are most notable in this regard) have the most to gain from emigration to the United States. Unskilled workers in countries with more equality of earnings are well paid compared to unskilled workers here and thus have less incentive to move, so immigrants to the United States from these countries are *positively selected* with respect to skills (that is, they are more skilled than the average worker who remains in the country of origin).

In countries with less equal distributions of earnings than are found in the United States, skilled workers do relatively well, but there are large potential gains to the unskilled from emigrating to the United States. These unskilled workers may be blocked from making human capital investments within their own countries (and thus from taking advantage of the high returns to such investments that are implied by the large earnings differentials). Instead, their human capital investment may take the form of emigrating and seeking work in the United States. Less-developed countries tend to have relatively unequal earnings distributions, so it is to be expected that immigrants from these countries (and especially Mexico, which is closest) will be *negatively selected* with regard to skills. That is, immigrants to the United States from countries with less equal earnings distributions will be disproportionately unskilled.[9] (Example 10.1 reports on the preponderance of unskilled immigrants to the United States from Puerto Rico.)

THE INDIVIDUAL RETURNS TO INTERNATIONAL AND DOMESTIC MIGRATION

The previous sections discussed the fact that the people most likely to move are the ones with the most to gain and the least to lose by migration, and that they move to areas where their net gains are likely to be largest. Another way to test our human capital theory of migration is to see if the earnings of *individual* immigrants are higher than they would have been without migration. One way to proceed with calculations of these "returns" to migration is to calculate the differences in earnings received by migrants and the earnings received by workers of comparable age and education in the areas from which the migrants came.

While the available studies of internal migration in the United States are somewhat old, they support the prediction that migrants earn more than they would have earned if they had not moved. One study of families that moved across state lines in 1971–1972, for example, found that increases in the present value of earnings over the four-year period just after the move averaged $4,254 for husbands.

---

[9]For a more thorough discussion of this issue, see George J. Borjas, *Friends or Strangers* (New York: Basic Books, 1990), especially Chapters 1 and 7.

EXAMPLE 10.1

Migration of Puerto Ricans to the United States

Tests of theories of migration using immigration flows are confounded by the fact that United States' immigration rules restrict the entry into the United States of individuals seeking permanent resident status. These restrictions occur because the total number of immigrants legally permitted is limited, and because immigration slots are allocated based on family reunification criteria, continent of origin, and an individual's skills. Thus, we cannot generally observe the supply of all people who want to immigrate; we only observe those lucky enough to be admitted.

Puerto Rico is a territory of the United States and its residents are U.S. citizens. Hence, Puerto Ricans are free to migrate to the mainland United States without any restrictions. Puerto Rico has a much more unequal wage distribution than the United

States, and the return to skill is also higher there. As such, in accordance with the theory in the text, one would expect to observe immigrants from Puerto Rico coming disproportionately from the lower-skilled, or lower-educated, groups of workers. A careful study of migration flows suggests that this is exactly what occurs. In 1980, for example, men who had never migrated from Puerto Rico averaged 10.8 years of schooling, whereas a group of men of comparable age who had migrated to the United States before 1975 averaged 9.4 years of schooling.

SOURCE: Fernando A. Ramos, "Outmigration and Return Migration of Puerto Ricans," *in Immigration and the Work Force,* ed. George J. Borjas and Richard B. Freeman (Chicago: University of Chicago Press, 1992).

This increase can be compared to an average increase of $1,648 for nonmoving husbands.[10]

Interestingly, while the *family* incomes of those who moved in 1971–1972 rose more than the incomes of those who did not, the *wives* in families experiencing moves did more poorly in terms of increased earnings than did wives in nonmoving families! The reason for this disparity is no doubt found in the way that the family migration decisions were made. Family income was apparently a major concern among movers, and because the husband was typically the dominant earner at that time, his earnings opportunities probably were given primary weight in the decision about whether (and where) to move. The husband was thus free to move where his earnings potential was best, and it would only be by

---

[10]Solomon W. Polachek and Francis W. Horvath, "A Life-Cycle Approach to Migration: Analysis of the Perspicacious Peregrinator," in *Research in Labor Economics,* vol. 1, ed. Ronald Ehrenberg (Greenwich, Conn.: JAI Press, 1977). Comparing the earnings of movers and nonmovers must be done carefully, because recent research indicates that those who move may be more productive, given their age and education, than those who stay. On this latter point, see Wim P. M. Vijverberg, "Labour Market Performance as a Determinant of Migration," *Economica 60* (May 1993): 143–160. For a recent study of internal migration in the United States, see George J. Borjas, Stephen G. Bronars, and Stephen J. Trejo, "Self-Selection and Internal Migration in the United States," *Journal of Urban Economics* 32, no. 2 (September 1992): 159–185.

coincidence that this same place would be optimal (in terms of earnings) for his wife. With more women now permanently attached to the labor force, however, and with women's wages now rising relative to men's (see Chapters 12 and 14), it would be interesting to know whether decisions about family migration are now made differently than they were in 1971–1972.

Comparing the earnings of *international* immigrants with what they would have earned had they not emigrated is generally not feasible, owing to a lack of data on earnings in the home country.[11] Thus, studies of the returns to immigration have focused on comparisons with native-born workers in the "host" country. Most of the published research has been done on the United States, and Table 10.3 contains data from different time periods on the wages, relative to those for native-born Americans, of three cohorts of male immigrants: those who came in the late 1960s, the late 1970s, and late 1980s.

One can observe three phenomena from Table 10.3. First, as can be seen from looking at the ratios printed in boldface type, immigrants earn substantially less than natives (including those who are ethnically similar) when they first arrive. Second, if one looks along the rows for the 1965–1969 and 1975–1979 cohorts, it is clear that relative wages increase from their initially low levels, which means that wages of immigrants rise faster than those of natives during at least the immigrants' first decade in this country. Increases in the second decade are generally smaller and less certain to be above those for natives. Third, from comparing the initial (boldface) ratios across the three cohorts, it is evident that each cohort of immigrants has done less well at entry than its predecessor.

The first phenomenon, that immigrants initially earn substantially less than natives, is hardly surprising. Even after controlling for the effects of age and education (the typical immigrant is younger and less-educated than the typical native), immigrants earn less owing to their difficulties with English, their unfamiliarity with American employment opportunities, and their lack of an American work history (and employers' consequent uncertainties about their productivity).

The second phenomenon, that earnings of immigrants rise relatively quickly, no doubt reflects their high rates of investment in human capital after arrival. After immigration, immigrants typically invest in themselves by acquiring work experience and improved proficiency in English, and these investments raise the wages they can command. These human capital investments, like others analyzed in this and the preceding chapter, are made with an eye on the expected net returns. For example, a recent study found that English fluency raises immigrant earnings by an average of 17 percent in the United States, 12 percent in Canada, and 9 percent in Australia; however, not all immigrants have the same incentives to become proficient in English. Those who live in "enclaves," where business is conducted in

---

[11]Barry R. Chiswick, *Illegal Aliens: Their Employment and Employers* (Kalamazoo, Mich.: W.E. Upjohn Institute for Employment Research, 1988), mentions two studies that compared the earnings or living standards of Mexican immigrants with the conditions under which they lived before they left. In one study it was found that living conditions, as indexed by the availability of running water and electricity, rose substantially. The other study reported that the earnings of Mexican apple harvesters in Oregon, even after deducting the costs of migration, were triple what they would have been in Mexico.

TABLE 10.3

Ratio of Wages, Immigrant to Native-Born Men, 1970–1990

	A. Comparison with All Native-Born Men, Ages 25–64		
	Wage Ratio in		
Immigrants Arriving in	**1970**	**1980**	**1990**
1965–1969	**0.834**	0.922	1.011
1975–1979	-	**0.724**	0.822
1985–1989	-	-	**0.683**
	B. Comparison with Ethnically Similar Natives, Ages 25–34 in Years Shown: Asians		
1965–1969	**0.824**	1.091	1.085
1975–1979	-	**0.803**	0.898
1985–1989	-	-	**0.757**
	C. Comparison with Ethnically Similar Natives, Ages 25–34 in Years Shown: Mexicans		
1965–1969	**0.735**	0.835	0.805
1975–1979	-	**0.662**	0.705
1985–1989	-	-	**0.661**

SOURCE: George Borjas, "The Economics of Immigration," *Journal of Economic Literature* 32, no. 4 (December 1994), Tables 3, 7.

one's native tongue, those who expect to return to their homeland, and those who immigrated for other than economic reasons are less likely to invest time and money in learning English.[12] (See Example 10.2 for a further analysis of immigrants' incentives to invest in human capital.)

Third, it appears that the immigrants of recent years have been increasingly less skilled than their predecessors. The overall wage ratio at entry has fallen from 0.834 in the late 1960s to 0.683 in the late 1980s, and careful analyses of this decline indicate that more-recent immigrants have come with relatively less human capital. For example, in 1970, immigrants were 22 percent more likely than natives to be high school dropouts, but they are now almost 150 percent more likely to be dropouts. It has been estimated that the changing mix of national origin among immigrants to the United States, with increased proportions coming from countries with relatively low average levels of educational attainment, accounts for almost all of this decline in the human capital of immigrants.[13]

---

[12]Barry R. Chiswick and Paul W. Miller, "The Endogeneity between Language and Earnings: International Analyses," *Journal of Labor Economics* 13, no. 2 (April 1995): 246–288.

[13]George Borjas, "The Economics of Immigration," *Journal of Economic Literature* 32, no. 4 (December 1994): 1667–1717.

One consequence of the decline in skill levels among immigrants is that, while at least some groups of those who immigrated in the late 1960s achieved wage parity with natives two decades later, it is unlikely that many recent immigrant groups will do so. For example, while Asians who immigrated in the late 1960s had wages that were 9 percent higher than those of Asian-Americans after a decade in the United States, their counterparts who immigrated in the late 1970s had wages 10 percent lower than those of Asian-Americans after a decade. Similarly, one study has estimated that Latin Americans who immigrated before 1975 could expect lifetime earnings only 12 percent below those of the average native (including non-Latinos); the most recent immigrants from Latin America can expect lifetime earnings some 27 percent lower![14]

Whether immigration is a good investment for immigrants, however, depends on the earnings they can attain in the host country relative to their country of origin. Thus, even if the typical Mexican immigrant can expect to earn only 73 percent of what is earned by the typical native-born American over a lifetime, the fact that the average resident of Mexico is able to consume only one-third as much as the typical resident of the United States implies that the migration investment still has a large monetary payoff.

RETURN MIGRATION

Migration, whether internal or international, is frequently accompanied by a later permanent return to the area of origin.[15] Twenty percent of all moves are to an area in which the person had *previously* lived, and about half of these are back to one's birthplace. Thus *return migration*—migrating back to a place from which one originated in some sense—is an important phenomenon of geographic mobility.

There are two major reasons for return migration. First, much of the migration across international borders may well be by people who intend to stay in the foreign country for only a limited period of time. These people live frugally, send much of their earnings back to their homeland, and return when their objectives are met.

Second, return migration may be a response by those who find either that job opportunities were not what they had expected or that the psychic costs of living without the social or economic "safety net" of friends and family were higher than they had anticipated. To say that, on average, migration is a good investment for those who decide to undertake it does not imply that it is a good investment for all. Clearly, most people *do not* migrate in any given year, presumably because

---

[14]George Borjas, *International Differences in the Labor Market Performance of Immigrants* (Kalamazoo, Mich.: W. E. Upjohn Institute for Employment Research, 1988), 62, 67.

[15]The discussion in this section is influenced by John Vanderkamp, "Migration Flows, Their Determinants and the Effects of Return Migration," *Journal of Political Economy* 79 (September/October 1971): 1012–1031; Fernando A. Ramos, "Outmigration and Return Migration of Puerto Ricans," in *Immigration and the Work Force*, ed. George J. Borjas and Richard B. Freeman (Chicago: University of Chicago Press, 1992); and Borjas, "The Economics of Immigration," 1691–1692.

EXAMPLE 10.2

"Economic" vs. "Political" Immigrants

Individuals who immigrate to a country like the United States presumably do so because they believe they will be improving their well-being. For some the decision is motivated primarily by economic considerations, and the timing of the move is both voluntary and planned. These individuals may be referred to as "economic" migrants. Others, however, may be forced to flee their countries because of *political* upheavals, and for these individuals the decision is likely to be less motivated by economic factors, not planned as far in advance, and somewhat less voluntary (given the life-threatening prospects they may face). The latter may be referred to as "political" migrants.

What differences might we expect in the economic success of the two groups when they arrive in the United States? On the one hand, since the economic migrants' decisions were motivated by expectations of improved economic welfare, one might expect that they would initially earn more than the political migrants, who were less prepared for the move. On the other hand, members of the latter group do not have the option of ultimately returning to their homelands as the economic migrants do. Because return migration is precluded for political migrants, they have stronger incentives than economic migrants to make human capital investments that have payoffs only in the United States (economic mi-

grants may want to preserve skills that will be useful to them if they return to their homelands). In addition, political migrants often leave all their physical or financial assets behind when they flee their homelands; as a result, they may prefer to concentrate a greater share of their subsequent investments in human (rather than physical) capital. For both reasons, one might expect political migrants to have steeper earnings profiles—more rapid earnings growth with years in the United States—than economic migrants.

In a carefully conducted study, George Borjas found substantial evidence to support these expectations. Other factors (such as age and education) held constant, Cuban male immigrants to the United States, many of whom fled their homeland after Fidel Castro came to power, appear to have lower earnings than other Hispanic male immigrants (primarily Mexicans and Puerto Ricans) in the early years after both groups arrive in the United States; however, in subsequent years they exhibit more rapid rates of earnings growth.

SOURCE: George Borjas, "The Economic Status of Male Hispanic Migrants and Natives in the U.S.," in *Research in Labor Economics*, vol. 6, ed. Ronald Ehrenberg (Greenwich, Conn.: JAI Press, 1984), 65–122.

they believe that, for them, it would not be a good investment. It is equally clear, however, that some migrants find out they have made a mistake. What they thought would be a good investment may turn out not to be. Interestingly, a recent study of return migration finds evidence consistent with the hypothesis that those most likely to return are those who were "closest to the margin" at the time they came (that is, they were the ones with the least to gain among those who decided to emigrate).[16]

---

[16]George J. Borjas and Bernt Bratsberg, "Who Leaves? The Outmigration of the Foreign-Born," *Review of Economics and Statistics*, 78, no.1 (February 1996): 165–176.

Policy Application: Restricting Immigration

Nowhere are the analytical tools of the economist more important than in the area of immigration policy; the lives affected by immigration policy number in the millions each year. After a brief outline of the history of U.S. immigration policy, this section will analyze in detail the consequences of illegal immigration, a phenomenon currently attracting widespread attention.

U.S. IMMIGRATION HISTORY

The United States is a rich country, a country whose wealth and high standard of living make it an attractive place for immigrants from nearly all parts of the world. For the first 140 years of its history as an independent country, the United States followed a policy of essentially unrestricted immigration (the only major immigration restrictions were placed on Asians and on convicts). The flow of immigrants was especially large after 1840, when U.S. industrialization and political and economic upheavals in Europe made immigration an attractive investment for millions. As one can see from Table 10.4, officially recorded immigration peaked in the first decade of the twentieth century, when the *yearly* flow of immigrants was more than 1 percent of the population.

In 1921, however, Congress adopted the Quota Law, which set annual quotas on immigration on the basis of nationality. These quotas had the effect of reducing immigration from eastern and southern Europe. This act was followed by other laws in 1924 and 1929 that further restricted immigration from southeastern Europe. These various revisions in immigration policy were motivated, in part, by widespread concern over the alleged adverse effect on native employment of the arrival of unskilled immigrants from eastern and southern Europe.

In 1965 the passage of the Immigration and Nationality Act abolished the quota system based on national origin that so heavily favored northern and western Europeans. Under this law, as amended in 1990, overall immigration is restricted to 675,000 people per year (as of 1995), with 480,000 spots reserved for family-reunification purposes, 140,000 reserved mostly for immigrants with exceptional skills who are coming for employment purposes, and 55,000 for "diversity" immigrants (from countries that have not recently provided many immigrants to the United States). Political refugees, who must meet certain criteria relating to persecution in their home countries, are admitted without numerical limit. While less overtly discriminatory than it once was, immigration law in the United States still imposes a ceiling on immigrants that is far below the numbers who wish to come. The fact that immigration to the United States is a very worthwhile investment for many more people than can legally come has created incentives for people to live in the country illegally.

Illegal immigration can be divided into two categories of roughly equal size: immigrants who enter legally but overstay or violate the provisions of their visas, and those who enter the country illegally. Over 20 million people enter the United States each year, usually as students or visitors, under nonimmigrant visas. Once here, the foreigner can look for work, although it is illegal to work at a job under a

TABLE 10.4

Officially Recorded Immigration: 1820 to 1994

Period	Number (in thousands)	Annual Rate (per thousand of U.S. population)	Year	Number (in thousands)	Annual Rate (per thousand of U.S. population)
1820–1830	152	1.2	1981	597	2.6
1831–1840	599	3.9	1982	594	2.6
1841–1850	1,713	8.4	1983	560	2.4
1851–1860	2,598	9.3	1984	544	2.3
1861–1870	2,315	6.4	1985	570	2.4
1871–1880	2,812	6.2	1986	602	2.5
1881–1890	5,247	9.2	1987	602	2.5
1891–1900	3,688	5.3	1988	643	2.6
1901–1910	8,795	10.4	*1989	1,091	4.4
1911–1920	5,736	5.7	*1990	1,536	6.1
1921–1930	4,107	3.5	*1991	1,827	7.3
1931–1940	528	0.4	*1992	974	3.8
1941–1950	1,035	0.7	*1993	904	3.5
1951–1960	2,515	1.5	*1994	804	3.1
1961–1970	3,322	1.7			
1971–1980	4,389	2.0			
1981–1990	7,338	3.1			

* Includes illegal immigrants granted amnesty under the Immigration Reform and Control Act of 1986.

SOURCE: U.S. Immigration and Naturalization Service, *Annual Report*; U.S. Bureau of the Census, *1992 Statistical Abstract of the United States*, Table 5; John W. Wright, ed., *The Universal Almanac 1990* (New York: Andrews and McNeel), 247; and *1996 Information Please Almanac* (Boston: Houghton Mifflin Company, 1996), 831, 835.

student's or visitor's visa. If the "student" or "visitor" is offered a job, he or she can apply for an "adjustment of status" to legally become a permanent resident, although the chances for approval as an employment-based immigrant are slim for the ordinary worker.

The other group of illegal immigrants enter the country without a visa. Immigrants from the Caribbean often enter through Puerto Rico, whose residents are U.S. citizens and thus, as noted in Example 10.1, are allowed free entry to the mainland. Others walk across the Mexican border. Still others are smuggled into the United States or use false documents to get through entry stations. For obvious reasons, it is difficult to establish the number of illegal immigrants who have come to the United States; however, the flow of illegals is believed to be 200,000 to 300,000 per year, and the total number residing in the United States in 1992 was estimated at 3.4 million.[17]

---

[17]Friedberg and Hunt, "The Impact of Immigrants on Host Country Wages, Employment, and Growth."

Despite the lack of precise knowledge about the dimensions of illegal immigration, the fact remains that by the 1980s it had become a very prominent policy issue. The Secretary of Labor estimated in late 1979 that if only *half* of the jobs held by illegal aliens were given to U.S. citizens, the unemployment rate would drop from 6 percent to 3.7 percent. Similar beliefs led Congress to pass the Immigration Reform and Control Act of 1986, which imposed penalties on *employers* who knowingly hire illegal aliens (previously, the penalty for illegal employment was deportation, which clearly fell only on the illegally employed worker). The sanctions against employers included fines that can range from $250 to $10,000 per illegal worker, with penalties escalating throughout that range for repeated offenses. Jail terms were prescribed for "pattern and practice" offenders. The reform act also granted amnesty (and legal immigrant status) to all those who had been in the United States illegally since the end of 1981, and illegal aliens who had worked in agriculture for over 90 days per year were granted the right to apply for immigrant status even if they came after 1981. All told, some 2.7 million people applied for amnesty under the provisions of the act.

The policies people advocate are based on their beliefs about the consequences of immigration for employers, consumers, taxpayers, and workers of various skill levels and ethnicities. Nearly everyone with an opinion on this subject has an economic model implicitly or explicitly in mind when addressing these consequences; the purpose of this section is to make these economic models explicit and to evaluate them.

NAIVE VIEWS OF IMMIGRATION

There are two opposing views of illegal immigration that can be considered naive. One view, which is widely held in the government, is that every illegal immigrant deprives a citizen or legal alien of a job. For example, a Department of Labor official told a House committee studying immigration, "I think it is logical to conclude that if they are actually employed, they are taking a job away from one of our American citizens."[18] According to this view, if x illegal aliens are deported and others kept out, the number of unemployed Americans would decline by x.

At the opposite end of the policy spectrum is the equally naive argument that the illegals perform jobs no American citizen would do:

> You couldn't conduct a hotel in New York, you couldn't conduct a restaurant in New York . . . if you didn't have rough laborers. We haven't got the rough laborers anymore. . . . Where are we going to get the people to do that rough work?[19]

Both arguments are simplistic because they ignore the slopes of the demand and supply curves. Consider, for example, the labor market for the job of "rough laborer"—any job most American citizens find distasteful. Without illegal

---

[18]Elliott Abrams and Franklin S. Abrams, "Immigration Policy—Who Gets In and Why?" *Public Interest* 38 (Winter 1975): 25.

[19]Ibid., 26.

FIGURE 10.1
Demand and Supply of "Rough Laborers"

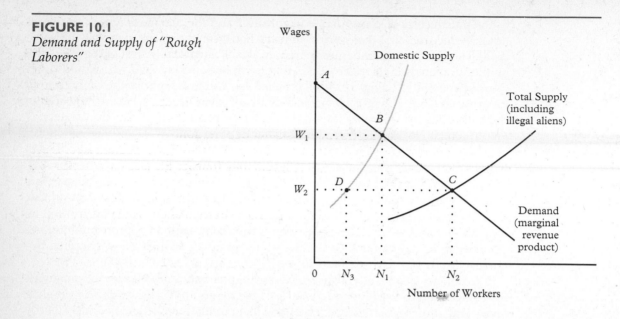

immigrants, the restricted supply of Americans to this market would imply a relatively high wage (W_1 in Figure 10.1). N_1 citizens would be employed. If illegal aliens entered the market, the supply curve would shift outward and perhaps flatten (implying that immigrants were more responsive to wage increases for rough laborers than citizens were). The influx of illegals would drive the wage down to W_2, but employment would increase to N_2.

Are Americans unwilling to do the work of rough laborers? Clearly, at the market wage of W_2, many more aliens are willing to work at the job than U.S. citizens are. Only N_3 citizens would want these jobs at this low wage, while the remaining supply ($N_2 - N_3$) is made up entirely of aliens. If there were no immigrants, however, N_1 Americans would be employed at wage W_1 as rough laborers. Wages would be higher, as would the prices of the goods or services produced with this labor, but the job would get done. The only "shortage" of American citizens is at the low wage of W_2; at W_1 there is no shortage (see Chapter 2 for further discussion of labor shortages).

Would deporting those illegal aliens working as rough laborers create the same number of jobs for U.S. citizens? The answer is clearly no. If the $N_2 - N_3$ aliens working as laborers were deported and all other illegal aliens were kept from the market, the number of Americans employed as laborers would rise from N_3 to N_1 and their wages would rise from W_2 to W_1 (Figure 10.1). $N_2 - N_1$ jobs would be destroyed by the rising wage rate associated with deportation. Thus, while deportation would increase the employment and wage levels of Americans in the laborer market, it would certainly not increase employment on a one-for-one basis.

There is, however, one condition in which deportation *would* create jobs for American citizens on a one-for-one basis: when the federal minimum wage law creates a surplus of labor. Suppose, for example, that the supply of American laborers is represented by ABS_1 in Figure 10.2 and the total supply is represented by ACS_2. Because an artificially high wage has created a surplus, only N of the N' workers willing to work at the minimum wage can actually find employment. If some of them are illegal aliens, sending them back—coupled with successful efforts to deny other aliens access to these jobs—would create jobs for a comparable number of Americans. However, the demand curve would have to intersect the domestic supply curve (ABS_1) at or to the left of point B to prevent the wage level from rising (and thus destroying jobs) after deportation.

The analyses above ignore the possibility that if low-wage immigrant labor is prevented from coming to the jobs, employers may transfer the jobs to countries with abundant supplies of low-wage labor. If this were to occur, unskilled workers in this country would continue to feel downward pressure on their wages and employment opportunities even if illegal immigration were to cease. Thus, it may well be the case that unskilled American workers are in competition with foreign unskilled workers anyway, whether those workers are employed in the United States or elsewhere. However, not all unskilled jobs can be moved abroad, because not all outputs can be imported (most unskilled services, for example, must be performed at the place of consumption); therefore, the analyses that follow will continue to focus on situations in which the "export" of unskilled jobs is infeasible or very costly.

AN ANALYSIS OF THE GAINERS AND LOSERS

Some claim that, while perhaps not reducing citizen-held jobs one-for-one, large immigrant flows are indeed harmful to American workers. This view is probably the dominant force behind our restrictive immigration policy and the consequent concern about illegal immigration.

FIGURE 10.2

Demand and Supply of "Rough Laborers" with a Minimum Wage

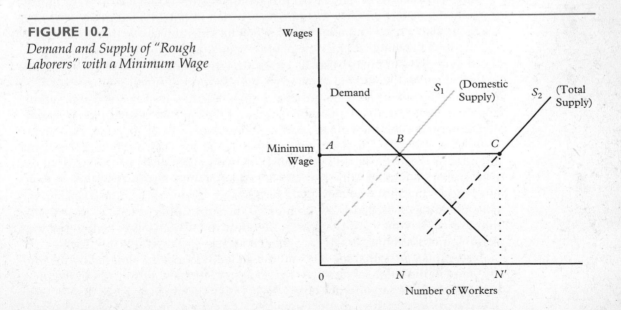

The argument is based primarily on a single-market analysis like that contained in Figure 10.1, where only the effects on the market for rough labor are examined. As far as it goes, the argument is plausible. When immigration increases the supply of rough laborers, both the wages and the employment levels of American citizens working as laborers are reduced. The total wage bill paid to American laborers falls from $W_1 0 N_1 B$ in Figure 10.1 to $W_2 0 N_3 D$. Thus, some American workers leave the market in response to the reduced wage, and those who stay earn less. If the Americans employed as laborers are the target of antipoverty efforts, the influx of immigrants could frustrate such efforts by reducing their wages, employment levels, or working hours.

Even if the immigration of unskilled labor were to adversely affect domestic laborers, however, it would be a mistake to conclude that it is necessarily harmful to Americans as a *whole*. First, immigration of "cheap labor" clearly benefits consumers using the output of this labor. As wages are reduced and employment increases, the goods and services produced by this labor are increased in quantity and reduced in price.

Second, employers of rough labor (to continue our example) are obviously benefited, at least in the short run. In Figure 10.1, profits are increased from $W_1 AB$ to $W_2 AC$. This rise in profitability will have two major effects. By raising the returns to capital, it will serve as a signal for investors to increase investments in plant and equipment (the investment funds could be attracted from overseas as well as from domestic sources). Increased profits will also induce more people to become employers. The increases in capital and the number of employers will eventually drive profits down to their normal level, but in the end the country's stock of capital is increased and opportunities are created for some workers to become owners.

Third, our analysis of the market for laborers assumed that the influx of immigrants had no effect on the demand curve (which was held fixed in Figure 10.1). This is probably not a bad assumption when looking at just one market, because the fraction of earnings immigrant laborers spend on the goods and services produced by rough labor may be small. However, immigrants do spend money in the United States, and this added demand creates job opportunities for others (see Figure 10.3). Thus, workers who are not close substitutes for unskilled immigrant labor may benefit from immigration because of the increase in consumer demand attendant on this addition to our working population.

(Note: Recall from Chapter 3 that if the demand for skilled workers increases when the wage of unskilled labor falls, the two grades of labor would be *gross complements*. Assuming skilled and unskilled labor are substitutes in the production process, the only way they could be gross complements is if the *scale effect* of a decline in the unskilled wage dominated the substitution effect. In the case of immigration one may suppose the scale effect to be very large, because as the working population rises, aggregate demand is increased. While theoretical analysis cannot *prove* that the demand for skilled workers is increased by the immigration of unskilled labor if the two grades of labor are substitutes in the production process, it can offer the above observation that an increase in demand for skilled workers remains a distinct possibility. Of course, for any type of labor that

FIGURE 10.3

Market for All Labor Except Unskilled

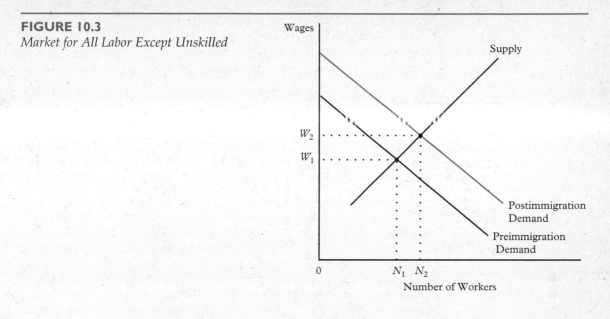

is *complementary* with unskilled labor in the production process—supervisory workers, for example—immigration does represent a clear-cut gain.)[20]

Given the *theoretical* implications that immigration can produce gains for some native workers and losses for others, estimating the *actual* effects of immigration on various groups of natives has been of considerable interest in recent years. Most research studies attempt to measure the effects of immigration on native wage and employment levels by using local labor markets as units of observation. These studies assume that the greater the influx of immigrants to an area, the greater will be the area's change in native wage and employment levels. Comparisons can be made of native wage and employment levels in the same area before and after an increase in immigration (as in Example 10.3), or they can be made for a given year among areas with very different immigrant compositions. No matter which kind of comparison is made, studies using local labor markets as units of observation estimate that the effects of immigration on native wages and employment levels—for both skilled and unskilled workers—are minimal.[21]

Possible explanations for the surprisingly negligible effects of immigration estimated from local labor market studies are that (*a*) immigrants may choose to locate in areas where jobs are expanding anyway, or (*b*) internal migration by natives may help to counteract the increased supply of immigrants (as natives avoid or

---

[20]For an empirical investigation of the substitutability between immigrants and nonimmigrant labor, see Jean B. Grossman, "The Substitutability of Natives and Immigrants in Production," *Review of Economics and Statistics* 64 (November 1982): 596–603.

[21]For comprehensive reviews of the empirical issues and findings on this subject, see George J. Borjas, "The Economic Benefits from Immigration," *Journal of Economic Perspectives* 9, no. 2 (Spring 1995): 3–22; Friedberg and Hunt, "The Impact of Immigrants on Host Country Wages, Employment, and Growth"; and Borjas, "The Economics of Immigration."

EXAMPLE 10.3

The Mariel Boatlift and Its Effects on Miami's Wage and Unemployment Rates

Between May and September of 1980, some 125,000 Cubans were allowed to emigrate to Miami from the port of Mariel in Cuba. These immigrants, half of whom permanently settled in Miami, increased Miami's overall labor force by 7 percent in under half a year. Because two-thirds of "the Mariels" had not completed high school, and because unskilled workers made up about 30 percent of Miami's workforce, it is likely that the number of *unskilled* workers in Miami increased by 16 percent or more during this short period! Such a marked and rapid increase in labor market size is highly unusual, but it provides an interesting "natural experiment" on the consequences of immigration for a "host" area.

As discussed in the text, the effects of immigration on host areas are more complex than those associated with a simple shift in supply. The demand for labor itself shifts as a result of an influx of consumers/workers, and there also may be adjustments in locational decisions by present or potential residents of an area. In the case of the Mariel boatlift, the effects on the wages and unemployment rates of unskilled workers in Miami were surprisingly small.

If immigration has negative effects on wages in the receiving areas, we would expect to observe that the wages of Miami's unskilled workers fell relative to the wages of its skilled workers and relative to the wages of unskilled workers in otherwise comparable cities. Neither relative decline occurred; in fact, the wages of unskilled black workers in Miami actually rose relative to wages of unskilled blacks in four comparison cities (Atlanta, Los Angeles, Houston, and Tampa). Similarly, the unemployment rate among low-skilled blacks in Miami improved, on average, relative to that in other cities during the five years following the boatlift. Among Hispanic workers, there was a predictable increase in Miami's unemployment rate relative to that in the other cities in 1981, but from 1982 to 1985 the Hispanic unemployment rate in Miami fell faster than in the comparison cities.

What accounts for the absence of adverse pressures on the wages and unemployment rates of unskilled workers in the Miami area? Concurrent rightward shifts in the demand curve for labor probably tended to offset the rightward shifts in labor supply curves. However, it also appears that some residents may have left Miami in response to the influx of immigrants and that other potential migrants went elsewhere; the rate of Miami's population growth after 1980 slowed considerably relative to that of the rest of Florida, so that by 1986 its population was roughly equal to what it was projected to be by 1986 *before* the boatlift. For locational adjustments of residents and potential in-migrants to underlie the lack of wage and unemployment effects, these adjustments would have to have been very rapid. Their presence reinforces the theoretical prediction, made earlier in this chapter, that migration flows are sensitive to economic conditions in both sending and receiving areas.

SOURCE: David Card, "The Impact of the Mariel Boatlift on the Miami Labor Market," *Industrial and Labor Relations Review* 43, no. 2 (January 1990): 245–257.

leave areas of heavy immigrant inflow). If not properly controlled for, both of these behaviors could mask the true effects of immigration on local labor markets. While there is some evidence that native internal migration rates do react to immigration (as seen in Example 10.3), for counteracting internal flows to explain many of the negligible estimates would require implausibly rapid responses on the part of native migrants. Thus, while the true effects of immigration on various groups of native workers remain something of a puzzle, they are most likely not very large.[22]

DO THE OVERALL GAINS FROM IMMIGRATION EXCEED THE LOSSES?

So far, we have used economic theory to analyze the likely effects of immigration on various groups of natives, including consumers, owners, and both skilled and unskilled workers. Theory suggests that some of these groups should be clear-cut gainers; among these are owners, consumers, and workers who are complements in production with immigrants. Native workers whose labor is highly substitutable in production with immigrant labor are the most likely losers from immigration, while the gains or losses for other groups of native workers are theoretically unpredictable owing to potentially offsetting influences of the substitution and scale effects. Further, as we have seen from empirical studies, the actual effects that have been estimated for several of the above groups are apparently quite small, but these effects still must be classified as uncertain.

In this subsection, we use economic theory to analyze a slightly different question: What does economic theory say about the *overall* effects of immigration on the host country? Put in the context of the *normative* criteria presented in Chapter 1, this subsection asks, "If there are both gainers and losers from immigration among natives in the host country, is it likely that the gainers would be able to compensate the losers and still feel better off?" The answer to this question will be yes if immigration increases the aggregate disposable income of natives.

Immigration potentially adds people who are both consumers and producers to the host country, so whether an influx of immigrants makes those already residing in the host country richer or poorer, in the aggregate, depends to a large extent on how much the immigrants *add* to overall production as compared to how much they *consume.* Let us take a simple example of elderly immigrants allowed into the country to reunite with their adult children. If these immigrants do not work, and if they are dependent on their children or on American taxpayers for their consumption, then clearly the overall per capita disposable income among natives must fall. (This fall, of course, could well be offset by the increased utility of the reunited families, in which case it would be a price the host country might be willing to pay.)

In the slightly more complicated case in which immigrants *work* after their arrival, our profit-maximizing models of employer behavior suggest that they are paid no more than the value of their marginal product. Thus, if they rely only on their own earnings to finance their consumption, immigrants who work do not reduce the per capita disposable income of natives in the host country. Moreover, if immigrant earnings are not equal to the *full* value of the output they add to the host country, then the total disposable income of natives will increase.[23]

---

[22]Borjas, "The Economics of Immigration," 1697–1700.

[23]Economic theory suggests this will be the case if the shift in labor supply is large enough to significantly lower the marginal revenue product of labor in the immigrants' labor market. If so, wages will fall, output will expand, and the *profits from the added output* are captured by owners, who are presumably natives.

Our analysis of the effects of working immigrants cannot end here, though, because most host countries (including the United States) have several government programs, financed by various taxes, that may distribute benefits to qualified immigrants. If the taxes paid by immigrants are sufficient to cover the benefits they receive from such programs, then the presence of these immigrants does not threaten the per capita disposable income of natives. Indeed, some government programs, such as national defense, are true "public goods" (whose costs are not increased by immigration), and any taxes paid by immigrants help natives defray the expenses of these programs. However, if immigrants are relatively high users of government support services, and if the taxes they pay do not cover the value of their benefits, then it is possible that the fiscal burden of immigration could be large enough to reduce the aggregate income of natives.

Given the declining skills of recent immigrant cohorts, and given that many government programs (public health, welfare, and unemployment insurance, for example) are aimed at subsidizing the poor, there is growing concern that recent immigration to the United States may be harmful to natives. Studies that have estimated the net fiscal effects of immigration differ in their findings, with some estimating that immigrants receive benefits in excess of what they pay in taxes, and others estimating the opposite.[24] Again, as with the estimated labor market effects on various groups of native workers, the inconclusive results so far are probably indicative of relatively small effects.

Illegal immigration has been the major focus of immigration policy in recent years, so it is interesting to consider how it, in particular, is likely to affect the overall disposable incomes of American citizens (and other legal residents). While the exact answer is unknown, three considerations suggest that *illegal immigration may be more likely to increase native incomes than legal immigration!*

First, illegal immigrants come mainly to work, not for purposes of family reunification. Therefore, they clearly add to the production of domestic goods and services. Second, while they tend to be poor, they are ineligible for many programs (welfare, food stamps, Social Security, unemployment insurance) that transfer resources to low-income citizens. Third, despite their wish to "hide" from the government, immigrants cannot avoid paying most taxes (especially payroll, sales, and property taxes); indeed, one study even indicated that 75 percent of illegal immigrants had income taxes withheld but that relatively few filed for a refund.[25]

Thus, one cannot rule out the possibility that, despite governmental efforts to prohibit it, the "transaction" of illegal immigration is—to use the normative terminology of Chapter 1—"Pareto-improving." That is, the immigrants themselves clearly gain (otherwise they would go back home), while as a group, natives may well not lose! The issue is clearly an empirical one, and the net effects of illegal immigration probably deserve more study before the country decides to allocate more resources to stopping it.

---

[24]For reference to these studies, see Borjas, "The Economic Benefits from Immigration," 9.

[25]Gregory DeFreitas, *Inequality at Work: Hispanics in the U.S. Labor Force* (New York: Oxford University Press, 1991), 228. The same study showed minimal use of public services by illegal immigrants.

Employee Turnover and Job Matching

While most workers who experience geographic mobility also change jobs (although perhaps not employers), these migrants are but one part of a wider group of workers who change jobs each year with or without a change of residence. Prior to 1982, the U.S. Department of Labor collected and published data on the percentage of employees who separated from their employers each year. Among American male workers in the 1976–1981 period, for example, 14 percent separated from their employers each year.[26] Some of these separations were voluntary in the sense that they were initiated by the employee, and some were involuntary (employer-induced). Voluntary separations are termed *quits* and involuntary separations are termed *layoffs*. Layoffs can be temporary separations for economic reasons or permanent discharges, whether for cause (firing) or for economic reasons. As we shall see below, however, the distinction between employer- and employee-initiated separation may be less clear than these categories suggest.

From the perspective of an individual worker, the human-capital model suggests that changing jobs is a costly transaction that will be undertaken voluntarily only if the expected benefits are relatively large. Workers, then, are seen as using job mobility as a means of improving their personal well-being. From a more global perspective, however, worker mobility performs the socially useful role of matching workers with the employers who value their skills most highly. We elaborate briefly below.

Workers are unique, in the sense that each one has skills and interests that are different from those of others. Employers, for their part, have differing demands for skills and other worker characteristics that are a function of consumer preferences for their products, available production technologies, and even such factors as their management practices. For example, some jobs have duties or work schedules that are highly structured and predictable, while similarly skilled workers in other firms face tight deadlines on short notice, making for a highly variable work schedule. Workers who favor predictable routines and dislike last-minute demands on their time will clearly be more productive in the former environment, while equally skilled workers who relish change and challenges may be more productive in the latter.

Given that the information workers and employers initially have about each other is both incomplete and costly to obtain, it is highly unlikely that the first "match" a worker is able to make with an employer will turn out to be the best one that is ultimately available; therefore, subsequent mobility plays a critical role in improving the job match for a given worker over time. Employers will desire to fire workers who are less productive than they believed them to be at the time of

---

[26]Jacob Mincer and Yoshio Higuchi, "Wage Structures and Labor Turnover in the U.S. and Japan," *Journal of the Japanese and International Economies* 2 (1988): 97–133. A more recent study of U.S. data from the same time period found even higher rates of job turnover; see Patricia M. Anderson and Bruce D. Meyer, "The Extent and Consequences of Job Turnover," *Brookings Papers on Economic Activity*: *Microeconomics* (1994): 177–248. Another recent contribution to the literature is Harry T. Holzer, "Job Vacancy Rates in the Firm: An Empirical Analysis," *Economica* 61, no. 241 (February 1994): 17–36.

hire, and workers will want to quit if their talents can command a higher wage (presumably because they are more productive) elsewhere. The economy thus edges toward the goal of good matches through a process of trial and error. When an error is made in matching a worker with an employer, the employment relationship is terminated and mobility occurs, but when a good match is made the relationship can be expected to endure.

THE PATTERNS OF JOB MOBILITY

We will see a bit later (in Table 10.6) that between the ages of 20 and 60, males in the United States work for an average of over seven different employers, and they work for three of those during their twenties alone. This average, however, masks considerable variation in personal mobility rates. One study, for example, found that 8 percent of American workers with ten years of work experience had worked that time for a single employer, while 28 percent had worked for six or more employers during that period.[27] In the subsections below, we employ human capital theory to analyze the patterns of job mobility that appear to exist.

WAGE EFFECTS   Human capital theory predicts that, *other things equal*, a given worker will have a greater probability of quitting a low-wage job than a higher-paying one. That is, workers employed at lower wages than they could obtain elsewhere are the most likely to quit. Indeed, a very strong and consistent finding in virtually all studies of worker quit behavior is that, holding worker characteristics constant, employees in industries with lower wages have higher quit rates. At the level of individual workers, research indicates that those who change employers have more to gain from a job change than those who stay and that, indeed, their wage growth after changing is faster than it would have been had they stayed.[28]

In thinking about the relationship between quit rates and wages, it is useful to bear in mind a constant theme throughout this text: market outcomes are the result of both worker *and* employer behavior. While workers may decide to quit if their wages fall below what they could get elsewhere, *employers* often have incentives to reduce quits by raising wages. We may talk of a quit as "worker-initiated," but the fact that an employer did not choose to take steps to retain potential quitters would seem to imply that the employer believed keeping them was not worth the cost. For example, Japanese firms offer more firm-specific training than U.S. firms

---

[27]Henry S. Farber, "The Analysis of Interfirm Worker Mobility," *Journal of Labor Economics* 12, no. 4 (October 1994): 554–593.

[28]Donald O. Parsons, "Models of Labor Market Turnover: A Theoretical and Empirical Survey," in *Research in Labor Economics*, vol. 1, ed. Ronald Ehrenberg (Greenwich, Conn.: JAI Press, 1977), 185–223; Michael G. Abbott and Charles M. Beach, "Wage Changes and Job Changes of Canadian Women: Evidence from the 1986–87 Labour Market Activity Survey," *Journal of Human Resources* 29, no. 2 (Spring 1994): 429–460; George Borjas and Sherwin Rosen, "Income Prospects and Job Mobility of Younger Men," in *Research in Labor Economics*, vol. 3, ed. Ronald Ehrenberg (Greenwich, Conn.: JAI Press, 1980); and Christopher J. Flinn, "Wages and Job Mobility of Young Workers," *Journal of Political Economy* 94, no. 3, pt. 2 (June 1986): S88–S110.

and offer their workers much larger wage increases as employee tenure with the firm increases; the result is an average yearly separation rate that is one-fourth the U.S. average. Thus, the distinction between worker-initiated and employer-induced quits is somewhat ambiguous.[29] To expand on this point, we shall briefly discuss the relationship between quit rates and firm-specific human capital investments in the context of both *firm size* and *gender* differences in quit rates.

From Table 10.5, it can be seen that *quit rates tend to decline as firm size increases.* One explanation for this phenomenon is that large firms offer more possibilities for transfers and promotions. Another, however, builds on the fact that large firms generally pay higher wages.[30] This explanation asserts that large firms tend to have highly mechanized production processes, where the output of one work team is highly dependent on that of production groups preceding it in the production "chain." Larger firms, it is argued, have greater needs for dependable and steady workers because employees who shirk their duties can impose great costs on a highly interdependent production process. Large firms, then, establish "internal labor markets" for the reasons suggested in Chapter 5; that is, they hire workers at entry-level jobs and carefully observe such hard-to-screen attributes as reliability, motivation, and attention to detail. Once having invested time and effort in selecting the best workers for its operation, a large firm finds it costly for such workers to quit. Thus, large firms pay high wages to reduce the probability of quitting because they have substantial firm-specific screening investments in their workers.[31]

It has been widely observed that women workers have higher quit rates, and therefore shorter job tenures, than men. To a large degree, this higher quit rate probably reflects lower levels of firm-specific human capital investments. We argued in Chapter 9 that the interrupted careers of "traditional" women workers rendered many forms of human capital investment less beneficial than would otherwise be the case, and lower levels of firm-specific training could account for lower wages, lower job tenures, and higher quit rates.[32] In fact, once the lower wages and shorter careers of women are controlled for, there appears to be no difference between the sexes in the propensity to quit a job.[33] Indeed, one study of

---

[29]Recent research indicates that employees who are fired experience a decline in wages, while those who quit for other than "family" reasons experience an increase; see Kristen Keith, "Reputation, Voluntary Mobility, and Wages," *Review of Economics and Statistics* 75, no. 3 (August 1993): 559–563. See Mincer and Higuchi, "Wage Structures and Labor Turnover in the U.S. and Japan," for the evidence on Japanese separation rates.

[30]Walter Oi, "The Fixed Employment Costs of Specialized Labor," in *The Measurement of Labor Cost*, ed. Jack E. Triplett (Chicago: University of Chicago Press, 1983).

[31]This argument is developed more fully and elegantly in Walter Oi, "Low Wages and Small Firms," in *Research in Labor Economics,* vol. 12, ed. Ronald Ehrenberg (Greenwich, Conn.: JAI Press, 1991).

[32]Jacob Mincer and Boyan Jovanovic, "Labor Mobility and Wages," in *Studies in Labor Markets,* ed. Sherwin Rosen (Chicago: University of Chicago Press, 1981).

[33]Francine Blau and Lawrence Kahn, "Race and Sex Differences in Quits by Younger Workers," *Industrial and Labor Relations Review* 34 (July 1981): 563–577, and Audrey Light and Manuelita Ureta, "Panel Estimates of Male and Female Job Turnover Behavior: Can Female Non-quitters Be Identified?" *Journal of Labor Economics* 10 (April 1992): 156–181.

TABLE 10.5
Monthly Quit Rates (per 100 Workers) by Firm Size, Selected Industries,
1977–1981 Averages

Industry	Number of Employees			
	<250 Employees	250–499	500–999	1000 and Over
All manufacturing	3.28	3.12	2.40	1.50
Food and kindred products	3.46	4.11	3.95	2.28
Fabricated metal products	3.33	2.64	2.12	1.20
Electrical machinery	3.81	3.12	2.47	1.60
Transportation equipment	3.90	2.78	2.21	1.41

SOURCE: Walter Oi, "The Durability of Worker-Firm Attachments," Report to the U.S. Department of Labor, Office of the Assistant Secretary for Policy, Evaluation, and Research, March 25, 1983, Table 1.

employee behavior at a single firm found that females were *less* likely to quit than otherwise identical, equally paid males employed in the same jobs.[34]

CYCLICAL EFFECTS   Another implication of human capital theory is that workers will have a higher probability of quitting when it is relatively easy for them to obtain a better job quickly. Thus, when labor markets are *tight* (jobs are more plentiful relative to job seekers), one would expect the quit rate to be higher than when labor markets are *loose* (few jobs are available and many workers are being laid off). This prediction is confirmed in studies of time-series data.[35] Quit rates tend to rise when the labor market is tight and fall when it is loose. One measure of tightness is the unemployment rate; the negative relationship between the quit rate and unemployment can be readily seen in Figure 10.4. Another measure of labor market conditions is the layoff rate, which tends to rise in recessions and fall when firms are expanding production. It, too, is inversely correlated with the quit rate, as Figure 10.4 shows.

One interesting issue is whether the "quality" of job matches rises or falls during a recession (quality is measured by the *likelihood that the employment relationship will not be permanently dissolved by either party*). On the one hand, when job openings are few and job seekers are plentiful, employers have more applicants for each open position and can be more selective in making offers of employment. This reasoning suggests that match quality might increase in a recession. On the

[34]Andrew Weiss, "Determinants of Quit Behavior," *Journal of Labor Economics* 2 (July 1984): 371–387. Weiss argues that to the extent that (*a*) males and females were treated equally in the firm, and (*b*) males faced better job alternatives outside the firm than did females (see Chapter 12 for evidence on gender discrimination), then (*c*) males at the firm should be expected to have higher quit rates than otherwise identical females in the firm.

[35]Parsons, "Models of Labor Market Turnover," 185–223.

FIGURE 10.4

The Quit Rate and Labor Market "Tightness"

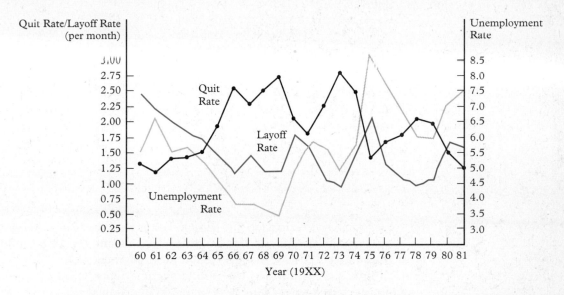

other hand, workers can expect fewer offers and may thus be more inclined during recessions to take the first offer that comes along; with workers being *less* selective, match quality might deteriorate. Recent research suggests that the latter influence dominates and that match quality during recessions is reduced.[36]

AGE AND JOB TENURE   A consistent theme in this and the preceding chapter is that younger workers are more likely to make human capital investments of all kinds. As Table 10.6 indicates, this appears to be true for job mobility investments as well. In both the United States and the United Kingdom, the number of new employers for whom the average employee works declines with age. In the United States, for example, men in their twenties change employers an average of three times, those in their thirties twice, and those in their fifties about once. In the United Kingdom, where job changing is less common, mobility also declines with age.

The decline of job mobility with age, though, potentially represents the effects of *two* forces. True, younger workers have a longer period over which to collect the benefits of job changing, and they may have lower investment costs as well. However, we also expect the *quality of job matches* to rise over the life cycle, as workers establish a work history, refine their skills, find out about their strengths and weaknesses, and are able to sequentially collect and evaluate more job offers. If match quality for a worker does improve over time, we would expect to find

---

[36]Audra J. Bowlus, "Matching Workers and Jobs: Cyclical Fluctuations in Match Quality," *Journal of Labor Economics* 13, no. 2 (April 1995): 335–350.

TABLE 10.6
Number of Employers For Whom an Employee Works from Ages 20 to 60, Men, United States and United Kingdom, 1983

Age Group	Number of New Employers During Age Interval		Cumulative Number of Employers	
	U.S.	U.K.	U.S.	U.K.
20–29	3.1	1.9	3.1	1.9
30–39	2.1	1.2	5.2	3.1
40–49	1.4	0.9	6.6	3.9
50–59	0.9	0.6	7.5	4.5

SOURCE: Adapted from S. W. Polachek and W. S. Siebert, *The Economics of Earnings* (Cambridge, Eng.: Cambridge University Press, 1993), 253.

that the longer one has been in a job, the less likely it is that he or she will separate from it. Recent studies do suggest that holding age constant, the longer one has been with an employer the less likely it is that the employment relationship will be ended in a future period; further, the results suggest that the influence of job matching may even be greater than the influence of age alone.[37]

COSTS OF QUITTING   Economic theory predicts that when the costs of quitting one's job are relatively low, mobility is more likely. This observation underlies our analysis of the rise in quit rates during periods of prosperity, for example, and we can also see the effects of mobility costs when looking at residential location and job turnover. Industries with high concentrations of employment in urban areas, where a worker's change of employer does not necessarily require investing in a change of residence, appear to have higher rates of turnover (holding wage rates and employee age constant) than industries concentrated in nonmetropolitan areas.[38]

Beyond the costs that can be associated with such measurable characteristics as age and residential location are those that are *psychic* in nature. These latter costs, though unobservable to the researcher, are very likely to differ widely across individuals (for example, some people adapt more quickly to new surroundings than others do). Recent studies have found considerable heterogeneity among workers

[37]Robert Topel and Michael Ward, "Job Mobility and the Careers of Young Men," *Quarterly Journal of Economics* 107 (May 1992): 439–480; and Farber, "The Analysis of Interfirm Worker Mobility." For theoretical analyses of job matching, see Boyan Jovanovic, "Job Matching and the Theory of Turnover," *Journal of Political Economy* 87 (October 1979): 972–990, and Kenneth J. McLaughlin, "Rent Sharing in an Equilibrium Model of Matching and Turnover," *Journal of Labor Economics* 12, no. 4 (October 1994): 499–523.

[38]Parsons, "Models of Labor Market Turnover," and Farrell E. Bloch, "Labor Turnover in U.S. Manufacturing Industries," *Journal of Human Resources* 14 (Spring 1979): 236–246.

TABLE 10.7
Average Job Tenure, Selected Countries, 1991

Country	Average Tenure (in Years) with Current Employer	
	Men	**Women**
Australia	7.0	5.4
Canada	8.9	6.5
France	10.6	9.6
Germany	12.1	8.0
Japan	12.5	7.3
United Kingdom	9.2	6.3
United States	7.5	5.9

SOURCE: Organisation for Economic Co-Operation and Development, *Employment Outlook: July 1993* (OECD: 1993), Table 4.1.

in their propensities to change jobs, with one study estimating that almost half of *all* permanent separations that took place over a three-year period involved a small number (13 percent) of workers who had three or more separations during the period (in contrast, 31 percent of workers had no separations at all during the period).[39]

It is also possible that the costs of job changing by employees vary internationally. Data we saw in Table 10.6, and earlier in Example 5.3 (Chapter 5), suggested that workers in the United States may well be more likely to change employers than workers elsewhere. Indeed, Table 10.7 confirms that, on average, American workers have been with their current employers fewer years than workers in most other developed economies, particularly those in Europe and Japan. We do not know why Americans are more mobile than others, but one possibility discussed in Chapter 5 related to the lower levels of company training received by American workers (which is both a cause and an effect of short expected job tenures).[40] Another possibility, however, is that the costs of mobility are lower in the United States (despite the fact that Japan and Europe are more densely populated and hence more "urban"). What would create these lower costs?

One hypothesis that has received at least some investigation is that housing policies in Europe and Japan increase the costs of residential, and therefore *job*, mobility. Germany, the United Kingdom, and Japan, for example, have controls on

---

[39]Patricia M. Anderson and Bruce D. Meyer, "The Extent and Consequences of Job Turnover," *Brookings Papers on Economic Activity: Microeconomics* (1994): 177–248; Farber, "The Analysis of Interfirm Worker Mobility."

[40]It has also been suggested that American job matches may be relatively poor; see John Bishop, "Improving Job Matches in the U.S. Labor Market," *Brookings Papers on Economic Activity: Microeconomics* (1993): 335–400.

the rent *increases* that landlords can charge to existing renters, while tending to allow them freedom to negotiate any mutually agreeable rent on their *initial* lease with the renter. Thus, it is argued that renters who move typically face very large rent increases in these countries. Similarly, subsidized housing is much more common in these countries than in the United States, but since it is limited relative to the demand for it, those British, German, or Japanese workers fortunate enough to live in subsidized units are reluctant (it is argued) to give them up. The empirical evidence on the implications of housing policy for job mobility, however, is both limited and mixed.[41]

One could also hypothesize that the United States, Australia, and Canada, all of which exhibit shorter job tenures than most European countries and Japan, are large, sparsely populated countries that historically have attracted people willing to immigrate from abroad or resettle internally over long distances. In a country of "movers," moving may not been seen by either worker or employer as an unusual or especially traumatic event.[42]

While questions remain about the *causes* of different job mobility rates across countries, the social desirability of greater mobility can also be debated. On the one hand, mobility can be seen as socially useful, because it promotes both individual well-being and the quality of job matches. In Chapter 8 we pointed out, for example, that mobility (or at least the *threat* of mobility) was essential to the creation of compensating wage differentials. Moreover, the greater the number of workers and employers "in the market" at any given time, the more flexibility an economy has in making job matches that best adapt to a changing environment. Indeed, when focusing on this aspect of job mobility, economists have long worried whether economies have *enough* mobility. A recent case in point is the concern whether employers have created "job lock" by adopting pension plans and health insurance policies that are not portable if the employee leaves the firm. [43]

On the other hand, lower mobility costs (and therefore greater mobility) among workers may well serve to *reduce* the incentives of their employers to provide job training. As discussed in Chapter 5, the high rate of job mobility among American workers apparently serves to frustrate the goal of upgrading their skills through company training.

---

[41] See Patrick Minford, Paul Ashton, and Michael Peel, "The Effects of Housing Distortions on Unemployment," *Oxford Economic Papers* 40, no. 2 (June 1988): 322–345; and Axel Borsch-Supan, "Housing Market Regulations and Housing Market Performance in the United States, Germany, and Japan," in *Social Protection Versus Economic Flexibility: Is There a Trade-Off?* ed. Rebecca M. Blank (Chicago: University of Chicago Press, 1994), 119–156.

[42] One recent study, for example, found no evidence that American employers stigmatized employees who frequently changed jobs; see Keith, "Reputation, Voluntary Mobility, and Wages."

[43] See Stuart Dorsey, "Pension Portability and Labor Market Efficiency: A Survey of the Literature," *Industrial and Labor Relations Review* 48, no. 2 (January 1995): 276–292; Alan C. Monheit and Philip F. Cooper, "Health Insurance and Job Mobility," and Jonathan Gruber and Brigitte C. Madrian, "Health Insurance and Job Mobility: The Effects of Public Policy on Job Lock," both in *Industrial and Labor Relations Review* 48, no. 1 (October 1994): 68–102. For a much earlier article, see Arthur Ross, "Do We Have a New Industrial Feudalism?" *American Economic Review* 48, no. 5 (December 1958): 914.

Whether the presence of job-changing costs is a social boon or bane, these costs and the mobility associated with them are factors with which all employers must contend. We comment in the next subsection on how these costs might alter our simple model of labor demand, and we then move on in the next chapter to a consideration of the various pay strategies employers can use both to recruit and retain the "right" employees and to provide them with the best set of production incentives.

COSTS OF TURNOVER AND THE MONOPSONY MODEL

In Chapters 3 and 4, we noted that some economists have begun to explore theoretical models that produce monopsony-like behavior by employers in situations in which they are not the sole buyers of labor in a particular market. These explorations are motivated partly by the desire to explain why it might be difficult to find the employment reductions that standard labor demand theory expects to occur when the minimum wage is increased. A deeper motivation for these explorations, however, is the desire to analyze whether more-complex models of employer and employee behavior yield important insights that are not produced by simpler models. We now briefly consider the implications for labor *demand* theory of the fact that employee turnover is costly. Further complexities and their implications for labor demand are analyzed in Chapter 11.

BACKGROUND ISSUES   The student will recall that in the standard model of labor demand, each employer is assumed to face a labor supply curve that is horizontal at the market wage rate. That is, any single firm is assumed to be a "wage taker" that can always hire additional workers at a constant (market) wage of, say, W^*. The firm has no incentive to pay *above* the market wage, because it can secure all the employees it wants at W^*, and if it paid *below* the market wage it would lose all its workers to other firms. This horizontal supply curve also means that the *marginal cost* of hiring labor is constant at W^*. With a downward-sloping marginal revenue product of labor curve, the profit-maximizing firm (which hires until marginal revenue product equals W^*) therefore has a downward-sloping labor demand curve.

From the standard model arises the "law of one price," which states that, in equilibrium, all firms in the market for workers of the same skill will pay the same wage rate, as long as conditions of employment are the same. Two points must be made concerning the law of one price. First, a major implication of this law is that, with the exception of compensating differentials for employment conditions of one sort or another, *wages will be determined by workers' human capital characteristics*. All firms would have to pay the market wage for each skill group regardless of their level of profitability, their industry, or their size. Under this model, then, *employer characteristics do not influence wages* except when either favorable or unfavorable employment conditions give rise to compensating wage differentials.

Second, *worker mobility* is what generates the "one price" for labor of a given skill. If workers of equal skill were paid different wages by employers with comparable working conditions, the standard, competitive model asserts that the lower-paid ones would quit their jobs and seek employment with higher-paying firms. Wages in the lower-paying firms thereby would be driven up, while wages in the higher-paying firms would be driven down, by worker mobility. The standard model, with its horizontal labor supply curve facing each firm, implicitly assumes that mobility is costless and that the quit rate among workers is infinitely elastic with respect to wages (that is, if a firm were to cut its wages below those paid elsewhere, all its workers would quit).

THE IMPLICATIONS OF MOBILITY COSTS   In this chapter, we have pointed out that job mobility is costly, and that the decision to change jobs can be analyzed as an investment in human capital. The human capital model of job mobility, as captured in equation (10.1), implies that a worker will *not* invest in mobility if the present value of the net benefits is negative. That is, even if the gross benefits of switching one's job are positive, making the change is not worthwhile if these benefits are small relative to the costs of searching for other offers, ending one's current employment relationship, possibly moving to a new residence, and settling into a new job.

If the costs of changing jobs make some wage (or utility) gains not worth capturing, and if these costs differ across individual workers, then we would not expect the quit rate to be infinitely responsive to wages. A small deviation from the market wage by a given firm might induce *some* workers to change employers, but a larger deviation would be required before others are induced to invest in mobility. Of course, one might reasonably expect supply to be more responsive to wages in the long run, because new entrants to the labor force are searching anyway and can choose the best opportunities (or avoid the worst) without having to incur the costs of severing ties with a current employer. However, if information is difficult to obtain and search is costly even in the long run, wage differences across workers with the same human capital characteristics and similar conditions of employment might persist more or less permanently.

Empirically, economists have estimated that quit rates respond to wages in the expected way (they rise when wages fall), but the estimated response is considerably less than infinitely elastic.[44] Moreover, there is also evidence of persistent wage differentials across *industries* and *firm-size* groups[45] that researchers have

---

[44]See David Card and Alan B. Krueger, *Myth and Measurement: The New Economics of the Minimum Wage* (Princeton, N.J.: Princeton University Press, 1995), 375, for a summary of evidence on quit rates.

[45]Steven G. Allen, "Updated Notes on the Interindustry Wage Structure, 1890–1990," *Industrial and Labor Relations Review* 48, no. 2 (January 1995): 305–321; Richard Freeman, "Does the New Generation of Labor Economists Know More Than the Old Generation?" in *How Labor Markets Work*, ed. Bruce E. Kaufman (Lexington, Mass.: Lexington Books, 1988), 205–223; and Richard Thaler, "Anomalies: Interindustry Wage Differentials," *Journal of Economic Perspectives* 3 (Spring 1989): 181–193. We discuss the wage effects of firm size more fully in Chapter 11.

not been able to explain by differences in workers' human capital or by conditions giving rise to compensating wage differentials. While there are other potential explanations for these findings, the evidence on quit rates and wage differentials is certainly consistent with the presence of search and relocation costs that impede worker mobility.

The presence of mobility costs implies that individual firms well might face upward-sloping labor supply curves over some range of wages and some finite time period. A firm could lower its wages (at least to some extent) without losing all its workers to other firms, and it could raise its wages by some amount without attracting all the workers from other firms. As was pointed out in Chapter 3, the essence of the monopsonistic model of employer demand for labor is an upward-sloping labor supply curve to individual employers. It is this upward-sloping supply curve that drives the firm's marginal cost of labor above its wage rate, thus creating uncertainty about how its desired level of employment will respond to a mandated wage increase. (The student will recall from Chapter 3 that when the marginal cost of labor is above the wage, small mandated wage increases can simultaneously raise the wage level and *reduce* the marginal cost of labor.) One possible source of monopsony-like behavior by firms, then, is the presence of costs associated with job changing.[46]

While monopsony-like behavior by an employer is rooted in an upward-sloping labor supply curve—which causes the firm's marginal costs of labor to lie above its wage rate—the *extent* to which this behavior deviates from that presumed by the standard labor demand model is a function of the *extent to which marginal costs of labor exceed the wage rate*. If marginal costs are substantially above the wage rate to begin with, for example, then even a relatively large mandated wage increase could still reduce the marginal costs of labor to the firm (and lead to theoretically ambiguous expectations about changes in the level of employment). However, if marginal costs were only slightly above the wage to begin with, the same mandated wage increase might *raise* the marginal costs of labor, which would lead us to expect the conventionally predicted fall in employment.

As illustrated in Figure 10.5, the degree to which a firm's marginal costs of labor exceed its wage rate depends on how steeply sloped its labor supply curve is.[47] When mobility costs are lower, the labor supply curve to an individual employer will be flatter (Figure 10.5a) and the associated marginal cost curve will rise relatively slowly. If mobility costs are higher, both the firm's labor supply curve and its

---

[46]Card and Krueger, *Myth and Measurement*, 373–381, summarizes, and provides references to, the literature on monopsony models that are based on mobility costs.

[47]It can be mathematically proven that, with a straight-line labor supply curve to the firm, such as the ones illustrated in Figure 10.5, the accompanying marginal cost of labor curve has a slope that is *twice* that of the labor supply curve.

FIGURE 10.5

Mobility Costs and the Extent to Which the Marginal Costs of Labor Exceed the Wage

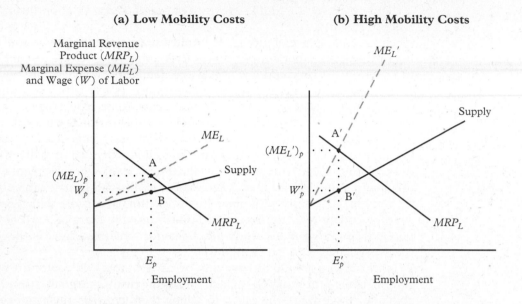

marginal costs of labor rise sharply (see Figure 10.5b). Given its marginal revenue product of labor curve, if the firm were faced with a labor supply curve such as the one in panel (a), it would have a profit-maximizing employment level of E_p, would pay a wage of W_p, and the extent to which its marginal costs of labor exceeded its wage rate would be given by the distance AB. If instead the firm faced a supply curve like the one in panel (b), the gap between its marginal costs of labor and its wage rate (W_p') at the profit-maximizing level of employment (E_p') would be equal to the distance A'B', which is greater than AB. Thus, the *extent* to which a firm behaves like a monopsonist is a function of how steeply sloped its labor supply curve is—which is, in turn, a function of mobility costs.

REVIEW QUESTIONS

1. You may know that *states* now license lawyers, teachers, pharmacists, nurses, doctors, and so forth. These licensing procedures operate in such a way that unless lawyers, teachers, etc., pass a state test and become licensed, they cannot work in their profession in that state. A recent letter to *USA Today* stated:

> Bill Clinton should remove state-to-state licensing barriers. Every time a lawyer, teacher or health-care worker moves, some bureaucrat tells him he can't work. One of

the biggest health care costs is all this ridiculous licensing.

Please answer the following questions:

a. From the perspective of positive economics, what are the labor market effects of having states, rather than the federal government, license professionals?

b. Who would gain and who would lose from federalization of occupational licensing?

2. As you know, thousands of illegal immigrants are working in the United States. Suppose the United States increases the penalties for illegal immigration to include long jail sentences for illegal *workers*. Analyze the effects of this increased penalty on the wages and employment levels of *all* affected groups of workers.

3. It has been said, "The fact that quit rates in Japan are lower than in the United States suggests that Japanese workers are inherently more loyal to their employers than are American workers." Assuming that quit rates are indeed lower in Japan than in the United States, evaluate this assertion that Japanese workers have stronger preferences for loyalty than do American workers.

4. One way for the government to facilitate economic growth is for it to pay workers in depressed areas to move to regions where jobs are more plentiful. What would be the labor market effects of such a policy?

5. Other things equal, firms usually prefer their workers to have low quit rates. However, from a social perspective, quit rates can be too low. Why do businesses prefer low quit rates, and what are the social disadvantages of having such rates "too low"?

6. For the last 100 years coal-mine operators in South Africa have recruited migrant workers from other African countries to work in their mines for a specified period (for example, three years). These miners have been housed in male-only dormitories and have not been permitted to live with their families. Recently, the migrant workers and their unions have resisted this policy of separating workers from their families, and in a few instances workers have defied company policy and moved their wives and children into their rooms. If the migrant workers are successful in their efforts to live with their families, what are the likely labor market consequences?

7. A recent television program examining the issue of Mexican immigration stated that most economists believe immigration is a benefit to the United States.

a. State the chain of reasoning underlying this view.

b. From a normative perspective, is the key issue wage effects on native workers or subsidies of immigrants by the host country? Why?

SELECTED READINGS

Abowd, John M., and Richard B. Freeman, eds. *Immigration, Trade, and the Labor Market*. Chicago: University of Chicago Press, 1991.

Borjas, George. "The Ecomics of Immigration." *Journal of Economic Literature* 32, no. 4 (December 1994): 1667-1717.

Borjas, George. *Friends or Strangers*. New York: Basic Books, 1990.

———. *International Differences in the Labor Market Performance of Immigrants*. Kalamazoo, Mich.: W.E. Upjohn Institute for Employment Research, 1988.

Borjas, George J., and Richard B. Freeman, eds. *Immigrants and the Work Force.* Chicago: University of Chicago Press, 1992.

Chiswick, Barry. *Illegal Aliens: Their Employment and Employers.* Kalamazoo, Mich.: W.E. Upjohn Institute for Employment Research, 1988.

——. "Illegal Immigration and Immigration Control." *Journal of Economic Perspectives* 2, no. 3 (Summer 1988): 101–115.

Parsons, Donald O. "Models of Labor Market Turnover: A Theoretical and Empirical Survey." In *Research in Labor Economics,* vol. 1, ed. Ronald Ehrenberg. Greenwich, Conn.: JAI Press, 1977. 185–223.

11

Pay and Productivity

In the simplest model of the demand for labor (presented in Chapters 3 and 4), employers had few managerial decisions to make; they simply *found* the marginal productivity schedules and market wages of various kinds of labor and hired the profit-maximizing amount of each kind. In a model like this, there was no need for employers to design a compensation policy.

Most employers, however, appear to give considerable attention to their compensation policies, and some of the reasons why have already been explored. For example, employers offering specific training (see Chapter 5) have a "zone" into which the wage can feasibly fall, and they must balance the costs of raising the wages of their specifically trained workers against the savings generated from a higher probability of retaining these workers. Likewise, when the compensation package is expanded to include such items as employee benefits or job safety (see Chapter 8), employers must decide on the mix of wages and other valued items in the compensation package. We have also seen that under certain conditions employers will behave monopsonistically, in which case they "set" their wages rather than "finding them out."

This chapter will explore in more detail the complex relationship between compensation and productivity. Briefly put, employers face a myriad of managerial decisions rooted in the following practical realities:

1. Workers differ from each other in work habits that greatly affect productivity but are often difficult (costly) to observe before, and sometimes even after, hiring takes place;
2. The productivity of a given worker with a given level of human capital can vary considerably over time or in different environments, depending on his or her level of motivation (see Example 11.1);

EXAMPLE 11.1

The Wide Range of Possible Productivities: The Case of the Factory That Could Not Cut Output

In 1987, a manufacturer of airguns ("BB guns") in New York State found that its sales were lagging behind production. Wanting to cut production by about 20 percent without engaging in widespread layoffs, the company decided to temporarily cut back from a five-day to a four-day workweek. To its amazement, the company found that, despite this 20 percent reduction in working hours, production levels were not reduced—its workers produced as many airguns in four days as they previously had in five!

Central to the problem of achieving its desired output reduction was that the company paid its workers on the basis of the number of items they produced. Faced with the prospect of a temporary cut in their earnings, its workers reduced time on "breaks" and increased their pace of work sufficiently to maintain their previous levels of output (and earnings). The company was therefore forced to institute artificial caps on employee production; when these individual output quotas had been met, the worker was not allowed to produce more.

The inability to cut output, despite cutting back on hours of work, suggests how wide the range of possible worker productivity can be in some operations. Clearly, then, careful attention by management to the motivation and morale of employees can have important consequences, both privately and socially!

3. Worker productivity over a given period of time is a function of innate ability, the level of effort, and the environment (the weather, general business conditions, or the actions of other employees);
4. Being highly productive is usually not just a matter of slavishly following orders, but rather of *taking the initiative* to help advance the employer's objectives.[1]

Employers, then, must choose management strategies and compensation policies to obtain the right (that is, profit-maximizing) kind of employees and offer them the optimum incentives for production. In doing so, they must weigh the costs of various policies against the benefits. The focus of this chapter is on the role of compensation policies in optimizing worker productivity. Because compensation policies involve a set of promises the firm makes to its workers, and because they exist within the larger context of a particular employment relationship, we begin our analysis with some general issues surrounding the form and the substance of employment "contracts."

---

[1] For a stimulating article from which much of the ensuing discussion draws, see Herbert A. Simon, "Organizations and Markets," *Journal of Economic Perspectives* 5 (Spring 1991): 24–44.

The Employment Contract

The employment relationship can be thought of as a contract between a principal (the employer) and an agent (the employee). The employee is hired to help advance the employer's objectives in return for receiving wages and other benefits. Often there are understandings or implied promises that if employees work hard and perform well they will be promoted to higher-paying jobs as their careers progress.

The agreement by an employee to perform tasks for an employer in return for current and future pay can be thought of as a contract. A *formal* contract, such as one signed by a bank and a homeowner for the repayment of a loan, lays out quite explicitly all that each party promises to do and what will happen if either party fails to perform as promised. Once signed, a formal contract cannot be abrogated by either party without penalty. Disputes over performance can be referred to courts of law or other third parties for resolution.

Unlike formal contracts, most employment contracts are *incomplete* and *implicit*. They are usually incomplete in the sense that rarely are all the specific tasks that may be required of employees spelled out in advance. Doing so would limit the flexibility of employers in responding to changing conditions, and it would also require that employers and employees renegotiate their employment contract when each new situation arises—which would be costly to both parties.

Employment contracts are often also implicit in the sense that they are normally a set of informal understandings that are too vague to be legally enforceable. For example, just what has an employee promised to do when she has agreed to "work hard," and how can it be proved she has failed to do so? Specifically what has a firm promised to do when it has promised to "promote deserving employees as opportunities arise"? Further, employees can almost always quit a job at will, and employers often have great latitude in firing employees; hence, the employment contract is one that usually can be abrogated by one party or the other without legal penalty.[2]

---

[2]The doctrine of *employment-at-will,* under which employers (and employees) have the right to terminate an employment relationship at any time, has historically prevailed in the United States. Those not subject to this doctrine in the United States have included unionized workers with contract provisions governing discharges, tenured teachers, and workers under some civil service systems.

Recently, however, a number of state courts have adopted public policy and/or implicit contract exceptions to the doctrine. The former prevent an employee from being discharged for an action that is consistent with public policy (e.g., reporting the violation of an OSHA standard), while the latter prevent discharges "without cause" if actions taken by an employer (e.g., oral statements, established past practices, or statements in a personnel manual) implicitly promise such protection. The adoption by the courts of implicit contract exceptions to the employment-at-will doctrine seems to make it less likely that employers will unilaterally break promises. However, since these exceptions increase employers' costs of discharging workers, they obviously will alter employers' behavior in a number of ways (e.g., hiring standards, employment levels). For a full discussion of these issues, see Ronald Ehrenberg, "Workers' Rights: Rethinking Protective Labor Legislation," in *Rethinking Employment Policy,* ed. Lee Bawden and Felicity Skidmore (Washington, D.C.: Urban Institute Press, 1989).

The severe limits on legal enforceability make it essential that implicit contracts be *self-enforcing*. We turn now to a discussion of the difficulties that must be surmounted in making employment contracts self-enforcing.

COPING WITH INFORMATION ASYMMETRIES

For markets to successfully promote mutually beneficial transactions, both buyers and sellers must have access to accurate information about the quality and price of the goods or services being traded. Further, if the transaction involves a contract, the contract must be enforceable, because it is often advantageous for one or both parties to cheat by reneging on their promises in one way or other.

Opportunities for cheating are enhanced when information is "asymmetric"— that is, when one party knows more than the other about its intentions or performance under the contract. For example, job applicants know far more about their own work ethic than do the employers who are interviewing them, while employers know more than applicants about the actual duties of the jobs being offered. Applicants thus have incentives to overstate the depth of their commitment to hard work, and employers have incentives to represent jobs as less demanding than they actually may be.

To take another example, suppose an insurance company promises a newly hired insurance adjuster that she will receive a big raise in four years if she "does a good job." The company may later decide to refuse her the raise she deserves by falsely claiming her work was not good enough. Alternatively, the adjuster, who works out of the office and away from supervisory oversight most of the time, may have incentives to "take it easy" by doing cursory or overly generous estimates of client losses. How can these forms of cheating be avoided?

There are, of course, a variety of formal sanctions against cheating that can be imbedded in the agreements made by employers and employees. Firms with federal contracts promise to make special efforts to hire and promote women and minorities; they can lose the right to compete for government contracts if this promise to the government, their applicants, and their employees is broken. Employees who lie about their qualifications on employment application forms can be fired. Employers who break the provisions of agreements they have signed with their unions can be sued or legally subjected to a strike. All these examples, however, require that cheating actually be *proved*. While formal sanctions will help to discourage cheating if there is at least a chance of its being discovered, ways can often be found to reduce one's chances of being cheated even in the absence of the threat of formal punishment.

One way to avoid being cheated is to transact with the "right kind" of person, and to do this one must find a way to induce the other party to reveal ("signal") the truth about its actual characteristics or intentions. Suppose, for example, that an employer wants to hire employees who are willing to defer current gratification for long-term gain (that is, it wants employees who do not highly discount the future). Simply asking applicants if they are willing to delay gratification might not evoke honest answers. There are two ways, however, in which an employer could cause applicants to signal their preferences indirectly. *deferred comp*

As pointed out in Chapter 8, the employer could offer its applicants relatively low current wages and a large pension benefit upon retirement. Potential applicants with relatively high discount rates would find this pay package less attractive than applicants with low discount rates, and they would be discouraged from either applying for the job or accepting an offer if it were tendered.

Another way this firm could induce applicants to signal something about their *schooling* true discount rate is to require a college degree or some other training investment as a hiring standard. As noted in Chapter 9, people with high discount rates are less likely to make investments of any kind, so the firm's hiring standard should discourage those with high discount rates from seeking offers.

The essence of signaling, then, is the voluntary revelation of truth about oneself in one's *behavior,* not just one's statements. Many of the compensation policies discussed in the remainder of this chapter are at least partially aimed at eliciting truthful signals from job applicants or employees.[3]

Even the "right kind" of people, of course, often have incentives to underperform on their promises. Economists have come to call this type of cheating *opportunistic behavior,* and it occurs not because people intend from the outset to be dishonest but because they generally try to advance their own interests by adjusting their behavior to unfolding opportunities. Thus, the challenge is to adopt compensation policies that more or less automatically induce both parties to adhere to their promises.[4]

The key to a self-enforcing agreement is that there be losses imposed on the cheater that do not depend on proving to a third party that a contract violation has occurred. In the labor market, the usual "punishment" for cheating on agreements is that the victim severs the employment relationship; consequently self-enforcement requires that *both employer and employee derive more gains from honest continuation of the existing employment relationship than from severing it.* If workers are receiving, or have honest expectations of receiving, more from the existing relationship than they expect to receive elsewhere, they will automatically lose if they shirk their duties and are fired as a consequence. If employers profit more from the continued employment of their existing workers than from hiring replacements, they will suffer losses by failing to promote "good" workers as promised and thereby inducing them to quit.

For workers to be paid more than they could get elsewhere, yet produce more profits for the employer than outsiders could, there must be a "surplus" generated by the employment relationship. An example of such a surplus was discussed in Chapter 5, in which it was pointed out that specific training raised workers'

---

[3]For a formal model that uses educational attainment as a signal for innate ability (which is difficult for an employer to observe directly), refer back to Chapter 9.

[4]See H. Lorne Carmichael, "Self-Enforcing Contracts, Shirking, and Life Cycle Incentives," *Journal of Economic Perspectives* 3 (Fall 1989): 65–84, for a more complete discussion of the importance of self-enforcement to implicit contracting.

marginal revenue productivity, but only within the employing firm. To discourage specifically trained employees from leaving (thereby destroying the human capital investment made by the firm), the employer must pay a wage above what its workers could receive elsewhere. To justify its investment decision, however, the firm must have expectations of recouping its investment costs, which means that its posttraining wage must be less than marginal revenue product.

The gap between workers' marginal revenue product with their current employer and the wage they can command *elsewhere* is a surplus that will be divided in some fashion by employers and employees. *Division* of the surplus is necessary for the self-enforcement of implicit contracts, because if one party receives the entire surplus the other party has nothing to lose by terminating the employment relationship. For example, if an employer tried to obtain the entire surplus generated by specific training by paying a wage equal to the wage its employees could get elsewhere, its employees would lose nothing by quitting (thereby "destroying" the employer's investment in their training). A graphic representation of the division of a surplus is given in Figure 11.1, where it can be seen that attempts by one party to increase its share of the surplus will reduce the other party's losses from terminating the employment relationship.

Surpluses are usually generated by some earlier investment, but the investment need not be in specific training. If a firm invests heavily in recruiting new employees, for example, it will insist on a gap between marginal revenue product and the wage so that its recruitment costs can be recouped. In doing so, however, it will want to set wages enough above the workers' alternative offers to discourage their quitting.

Firms can also create a surplus by investing in their *reputations*. For example, an employer that is well known for keeping its promises about future promotions or raises can attract workers of higher productivity at lower cost than can employers with poor reputations.[5] Because the good reputation increases productivity relative to the wage paid, a surplus is created that can be divided between the firm and its workers. If the firm cheats and loses its good reputation, it will either have to pay more for the same quality of worker or pay the current wage and expect to obtain workers with lower productivity; in either case, cheating causes it to lose its part of the surplus.

MOTIVATING WORKERS

To this point we have discussed primarily the *form* of the employment contract: such contracts are implicit and thus must be structured in such a way that the parties signal their true intentions and that their agreement is self-enforcing. We turn now to an issue of contractual *substance:* the difficulties of aligning the goals of the agent with those of the principal. Putting it differently, we will examine some gen-

---

[5]A firm with a poor reputation for performing on its promises must pay a compensating wage differential to attract workers of given quality away from employers with good reputations.

FIGURE 11.1

Two Alternative Divisions of the Surplus

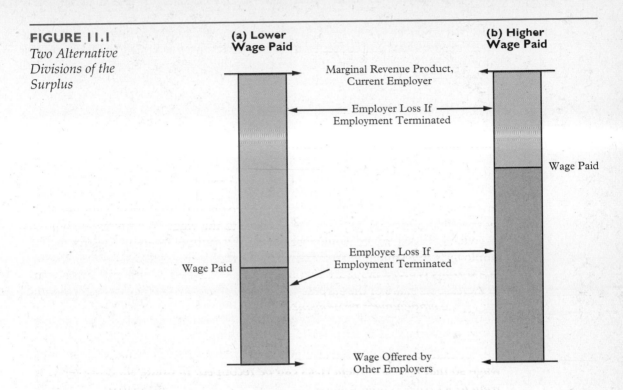

(a) Lower Wage Paid

(b) Higher Wage Paid

Marginal Revenue Product, Current Employer

Employer Loss If Employment Terminated

Wage Paid

Employee Loss If Employment Terminated

Wage Paid

Wage Offered by Other Employers

eral issues in motivating workers to put forth their best efforts toward maximizing the profits of their employers.

Workers, it will be recalled, can be viewed as utility maximizers. They are primarily motivated by self-interest, and they value both leisure and the goods and services money can buy. Likewise, they seek to avoid unpleasant or otherwise costly activities. "Putting forth their best efforts" may entail working when they do not feel like it or engaging in activities that, other things equal, they would rather avoid. What policies can employers devise to induce a high level of effort from their employees?

SUPERVISION   One way to motivate high levels of effort is to closely supervise employees. While virtually all employees work under some form of supervision, close and detailed supervision is costly. Tasks in any production process are divided so that the economies afforded by specialization are possible. In all but the most manual, repetitive tasks, the worker must make decisions or adjustments in response to changing conditions. To insist on extremely close supervision would mean that the supervisor must have all the information at exactly the same time as the worker—in which case the supervisor might just as well make the decision!

In short, detailed supervision destroys the advantages of specialization in some cases and in other cases is just not feasible; supervisors cannot be in all places at all times with all the relevant pieces of information. In addition, supervisors are usually employees (agents) themselves, so a way must be found to motivate *them* to do their jobs well. If such motivation is lacking, they may try to make life easy for themselves by colluding with their supervisees against the interests of the employer.

PAY FOR PERFORMANCE   If supervision cannot be close enough to ensure the alignment of the agent's interests with those of the principal, the economist naturally thinks of *pay* as a motivator. Linking pay to output presumably provides strong incentives to put forth effort, but there are two general problems that incentive-pay schemes must confront.[6]

One problem arises from the need for any system of compensation to satisfy the desires of both employer and employee. Basing one's pay on one's current output places employees at the risk of having earnings that are variable over time. There are factors affecting output that are beyond the control of even the hardest-working employees: illness, machinery breakdowns, and interruptions or delays in the supply of needed materials come quickly to mind. If employees are paid solely on the basis of their current output, they bear *all* the risk of fluctuations in output, even those caused by events that are beyond their control. As a result, they may be unwilling, without extra pay, to subject themselves to a compensation scheme that provides an unstable income.

(If employers seek to satisfy workers' desires for earnings stability by paying wages that are wholly or largely independent of output, they run up against the problem of *moral hazard*. Moral hazard is a problem of insurance: insuring people against a loss over which they have some control causes them to reduce their efforts to prevent the loss. For example, homeowners insured against lawsuits by people who slip and fall on their property are less likely to shovel their walks after a snowstorm, and drivers insured against theft are less likely to lock their cars. Similarly, unless long-term incentives are in place, workers insured against low current productivity are less likely to put forth high levels of effort. Example 11.2 illustrates this problem of moral hazard.)

A second class of problems arises from the need to base performance pay on measures that correlate well with both the *employee's effort* and the *employer's objectives*. That is, paying for performance requires basing pay on measures that meet two requirements. Because the employer is trying to elicit *effort* from its employees, one requirement is that the measures upon which pay is based be sensitive to employee effort. The more that factors beyond the control of individual employees affect an individual's pay, the smaller will be employees' incentives to put forth effort. Put somewhat differently, to the extent that pay is unrelated to individual effort, the moral hazard problem noted above implies reduced effort levels among employees.

The other requirement for a pay-for-performance measure to be effective is that it capture, or at least correlate well with, the employer's ultimate objectives. Here,

---

[6]This subsection draws heavily on David E. Sappington, "Incentives in Principal–Agent Relationships," *Journal of Economic Perspectives* 5 (Spring 1991): 45–66, and George P. Baker, "Incentive Contracts and Performance Measurement," *Journal of Political Economy* 100 (June 1992): 598–614.

EXAMPLE 11.2

Calorie Consumption and the Type of Pay

We noted in the text that time-based pay raises the question of "moral hazard": that is, because workers are paid regardless of their output, they may not put forth their best efforts. An interesting examination of this question comes from Bukidon in the Philippines, where it is common for workers to hold several different farming jobs during a year. In some of these jobs they are paid for their time (their pay is by the hour), and in some they are paid directly for their output. Therefore, we are able to observe how hard the same individual works under the two different types of pay system.

A recent study discovered clear-cut evidence that the workers put forth much less effort in these physically demanding jobs when paid by the hour rather than for their output. Measuring effort expended by both weight change and calorie consumption, the study found that workers consumed *23 percent fewer calories* and *gained more weight per calorie consumed* when they were paid by the hour! Both facts suggest that less physical effort was put forth when workers were paid by the hour than when they were paid a piece rate.

SOURCE: Andrew D. Foster and Mark R. Rosenzweig, "A Test for Moral Hazard in the Labor Market: Contractual Arrangements, Effort, and Health," *Review of Economics and Statistics* 76, no. 2 (May 1994): 213–227.

---

the problem is that some of the qualitative aspects of performance are either unobservable or unmeasurable. Of what value to a retail clothing store is a billing clerk who is friendly, works quickly, and makes few mistakes? What is the "output" of a teacher who cares enough about students to visit them at home when they are sick or troubled? Clearly, such employees exhibit qualities of dedication or competence that have great value to the employer but, equally clearly, that value is almost impossible to measure. Imperfectly designed performance measures run the risk of inducing employees to emphasize that part of their performance that is measurable ("quantity," usually) and to ignore the other aspects.

MOTIVATING THE INDIVIDUAL IN A GROUP

The simplest model of worker behavior, outlined in Chapters 6 through 9, assumed that each worker's utility was a function of his or her *own* consumption of goods, services, leisure time, and job characteristics. If workers seek to maximize utility by increasing their own consumption of valued goods, then focusing on the link between each individual's pay and performance is sufficient in developing company policy. As noted briefly in Chapter 8 (Example 8.1), however, the concern for one's standing in a reference group is often a factor that affects a worker's utility. The concern for one's standing relative to others suggests that the simplest model of worker behavior may be an inadequate guide to establishing compensation policies that effectively motivate workers. The importance of the *group* in motivating *individuals* presents both problems and opportunities for the employer.

ISSUES OF FAIRNESS   People's concern about their treatment *relative to others* in their reference group means that fairness is an issue that pervades the employment relationship. Workers want a "fair" wage and "fairness" in promotion, layoff, or grievance procedures. Employers want a "fair day's work" from their workers and the freedom to earn a "fair return" on their invested capital. Notions of what is fair differ, of course, but they are usually based on how others in one's reference group are (or were) treated.

The concern with fairness, despite our inability to define it precisely, is probably greater in the labor market than in any other market. As noted in Chapter 1, the item being traded in the labor market (one's labor services) cannot be detached from its owner (the worker). Thus, the conditions of work, the process by which decisions about the employment contract are made, and one's earnings relative to others take on great importance.

A worker who obtains a 7 percent wage increase during a year in which both price and wage increases average 4 percent might be quite happy until she finds out that a colleague working in the same job for the same employer received a 10 percent increase! Likewise, a worker who has been disciplined after a formal hearing in front of a neutral third party may believe he has been more fairly treated than if he had received the *same* punishment from management without a formal hearing.

Employers designing compensation policies with an eye toward worker productivity cannot ignore workers' perceptions of fairness.[7] Workers who feel unfairly treated may quit, reduce their effort level, steal from the employer, or even sabotage output in order to "settle the score." Unfortunately for employers, however, the fairness of identical policy decisions often can be perceived differently depending on their context or presentation.

The *framing* of a decision, or how it is presented, often affects how fair it is perceived to be. For example, a survey by three researchers asked respondents to consider a situation in which two small companies, neither one growing as planned, paid their workers $X in yearly compensation, with the first paying its compensation entirely in salary and the second paying a salary of $0.9X and a "bonus" of 10 percent. Their survey found that 61 percent of the respondents thought it would be unfair if the first company cut its workers' salaries by 10 percent, but only 20 percent thought it would be unfair if the second company eliminated its bonus.[8] Apparently, pay framed as "salary" connotes a greater entitlement than pay framed as "bonus."

---

[7]Interviews with managers often suggest that the perception of "fairness" is an important motivational tool; see, for example, Alan S. Blinder and Don H. Choi, "A Shred of Evidence on Theories of Wage Stickiness," *Quarterly Journal of Economics* 105, no. 4 (November 1990): 1003–1015. For a similar study, see David I. Levine, "Fairness, Markets, and the Ability to Pay: Evidence from Compensation Executives," *American Economic Review* 83, no. 5 (December 1993): 1241–1259.

[8]Daniel Kahneman, Jack L. Knetsch, and Richard Thaler, "Fairness as a Constraint on Profit-Seeking: Entitlements in the Market," *American Economic Review* 76 (September 1986): 728–741.

The *reference point* for judging a compensation decision also affects its perceived fairness. The survey mentioned above discovered that 83 percent thought it would be unfair for a successful house painter who was paying his workers $9 per hour to cut their wages to $7 if he discovered that reliable help could be obtained for less. Only 37 percent thought it would be unfair of him to cut wages, however, if he decided to quit the painting business and instead go into landscaping, an industry with lower wages. Moreover, while the vast majority surveyed thought it was unfair for a profitable business to cut wages, most thought it was fair if an unprofitable company did. Clearly, the context of a given decision matters.

In the examples discussed above, the reference group is either one's immediate work group or some larger group, such as those in one's industry, occupation, or labor market status (that is, whether one is an employee or an employer). In all cases, however, the critical elements in one's perception of fairness are how others in the group are treated and whether one's *relative* standing is being safeguarded or diminished.

GROUP LOYALTY   An issue of employee motivation that cannot be ignored is group loyalty and organizational pride. As suggested above, human beings often define themselves and their welfare by reference to a group to which they see themselves as belonging. Besides concern for their own levels of consumption and their relative standing in the group, they are also typically concerned with the status or well-being of the entire group. Most people are willing, for example, to make at least some personal sacrifices for their team, school, employing organization, community, or country.

The sacrifices each is willing to make are limited by the "free rider" problem. That is, if person A works hard to advance the goals of an organization to which persons B through Z also belong, the others may take advantage of A by enjoying the benefits of the organization's enhancement without any extra effort of their own. Recognizing that this free-rider problem limits the sacrifices each individual is willing to make, it is nonetheless true that many workers are ready and able to identify strongly with their employing organization.

Because the essence of "doing a good job" so frequently means taking the initiative in many small, unnoticeable ways to advance the organization's interests, employers with highly productive workers almost universally pay attention to policies that foster organizational loyalty. The widespread human tendency to identify with the group can thus be a powerful motivator for high productivity.[9] Policies designed to align the interests of employees with those of their employers are likely to be seriously flawed if they exist in an environment that ignores issues of group loyalty. While many steps employers can take to nurture organizational loyalty go beyond the bounds of economics, we will analyze below compensation schemes that base an individual's pay on the performance of the *group*.

---

[9] Simon, "Organizations and Markets," 34–38.

COMPENSATION PLANS: OVERVIEW AND GUIDE TO THE REST OF THE CHAPTER

As discussed above, an employer's compensation plan is an important part of the employment contract. It represents a large part of what the employer promises its employees in return for their effort. Along with the employer's hiring standards, supervisory policies, and general managerial philosophy, the structure of the compensation plan greatly affects incentives of employees to put forth effort. While a detailed discussion of many managerial policies is outside the scope of this text, the incentives created by compensation schemes fall squarely within the purview of modern labor economics. In what follows, therefore, we use economic concepts to analyze the major characteristics of compensation plans.

There are three elements that broadly characterize an employer's compensation scheme: the *basis* on which pay is calculated, the *level* of pay in relation to pay for comparable workers elsewhere, and—for employers with internal labor markets—the *sequencing* of pay over workers' careers. The remainder of the chapter is devoted to analyses of these elements. Especially important to these analyses is an evaluation of how the elements under scrutiny are shaped to deal with the general problems of contracting and worker motivation raised so far in this chapter. The chapter ends with a section that applies some of the concepts covered to achieve a better understanding of three labor market "puzzles."

Productivity and the Basis of Yearly Pay

Broadly speaking, workers can be paid for their *time,* their *output,* or some hybrid of the two. If paid solely for their time, employees usually must be motivated by future considerations, close supervision, or organizational loyalty to put forth their best efforts. The alternative of paying them on the basis of their output would appear to alleviate motivational problems by aligning the interests of workers and the employer without the need for much supervision or management. Given that over 80 percent of U.S. employees are paid for their time, not their output, one must ask why output-based pay is not more widely used. Because compensation plans must satisfy both the employer and the employee, we organize our analysis around the considerations relevant to each side of the labor market.

EMPLOYEE PREFERENCES

Piece-rate pay, under which workers earn a certain amount for each item produced, is the most common form of individually based incentive pay for production workers. Another system linking earnings to individuals' output is payment by *commission,* under which workers (usually salespeople) receive a fraction of the value of the items they sell. *Gainsharing* plans, which have grown in popularity recently, are *group*-incentive plans that at least partially tie earnings to gains in group productivity, reductions in cost, increases in product quality, or other measures of group success. *Profit-sharing* and *bonus* plans attempt to relate workers' pay to the profits of their firm or subdivision; this form of pay also rewards work groups rather than individuals. Under all these systems, workers are paid at least somewhat proportionately to their output or to the degree their employer prospers.[10]

If employees were told that their average earnings over the years under a time-payment system would be equal to their earnings under an output-based pay plan, they would probably prefer to be paid on a *time* basis. Why? Earnings under output-based pay plans clearly vary with whatever measure of output serves as the basis for pay. As mentioned earlier, many things that affect individual or group output depend on the external environment, not just on the level of energy or commitment the individual worker brings to the job. Thinking of piece-rate pay, for example, the number of items an individual produces in a given day is affected by the age and condition of machinery, interrupted flows of supplies owing to strikes or snowstorms, and the worker's own illness or injury. Commissions earned by salespeople, to take another example, are clearly affected by the overall demand for the product being sold, and this demand can fluctuate for a number of reasons well beyond the control of the individual salesperson. Earnings that are dependent on some measure of *group* output will vary with the level of effort expended by others in the group as well as with the external environmental factors mentioned above.

The variations in earnings that are inherently possible under output-based pay are thought to be unappealing to workers because of their presumed *risk aversion* (that is, workers' preference for earnings certainty, even if it means somewhat lower pay). Most workers have monthly financial obligations for rent, food, insurance, utilities, and so forth. If several low-income pay periods are strung together they might have difficulty in meeting these obligations, even if several high-income pay periods were to follow. They may also believe it is unfair that their earnings can vary with the performance of *others*.

Because of their anxiety about periods of lower-than-usual pay, employees might prefer the certainty of time-based pay to the uncertainty of output-based pay, other things (such as the average level of earnings) equal. To induce risk-averse employees to accept output-based pay, employers would have to pay higher average wages over time; that is, a compensating differential would have to exist to compensate workers for the anxiety associated with variations in their earnings. Conversely, to obtain more certainty in their stream of earnings, employees would probably be willing to accept a somewhat lower average wage.

Worker risk aversion aside, it is interesting to consider *which* workers will be attracted to piece-rate or commission pay schemes. The analysis reveals an example of a situation in which signaling can be exploited: the workers most attracted to individually based incentive-pay plans are those whose earnings would exceed what they could earn under a time-based plan. Because time-based plans pay the

---

[10]A variant of piece-rate pay is the allowance of a *standard time* to complete a given task. A worker who finishes the task more *quickly* is paid for the full standard time regardless of how little time was actually spent; if the worker takes *longer* to complete the task, pay reverts to an *hourly* basis. One survey of employers in the United States indicated that 14 percent had gainsharing plans and 45 percent had profit-sharing; see Paul Osterman, "How Common Is Workplace Transformation and Who Adopts It?" *Industrial and Labor Relations Review* 47, no. 2 (January 1994): 173–188.

same, at least in the short run, to high and low producers alike, <u>workers who gain most from piece rates or commissions are those whose levels of motivation or ability are above average.</u> Thus, employees who choose to work under compensation plans that reward individual productivity signal (that is, communicate by their *behavior*) that they believe themselves to be above-average producers.

Both worker risk aversion and the signaling aspects of individual incentive-pay plans imply that workers receiving incentive pay earn more than comparable workers paid on the basis of time. Although there are few studies of this issue, the prediction that incentive-pay workers earn more appears to hold up. A 1960s study of punch-press operators in Chicago found that piece-rate workers earned about 9 percent more per hour of work than did those paid an hourly wage. Research by the Bureau of Labor Statistics found that auto-repair workers paid on an incentive basis earned 20–50 percent more per hour than those paid on a time basis. Finally, another study estimated that piece-rate workers in the footwear and men's and boys' suit and coat industries earned 14–16 percent more than comparable workers receiving time-based pay. Only a small part of this latter differential could be attributed to a compensating wage differential; most of the differential was associated with greater productivity.[11]

EMPLOYER CONSIDERATIONS

The willingness of employers to pay a premium in order to induce employees to accept piece rates depends on the costs and benefits to employers of incentive-pay schemes. If workers are paid with piece rates or commissions they bear the consequences of low productivity, as noted above; thus, employers can afford to spend less time screening and supervising workers. <u>If workers are paid on a *time* basis, the *employer* accepts the risk of variations in their productivity.</u> When they are exceptionally productive, profits increase; when they are less productive, profits decline. Employers, however, may be less anxious about these *variations* than employees are. They typically have more assets and can thus weather the lean periods more comfortably than individual workers can. Employers also usually have several employees, and the chances are that not all will suffer the same swings in productivity at the same time (unless there is a morale problem in the firm). Thus, employers may not be as willing to pay for income certainty as workers are.

The other major employer consideration in deciding on the basis for pay concerns the incentives for employee effort. The considerations related to three major types of incentive plans in use are discussed below.

PAY FOR OUTPUT: INDIVIDUAL INCENTIVES   From the employer's perspective, the big advantage of individually based output pay is that it induces employees to adopt a set of work goals that are consistent with those of their

---

[11]John Pencavel, "Work Effort, On-the-Job Screening, and Alternative Methods of Remuneration," in *Research in Labor Economics,* vol. 1, ed. Ronald Ehrenberg (Greenwich, Conn.: JAI Press, 1977), 225–258; Sandra King, "Incentive and Time Pay in Auto Dealer Repair Shops," *Monthly Labor Review* 98 (September 1975): 45–48; and Eric Seiler, "Piece Rate vs. Time Rate: The Effect of Incentives on Earnings," *Review of Economics and Statistics* 66 (August 1984): 363–376.

employer. Employees paid a piece rate are motivated to work quickly, while those paid by commission are induced to very thoroughly evaluate the needs of the firm's customers. Moreover, these inducements exist without the need for, and expense of, close monitoring by the firm's supervisors. There are several disadvantages, however, to individually based incentive-pay schemes. These general problems have to do with maintaining quality standards and a "team" commitment, proper use of equipment, setting the rate, and measuring output.

Workers paid strictly by the piece are motivated to work quickly, but they are also motivated to have minimal regard for quality, for the performance of others on their immediate work term, or for the firm as a whole. Workers paid by commission also have a temptation to put their own interests in a sale ahead of the customer's, an incentive that may work against the long-run interest of the employer.[12] Thus, both piece rates and commissions can weaken the group loyalty so frequently needed to advance the employer's interests. They also create a need for close supervisory attention to the quality of work performed, a need and an expense that in many cases will offset other supervisory savings associated with incentive pay.

Allied to the problem of work quality is the problem of equipment misuse. Workers receiving incentive pay are motivated to work so quickly that machines or tools are often damaged or otherwise misused. It is often asserted, for example, that piece-rate workers disengage safety devices on machinery in their desire to maximize output. This problem is mitigated to the extent that equipment damage causes *downtime* that results in lost employee earnings. Many firms using piece rates require workers to provide their *own* machines or tools.

A third problem, probably more often associated with piece rates than with commissions, is setting the rate. For example, it may be standard practice in the auto-repair industry to assume that an engine tune-up will require two hours of work and to translate this time requirement into a "per job" piece rate. Suppose, however, that some new tool or electronic device is adopted that reduces the time required for a tune-up. A new piece rate will have to be adopted, but how do the shop's owners determine the standard time requirement for tune-ups now? The best way may be to observe mechanics using the new devices, but if these workers know they are being observed for purposes of setting a new rate, they will probably deliberately work slowly so that the time requirement is overestimated. The problem is compounded in industries facing frequent changes in products or technology.

A fourth reason why individual incentive-pay schemes are not more widely used is the problem of measuring individual *output*. The already mentioned problem of unwittingly inducing piece-rate employees to emphasize quantity over

---

[12]The piece rate's inducement to emphasize quantity over quality is antithetical to a "quality revolution," associated with W. E. Deming, that has attracted much interest in the last decade or two. For a summary of the managerial philosophy that emphasizes quality, including the use of statistical process control techniques, see Alan Hodgson, "Deming's Never-Ending Road to Quality," *Personnel Management* (July 1987): 40–44. Some high-profile examples of the problems that can be caused by commissions are cited in George Baker, Robert Gibbons, and Kevin J. Murphy, "Subjective Performance Measures in Optimal Incentive Contracts," *Quarterly Journal of Economics* 109, no. 4 (November 1994): 1125–1156.

quality is not really inherent in the method of basing pay on individual output; it is the result of the larger problem of measuring output. A typist, for example, could be paid by the number of *error-free* pages produced. In most jobs in which at least a major dimension of output can be measured, however, quantity is more objectively measured than quality—and "selling" workers on the *fairness* of an individual incentive-pay plan usually necessitates the use of measures that are free of subjective judgment.

The emphasis on quantity over quality is just one example of the distortions that can be caused by individual incentive-pay plans in an environment in which not all aspects of output can be measured. (For others, see Example 11.3.) A more general example arises when the worker has several tasks to perform, only some of which are objectively measurable. Basing pay on the measurable components of one's job may cause workers to ignore the unmeasurable tasks; for example, basing the pay of teachers on students' national standardized test scores may cause them to "teach to the test" and deemphasize activities that foster creative thinking or improve writing skills. [13]

In many operations, however, even the quantity of output is difficult to measure objectively. The output of goods or services produced by an auto mechanic, a salesperson, or a dressmaker is relatively easy to measure in terms of quantity, but what about that of an office manager or an auto assembly-line worker? The manager has a number of duties and deals with a multitude of problems; combining them into a single index of output would be next to impossible. Assembly-line workers, on the other hand, may have an easily counted output, but it is not individually controlled. In both cases, *individual* incentive pay would be arbitrary or useless; however, *group* incentives might be attractive in these situations.

PAY FOR OUTPUT: GROUP INCENTIVES   When individual output is difficult to monitor, when individual incentive plans are detrimental to output quality, or when output is generated by "teams" of interdependent workers, firms sometimes adopt group incentive-pay schemes to more closely align the interests of employer and employee. These plans may tie at least a portion of pay to some component of profits (group productivity, product quality, cost reductions), or they may directly link pay with the firm's overall profit level. In still other cases workers might *own* the firm and split the profits among themselves. [14]

One drawback to group incentives is that group are composed of individuals, and it is at the individual level that decisions about shirking are ultimately made. A person who works very hard to increase group output or the firm's profits winds up splitting the fruits of his or her labor with all the others, who may not have put out extra effort. Group incentives, then, are sometimes no incentive at

---

[13]Bengt Holmstrom and Paul Milgrom, "Multitask Principal–Agent Analyses: Incentive Contracts, Asset Ownership, and Job Design," *Journal of Law, Economics, and Organization* 7 (Special Issue, 1991): 24–52.

[14]For a review of the literature on productivity in worker-owned or worker-managed firms, see James B. Rebitzer, "Radical Political Economy and the Economics of Labor Markets," *Journal of Economic Literature* 31, no. 3 (September 1993): 1405–1409, and Michael A. Conte and Jan Svejnar, "The Performance Effects of Employee Ownership Plans," in *Paying for Productivity*, ed. Alan S. Blinder (Washington, D.C.: Brookings Institution, 1990), 142–181.

EXAMPLE 11.3

Incentive Pay and Output—or "You Get What You Pay For"

The effects of incentive-pay schemes depend on just what "output" is being paid for. To take one example, instead of paying dentists on the basis of "contact hours" with patients, the British National Health Service decided (for a while) to compensate them on the basis of cavities filled. The result was that the incidence of tooth decay identified by dentists increased substantially and the time it took to fill cavities dropped from 18 to 6 minutes per filling. It is obvious that this new basis for payment was of questionable benefit to patients.

Another example comes from a study of lawyers to see how the time they spent on civil cases was affected by the basis upon which their fee was calculated. The study compared the behavior of lawyers who charge an hourly fee with that of lawyers who charge on a contingency basis (that is, charge the client a percentage of the damages they are able to win from the party they are suing). In cases involving modest sums of money ($10,000 or less), lawyers who were paid an hourly fee tended to put in more preparation time than did contingent-fee lawyers; the reverse was true in cases in which the sums involved were greater. This pattern of effort is to be expected: the payment to lawyers charging hourly fees is independent of outcome, whereas the payoffs to contingent-fee lawyers—and hence their efforts—rise with the stakes involved.

SOURCES: John Pencavel, "Piecework and On-the-Job Screening" (Department of Economics, Stanford University, June 1975), 4; Herbert M. Kritzer, William L. F. Felstiner, Austin Sarat, and David M. Trubek, "The Impact of Fee Arrangement on Lawyer Effort," *The Law and Society Review* 19, no. 2 (1985): 251–278.

---

all. People come to realize that they can reap the rewards of someone else's hard work without doing any extra work of their own, and that if they do put out extra work, the rewards mainly go to others. Thus, these *free-rider* problems give workers incentives to cheat on their fellow employees by shirking.[15]

In very small groups cheating may be easy to detect, and group punishments, such as ostracism, can be effectively used to eliminate it. In these cases, group incentive-pay systems can accomplish their aims. When the group of workers receiving incentive pay is large, however, employers may have to devote managerial resources to building organizational loyalties if shirking is to be discouraged. Interestingly, studies have found that there is a positive correlation between profit sharing and organizational output.[16]

---

[15]For a more in-depth analysis of this problem, see Haig R. Nalbantian, "Incentive Contracts in Perspective," in *Incentives, Cooperation, and Risk Sharing,* ed. Haig R. Nalbantian (Totowa, N.J.: Rowman & Littlefield, 1987), and Eugene Kandel and Edward Lazear, "Peer Pressure and Partnerships," *Journal of Political Economy* 100, no. 4 (August 1992): 801–817.

[16]Martin Weitzman and Douglas Kruse, "Profit Sharing and Productivity," in *Paying for Productivity,* ed. Alan S. Blinder (Washington, D.C.: Brookings Institution, 1990); Douglas L. Kruse, *Profit-Sharing: Does It Make a Difference?* (Princeton: Industrial Relations Section, Princeton University, 1993); and Sandeep Bhargava, "Profit Sharing and the Financial Performance of Companies: Evidence from U.K. Panel Data," *Economic Journal* 104, no. 426 (September 1994): 1044–1056.

A common example of incentive pay based on group results is the widespread use of profit-based bonuses in the compensation of top executives. With these plans one major issue is the familiar one of measurement: over what time period should profits be measured? Consider a firm wishing to maximize profits over the *long run* and trying to decide how to compensate its executives in such a way that this long-term goal will be achieved. If it adopts a yearly profit-sharing plan in which a fraction of year-end profits is given to each executive, its executives may be induced to pursue strategies designed to maximize profits in the current period. These short-run strategies may not be consistent with long-run profit maximization, but the executives involved may use their short-run performances to obtain positions with other firms before the long-run consequences of their strategies are fully observed.

Perhaps for these reasons, most corporations in the United States tie at least a portion of their senior executives' compensation to company performance over a *multiyear* period. Most of these long-term "performance attainment" plans base their awards on some measure of company prosperity over a period of three to five years, apparently in the belief that a period of less than three years is too short to measure long-term performance, while more than five years would represent so long a delay in receiving rewards that their motivational effects would be weakened.

The strongest way to align the interests of corporate executives and company shareholders (the *owners* of corporations) would be to tie their pay to the value of the company's shares of stock. Corporate shareholders are clearly interested in maximizing the returns on their investments, and actions that executives can take to increase the company's long-run profitability presumably will be reflected in its stock prices. Basing executive compensation on the value of corporate stock is done both indirectly, through bonuses tied to the performance attainment measures noted above, and through the direct ownership of (or rights to buy) corporate stock.

In practice, executive pay in the United States is clearly affected by changes in shareholder wealth, but perhaps not by as much as one might expect. One study of over 1,000 corporations found that, directly or indirectly, the *yearly pay* of their chief executive officers (CEOs) went up only two cents for each $1,000 increase in total shareholder wealth; however, because the typical CEO personally owned an average of $3.5 million in company stock, his or her *wealth* went up $2.50 for each $1,000 increase in total shareholder wealth (CEOs owned about 0.25 percent of their company's stock).[17]

It is interesting that personal ownership of company stock offers far and away the strongest monetary incentives for CEOs to act on behalf of shareholders, but it is also interesting that their yearly pay is not much affected by changes in shareholder wealth. One reason may be rooted in the phenomenon of risk aversion noted earlier among other employees. Stock prices are influenced by forces other than a

---

[17]Michael C. Jensen and Kevin J. Murphy, "Performance Pay and Top-Management Incentives," *Journal of Political Economy* 98 (April 1990): 225–264.

company's current or future profitability; such factors as "investor psychology," inflation, the attractiveness of alternative investments (savings accounts or bonds, for example), and changes in government tax policies can affect stock prices independently of firm performance. Stock prices also fluctuate considerably over time, and these fluctuations, especially those beyond the control of the CEO, may serve to make performance-based pay too variable to be attractive to prospective CEOs.

Studies that have investigated the effects of incentive pay for top executives have found that firms whose executive compensation was at least implicitly tied to the firm's long-run performance outperformed other firms.[18] Other studies show that the adoption of executive performance attainment plans leads to improved short-run stock market performance of these firms. Apparently the stock market believes that performance attainment plans will increase profits.[19]

PAY FOR TIME, WITH MERIT INCREASES   Given the difficulties of risk aversion and measurement inherent in output-based pay, most employers opt for some form of time-based pay. While satisfying the desires of employees for stability in pay, basing pay on hours of work raises the issue of moral hazard: because workers' pay is unaffected by their output, the incentives to produce are reduced. What can be done to overcome this problem?

Time-based pay schemes are accompanied by the need for supervision, but as noted earlier, detailed supervision is usually not feasible. In motivating their workers, therefore, many employers relying on time-based pay use *merit-pay* plans, which award larger pay increases each year to their better performers. Performance is judged by supervisors, who are often required to submit annual performance evaluations of the employees who work for them.

The problems facing merit-pay plans are rooted in the by now familiar issue of measuring individual performance. Even when outcome-based measures are feasible, they fail to take account of factors in the external environment that affect an individual's output. Because these outcome-based measures may have a low correlation with the effort of individual workers, the incentives for effort are reduced by the presence of external influences on performance. In addition, workers may find outcome-based merit pay unappealing or unfair because their earnings vary with factors beyond their control.

One way to remove the effects of external factors in merit-pay schemes is to rate workers *relative to* their peers. Because their peers face the same external forces, a system of relative rankings is one way to increase the connection between individual

---

[18]Jonathan S. Leonard, "Executive Pay and Firm Performance," *Industrial and Labor Relations Review* 43 (February 1990): 13S–29S, and John M. Abowd, "Does Performance-Based Managerial Compensation Affect Corporate Performance?" *Industrial and Labor Relations Review* 43 (February 1990): 52S–73S.

[19]See, for example, J. Brickley, S. Bhagat, and R. Lease, "The Impact of Long-Run Managerial Compensation Plans on Shareholder Wealth," *Journal of Accounting and Economics* 7 (April 1985): 115–129. An alternative explanation for these findings, however, is that executives may push for the adoption of these plans only when they believe the performance of the firm is likely to be good. If this occurs, adoption may *signal* to the stock market that the firm expects "good times" ahead. The resulting observed improvement in stock market performance may reflect only this signal, not any anticipated incentive effects.

effort and pay. In principle, at least, workers who put forth the most effort relative to their peers will receive the highest ratings and the largest pay increases, regardless of the effects on output of external events.

The problem of relative rankings for merit-pay purposes is that the "effort" induced among employees may not be consistent with the employer's interests. For example, one way to enhance one's *relative* status is to sabotage the work of others. Finding pages torn out of library books on reserve shortly before major examinations is not unknown at colleges or universities, where grading is often based on relative performance; similar efforts to undercut one's rivals can occur in the workplace as well.

Because relative performance ratings usually have a subjective component, another kind of counterproductive effort may take place: politicking. Workers may spend valuable work time "marketing" their services or otherwise ingratiating themselves with their supervisors.[20] Thus, efforts are directed away from productivity itself to generate what is, at best, the *appearance* of productivity. Further, because of their subjectivity, rankings of employees by their supervisors are often perceived as arbitrary and therefore unfair by those being rated.[21] These perceptions underlie the two major explanations given when merit-pay plans are judged to have failed: the lack of consistency in ratings among different managers and the "bunching" of ratings in the middle categories. Merit-pay plans are particularly distrusted by nonmanagerial employees.[22]

Productivity and the Level of Pay

Given the difficulties created for both employer and employee by pay-for-performance plans (including merit pay), employers are often driven to search for other monetary incentives that can be used to motivate their workers. In this section we discuss motivational issues related to the *level* of pay.

We began this chapter by reiterating that, for many employers, setting a compensation policy consists of more than just "finding out" the market wage for given jobs. Many employers and employees exchange a set of informal promises regarding their current and future behavior, and to make these implicit contracts

---

[20]Paul Milgrom, "Employment Contracts, Influence Activities, and Efficient Organization Design," *Journal of Political Economy* 96 (February 1988): 42–60; Canice Prendergast, "A Theory of 'Yes Men'," *American Economic Review* 83, no. 4 (September 1993): 757–770.

[21]For a theoretical analysis incorporating the important element of trust between workers and supervisors, see Baker, Gibbons, and Murphy, "Subjective Performance Measures in Optimal Incentive Contracts."

[22]Charles Peck, *Pay and Performance: The Interaction of Compensation and Performance Appraisal*, Conference Board Research Bulletin 155 (New York: Conference Board, 1984), 13; and Fred Foulkes, *Personnel Policies in Large Nonunion Companies* (Englewood Cliffs, N.J.: Prentice Hall, 1980), Chapter 9.

While we discuss individually the tools that can be used to motivate workers—incentive pay, supervision, stock ownership, or profit sharing, for example—they should all be seen as part of a firm's *system* for motivating its workers. This point is made by Bengt Holmstrom and Paul Milgrom, "The Firm as an Incentive System," *American Economic Review* 84, no. 4 (September 1994): 972–991.

self-enforcing the employer and employee must divide a surplus. If the employee is paid more than he or she could command elsewhere, but generates more profits for the employer than a replacement would, then both parties stand to lose if the employment contract is dishonestly abrogated. Many alternative divisions of the surplus are possible, some more favorable to the employer and some more favorable to the employee; thus, the employer must decide which of many compensation levels to offer applicants and employees in an effort to assemble a productive, profitable workforce.

Complicating employers' compensation-policy decisions further is the possibility that the *size* of the surplus to be divided is itself a function of the level of compensation. For reasons to be noted shortly, it is widely believed that workers' efforts rise with their level of pay. Because the upper limit of what employers can pay their workers is a function of workers' marginal revenue product (*MRP*), and because *MRP* may rise with pay level, an employer's choice of pay level may influence the size of the surplus as well as its division.

There are several reasons why higher wages are thought to increase worker productivity, one involving the *type* of worker the firm can attract and the others relating to the productivity that can be elicited from *given* workers. High wages are thought to attract better employees because they enlarge the employer's applicant pool and enable the firm to be more selective in its choice of workers. Higher wages allow it to select more experienced, dependable, and highly motivated employees, because it can "skim the cream" off the top of a large pool of applicants.

The reasons why higher wages are thought to generate greater productivity from given workers all relate to the commitment to the firm they build. The higher the wages are relative to what workers could receive elsewhere, the less likely it is that the workers will quit; knowing this, employers are more likely to offer training and more likely to demand longer hours and a faster pace of work from their workers. Employees, on their part, realize that even though supervision may not be detailed enough to detect shirking with certainty, if they are caught cheating on their promises to work hard and are fired as a result, the loss of a job paying above-market wages is costly both now and over their remaining work life.

Another reason given for the assertion that higher wages generate more productivity from given employees comes out of workers' concerns that treatment be fair. Workers who believe they are being fairly treated are more likely to put forth effort and commitment; those who perceive themselves as unfairly treated will withhold effort, resist change, or sabotage output in an attempt to "get even."[23] Workers with implicit employment contracts are likely to perceive that employers have at least some discretion over the level of pay, and generally speaking, the higher the level chosen the more likely workers are to regard their employers as treating them fairly.

---

[23]This assertion is based on what psychologists call equity theory. For recent works by economists that employ this theory, see George A. Akerlof and Janet Yellen, "The Fair Wage–Effort Hypothesis and Unemployment," *Quarterly Journal of Economics* 105 (May 1990): 255–283, and Robert M. Solow, *The Labor Market as a Social Institution* (Cambridge, Mass.: Basil Blackwell, 1990).

What employees regard as a fair wage, however, depends more particularly on three comparisons. One is the extent to which the employer is seen as profiting from their services. It is often considered unfair if a highly profitable employer is ungenerous in "sharing" its good fortune with its workers, even if the wages it pays already are relatively high. Likewise, workers who are asked to sacrifice leisure and put forth extraordinary effort on the job are likely to expect the firm to make an extraordinary financial sacrifice (that is, the offer of high pay) to them in return.

Second, employees frequently compare their pay with that of others (especially those of the same age) in the organization, and employers just as frequently expend considerable resources to ensure that pay differences across jobs in their organizations are perceived as the result of objective and evenhanded analysis. Almost all large and medium-sized companies use job evaluation plans in setting internal pay differentials. These plans rate jobs according to such factors as skill, responsibility, effort, and working conditions, and then relate internal pay differentials to differences in the point ratings assigned to each job. Market wage surveys are used in setting wage levels for jobs into which external applicants are hired, and the wages in these jobs then serve as the reference points to rate the firms' other jobs. While the points awarded for each job's tasks are themselves subjective, the process and standards for the determination of pay are intended to reduce employees' concerns about arbitrary and unfair treatment.[24] (For more on this topic, see Appendix 12A.)

Third, and of most interest to economists because it is most objectively measurable, employees judge the fairness of their pay by comparing it to what they could obtain elsewhere. Raising compensation above the level that workers can earn elsewhere, of course, has both benefits and costs to the employer. While initial increases in pay may well serve to increase productivity and therefore the profits of the firm, after a point the costs to the employer of further increases will exceed the benefits. The above-market pay level at which the marginal revenues to the employer from a further pay increase equal the marginal costs is the level that will maximize profits; this has become known as the *efficiency wage* (see Example 11.4).[25]

The theory of efficiency wages has a wide set of implications that, in recent years, have begun to be explored by economists. For example, the persistence of

---

[24]Robert Flanagan, Lawrence Kahn, Robert Smith, and Ronald Ehrenberg, *Economics of the Employment Relationship* (Glenview, Ill.: Scott, Foresman, 1989), 44; David I. Levine, "The U.S. Labor Market: 'Institutions' ≠ Rigid and 'Unregulated' ≠ Market-Clearing," *Proceedings of the Industrial Relations Research Association* (January 1994): 177–185; and George Baker and Bengt Holmstrom, "Internal Labor Markets: Too Many Theories, Too Few Facts," *American Economics Review* 85, no. 2 (May 1995): 255–259.

[25]It should be clear that the efficiency wage refers to all forms of compensation, not just cash wages. Lawrence Katz, "Efficiency Wage Theories: A Partial Evaluation," in *NBER Macroeconomics Annual, 1986,* ed. Stanley Fischer (Cambridge, Mass.: MIT Press, 1986); Joseph E. Stiglitz, "The Causes and Consequences of the Dependence of Quality on Price," *Journal of Economic Literature* 25, no. 1 (March 1987): 1–48; and Kevin M. Murphy and Robert H. Topel, "Efficiency Wages Reconsidered: Theory and Evidence," in *Advances in Theory and Measurement of Unemployment,* ed. Yoram Weiss and Gideon Fishelson (London: Macmillan, 1990), offer detailed analyses of efficiency-wage theories.

EXAMPLE 11.4

Did Henry Ford Pay Efficiency Wages?

The 1908–1914 period saw the introduction of "scientific management" and assembly line production processes at the Ford Motor Company. The change in production methods led to a change in the occupational composition of Ford's workforce, and by 1914 most of its workers were relatively unskilled and foreign-born. Although these changes proved extremely profitable, worker dissatisfaction was high. In 1913 turnover rates reached 370 percent (370 workers had to be hired each year to keep every 100 positions filled), which was high even by the standards of the Detroit automobile industry at the time. Similarly, absenteeism typically averaged 10 percent a day. However, while Henry Ford was obviously having difficulty retaining and eliciting effort from workers, he had little difficulty finding replacements: there were always long lines of applicants at the factory gates. Hence, Ford's daily wage in 1913 of about $2.50 was at least at the competitive level.

In January of 1914, Ford instituted a $5.00-a-day wage; this doubling of pay was granted only to workers who had been employed at the company for at least six months. At roughly the same time, residency in the Detroit area for at least six months was made a hiring standard for new job applicants. Since the company was limiting the potential applicant flow and was apparently not screening job applicants any more carefully after the pay increase, it appears the motivation for this extraordinary increase in wages was not to increase the quality of new hires.

It is clear, however, that the increase *did* affect the behavior of existing employees. Between March of 1913 and March of 1914, the quit rate of Ford employees fell by 87 percent and their discharges by 90 percent. Similarly, the absentee rate fell by a factor of 75 percent during the October 1913 to October 1914 period. Morale and productivity increased and the company continued to be profitable.

There is some evidence that at least initially, however, Ford's productivity gains were less than the wage increase. Historians have pointed to the noneconomic factors that influenced Ford's decision, including his paternalistic desire to teach his workers good living habits. (For workers to receive these increases, investigators from Ford first had to certify that they did not pursue lifestyles that included behavior like excessive gambling or drinking.) While the wage increase thus probably did not lead to a wage level that maximized the company's profits (a smaller increase probably would have done that), the policy did have a substantial positive effect on worker turnover, effort, morale, and productivity.

SOURCE: Daniel Raff and Lawrence Summers, "Did Henry Ford Pay Efficiency Wages?" *Journal of Labor Economics* 5 (October 1987): S57–S86.

---

unemployment is thought by some to result from the widespread payment of above-market wages (see Chapter 15).[26] Further, persistently different wage rates paid to qualitatively similar workers in different industries are the hypothesized result of efficiency-wage considerations.[27]

For our purposes here, however, the most important implications of efficiency wages relate to their effects on productivity, and two types of empirical studies are

---

[26]Janet Yellen, "Efficiency Wage Models of Unemployment," *American Economic Review* 74 (May 1984): 200–208, and Andrew Weiss, *Efficiency Wages: Models of Unemployment, Layoffs, and Wage Dispersion* (Princeton: Princeton University Press, 1990).

[27]Richard Thaler, "Anomalies: Interindustry Wage Differentials," *Journal of Economic Perspectives* 3 (Spring 1989): 181–193; Surendra Gera and Gilles Grenier, "Interindustry Wage Differentials and Efficiency Wages: Some Canadian Evidence," *Canadian Journal of Economics* 27, no. 1 (February 1994): 81–100.

of interest. One set of studies *infers* the effects of efficiency wages on productivity from the types of firms that pay these wages. That is, if some firms raise wages above the market level for profit-maximizing purposes, we ought to observe that those who do are the ones that (*a*) stand to gain the most from enhancing worker reliability (perhaps because they have a lot invested in expensive equipment), or (*b*) find it most difficult to properly motivate their workers through output-based pay or supervision.[28] The other kind of study directly relates the effects of efficiency wages to measures of productivity, rates of disciplinary dismissals, or changes in the employer's product market share.[29] The studies so far are limited in number, but they are generally supportive of efficiency-wage theory.

Note that the payment of wages above what workers could earn elsewhere makes sense only because workers expect to have long-term employment relationships with firms. If workers switched jobs every period they would face no incentive to reduce shirking when a firm paid above-market wages, because firing someone who is going to quit anyway is not an effective penalty; as a result, firms would have no incentive to pursue an efficiency-wage policy. Thus, efficiency wages are likely to arise only in situations where structured internal labor markets exist. The existence of internal labor markets, however, raises *other* possibilities for using pay to motivate workers, and it is to these possibilities that we now turn.

Productivity and the Sequencing of Pay

Employers with internal labor markets have options for motivating workers that grow out of their employees' expected *careers* with the organization. Applicants to, and employees of, employers with internal labor markets are concerned with the present value of *career* compensation. This "lifetime" perspective increases employers' options for developing compensation policies, because both the pay levels at each step in one's career and the swiftness of promotion to given steps can be varied by the firm while still living within the constraint of having to offer an attractive present value of career compensation. In this section we analyze several possibilities for sequencing pay over workers' careers that are thought to provide incentives for greater productivity.

---

[28]Alan B. Krueger, "Ownership, Agency and Wages: An Examination of Franchising in the Fast Food Industry," *Quarterly Journal of Economics* 106 (February 1991): 75–101; Erica L. Groshen and Alan B. Krueger, "The Structure of Supervision and Pay in Hospitals," *Industrial and Labor Relations Review* 43 (February 1990): 134S–146S; and Carl M. Campbell III, "Do Firms Pay Efficiency Wages? Evidence with Data at the Firm Level," *Journal of Labor Economics* 11, no. 3 (July 1993): 442–470.

[29]Peter Cappelli and Keith Chauvin, "An Interplant Test of the Efficiency Wage Hypothesis," *Quarterly Journal of Economics* 106 (August 1991): 769–787; Jozef Konings and Patrick P. Walsh, "Evidence of Efficiency Wage Payments in U.K. Firm Level Panel Data," discussion paper no. 138, London School of Economics, Centre for Economic Performance, April 1993; and Levine, "The U.S. Labor Market."

UNDERPAYMENT FOLLOWED BY OVERPAYMENT

It may be beneficial to both employer and employee to arrange workers' pay over time so that employees are "underpaid" early in their careers and "overpaid" later on.[30] This sequencing of pay, it can be argued, will increase worker productivity and enable firms to pay *higher* present values of compensation than otherwise, for two reasons. An understanding of these reasons takes us back to the problem of creating self-enforcing contracts in the presence of asymmetric information.

First, employment contracts that underpay workers in the early years of their careers and overpay them later on will appeal most to workers who intend to establish long-term relationships with their employers and work diligently enough to avoid being fired before their deferred rewards can be collected. Thus, in the absence of knowledge by employers of which applicants are diligent and not likely to quit, a pay scheme featuring deferred compensation appears to be a signaling mechanism to force employees to reveal information about themselves that employers otherwise could not obtain.[31]

Second, a company that pays poorly to begin with but well later on increases the incentives of its employees to work industriously. Once in the job, an employee has incentives to work diligently in order to qualify for the later overpayment. The employer need not devote as many resources to supervision each year as would otherwise be the case, because the firm has several years in which to identify shirkers and withhold from them the reward. Workers are less likely to take chances and shirk their responsibilities, because the penalties for being caught and fired are forfeiture of a large future reward. Because all employees work harder than they otherwise would, their total compensation tends to be higher also.

One feasible compensation-sequencing scheme would pay workers *less* than their marginal product early in their careers and *more* than their marginal product later on. This scheme, however, must satisfy two conditions. First, the present value of the earnings streams offered to employees must be at least equal to alternative streams offered to workers in the labor market; if not, the firm cannot attract the workers it wants. Since pay that is deferred into the future is discounted, deferred sums must be larger the higher is the discount rate, or *present-orientedness*, of workers (see Chapter 9). Second, the scheme must also satisfy the equilibrium conditions that firms maximize profits and do not earn supernormal profits. If profits are not maximized, the firm's existence is threatened; if firms make supernormal profits, new firms will be induced to enter the market. Thus, in neither case would equilibrium exist.

These two conditions will be met if hiring is done until the present value of one's career-long marginal product equals the present value of one's career earnings stream. (This career-long condition is the multiyear analogue of the single-year

---

[30] Our discussion here draws on Edward Lazear, "Why Is There Mandatory Retirement?" *Journal of Political Economy* 87, no. 6 (December 1979): 1261–1284. For a review of issues raised in this and succeeding sections, see H. Lorne Carmichael, "Self-Enforcing Contracts, Shirking, and Life Cycle Incentives."

[31] The lower turnover rate among workers who have been promised larger pensions upon retirement is apparently mostly the result of self-selection, not the threat of lost pension wealth; see Steven G. Allen, Robert L. Clark, and Ann A. McDermed, "Pensions, Bonding, and Lifetime Jobs," *Journal of Human Resources* 28, no. 3 (Summer 1993): 463–481.

profit conditions discussed in Chapter 3 and the two-year profit-maximization criteria discussed in Chapter 5.) Thus, for firms choosing the "underpayment now, overpayment later" compensation scheme to be competitive in both the labor and the product markets, the present value of the yearly amounts by which marginal revenue product (*MRP*) *exceeds* compensation early on must equal the present value of the later amounts by which *MRP falls short* of pay.

The above compensation plan is diagrammed in Figure 11.2. We assume that *MRP* rises over one's career, but that in the first *t** years of employment one's compensation remains below *MRP*. At some point in one's career with the firm—year *t** in the diagram—compensation begins to exceed *MRP*. From *t** until retirement in year *r* is the period during which diligent employees are rewarded by receiving compensation in excess of what they could receive elsewhere (namely, their *MRP*). For the firm to be competitive in both the labor and the product markets, the *present value* of area *A* in the diagram must equal the *present value* of area *B*. (Area *B* is larger than area *A* in Figure 11.2 because sums received further in the future are subjected to heavier discounting when present values are calculated.)

To be sure, there are risks to both parties in making this kind of agreement. On the one hand, employees agreeing to this compensation scheme take a chance that they may be fired without cause or that their employer may go bankrupt before they have collected their reward in the years beyond *t**. It is easy to see that employers will have some incentives to renege, since older workers are being paid a wage that exceeds their immediate value (at the margin) to the firm.

On the other hand, employers who do not wish to fire people face the risk that older, "overpaid" employees will stay on the job longer than is necessary to collect their reward—that is, stay on longer than time *r* in Figure 11.2. Knowing that their current wage is greater than the wage they can get elsewhere, since it reflects payment for more than current output, older employees will have incentives to keep working longer than is profitable for the firm.

Some safeguards for *employees* can be built into the employment contract when this type of pay sequencing is utilized. Employers can protect older employees from arbitrary discharge by stipulating the grounds on which employees can be discharged and guaranteeing seniority rights for older workers. According to these seniority provisions, workers with the shortest durations of employment with the firm are usually laid off first when the firm cuts back its workforce. Without these seniority rights, firms might be tempted to lay off older workers, whose wages are greater than *MRP*, and keep the younger ones, who are paid less than *MRP* at this point in their careers.

Employees can also be protected from employer "cheating" later in their careers by obtaining part of their "overpayment" in the form of vested pension rights. Once vested (within five years of service, under federal law), employees covered by pension plans have rights to a benefit upon retirement even if they are separated from their employer before retirement age (see Chapter 8).

Ultimately, however, the best protection older workers have from employer cheating may be the employer's need to recruit *other* workers. If a certain employer gains a reputation for firing older workers despite an implicit agreement not to do so, that employer will have trouble recruiting new employees. However, if the

FIGURE 11.2

A Compensation Sequencing Scheme to Increase Worker Motivation

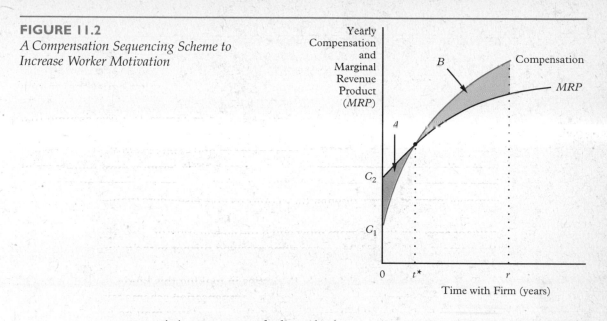

company is in permanent decline, if it faces an unusually adverse market, or if information on its employment policies is not easily available, incentives to renege on its promises could be very strong.

Federal legislation in recent years has made it more difficult for *employers* to avoid the problem of having older employees who elect to stay on the job past the point (*r* in Figure 11.2) at which they have collected their reward. Before 1978, many employers had mandatory retirement ages for their employees, so that they could enforce retirement at point *r*, for example. However, amendments to the Age Discrimination in Employment Act in 1978 and 1986 precluded mandatory retirement for most workers. Age discrimination legislation also makes it very difficult for employers to reduce the wages of workers who stay past point *r*. Therefore, in facing this problem, the best employers can do is offer large inducements for workers to retire at a certain age. For example, a study of pension plans in 190 of the largest companies in the United States (employing about one-quarter of all workers) found that it is common for the present value of pension benefits, summed over the expected lifetime of the retirees, to decline as retirement is postponed. This study discovered that for workers with typical earnings and years of service, the present value of pension benefits was over 25 percent greater if retirement occurred five years before, rather than at, normal retirement age.[32]

One implication of the "underpayment-then-overpayment" compensation scheme is that it is more likely to exist for jobs in which close supervision of workers is not feasible. Indeed, a study that separated jobs into those that were conducive to close supervision and those that were not found that jobs in the latter

---

[32]Edward Lazear, "Pensions as Severance Pay," in *Financial Aspects of the United States Pension System*, ed. Zvi Bodie and John Shoven (Chicago: University of Chicago Press, 1983). Since benefits are expressed nominally, Lazear uses a discount rate of 10 percent.

category were more likely to have relatively high wages for older workers, pensions, and (in the past, at least) mandatory retirement rules.[33]

PROMOTION TOURNAMENTS

Another form of worker motivation within the context of internal labor markets might best be called a *promotion tournament.* Tournaments have three central features: who will win is uncertain, the winner is selected based on *relative* performance (that is, performance compared to that of the other "contestants"), and the rewards are concentrated in the hands of the winner, so that there is a big difference between winning and losing. Not all promotions within firms satisfy this definition, largely because the rewards are relatively small and the "winners" are easy to predict. For example, one study found that promotions were typically associated with increased wage growth of 2 to 3 percent, and those who received their first promotion most quickly tended to be promoted most quickly later on as well.[34]

Promotions to very senior leadership positions, however, often take place through a process that fits the description of a tournament. Suppose, for example, a group of entering management trainees were hired with the expectation that *one* of them would become a high-ranking corporate officer and make an extraordinary sum of money each year. The employees who did not make it to the top would be guaranteed a spot in the firm somewhere, but they would not achieve such high earnings.

Now, if everyone knew in advance who would be promoted, this scheme would not be incentive-producing nor would it have aspects of a tournament. However, if no one knew in advance who would "win" but all were told that winning the top job depended on hard work, all would be attracted by the large salary (or prestige) and work hard to get it. Here, as in the previous schemes, the prospect of obtaining large sums toward the end of one's career offers incentives for diligent work throughout earlier years.

In this scheme, however, not all diligent workers get the prize at career's end; only the winner does. Further, once the prize has been awarded and the winners and losers are known, the winners may "rest on their laurels" and the losers no longer have the same strong incentives to work hard (see Example 11.5). Moreover, the employer, knowing the losers have reduced incentives, has every reason to want to get rid of them. Dangling a lucrative future job in front of everyone increases the incentives of all, even the eventual losers, to work hard; once the prize has been awarded, the losers are of substantially less value to the firm.

The problem for the employer is that employees may not be willing to enter this tournament unless even the losers are treated relatively well. A firm known for firing older mid-level managers may not be able to attract a large enough pool of young management trainees from which to produce an excellent corporate officer

---

[33]Robert Hutchens, "A Test of Lazear's Theory of Delayed Payment Contracts," *Journal of Labor Economics* 5 (October 1987): S153–S170.

[34]Baker and Holmstrom, "Internal Labor Markets: Too Many Theories, Too Few Facts."

EXAMPLE 11.5

Demanding Employers, Overworked Employees, and Neglected Families

Salaried workers often put in very long hours at work, frequently on short notice, or are expected to travel or even relocate their families at the wishes of their employers. Many end up feeling that they are required to enthusiastically respond to the unanticipated needs of their employers without the employers feeling a reciprocal obligation to fully support them when needs arise at home. Is this imbalance the result of powerful employers exploiting helpless workers? Maybe, but the considerations of this chapter suggest that there is an alternative explanation: perhaps these workers are receiving efficiency wages or have chosen to compete in promotion tournaments.

There are two reasons why employees who are receiving efficiency wages or who are in promotion tournaments work so hard. One reason is that their employers have the *ability* to make heavy demands, and the other is that their employers have an *incentive* to be demanding. Their employers have the *ability* to demand long hours on short notice, say, because the employees receive a "reward" for remaining with the firm. Workers who quit a firm that offers efficiency wages are likely to face either unemployment or the prospect of another job at a lower wage, and those who quit a tournament obviously forfeit their chances of winning.

Incentives for the employers to be demanding stem from their need to distinguish applicants who are inherently work-oriented from those who are not. Firms offering *tournaments* need to attract those who are inherently work-oriented, because they do not want either the winners or the losers to "slack off" much after the competition is over and the winner is announced. Firms paying *efficiency wages* must

be careful to employ only those who will become worth their above-market wages with relatively little supervisory effort. The problem for both firms is how to identify those who are truly work-oriented, either at the time of application or shortly thereafter.

All applicants will claim to be hard workers, of course, and even those who have strong preferences for leisure can pretend to be work-oriented for a time after hire. Employers therefore need to elicit a "signal" from their applicants or employees about their true work orientation, and one way to do this is to announce to all applicants that long hours and uncompromising loyalty are expected. The expectations obviously must be reasonable enough that the firms can generate applicants, but in terms of our signaling discussion in Chapter 9, the announced work requirements must be demanding enough to discourage pretenders from applying for, or accepting, employment with these firms. Unfortunately, however, while employers offering efficiency wages and promotion tournaments will strive to make themselves unattractive to those with relatively strong preferences for leisure, they will also make themselves unattractive to anyone with significant *household* responsibilities!

SOURCES: James B. Rebitzer and Lowell J. Taylor, "Do Labor Markets Provide Enough Short-Hour Jobs? An Analysis of Work Hours and Work Incentives," *Economic Inquiry* 33, no. 2 (April 1995): 257–273; and Melvin W. Reder, "On Labor's Bargaining Disadvantage," in *Labor Economics and Industrial Relations: Markets and Institutions,* ed. Clark Kerr and Paul D. Staudohar (Cambridge, Mass.: Harvard University Press, 1994), 237–256.

in the future. For this reason, a firm may be tempted to agree to essentially guarantee the losers desirable jobs somewhere in the organization.

Since workers whose wages are less than or equal to their marginal revenue product do not need any guarantee of job security, it is most likely true that the losers of promotion tournaments have wages or salaries that *exceed* marginal product. If this is the case, the employer will obviously want to offer strong incentives for these employees to retire at a certain point. Again, then, a mandatory retirement clause or inducements to retire voluntarily may be an essential ingredient in the running of a promotion tournament.

Promotion tournaments, like golf tournaments, are contests in which an individual's ultimate compensation depends on his or her performance relative to that of other competitors.[35] The winner may perform only slightly better than the runner-up yet receives much more compensation (if this were not the case, winning would not be as valuable and the effort expended by the contestants would not be as great).[36] A disadvantage of tournaments, then, is that with compensation tied to *relative* performance, some of the contestants' efforts (as we pointed out when discussing merit-pay evaluations based on relative performance) may be directed more toward reducing the productivity of others than toward increasing their own output.[37]

Promotion-related incentive plans face additional problems, however, when employees find it feasible to seek careers outside their current organization and are able to send at least some signals of their productivity to other potential employers. We turn now to an analysis of situations in which the career concerns of employees might lead them to seek employment elsewhere.

CAREER CONCERNS AND PRODUCTIVITY

Employees often define themselves more as members of a profession or field than as members of a particular organization. As such, they may be as motivated to impress *other* employers (in the hopes of receiving future offers) as they are their own. What are the implications of these "career concerns"?

THE DISTORTION OF EFFORT   Other employers can observe objective measures of performance more easily than either subjective measures ("quality," for example) or levels of effort. As a result, employees with career concerns have an incentive to allocate their efforts toward measurable areas of performance and

---

[35]For an analysis of how prizes affect performances in golf tournaments, see Ronald G. Ehrenberg and Michael L. Bognanno, "Do Tournaments Have Incentive Effects?" *Journal of Political Economy* 98 (December 1990): 1307–1324, and Ehrenberg and Bognanno, "The Incentive Effects of Tournaments Revisited: Evidence from the European PGA Tour," *Industrial and Labor Relations Review* 43, no. 3 (February 1990): 74S–88S.

[36]Edward Lazear and Sherwin Rosen, "Rank-Order Tournaments as Optimum Labor Contracts," *Journal of Political Economy* 89 (October 1981): 841–864, and Sherwin Rosen, "Prizes and Incentives in Elimination Tournaments," *American Economic Review* 76 (September 1986): 701–715.

[37]The growth of "tournaments" in a variety of economic sectors, and the social disadvantages of huge gains tied to what may be small relative differences in productivity, are accessibly analyzed in Robert H. Frank and Philip J. Cook, *The Winner-Take-All Society* (New York: Free Press, 1995).

deemphasize areas that other employers cannot observe. As discussed in the section on pay for performance, for example, executives looking for opportunities elsewhere have incentives to pursue strategies that yield short-run profits (which are highly visible) even if doing so harms the long-term interests of their current employer.[38]

PIECE RATES AND EFFORT   While job possibilities with other employers can distort workers' allocations of their effort, they can also solve a problem with piece-rate pay that was mentioned earlier but not fully discussed. In a world in which products and technologies are constantly changing, piece rates must be continually reset. In establishing a piece rate, the employer makes a guess about how long it takes to complete the task and calibrates the piece rate so that the average hourly earnings of its workers are attractive enough to recruit and retain a workforce.

Management, however, can never know for sure just how long it takes to complete a task, given a reasonably high level of effort by production workers. Supervisors are rarely expert production workers themselves, and even the latter go through a learning period and become more productive with practice. Moreover, as noted earlier, workers have incentives to "go slow" in trial runs so that management will overestimate the time it takes to complete the task and set a relatively high piece rate.

If workers know that the estimated time for task completion, and therefore the piece rate, is too high, they may withhold effort and deliberately work slowly out of fear that the firm will later reduce the piece rate if it finds out the truth. If employees are mobile across firms, however, they will be less concerned about their *current* employer's future actions. They are more likely to decide to work at top speed, so that other employers are sufficiently impressed to hire them in the future. Where workers' pay is at least partially based on a piece rate, then, career concerns can be helpful in eliciting maximum effort from one's employees.

THE SEQUENCING OF EFFORT   For employees who are concerned about future promotions, whether with their current employer or elsewhere, there are usually two general incentives for high productivity: one's current pay and the chances of future promotion. When career (that is, promotion) concerns are strong, employers may not need much in the way of current pay-for-performance incentives to motivate their employees. As career concerns weaken, firms may need to adopt more-current incentives to maintain worker effort.[39]

---

[38]When workers' current employers can observe their true productive characteristics better than outsiders can, outsiders (that is, other employers) wanting to make "talent raids" may reasonably infer who are the most valuable employees from observing who is promoted. Thus, promotion itself sends information to other employers, which may help the employee who is promoted but harm his or her current employer. Several papers have recently addressed this issue, among which are Dan Bernhardt, "Strategic Promotion and Compensation," *Review of Economic Studies* 62, no. 2 (April 1995): 315–339, and Derek Laing, "Involuntary Layoffs in a Model with Asymmetric Information Concerning Worker Ability," *Review of Economic Studies* 61, no. 2 (April 1994): 375–392.

[39]Robert Gibbons and Kevin J. Murphy, "Optimal Incentive Contracts in the Presence of Career Concerns: Theory and Evidence," *Journal of Political Economy* 100 (June 1992): 468–505.

Workers are more likely to be motivated by career concerns, and less likely to be motivated by current performance incentives, when they are relatively young. When workers are inexperienced, neither the employer nor the employees themselves know their true ability to perform the job. Performance is a function of ability, effort, and luck, and as enough time passes so that random factors cancel out and the correlations of effort and performance become clearer, both their current employers and the workers themselves will be able to draw inferences about their abilities. When workers' abilities are completely or largely unknown, even by the workers, relating pay to performance is not likely to increase effort much because the connection between effort and output is so unclear. As workers' abilities become clearer and they are sorted into the most appropriate jobs, current performance-pay incentives make more sense.

The relatively low level of reliance on current pay-for-performance plans among younger workers should not reduce their relative productivity, however, because they have unusually strong incentives to put forth effort. At the beginning of their careers, all workers are unknowns in terms of both their abilities and the effort they are willing to expend. As time goes on, employers learn more about their workers and continually update their earlier impressions. Therefore, the effects of a good first impression are very important to a worker's future promotion possibilities, because it is the first impression to which future updates are applied. Thus, extraordinary effort among inexperienced workers with career concerns can be anticipated.

Moreover, the inability of employers—especially outside employers—to closely monitor workers' efforts can, in the presence of career concerns, lead to *more* effort. Employees realize that future promotions depend in large part on employers' beliefs about their *ability*. Because some of their efforts can be hidden, particularly from outside employers, inexperienced workers have incentives to put in extra, hidden effort in an attempt to mislead employers about their ability. For example, an employee expected to work 50 hours a week may put in an extra 20 hours at home to boost performance in an attempt to raise employers' perceptions of his or her ability.

As one's career progresses, however, ability becomes known with more certainty and the career-based incentives for extraordinary effort decline. Fortunately, as noted above, the case for performance-based current pay also becomes stronger. Indeed, one study found that older CEOs were paid more on the basis of current performance than younger CEOs.[40]

Applications of the Theory: Explaining Three Puzzles

The conceptual issues outlined in this chapter can help to shed light on three questions that puzzle labor economists: why pay increases with seniority, why larger employers pay higher wages, and why employment reductions in the face of mandated wage increases are not observed as readily as simple theory would suggest.

---

[40]Gibbons and Murphy, "Optimal Incentive Contracts in the Presence of Career Concerns."

In all three cases, there are multiple theoretical or data-related reasons that can be called upon to "explain" the empirical phenomenon; some of these were presented in this chapter and some were introduced earlier. This section briefly summarizes these reasons and, where relevant, reviews the results of empirical studies to evaluate which ones seem most relevant. As we will see, definitive solutions to all three puzzles await further work.

WHY DO EARNINGS INCREASE WITH JOB TENURE?

Earnings tend to rise with age, as we saw in Chapter 9, but in addition, they also rise as *tenure* with one's employer increases. There are three sets of explanations for why wage increases should be associated with job tenure, all of which have different implications.[41] The simplest explanation is that workers are paid wages equal to their marginal revenue product, and their wages therefore rise because their productivity increases. Increasing productivity might result from workers' investments in on-the-job *general* training, which depresses their earnings initially but increases productivity later on (see Chapter 9). If this simplest explanation is the "correct" one, then wages and productivity rise together at the same rate, as shown in panel (a) of Figure 11.3.

The second explanation for rising wages asserts that *firm-specific* investments are jointly undertaken by workers and their employers. As will be recalled from Chapter 5, the joint investment creates a "surplus" that is *shared* by the worker and the firm; therefore, workers generally receive wage increases that are *less* than the increase in their productivity. As illustrated in panel (b) of Figure 11.3, with firm-specific human capital investments, wages are below—and rise more slowly than—marginal revenue productivity.

Finally, this chapter has offered yet a third explanation for rising wage profiles: they may be part of a delayed-compensation incentive system designed to attract and motivate workers who have long-term attachments to their employers. Under this third explanation, which is depicted in panel (c), wages rise *faster* than marginal revenue productivity and ultimately rise above it.[42]

Economists have been interested in devising empirical analyses that distinguish among these competing theories, but directly measuring *productivity* is not generally feasible. Therefore, most studies have identified workers for whom theory suggests that one or another of the above explanations is very likely (or unlikely), and then compares their wage profiles with those of other workers. Support for an

---

[41]A review of this puzzle and the early empirical work on it can be found in Robert Hutchens, "Seniority, Wages, and Productivity: A Turbulent Decade," *Journal of Economic Perspectives* 3, no. 4 (Fall 1989): 49–64.

[42]A variant of this third explanation is that employers offer rising wage profiles because employees *prefer* them. It is argued in Robert H. Frank and Robert M. Hutchens, "Wages, Seniority, and the Demand for Rising Consumption Profiles," *Journal of Economic Behavior and Organization* 21, no. 3 (August 1993): 251–276, that employees' utility is in part a function of their wage *increases* (not only their wage level). Therefore, to be competitive in the labor market, employers are induced to offer them wage profiles that start lower and rise faster than they otherwise would.

FIGURE 11.3

Alternative Explanations for the Effect of Job Tenure on Wages

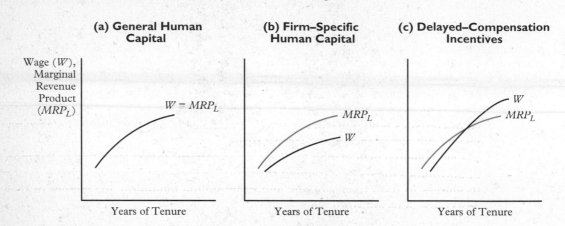

explanation can be inferred if the relative wage profiles display their predicted patterns. For example, delayed-compensation plans are unnecessary if the output of a worker is easily monitored or if the worker is self-employed; therefore, if some employees work under delayed-compensation pay plans, we should find (as two studies have) that the wage profiles of the self-employed and workers with easily monitored outputs rise more slowly than average.[43] The human capital explanations receive support from a study that found more steeply rising payoffs to job tenure among workers who were most likely to invest in human capital.[44]

The most direct attempt to distinguish among the three explanations discussed above came in a recent study that was able to estimate productivity profiles, which were then compared to wage profiles. The results seemed to suggest that wage and productivity profiles rose at the same rate, which supports the first explanation discussed above, but the authors acknowledged that their estimates of productivity were sufficiently imprecise that they could not rule out either of the other two explanations.[45] Thus, it is fair to say that the best of the explanations for rising tenure profiles has by no means been discovered—and, of course, it may well be

---

[43]Edward P. Lazear and Robert L. Moore, "Incentives, Productivity, and Labor Contracts," *Quarterly Journal of Economics* 99, no. 2 (May 1984): 275–296; Robert Hutchens, "A Test of Lazear's Theory of Delayed Payment Contracts," *Journal of Labor Economics* 5 (October 1987, pt. 2): S153–S170.

[44]James N. Brown, "Why Do Wages Increase with Tenure?" *American Economic Review* 79, no. 5 (December 1989): 971–991. For somewhat similar studies, see Sheldon E. Haber and Robert S. Goldfarb, "Does Salaried Status Affect Human Capital Accumulation?" *Industrial and Labor Relations Review* 48, no. 2 (January 1995): 322–337, and David Neumark and Paul Taubman, "Why Do Wage Profiles Slope Upward? Tests of the General Human Capital Model," *Journal of Labor Economics* 13, no. 4 (October 1995): 736–761.

[45]Judith K. Hellerstein and David Neumark, "Are Earnings Profiles Steeper Than Productivity Profiles? Evidence from Israeli Firm-Level Data," *Journal of Human Resources* 30, no. 1 (Winter 1995): 89–112.

that each correctly provides a *partial* explanation for the increase of earnings with job tenure.

WHY DO LARGE FIRMS PAY MORE?[46]

Roughly one-fourth of all American employees work in firms with fewer than 25 workers, while another one-third work in firms with more than 1,000. Workers in the latter group, however, are much better paid; it has been estimated that they earn 12 percent more than those with the same measured human capital characteristics who work in the smallest firms. It also is the case that wages rise faster with experience in the largest firms.

One potential explanation for these wage patterns is that large firms offer more opportunities for specific training than smaller firms, and they thus have greater incentives to train their workers and promote the long-term attachment of their workforce. A recent study finds evidence supporting this explanation.[47]

A second possible explanation is that large firms more often use highly interdependent production processes, which require that workers be exceptionally dependable and disciplined (one shirking worker can reduce the output of an entire team). Workers in a highly interdependent production environment are more regimented and have less ability to act independently, and their higher wages can be seen as a compensating wage differential for the unattractiveness of a job requiring rigid discipline.

A third hypothesis is that large firms make available to workers many steps in a career "job ladder," so that long-term attachments between worker and employer are more attractive than in smaller firms. As has been noted in this chapter, employers whose workers are seeking long-term attachments have more options for using pay to motivate productivity. Efficiency wages are a more effective motivator when there is an expected long-term attachment, because workers' losses from being terminated rise with both their wage level *and* the length of their future expected tenure. Deferred-compensation schemes and promotion tournaments obviously can *only* be used in the context of long-term attachment. While large firms have more *opportunities* for adopting efficiency wages, deferred-compensation plans, or promotion tournaments, they may also have a greater *need* to adopt one or more of these schemes. Owing to sheer size, it is argued, they find it more difficult to monitor their employees and thus must turn to other

---

[46]Two papers that summarize the literature on this topic are Walter Y. Oi, "Employment Relations in Dual Labor Markets ('It's Nice Work If You Can Get It')," *Journal of Labor Economics* 8 (January 1990): S124–S149, and James E. Pearce, "Tenure, Unions, and the Relationship Between Employer Size and Wages," *Journal of Labor Economics* 8 (April 1990): 251–269.

[47]Kevin T. Reilly, "Human Capital and Information: The Employer Size–Wage Effect," *Journal of Human Resources* 30, no. 1 (Winter 1995): 1–18.

methods to motivate high levels of effort. One recent study concluded that the firm-size effect is more related to the presence of efficiency wages than to compensating wage differentials for a demanding work environment.[48]

Finally, it has been argued that larger firms find job vacancies more costly. They tend to be more capital-intensive and, as noted above, have more interdependent production processes. Therefore, an unfilled job or an unexpected quit could more severely disrupt production in larger firms and, by idling much of its labor and capital, impose huge costs on the firm. In an effort to reduce quits and ensure that vacancies can be filled quickly, larger firms thus decide to pay higher wages—even when the work environment is not unattractive and efficiency wages are otherwise unnecessary (because other work incentives exist).[49]

MONOPSONISTIC BEHAVIOR BY EMPLOYERS

We noted in Chapter 4 that employment reductions in the face of minimum wage increases have been puzzlingly difficult to observe in a clear and convincing way. One explanation is essentially that the basic theory of labor demand is "correct," but measuring the employment changes caused just by the minimum wage is difficult. Another explanation is that the simple model of employer behavior is incomplete. As we saw in Chapter 3's discussion of monopsony, if the labor supply curves facing *individual firms* are upward-sloping instead of horizontal, then firms have marginal costs of labor that exceed the wage rate; in this situation, a mandated wage can simultaneously increase average pay while reducing the *marginal* cost of labor to a firm.

In Chapter 10 we discussed how the presence of search costs can create circumstances in which firms behave monopsonistically even when they are not the sole buyers of labor services in a market. The considerations of this chapter suggest another reason why the labor supply curve to a firm might slope upward. As firms grow in size, they find it more costly to monitor worker effort or to measure an individual worker's contribution to profits. To cope with the increased difficulties of ensuring employee effort, the larger a firm becomes the more it must pay in efficiency-wage premiums to elicit this effort. The need for an increased wage as a firm hires more workers means, of course, that firms face an upward-sloping labor supply curve.

Because the essence of labor market monopsony is the presence of an upward-sloping labor supply curve to individual firms, monopsonistic behavior can be produced by these rising monitoring costs. In the case of mandated wage

---

[48]David Fairris and Lee J. Alston, "Wages and the Intensity of Labor Effort: Efficiency Wages Versus Compensating Payments," *Southern Economic Journal* 61, no. 1 (July 1994): 149–160. An extensive review of papers on both the "monitoring" and the "compensating differentials" explanations can be found in Rebitzer, "Radical Political Economy and the Economics of Labor Markets," 1417–1419.

[49]For some evidence along the lines of this argument, see James B. Rebitzer and Lowell J. Taylor, "Efficiency Wages and Employment Rents: The Employer Size–Wage Effect in the Job Market for Lawyers," *Journal of Labor Economics* 13, no. 4 (October 1995): 678–708.

increases, then, the firm's total costs rise and its profits fall, but the net *marginal* cost of hiring labor might go down. Marginal labor costs can fall because, with higher wages, workers are more afraid of losing their jobs and thus need *less supervision* to be more productive. The possibility that the *marginal* costs of labor might fall imparts some uncertainty to predictions about how employment levels will respond to mandated wage increases.[50] (A careful rereading of the monopsony section of Chapter 3, however, will remind students that this uncertainty is greatest for relatively small mandated increases and for those employment changes observed in the short run. Mandated wage changes large enough to *increase* the marginal cost of labor are expected to have the conventional effects of reducing employment. Further, the fact that profits are reduced by any mandated wage increase creates further employment-reducing forces in the long run.)

REVIEW QUESTIONS

1. "The way to get power over workers is to underpay them." Comment.

2. The earnings of piece-rate workers usually exceed those of hourly paid workers performing the same tasks. Theory suggests three reasons why. What are they?

3. Suppose that as employment shifts out of manufacturing to the service sector, a higher proportion of workers are employed in small firms. What effect would this growth of employment in small firms have on the types of compensation schemes used to stimulate productivity?

4. Suppose two soft-drink bottling companies employ drivers whose job it is to deliver cases of drinks to stores, restaurants, businesses, schools, and so forth. One company pays its drivers an hourly wage, and the other pays them by the number of cases delivered each day (which can be affected by efforts of drivers to visit and sell to new customers). Which company is more likely to experience higher rates of traffic accidents and back injuries (from the lifting of heavy cases) among its drivers? Why?

5. Most real estate agents are paid entirely by *commission*. Commissions are usually paid by the person whose property has been sold, and it is normally calculated as a percentage of the sales price. Roughly half of the commission goes to the agent and half to the broker for whom the agent works. What is the likely connection between this compensation scheme and the fact that brokers never lay off their agents?

6. Some real estate brokers split the commission revenues generated by each sale with the responsible agent, as described in question 5. Others, however, require their agents to pay *them* (the brokers) money upfront, and then allow the agents to keep the *entire* commission from each sale they make. Which agents would you predict to have the larger volume of sales, those who split all commissions with their employer or those who pay an up-front fee to their

---

[50]A more formal presentation of this "supervisory" model of monopsonistic behavior can be found in James B. Rebitzer and Lowell J. Taylor, "The Consequences of Minimum Wage Laws: Some New Theoretical Ideas," *Journal of Public Economics* 56 (1995): 245–255.

employer and then keep the entire commission? Explain.

7. Suppose mandatory retirement rules were abolished and firms undertook various strategies to induce *voluntary* retirements at age 65. Some of these possible strategies are listed below. The firm's objectives are to unambiguously increase the incentives for people over 65 to retire, but to do so in a way that offers the strongest incentives to the *least productive* of the older workers to retire. (For our purposes, the least productive will be defined as the workers no other firm would want at anything close to their current wage. Productive workers, even though elderly, could get jobs elsewhere at close to their current wage.) Evaluate each of the following strategies to determine whether it will accomplish the firm's objectives:

a. Cut the wages of all workers after the age of 65.

b. Provide a large lump-sum payment to anyone who quits his or her employment *at the firm* at age 65.

c. Increase the monthly pension benefit of anyone who *retires* (and does not work elsewhere) at age 65.

8. An amusement park open only in the summer hires teenagers to operate its rides and concession stands, paying them $3.00 per hour and putting aside $1.50 per hour into a fund that they will receive as a lump-sum payment if they work through Labor Day (typically, its biggest day of the year).

a. What problem is the amusement park apparently trying to solve with its compensation plan, and in what two ways does this plan help to solve the problem?

b. Suppose the government rules that the compensation plan violates minimum wage laws because workers who quit before Labor Day receive only $3.00 per hour. How can the park now address the problem mentioned in your answer to (a)?

SELECTED READINGS

Akerlof, George A., and Janet L. Yellen, eds. *Efficiency Wage Models of the Labor Market.* New York: Cambridge University Press, 1986.

Carmichael, H. Lorne, "Self-Enforcing Contracts, Shirking, and Life Cycle Incentives." *Journal of Economic Perspectives* 3 (Fall 1989): 65–84.

Frank, Robert H., and Philip J. Cook. *The Winner-Take-All Society.* New York: The Free Press, 1995.

Lazear, Edward P. "Compensation, Productivity, and the New Economics of Personnel." In *Re-*search *Frontiers in Industrial Relations,* ed. David Lewin, Olivia S. Mitchell, and Peter D. Sherer. Madison, Wis.: Industrial Relations Research Association, 1992.

Sappington, David E. "Incentives in Principal–Agent Relationships." *Journal of Economic Perspectives* 5 (Spring 1991): 45–66.

Simon, Herbert A. "Organizations and Markets." *Journal of Economic Perspectives* 5 (Spring 1991): 24–44.

12

Gender, Race, and Ethnicity in the Labor Market

The American labor force has gone through a period of remarkable demographic change in the past three decades. Some forces for change have been rooted in the different expectations of women regarding the balance between household and market work. Other forces for change have arisen from immigration, both legal and illegal, and from different birth rates among racial/ethnic groups. The result has been a pronounced and continuing change in the mix of groups in the labor force.

Table 12.1 contains both changes occurring from 1976 to 1992 and projections that are foreseeable by the year 2005. White males, who were 53 percent of the civilian labor force in 1976, constituted less than half (43 percent) by 1992, and their share is projected to fall to 38 percent by the year 2005. All other major demographic groups have experienced—and will continue to experience—relative growth. Women are estimated to comprise 48 percent of the labor force by the turn of the century, and the growth rates among Asians and Hispanics are so great that their shares will almost triple over the period from 1976 to 2005.

With the exception of Asians, the groups in the labor force that are growing most rapidly are those whose members earn substantially less, on average, than white males for full-time work. A glance at Figure 12.1 suggests that, as of 1992, none of the non-Asian groups with rapid growth rates averaged more than 71 percent of white male earnings for full-time work; the full-time earnings of black and Hispanic women averaged less than 60 percent of white male earnings. (Because

TABLE 12.1

Shares of the Civilian Labor Force for Major Demographic Groups: 1976, 1992, 2005

	Year		
	1976	**1992**	**2005** (projected)
White males (non-Hispanic)	53%	43%	38%
Women (all races)	41	46	48
Blacks (both genders)	10	11	11
Asians and Native Americans (both genders)[a]	2	3	5
Hispanics (all races, both genders)	4	8	11

[a]Includes Alaskan Natives and Pacific Islanders.

SOURCE: Howard N. Fullerton Jr., "New Labor Force Projections, Spanning 1988 to 2000," *Monthly Labor Review* 112 (November 1989): 3–12, and Fullerton, "Another Look at the Labor Force," *Monthly Labor Review* 116, no. 11 (November 1993): 31–40.

Asians comprise a relatively small proportion of the population, published data on their earnings are not available on a yearly basis. In 1979, however, men of Japanese and Chinese ancestry earned 13 and 15 percent more, respectively, than the average male worker.)[1]

The growing numerical significance of demographic groups whose members are relatively poorly paid has heightened interest in understanding the sources of earnings differences across groups. The purpose of this chapter is to analyze such differences, with special attention to the topic of discrimination. In the next section we more carefully analyze earnings differentials by gender, race, and ethnicity, with emphasis on the definition of, and problems in measuring, labor market discrimination. We follow with a section that presents various theories of discrimination, and then end the chapter with a section that describes and evaluates various programs to combat discrimination in the labor market.

Measured and Unmeasured Sources of Earnings Differences

This section focuses on explaining the earnings differentials for three of the larger (and partially overlapping) groups whose members have been targeted by government policy as potential victims of employment discrimination: women, blacks, and Hispanics. The focus is on these groups because data and studies are more readily available for them than for groups defined by such characteristics as

[1]Reynolds Farley, "Blacks, Hispanics, and White Ethnic Groups: Are Blacks Uniquely Disadvantaged?" *American Economic Review* 80 (May 1990): 237–241.

FIGURE 12.1

Earnings as a Percentage of White Male Earnings, Various Demographic Groups, Full-Time Workers over 15 Years Old, 1992

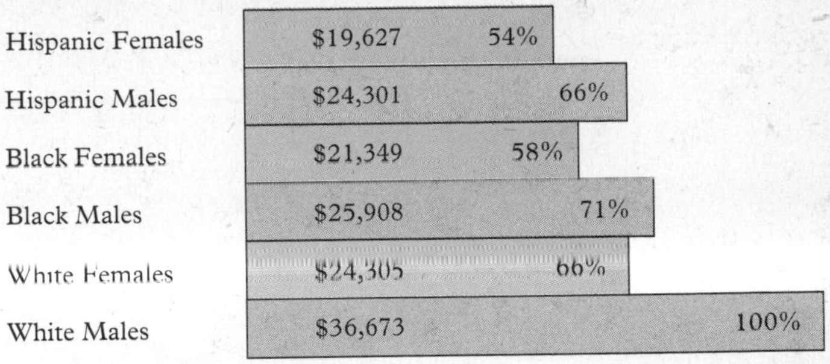

Hispanic Females	$19,627	54%
Hispanic Males	$24,301	66%
Black Females	$21,349	58%
Black Males	$25,908	71%
White Females	$24,305	66%
White Males	$36,673	100%

SOURCE: U.S. Bureau of the Census, *Money Income of Households, Families, and Persons in the United States, 1992,* Series P-60, no. 184 (Washington, D.C.: U.S. Government Printing Office, 1993), Table 31.

physical limitation or sexual preference.[2] We analyze *earnings* rather than *total compensation* (which would be preferable), for the practical reason that data on the value of employee benefits are not generally available by demographic group.

EARNINGS DIFFERENCES BY GENDER

Combining all races, women over the age of 18 who worked full-time earned an average of just 67 percent of what males earned in 1992. While this percentage is an increase from the percentages that were obtained in 1970 (50 percent), 1980 (59 percent), and 1990 (65 percent), it still suggests a huge difference in average pay.[3] Understanding the sources of this difference is critical to a determination of what policies, if any, might be needed to address the gap in pay.

The first step in analyzing earnings differentials is to think of potential *sources* of difference, many of which can be measured. We know from Chapter 9 that two important and measurable factors that influence earnings are education and age. While the most recent cohorts of women have levels of schooling at least equal to those of men, the same cannot be said of older cohorts. Moreover, we also know that the age/earnings profiles for women are flatter than the ones for men. Therefore, we would expect that controlling for age and education would account for at least some of the female/male differences in earnings.

The data in Table 12.2, which categorizes women and men by age and education, suggest that, as expected, female/male earnings ratios tend to fall with age. Even for

---

[2]For papers on these two topics, see Marjorie L. Baldwin, Lester A. Zeager, and Paul R. Flacco, "Gender Differences in Wage Loss from Impairments: Estimates from the Survey of Income and Program Participation," *Journal of Human Resources* 29, no. 3 (Summer 1994): 865–887; and M. V. Lee Badgett, "The Wage Effects of Sexual Orientation Discrimination," *Industrial and Labor Relations Review* 48, no. 4 (July 1995): 726–739.

[3]As noted, the pay differences presented and analyzed in this chapter relate to wages and earnings, not to measures of total compensation (which would include employee benefits). There is some indication that women are less likely than comparable men to have pension, health insurance, or disability benefits; see Janet Currie, "Gender Gaps in Benefits Coverage," working paper no. 4265, National Bureau of Economic Research, Cambridge, Mass., January 1993.

TABLE 12.2

Female Earnings as a Percentage of Male Earnings, by Age and Education, Full-Time Workers, 1992

Age	High School Graduate	Bachelor's Degree	Master's Degree
25–34	77%	77%	77%
35–44	61	68	67
45–54	64	63	66
55–64	53	66	77

SOURCE: U.S. Bureau of the Census, *Money Income of Households, Families, and Persons in the United States: 1992*, Series P-60, no. 184 (Washington, D.C.: U.S. Government Printing Office, 1993), Table 29.

the youngest cohort of women in the table, however, these ratios are so low (0.77) that we must look elsewhere for explanations of the female/male earnings difference.

A measurable factor that could help to explain female/male earnings ratios is occupation. As can be seen in Table 12.3, women tend to be "overrepresented" in low-paying occupations and "underrepresented" in high-paying ones; thus, at least some of the difference between the average pay of women and men is the result of different occupational distributions. Moreover, Table 12.3 also suggests that even in the *same* occupations women earn substantially less than men. Since the higher-paying occupations selected for inclusion in Table 12.3 generally require specialized college or postgraduate education, it can be reasonably assumed that women and men entering them share a "career" orientation—yet even for these occupations in 1994, the female/male earnings ratios lay in the range of 0.74 to 0.87!

Within occupations, of course, earnings are affected by one's hours of work and one's years of experience. We saw in Chapter 9 that women average fewer hours of "market" work per week than do men in the same occupation. Putting aside the effects of part-time employment by focusing on those working full-time, Table 9.2 indicated that women in given occupations average 5 to 10 percent fewer hours per week than do men. Because salaried workers presumably receive a compensating wage differential for longer hours of work, some of the earnings differentials in Table 12.3 could be associated with lower hours of work among women.

Recent analyses suggest that, within occupations, women typically have less (and sometimes, interrupted) work experience and are less likely to be promoted.[4]

---

[4]Edward P. Lazear and Sherwin Rosen, "Male-Female Wage Differentials in Job Ladders," *Journal of Labor Economics* 8 (January 1990 supplement): S106–S123, and Erica L. Groshen, "The Structure of the Female/Male Wage Differential: Is It Who You Are, What You Do, or Where You Work?" *Journal of Human Resources* 26 (Summer 1991): 457–472; and Stephen J. Spurr and Glenn J. Sueyoshi, "Turnover and Promotion of Lawyers: An Inquiry into Gender Differences," *Journal of Human Resources* 29, no. 3 (Summer 1994): 813–842.

TABLE 12.3
Female/Male Earnings Ratios and Percentages of Female Jobholders, Full-Time Wage and Salary Workers, by Selected High- and Low-Paying Occupations, 1994

	Percentage Female in Occupation	Female-to-Male Earnings Ratio
High-Paying[a]		
Chemists, except biochemists	37	0.85
College/university teachers	36	0.87
Computer systems analysts	31	0.86
Lawyers	31	0.74
Management analysts	43	0.83
Physicians	23	0.77
Low-Paying[a]		
Cashiers	78	0.83
Cooks, except short-order	38	0.87
Food preparation, other	42	1.00
Hand packers and packagers	61	0.96
Laundering machine operators	58	0.91
Stock handlers and baggers	26	0.89
Textile sewing machine operators	85	0.88
Waiters and waitresses	71	0.79

[a]"High-paying" occupations are those in which women earned more than $700 per week in 1994; "low-paying" ones are those in which men earned less than $300 per week. Occupations in which so few of either gender were employed that earnings data were not published are omitted.

SOURCE: U.S. Bureau of Labor Statistics, *Employment and Earnings* 42 (January 1995), Table 38.

One study of lawyers who graduated from the same law school at the same time, for example, found that women earned about 7 percent less than men initially, but after 15 years they earned 40 percent less.[5] Some of this difference at 15 years could be associated with fewer current hours of work, and some was associated with less accumulated experience (women in the sample had fewer total months of experience, and more months of *part-time* work, than did their male counterparts). Given the primary role women have typically played in child-rearing, the authors attributed much of this "experience gap" to child care. Indeed, another recent study reports that in 1991, among all women working at age 30, those who were mothers

---

[5]Robert G. Wood, Mary E. Corcoran, and Paul N. Courant, "Pay Differences Among the Highly Paid: The Male-Female Earnings Gap in Lawyers' Salaries," *Journal of Labor Economics* 11, no. 3 (July 1993): 417–441.

earned 25 percent less than 30-year-old men, while those who were not mothers earned only 5 percent less.[6]

Clearly, controlling for occupation, education, age, experience, and hours of work probably goes a long way toward explaining earnings differentials by gender, and other measurable variables added to this list could explain some of the rest. It is possible, however, that some differences would remain "unexplained" even if all measurable factors were included in our analysis. If so, there are two possible interpretations. One is that these remaining differences are the result of characteristics affecting productivity that might differ by gender but *cannot be observed or measured* by the researcher (for example, the relative priorities men and women typically assign to market and household activities, if the two conflict). Alternatively, the unexplained differential could be interpreted as resulting from *discriminatory treatment* in the labor market.

Raising the issue of discrimination demands that it be defined and that we explore the methods used to identify its presence. The next three subsections deal with these issues.

DEFINING DISCRIMINATION   *Labor market discrimination* is said to *currently* exist if individual workers who have identical productive characteristics are treated differently because of the demographic groups to which they belong. There are two prominent forms that gender discrimination is alleged to take. First, employers are sometimes suspected of paying women less than men with the same experience and working under the same conditions in the same occupations; this is labeled *wage discrimination*. Second, women with the same education and productive potential are seen as shunted into lower-paying occupations or levels of responsibility by employers, who reserve the higher-paying jobs for men. This latter form of discrimination has been called *occupational discrimination.*

Basic to the concept of labor market discrimination is that workers' wages are a function of both their *productive characteristics* (their human capital, the size of the firm for which they work, and so on) and the *"price"* each characteristic commands in the labor market. Thus, economic theory suggests that the wages of women and men might differ because of differences in their levels of job experience, for example, or they might differ because men and women are compensated differently for each added year of experience. *Discrimination is said to be present when the prices paid by employers for given productive characteristics are systematically different for different demographic groups.* Put differently, if men and women (or minorities and nonminorities) with equal productive characteristics are paid unequally, even in the same occupations, then discrimination in the labor market exists.

Emphasizing gender differentials in the "prices" paid for human capital characteristics, however, does not present a total picture of labor market discrimina-

---

[6]Jane Waldfogel, "Working Mothers Then and Now: A Cross-Cohort Analysis of the Effects of Maternity Leave on Women's Pay," paper prepared for the ILR-Cornell Institute for Labor Market Policies Conference on Gender and Family Issues in the Workplace, April 1995.

tion. In particular, it does not address a major question that arises in the context of occupational choice: *Why might members of different demographic groups acquire different productive characteristics, especially in the preparation for, or choice of, different occupations?* The choices of some groups might be directly limited by occupational discrimination, as implied above, but what are we to think if women (say) tend to choose the teaching of high school science rather than teaching biophysics in a university? Does this choice reflect different preferences? Does it reflect a rational, human capital decision to invest in skills that do not depreciate very quickly if one drops out of the labor market for a time, perhaps to start a family? Or does it reflect the *expectation* that educational investments will have a lower payoff for women, so that spending the extra years studying biophysics is not deemed to be worth it?

Whatever the cause, *occupational segregation* is said to exist when the distribution of occupations within one demographic group is very different than the distribution in another. With respect to gender, occupational segregation is reflected in there being "female-dominated" occupations and "male-dominated" ones. The problem is that occupational segregation is not necessarily a reflection of occupational *discrimination.*

If occupational choices are directly limited, or if they are influenced by lower payoffs to given human capital characteristics, then occupational segregation certainly reflects labor market discrimination. If these choices reflect different preferences, however, or different household responsibilities (particularly related to child care), then two arguments can be made. One is that there is no particular problem, that occupational preferences—including those toward household work—form naturally from one's life experiences and should be respected in a market economy. The other view is that these preferences are the result of *premarket* discrimination—differential treatment by parents, schools, and society at large that points girls toward lower-paying (including household) pursuits long before they reach adulthood and enter the labor market.

This brief discussion of occupational segregation suggests that measuring what we define as "current labor market discrimination" might understate the overall problem of discrimination. Taking productive characteristics as *given* and focusing on differences in the "prices" paid for each characteristic to members of different demographic groups ignores the effects of *past* discrimination or any *current premarket* discrimination on occupational choice. As we have pointed out, however, to attribute *all* differences in occupational choice to discrimination might be going too far, because it would involve asserting that differences in *preferences* are necessarily the result of discriminatory treatment.

The above ambiguities, and some others as well, will be evident as we move to a discussion of how discrimination is *measured.* We begin with a discussion of the most pronounced and easily measured labor-market difference between women and men: differences in their occupational distributions.

MEASUREMENT: OCCUPATIONAL SEGREGATION   As was seen in Table 12.3, women and men are not equally represented in the various occupations. While dramatic changes have occurred since 1970, women are still underrepresented in higher-paying jobs and overrepresented in the lower-paying ones. Various measures are used to summarize the inequality of gender representation across detailed occupational categories, all of which are based on comparing the existing distribution of men and women in occupations to the distribution that would exist if "assignment" to occupations were random with respect to gender.[7]

One measure, for example, is the *index of dissimilarity.* Assuming workers of one gender remain in their jobs, this index indicates the percentage of the other that would have to change occupations for the two genders to have equal occupational distributions. If all occupations were completely segregated, the index would equal 100, while if men and women were equally distributed across occupations it would equal zero. One study of narrowly defined occupations (such as those in Table 12.3) placed the index of occupational dissimilarity by gender at 57 percent in 1988—down from around 66 percent in 1970.[8] Studies using other measures likewise indicate a continuing decline in occupational segregation, particularly among professionals, managers, and sales and administrative support workers.[9]

Despite a decline in occupational segregation, studies generally find that its effects on women's wages are substantial. It is typically estimated that if American women with given educational attainment and experience levels were in the same occupations as their male counterparts, their wages would rise by as much as 10 percent.[10] These effects of occupational segregation on the earnings of women are more pronounced than in many European countries. The reason, pointed out in Example 12.1, is that the wage differentials (for both men and women) between high-and low-paying occupations are relatively larger in the United States, so the penalty for being in a low-wage job is generally greater than in Europe. We will see in Chapter 14, however, that during the 1980s wages in "women's jobs" advanced markedly relative to those in "men's jobs" in the United States, and these occupational wage changes played a large role in reducing the earnings gap during that period, especially among the less-educated.[11]

---

[7]Dale Boisso, Kathy Hayes, Joseph Hirschberg, and Jacques Silber, "Occupational Segregation in the Multidimensional Case: Decomposition and Tests of Significance," *Journal of Econometrics* 61, no. 1 (March 1994): 161–171; Martin Watts, "Divergent Trends in Gender Segregation by Occupation in the United States: 1970–92," *Journal of Post-Keynesian Economics* 17, no. 3 (Spring 1995): 357–379.

[8]Mary C. King, "Occupational Segregation by Race and Sex, 1940–88," *Monthly Labor Review* 115 (April 1992): 30–37.

[9]Boisso, Hayes, Hirschberg, and Silber, "Occupational Segregation in the Multidimensional Case," and Watts, "Divergent Trends in Gender Segregation by Occupation in the United States."

[10]Francine D. Blau and Marianne A. Ferber, *The Economics of Women, Men and Work*, 2d ed. (Englewood Cliffs, N.J.: Prentice-Hall, 1992), 191–193, and Elaine Sorenson, "The Crowding Hypothesis and Comparable Worth," *Journal of Human Resources* 25 (Winter 1990): 55–99. Slightly larger effects of segregation are found in Groshen, "The Structure of the Female/Male Wage Differential," and smaller ones are reported in David Macpherson and Barry T. Hirsch, "Wages and Gender Composition: Why Do Women's Jobs Pay Less?" *Journal of Labor Economics* 13, no. 3 (July 1995): 426–471.

[11]Francine D. Blau and Lawrence M. Kahn, "Rising Wage Inequality and the U.S. Gender Gap," *American Economic Review* 84, no. 2 (May 1994): 23–28.

EXAMPLE 12.1

The Gender Earnings Gap Across Countries

How do gender wage differentials in the United States compare to those in other developed countries? Put succinctly, data from eight countries on the relative wages of women and men suggest that women in the United States do comparatively poorly. The ratios of female wages in the mid-1980s, ranked from high to low, are as follows:

Sweden	0.77
Austria	0.74
Australia	0.73
Norway	0.71
Germany	0.71
United States	0.67
Switzerland	0.65
United Kingdom	0.61

The irony of the relatively low wage ratio in the United States is that women's productive characteristics are closer to those of men in the United States than in any other of the countries. Further, American women are less occupationally segregated, and American legislation concerning equal employment opportunity generally predated laws elsewhere. What seems to be the cause of this relatively large gender gap is the wider pay differentials between high- and low-paid workers in the United States. In a word, it appears that wage differentials across and within occupations in the United States are larger than in other countries, so that *all* groups of workers with less experience or in lower-paid occupations are relatively worse off here than in other countries.

SOURCE: Francine D. Blau and Lawrence M. Kahn, "The Gender Earnings Gap: Some International Evidence," in *Differences and Changes in Wage Structures,* ed. Richard Freeman and Lawrence Katz (Chicago: University of Chicago Press, 1995).

As noted previously, however, not all gender segregation is the result of labor market discrimination; at least some may be the result of either preferences formed before labor market entry or choices made later in the context (say) of family decision making. There is as yet no measure that has been devised to estimate that portion of occupational segregation that can be attributed to unequal treatment by employers.

Our inability to measure the extent to which discriminatory employer behavior affects the occupational distribution of women does not imply that such discrimination is absent, nor does it imply that such discrimination is impossible to prove. What it does suggest is that other types of information—usually pertaining to specific cases—must be gathered. For example, one study found that the percentage of insurance adjusters who were women more than doubled from 1970 to 1989, but that women were predominantly employed as "inside" adjusters and men as "outside" adjusters (who have more discretionary authority, more prestige, and better pay).[12] Whether this pattern of job assignment represents current discrimination

---

[12]See Blau and Ferber, *The Economics of Women, Men, and Work,* 129.

depends on facts particular to the insurance industry—especially on whether outside adjusters require more experience and whether the women involved had less experience than men.

MEASUREMENT: WAGE DISCRIMINATION   Measuring wage discrimination presents analogous problems. We pointed out earlier that average earnings can differ between women and men either because of differences in average levels of productive characteristics or because of differences in what women and men are paid for possessing each characteristic. The latter source of difference is what we interpret as current labor market discrimination. Ideally, wage discrimination could be identified and measured in the following four-step process.[13]

1. We would collect data, for men and women separately, on *all* human capital and other characteristics that are theoretically relevant to the determination of earnings. Based on discussions in earlier chapters, the characteristics of age, education and training, experience, tenure with current employer, hours of work, firm size, region, intensity of work effort, industry, and the job's duties, location and working conditions come readily to mind.
2. We would then estimate (statistically) how each of these characteristics contributes to the earnings of women. That is, we would use statistical techniques to estimate the "payoffs" to women associated with each characteristic. (The basic statistical technique used is called "regression analysis," and it allows us to estimate how changes in a productive characteristic affect earnings, holding other productive characteristics constant. A computer must be used to make these estimates when, as in the case at hand, there are *several* relevant productive characteristics to be jointly analyzed. However, the general idea behind this technique is graphically illustrated in Appendix 12A, using the simple example of estimating how wages are affected by changes in a single composite measure of job "difficulty.")
3. Having measured levels of the productive characteristics typically possessed by men and women (step 1), and having estimated how changes in each productive characteristic affect the earnings of women (step 2), we would next estimate how much women *would* earn *if* their productive characteristics were exactly the same as those of men. This would be done by applying the payoffs *women* receive for each productive characteristic to the average level of those characteristics possessed by *men*.

---

[13]This procedure was first described in Ronald Oaxaca, "Male-Female Wage Differentials in Urban Labor Markets," *International Economic Review* 14 (October 1973): 693–709. For recent refinements, see Ronald L. Oaxaca and Michael R. Ransom, "On Discrimination and the Decomposition of Wage Differentials," *Journal of Econometrics* 61, no. 1 (March 1994): 5–21, and Moon-Kak Kim and Solomon W. Polachek, "Panel Estimates of Male-Female Earnings Functions," *Journal of Human Resources* 29, no. 2 (Spring 1994): 406–428.

4. Finally, we would compare the *hypothetical* average earnings level calculated for women (in step 3) with the *actual* average earnings of men. This latter comparison would yield an estimate of wage discrimination, because it reflects the effects of the different prices for productive characteristics paid to men and women. (In the absence of discrimination, women and men who have identical productive characteristics should have identical earnings.)

There are two problems with this "ideal" measure of wage discrimination: not all potentially measurable productive characteristics are included in available data sets, and some important characteristics are inherently unmeasurable. Such characteristics as native intelligence or the presence of emotional disorders are randomly distributed across the population, so that their effects on women's average earnings are expected to be about the same as they are on men's. Other unobserved characteristics may be differently distributed between women and men. Because of greater household responsibilities, for example, women may be more likely to seek work closer to home, may be less available for work outside normal business hours, or may more often be the parent "on call" if a child becomes ill at school. These factors reduce the earnings of women, but because they are unmeasured they tend to show up statistically as reduced payoffs to the observed characteristics.

Thus, not all of the wage differences that would remain if observed productive characteristics were equalized between women and men can be unambiguously identified as the result of discrimination in the labor market. As with occupational segregation, some of the differences may reflect choices on the supply side of the market.

These measurement problems notwithstanding, it is interesting to follow the four-step procedure outlined above and see what the earnings gap between women and men would be if observed productive characteristics were equalized. Using mid-1980s data that included unusual details on labor force experience, vocational preparation, and firm size, one study found that women's earnings per hour of work would have averaged between 88 and 90 percent of men's if their productive characteristics (including occupation) were equalized.[14] Recent studies try to account for the effects of some *unobserved* characteristics (preferences, for example) by using data on *changes* in wages and productive characteristics over time for the *same*—presumably unchanging—individuals. Studies taking this latter approach find that the level of possible wage discrimination is cut roughly in half, but this implies, of course, that some wage discrimination may remain.[15]

---

[14]Blau and Ferber, *The Economics of Women, Men, and Work,* 191–193.

[15]Kim and Polachek, "Panel Estimates of Male-Female Earnings Functions," Sharmila Choudhury, "Reassessing the Male-Female Wage Differential: A Fixed Effects Approach," *Southern Economic Journal* 60, no. 2 (October 1993): 327–340.

The observed productive characteristic that contributes most to the wage gap between women and men in the same occupation is labor market *experience.* Women typically have *less* work experience than men of comparable age, education, and occupation; further, an extra year of total experience also appears to have a *lower payoff* to women. One study, however, suggests that we need to go beyond measuring total years of experience to analyze the effects on wages of the *frequency* and *timing* of periods when women (and men) are out of the labor force.[16] Thus, in the absence of data on the frequency and timing of nonwork spells (data not normally available to the researcher), at least some of the lower payoff to work experience for women may be the result of an unmeasured productive characteristic.

Overall, the *combined* effects of occupational segregation and wage discrimination could possibly reduce women's wages by up to 15 or 20 percent. These estimates are interesting, but they are hardly a precise measure of the effects of discrimination. On the one hand, current labor market discrimination of this magnitude could discourage women from making certain human-capital investments that men might find attractive, thus affecting the level of the productive characteristics women bring with them to the labor market.[17] On the other hand, there is as yet no completely satisfactory way to distinguish the effects of discrimination from those caused by unmeasured differences that are associated with gender. Therefore, we do not know whether the 15 to 20 percent differential that apparently would remain if measured productive characteristics were equalized over- or understates the magnitude of discrimination against women.

EARNINGS DIFFERENCES BETWEEN BLACK AND WHITE AMERICANS

We saw in Figure 12.1 that black males who worked full-time in 1992 earned just 71 percent as much as white males; black females earned just 58 percent as much. These percentages represent increases from their levels in 1970, but as the data in Table 12.4 indicate, the patterns and magnitudes of increase are different for women and men. For men, the increase occurred entirely before 1975; since 1975 the overall earnings ratio has remained essentially unchanged. Black women experienced a continued increase throughout the 1970 to 1990 period, although the

---

[16]Audrey Light and Manuelita Ureta, "Early-Career Work Experience and Gender Wage Differentials," *Journal of Labor Economics* 13, no. 1 (January 1995): 121–154. A recent study by Francine D. Blau and Lawrence M. Kahn, "Swimming Upstream: Trends in the Gender Wage Differential in the 1980s," *Journal of Labor Economics* (forthcoming) finds that women's returns to *full-time* experience were lower than men's in 1979 but similar by 1988.

[17]One attempt to measure the effects of current labor market discrimination on subsequent human capital accumulation is reported in David Neumark and Michele McLennan, "Sex Discrimination and Women's Labor Market Outcomes," *Journal of Human Resources* 30, no. 4 (Fall 1995): 713–740.

TABLE 12.4

Earnings Ratios of Full-Time, Full-Year Workers, by Race and Gender, 1970–1992

	Earnings Ratios		
Year	Black Men/ White Men	Black Women/ White Men	Black Women/ White Women
1970	.65	.47	.84
1975	.69	.51	.92
1980	.70	.53	.92
1985	.71	.55	.90
1990	.70	.58	.90
1992	.71	.58	.88

SOURCES: U.S. Bureau of the Census, *Money Income of Households, Families and Persons*, Series P–60, no. 80 (1971), Table 52; no. 105 (1977), Table 48; no. 132 (1982), Table 58; no. 156 (1987), Table 40; no. 174 (1991), Table 31; no. 184 (1993), Table 31.

slight fall in their earnings relative to those for white women after 1975 suggests that their gains relative to white men were associated more with their gender than with their race.

The earnings of full-time workers, however, do not tell the whole story of the economic disparities between black and white Americans. There is no major difference in the fraction of adult male employees in the two groups who work part-time, and there is a *lower* percentage of black women (18 percent) than white women (26 percent) who work part-time. There are significant disparities, however, in the *employment-to-population ratios* (the ratios of employed adults to the entire population of adults in a particular demographic group). It can be seen in the first two columns of Table 12.5 that, as compared to the white population, a much lower percentage of the black population is employed. The differences are particularly striking for males. We begin our analysis of black/white disparities by first considering these differences in the employment ratios.

DIFFERENCES IN EMPLOYMENT RATIOS   The employment ratio for a given demographic group is completely determined by the percentage of the group seeking employment (the labor force participation rate) and the percentage of those seeking employment who find it. Because the latter is equal to 100 percent minus the group's unemployment rate, the employment ratio can be expressed as a function of two widely published rates: the group's labor force participation rate and its unemployment rate.

Table 12.5 contains data on labor force participation rates and unemployment rates by race and gender. Looking first at labor force participation, we see that black women had *higher,* but more slowly growing, labor force participation rates than white women over the 1970 to 1990 period. By 1994, the labor force participation rates of white women were slightly higher. Among men, however, the picture is much different. Black men have had consistently lower participation rates than white men, and while both groups of men experienced reductions in labor force participation rates from 1970 to 1994, the reductions were greater for blacks.

The declining labor force participation rates of men are not just the result of earlier retirement among older men or more postsecondary schooling by the young (although as we saw in Chapter 6, both phenomena have played a role) The participation rates even of men aged 35 to 44 have dropped for both blacks and whites, with these reductions being more or less confined to those with a high school education or less. As we saw in Chapter 9, and will come to again in Chapter 14, the wages of poorly educated workers—especially men—have fallen in recent years, and many of these men apparently have become "discouraged" and dropped out of the labor force. It appears that at least some of the larger declines in labor force participation among black males are a consequence of their lower average levels of education.[18]

Table 12.5 also suggests that the higher unemployment rates of blacks are a cause of their lower employment-to-population ratios. Before 1980, the unemployment rates of black men and women were 1.6 to 1.9 times higher than those of whites, and since 1980 unemployment rates among blacks have been over *twice* as high. These patterns are *not* just a function of differences in education, age, experience, or region of residence; the black unemployment rate is roughly double the rate for whites in *every* group.[19]

The relative constancy of the black/white *ratio* of unemployment rates suggests that this ratio is not affected much by the business cycle. In both prosperous years and recessions, the unemployment rate of blacks has remained double that of comparable whites. It would be erroneous to conclude from this constancy, how-

---

[18]Finis Welch, "The Employment of Black Men," *Journal of Labor Economics* 8 (January 1990 supplement): S26–S74; for a related article in the same issue, see Glen G. Cain and Ross E. Finnie, "The Black–White Difference in Youth Employment: Evidence for Demand-Side Factors," S364–S395. Chinhui Juhn, "Decline of Male Labor Force Participation: The Role of Declining Market Opportunities," *Quarterly Journal of Economics* 107 (February 1992): 79–121, finds that all of the decline in white male labor force participation rates, but only *half* of the decline in black male participation, can be attributed to declining wages. This article concludes that preferences among less-educated black males for nonmarket activities must have increased since the 1970s. John Bound and Richard B. Freeman, "What Went Wrong? The Erosion of Relative Earnings and Employment of Young Black Men in the 1980s," *Quarterly Journal of Economics* 107 (February 1992): 202–232, point to a huge increase in the incarceration rate among young black high school dropouts during the 1980s. It is difficult to tell, however, whether returns to criminal activities improved, or whether declining job market opportunities drove young dropouts into criminal activities.

[19]Steven Shulman, "Why Is the Black Unemployment Rate Always Twice As High As the White Unemployment Rate?" in *New Approaches to Economic and Social Analyses of Discrimination,* ed. Richard R. Cornwall and Phanindra V. Wunnava (New York: Praeger, 1991), 5–38, and Steven G. Rivkin, "Black/White Differences in Schooling and Employment," *Journal of Human Resources* 30, no. 4 (Fall 1995): 826–852.

TABLE 12.5

Employment Ratios, Labor Force Participation Rates, and Unemployment Rates, by Race and Gender[a]

Year	Employment Ratio		Labor Force Participation Rate		Unemployment Rate	
	Blacks	Whites	Blacks	Whites	Blacks	Whites
			Men			
1970	71.9%	77.8%	77.6%	81.0%	7.3%	4.0%
1975	62.7	73.6	72.7	79.3	13.7	7.2
1980	62.5	74.0	72.1	78.8	13.3	6.1
1985	60.0	72.3	70.8	77.0	15.3	6.1
1990	61.8	73.2	70.1	76.9	11.8	4.8
1994	60.8	71.8	69.1	75.9	12.0	5.4
			Women			
1970	44.9	40.3	49.5	42.6	9.3	5.4
1975	42.4	42.0	49.3	46.0	14.0	8.6
1980	46.6	48.1	53.6	51.4	13.1	6.5
1985	48.1	50.7	56.5	54.1	14.9	6.4
1990	51.5	54.8	57.8	57.5	10.8	4.6
1994	52.3	55.8	58.7	58.9	11.0	5.2

[a]For 1970, 1975, and 1980, data on blacks include other racial minorities. Data in all years are for persons age 16 or older.

SOURCES: U.S. Bureau of Labor Statistics, *Employment and Earnings* 17 (January 1971), Table A-1; 22 (January 1976), Table I; 28 (January 1981), Table 3; 33 (January 1986), Table 3; 38 (January 1991), Table 3; 42 (January 1995), Table 3.

ever, that recessions have equal proportionate effects on black and white employment; in fact, the constant ratio means that black workers suffer *disproportionately* in a recession.

Suppose, for example, that the white unemployment rate were 5 percent and the black unemployment rate were 10 percent; these rates imply, of course, that 95 percent of the white labor force, and 90 percent of the black labor force, is employed. Suppose in addition that a recession occurs, and that the white and black unemployment rates rise to 8 and 16 percent, respectively. Among whites, the employment rate falls from 95 to 92 percent, which implies that a bit over 3 percent of whites who had jobs lost them (3/95 = .032). Among blacks, however, the employment rate falls from 90 to 84 percent, indicating that almost 7 percent of employed blacks lost their jobs (6/90 = .067).

The greater sensitivity of black employment to aggregate economic activity has led many observers to conclude that blacks are the last hired and first fired. In view of the findings that the racial patterns in unemployment rates are not affected much by observed productive characteristics, it would appear that these patterns are caused either by discrimination or by unmeasured productive characteristics (such as the *quality* of schooling, for example). As noted above, it is difficult to distinguish the effects of unmeasured differences from those of discrimination, although recent studies of wage discrimination have come closer to measuring a complete set of productive characteristics. These studies will be discussed in the following subsection.

OCCUPATIONAL SEGREGATION AND WAGE DISCRIMINATION   Among black workers who are employed, analyses similar to those for women can be made to measure the extent of occupational segregation and the degree to which measurable productive characteristics explain the black/white gap in earnings. Occupational segregation appears to be less prevalent by race than by gender. Recent studies that calculated indices of occupational dissimilarity by both race and gender found that the indices comparing black and white occupational distributions had values roughly *half* the size of indices comparing male/female occupational distributions. While racial occupational dissimilarities are smaller and have fallen faster over time than gender-related ones, economists continue to study what role, if any, discrimination plays in generating occupational differences by race.[20]

Turning to the issue of *wage discrimination*, researchers have attempted to determine what factors are most responsible for the large gap that exists between blacks and whites. Analyses that use conventional data on education, experience, age, hours of work, region, occupation, industry, and firm size conclude that these easily measured factors account for much, but clearly not all, of the observed earnings gap between black and white men. One study, for example, estimated that if black men had the same conventionally measured productive characteristics (including occupation) as white men, they would receive earnings 89 percent of those received by whites.[21] As in the case of gender earnings differentials, however, one is left with the question of whether the remaining 11 percent differential reflects current wage discrimination or unmeasured productive characteristics.

One normally unmeasured productive characteristic that plays a key role in "explaining" black/white wage differentials is cognitive achievement, as measured by scores on the Armed Forces Qualification Test (AFQT). Black Americans have lower AFQT scores, on average, which one study attributes to poorer-quality

---

[20]Andrew M. Gill, "Incorporating the Cause of Occupational Differences in Studies of Racial Wage Differentials," *Journal of Human Resources* 29, no. 1 (Winter 1994): 20–41. Also see James S. Cunningham and Nadja Zalokar, "The Economic Progress of Black Women, 1940–1980: Occupational Distribution and Relative Wage," *Industrial and Labor Relations Review* 45 (April 1992): 540–555, and Mary C. King, "Occupational Segregation by Race and Sex."

[21]Francine D. Blau and Lawrence M. Kahn, "Race and Gender Pay Differentials," in *Research Frontiers in Industrial Relations and Human Resources,* ed. David Lewin, Olivia S. Mitchell, and Peter D. Sherer (Madison, Wis.: Industrial Relations Research Association, 1992), 381–416.

schooling and the influences of poverty on home and neighborhood characteristics.[22] Studies that are able to include AFQT scores among their measures of productive characteristics have been limited to young people, but they generally estimate that differences in cognitive achievement alone explain at least two-thirds of the overall black/white earnings gap. Typically, these analyses conclude that if AFQT scores and other productive characteristics were equalized, the wages of young black Americans would fall somewhere in the range of 8 percent less to 8 percent more than those of comparable whites.[23]

The effects of differences in cognitive achievement levels are clearly serious. Gaps between black and white Americans in schooling attainment and measured school quality (expenditures per pupil, for example) have narrowed considerably in recent decades, although the effects of these gains have been masked by increased relative wages of workers with the highest levels of educational attainment.[24] Differences in AFQT scores remain substantial, however, and the uncertain ability of additional schooling resources to influence cognitive achievement (see Chapter 9) raises questions about how public policies can now help to equalize achievement scores. Moreover, as long as black unemployment rates are twice those of whites, blacks will continue to fall short of whites, on average, in terms of job experience and the tenure-related benefits of on-the-job training.[25]

EARNINGS DIFFERENCES BY ETHNICITY

Increased immigration has sparked a renewed interest in the relative earnings of various ancestral groups in the United States, most especially because the earnings differences are so pronounced. Table 12.6 contains earnings data on men, aged 25 to 54, from the 1980 *Census of Population*. The first column displays full-time earnings of American-born men from selected ancestral groups relative to the

---

[22]Derek Neal and William Johnson, "The Role of Premarket Factors in Black-White Wage Differences," working paper no. 5124, National Bureau of Economic Research, Cambridge, Mass., May 1995. Independent studies have shown the AFQT to be an unbiased measure of basic cognitive skills.

[23]June O'Neill, "The Role of Human Capital in Earnings Differences Between Black and White Men," *Journal of Economic Perspectives* 4 (Fall 1990): 25–46; Gill, "Incorporating the Cause of Occupational Differences in Studies of Racial Wage Differentials"; and Nan L. Maxwell, "The Effect on Black-White Wage Differences of Differences in the Quantity and Quality of Education," *Industrial and Labor Relations Review* 47, no. 2 (January 1994): 249–264.

[24]O'Neill, "The Role of Human Capital in Earnings Differences Between Black and White Men," 29–32; James P. Smith and Finis Welch, "Black Economic Progress After Myrdal," *Journal of Economic Literature* 27 (June 1989): 519–564; David Card and Alan Krueger, "School Quality and Black-White Relative Earnings: A Direct Assessment," *Quarterly Journal of Economics* 107 (February 1992): 151–200; and Francine D. Blau and Andrea H. Beller, "Black–White Earnings Over the 1970s and 1980s: Gender Differences in Trends," *Review of Economics and Statistics* 74 (May 1992): 276–286.

[25]Edwin A. Sexton and Reed Neil Olsen, "The Returns to On-the-Job Training: Are They the Same for Blacks and Whites?" *Southern Economic Journal* 61, no. 2 (October 1994): 328–342.

TABLE 12.6

Earnings Differences, by Ancestry, of U.S.-Born Males, Ages 25 to 54, 1979

Ancestral Group	Earnings as a Percent of U.S. Average	Estimated Earnings as a Percent of U.S. Average If Productive Characteristics of Group Were Average
U.S. total	100	100
Mexican	83	94
Puerto Rican	84	97
Other Spanish (incl. Cuban)	91	93
Chinese	115	87
Japanese	113	94
Native American	82	88
Austrian	126	106
Canadian	101	100
English	103	101
German	104	101
Hungarian	119	108
Irish	105	103
Italian	109	106
Russian	139	108

SOURCE: Reynolds Farley, "Blacks, Hispanics, and White Ethnic Groups: Are Blacks Uniquely Disadvantaged?" *American Economic Review* 80 (May 1990): 239 (Table 2).

U. S. average, and from it one can note the relatively high earnings of men whose ancestry was Russian, Austrian, Hungarian, Chinese, or Japanese. Conversely, men whose ancestry is Native American, Mexican, or Puerto Rican had especially low earnings.

Drawing upon our discussion of earnings differences across gender and race, we must ask to what extent these differences resulted from different levels of productive characteristics. Educational attainment, for example, across ethnic groups is widely divergent. Men of Austrian, Chinese, and Russian ancestry had average levels of college attainment twice the national average of 1.7 years in 1980, while men from Puerto Rican and Mexican backgrounds had average levels that were under half the national average. The second column in Table 12.6 presents estimates of what earnings in each group would have been if observed productive characteristics, including education, were equalized across all groups. The results suggest that if observed productive characteristics were equalized, men of Hungarian and Russian ancestry would have earned 8 percent more than average, while those of Chinese and Native American ancestry would have earned roughly 12 percent less.[26]

Because of social concern about labor market discrimination, it is natural to focus on groups whose earnings appear to be low, given their productive characteristics. In recent years, however, there has also been interest in the diversity of earnings across white ethnic groups, for which discrimination is of less concern. Of particular interest is whether there are unmeasured qualitative differences in education or background that differ across ethnic groups. Indeed, recent studies have found evidence that there are important intergenerational transfers of "ethnic human capital," some of which is manifest in divergent rates of return to education.[27]

Research interest in ancestral groups that are suspected victims of labor market discrimination have centered on "Hispanics," a categorization including people from such diverse backgrounds as Mexican, Puerto Rican, Cuban, and Central and South American. While these groups share a common linguistic heritage, one can see from Table 12.6 that they have somewhat different earnings and human capital levels, even if American-born. Aggregating these groups into one is convenient for purposes of research, because it permits samples of *yearly* data large enough to support research, but it misses some of the cultural differences highlighted just above when discussing earnings by ancestry.

The influx of Spanish-speaking immigrants into the United States in the past two decades or so has resulted in the growth of a group of workers characterized by its youth, low levels of education, inexperience in the American labor market, and relatively low levels of proficiency in English. Motivated in part by concerns about discrimination, recent research on earnings differences between Hispanics and non-Hispanic whites has focused on the effects of English-language proficiency on earnings. Language proficiency is not measured in the data sets normally used to analyze earnings, yet it clearly affects one's productivity in just about any job; hence, if measures of it are omitted from the analysis, one cannot conclude anything about the presence or absence of discrimination against immigrant groups.

The handful of studies that have had access to data on language proficiency estimate that equalizing all productive characteristics, including language profi-

---

[26]An analysis of wage differences in rural America estimates that equalizing the productive characteristics of Native Americans would result in their earning 3 to 7 percent less than rural whites. See Jean Kimmel, "Rural Wages and Returns to Education: Differences Between Whites, Blacks, and American Indians," staff working paper no. 94–27, W. E. Upjohn Institute for Employment Research, July 1994. Similar findings come from a study of native groups in Canada; see Peter George and Peter Kuhn, "The Size and Structure of Native–White Wage Differentials in Canada," *Canadian Journal of Economics* 27, no. 1 (February 1994): 20–42.

[27]George J. Borjas, "Ethnic Capital and Intergenerational Mobility," *Quarterly Journal of Economics* 107 (February 1992): 123–150, and Barry R. Chiswick, "The Skills and Economic Status of American Jewry: Trends Over the Last Half-Century," *Journal of Labor Economics* 11, no. 1, pt. 1 (January 1993): 229–242. Chiswick finds that rates of return to education among Jewish workers are especially high, which could help to account for the earnings "premiums" received by those of Hungarian and Russian ancestry.

ciency, would bring the earnings of Hispanics up to within 3 to 6 percent of those received by non-Hispanic whites.[28] Reading proficiency appears to be a more important determinant of earnings than speaking proficiency.

Taken together, various recent studies of Hispanic earnings suggest modest, but notable, effects on earnings of either unmeasured differences or labor market discrimination, once English proficiency is accounted for. The 3 to 6 percent difference noted above roughly matches the 3 to 7 percent differentials noted in Table 12.6 for American-born Hispanic men, for whom English proficiency can be presumed.

Theories of Market Discrimination

As argued in the previous section, we cannot rule out the presence of discrimination against women and minorities in the labor market. Before designing policies to end discrimination, however, we must understand the *sources* and *mechanisms* causing it. The goal of this section is to lay out and evaluate the different theories of discrimination proposed by economists.

Three general sources of labor market discrimination have been hypothesized, and each source suggests an associated model of how discrimination is implemented and what its consequences are. The first source of discrimination is *personal prejudice*, wherein employers, fellow employees, or customers dislike associating with workers of a given race or sex.[29] The second general source is *statistical prejudgment*, whereby employers project onto *individuals* certain perceived *group* characteristics. Finally, there are models based on the presence of *noncompetitive* forces in the labor market. While all the models generate useful, suggestive insights, we will see that none has been convincingly established as superior.

PERSONAL-PREJUDICE MODELS

The models based on personal prejudice assume that either employers, customers, or employees have "prejudicial tastes"; that is, they have preferences for not associating with members of certain demographic groups. Such models assume the existence of competitive labor markets, in that firms are seen as "wage takers," and they analyze the wage and employment implications of these prejudicial tastes. We begin with a discussion of the model in which employer tastes are the source of the discrimination.

---

[28]David E. Bloom and Gilles Grenier, "The Earnings of Linguistic Minorities: French in Canada and Spanish in the United States," *Quarterly Journal of Economics* 106 (May 1991): 557–586, Francisco L. Rivera-Batiz, "English Language Proficiency and the Economic Progress of Immigrants," *Economic Letters* 34 (1990): 295–300; and Barry R. Chiswick, "Speaking, Reading and Earnings Among Low-Skilled Immigrants," *Journal of Labor Economics* 9 (April 1991): 149–170. See also Barry R. Chiswick and Paul W. Miller, "The Endogeneity Between Language and Earnings: International Analyses," *Journal of Labor Economics* 13, no. 2 (April 1995): 246–288.

[29]The models of personal prejudice are based on Gary S. Becker, *The Economics of Discrimination*, 2d ed. (Chicago: University of Chicago Press, 1971).

EMPLOYER DISCRIMINATION Suppose that white male *employers* are prejudiced against women and minorities but (for simplicity's sake) that customers and fellow employees are not prejudiced. This prejudice may take the form of aversion to associating with women and minorities, it may be manifested as a desire to help fellow white males whenever possible, or it may be motivated by status considerations and take the form of occupational segregation. In whatever form, this prejudice is assumed to result in the discriminatory treatment of women and minorities. Further, we assume for the purposes of this model that the women and minorities in question have the same productive characteristics as white males. (This assumption directs our focus to market discrimination by putting aside premarket factors.)

If employers have a decided preference for hiring white males in high-paying jobs despite the availability of equally qualified women and minorities, they will act *as if* the latter were less productive than the former. By virtue of our assumption that the women and minorities involved are equally productive in every way, the devaluing of their productivity by employers is purely subjective and is a manifestation of personal prejudice. The more prejudiced an employer is, the more actual productivity will be discounted.

Suppose that MRP stands for the actual marginal revenue productivity of all workers in a particular labor market and d represents the extent to which this productivity is subjectively devalued for minorities and women. In this case, market equilibrium for white males is reached when their wage (W_M) equals MRP:

$$MRP = W_M \tag{12.1}$$

For the women and minorities, however, equilibrium is achieved only when their wage (W_F) equals their *subjective* value to firms:

$$MRP - d = W_F, \tag{12.2}$$

or

$$MRP = W_F + d \tag{12.2a}$$

Since the actual marginal revenue productivities are equal by assumption, equations (12.1) and (12.2a) are equal to each other, and one can easily see that W_F must be less than W_M:

$$W_M = W_F + d, \tag{12.3}$$

or

$$W_F = W_M - d \tag{12.3a}$$

What this says algebraically has a very simple economic logic: if the actual productivity of women and minorities is devalued by employers, workers in these

FIGURE 12.2

Equilibrium Employment of Women or Minorities in Firms That Discriminate

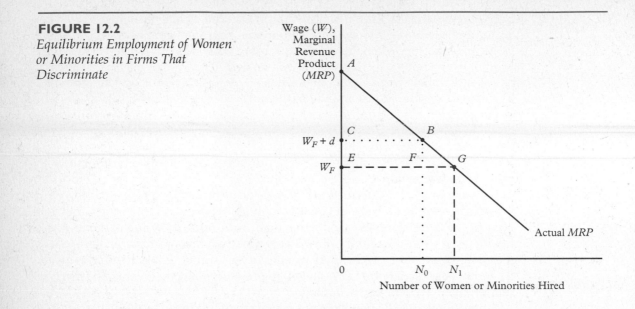

groups must offer their services at lower wages than white males to compete for jobs.

This model of employer discrimination has two major implications, as illustrated by Figure 12.2, which is a graphic representation of equation (12.2a). Figure 12.2 shows that a discriminatory employer faced with a market wage rate of W_F for women and minorities will hire N_0, for at that point $MRP = W_F + d$. *Profit-maximizing* employers, however, will hire N_1; that is, they will hire until $MRP = W_F$. The effects on profits can be readily seen in Figure 12.2 if one remembers that the area under the MRP curve represents total revenues of the firm, with capital held constant. Subtracting the area representing the wage bill of the discriminatory employer ($0EFN_0$) yields profits for these employers equal to the area $AEFB$. Profits for a nondiscriminatory employer, however, are AEG. These latter employers hire women and minorities to the point where their marginal product equals their wage, while the discriminators end their hiring short of that point. Discriminators thus give up profits in order to indulge their prejudices.

The second implication of our employer discrimination model concerns the size of the gap between W_M and W_F. The determinants of this gap can best be understood by moving from the analysis of a firm to an analysis of the *market* demand curve for women or minorities. In Figure 12.3, the market's demand for women or minorities is expressed in terms of their wage rate *relative* to the wage for white males. The figure assumes that there are a number of nondiscriminatory employers, who will hire up to N_a women or minorities at a relative wage of unity (that is, at $W_F = W_M$). For those employers with discriminatory preferences, W_F must fall below W_M to induce them to hire women or minorities. These employers are assumed to differ in their preferences, with some willing to hire women or minori-

FIGURE 12.3
Market Demand for Women or Minorities as a Function of Relative Wages

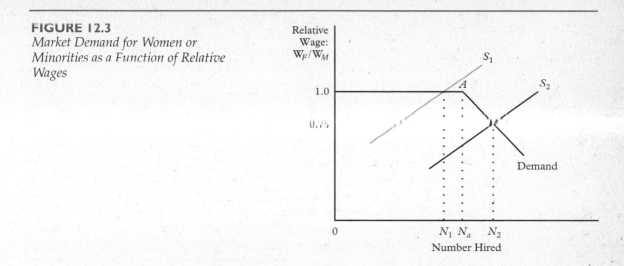

ties at small wage differentials and others requiring larger ones. Thus, the market's relative demand curve is assumed to bend downward at point *A*, reflecting the fact that to employ an increased number of women or minorities would require a fall in W_F relative to W_M.

If the supply of women or minorities is relatively small (supply curve S_1 in Figure 12.3), then such workers will all be hired by nondiscriminatory employers and there will be no wage differential. If the number of women or minorities seeking jobs is relatively large (see supply curve S_2), then some discriminatory employers will have to be induced to hire women or minorities, driving W_F down below W_M. In Figure 12.3, combining supply curve S_2 with the demand curve drives the relative wage down to 0.75.

Besides changes in the labor supply curves of women or minorities, there are two other factors that can cause the "market" differential between W_F and W_M to change. First, given the supply curve, if the number of nondiscriminators were to increase, as shown in Figure 12.4, the wage differential would decrease. The increase in the nondiscriminators shows up graphically in the figure as an extension of the horizontal segment of the demand curve to *A'*, and the relative wage is driven up (to 0.85 in the figure). Behaviorally, the influx of nondiscriminators absorbs more of supply than before, leaving fewer workers who must find employment with discriminatory employers. Moreover, the few who must still find work with discriminatory employers are able to bypass the worst discriminators and can go to work for those with smaller preferences for discrimination.

Second, the same rise in W_F relative to W_M could occur if the number of prejudiced employers stayed the same but their discriminatory preferences were reduced. Such reduction would show up graphically as a flattening of the downward-sloping part of the market's relative demand curve, shown in Figure 12.5. The changes hypothesized in this figure cause W_F to rise relative to W_M, because the inducement required by each discriminatory employer to hire women or minorities is now smaller.

The most disturbing implication of the employer discrimination model is that discriminators seem to be maximizing *utility* (satisfying their prejudicial preferences) instead of *profits*. This practice should immediately raise the question of how they survive. Firms in competitive product markets *must* maximize profits just to make a normal rate of return on invested capital. Those who do not make this return will find they can earn a better return by investing some other way—a way, perhaps, that does not involve hiring workers. Conversely, since profit-maximizing (nondiscriminatory) firms would normally make more money from a given set of assets than would discriminators, we should observe nondiscriminatory firms buying out others and gradually taking over the market. In short, if competitive forces were at work in the product market, firms that discriminate would be punished and discrimination could not persist unless their owners were willing to accept below-market rates of return.

Because a firm that discriminates will have higher costs than one that doesn't, theory suggests that employer discrimination is most likely to persist when owners or managers have the ability and the incentive to pursue a goal other than profit maximization. Firms with the "luxury" of not having to maximize profits in order to stay in business are those that have at least some degree of monopoly power in their product markets, and these very same firms are likely to have their prices (or key practices) regulated by a public agency. Thus, firms with product-market monopoly power have both the opportunity and the *incentive* to indulge in utility-maximizing—as opposed to profit-maximizing—behaviors, because by indulging in wasteful practices they can "hide" excess profits from the public.

Studies have found evidence of more discrimination in regulated, monopolized product markets.[30] One, for example, found that in the regulated banking industry, the fewer banks there were competing in a geographical area, the smaller the share of female employment was. Another found that when the federal government deregulated the trucking industry by eliminating restrictions on the entry of new firms, the increased competition among trucking firms was associated with a reduction in the wage premium received by white relative to black drivers. These findings are consistent with the implications of the employer discrimination model.

CUSTOMER DISCRIMINATION A second personal-prejudice model stresses *customer* prejudice as a source of discrimination. Customers may prefer to be

---

[30]Orley Ashenfelter and Timothy Hannan, "Sex Discrimination and Product Market Competition: The Case of the Banking Industry," *Quarterly Journal of Economics* 101 (February 1986): 149–173; and James Peoples Jr. and Lisa Saunders, "Trucking Deregulation and the Black/White Wage Gap," *Industrial and Labor Relations Review* 47, no. 1 (October 1993): 23–35. Also see James Peoples Jr., "Monopolistic Market Structure, Unionization, and Racial Wage Differentials," *Review of Economics and Statistics* 76, no. 1 (February 1994): 207–211.

FIGURE 12.4

Effects on Relative Wages of an Increased Number of Nondiscriminatory Employers

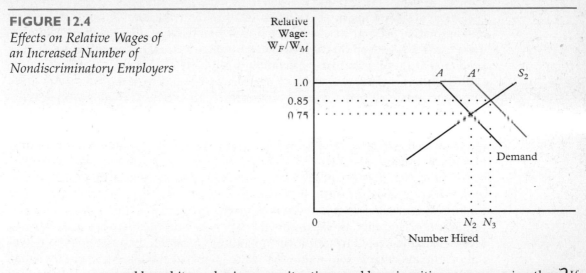

served by white males in some situations and by minorities or women in others. If their preferences for white males extend to jobs requiring major responsibility, such as physician or airline pilot, and their preferences for women and minorities are confined to less responsible jobs—receptionist or flight attendant, say—then occupational segregation that works to the disadvantage of women and minorities will occur. Further, if women or minorities are to find employment in the jobs for which customers prefer white males, they must either accept *lower wages* or be *more qualified* than the average white male. The reason for this is that their value to the firm is lower than that of *equally qualified* white males because of customers' preferences for white males.

One of the implications of customer discrimination is that it will lead to segregated workplaces, at least in the occupations with high customer contact. Firms

FIGURE 12.5

Effects on Relative Wages of a Decline in the Discriminatory Preferences of Employers

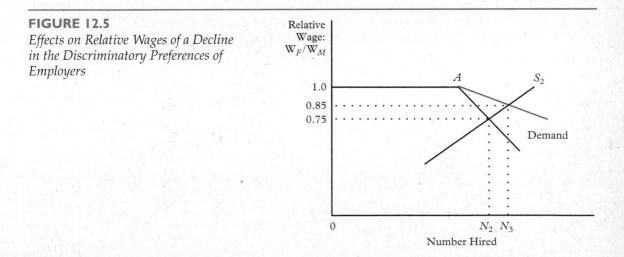

that cater to discriminatory customers will hire the "preferred" group of workers, pay higher wages, and charge higher prices than firms that employ workers from disfavored groups and that serve nondiscriminatory customers. While one might predict that the discriminatory customers would be driven by higher prices to change their behavior, the goods or services associated with their discriminatory preferences may represent a small proportion of their overall consumption expenditures. Hence, they may not find it sufficiently attractive to change their ways, and customer discrimination may continue despite the costs to both the discriminators and the victims. (See Example 12.2 for a discussion of customer discrimination in professional sports.)

It is clear that the presence of customer discrimination will reduce earnings for disfavored groups differently in different occupations, depending on customers' prejudices regarding each. An obvious group to analyze is the self-employed, a group whose incomes are both directly dependent on the behavior of customers and clearly unaffected by employer prejudices. A careful analysis of 1980 census data estimated that if self-employed black men had the same characteristics as self-employed white men in 1980, they would have earned about 19 percent less.[31] Customer discrimination thus cannot be ruled out. Moreover, it is notable that this 19 percent "residual" gap among the self-employed was greater than the 11 percent gap the same study estimated for otherwise comparable black and white salaried employees!

EMPLOYEE DISCRIMINATION A third source of discrimination based on personal prejudice might be found on the supply side of the market, where white male workers may avoid situations in which they will have to interact with minorities or women in ways they consider distasteful. For example, they may resist taking orders from a woman, sharing responsibility with a minority member, or working where women or minorities are not confined to low-status jobs.

If white male workers, for example, have discriminatory preferences, they will tend to quit or avoid employers who hire and promote on a nondiscriminatory basis. Employers who wish to employ workers in a nondiscriminatory fashion, therefore, would have to pay white males a wage premium (a compensating wage differential) to keep them.

If employers were nondiscriminatory, however, why would they pay a premium to keep white males when they could hire equally qualified and less expen-

---

[31]George Borjas and Stephen G. Bronars, "Consumer Discrimination and Self-Employment," *Journal of Political Economy* 97 (June 1989): 581–605. Stephen Coate and Sharon Tennyson, "Labor Market Discrimination, Imperfect Information and Self-Employment," *Oxford Economic Papers* 44, no. 2 (April 1992): 272–288, argues that part of the lower returns to self-employment could represent a "spillover" from labor market discrimination, whatever its source.

EXAMPLE 12.2

Customer Discrimination and Professional Sports

Evidence of customer discrimination by sports fans has recently been documented. The most direct evidence comes from a study of baseball card prices. Controlling for player performance along a variety of dimensions, it was found that the cards for retired white players sold for 10 to 13 percent more than the cards for retired nonwhite players with comparable performance measures. (Happily, a study of "rookie" cards for current players shows no race-related price differentials, which may imply that younger fans do not have prejudicial tastes.)

Although the effects of discrimination on sports card prices are hardly one of society's larger problems, fan discrimination appears to have a more serious effect on the salaries paid by National Basketball Association teams. While 72 percent of NBA players are black, and while overall average salaries are equal for blacks and whites, there is evidence from two studies that if black and white players were equally skilled, the white players would earn from 16 to 23 percent more. That is, if white and black players are matched, so that they have the same offensive and defensive statistics and the same experience, white players average from one-sixth to one-fourth more in salary. Why?

Discrimination among basketball fans may be at least part of the answer. These same studies found that replacing a black player with a white one of equal skill raised attendance and revenues by amounts roughly comparable to the 16–23 percent premium paid to whites! Moreover, teams appeared to respond to fan prejudice in another way: in the three NBA cities with the largest proportion of white residents, 39 percent of the players were white; in the three NBA cities with the lowest proportion of white residents, only 18 percent of the players were white.

SOURCES: Clark Nardinelli and Curtis Simon, "Customer Racial Discrimination in the Market for Memorabilia: The Case of Baseball," *Quarterly Journal of Economics* 105 (August 1990): 575–595; Paul E. Gabriel, Curtis Johnson, and Timothy J. Stanton, "An Examination of Customer Racial Discrimination in the Market for Baseball Memorabilia," *Journal of Business* 68, no. 2 (April 1995): 215–230; Lawrence Kahn and Peter Sherer, "Racial Differences in Professional Basketball Players' Compensation," *Journal of Labor Economics* 6 (January 1988): 40–61; Timothy Tregarthen, "Racism in the NBA: The Premium for White Players," *The Margin* 4 (March/April 1989): 4–6.

sive women or minorities? Put differently, how can *employee* discrimination survive if firms are profit-maximizing organizations? One answer is that white males constitute a large fraction of the labor force, so it is difficult to imagine producing without them. Moreover, the pressure for women and minorities to be employed outside of certain "traditional" occupations is relatively recent, so white males hired under one set of implicit promises relating to their future promotion possibilities now must adjust to a new set of competitors for positions within the firm. Firms realize that changing their practices involves reneging on past promises, and the loss of morale among long-time employees can impose costly losses on them if productivity or commitment to the firm declines. Thus, firms may seek to accommodate to the preferences for discrimination among their workers.[32] Put differently, employee discrimination may be costly to employers, but so is getting rid of it.

One way to accommodate to employee discrimination is to hire on a segregated basis, so that employees of different demographic backgrounds do not have to associate. While it is usually not economically feasible to completely segregate a plant, it *is* possible to segregate workers by job title. Thus, both the employee and the customer models of discrimination can help to explain the finding of one study that employers usually hire only women or only men into any single job title—even if *other* employers hire members of the opposite sex into that job title.[33]

As was the case for both the employer and the customer models of discrimination, there is also modest empirical support for the employee-discrimination model. The most direct test using contemporary data, for example, found that young whites in *racially integrated* workplaces earned higher wages than otherwise comparable white workers in segregated plants; interestingly, the study found that minorities *also* appear to demand higher wages when they must work with members of other racial or ethnic groups. However, the authors did not find corresponding wage differentials associated with integration by gender.[34]

STATISTICAL DISCRIMINATION

We discussed in Chapter 5 the need for employers to acquire information on their job applicants in one way or another, all of which entail some cost. Obviously, the firm will evaluate the *personal* characteristics of its applicants, but in seeking to guess their potential productivity it may also utilize information on the average characteristics of the *groups* to which they belong. If group characteristics are factored into the hiring decision, statistical discrimination can result (at least in the short run) even in the absence of personal prejudice.[35]

---

[32]For a more complete statement of this source of discrimination, see Steven Schulman, "Why Is the Black Unemployment Rate Always Twice As High As the White Unemployment Rate?"

[33]Erica Groshen, "The Structure of the Male/Female Wage Differential."

[34]James F. Ragan Jr. and Carol Horton Tremblay, "Testing for Employee Discrimination by Race and Sex," *Journal of Human Resources* 23, no. 1 (Winter 1988): 123–137. A recent study of employee discrimination in a historical setting can be found in David Buffum and Robert Whaples, "Fear and Lathing in the Michigan Furniture Industry: Employee-Based Discrimination a Century Ago," *Economic Inquiry* 33, no. 2 (April 1995): 234–252.

[35]The considerations developed in this section are more formally and completely treated in Dennis J. Aigner and Glen G. Cain, "Statistical Theories of Discrimination in Labor Markets," *Industrial and Labor Relations Review* 30, no. 2 (January 1977): 175–187. A similar theory is developed in M. A. Spence, "Job Market Signaling," *Quarterly Journal of Economics* 87, no. 3 (August 1973): 355–374. Shelly J. Lundberg and Richard Startz, "Private Discrimination and Social Intervention in Competitive Labor Markets," *American Economic Review* 73, no. 3 (June 1983): 340–347, consider the social gains that can theoretically be obtained from regulating a labor market characterized by statistical discrimination.

Employers rarely know what the actual productivity of an individual applicant will be. The only information available to them at the time of hire is information that is thought to be *correlated* with productivity: education, experience, age, test scores, and so forth. These correlates are imperfect predictors of actual productivity, however, and employers realize this. To some extent, then, they supplement information on these correlates with a subjective element in making hiring decisions, and this subjective element could have the effects of discrimination even though it might not be rooted in personal prejudice.

Statistical discrimination can be viewed as a part of the *screening problem,* which arises when observable personal characteristics that are correlated with productivity are not perfect predictors. By way of example, suppose two types of workers apply for a secretarial job: those who can type 70 words per minute (wpm) over the long haul and those who can type 40 wpm. These actual productivities are unknown to the employer, however. All the employer observes are the results of a five-minute typing test administered to all applicants. What are the problems created by the use of this test as a screening device?

The problems relate to the fact that some typists who can really type only 40 wpm on the job will be lucky and score higher than 40 on the test. Others who can really type 70 wpm on the job will be unlucky and score less than 70 on the test. The imperfection of the test as a predictor will cause two kinds of errors in hiring decisions: some "good" applicants will be rejected, and some "bad" workers will be hired.

Figure 12.6 shows the test-score distributions for both groups of workers. Those who can actually type 70 wpm score 70 on average, but half score less. Likewise, half of the other group score better than 40 on the test. If an applicant scores 55, say, the employer does not know if the applicant is a good (70 wpm) or bad (40 wpm) typist. If those scoring 55 are automatically rejected, the firm will be rejecting some good workers, and if it needs workers badly, this policy will entail costs. Likewise, if it accepts those scoring 55, some bad workers will be hired.

In an effort to avoid the above dilemma, suppose the employer does some research and finds out that applicants from a particular business school are specifically

FIGURE 12.6
The Screening Problem

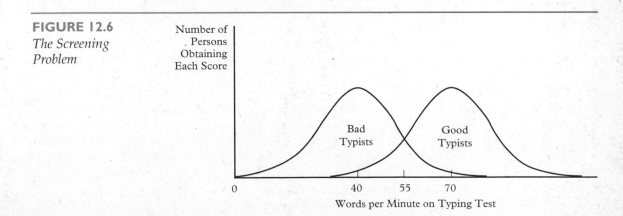

coached to perform well on five-minute typing tests. Thus, applicants who can actually type X words per minute over a normal day will tend to score *higher* than X wpm on a five-minute test because of the special coaching (that is, they will appear better than they really are). Recognizing that students from this school will have average test scores above their long-run productivity, the firm might decide to reject all applicants from this school who score 55 or below (on the grounds that, for most, the test score overestimates their ability), even though some who score less than 55 really can do better.

The general lesson of this example is that, in effect, firms will use both *individual* data (test scores, educational attainment, experience) and *group* data in making hiring decisions when the former are not perfect predictors of productivity. However, this use of group data can give rise to market discrimination because people with the same *measured productive characteristics* (test scores, education, etc.) will be treated differently on a systematic basis depending on *group* affiliation.

The relevance of the above discussion to the problem of discrimination against minorities and women is that race and gender may well be the group information used to supplement individual data in making hiring decisions. If the group data bear no relationship to actual productivity, or if the screening devices used are known to be less predictive for some groups than others, then we really have a case of discrimination rooted in personal prejudice. However, we have shown that the use of group data to modify individual information may be based on nonmalicious grounds. Might these grounds legitimately apply from an employer's perspective to minorities and women?

Suppose that, *on average*, minorities with high school educations are discovered to be less productive than white males with high school educations owing to differences in schooling quality. Or suppose that, because of shortened career lives, women with a given education level are, *on average*, less valuable to firms than men of equal education (refer to our discussion of women and job training in Chapters 5 and 9). Employers might employ this group information to modify individual data when making hiring decisions, just as they did in our hypothetical example of the business school above. The result would be that white males with given measured characteristics would be systematically preferred over women or minorities with the same characteristics, a condition that would be empirically identified as labor market discrimination.

One unfortunate side effect of using group data to supplement individual data is that, while it could lead employers to the correct hiring decisions on average, it assigns a group characteristic to people who may not be typical of the group. There are women who will have long, uninterrupted careers, just as there undoubtedly would be graduates of the business school mentioned above who do not test well and thus perform more poorly on tests than they could do on the job. There will also be minority high school graduates of substantial ability who would have gone to college had not family poverty intervened. These atypical group members are stigmatized by the use of group data. They may have actual productivity equal to that of those who are hired, but because of the group association they do not get the job.[36]

Thus, *statistical discrimination* could lead to a systematic preference for white males over others with the same *measured* characteristics, and it could also create a situation in which minorities or women who are the equals of white males in *actual* productivity are paid less because of the above-mentioned group stigma. Both problems are caused by the use of group data in making hiring decisions, but this use need not be motivated by prejudice. The results, however, have the same appearance and effects as if prejudice were present.

An important implication of this model of statistical discrimination is that the use of group data will become a more costly screening device as members of each group become more dissimilar. For example, as greater proportions of women desire to work in full-time, year-round careers and do not intend to drop out of the labor force to raise children, employers using gender as a handy index of labor force attachment will find themselves making costly mistakes. They will reject many female applicants who have a permanent labor force attachment (in whom an investment in specific training would be very worthwhile), and they may accept male applicants who are less productive. In either case, firms using incorrect screening devices will have lower profits than those that adopt appropriate screens. Thus, as unmeasured differences within the relevant demographic groups widen, the use of race or sex *group* data should lessen and statistical discrimination should gradually disappear.

NONCOMPETITIVE MODELS OF DISCRIMINATION

The discriminatory models discussed so far have traced out the wage and employment implications of personal preferences or informational problems for labor markets in which firms were assumed to be wage takers. The rather diverse models to which we now turn are all based on the assumption that individual firms have some degree of influence over the wages they pay, either through *collusion* or through some source of *monopsonistic* power.

CROWDING [The existence and extent of occupational segregation, especially by gender, have caused some to argue that it is the result of a deliberate *crowding* policy intended to lower wages in certain occupations. Graphically, the "crowding hypothesis" is very simple and can be easily seen in

---

[36]The discussion here has obvious relevance to the "signaling" issue discussed in Chapter 9. Minorities, for example, may be *too poor* to acquire the necessary "signal" in many cases where their ability would indicate they should. See Edward P. Lazear and Sherwin Rosen, "Male-Female Wage Differentials in Job Ladders," for an application of a statistical discrimination model to *promotion* (but not the hiring) of women.

FIGURE 12.7
Labor Market "Crowding"

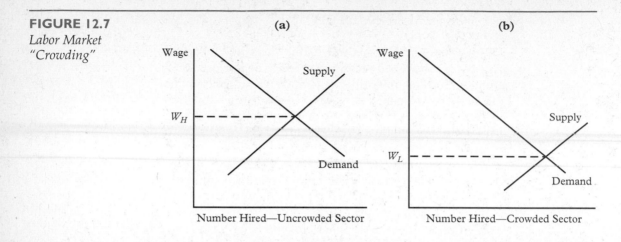

Figure 12.7. Panel (a) illustrates a market in which supply is small relative to demand and the wage (W_H) is thus relatively high. Panel (b) depicts a market in which crowding causes supply to be large relative to demand, resulting in a wage (W_L) that is comparatively low.

While the effects of crowding are easily seen, the phenomenon of crowding itself is less easily explained. If men and women were equally productive in a given job or set of jobs, for example, one would think that the lower wage of women caused by their being artificially crowded into certain jobs would make it attractive for firms now employing men in *other* jobs to replace them with less-expensive women workers; this profit-maximizing behavior should eventually eliminate any wage differential. The failure of crowding, or occupational segregation, to disappear suggests the presence of noncompeting groups (and therefore barriers to employee mobility), but we are still left with trying to explain why such groups exist in the first place. Over the past seventy years various possible explanations have been put forth: the establishment of some jobs as "male" and others as "female" through social custom, differences in aptitude that are either innate or acquired, and different supply curves of men and women to monopsonistic employers (discussed later). None of these explanations is complete in the sense of getting at the ultimate source of discrimination, but it is undeniable that the more female-dominated an occupation is, the lower its wages are, even after controlling for the human capital of the workers in it.[37]

---

[37]See Elaine Sorenson, "The Crowding Hypothesis and Comparable Worth." An excellent history of crowding theories is provided in Janice F. Madden, *The Economics of Sex Discrimination* (Lexington, Mass.: Lexington Books, 1973), 30–36. The crowding hypothesis is nicely advanced also in Barbara Bergmann, "The Effect on White Incomes of Discrimination in Employment," *Journal of Political Economy* 79 (March-April 1971): 294–313. For results related to the racial composition of occupations, see Barry T. Hirsch and Edward J. Schumacher, "Labor Earnings, Discrimination, and the Racial Composition of Jobs," *Journal of Human Resources* 27, no. 4 (Fall 1992): 602–628.

DUAL LABOR MARKETS A variant of the crowding hypothesis with more recent origins is the view, held by some economists, that there is a *dual labor market*. Dualists see the overall labor market as divided into two noncompeting sectors: a *primary* and a *secondary* sector. Jobs in the primary sector offer relatively high wages, stable employment, good working conditions, and opportunities for advancement. Secondary-sector jobs, however, tend to be low-wage, unstable, dead-end jobs with poor working conditions; the returns to education and experience are thought to be close to zero in this sector. Of key importance to the dualists' approach is that mobility between sectors is thought to be limited. Workers relegated to the secondary sector are tagged as unstable, undesirable workers and are thought to have little hope of acquiring primary-sector jobs.

Historically, dualists continue, a large proportion of minorities and women have been employed in the secondary sector, and this leads to perpetuation of discrimination against them. Minorities and women, it is argued, are discriminated against because they tend (as a group) to have unstable work histories, but these histories are themselves a result of being unable to break into the primary labor market.

The dual labor market description of discrimination does not really explain what initially caused women and minorities to be confined to secondary jobs. Some Marxist economists view the existence of noncompeting sectors as at least partially due to attempts by capitalists to divide labor and thus to discourage organized opposition to the capitalist system; this theory of discrimination is discussed later in the section on collusive behavior. Some economists operating within more neoclassical frameworks view the existence of two sectors, and the assignment of workers to the two sectors, as arising because of differences in monitoring costs between categories of workers.[38] As discussed in Chapter 11, firms may use "efficiency wages" or steeply sloped age/earnings profiles (characteristics of the primary sector) as compensation strategies to motivate workers and discourage shirking. These strategies deliberately encourage—and are predicated upon—a long-term relationship between workers and the firm. For workers with relatively short expected tenure, direct monitoring of work effort is required; there are no incentives for firms to adopt high-wage or deferred-compensation strategies.

To the extent that females have historically entered and left the labor force frequently (because of marriage and/or childbearing), an explanation of why they might initially have been assigned to the secondary sector is self-evident.[39] Why minorities were initially confined to the secondary sector is less obvious, especially since there is no theoretical or empirical evidence that, other things equal, turnover rates are higher or desired hours of work are lower among minorities.[40]

---

[38]See, for example, Jeremy Bulow and Lawrence Summers, "A Theory of Dual Labor Markets with Application to Industrial Policy, Discrimination, and Keynesian Unemployment," *Journal of Labor Economics* 4 (July 1986): 376–414.

[39]See Claudia Goldin, "Monitoring Costs and Occupational Segregation by Sex: A Historical Analysis," *Journal of Labor Economics* 4 (January 1986): 1–27.

[40]James Rebitzer, "Radical Political Economy and the Economics of Labor Markets," *Journal of Economic Literature* 31, no. 3 (September 1993): 1417.

Empirical evidence does suggest, however, that there are two distinct sectors of the labor market—one in which education and experience are associated with higher wages and one in which they are not—and that nonwhites are more likely to be in the latter sector.[41]

Such evidence in favor of the dual labor market hypothesis offers an explanation of why discrimination persists. It calls into question the levels of competition and mobility that exist and suggests that the initial existence of noncompeting race/sex groups will be self-perpetuating.[42] In short, the dual labor market hypothesis is consistent with any of the models of discrimination analyzed above; what it does suggest is that if any of these theories *are* applicable, we cannot count on natural market forces to eliminate the discrimination that results.

SEARCH-RELATED MONOPSONY The crowding and dual labor market explanations for discrimination are grounded in the assumption that workers are "assigned" to occupational groups from which mobility to other groups is severely restricted; how or why assignments are made is not entirely clear. A third model of restricted mobility, which was hinted at in discussions of both crowding and the dual labor market, is built around the presence of job search costs for employees.[43] This model combines a monopsonistic model of firm behavior, such as the one discussed in the final section of Chapter 10, with the phenomenon of prejudice discussed earlier.

Suppose that some, but not all, employers refuse to hire minorities or women owing to their own prejudices, those of their customers, or those of their employees. In contrast, no employers rule out the hiring of white males. Minorities and women looking for jobs do not readily know who will refuse them out of hand, so they have to search longer and harder than do white men to generate the same number of job offers. Put differently, the existence of at least some discriminatory employers increases the search costs of minorities and women, making them less mobile (other things equal) than white men. We saw at the end of Chapter 10 that employee search costs could create upward-sloping labor supply curves to individual employers, which increases the marginal costs of labor above the wage and induces monopsonistic behavior even in labor markets with many employers. We also saw that labor supply cuves that are more steeply sloped create a larger divergence between wages and marginal labor costs. Therefore, because profit-maximizing employers select employment levels at which marginal costs and marginal revenues of labor are equalized, groups of workers with more

---

[41]William Dickens and Kevin Lang, "A Test of Dual Labor Market Theory," *American Economic Review* 75 (September 1985): 792–805.

[42]That the forces of competition should at least gradually end arbitrary wage differentials is a consistent theme in economic analysis. However, the persistence of wage differentials across industries, even when all other measurable factors affecting wages are accounted for, represents another area in which some have argued that labor market outcomes are inconsistent with economic theory. See footnote 27 in Chapter 11 and William T. Dickens and Kevin Lang, "The Reemergence of Segmented Labor Market Theory," *American Economic Review* 78 (May 1988): 129–134.

[43]For a more rigorous discussion of this model, see Dan H. Black, "Discrimination in an Equilibrium Search Model," *Journal of Labor Economics* 13, no. 2 (April 1995): 309–334.

FIGURE 12.8
Search-Related Monopsony and Wage Discrimination

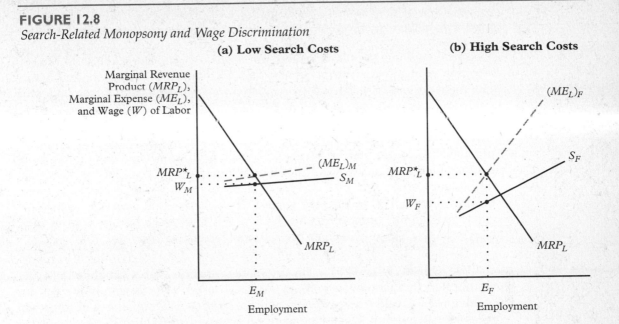

steeply sloped supply curves receive wages that are lower, relative to their marginal revenue product, than workers with flatter supply curves.

Figure 12.8 graphically illustrates the implications of a situation in which two groups of workers have the same productivity (that is, they both have a marginal revenue product of labor equal to MRP_L^*), but one group has higher search costs than the other. Panel (a) depicts the supply and the marginal-revenue-product-of-labor curves for the group (white males, presumably) with relatively low search costs. Because their search costs are low, a small wage cut would result in many workers leaving the firm, while a small wage increase would encourage many additional applicants from other firms. Therefore, the labor-supply curve of this group to their employers (S_M) is relatively flat, which also means that the associated *marginal* expense of labor curve, $(ME_L)_M$, is relatively flat. Profit-maximizing employers will hire E_M workers from this group and pay them a wage of W_M, which is only slightly below MRP_L^*.

Panel (b) illustrates the relevant curves for a group (minorities or women) with higher search costs created by the existence of prejudicial employers. These workers are assumed to have exactly the same marginal revenue product of labor, but their higher search costs imply a more steeply sloped labor-supply curve (S_F), a more steeply sloped marginal expense of labor curve, $(ME_L)_F$, and a greater divergence between marginal revenue product and the wage rate. E_F workers in this group are hired, and they are paid a wage of W_F. Comparing panels (a) and (b), it is readily seen that despite having the same marginal productivity, workers with higher search costs are paid lower wages (that is, $W_F < W_M$). At a practical level, if members of both groups are hired by a given firm, those with higher search costs may be placed into lower job titles.

Our discussion of search-related monopsony invites two comments. First, in Chapters 3 and 4 we introduced the monopsony model of labor demand as a potential source for the small and apparently uncertain responses of employment to *mandated* wage increases under minimum-wage laws, at least in the short run. Interestingly, the monopsony model has *also* been invoked to explain the lack of employment declines associated with mandated wage increases for women under the United Kingdom's Equal Pay Act of 1970.[44]

Second, if prejudice increases the job search costs for women and minorities, so that members of these groups are less likely to search for alternative offers of employment, their "job matches" (as discussed in Chapter 10) will be of lower quality than the job matches for white men. Higher search costs, then, mean that individual women and minority-group members are less likely to find the employers who can best utilize their talents. Thus, even within narrowly defined occupational groups, minorities and women will tend to be less productive, and receive less pay, than white men owing to poorer-quality matches.

COLLUSIVE BEHAVIOR Finally, some theories are grounded in an assumption that employers collude with each other to subjugate minorities (or women), thus creating a situation in which monopsonistic wages can be forced on the subjugated group. One of the more cogent and complete collusive theories of discrimination argues that prejudice and the conflicts it creates are inherent in a capitalist society because they serve the interests of owners.[45] Even if the owners of capital did not conspire to *create* prejudice, they nevertheless find that if it continues they can enhance their profits. Workers divided by race or gender are harder to organize and, if they *are* unionized, are less cohesive in their demands. Further, antagonisms on the shop floor deflect attention from grievances related to working conditions. Hence, it is argued that owners of capital gain, while *all* workers—but particularly minorities and women—lose from discrimination.

The collusive-behavior model raises some immediate questions. If discrimination is created or at least perpetuated by capitalists, how does one account for its existence in precapitalist or socialist societies? Further, it may be true that if all white employers conspire to keep women and minorities in low-wage, low-status jobs, they can all reap monopoly profits. However, if employers A through Y adhere to the agreement, employer Z will always have incentives to *break* the agreement! Z can hire women or minorities cheaply because of the agreement among *other* employers not to hire them, and Z can enhance profits by hiring these otherwise equally productive workers to fill jobs that A through Y are staffing with high-priced white males. Since every other employer has the same incentives as Z, the conspiracy will tend to break down unless cheaters can be disciplined in some

---

[44]Alan Manning, "The Equal Pay Act as an Experiment to Test Theories of the Labour Market," discussion paper no. 153, London School of Economics, Centre for Economic Performance, June 1993.

[45]Michael Reich, "The Economics of Racism," in *Problems in Political Economy: An Urban Perspective*, ed. David M. Gordon (Lexington, Mass.: D.C. Health, 1971), 107–113.

way. The collusive-behavior model does not tell us how the conspiracy is maintained and coordinated among the millions of U.S. employers.

EVALUATION OF DISCRIMINATION THEORIES

Our analysis of the different theories of discrimination suggests that current labor market discrimination is the result of forces that hinder *competition* or labor market *adjustments* to competitive forces. Some theories postulate the existence of noncompetitive elements at the outset. The "personal prejudice" theories do not, but they have trouble explaining how current labor market discrimination can persist in competitive markets. For example, the product market should punish those employers who discriminate or who fail to change their screening methods as the average characteristics of minorities or women change. In considering the persistence of practices that are costly, however, one must remember that there are costs of *eliminating* such practices as well; as noted earlier, firms that have hired whites or males with certain implied promises about their favored status regarding promotions may find it costly to renege on these promises by changing their employment practices.

It would thus appear that all models of discrimination agree on one thing: any persistence of labor market discrimination is the result of forces or motivations that are either noncompetitive or very slow to adjust to competitive forces. While no one model yet can be demonstrated to be superior to the others in explaining the facts, the various theories and the facts they seek to explain suggest that government intervention might be useful in eliminating the noncompetitive (or sluggish) influences.

Federal Programs to End Discrimination

The federal government has enforced two sets of rules in an attempt to eliminate market discrimination. One is a *nondiscrimination* requirement imposed on almost all employers. The other is a requirement that federal contractors engage in *affirmative action*—that is, actively seek out minorities and women to staff their vacancies.

EQUAL PAY ACT OF 1963

Over the years prior to the 1960s, sex discrimination was officially sanctioned by so-called *protective labor laws,* which limited women's total hours of work and prohibited them from working at night, lifting heavy objects, and working during pregnancy. Not all states placed all these restrictions on women, but the effect of these laws was to limit the access of women to many jobs. These laws were overturned by the Equal Pay Act of 1963, which also outlawed separate pay scales for men and women using similar skills and performing work under the same conditions.

The act was seriously deficient as an antidiscrimination tool, however, because it said nothing about equal opportunity in hiring and promotions. This flaw can be easily understood by a quick review of our theories of discrimination. If there is prejudice against women from whatever source, employers will treat female employees as if they were less productive or more costly to hire than equally productive males. The market response is for female wages to fall below male wages, because otherwise women cannot hope to be able to successfully compete with men in obtaining jobs. The Equal Pay Act took a step toward the elimination of wage differentials, but in so doing it tended to suppress a market mechanism that helped women obtain greater access to jobs.[46] The act failed to acknowledge that if labor market discrimination is to be eliminated, legislation must require *both* equal pay *and* equal opportunities in hiring and promotions for people of comparable productivity.

TITLE VII OF THE CIVIL RIGHTS ACT

Some defects in the Equal Pay Act of 1963 were corrected the next year. Title VII of the Civil Rights Act of 1964 made it unlawful for any employer "to refuse to hire or to discharge any individual, or otherwise to discriminate against any individual with respect to his compensation, terms, condition, or privileges of employment, because of such individual's race, color, religion, sex or national origin." Union practices were also addressed by the new legislation. Historically, it had been very difficult for racial minorities to obtain admission into certain craft unions representing workers in the skilled trades, an exclusion that denied minorities access to both the skills training provided through union apprenticeship programs and the employment opportunities dispensed through union hiring halls. Unions representing workers in large industries were generally more integrated, although in a few unions the quality of representation in collective bargaining and in the administration of the labor agreement varied by race. Title VII made it unlawful for any labor organization to exclude individuals from membership, to segregate membership, to refuse to refer for employment, or to discriminate in admission to apprenticeship programs on the basis of race, color, religion, sex, or national origin.

This broad statement of a national policy favoring nondiscriminatory employment practices was qualified in certain respects, however. First, Title VII was not retroactive; it was written to apply to acts of discrimination occurring after its effective date of July 2, 1965. Second, the law permits exceptions to its general requirement of nondiscrimination "where religion, sex, or national origin is a bona fide occupational qualification reasonably necessary to the normal operation of a business." In practice this applies to a limited number of situations (for example,

---

[46]Some critics of the Equal Pay Act of 1963 argued that its motivation was to help men compete with lower-paid women. See Nancy Barrett, "Women in the Job Market: Occupations, Earnings, and Career Opportunities," in *The Subtle Revolution*, ed. Ralph E. Smith (Washington, D.C.: Urban Institute, 1979), 55.

certain jobs in religious organizations, nursing homes in which the patients are of predominantly one sex, etc.). Third, Title VII permits an employer to differentiate wages and other employment conditions "pursuant to a bona fide seniority system . . . provided that such differences are not the result of an intention to discriminate." Finally, no party subject to the statute is required to grant preferential treatment to any group because of existing imbalances in the workforce. As will become clear below, the last two qualifications have raised difficult issues for the application of the law.

Title VII applies to all employers in interstate commerce with at least 15 employees and is enforced by the Equal Employment Opportunity Commission (EEOC), which has the authority to mediate complaints, encourage lawsuits by private parties or the U.S. attorney general, or (since 1972) bring suits itself against employers that have violated the law. In order to expand the impact of the law, the courts permitted individual plaintiffs to expand their suits into "class actions" in which the potential discriminatory impact of an organization's employment practices on an entire group of workers is assessed by the courts.

Over the years, the federal courts have fashioned two standards of discrimination that may be applied when discriminatory employment practices are alleged—*disparate treatment* and *disparate impact*. Disparate treatment occurs under Title VII if individuals are treated differently (for example, paid different wages or benefits) because of their race, sex, color, religion, or national origin, and if it can be shown that there was an intent to discriminate. While this is probably the more obvious approach to defining discrimination, it is not the definition that the courts have relied on most frequently. The difficulty raised by this standard is that personnel policies that appear to be neutral in the sense that they ignore race, gender, etc., may nevertheless perpetuate the effects of past discrimination. For example, word-of-mouth recruiting (a seemingly neutral policy) in a plant with a largely white workforce would be suspect under Title VII even if the selection of new employees from among the applicants was done on a nondiscriminatory basis, since the racial composition of the applicants is likely to be influenced by the recruiting method.

The concern with addressing the present effects of past discrimination led to the disparate impact standard. Under this approach it is the result, not the motivation, that matters. Personnel policies that appear to be neutral but lead to different impacts by race, gender, etc., are prohibited under Title VII unless they can be related to job performance.[47] For example, employers may use tests and educational standards to screen applicants, but these tests must be validated against job performance. In the words of the Supreme Court, "Tests must measure the person for the job; not the person in the abstract." Job application forms may ask about *convictions* but not *arrests* (arrest rates among minorities tend to be higher, but the courts reason that it is conviction that is important to the employer). Marital status cannot be

---

[47]*Griggs* v. *Duke Power Company* 401 U.S. 424 (1971). The Civil Rights Act of 1991 requires employers responding to demonstrations of disparate impact to prove that the policies having such impact are both job-related and serve a business necessity.

used as a screening device unless it is applied uniformly to both sexes and is clearly a job-related requirement. In interpreting Title VII, the federal courts have generally taken the position that neutral (for example, colorblind or sexblind) personnel practices that carry forward the effects of past discrimination constitute present discrimination. As a result, plaintiffs, employers, and the courts have become interested in how closely the race or gender composition of groups selected for employment, promotion, training, or termination accords with the race or gender composition of the pool of workers available for selection.

The adoption of the disparate impact standard by the courts as a standard of discrimination has mounted a significant challenge to employer personnel screening devices. As noted in Chapter 5, when it is extremely costly to ascertain the qualifications of individual applicants, employers have an incentive to rely on screening devices that sort job applicants on the basis of the "average" characteristics of a group, rather than according to individual merit. While the use of screening devices often results in lower costs of personnel administration, it also gives rise to the statistical discrimination discussed earlier in this chapter. In taking the position that workers must be judged on the basis of their individual abilities, rather than average group characteristics, the courts have launched a strong assault against mechanisms of statistical discrimination, and one consequence of this assault has been higher private costs of human resource management.[48]

In certain instances, the application of the disparate impact standard and other efforts to combat labor market discrimination have been limited by some of the express qualifications written into Title VII. In recent years two particularly difficult issues have arisen in the application of the law: the treatment of seniority arrangements perpetuating the effects of past discrimination and the adoption of a "comparable worth" standard by which to judge pay equality when occupations are segregated.

SENIORITY   Most unionized firms and many nonunion firms use seniority as a consideration in allocating promotion opportunities. Moreover, employees are frequently laid off in order of reverse seniority, the least-senior first, in a recession. It was partially in recognition of the historically important role of seniority in American personnel arrangements that Congress appeared to exempt seniority systems from challenge under Title VII. Yet seniority systems have the strong potential for perpetuating the effects of past discrimination. We have seen how occupational segregation—the tendency of women or minorities to be restricted to

---

[48]One must be careful to distinguish here between the costs to employers (*private* costs) and the costs to society (*social* costs) of statistical discrimination. Although employers' private costs for human resource management may be low because of statistical discrimination, the costs to society may be high if qualified applicants are rejected simply because of the group they are members of. While prohibiting statistical discrimination may increase the private costs of human resource management, it may decrease the social costs.

relatively low-wage jobs despite qualifications for higher positions—has been one historical mechanism of discrimination in the labor market.

In many instances, particularly in the South, job segregation was accompanied by departmental seniority arrangements. That is, seniority was computed as time employed in a department, not as time employed in the plant or company. When companies sought to break down historical patterns of job segregation to comply with Title VII, two types of adjustment occurred: women and minorities were moved within a company from low-wage jobs to higher-wage jobs in other departments, and women and minorities were hired by companies into some jobs for the first time. Under either mechanism, women and minorities ended up with relatively low seniority under departmental seniority systems.

Many of these adjustments occurred during the late 1960s, when the general demand for labor was high. With the less favorable economic circumstances of the 1970s, however, firms began to lay off workers, and under departmental seniority arrangements a disproportionate number of those laid off were minorities and women. In many of these cases, individuals with very little departmental seniority had more *plant* seniority than workers who retained their jobs in the high-wage departments, and they might have been able to retain their jobs if they had the seniority that they had accrued in their former departments. Departmental seniority arrangements resulted in a disparate impact on women and minorities and perpetuated the effects of past discrimination. The resulting Title VII litigation presented the courts with a quandary. Under the disparate impact standard, the seniority systems were discriminatory, but the language of Title VII explicitly permitted "bona fide seniority systems." The lower courts tended to resolve the quandary by taking the position that a seniority systems was not bona fide if it discriminated, and that under the prevailing definition of discrimination, only plant-wide seniority systems were bona fide. When the Supreme Court considered the issue, however, it reversed the appellate courts and held that the language in Title VII permitted even departmental seniority systems that perpetuated the effects of discrimination.[49]

Minorities and women who were hired for the first time following passage of Title VII were susceptible to layoff under either plant or departmental seniority. Some were individuals who had been victims of hiring discrimination prior to the passage of the law or who did not apply for employment earlier because the company had a reputation for discriminating. In litigation arising out of these cases, plaintiffs often argued that the appropriate remedy was an award of seniority retroactive to the date when the individual would have been hired if the company had not practiced discrimination. (This is sometimes referred to as "fictional seniority.") On this issue the Supreme Court has ruled that fictional seniority is an appropriate remedy for individuals who can demonstrate that they were victims of

---

[49]*International Brotherhood of Teamsters* v. *United States* 431 U.S. 324, 14 FEP 1514 (1977).

unlawful discrimination. However, the Supreme Court has argued that it is not appropriate to dismiss current employees as part of the remedy for past discrimination. It has also ruled that laying off more-senior white employees instead of more recently hired minorities in order to preserve racial balance is unconstitutional.[50]

COMPARABLE WORTH   Many contend that achieving "equal pay for equal work" would be a rather hollow victory, since occupations are so segregated by gender that men and women rarely do "equal work." As a result some have come to support the goal of equal pay for jobs of "comparable worth." Proponents of comparable worth can point to the fact that the "male" occupation of maintaining *machines* (general maintenance mechanic) pays $10 per hour, for example, while the "female" job of maintaining *children* (child-care worker) pays half that. Why, they might ask, should those who take care of human beings be paid less than those who take care of machines?

The stated goal of equalizing the pay of women and men according to the intrinsic "worth" of their jobs has rekindled an ancient debate on just how it is that the value of an economic resource is established. Some two hundred years ago Adam Smith addressed the "water–diamonds" paradox in his famous treatise on economics, *The Wealth of Nations.* Smith asked why water, a resource so valuable that life on earth would be impossible without it, sells for a much lower price than diamonds, which are merely decorative. The resolution of the paradox offered by economic theory is that prices are established by supply and demand, and that the *marginal* value of a resource is a function of its price. Water sells for a very low price because it is abundant relative to the demand for it. While its *total* value is incalculable, water's low price induces people to use it in ways that have low *marginal* value. That is, if water were relatively scarce and therefore sold at a high price, people would use it only in ways that are life-sustaining (and therefore are of high value). Because it is relatively abundant and sells for almost nothing, however, water is used in ways that go beyond the essential to the merely *decorative*: We see it being sprayed on golf-course putting greens and in the air by downtown water fountains.

When asked to answer why it is, then, that mechanics are paid more than child-care workers, economists tend to answer in terms of market forces: for some reason, the supply of mechanics must be smaller relative to the demand for them than the supply of child-care workers. Perhaps this reason has to do with working conditions, or perhaps it is more difficult to learn and keep abreast of the skills required of a mechanic, or perhaps occupational crowding increases the supply of child-care workers. *Whatever* the reason, it is argued, wages are the price of labor—and prices play such a critical *practical* role in the allocation of resources that they are best left unregulated.

---

[50]*Franks* v. *Bowman Transportation* 424 U.S. 747, 12 FEP Cases 549 (1976), and *Fire Fighters Local 1784* v. *Stotts*, U.S. S. Ct. no. 82–206, June 12, 1984, and *Wygant* v. *Jackson Board of Education*, U. S. S. Ct. no. 84–1340, May 19, 1986.

Thus, in fighting discrimination, most economists would advise modifying the demand or supply behaviors that *cause* unequal outcomes rather than treating the *symptoms* by regulating wages. If the wages of child-care workers were to be raised above their market-clearing level, to take the case at hand, a surplus could be created in that labor market. As implied by our analysis of the minimum wage back in Chapter 4, above-equilibrium wages in the market for child-care workers would mean fewer jobs and many unemployed applicants—hardly the outcome envisioned by those wanting to end discrimination. (A lengthy analysis of these unintended side effects is given in Example 12.3, in the context of equalizing the pay of university professors across the various disciplines.)

The proponents of comparable-worth wage adjustments tend to dismiss the predictions that "women's jobs" will be lost or that labor surpluses in these jobs will be created. These proponents tend to view employers not as the passive wage takers assumed by the simple economic model of labor demand, but as institutions that have the power to *set* their wages. As we saw in Chapter 11, many employers are believed to pay efficiency wages and are apparently very concerned with their employees' perceptions of fairness in compensation; indeed, we observe that large employers often use complex job-rating schemes to determine the internal pay differentials associated with various job titles and the promotion steps within each. It is precisely these job-rating systems that comparable-worth advocates propose to use in bringing the pay in women's jobs up to the levels observed for men's. (A brief review of how these systems work is given in Appendix 12A.)

Generally speaking, comparable worth is a policy that involves using "experts" to assign points to each job according to the knowledge and problem-solving abilities required, its level of accountability, the physical conditions of work, and perhaps other characteristics. Jobs with equal point values would receive equal pay and, of course, jobs assigned more points would receive higher pay. The process by which points are awarded to each job is obviously critical, and both sides of the comparable-worth issue see "expert bias" as a problem. Opponents claim that job ratings can be used to unjustifiably raise the pay in targeted jobs above market levels, while proponents argue that the job ratings now used within firms unfairly lower the value of women's jobs.[51]

In Australia, where federal and state tribunals have historically decided wage cases affecting some 85 percent of union and nonunion workers, informal types of job rating have been used to attempt the equalization of wages in men's and women's jobs across the *entire economy*.[52] The relatively few cases in which

---

[51]See Donald J. Treiman and Heidi L. Hartmann, eds., *Women, Work and Wages: Equal Pay for Jobs of Equal Value* (Washington, D.C.: National Academy Press, 1981), and Steven E. Rhoads, *Incomparable Worth* (Cambridge, Eng.: Cambridge University Press, 1993), 160–165. For discussions of comparable worth that span a variety of disciplines, and both proponents and opponents, see M. Anne Hill and Mark R. Killingsworth, eds., *Comparable Worth: Analyses and Evidence* (Ithaca, N.Y.: ILR Press, 1989); Robert T. Michael, Heidi L. Hartmann, and Brigid O'Farrell, eds., *Pay Equity: Empirical Inquiries* (Washington, D.C.: National Academy Press, 1989); Mark R. Killingsworth, *The Economics of Comparable Worth* (Kalamazoo, Mich.: W. E. Upjohn Institute for Employment Research, 1990); and Paula England, *Comparable Worth: Theories and Evidence* (New York: Aldine DeGruyter, 1993).

[52]Rhoads, *Incomparable Worth*, 183–190, 200–212.

EXAMPLE 12.3

Comparable Worth and the University

Some of the difficulties involved with the concept of *comparable worth* can be illustrated by an example in which gender does not even enter. Consider the labor market for university professors in the fields of computer science and English, and suppose that initially the demand and supply curves for both are given by D_{0C} and S_{0C}, and D_{0E} and S_{0E}, respectively. As the figure indicates, in this circumstance the same wage (W_0) will prevail in both markets, and N_{0C} computer science professors and N_{0E} English professors will be hired. Suppose also that in some objective sense the quality of the two groups of professors is equal.

Presumably this is a situation that advocates of comparable worth would applaud. Both types of professors require the same amount of training, represented by a Ph.D., and both are required to engage in the same activities, teaching and research. Unless one is willing to assign different values to the teaching and research produced in different academic fields, one must conclude that the jobs are truly comparable. Hence, if the two groups are equal in quality, equal wages would be justified according to the concept of comparable worth.

Suppose now, however, that the demand for computer science professors rises to D_{1C} as a result of the increasing numbers of students who want to take computer science courses. Suppose at the same time the demand for English professors falls to D_{1E} because fewer students want to take elective courses in English. At the old equilibrium wage rate there is now an excess demand for computer science professors of $N_{1C} - N_{0C}$ and an excess supply of English professors of $N_{0E} - N_{1E}$.

How can universities respond? One possibility is to let the market work; the wage of computer science professors will rise to W_{1C} and that of English professors will fall to W_{1E}. Employment of the former will

rise to N_{2C} while employment of the latter will become N_{2E}.

Another possibility is to keep the wages of the two groups of professors equal at the old wage rate of W_0. Universities could respond to the excess demand for computer scientists and the excess supply of English professors by lowering hiring standards for the former and raising them for the latter. Since the average quality of English professors would then exceed the average quality of computer scientists, the wage paid per "quality-unit" would now be higher for the computer scientists. Hence, true comparable worth—equal pay for *equal-quality* workers performing comparable jobs—would not be achieved. Moreover, employment and course offerings in this situation would not change to meet changing student demands.

Alternatively, some advocates of comparable worth might argue that universities should respond by raising the wages of *all* professors to W_{1C}. While this would eliminate the shortage of computer science professors, it would exacerbate the excess supply of English professors, raising it to $N_{4E} - N_{3E}$. Universities would respond by drastically reducing the employment of English professors even further to N_{3E} (and reducing course offerings). Moreover, the excess supply again would permit universities to raise hiring standards for English professors, so again average quality would rise. As a result, once more the wage per quality-unit of English professors would be less than that of computer science professors, and again true comparable worth would not be achieved.

The message one takes away from this example is that it is difficult to "trick the market." In the face of

(continued on next page)

EXAMPLE 12.3, *continued*

(a)

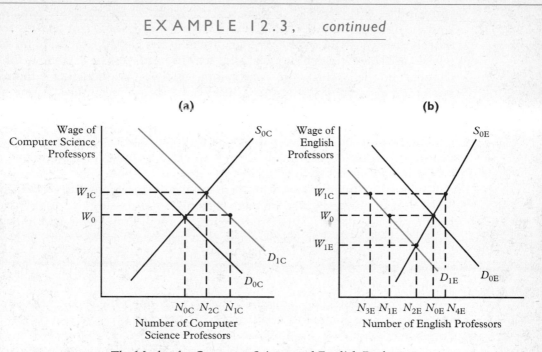

(b)

The Market for Computer Science and English Professors

changing relative demand conditions, either wage differentials for the two types of professors must be allowed to arise or quality differentials will arise. In neither case, however, can comparable worth be achieved. Put another way, the value of a job cannot be determined independently of market conditions.

How have universities actually responded to the changing relative demand conditions for faculty in the fields portrayed in this example? Some evidence can be found from data on faculty salaries, by academic field, obtained each year from a survey of public universities and colleges conducted by Oklahoma State University. In the academic year 1976–77 respondents reported average salaries for new assistant professors of $15,526 in computer science and $13,321 in English and literature. By 1991–92, average salaries of

the former had risen by 201 percent to $46,778, while those for the latter had risen only 137 percent to $31,567. As a result, while the typical assistant professor in English and literature earned *85.8* percent of what the average new assistant professor in computer science earned in 1976–77, he or she earned only *67.5* percent by 1991–92. Relative salaries of assistant professors in academia did adjust substantially to changing relative demand conditions.

SOURCE: Data are from W. Lee Hansen, "Changing Faculty Salaries," in *American Professors,* ed. H. Bowen and J. Schuster (New York: Oxford University Press, 1986), Table 6.10, and Daniel Hamermesh, "Diversity Within Adversity," *Academe* 78 (March-April 1992), Table III.

comparable-worth policies have been used to address unequal pay in the United Kingdom and the United States have required equalization only *within the boundaries of a single employer*. In contrast to the United Kingdom, however, where cases involving both public and private employers have come before the tribunals specially created to hear comparable-worth complaints,[53] the major push for comparable worth in the United States has come in the state and local government sector. A number of state and local governments have conducted formal job evaluation surveys to see if "female" occupations are "underpaid," and on the basis of these evaluations, many government sector employers have begun to implement comparable-worth salary adjustments through collective bargaining or the legislative process.

To date, the initial effects of implementing comparable worth in the United States and the United Kingdom have been neither as positive as its proponents had hoped nor as dire as its critics had portended. Proponents had hoped for large increases in female wages, but by the time comparable-worth, or pay equity, adjustments have been filtered through the collective bargaining or legislative process, their estimated effect on male/female wage differentials has been small.[54]

Critics had argued that comparable-worth wage adjustments, by increasing the wages in female-dominated occupations, should lead employers to reduce their employment in these occupations and hence to reduce female employment. However, empirical studies of a number of cases in which comparable-worth adjustments were implemented suggest that if the adjustments did have a negative effect on female employment, these effects were quite small, and some studies find no evidence of negative effects.[55]

Other critics have expressed concern that raising the wages of traditional female occupations would reduce the incentive of women to seek occupational advancement and thus would leave job segregation unchanged. Again, however, the limited analyses that have been done suggest that the comparable-worth wage adjustments did not slow down the flow of women into traditionally male occupations in the state and local sector.[56]

While the comparable-worth adjustments in the United States and United Kingdom, which are administered at the employer level, have had rather modest effects on women's wages, the economy-wide applications of comparable worth in Australia are

[53]Rhoads, *Incomparable Worth*, 148–160.

[54]See, for example, Peter E. Orazem, J. Peter Mattila, and Sherry K. Welkum, "Comparable Worth and Factor Point Pay Analysis in State Government," *Industrial Relations* 31 (Winter 1992): 195–215; Mark Killingsworth, *The Economics of Comparable Worth*; and Rhoads, *Incomparable Worth*, 166.

[55]See, for example, Mark Killingsworth, *The Economics of Comparable Worth*; Shulamit Kahn, "Economic Implications of Public Sector Comparable Worth: The Case of San Jose, California," *Industrial Relations* 31 (Spring 1992): 270–291; Ronald G. Ehrenberg and Robert S. Smith, "Comparable Worth Wage Adjustments and Female Employment in the State and Local Sector," *Journal of Labor Economics* 5 (January 1987): 43–62; and Manning, "The Equal Pay Act as an Experiment to Test Theories of the Labor Market."

[56]Shulamit Kahn, "Economic Implications of Public Sector Comparable Worth."

believed to have narrowed the pay gap between men and women by some 18 percentage points. Standard economic theory predicts that a mandated increase of this magnitude should be followed by a fall in the relative employment of women, and indeed there was such a decline; however, the decline in the employment of women relative to men was minimal. While some have concluded that, as with minimum wage increases, the predictions of economists were based on a model of the labor market that is too simple, others argue that if one looks at the *hours* of work or at the *overall* level of unemployment in Australia one can see the predicted *scale* and *substitution* effects of these wage increases in action.[57]

THE FEDERAL CONTRACT COMPLIANCE PROGRAM

In 1965 the U. S. Office of Federal Contract Compliance Programs (OFCCP) was established to monitor the hiring and promotion practices of federal contractors (firms supplying goods or services to the federal government). OFCCP requires contractors above a certain size to analyze the extent of their underutilization of women and minorities and to propose a plan to remedy any such underutilization. Such a plan is called an *affirmative action plan.* Contractors submitting unacceptable plans or failing to meet their goals are threatened with cancellation of their contracts and their eligibility for future contracts, although these drastic steps are rarely taken.

Affirmative action planning is intended to commit firms to a schedule for rapidly overcoming unequal career opportunities afforded women and minorities. Such planning affects both *hiring* and *promotion* practices, but it also raises numerous philosophical and practical questions that tend to make the planning process highly controversial.

Suppose an insurance company is attempting to construct an affirmative action plan with regard to secretaries. Its first step in setting hiring goals is to decide what number of minorities are "available" and what fraction they constitute of all available workers. If blacks, say, constitute 9 percent of the labor supply available to the firm, then it might seem to be a simple matter of setting a goal of 9 percent. However, the planner must resolve some serious questions.

First, should the pool of black secretaries be estimated based on the firm's *actual applicant* pool? The answer is probably no, since any discriminatory practices in the past will discourage black applicants currently. Further, affirmative action planning is intended to force companies to *change* their hiring practices. On the other hand, a firm's location within a city can attract more or fewer black applicants, depending on how far from the firm blacks live and the level of compensation offered. Moreover, as we saw in Chapter 8, the mix of employee benefits in the total compensation package can alter the attractiveness of an employer to women,

---

[57]Rhoads, *Incomparable Worth*, 201–204.

the young, and the poor.[58] Thus, to some extent the *potential* pool of *interested* applicants is a legitimate consideration.

Should the potential pool be estimated from the fraction of all *trained secretaries* in the area who are black? If we are interested in eradicating *market* discrimination, this may be the logical measure, since it would force firms to hire black secretaries in the same proportion as they are found in the labor market. However, years of discrimination may have induced blacks to avoid training for this occupation, with the result that blacks may be substantially underrepresented in the secretarial labor market.

Should firms then be compelled to hire black secretaries in proportion to their numbers in the adult *population* of the city at large? This goal implicitly sets out to eliminate all discrimination, both in the labor market and outside of it, but if blacks are underrepresented in the occupation, the attainment of this goal is impractical in the short run. Firms attempting to hire more black secretaries than are available would have two choices. They could hire black high school graduates and train them in secretarial skills. Remember, however, that such training is *general* in nature, so the firms would not offer it unless the workers involved paid for it in some way. Without training as an option, firms would simply try to bid against each other for the services of existing black secretaries, which would drive up their wages. The higher wage rates would induce more blacks to seek secretarial training, and their underrepresentation in the occupation would disappear in the long run.

While population-based goals would appear to fight all kinds of discrimination, they might in fact fight none. It stands to reason that if hiring goals are set beyond the immediate reach of firms, each will individually fail to meet them. Can the government reasonably punish firms for failing to hire beyond the numbers currently available? If it cannot, then failure to meet goals will not result in punishment, which seems to remove the incentive for firms to take energetic steps to integrate their workforces.

A final issue in hiring has to do with how the goals are applied. If black secretaries, to continue our example, are 9 percent of the available pool, does that mean that 9 percent of all *newly hired* secretaries should be black? This goal might seem reasonable from a firm's point of view, but if labor turnover is low it would take a very long time for the 9 percent of *new hires* to accumulate to the point where blacks were 9 percent of the firm's total secretarial workforce. Since the Civil Rights Act of 1964 prohibits workers of one race from being fired to make room for those of another, getting rid of employment imbalances must occur through new hiring. However, only if aggrieved groups are *favored* in hiring can the effects of past discrimination be eradicated quickly.

---

[58]For a review of the economic factors affecting "availability," see Ronald Ehrenberg and Robert Smith, "Economic and Statistical Analysis of Discrimination in Hiring," *Proceedings of the Thirty-Sixth Annual Meeting of the Industrial Relations Research Association* (Madison, Wis.: Industrial Relations Research Association, 1984).

Favoritism in hiring not only raises the issue of *reverse discrimination,* wherein whites or males can assert they are being discriminated against because of race or sex, but also raises the issue of how firms, as a whole, can hire women or blacks in proportions greater than their current availability. The courts have yet to resolve the considerable tension between Title VII's standard of nondiscrimination, which protects all groups from disparate treatment, and the OFCCP's standard of affirmative action.

It is testimony to the difficulty of these questions about affirmative action planning that the government's requirements for calculating "availability" are rather vague. The OFCCP requires federal contractors to consider eight factors when calculating the availability of women and minorities in the process of affirmative action planning:

1. The minority population in the "immediate labor area" (the geographic area from which employees may reasonably commute);
2. The availability of women seeking employment in the immediate labor area or in the area from which a contractor can reasonably recruit (which may include the region or the nation in some occupations);
3. The size of the minority or female unemployed labor force in the immediate labor area;
4. The percentage of minorities and women in the workforce in the immediate labor area;
5. The availability of minorities and women with the requisite skills in the immediate labor area or in the area from which the contractor can reasonably recruit;
6. The availability of women and minorities in the contractor's organization who are promotable;
7. The existence of training institutions capable of training persons in the area with the requisite skills; and
8. The degree of training the contractor is reasonably able to undertake.[59]

While the OFCCP requires contractors to demonstrate that they have *considered* each factor, only those factors relevant to the job under evaluation need to be used.

A brief analysis of the above requirements will show that they raise several questions. First, the factors that emphasize the "immediate labor area" appear to assume all workers in the area are equally interested in work at the plant, independent of commuting distance. Given that commuting is costly, in terms of both cash outlays and time, shouldn't people closer to the plant be considered more "available" than those farther away?

Second, factors 1 and 2 differ from factor 5 in the attention given to *existing* skills, raising the issue discussed above concerning the goals of the contract compliance program. Is the aim of the program to eliminate only current *market*

---

[59]Bureau of National Affairs, *Affirmative Action Compliance Manual for Federal Contractors,* Binder 1, Chapter 2 (Washington, D.C.: Bureau of National Affairs, March 1993).

discrimination against those already in a given skill group, or should it directly address the issue of *premarket* differences in skill acquisition among race or sex groups?

Third, factor 5 is intended to apply to firms hiring in occupations that have regional or national labor markets. However, if contractors are required, as a matter of course, to adopt nontraditional hiring practices that are likely to yield more female or minority applicants, is it unreasonable to expect them to recruit regionally or even nationally for workers they normally recruit locally?

Finally, several questions can be raised about factors 6 and 8. If few minorities or women are at the office-manager rank in an organization, is the firm obliged to offer special managerial training courses for them? Should such training be equally available to interested white males? What if the interest in managerial positions varies by race or sex? Are companies supposed to promote on a nondiscriminatory basis, with the result that imbalances in its *higher*-level jobs will remain for years into the future (see Example 12.4)? Or instead, must employers hurry women and minorities along the promotional ladder faster than normal so that these higher-level imbalances will go away more quickly? These are some of the dilemmas inherent in the government's contract compliance program.

EFFECTIVENESS OF FEDERAL ANTIDISCRIMINATION PROGRAMS

A question of obvious interest is just how effective the two federal antidiscrimination programs have been in increasing the relative earnings of minorities and women. The question is not easy to answer, however, because we must make some guesses as to what earnings differentials *would have been* in the absence of these programs.

The ratio of black to white incomes has risen since 1960, and it is natural to ask if this rise was a result of government efforts, or were other forces working to accomplish this result? Three other forces are commonly cited. First, an improvement in the *educational attainment* of black workers relative to that of whites during this period is thought to have played an important role in raising the ratio of black to white earnings; in fact, one study estimated that increased educational attainment accounts for 20–25 percent of the post-1960 gain in the earnings ratio.[60] Second, there is evidence that the *quality* of schooling improved more after 1960 for blacks than whites, and one study has estimated that from 15 to 20 percent of the increased earnings ratio can be attributed to enhanced school quality.[61] Finally, it has been argued that because the relatively large reduction in labor force participation rates among blacks was centered in the least-educated group of workers, the average earnings of those who remained employed were thereby increased, giving the *appearance* of

---

[60]Smith and Welch, "Black Economic Progress After Myrdal."
[61]Card and Krueger, "School Quality and Black-White Relative Earnings."

EXAMPLE 12.4

How Fast Can Discrimination Be Eradicated?

To illustrate the possible rate of progress in minority employment within a firm, let us take a numerical example. Suppose there is a job group that contains 1,600 employees, 100 (6.25) percent of whom are black. Suppose, further, that this is an entry-level job group (so that all replacements come from new hires) and that the yearly turnover rate is 20 percent. Finally, assume that blacks represent 12 percent of the firm's available labor pool for this job.

The firm in question must hire 320 new workers for this job group each year. If 12 percent (about 38) of those hired each year are black, how long will it take before 12 percent (192) of the 1,600-person work group is black? Another, perhaps more significant, question is: How fast will the racial composition of the work group change? These questions have no obvious answers because if blacks and whites have the same turnover rate (of 20 percent), the organization is both losing and hiring blacks each year.

One way to answer the above questions is to simulate employee turnover each year. The accompanying table shows that in the first year 20 blacks quit and 38 (12 percent of the 320 new hires) are hired. The net gain in blacks raises their level of employment in the group to 118 and their percentage of employment to 7.37 (from 6.25). In the second year, 38 blacks are again hired and about 24 quit, representing a net gain of 14, and by the end of the year the work group is 8.25 percent black. As this process continues, there are net additions to the black component of the workforce each year, but these additions get smaller and smaller.

Of special interest in this example is the fact that it takes about 10 years of *nondiscriminatory hiring* for the percentage of blacks in the work group to get close to the goal of 12 percent. (The rate of progress would be approximately cut in half if the turnover rate were 10 percent instead of 20 percent.) Thus, if the proportion of blacks among new hires is equal to their proportion in the available labor pool and if their turnover rates are no lower than those of whites, the long-run goal of employment equality will take many years to achieve once nondiscriminatory hiring is begun. This mathematical fact illustrates why those charged with administering antidiscrimination programs are simultaneously besieged by shouts of frustration and calls for patience.

*Change in the Racial Composition of a 1,600-Person Job Group
(20% yearly turnover rate)*

	Year						
	0	1	2	3	4	5	10
Number of blacks							
Loss		20	24	26	29	31	36
New hires		38	38	38	38	38	38
Net gain		18	14	12	11	7	2
Cumulative level	100	118	132	144	155	162	181
Percent black	6.25	7.37	8.25	9.00	9.69	10.12	11.31

overall improvement. Roughly 10 to 20 percent of the improved earnings ratio has been attributed to this last factor.[62]

Taking the upper estimates of the three sources of earnings increases cited above, there is at least a third of the improvement in the black/white earnings ratio for men that remains to be explained. Is it possible that federal efforts to reduce discrimination in the labor market were responsible? One comprehensive review of the literature and the evidence on this issue has concluded that federal efforts were successful in raising black earnings levels.[63]

One important fact about black economic progress is that there was a discontinuous jump in the black/white earnings ratio between 1960 and 1975. This sudden improvement coincided with the onset of federal antidiscrimination programs, and it cannot be explained by the rather continuous increases taking place in such other factors as schooling quality or attainment. A second important fact is that the greatest gains in the black/white earnings ratio during the 1960–1975 period were in the South, where segregation was most blatant and where federal antidiscrimination efforts were greatest.

The conclusion that federal antidiscrimination efforts were at least partially successful in raising the relative earnings of blacks must be acknowledged as somewhat surprising, because many studies of individual programs (such as the contract compliance program) have estimated rather meager results. The paradox of overall improvement resulting from programs that appear to have been individually weak may be resolved by noting that each program was part of a comprehensive set of programs—largely aimed at the South—to dismantle all forms of racial segregation, register blacks to vote, and provide legal remedies for victims of discrimination. In the words of one analyst:

> There is evidence that southern employers were eager to employ blacks if they were given the proper excuse. This produced a strong leverage effect for the new laws. . . . An entire pattern of racial exclusion was challenged. This helps to explain how an apparent straw (the Equal Employment Opportunity Commission and the Office of Federal Contract Compliance) could have broken the back of southern employment discrimination. They were only the tip of a federal iceberg launched against the South.[64]

While optimism about the effects of federal antidiscrimination programs in the 1960s and 1970s is warranted, it is not clear that such programs were successful in

---

[62]John J. Donohue III and James Heckman, "Continuous Versus Episodic Change: The Impact of Civil Rights Policy on the Economic Status of Blacks," *Journal of Economic Literature* 29 (December 1991): 1603–1643.

[63]Donohue and Heckman, "Continuous Versus Episodic Change." For a thumbnail sketch of this comprehensive review, see James Heckman, "Accounting for the Economic Progress of Black Americans," in *New Approaches to Economic and Social Analyses of Discrimination*, ed. Cornwall and Wunnava, 331–337. A recent paper by Kenneth Y. Chay, "The Impact of Federal Civil Rights Policy on Black Economic Progress: Evidence from the Equal Employment Opportunity Act of 1972," working paper no. 346, Industrial Relations Section, Princeton University, August 1995, supports the view that federal efforts helped to reduce the black/white pay gap.

[64]Heckman, "Accounting for the Economic Progress of Black Americans," 336.

the 1980s, when the market for less-educated workers turned poor. It might be possible to argue that the earnings of blacks in the 1980s would have been even *lower* were it not for federal efforts, but the evidence so far is that once the most blatant forms of discrimination were attacked the effects of federal efforts have weakened.[65] Moreover, there is only slim evidence that federal antidiscrimination efforts have directly helped women; what evidence there is of positive effects associated with specific programs suggests they were smaller than the effects for blacks.[66] Whether the *totality* of federal laws and programs to reduce gender discrimination has played a role in the gains made by women in the past two decades has not been studied. Also yet to be studied are the effects of federal antidiscrimination efforts on other minority groups.

REVIEW QUESTIONS

1. Assume that women live longer than men, on the average. Suppose an employer hires men and women, pays them the same wage for the same job, and contributes an equal amount per person toward a pension. However, the promised monthly pension after retirement is smaller for women than for men because the pension funds for them have to last longer. According to the *Manhart* decision by the Supreme Court, the above employer would be guilty of discrimination because of the unequal monthly pension benefits after retirement.

   a. Comment on the Court's implicit definition of discrimination. Is it consistent with the definition normally used by economists? Why or why not?

   b. Analyze the economic effects of this decision on men and women.

2. Assume there is a central city school district in which the student population is predominantly black. Surrounding the central city are predominantly white suburban school districts. Together, the central city and suburban school districts can be thought of as a local labor market for teachers. Other things being equal, black teachers in this labor market are equally willing to work in central city and suburban schools, but white teachers prefer suburban schools and are reluctant to accept jobs in the central city. There are too few black teachers to completely staff central city schools, and teachers generally have choices in the jobs they can accept.

   If federal law requires equal salaries for teachers of all races *within* a given school district but allows salaries to vary across school districts, will black teachers earn more, less, or the same salary as they would if white teachers were not prejudiced against black students? (Note: The prejudice of white teachers extends only to students, not to black teachers as co-workers. Note also: The chain of reasoning required in this answer should be made explicit in your answer.)

---

[65]Donohue and Heckman, "Continuous Versus Episodic Change," 1640.

[66]See Jonathan S. Leonard, "Women and Affirmative Action," *Journal of Economic Perspectives* 3 (Winter 1989): 61–75, and Blau and Ferber, *The Economics of Women, Men, and Work*, 224–225.

3. Suppose government antidiscrimination laws require employers to disregard marital status and gender in screening and hiring workers.
   a. Disregarding the employers who are engaged in discrimination, which employers will be most affected by this ruling?
   b. What alternatives do these employers have in coping with the problems created by this decision?
   c. What are the likely consequences of each alternative on employment levels and job stability among these employers?

4. Suppose the government has two methods of awarding contracts to firms. One is competitive, with the award going to the lowest bidder (who cannot then charge more than his or her bid). The other is noncompetitive, with the award going to a selected contractor who is reimbursed for actual costs incurred plus a certain percentage for profits. Suppose, too, that government contractors must hire a certain quota of minorities, many of whom require general training to be fully productive. Suppose also that federal legislation prevents the employer from shifting the costs of this general training to the minority employees. If you were an already trained minority worker, which method of contract award would you prefer? Why?

5. A recent Associated Press article quoted a report saying that male high school teachers were paid more than female high school teachers. Assuming this is true, what information would you require before judging this to be evidence of wage discrimination? (In your answer, define wage discrimination and explain how the required information relates to this definition.)

6. You are involved in an investigation of charges that a large university in a small town is discriminating against female employees. You find that the salaries for professors in the nearly all-female School of Social Work are 20 percent below average salaries paid to those of comparable rank elsewhere in the university. Is this university exhibiting behavior associated with *employer* discrimination?

7. Suppose a city pays its building inspectors $12 an hour and its public health nurses $8 an hour. Assume that building inspectors are all male, that the nurses are all female, and that the wages paid to each occupation reflect the forces of supply and demand (which themselves may reflect discrimination in the labor market at large). Suppose that the city council passes a comparable-worth law that in effect requires the wages of public health nurses to be equal to the wages of building inspectors. Evaluate the assertion that this comparable-worth policy would primarily benefit high-quality nurses and low-quality building inspectors.

8. In the 1920s South Africa passed laws that effectively prohibited black Africans from working in jobs that required high degrees of skill; skilled jobs were reserved for whites. Analyze the consequences of this law for black and white South African workers.

9. Suppose that the United States were to adopt, on a permanent basis, a wage subsidy to be paid to employers who hire black, disadvantaged workers (those with relatively little education and few marketable skills). Analyze the potential effectiveness of this subsidy in overcoming (*a*) current labor market discrimination against blacks, and (*b*) premarket differences between blacks and whites in the long run.

SELECTED READINGS

Aigner, Dennis J., and Glen G. Cain. "Statistical Theories of Discrimination in Labor Markets." *Industrial and Labor Relations Review* 30 (January 1977): 175–187.

Becker, Gary. *The Economics of Discrimination.* 2d ed. Chicago: University of Chicago Press, 1971.

Blau, Francine D., and Marianne A. Ferber. *The Economics of Women, Men, and Work.* 2d ed. Englewood Cliffs, N.J.: Prentice-Hall, 1992.

Borjas, George, and Mary Tienda, eds. *Hispanics in the U.S. Economy.* New York: Academic Press, 1985.

Cain, Glen G. "The Challenge of Segmented Labor Market Theories to Orthodox Theory: A Survey." *Journal of Economic Literature* 14 (December 1976): 1215–1257.

Cornwall, Richard R., and Phanindra V. Wunnava, eds. *New Approaches to Economic and Social Analyses of Discrimination.* New York: Praeger, 1991.

Donohue, John H. III, and James Heckman. "Continuous Versus Episodic Change: The Impact of Civil Rights Policy on the Economic Status of Blacks." *Journal of Economic Literature* 24 (December 1991): 1603–1643.

Ehrenberg, Ronald, and Robert Smith. "Economic and Statistical Analysis of Discrimination in Hiring." *Proceedings of the Thirty-Sixth Annual Meeting of the Industrial Relations Research Association.* Madison, Wis.: Industrial Relations Research Association, 1984.

Fuchs, Victor R. "Women's Quest for Economic Equality." *Journal of Economic Perspectives* 3 (Winter 1989): 25–41.

Goldin, Claudia. *Understanding the Gender Gap: An Economic History of American Women* (New York: Oxford University Press, 1990).

Hill, M. Anne, and Mark R. Killingsworth, eds. *Comparable Worth: Analyses and Evidence.* Ithaca, N.Y.: ILR Press, 1989.

Killingsworth, Mark R. *The Economics of Comparable Worth.* Kalamazoo, Mich.: W. E. Upjohn Institute for Employment Research, 1990.

Smith, James P., and Finis R. Welch. "Black Economic Progress After Myrdal." *Journal of Economic Literature* 27 (June 1989): 519–564.

APPENDIX 12A

Estimating "Comparable Worth" Earnings Gaps: An Application of Regression Analysis

Although many economists have difficulty with the notion that the "worth" of a job can be established independently of market factors, formal job evaluation methods have existed for a long time. The state of Minnesota is one of the few states that have actually begun to implement "comparable worth" pay adjustments for their employees based on such an evaluation method. The purpose of this appendix is to give the reader an intuitive feel for how one might use data from job evaluations to estimate whether discriminatory wage differentials exist.[1]

Minnesota, in conjunction with Hay Associates, a prominent national compensation consulting company, began an evaluation of state government jobs in 1979. Initially evaluated were 188 positions in which at least ten workers were employed and which could be classified as either *male* (at least 70 percent male incumbents) or *female* (at least 70 percent female incumbents) positions. Each position was evaluated by trained job evaluators and awarded a specified number of *Hay Points* for each of four job characteristics or factors: required know-how, problem solving, accountability, and working conditions. The scores for each factor were then added to obtain a total Hay Point, or job evaluation, score for each job. These scores varied across the 188 job titles from below 100 to over 800 points.

---

[1]For a more complete discussion of the Minnesota job evaluation and comparable-worth study, see *Pay Equity and Public Employment* (St. Paul, Minn.: Council on the Economic Status of Women, March 1982).

FIGURE 12A.1

Estimated Male "Comparable Worth" Salary Equation

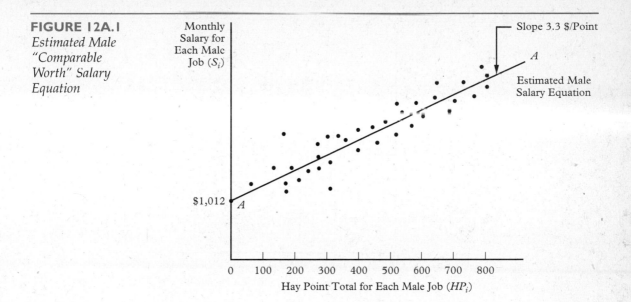

Given these objective job evaluation scores, the next step is to ask what the relationship is between the salary (S_i) each male job pays and its total Hay Point (HP_i) score. Each dot in Figure 12A.1 represents a male job, and this figure plots the monthly salary for each job against its total Hay Point score. On average, it is clear that jobs with higher scores receive higher pay.

Although these points obviously do not all lie on a single straight line, it is natural to ask what straight line fits the data best. An infinite number of lines can be drawn through these points, and some precise criterion must be used to decide which line fits best. As discussed in Appendix 1A, the procedure typically used by statisticians and economists is to choose that line for which the sum (across data points) of the squared vertical distances between the line and the individual data points is minimized. The line estimated from the data using this method—the *method of least squares*—has a number of desirable statistical properties.[2]

Application of this method to data for the *male* occupations contained in the Minnesota data yielded the estimated line:[3]

$$S_i = 1012 + 3.3 \, HP_i \tag{12A.1}$$

---

[2]See Appendix 1A.

[3]These estimates are obtained in Ronald Ehrenberg and Robert Smith, "Comparable Worth in the Public Sector," in *Public Sector Payrolls*, ed. David Wise (Chicago: University of Chicago Press, 1987).

FIGURE 12A.2

Using the Estimated Male "Comparable Worth" Salary Equation to Estimate the Extent of Underpayment in Female Jobs

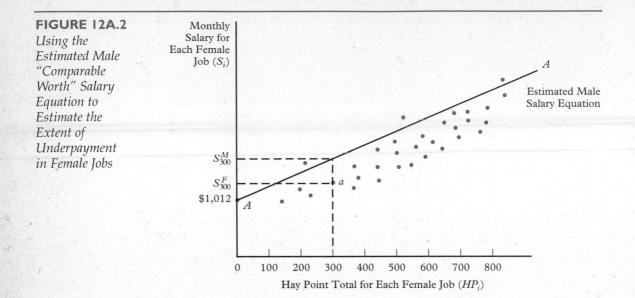

So, for example, if male job i were rated at 200 Hay Points, we would predict that the monthly salary associated with job i would be $1,012 + (3.3)(200)$, or $1,672. This estimated male salary equation is drawn in Figure 12A.1 as line AA.

Now, if the value of a job could be determined solely by reference to its job evaluation score, one would expect that, in the absence of wage discrimination against women, male and female jobs rated equal in terms of total Hay Point scores would pay equal salaries (at least on average). Put another way, the same salary equation used to predict salaries of male jobs could be used to provide predictions of salaries for female jobs, and any inaccuracies in the prediction would be completely random. Hence, a test of whether female jobs are discriminated against is to see if the salaries they pay are systematically less than the salaries one would predict they would pay, given their Hay Point scores and the salary equation for male jobs.

Figure 12A.2 illustrates how this is done. Here each dot represents a salary/Hay Point combination for a female job. Superimposed on this scatter of points is the estimated male job salary equation, AA, from Figure 12A.1. The fact that the vast majority of the data points in Figure 12A.2 lie below the male salary line suggests that female jobs tend to be underpaid relative to male jobs with the same number of Hay Points. For example, the female job that is rated at 300 Hay Points (point a) is paid a salary of S_{300}^F. However, according to the estimated male salary line, if that job were a male job it would be paid S_{300}^M. The difference in percentage terms between S_{300}^M and S_{300}^F is an estimate of the comparable-worth earnings gap—the extent of underpayment—for the female job. Indeed, calculations suggest that the average (across all the female occupations) comparable-worth earnings gap in the Minnesota data was over 16 percent.[4]

This brief presentation has glossed over a number of complications that must be addressed before such estimates can be considered estimates of wage discrimination against female jobs.[5] These include issues relating to the reliability and/or potential sex bias in the evaluation methods, whether salaries and Hay Point scores may be related in a nonlinear fashion, whether the *composition* of any given total Hay Point score (across the four sets of job characteristics) affects salaries, and whether variables other than the job evaluation scores can legitimately affect salaries. Nonetheless, it should give the reader a sense of how "comparable worth wage gap" estimates are computed.

[4]See Ehrenberg and Smith, "Comparable Worth in the Public Sector." Analogous estimates for four other states are presented there and in Elaine Sorensen, "Implementing Comparable Worth: A Survey of Recent Job Evaluation Studies," *American Economic Review* 76 (May 1986): 364–367.

[5]For a more complete discussion of these issues and empirical studies relating to comparable worth, see Ehrenberg and Smith, "Comparable Worth in the Public Sector"; Hill and Killingsworth, eds., *Comparable Worth: Analyses and Evidence;* Michael, Hartmann, and O'Farrell, eds., *Pay Equity: Empirical Inquiries;* and Killingsworth, *The Economics of Comparable Worth.*

13

Unions and the Labor Market

Our analysis of the workings of labor markets has, for the most part, omitted any mention of the role of labor unions and collective bargaining. Because many people have strong and conflicting opinions about the role of unions in our society, it is often difficult to remain objective when discussing them. Some people view labor unions as forms of monopolies that, while benefiting their own members, impose substantial costs on other members of society. In contrast, others view unions as *the* major means by which working persons have improved their economic status and as important forces behind much social legislation.

The purpose of this chapter is to analyze the goals, major activities, and overall effects of unions in the context of economic theory. We begin with some general descriptive material on unions internationally, with a more comprehensive description of unions in the United States, and then move to a fundamental theoretical question: What are the economic forces on the demand side of the market that constrain unions in their desire to improve the welfare of their members? With these constraints in mind, we devote the last half of the chapter to analyzing the primary activities of the collective bargaining process and to discussing empirical evidence on how unions affect wages, employment, labor productivity and profits. We close the chapter with a brief normative analysis of unions.

Union Structure and Membership

Labor unions are organizations of workers whose primary objectives are to improve the pecuniary and nonpecuniary conditions of employment among their members. Unions can be classified into two types: an *industrial* union represents most or all of the workers in an industry or firm regardless of their occupations, and a *craft* union represents workers in a single occupational group. Examples of industrial unions are the unions representing automobile workers, steel workers, bituminous-coal miners, and rubber workers; craft unions include those representing the various building trades, printers, and dockworkers.

Unions bargain with employers over various aspects of the employment contract, including pay and employee benefits; conditions of work; policies regarding hiring, overtime, job assignment, promotion, and layoff; and the means by which grievances between workers and management are to be resolved. Bargaining can occur at different levels. In Sweden before 1984, for example, a *national* confederation of unions bargained with a *national* association of employers over wage increases and other issues that were then recommended to their individual affiliates. Some issues were bargained by these affiliates at the *industry* level, and the resulting contract provisions were thus binding on all employers in the industry. Other issues were bargained at the *company* level.[1]

Thus, at one end of the spectrum, bargaining can be highly *centralized*, with representatives of entire industries sitting at the bargaining table to decide on contracts that bind multiple employers. At the *decentralized* end of the spectrum, bargaining can take place between a union and a single company—or even between the workers and management at a single plant within a company. In the middle are multiemployer agreements reached at the local level between a union and several employers; an example of such agreements would be the ones typically signed between construction craft unions (plumbers, say) and the construction contractors that operate in a given metropolitan area.

As large collective organizations, unions also represent a *political* force in democratic countries. Often, unions will use the political process in the attempt to gain benefits they could not as easily win through collective bargaining. In some countries (Great Britain, for example), unions have their own political party. In others, such as the United States, unions are not affiliated with any single political party; rather, they act as lobbyists for various bills and policies at the federal, state, and local levels of government.

INTERNATIONAL COMPARISONS OF UNIONISM

Table 13.1 displays international comparative data on union membership as a percentage of employment. The differences across countries are remarkable, especially in the very low rates of unionization we see for the United States. Reasons for these differences are not immediately obvious. For example, as of 1980, bargaining was highly centralized in the countries with the three highest membership rates (Sweden, Austria, and Australia), moderately centralized in the "mid-range" countries of Italy and Germany, and very decentralized in the United States. What might appear to be a correlation between centralization of bargaining and union membership, however, is called into question by the relatively high rates of union

---

[1]Harry Katz, "The Decentralization of Collective Bargaining: A Literature Review and Comparative Analysis," *Industrial and Labor Relations Review* 47, no. 1 (October 1993): 3–22

TABLE 13.1
Union Membership, Selected Countries, 1987–1989

Country	Membership as a Percentage of		
	Nonagricultural Employment	Full-Time Workers	Full-Time Manual Workers
Sweden	96	na	na
Austria	61	52	57
Australia	56	70	69
Ireland	51	48	49
United Kingdom	50	47	53
Italy	45	33	37
Germany	43	34	39
Canada	36	na	na
Netherlands	35	42	47
Switzerland	33	37	37
France	28	na	na
Japan	28	na	na
United States	17	19	27

Source: David G. Blanchflower and Richard B. Freeman, "Unionism in the United States and Other Advanced O.E.C.D. Countries," *Industrial Relations* 31 (Winter 1992): 56–79; Richard B. Freeman, "American Exceptionalism in the Labor Market: Union-Nonunion Differentials in the United States and Other Countries," in *Labor Economics and Industrial Relations: Markets and Institutions*, ed. Clark Kerr and Paul D. Staudohar (Cambridge, Mass.: Harvard University Press, 1994), 279.

membership in the United Kingdom, where bargaining was relatively decentralized by 1980.[2] Thus, it is likely that the historical and legal contexts within which unions operate in each country are critical to an understanding of the differing levels of membership.

These different legal contexts across countries also mean that union membership levels and union power are not easily correlated. In Sweden, for example, where almost everyone is in a union, some unions are much weaker in bargaining power than others. In Germany, to take another example, both union and nonunion workers are represented on workplace councils, which decide at the plant level on various personnel issues that in other countries are addressed by

---

[2]Katz, "The Decentralization of Collective Bargaining," 3.

local collective bargaining agreements. Finally, government tribunals play an important role in the Australian system of wage determination, with collective bargaining used to negotiate supplements to the governmental wage awards.[3]

Much of the empirical work on unions has been done on the United States, where bargaining is decentralized and, as we have seen, the majority of workers are nonunion. While the study of unions in one country does not easily generalize to others, given the different legal and historical environments, this empirical work may be of growing interest elsewhere owing to a trend toward a greater decentralization of bargaining in most developed economies during the last decade.[4] No matter how well (or poorly) studies of U.S. unions generalize, however, their results must still be understood within the context of American institutions. We therefore turn to a brief history of the legal structure within which American unions have operated.

THE LEGAL STRUCTURE OF UNIONS IN THE UNITED STATES

Public attitudes and federal legislation have not always been favorably disposed toward labor unions and the collective bargaining process in the United States. For example, during the early part of the twentieth century, employers were often able to claim that unions acted like monopolies in the labor market and hence were illegal under existing antitrust laws. Such employers were often able to get court orders or injunctions that prohibited union activity and aided them in stopping union organization drives. In addition, employers were often able to require potential employees to sign *yellow dog contracts*, contracts in which employees agreed not to join a union as a condition of accepting employment. Given this environment, it is not surprising that the fraction of the labor force who were union members stood at less than 7 percent in 1930.

Since that date, four major pieces of federal labor legislation have shaped the collective bargaining process in the private sector, the ability of unions to increase their membership, and the way unions operate.

Two laws were products of the Depression. The Norris-LaGuardia Act, enacted in 1932, for all practical purposes outlawed the antiunion practices of employers discussed above. The National Labor Relations Act (NLRA), or Wagner Act, of 1935 went far beyond the earlier act by requiring employers to bargain with unions that represented the majority of their employees and by asserting that it was illegal for employers to interfere with their employees' right to organize collectively. The National Labor Relations Board (NLRB) was established by the NLRA and given power both to conduct elections to see which union, if any, employees wanted to represent them ("certification elections") and to investigate

---

[3]Katz, "The Decentralization of Collective Bargaining," and Richard B. Freeman, "American Exceptionalism in the Labor Market: Union–Nonunion Differentials in the United States and Other Countries," in *Labor Economics and Industrial Relations: Market and Institutions*, ed. Clark Kerr and Paul D. Staudohar (Cambridge, Mass.: Harvard University Press, 1994), 272–299.

[4]Katz, "The Decentralization of Collective Bargaining."

claims that employers were either violating election rules or refusing to bargain with elected unions.[5] In the event violations were found, the NLRB was given further power to order violators to "cease and desist"; these orders were to be enforced by the courts.

After World War II the pendulum shifted decidedly in an antiunion direction. The Labor–Management Relations Act of 1947 (better known as the Taft–Hartley Act) restricted some aspects of union activity and permitted workers to vote in elections that could decertify a union from representing them in collective bargaining. Perhaps its most famous provision is Section 14B, which permits individual states to pass *right-to-work laws*. These laws prohibit the requirement that a person become, or promise to become, a union member as a condition of employment. As of the early 1990s, twenty-one states, located primarily in the South, Southwest, and Plains areas, had passed such laws.

Finally, in 1959 Congress passed the Labor–Management Reporting and Disclosure Act (the Landrum–Griffin Act). This law, which was designed to protect the rights of union members in relation to their leaders, contained provisions that increased union democracy. As argued below, such provisions may well have had the side effect of increasing the level of strike activity in the economy.

The laws that have been discussed to this point relate only to the private sector, where unionism in the United States first flourished. Indeed, prior to the 1960s public sector workers were prohibited from organizing. In 1962, however, President Kennedy signed Executive Order 10988, which gave federal workers the right to organize and bargain over working conditions, but not wages.[6] The influence of federal unions on wages, then, operates primarily through the political pressure they can exert on the president to recommend, or on Congress to approve, pay increases.

Beginning with Wisconsin in 1959, a number of states have extended to employees of state and local governments (including teachers) the rights to organize and collectively bargain. Generally speaking, public sector unions are barred from going on strike, so that laws permitting their right to bargain were accompanied by provisions for some form of binding arbitration (through which neutral parties would ultimately decide on disputes that could not be voluntarily resolved).[7]

Table 13.2 presents data on union membership from 1930 through 1994. For the years since 1970 the table also includes data on membership in employee associations, such as the National Education Association, which did not start out as

---

[5]Actually, the NLRA was much less prolabor than our brief discussion indicates; the NLRA also gave the NLRB power to investigate employers' claims that their employees, or unions, were violating provisions of the act.

[6]There were some major exceptions—namely, postal workers and employees of federal government authorities, such as the Tennessee Valley Authority (TVA). In each of these cases the prices of the products or services produced (mail delivery, hydroelectric power) can be raised to cover the cost of the contract settlement. In other federal agencies, salaries are paid out of general revenues.

[7]See Richard B. Freeman, "Unionism Comes to the Public Sector," *Journal of Economic Literature* 24 (March 1986): 41–86, for a more complete discussion of the evolution of legislation governing bargaining in the public sector.

TABLE 13.2

Union and Association Membership in the United States, 1930–1994

Year	Union Membership Only			Union and Association Membership		
	Total (in thousands)	Percentage of Labor Force	Percentage of Nonagricultural Employment	Total (in thousands)	Percentage of Labor Force	Percentage of Nonagricultural Employment
1930	3,401	6.8	11.6			
1934	3,088	5.9	11.9			
1938	8,034	14.6	27.5			
1942	10,380	17.2	25.9			
1946	14,395	23.6	34.5			
1950	14,300	22.3	31.5			
1954	17,022	25.4	33.7			
1958	17,029	24.2	33.2			
1962	16,586	22.6	29.9			
1966	17,940	22.7	28.1			
1970	19,381	22.6	27.3	21,248	24.7	30.0
1974	20,119	21.7	25.8	22,809	24.5	29.1
1978	20,246	19.7	24.0	22,880	22.3	27.1
1980				22,366	20.9	24.7
1982				19,763	17.9	22.1
1984				17,340	15.3	18.8
1986				16,975	14.4	17.5
1988				17,002	14.0	16.8
1992				16,353	12.9	16.0
1994				16,748	12.8	15.5

SOURCE: U.S. Bureau of Labor Statistics, *Directory of National Unions and Employee Associations, 1979,*. Bulletin 2079 (Washington, D.C.: U.S. Government Printing Office, 1980); U.S. Bureau of the Census, *Historical Statistics of the United States: Colonial Times to 1970* (Washington, D. C.: U.S. Government Printing Office, 1975); Bureau of National Affairs, *Directory of U.S. Labor Organizations,* 1984–85 ed. (Washington, D.C.: BNA Books, 1984); U.S. Department of Labor, *Employment and Earnings* (January 1985, 1987, 1989, 1993, 1995).

unions but have become increasingly involved in the collective bargaining process. Clearly, union membership as a percentage of nonagricultural employment grew rapidly during the 1930s and 1940s, but it has been more or less in decline since the mid–1950s. Public sector unionization added to total membership in the 1970s, but after 1978 the absolute number of union members has declined so rapidly that the percentage of employees who are unionized has been cut almost in half. One of the tasks of this chapter is to analyze the causes of this remarkable decline.

Unionized workers in the United States are members of "local" unions, organized at the level of the plant, the employer, or (especially for construction unions) the metropolitan area. We have noted that in the United States bargaining is relatively decentralized, so it is local unions that bear the brunt of negotiations. These locals, however, are usually members of larger "national" or "international" (usually meaning they include Canadian workers) unions, which provide help and advice to the locals with their organization drives and, later, their negotiations. If bargaining is being done at the industry level, or with one firm at the national level, it is representatives of the national or international union who sit at the bargaining table.

In turn, most of the nationals and internationals (and therefore some 72 percent of all union members) are affiliated with the AFL-CIO, which stands for the American Federation of Labor and Congress of Industrial Organizations. The AFL-CIO is not a union, but rather an association of unions organized both nationally and at the state level. Its main functions are to provide a unified political voice for its diverse member unions, to recommend and coordinate membership initiatives among its affiliates, and to provide research and information to its members. It does not directly negotiate with employers.

Table 13.3 provides another way of looking at union membership in the United States. From this table one can note, first, that the public sector is far more unionized than any major private sector industry, with a rate of membership that is double that in manufacturing. Second, men are more likely to be unionized than women, and blacks are more highly unionized than whites or Hispanics. Third, younger workers are less unionized than older workers under the age of 65.

Constraints On The Achievement Of Union Objectives

The founder of the American Federation of Labor, Samuel Gompers, was once asked what unions wanted. His answer was quite simple: "More." Hardly anyone who has studied union behavior believes unions' objectives are quite that simple, but it is self-evident that unions want to advance the welfare of their members in one way or another. Some of their objectives are *procedural*; they want to give workers some voice in the way employers manage the workplace, especially in the handling of various personnel issues such as job assignment, the allocation of overtime, the handling of worker discipline and grievances, and the establishment of joint labor–management safety committees and work teams. Procedural objectives are not always costly to the employer, who (especially with modern management techniques) may want a mechanism through which employee participation in management decisions can be achieved.[8] Other procedural objectives, however, put constraints on managerial prerogatives that, while difficult to quantify, are often seen by employers as costly.

---

[8] See William N. Cooke, "Employee Participation Programs, Group-Based Incentives, and Company Performance: A Union–Nonunion Comparison," *Industrial and Labor Relations Review* 47, no. 4 (July 1994): 594–609.

TABLE 13.3
Percentage of U.S. Wage and Salary Workers Who Are Union Members, by Selected Characteristics, 1994

Overall	15.5
Men	17.9
Women	12.9
Black	20.5
Hispanic	14.2
White	14.8
By Age	
16–24	6.2
25–34	12.7
35–44	18.5
45–54	22.5
55–64	20.3
65 and over	8.9
Industry	
Public Sector	38.7
Private Sector, all	10.9
Mining	15.6
Construction	18.8
Manufacturing	18.2
Transportation, Public Utilities	28.4
Wholesale, Retail Trade	6.2
Finance, Insurance	2.3
Services	6.2

Source: U.S. Bureau of the Census, *Statistical Abstract of the United States: 1995* (Austin, Tex.: The Reference Press, 1994), Table 698.

Wanting "more" is usually associated with the union goal of increasing the *compensation* levels of its members. The most visible element of compensation is the wage rate, but bargaining in the United States also occurs over such employee benefits as pensions, health insurance, and vacations. (In many other developed countries, these benefits are mandated by the government and therefore are not subject to collective bargaining.) The attempts to achieve "more," of course, take place in the context of *constraints*. Employers are on the other side of the bargaining table, and they must make agreements that permit them to operate successfully both with their workers *and* within their product markets. Increased compensation for their workers will give them incentives to *substitute* capital for labor, and to the extent that their costs of production rise, there also will be pressures to reduce the *scale* of operations. In short, unions must ultimately reckon

FIGURE 13.1

Effects of Demand Growth and the Wage Elasticity of Demand on the Market Constraints Faced by Unions

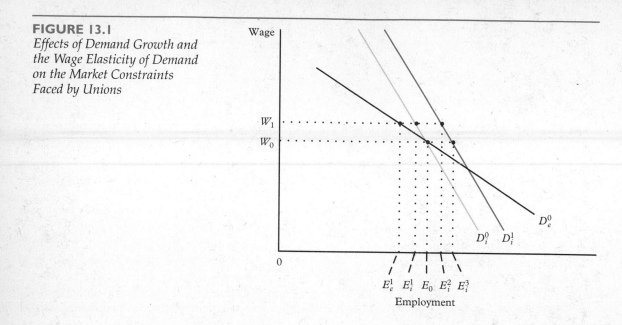

with the downward-sloping demand curve for labor. As a result, both the position and the elasticity of this curve become fundamental market constraints on the ability of unions to accomplish their objectives.

To see this, ignore employee benefits and working conditions for the moment and consider Figure 13.1, which shows two demand curves, D_e^0 and D_i^0 that intersect at an initial wage W_0 and employment level E_0. Suppose a union seeks to raise the wage rate of its members to W_1. To do so would require employment to fall to E_e^1 ijf the union faced the relatively elastic demand curve D_e^0, or to E_i^1 if it faced the relatively inelastic demand curve D_i^0. Other things equal, the more elastic the demand curve for labor is, the greater will be the reduction in employment associated with any given increase in wages.

Suppose now that the demand curve D_i^0 shifts out to D_i^1 while the negotiations are under way, owing perhaps to growing demand for the final product. If the union succeeds in raising its members' wage to W_1, there will be no absolute decrease in employment in this case. Rather, the union will have only slowed the rate of growth of employment to E_i^2 instead of E_i^3. More generally, other things equal, the more rapidly the labor demand curve is shifting out (in), the smaller (larger) will be the reduction *in employment* or the reduction *in the rate of growth of employment* associated with any given increase in wages. Hence, unions' ability to raise their members' wages will be strongest in rapidly growing industries with inelastic labor demand curves. Conversely, unions will be weakest in industries in which the wage elasticity of demand is highly elastic and in which the demand curve for labor is shifting in.

We now turn to two alternative models of how unions and employers behave in their agreements about wages and benefits, given the market constraints they face.

Each of the models analyzes the interaction of—and trade-offs between—wages and employment.

THE "MONOPOLY-UNION" MODEL

The simplest model of the union–employer relationship has been called one of "monopoly" unionism, whereby the union sets the price of labor and the employer responds by adjusting employment to maximize profits, given the new wage rate with which it is confronted. This model is formally illustrated by Figure 13.2, which shows the labor demand curve facing workers as a simple function of the wage rate (for simplicity, we abstract from other elements in the compensation package).

In Figure 13.2, we assume that the union values both the wages and the employment levels of its members and that it can aggregate its members' preferences so that we can meaningfully speak of a union utility function that depends on these two variables. This utility function is summarized by the family of indifference curves U_0, U_1, U_2, U_3. Each curve represents a locus of employment/wage combinations about which the union is indifferent. The indifference curves are negatively sloped, because to maintain a given utility level the union must be compensated for a decline in one variable (employment or wages) by an increase in the other. They exhibit the property of diminishing marginal rates of substitution (they are convex to the origin) because it is assumed that the loss of employment unions are willing to tolerate in return for a given wage increase grows smaller as employment falls. Finally, higher indifference curves represent higher levels of union utility.

Suppose that, in the absence of a union, market forces would cause the wage to be W_0 and employment to be E_0 (point a in Figure 13.2). How does collective

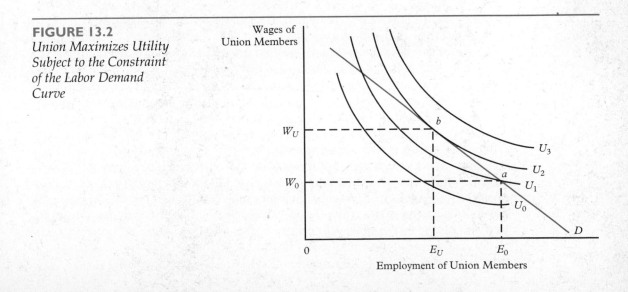

FIGURE 13.2
Union Maximizes Utility Subject to the Constraint of the Labor Demand Curve

bargaining affect this solution? One possibility is that the union and employer will agree on a higher wage rate and then, given the wage rate, the employer will determine the number of union members to employ. Given a bargained wage rate, the employer will maximize profits and determine employment from the demand curve. Since the union presumably knows this, its goal is to maximize its utility function subject to the constraint that its wage/employment combination will lie on the demand curve.

In terms of Figure 13.2 the union will seek to move to point *b*, where indifference curve U_2 is just tangent to the labor demand curve. At this point wages would be W_U and employment E_U. Given the constraint of the labor demand curve, point *b* represents the highest level of utility the union can attain.

THE "EFFICIENT-CONTRACTS" MODEL

An interesting feature of the simple monopoly-union model is that it is not "efficient." Instead of having unions set the wage and then having employers determine employment, both parties could be better off if they agreed to jointly determine wages and employment. Put succinctly in terms of Figure 13.2, there is a whole set of wage/employment combinations that at least one of the parties would prefer and that would leave the other no worse off; these combinations have been called "efficient contracts." (While the term "efficient" recalls our discussion of *Pareto efficiency* in Chapter 1, it is being used more narrowly here. Pareto efficiency refers to *social* welfare, and a transaction is said to be "Pareto-improving" if *society* is made better off—that is, some gain and no one else loses. "Efficiency" in the current context denotes only that the welfare of the two parties can be improved; it does not imply that society as a whole gains. Indeed, we will see in the next subsection that, in general, these "efficient" contracts lead to a socially wasteful use of labor.)

THE FORMAL MODEL   To begin our analysis, we must recall from Chapter 3 that the labor demand curve is defined by the employer's choosing an employment level that maximizes profits at each wage rate. Now, starting at a point like point *a* on the demand curve with the wage set at W_0, if the employer were to expand or contract employment, profits would fall. To keep profits from falling would require a lower wage rate. Expanding or contracting employment further would require a still lower wage rate to keep profits at the same level.

One can formalize this by reintroducing the concept of *isoprofit curves*, first discussed in Chapter 8. Here an isoprofit curve is a locus of wage/employment combinations along which an employer's profits are unchanged. Figure 13.3 shows three isoprofit curves for the employer whose labor demand curve is *D*. As discussed above, each curve reaches a maximum at its intersection with the demand curve; as we move along a given isoprofit curve in either direction away from the demand curve, wages must fall to keep profits constant. A higher isoprofit curve

FIGURE 13.3
Employer Isoprofit Curves

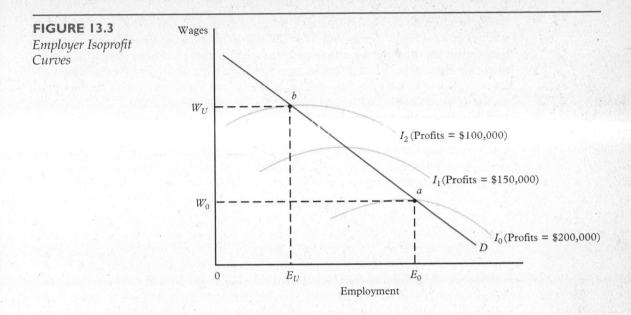

represents a lower level of employer profits because the wage associated with each level of employment is greater along the higher curve. So, for example, the employer would prefer any point on I_0, which includes the original wage/employment combination (point a), to any point on I_2, which includes the monopoly–union wage/employment solution (point b).

Figure 13.4 superimposes the family of employer isoprofit curves from Figure 13.3 onto the family of union indifference curves from Figure 13.2 and illustrates why the monopoly-union solution, point b, is not an *efficient contract*. Suppose, rather than locating at point b, the parties negotiated a contract that called for them to locate at point d, where the wage rate (W_d) would be lower but employment of union members (E_d) higher. At point d the union would be better off since it would now be on a higher indifference curve, U_3, while the firm would be no worse off, since it still would be on isoprofit curve I_2.

Similarly, suppose that rather than negotiating a contract to wind up at b, the parties agreed to a contract that called for them to locate at point e, with a wage rate of W_e and an employment level of E_e. Compared to the monopoly-union solution (point b) the union is equally well off, since it remains on indifference curve U_2, but now the firm is better off because it has been able to reach isoprofit curve I_1. Because I_1 lies below I_2, it represents a higher level of profits.

In fact, there is a whole set of contracts that both parties will find at least as good as point b; these are represented by the shaded area in Figure 13.4. Among this set, the ones that are efficient contracts—contracts in which no party can be made better off without hurting the other—are the ones in which employer isoprofit curves are just tangent to union indifference curves, such as points *d* and *e*. Indeed, there is a whole locus of such points, and they are represented in the figure by the curve *ed*. Each point on *ed* represents a tangency of a union indifference curve and an employer isoprofit curve; these are points at which the employer and the union are equally willing to substitute wages for employment at the margin (so that no more mutually beneficial trades of wages for employment are possible).

All of the points on *ed*, which is often called the *contract curve* (or locus of efficient contracts), will leave both parties at least as well off as at point *b*, and at least one party better off. However, the parties are not indifferent to where along *ed* the settlement is reached. Obviously the union would prefer to be close to *d* and the employer close to *e*. Where on the contract curve a settlement actually occurs in this model depends upon the bargaining power of the parties.[9]

THE CONTRACT CURVE   Two points need to be made about the contract curve. First, as shown in Figure 13.4, it lies "off" and to the right of the firm's labor demand curve. This implies that the firm is using more labor at any given wage rate than it would if it had unilateral control over employment, and it implies that the collective bargaining agreement will contain clauses that "create" (more precisely, ratify the use of) excess labor in the plant. For example, there may be clauses pertaining to minimum crew sizes or to rigid rules governing which workers must do specific tasks; some agreements may even have no-layoff clauses for certain workers. While the employer may be better off with these clauses, because it can induce the union to agree to a lower wage, its failure to minimize costs is socially wasteful (society could increase its aggregate output if labor were reallocated and used more productively).

Second, the contract curve will slope upward, but it is not necessary that it slope up and to the *right*, as shown in Figure 13.4. Depending on the shapes of the union's indifference curves and the firm's isoprofit curves, the contract curve could slope up and to the *left* or even be *vertical*.

An interesting special case involving a vertical contract curve is created when the curve is *vertical at the original (preunion) level of employment*. In this case, the firm agrees to maintain employment at the level that *maximizes profits*, given the *market wage rate*. The union and firm in effect bargain over how these profits are split; every dollar gained by the union is a dollar lost by the employer and there are no changes in output or employment. If the union succeeds in raising wages above their original (market) level, however, it is reasonable to ask how the firm could afford to pay higher wages, maintain its original employment level, and still operate successfully in the product market. The answer must be that it is in a *noncompetitive* product market and is therefore receiving profits in excess of those required for

---

[9]For an attempt to model how bargaining power affects the nature of contract settlements, see Jan Svejnar, "Bargaining Power, Fear of Disagreement, and Wage Settlements: Theory and Empirical Evidence from U.S. Industry," *Econometrica* 54 (September 1986): 1055–1078.

FIGURE 13.4

The Conract Curve–The Locus of "Efficient Contracts"

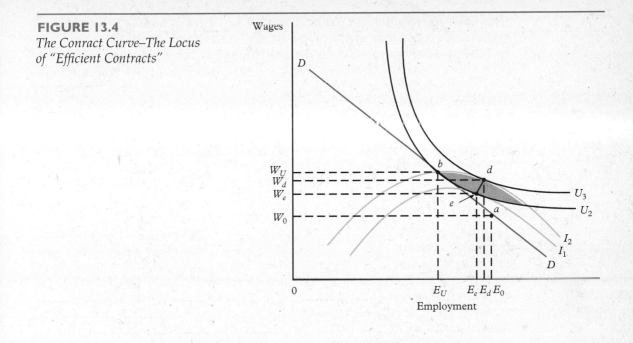

it to remain in business; a reduction in these excess profits might make management unhappy, but it does not cause the employer to change its behavior.[10] Further implications of a vertical contract curve are discussed in the final section of this chapter, in which the social gains or losses of unionization are considered.

ARE CONTRACTS REALLY "EFFICIENT?" How realistic is the efficient–contracts model as a description of the wage-determination process in unionized workplaces in the United States? The most obvious way to answer this question would be to look at the language of collective bargaining agreements to see if there is evidence of joint agreement on employment levels. Many contracts covering public school teachers specify maximum class sizes or minimum teacher/student ratios, and a few private sector contracts include no-layoff provisions for certain "core" workers, but the world is too uncertain for an employer to explicitly guarantee a certain *level* of employment.

Contracts, however, often contain language that perpetuates the use of excess labor. Many require that duties cannot be performed "out of job title," so that a

---

[10]Brian E. Becker, "Union Rents as a Source of Takeover Gains Among Target Shareholders," *Industrial and Labor Relations Review* 49, no. 1 (October 1995): 3–19. An empirical test for a vertical contract curve can be found in John M. Abowd, "The Effect of Wage Bargains on the Stock Market Value of the Firm," *American Economic Review* 79, no. 4 (September 1989): 774–800.

custodian, for example, could not paint a scuffed wall (a painter would be required), or an off-stage actress could not perform any of the duties of a lighting technician. These rigidities in job assignment clearly are designed to protect jobs even though the level of employment is not explicitly determined in the contract.

There are also *indirect* tests of the efficient-contracts model. This model and the monopoly–union model yield different implications about how wages and employment will vary in response to changes in variables that affect either the demand for labor or union preferences. A number of studies have analyzed these implications, and it is fair to say that at the moment there is evidence that both supports and goes against the efficient–contracts model.[11]

The Activities and Tools of Collective Bargaining

Having analyzed the general constraints facing unions as they seek to accomplish their goals, we turn now to an economic analysis of several activities that affect their power. We begin with a simple model of union *membership*, and use it to help understand the decline in membership faced by U.S. unions in recent decades. Next, we briefly discuss the ways in which unions use the *political* process in an attempt to alter the market constraints they face. Finally, we analyze the ultimate threats—of calling a *strike* or having an unresolved dispute decided by third-party *arbitration*—that unions can carefully use in the collective bargaining process.

UNION MEMBERSHIP: AN ANALYSIS OF DEMAND AND SUPPLY

A simple model of the demand for and supply of union activity can be used to explain the forces that influence union membership.[12] On the demand side, employees' demand to be union members will be a function of the "price" of union membership; this price includes initiation fees, monthly dues, the value of the time

[11]Orley Ashenfelter and James Brown, "Testing the Efficiency of Employment Contracts," *Journal of Political Economy* 94, no. 3, pt. 2 (June 1986): S40–S87; Thomas MaCurdy and John Pencavel, "Testing Between Competing Models of Wage and Employment Determination in Unionized Markets," *Journal of Political Economy* 94, no. 3, pt. 2 (June 1986):S3–S39; Randall Eberts and Joe Stone, "On the Contract Curve: A Test of Alternative Models of Collective Bargaining," *Journal of Labor Economics* 4 (January 1986): 66–81; David Card, "Efficient Contracts with Costly Adjustment: Short-Run Employment Determination for Airline Mechanics," *American Economic Review* 76 (December 1986): 1045–1071; Jan Svejnar, "Bargaining Power . . ."; John Abowd, "The Effect of Wage Bargains on the Stock Market Value of the Firm"; Janet Currie, "Employment Determination in a Unionized Public Sector Labor Market: The Case of Ontario's School Teachers," *Journal of Labor Economics* 9 (January 1991): 45–66; and Walter J. Wessels, "Do Unions Contract for Added Employment?" *Industrial and Labor Relations Review* 45 (October 1991): 181–193.

John Pencavel, *Labor Markets Under Trade Unionism* (Cambridge, Mass.: Basil Blackwell, 1991), Chapter 4, presents an analysis of the results on this topic, most especially of the evidence for a vertical contract curve.

[12]This model is based upon the approach found in Orley Ashenfelter and John Pencavel, "American Trade Union Growth, 1900–1960," *Quarterly Journal of Economics* 83 (August 1969):434–448, and John Pencavel, "The Demand for Union Services: An Exercise," *Industrial and Labor Relations Review* 24 (January 1971): 180–191.

FIGURE 13.5

The Demand for and Supply of Unionization

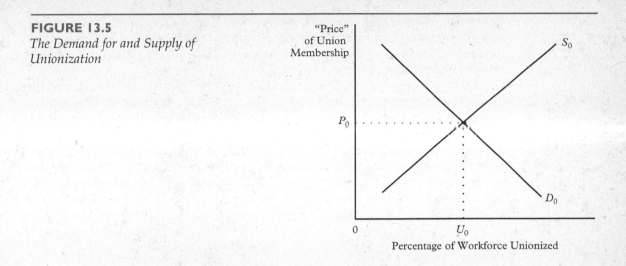

an individual is expected to spend on union activities, etc. Other things equal, the higher the price, the lower the fraction of employees that will want to be union members, as represented by the demand curve D_0 in Figure 13.5.

It is costly to represent workers in collective bargaining negotiations and to supervise the administration of union contracts. Moreover, union organizing campaigns require resources, and as unions move from organizing workers who are the most favorably inclined towards unions to those who are the least favorably inclined, the cost of making a sufficiently strong case to win a union representation election increases. Therefore, it is reasonable to conclude that, other things equal, the willingness of unions to provide union services is an upward-sloping function of the price of union membership, as represented by the supply curve S_0 in Figure 13.5. The intersection of these demand and supply curves yields an equilibrium percentage of the workforce that is unionized (U_0) and an equilibrium price of union services (P_0).

What are the forces that determine the *positions* of the demand and supply curves? Anything that causes either the demand curve *or* the supply curve to shift to the right will increase the level of unionization in the economy, other things equal. Conversely, if either of these curves shifts to the left, other things equal, the level of unionization will fall. Identifying the factors that shift these curves enables one to explain *changes* in the level of unionization in the economy over time.

On the demand side, it is likely that individuals' demand for union membership is positively related to their perceptions of the *net benefits* from being union members. For example, the larger the wage gain they think unions will win for them, the further to the right the demand curve will be and the higher the level of unionization. Another factor is *tastes;* if individuals' tastes for union membership increase, perhaps because of changes in social attitudes or the introduction of labor legislation that protects the rights of workers to join unions, the demand curve will also shift to the right.

On the supply side, anything that changes the *costs* of union organizing activities will affect the supply curve. Introduction of labor legislation that makes it easier (harder) for unions to win representation elections will shift the supply curve to the right (left). Changes in the industrial structure that make it more difficult to organize the workforce will also shift the curve to the left and reduce the level of unionization.[13]

The rapid growth in unionization that Table 13.2 suggests took place during the 1930s was a product of both the changing legal environment (the Norris-LaGuardia and Wagner Acts) and changing social attitudes towards unions induced by the Great Depression, which shifted both the demand and the supply curves to the right. The growth continued during the World War II years as low unemployment rates reduced workers' fears of losing their jobs if they indicated prounion sentiments (shifting the demand curve to the right). Unemployment increased after the end of World War II, shifting the demand curve back to the left, while the passage of the Taft-Hartley Act made it more difficult for unions to increase membership in right-to-work states and shifted the supply curve further to the left. Both shifts served to decrease the percentage unionized.

The decline in unionization rates that has taken place in the United States since the mid-1950s, and the recent acceleration in that decline, is hypothesized to be at least partially explained by five factors related to the demand for, or supply of, union services: demographic changes in the labor force, a shifting industrial mix, a heavier mix of employment in states in which the environment is not particularly favorable for unions, increased competitive pressures, and increased employer resistance to union organizing efforts.[14]

DEMOGRAPHIC CHANGES   The fraction of the labor force that is female has increased substantially (see Chapter 6), and women historically have tended not to join unions. The benefits from union membership are a function of individuals' expected tenure with firms; seniority provisions, job security provisions, and retirement benefits are not worth much to individuals who expect to be employed at a firm for only a short while. *In the past,* women tended to have shorter expected job tenure than men and to have more intermittent labor force participation. As a result, their expected benefits from joining unions were lower; an increase in their share in the labor force would shift the aggregate demand curve for union

---

[13]Rebecca S. Demsetz, "Voting Behavior in Union Representation Elections: The Influence of Skill Homogeneity and Skill Group Size," *Industrial and Labor Relations Review* 47, no. 1 (October 1993): 99–113, finds that plants with more homogeneously skilled workers are more supportive of unions, other things equal.

[14]For a recent discussion of the factors underlying the rise and fall of unionization rates in the United States, see the essays by Edward P. Lazear, Richard B. Freeman, and Melvin W. Reder in *The Journal of Economic Perspectives* 2, no. 2 (Spring 1988): 59–110. For quantitative estimates of the extent to which the factors discussed in this section are responsible for the decline in unionization, see Henry Farber, "The Decline of Unionization in the United States: What Can Be Learned from Recent Experience?" *Journal of Labor Economics* 8, no. 1, p. 2 (January 1990): S75–S105, and Henry Farber and Alan Krueger, "Union Membership in the United States: The Decline Continues," working paper no. 306, Industrial Relations Section, Princeton University, August 1992. For an analysis of declines in British unionization, see Martyn Andrews and Robin Naylor, "Declining Union Density in the 1980s: What Do Panel Data Tell Us?" *British Journal of Industrial Relations* 32, no. 3 (September 1994): 413–431.

membership to the left. Given the continually growing labor force attachment of women, however, demographic changes are an unlikely explanation for the decline in union membership.[15]

CHANGING INDUSTRIAL MIX A second possible factor in the decline of union membership is the shift in the industrial composition of employment, first discussed in Chapter 2. The fraction of workers in government, the most heavily unionized sector in the United States, has held more or less constant since the mid-1970s, while there has been a substantial decline in the employment shares of the most heavily unionized industries in the *private* sector (see Table 13.3): manufacturing, mining, construction, transportation, and public utilities. Employment has increased most notably in wholesale and retail trade, in finance, insurance and real estate, and in the service industries—all of which are the least-unionized sectors of the economy.

Why do the latter industries tend not to be unionized? These industries tend to be highly competitive, with high price elasticities of product demand. As discussed in Chapter 4, other things equal, industries with high price elasticities of demand also have high wage elasticities of labor demand. High wage elasticities limit unions' abilities to increase their members' wages without substantial employment declines also occurring. For this reason, the net benefits individuals perceive from union membership may be lower in these industries, and an increase in their importance in the economy would shift the demand for union services to the left in Figure 13.5, thereby reducing the percentage of the workforce that is unionized.

These industries also tend to be populated by small establishments. The demand for unionization is thought to be lower for employees who work in small firms, since they often feel less alienated from their supervisors. Similarly, since it is more costly to try to organize 1,000 workers spread over 100 firms than it is to organize 1,000 workers at one plant, it is often thought that the supply of union services would shift left as the share of employment going to small firms increases. Both of these factors tend to suggest (in terms of Figure 13.5) that unionization will decline as the share of employment in small establishments increases, providing another reason why the shift in industrial distribution of employment may have affected the extent of unionization.

REGIONAL SHIFTS IN EMPLOYMENT A third factor that may have contributed to the decline in union strength is the movement in population and employment that has occurred since 1955 from the industrial Northeast and Midwest—the Snowbelt—to the Sunbelt of the South. As noted earlier, the Taft-Hartley Act permitted states to pass right-to-work laws, and as of 1994, twenty-one states had done so. Such laws raise the costs of increasing union membership, since individuals who accept employment with a firm cannot be compelled to

---

[15]Farber and Krueger, "Union Membership in the United States: The Decline Continues," argue that demographic changes have played almost no role in the decline.

become union members as a condition of employment. In terms of Figure 13.5, these laws shift the supply curve of union services to the left, thereby reducing the level of unionization. Most Sunbelt states have right-to-work laws, and between 1955 and 1994 the proportion of employees working in right-to-work states increased from 24 to over 36 percent. This shifting geographic distribution of the workforce, coupled with the existence of these laws, undoubtedly had the effect of depressing union membership.

It is not at all obvious, however, that the decline in unionization occasioned by the move to the Sunbelt can be attributed to right-to-work laws per se. The extent of unionization in right-to-work states tended to be lower than that in other states even before the passage of the laws. These laws may only reflect attitudes towards unions that already exist in these communities.[16] The increasing influx of Snowbelters into the Sunbelt may eventually lead to a change in public attitudes *and* the repeal of some of these laws.

COMPETITIVE PRESSURES   A fourth factor is increased foreign competition in manufacturing and the deregulation of the airline, trucking, and telephone industries (see Example 13.1). In these industries, which tended to be highly unionized, increased product market competition has served to increase the price elasticities of product demand, and hence the wage elasticities of labor demand. To the extent that union members' wages did not fall substantially in the face of increased product market competition, unionized employment within these industries could have been expected to fall. Indeed, the share of unionized employment in these previously heavily unionized industries has fallen substantially in the past decade as competition from both foreign firms and new, nonunion employers in the deregulated industries has increased.[17]

By making labor demand curves more elastic, increased competitive pressures reduce the benefits to workers of collective action, hence shifting the demand curve for union membership to the left. Moreover, increased product market competition may well call forth *employer* responses that affect workers' demand for unions. For example, if firms find that foreign competition has intensified, they may seek to re-

---

[16]Numerous econometric studies have sought to estimate the effect of right-to-work laws on union strength, wages, and industrial conflict. A good survey of these studies is William Moore and Robert Newman, "The Effect of Right-to-Work Laws: A Review of the Literature," *Industrial and Labor Relations Review* 38 (July 1985): 571–586. While most analysts conclude that these laws have little or no effect, some, such as David Ellwood and Glenn Fine, in "The Impact of Right-to-Work Laws on Union Organizing," *Journal of Political Economy* 95 (April 1987): 250–273, find a substantial effect from the laws. Farber and Krueger, "Union Membership in the United States," find evidence of an overall decrease from 1977 to 1991 in the desire of workers to be unionized.

[17]For example, unionized employees were approximately 40 percent of manufacturing employment a decade ago, whereas in 1993, they constituted only 19 percent. Evidence that the effects of foreign competition are felt primarily in union members' employment levels, not in their wages, is found in John Abowd and Thomas Lemieux, "The Effects of International Trade on Union Wages and Employment: Evidence from the U.S. and Canada," in *Immigration, Trade, and the Labor Market,* ed. John Abowd and Richard Freeman (Chicago: University of Chicago Press, 1991).

EXAMPLE 13.1

Deregulation and the Airlines

Prior to 1978, regulation of the airline industry prohibited price competition between airlines that flew the same route, and it granted airlines that had no competitors on a route a form of monopoly power by limiting the entry of new carriers. Such regulation tended to reduce the price elasticity of demand for each airline's flights, which in turn strengthened unions in the industry by reducing the wage elasticity of demand for airline employees. Under the Airline Deregulation Act of 1978, however, price competition was permitted on routes with more than one carrier, and new airlines, which were often nonunion and had lower labor costs, began to compete with the existing carriers. As a result, revenue and employment fell substantially for the established, unionized carriers; one study suggests that their employment of mechanics had fallen by 15 to 20 percent as of 1983 because of deregulation.

These forces led the established airlines to "request" that their unions make *concessions,* in the form of reduced compensation and longer workweeks, in exchange for at least implicit promises that employment levels would be maintained. In some cases new contracts were written that agreed to temporary or permanent concessions. In other cases, however, airlines filed for bankruptcy and unilaterally reduced employees' wages.

Concessions often took the form of *two-tier wage structures,* in which newly hired employees were temporarily or permanently paid according to a lower wage scale than previously hired employees. Over 60 percent of the settlements negotiated in 1985 by the established airline carriers contained such provisions. These provisions had the effect, of course, of reducing the costs of newly hired employees relative to more-senior employees.

By 1987, the real earnings of pilots had fallen 17 percent below their levels in 1978, while the real earnings of airline mechanics had fallen by about 13 percent. Because the decline in real earnings among U.S. full-time male workers in this period was 4 percent, and among all nonsupervisory workers was 10 percent, one might conclude that, as expected, increased product market competition in the airline industry reduced the relative wages of pilots and mechanics. The real earnings of flight attendants, however, fell only by 5 percent, perhaps because of increased opportunities in other occupations for the women who typically had been recruited for these jobs. In fact, formal econometric studies that control for other factors suggest that, on balance, deregulation had only a *modest* effect on employees' earnings.

SOURCES: David Card, "The Impact of Deregulation on the Employment and Wages of Airline Mechanics," *Industrial and Labor Relations Review* 39 (July 1986): 527–538; Sanford Jacoby and Daniel Mitchell, "Management Attitudes Toward Two-Tier Pay Plans," *Journal of Labor Research* 7 (Summer 1986): 221–237; David Card, "Deregulation and Labor Earnings in the Airline Industry," working paper no. 247, Industrial Relations Section, Princeton University, January 1989; Nancy Brown Johnson, "Airline Workers' Earnings and Union Expenditures Under Deregulation," *Industrial and Labor Relations Review* 45 (October 1991): 154–165.

locate in areas where workers are less likely to unionize; similarly, they may seek to employ workers in demographic groups whose demands for union membership are relatively low. Both of these employer responses may at least partially underlie factors discussed above. Moreover, increased competition may cause employers to resist union organizing efforts more vigorously, which could well increase the costs of such efforts and shift the supply curve of union services to the left.

EMPLOYER RESISTANCE   U.S. employers can, and often do, play an active role in opposing union organizing campaigns, using both legal and illegal means. For example, under the National Labor Relations Act it is legal for employers to present arguments to employees detailing why they think it is in the workers' best interests to vote against a union and for employers to hire consultants to advise them how to best conduct a campaign to prevent a union from winning an election. On the other hand, it is illegal for an employer to threaten to withhold planned wage increases if the union wins the election or for a firm to discriminate against employees involved in the organizing effort. If a union believes an employer is involved in illegal activities during a campaign, it can file an unfair labor practices charge with the National Labor Relations Board which, if sustained, can lead the NLRB to issue a formal complaint. Although the evidence is somewhat ambiguous, it appears that both legal and illegal employer resistance to union organizing efforts reduces the chance that such efforts will succeed.

Table 13.4 chronicles, from 1970 to 1994, the number of union representation elections, the percent won by the union, and the number of unfair labor practice complaints filed by the NLRB against employers. While not all unfair practices occur during representation elections, the ratio of such complaints to the number of elections held gives us at least some idea of the intensity of employer resistance. This ratio has risen steadily since 1970, and during this same period, the percentage of elections won by unions declined from above 50 percent in 1970 to below it in every year thereafter (although it may have bottomed out in the mid-1980s). While many interpret these data to mean that increased employer resistance reduces the chances that the union will win an election, there is disagreement over what has caused the increased resistance by employers.

Some argue that employers are now more disposed, on purely ideological grounds, to maintain union-free workplaces. Others suggest, however, that the change in employer behavior was the result of an increase in the costs that employers expected to face if the unions won. During the 1970s and early 1980s wages of unionized workers grew more rapidly than the wages of nonunion workers just as competition from foreign producers increased sharply. Thus, the perceived economic benefits to nonunion employers of keeping their workplaces nonunion increased. This factor, it is argued, encouraged them to increasingly and aggressively combat union election campaigns, through both legal and illegal means (the "penalty" for committing an unfair labor practice is virtually nonexistent for first offenders).[18]

UNION ACTIONS TO ALTER THE LABOR DEMAND CURVE

Many actions that unions take are direct attempts to relax the market constraints they face: either to increase the demand for union labor or to reduce the wage elasticity of demand for their members' services. The laws of derived demand discussed

---

[18]William T. Dickens, "The Effect of Company Campaigns on Certification Elections: Law and Reality Once Again," *Industrial and Labor Relations Review* 36 (July 1983): 560–575; Robert Flanagan, *Labor Relations and the Litigation Explosion* (Washington, D.C.: Brookings Institution, 1987); and Henry Farber, "The Decline in Unionization in the United States."

TABLE 13.4
Union Representation Elections and Unfair Labor Practice Complaints Issued by NLRB, 1970–1994

| Year | Representation Elections | | NLRB Complaints Against Employers | |
	Number	Percent Won by Union	Number	Ratio: Complaints to Elections
1970	8,074	55.2	1,474	0.183
1975	8,577	48.2	2,335	0.272
1980	8,198	45.7	5,164	0.630
1985	4,614	42.4	2,840	0.616
1990	4,210	46.7	3,182	0.756
1994	3,752	46.6	3,162	0.843

SOURCE: *Annual Report of the National Labor Relations Board*, Appendix Tables 3A, 13 (various years).

in Chapter 4 implied that three important determinants of the wage elasticities of demand were the price elasticity of demand for the final product, the ease of substituting other inputs for union members in the production process, and the responsiveness of the supply of other inputs to their prices. Other things equal, if price elasticities of demand for the final product are less elastic, if it is difficult to substitute other inputs for union labor, and if the supplies of other inputs are relatively unresponsive to their prices, a more inelastic demand for union labor will result.

As noted in Chapter 4, the wage elasticity of demand for labor is more elastic in the long run. In the short run there may be only limited foreign competition in the output market; in the long run, as American automobile manufacturers realized in the late 1970s and the 1980s, foreign competition may increase, increasing the price elasticity of demand for output. In the short run, production technologies may be fixed; in the long run, labor-saving technologies may be introduced. Finally, in the short run the supplies of alternative inputs may be fixed, while in the long run— because of immigration, the training of other nonunion workers, or the production of new capital equipment—they may be more responsive to price. As a result, the market constraints unions face are more severe in the long run than in the short run.

Attempts by unions to shift the demand curve for union labor to the right and to reduce the wage elasticity of demand have taken many forms. Many of these attempts have *not* occurred through the collective bargaining process per se. Rather, they have occurred through union support of legislation that at least indirectly achieved union goals and through direct public relations campaigns to increase the demand for products produced by union members.

Turning first to policies to shift the demand for the final product, unions have lobbied for import quotas, which restrict the quantities of foreign-made goods that can be imported into the United States, and for *domestic content* legislation, which requires goods from abroad to have a certain percentage of American-made components. Unions have also lobbied strongly against legislation, such as the North American

Free Trade Act, that reduces tariffs on imported goods. Some unions have sought to directly influence people's tastes for the products they produce. The International Ladies Garment Workers' Union (ILGWU) sought, for many years, to encourage people to "Buy American," featuring the song "Look for the Union Label" in some of its television ads.

Unions have also sought, by means of legislation, to pursue strategies that increase the costs of other inputs that are potential substitutes for union members. For example, labor unions have been among the primary supporters of higher minimum wages.[19] While such support may be motivated by a concern for the welfare of low-wage workers, increases in the minimum wage also raise the relative costs to employers of less-skilled nonunion workers, thereby both increasing the costs of the products they produce and reducing employers' incentives to substitute nonunion workers for more-skilled union workers.

Another example of how unions can influence the demand for union labor is the union position on immigration policy. The AFL-CIO has been quite explicit, both historically and in recent years, about its concern that immigrants depress wages and provide competition for unionized American workers. With respect to the problem of illegal immigration in the early 1980s, the AFL-CIO asserted that

> while the nation should continue its compassionate and humane immigration policy, it is apparent that large numbers of illegal immigrants are being exploited by employers, thus threatening hard-won wages and working conditions. U.S. immigration policy should foster re-unification of families and provide haven for refugees from persecution, while taking a realistic view of the job opportunities and the needs of U.S. workers.[20]

It is not surprising, then, that unions have historically supported legislation restricting immigration.

Union attempts to restrict the substitution of other inputs for union labor typically occur by means of the collective bargaining process. Some unions, notably those in the airline, railroad, and printing industries, sought and won guarantees of minimum crew sizes (for example, at least three pilots were required to fly certain jet aircrafts). Such *staffing requirements* prevented employers from substituting capital for labor.[21] Other unions have won contract provisions that prohibit employers from *subcontracting* for some or all of the services they provide. For example, a union representing a company's janitorial employees may win a contract

---

[19]For evidence that union support for minimum wage legislation is often transformed into pro-minimum wage votes by members of Congress, see James Cox and Ronald Oaxaca, "The Determinants of Minimum Wage Levels and Coverage in State Minimum Wage Laws," in *The Economics of Legal Minimum Wages,* ed. Simon Rottenberg (Washington, D.C.: American Enterprise Institute for Public Policy Research, 1981).

[20]*The AFL-CIO Platform Proposals: Presented to the Democratic and Republican National Conventions 1980* (Washington, D.C.: AFL-CIO, 1980), 14.

[21]In cases in which these requirements call for the employment of employees whose functions are redundant—for example, fire stokers in diesel-operated railroad engines—*featherbedding* is said to take place. For an economic analysis of this phenomenon, see George Johnson, "Work Rules, Featherbedding and Pareto Optimal Union Management Bargaining," *Journal of Labor Economics* 8 (January 1990, pt. 2): S237–S259.

provision preventing the firm from hiring external firms to provide it with janitorial services. Such provisions may limit the substitution of nonunion for union workers. Craft unions, especially those in the building and printing trades, often negotiate specific contract provisions that restrict the functions that members of each individual craft can perform, thereby limiting the substitution of one type of union labor for another. Finally, craft unions also limit the substitution of unskilled union labor for skilled union labor by establishing rules about the maximum number of *apprentice* workers—workers who are learning the skilled trades—that can be employed relative to the experienced *journeymen* workers.

Apprenticeship rules also limit the supply of skilled workers to a craft. Indeed, they represent only one of several ways in which unions or employee associations may restrict entry into an occupation. Another way is to control the accreditation of outside institutions that provide training; the American Medical Association's accreditation of medical schools is an example. A third way of restricting entry into an occupation is to lobby for state occupational licensing laws.[22]

BARGAINING AND THE THREAT OF STRIKES

How do unions persuade employers to agree to changes that reduce the wage elasticity of demand or shift the demand curve for union labor to the right? Given the elasticity and position of demand curves, how are unions able to bargain for, and win, real wage increases when in most cases an increase in the price of an input reduces a firm's profits?

In some cases a union and an employer may agree to a settlement in which real wages are increased in return for the union's agreeing to certain work-rule changes that will result in increased productivity. If such an agreement is explicit and is tied to the resulting change in productivity, the process is often referred to as *productivity bargaining*. More typically, however, unions are able to win management concessions at the bargaining table because of the unions' ability to impose costs on management. These costs typically take the form of work slowdowns and strikes. A *strike* is an attempt to deny the firm the labor services of all union members.

Strikes, for all the publicity generated when they occur, are actually relatively rare in the United States. In the 1970s, for example, when data were available for *all* strikes, roughly 0.16 percent (less than one-fifth of 1 percent) of total work hours were lost to strikes. In recent years, we have data only on strikes involving 1,000 or more employees. In 1993, for example, there were 35 such strikes nationwide, involving some 182,000 workers, which cost the U.S. economy about one-hundredth of 1 percent of total work time.[23] Despite their infrequency, the *threat* of a strike hangs over virtually every bargaining situation in the private sector, and therefore models of the bargaining process and its outcomes must address this threat.

---

[22]See, for example, Morris Kleiner, "Are There Economic Rents for More Restrictive Occupational Licensing Practices?" *Proceedings of the 42nd Annual Meeting of the Industrial Relations Research Association* (Madison, Wis.: Industrial Relations Research Association, 1990): 170–185.

[23]U.S. Bureau of the Census, *Statistical Abstract of the United States: 1994* (Austin, Tex: The Reference Press, 1994), Table 681.

FIGURE 13.6
Hicks's Bargaining Model and
Expected Strike Length

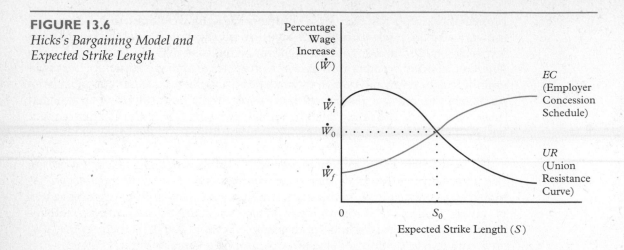

A SIMPLE MODEL OF STRIKES AND BARGAINING   The first, and also simplest, model of strikes in the bargaining process was developed by Sir John Hicks.[24] Suppose that management and labor are bargaining over only one issue: the size of the wage increase to be granted. How would the percentage increase that the union demands and the increase that the employer is willing to grant vary with the expected duration of a strike? Hicks analyzed this question with a diagram like the one shown in Figure 13.6, in which $\dot{W}$ is the percentage wage increase over which labor and management are bargaining.

On the employer side, the firm's highest pre-strike wage offer is assumed to be $\dot{W}_f$. If that offer is rejected and a strike ensues, the employer may be able to service its customers for a relatively short period of time through accumulated inventories or the use of nonstriking employees (including managers) in production jobs. As a strike progresses, however, the costs of lost business or dissatisfied customers mount, and the employer can be expected to increase its wage offer in an effort to end the strike. The expected willingness of employers to increase their wage offers as a strike lengthens is depicted by the upward-sloping *employer concession schedule, EC*, in Figure 13.6.

The union is assumed initially willing to accept some wage increase ($\dot{W}_i$) without a strike, but after a strike begins worker attitudes may harden, and the union may actually increase its wage demands early on. After some point in the strike, however, the loss of income workers are suffering begins to color their attitudes, and the union will begin to reduce its wage demands. This reduction is indicated by the *union resistance curve, UR*, in Figure 13.6, which eventually becomes downward-sloping.

As the strike proceeds, we expect the union's demands to decrease and the employer's offer to increase, until at strike duration S_0 the two will coincide. At this point a settlement is reached on a wage increase of $\dot{W}_0$, and the strike is expected to end. This simple model has several implications.

---

[24]John R. Hicks, *The Theory of Wages*, 2d ed. (New York: St. Martin's Press, 1966), 136–157.

First, holding the *EC* schedule constant, anything that shifts the *UR* schedule upward (that is, increases union resistance to management) will both lengthen the expected strike duration and raise the wage increase that can be expected. This heightened resistance may be manifest in either a higher "no-strike" wage demand (an increase in $\dot{W}_i$) or a flatter slope to the *UR* curve, which would indicate that the union is less willing to modify its wage demands as the strike proceeds.[25] Union resistance can be expected to increase, for example, if the costs to workers of being on strike were to fall. More particularly, if the unemployment rate is so low that strikers can easily obtain temporary jobs, or if union members are able to collect some form of unemployment benefits (either from the government or from the union) during the strike, then their willingness to strike or to remain on strike will increase. Indeed, we do find that strikes are both more likely and of longer duration in periods of relative prosperity; the availability to strikers of unemployment benefits similarly affects strike activity.[26]

A second implication of the simple Hicks model is that anything strengthening the resistance of employers will lower the *ER* curve, thereby lengthening expected strike duration and reducing the expected wage settlement. Thus, firms will be more likely to resist—and less likely to raise their wage offers very much as the strike progresses—if they are less profitable, face an elastic product demand curve, can stockpile product inventories in advance of a strike, can easily hire replacement workers (see Example 13.2), or receive "strike insurance" from other firms in the industry.[27]

---

[25]For evidence on the hypothesized downward slope to the *UR* curve, see Sheena McConnell, "Strikes, Wages, and Private Information," *American Economic Review* 79 (September 1989): 801–815, and David Card, "Strikes and Wages: A Test of an Asymmetric Information Model," *Quarterly Journal of Economics* 105 (August 1990): 625–659.

[26]Orley Ashenfelter and George Johnson, "Bargaining Theory, Trade Unions, and Industrial Strike Activity," *American Economic Review* 59 (March 1969): 35–49, Susan B. Vroman, "A Longitudinal Analysis of Strike Activity in U.S. Manufacturing: 1957–1984," *American Economic Review* 79 (September 1989): 816–826, and Peter C. Cramton and Joseph S. Tracy, "The Determinants of U.S. Labor Disputes," *Journal of Labor Economics* 12, no. 2 (April 1994): 180–209. For similar evidence on strikes and the business cycle in Canada and Great Britian, see Alan Harrison and Mark Stewart, "Is Strike Behavior Cyclical?" *Journal of Labor Economics* 12, no. 4 (October 1994): 524–553, and A. P. Dickerson, "The Cyclicality of British Strike Frequency," *Oxford Bulletin of Economics and Statistics* 56, no. 3 (August 1994): 285–303.

Two states, New York and Rhode Island, allow all workers on strike to collect unemployment benefits (after a waiting period), while other states allow strikers to receive benefits if certain conditions prevail. For evidence that rules governing strikers' eligibility for unemployment benefits influence the level of strike activity, see Robert Hutchens, David Lipsky, and Robert Stern, "Unemployment Insurance and Strikes," *Journal of Labor Research* 13 (Fall 1992): 337–354.

[27]Melvin W. Reder and George R. Neumann, "Conflict and Contract: The Case of Strikes," *Journal of Political Economy* 88, no. 5 (October 1980): 867–886; John F. Schnell and Cynthia L. Gramm, "The Empirical Relations Between Employers' Striker Replacement Strategies and Strike Duration," *Industrial and Labor Relations Review* 47, no. 2 (January 1994): 189–206. An example of employer strike insurance can be found in the airline industry, which had a "Mutual Aid Agreement" between 1958 and 1978. If one airline was struck, the pact called for other airlines to make payments to help defray its lost revenue. As the generosity of the plan increased over time, and hence the costs of a strike to any given airline declined, not surprisingly the frequency and duration of strikes in the industry increased. For a discussion of this pact, including why it ultimately broke down, see S. Herbert Unterberger and Edward C. Koziara, "The Demise of Airline Strike Insurance," *Industrial and Labor Relations Review* 34 (October 1980): 82–89.

EXAMPLE 13.2

Permanent Replacement of Strikers

The collective bargaining laws of most nations permit a company whose workforce is on strike to hire *temporary* replacement workers to keep the business operating. The United States is one of the few nations that permit firms to hire *permanent* replacement workers. That is, workers on strike in the United States are at risk of permanently losing their jobs.

Although the right of companies to hire permanent replacements dates back to a 1938 Supreme Court decision, only since the early 1980s are large companies doing so, or seriously threatening to do so. In 1981, the Reagan administration "broke" the air traffic controllers' union by permanently replacing striking controllers. Subsequently a number of large companies, including Phelps Dodge, Eastern Airlines, and the Greyhound Bus Lines, all permanently replaced striking workers. The threat by Caterpillar, Inc., in 1992 to permanently replace its 12,000 striking workers was sufficient to end a long-term strike on terms favorable to the company.

A recent study suggests that the greater likelihood replacements will be used has clearly reduced the willingness of unions to go on strike. Indeed, this study indicated that if the use of replacement workers had been prohibited, the number of strikes in the 1980s would have been 13 percent greater.

Why did large companies begin using permanent replacement workers in the 1980s and early 1990s when they had typically failed to do so during the previous four decades? Some attributed it to increasingly antiunion attitudes on the part of the federal government that were demonstrated by the Reagan administration's actions during the air controller strike. Others attributed it to the real wage stagnation that occurred in the 1980s for workers with less than a college education (see Chapter 14), which, together with a declining number of high-wage union jobs and relatively high unemployment rates, led many nonunion and unemployed workers to apply for permanent replacement positions, even at the risk of being called "scabs." Still others attributed it to the pressures of international competition and domestic deregulation, which increased employers' needs to cut costs and made them less willing to bow to union demands.

Does the increased use of permanent replacements, which reduced union bargaining power, portend the end of unions in the United States? The answer is probably no. In 1992 Congress considered legislation that would have prohibited the use of permanent replacements and, while the legislation wasn't passed, it is likely to be reconsidered in the future.

Furthermore, while employers may derive benefits from the use of permanent replacements, they also face costs. In situations in which employers heavily invest in specific training for their workers (see Chapter 5), they must bear the costs again if they hire replacement workers and suffer losses in productivity until the replacement workers are fully trained. If some former workers are rehired, relations between them and the replacement workers are likely to be strained, which will also adversely affect productivity. Finally, all workers will know that they face replacement if a future strike arises; this is likely to adversely affect their morale, their commitment to the firm, and hence their productivity. These costs all place a limit on employers' abilities to hire permanent replacements.

SOURCES: Peter Cramton and Joseph Tracy, "The Use of Replacement Workers in Union Contract Negotiations: The U.S. Experience, 1980–9," working paper no. 5106, National Bureau of Economic Research, Cambridge, Mass., 1975, and Louis Uchitelle, "Ousting Strikers: A Costly Tactic," *New York Times,* April 12, 1992, D2.

A final implication is that strikes appear to be unnecessarily wasteful. Had the expected settlement of $\dot{W}_0$ been reached *without* a strike, or with a *shorter* strike, both sides would have been spared some losses. When strikes are likely to be very costly to both parties, the two might agree in advance to certain *bargaining protocols* that will help to avert future strikes. For example, the parties might agree to start bargaining well in advance of a contract's expiration date, to limit the number of contract items they will discuss, or to submit the dispute to binding arbitration if they fail to reach agreement on their own. Indeed, there is some evidence that strikes are less frequent, and shorter, when the *joint costs* of any strike are likely to be greater.[28]

If strikes are costly, and if they can be averted in advance, why do they occur at all? Some argue that, to enhance their bargaining positions and retain the credibility of the *threat* of a strike, unions have to periodically use the strike weapon; that is, a strike may be designed to influence *future* negotiations.[29] Strikes also may be useful devices by which the internal solidarity of a union can be enhanced against the common adversary—the employer.

More fundamentally, however, strikes are thought to occur because the information that both sides have about each other's goals and intentions to resist may be imperfect. In this situation, economists say that information is "asymmetric," meaning that one side knows more about its own goals and intentions than does the other side. Strikes can occur when information is asymmetric, then, either because one party *mistakes* the other's true position,[30] or because only by striking can one party acquire a *signal* about the other's actual "needs."

STRIKES AND ASYMMETRIC INFORMATION Most recent economic analyses of strike activity in the United States are based on some kind of information asymmetry. Workers may want to share in the firm's profits, for example, but they will doubt management's willingness to be completely truthful about current and expected profit levels. The reason is not difficult to understand: management knows more about the firm's profitability than does labor, and if it can convince workers that the enterprise is not very profitable, the union can be expected to moderate its wage demands.

Knowing management's informational advantages and its incentives to understate profitability, the union may try to elicit a "signal" from management about the true level of profits. A strike would be one such signal. If the firm is lying, and profits are greater than stated, the firm may be unwilling to put up a

[28]John Kennan, "Strikes and Bargaining," in *Handbook of Labor Economics*, ed. Orley Ashenfelter and Richard Layard (Amsterdam: North-Holland, 1986), and Melvin Reder and George Neumann, "Conflict and Contract: The Case of Strikes."

[29]Richard Walton and Robert McKersie, *A Behavioral Theory of Labor Negotiations*, 2d ed. (Ithaca, N.Y.: ILR Press, 1991).

[30]Edward Montgomery and Mary Ellen Benedict, "The Impact of Bargainer Experience on Teacher Strikes," *Industrial and Labor Relations Review* 42, no. 3 (April 1989): 380–392, find that strikes are shorter and less likely to occur in situations in which the chief bargainers are more experienced, and thus less likely to inaccurately communicate their positions to each other.

fight (management may figure that, since giving in is financially feasible, it is better off avoiding the costs of a strike). If, however, the firm is telling the truth about its low level of profits, giving in may not be feasible; "taking" a strike, then, sends a signal that the firm believes labor's demands are far enough above what it can feasibly pay that they must be strongly resisted.

An implication of the asymmetric-information model of strike activity is that greater uncertainty about an employer's willingness and ability to pay for wage increases should raise both the probability that a strike will occur and the duration of the strike. It does appear that the more variable a firm's profitability is over time, other things equal, the greater this uncertainty will be and the greater will be the expected incidence and duration of strike activity.[31] If the parties realize this, however, they may avert a strike by establishing a reputation for revealing their true positions rather quickly.

One barrier to elimination of the misunderstandings caused by asymmetric information is that there are really *three* major parties to a negotiation, not just two. On the employee side of the negotiations are two groups: union *leaders* and the *rank-and-file* union members, who rely on their leaders for information.[32] The rank-and-file may understandably suspect their leaders of withholding information from them so that their negotiations are less stressful; put differently, the rank and file may suspect their leaders will "sell them out." Conversely, the leadership may be unsure just how strongly their members feel about certain demands being made of management. Thus, there are also information asymmetries (and hence possibilities for misunderstandings) within the *employee* side of the negotiating table.

Union leaders, who have been actively involved with management in the bargaining process, have much better information than rank-and-file union members about the employer's true financial position and the maximum wage settlement the union will be able to extract. If this settlement is smaller than the settlement the membership wants, the union leaders face two options.

On the one hand, union leaders can return to their members, try to convince them of the employer's true financial picture, and recommend that management's last offer (the maximum that they know they can achieve) be accepted. The danger they face with this option is that the members may vote down the recommendation, accuse the leaders of selling out to management, and ultimately vote them out of office.

On the other hand, union leaders can return to their members and recommend that the members go out on strike. This recommendation will allow them to appear to be strong, militant leaders, even though the leaders themselves know that the strike will not lead to a larger settlement. After a strike of some duration, however, in accordance with the notion of the union resistance curve in Figure 13.6,

---

[31]Joseph Tracy, "An Empirical Test of an Asymmetric Information Model of Strikes," *Journal of Labor Economics* 5 (April 1987): 149–173, and "An Investigation into the Determinants of U.S. Strike Activity," *American Economic Review* 76 (June 1986): 423–436.

[32]The model described here was put forth by Ashenfelter and Johnson, "Bargaining Theory, Trade Unions, and Industrial Strike Activity."

union members will begin to moderate their wage demands, and ultimately a settlement for which the union leaders will receive credit will be reached. Since the latter strategy is the one that is more likely to maintain the union's strength *and* keep the leaders in office, it is the strategy leaders may opt for even though it is clearly not in their members' best interests in the short run (the members have to bear the costs of the strike). Interestingly, strike activity rose markedly right after passage of the Landrum-Griffin Act in 1959, possibly because this act increased union democracy—thereby giving the wishes of the rank and file greater weight in the bargaining process.[33]

BARGAINING IN THE PUBLIC SECTOR: THE THREAT OF ARBITRATION

Although some states have granted to selected public sector employees the right to strike in one form or another, most have continued historic prohibitions against strikes by state and local government workers. When strikes are forbidden, however, laws often provide for third parties to enter the dispute-resolution process if bargaining between the parties comes to an impasse. The first step in this process is typically some form of *mediation*, in which a neutral third party attempts to facilitate a settlement by listening to each party separately, making suggestions on how each might modify its position to have more appeal to the other, and doing anything else possible to bring the parties to a voluntary settlement.

If a mediator is unable to bring the parties to a settlement, the dispute-resolution process sometimes calls for the next step to be *fact-finding*, in which a neutral party, after listening to both sides and gathering information, writes a report that proposes a settlement. The report is not binding on either party, but it may be considered by each to be a forecast of the settlement that binding arbitration would impose if the impasse were to continue.

If noncoercive methods fail to bring a voluntary settlement, *arbitration* becomes the final step of the dispute-resolution process. A single arbitrator may hear the case, or the case may be heard by a panel, usually consisting of one representative from labor, one from management, and one "neutral." Whether the parties *choose* to go to arbitration to settle their dispute, or whether by law they *must* go to arbitration, once the arbitration report is issued the parties are bound by its contents. (Arbitration associated with the bargaining process is called *interest arbitration* to distinguish it from the *grievance*-arbitration process so widely used in resolving contract-administration disputes during the life of a contract.)

There are two forms that interest arbitration can take. With *conventional arbitration*, the arbitrators are free to decide on any wage settlement of their choosing. They listen to both sides make their case and then render their own decision. Some have suspected that under this conventional procedure arbitrators tend to "split the difference" between the two parties, thereby encouraging the parties to take extreme positions (in the hope of "dragging" the arbitrator toward their true goal). This belief has led some jurisdictions to adopt *final-offer arbitration*, in which

[33]Ashenfelter and Johnson, "Bargaining Theory, Trade Unions, and Industrial Strike Activity."

the arbitrator is constrained to choose the final, prearbitration offer either of the union or of management; no other option is possible for the arbitrator. Final-offer arbitration, it was theorized, would induce the parties to make more reasonable final offers to each other, because by so doing they would increase the chances of their offer being the one accepted by the arbitrator.

Economists have been concerned with modeling how the possibility of arbitration affects negotiations between the two parties. As demonstrated by the formal model in Appendix 13A, two major considerations are thought to influence the parties: *uncertainty* about what the arbitrator will decide if the impasse continues, and their own *aversion to the risk* of this uncertainty.

Put succinctly, because the arbitrator's decision is unknown in advance, going to arbitration is a gamble. A party "wins" the gamble only if the arbitrator's decision grants a higher wage increase than it could get through voluntary agreement. Thus, in deciding whether to continue bargaining—or, instead, take a rigid position and let the dispute go to arbitration—a party needs to develop expectations of various possible arbitrator decisions. By calculating the likelihood of each possible outcome *and* the utility associated with it, the party can develop a set of voluntary agreements it would prefer over taking its chances with arbitration. If the "preferred sets" of the two parties happen to overlap, there is a *contract zone* of possible voluntary agreements that *both* parties will prefer to the gamble of arbitration. If there is no overlap, the parties cannot agree voluntarily and the dispute will definitely go to arbitration.

The contract zone can be *widened*, other things equal, by a party's *increased aversion to risk*. People are said to be risk averse if their *increased* utility from winning a $100 bet, for example, is smaller than their *decreased* utility if the bet is lost. That is, risk-averse parties put more weight on possible losses than on possible gains of equal magnitude, and therefore in many situations they will avoid gambling. The more a party wants to avoid "gambling" with arbitration, the wider will be its set of acceptable voluntary agreements.

Also, in the presence of risk aversion, if it becomes *more difficult to predict the arbitrator's decision,* the contract zone will tend to widen. If it is entirely possible, for example, that the arbitrator would come up with a decision that diverges wildly from a risk-averse party's best interests, the party's set of preferred voluntary agreements would be expanded! Thus, the contract zone will be widened both by increased risk aversion and by increased uncertainty about what the arbitrator will do.

While logic dictates that a bargaining situation with *no* contract zone will produce no voluntary agreement, it is not obvious that a wider contract zone will make reaching a voluntary agreement more likely.[34] A wider contract zone opens up more feasible outcomes to the two parties, so one might think that the chances of voluntary agreement are enhanced, but it also gives the parties more to argue about. To take an extreme example, if there were only one wage increase that both

---

[34] Vincent Crawford, "Arbitration and Conflict Resolution in Labor–Management Bargaining," *American Economic Review* 71 (May 1981): 205–210.

parties preferred to arbitration, then perhaps agreement would be reached more quickly and with more certainty than if there were several possible outcomes to be thoroughly debated.

While going to arbitration is clearly risky, the parties are not helpless in their abilities to influence the arbitrator's decision. If they are going to final-offer arbitration, they can improve their chances of "winning" by developing a final, prearbitration offer that the arbitrator is likely to regard as reasonable. The "influence" they exert in final-offer arbitration, then, amounts to guessing what the arbitrator thinks the outcome should be and then crafting an offer that approaches it. (Obviously, the union will approach it from *above* and management will approach it from *below,* as each tries to drag the arbitrator in its direction.)

If the parties are going to conventional arbitration, it is less certain how their offers can influence the arbitrator's decision. Some people might reason that the arbitrator will decide on a wage increase that lies between those of the two parties, or in the extreme, simply split the difference. If so, the parties might then be tempted to make final offers that are far from where they eventually expect to end up.

It might be more reasonable to believe, however, that arbitrators initially have their own views of a proper settlement, which can then be modified by listening to the arguments and positions of each party. Their own beliefs of what constitutes a reasonable outcome are not easily changed, and if a party's position (offer) is far from the outcome they consider appropriate, little weight will be given to it.[35] This latter view of how arbitrators behave implies that the parties can gain influence only by making offers that are close to what they think the arbitrator will decide. If both parties make the same (correct) guess about the arbitrator's preferred outcome, their final offers will bracket the arbitrator's decision. To outsiders it will look as though the arbitrator followed a simple, split-the-difference rule, but what really happened was that the parties strategically placed their offers around the arbitrator's expected position.[36]

If arbitrators have their own, strongly held views on the appropriate outcome in a particular case, and if the parties position their offers around that they expect to be the arbitrator's preferred outcome, then whatever form of arbitration is used, the behavior of the parties and the arbitrator should be more or less the same. This observation has been tested with data for 1978 to 1980 on police officers' contracts in New Jersey, where unresolved disputes go to final-offer arbitration unless both parties agree to submit to conventional arbitration. In the typical final-offer case during this period, the employer offered an increase of 5.7 percent, the union's offer was 8.5 percent, and the union won about two-thirds of the time. In cases that went to conventional arbitration, the typical decision was to award an 8.3 percent increase. Thus, there was almost no difference between outcomes under the two

---

[35]For experimental evidence in support of this view of arbitrator behavior, see Henry S. Farber and Max H. Bazerman, "The General Basis of Arbitrator Behavior: An Empirical Analysis of Conventional and Final-Offer Arbitration," *Econometrica* 54, no. 4 (July 1986): 819–844.

[36]Henry S. Farber, "Splitting-the-Difference in Interest Arbitration," *Industrial and Labor Relations Review* 35 (October 1981): 70–77.

forms of arbitration. Further, if the decisions under conventional arbitration are taken as an indication of the "preferred" wage increase, unions were clearly making more reasonable final offers than management in the cases going to final-offer arbitration.[37]

The Effects of Unions

Economists have long been interested in the effects of unions on wages, and recently attention has also been given to their effects on total compensation (including employee benefits), employment levels, hours of work, productivity, and profits. In this section we review the theory and the evidence on these effects.

THE THEORY OF UNION WAGE EFFECTS

Suppose one had data on the wage rates paid to two groups of workers identical in every respect except that one group was unionized and the other was not. Let W_u denote the wage paid to union members and W_n the wage paid to nonunion workers. If the difference between the two could be attributed solely to the presence of unions, then the *relative wage advantage (R)* that unions would have achieved for their members would be given, in percentage terms, by

$$R = (W_u - W_n)/W_n \tag{13.1}$$

Contrary to what one might expect, this relative wage advantage does *not* represent the absolute amount, in percentage terms, by which unions would have increased the wages of their members, because unions both directly and indirectly affect *nonunion* wage rates also. Moreover, one cannot a priori state whether estimates of R will overstate or understate the absolute effect of unions on their members' real wage levels. To illustrate the difficulties in interpreting union-nonunion wage differentials, we begin with the simple model of the labor market depicted in Figure 13.7.

Figure 13.7 represents two sectors of the labor market, both of which hire similar workers. Panel (a) is the union sector and panel (b) is the nonunion sector. Suppose *initially* that both sectors are nonunion and that mobility between them is costless. Workers will therefore move between the two sectors until wages are equal in both. With demand curves D_u and D_n, workers will move between sectors until the supply curves are S_u^0 and S_n^0, respectively. The common equilibrium wage will be W_0, and employment will be E_u^0 and E_n^0, respectively, in the two sectors.

Once one sector becomes unionized, and its wage rises to W_u^1, what happens to wages in the other sector depends on the responses of employees who are not em-

[37]Orley Ashenfelter and David Bloom, "Models of Arbitrator Behavior: Theory and Evidence," *American Economic Review* 74 (March 1984): 111–124. Evidence in Orley Ashenfelter, "Arbitrator Behavior," *American Economic Review* 77 (May 1987): 342–346, indicates that in other states with final-offer arbitration, unions did not always win more than half the time.

FIGURE 13.7

Spillover Effects of Unions on Wages and Employment

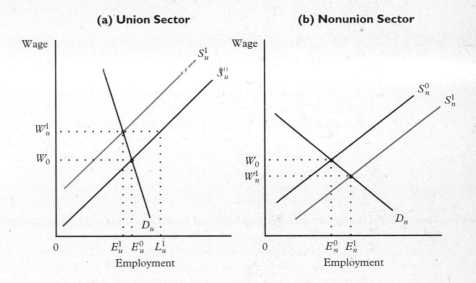

ployed in the union sector. In the subsections below, we discuss <u>four possible re-</u>
actions.[38]

SPILLOVER EFFECTS If the union succeeds in raising wages in the union
sector to W_u^1, this increase will cause employment to decline to E_u^1 workers,
resulting in $L_u^1 - E_u^1$ unemployed workers in that sector. If all the unemployed
workers *spill over* into the nonunion sector, the supply curves in the two sectors
will shift to S_u^1 and S_n^1, respectively. Unemployment will be eliminated in the union
sector; in the nonunion sector, however, an excess supply of labor will exist at the
old market-clearing wage, W_0. As a result, downward pressure will be exerted on
the wage rate in the nonunion sector until the labor market in that sector clears at
a *lower* wage, W_n^1, and a higher employment level, E_n^1.

<u>In the context of this model, the union has succeeded in raising the wages of its</u>
<u>members who kept their jobs. However, it has done so by shifting some of its</u>
<u>members to lower-wage jobs in the nonunion sector and, because of this spillover</u>
<u>effect, by actually lowering the wage rate paid to individuals initially employed in</u>

---

[38]Much of the discussion in this section is based upon the pioneering work of H.G. Lewis, *Unionism
and Relative Wages in the United States* (Chicago: University of Chicago Press, 1963). In Figure 13.7, our
analysis employs a two-sector model with labor supply curves to each sector. Remember that a labor supply curve to one sector is drawn holding the wages in other sectors (the "alternative wages") constant;
whenever the wage in one sector changes, the labor supply curve to the other sector may shift. We *sometimes* ignore this complexity below to keep our exposition as simple as possible and to highlight the various behaviors that might occur in either sector in response to unionization.

the nonunion sector. As a result, the observed union *relative wage* advantage (R_1), computed as

$$R_1 = (W_u^1 - W_n^1)/W_n^1 \qquad (13.2)$$

will tend to be greater than the true *absolute* effect of the union on its members' real wage. This true absolute effect (A), stated in percentage terms, is defined as

$$A = (W_u^1 - W_0)/W_0 \qquad (13.3)$$

Because W_n^1 is lower than W_0, R_1 is greater than A.

THREAT EFFECTS   Another possible response by nonunion employees is to want a union to represent them as well! Nonunion employers, fearing that a union would increase labor costs and place limits on managerial prerogatives, might seek to "buy off" their employees by offering them above-market wages.[39] Because there are costs to workers (as noted earlier) of union membership, some wage less than W_u^1 but higher than W_0 would presumably be sufficient to assure employers that the majority of their employees would not vote for a union (assuming that the employees are happy with their nonwage conditions of employment).

The implications of such *threat effects*—nonunion wage increases resulting from the threat of union entry—are traced in Figure 13.8. The increase in wage in the union sector, and resulting decline in employment there, is again assumed to cause the supply of workers to the nonunion sector to shift to S_n^1. In response to the threat of union entry, however, nonunion employers are assumed to *increase* their employees' wages to W_n^*, which lies between W_0 and W_u^1. This wage increase causes employment to decline to E_n^*; at the higher wage nonunion employers demand fewer workers. Moreover, since the nonunion wage is now not free to be bid down, an excess supply of labor, $L_n^* - E_n^*$, exists, resulting in unemployment. Finally, because the nonunion wage is now higher than the original wage, the observed union relative wage advantage:

$$R_2 = (W_u^1 - W_n^*)/W_n^* \qquad (13.4)$$

is smaller than the absolute effect of unions on their members' real wages.

WAIT UNEMPLOYMENT   One might question whether workers who lose (or do not have) a union job will necessarily leave the union sector and take jobs in the nonunion sector. Even with a fixed employment level in the union sector, job vacancies occur as a result of retirements, deaths, and voluntary turnover. Some of those who do not have union jobs will find it attractive to search for work in the union sector, and their search might be more effective if they are not

---

[39]For a more formal discussion of this possibility, see Sherwin Rosen, "Trade Union Power, Threat Effects, and the Extent of Organization," *Review of Economic Studies* 36 (April 1969): 185–196.

FIGURE 13.8

Threat Effects of Unions on Wages and Employment in Nonunion Sector

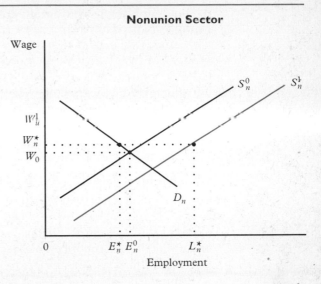

Nonunion Sector

simultaneously employed elsewhere. Workers who reject lower-paying nonunion jobs so that they can search for higher-paying union ones create the phenomenon of *wait unemployment* (they are waiting for union jobs to open up).[40]

The main behavior behind the wait-unemployment response is that workers will move from one sector to another if the latter offers higher *expected* wages. Expected wages in a sector are equal to the sector's wage rate multiplied by the probability of obtaining a job in that sector. Thus, even if one were always able to find a job in the nonunion sector, rejecting employment there might be beneficial if there were a reasonable chance (even if it were less than 100 percent) of obtaining a higher-paying union job. The importance of the resultant wait unemployment for our current discussion is that not everyone who loses a job in the union sector will spill over into the nonunion sector; in fact, it is even theoretically possible that some workers originally in the nonunion sector would quit their jobs to take a chance on finding work in the union sector!

The presence of wait unemployment in the union sector will reduce the spillover of workers to the nonunion sector, thus moderating downward pressure on nonunion wages. Moreover, if enough nonunion workers decide to search for union jobs, the labor supply curve to the nonunion sector could even shift to the left. In this case, unionization in one sector could cause wages in the nonunion sector to rise, just as with the threat effect (in fact, there is a "threat" here that is being carried out: workers are leaving the nonunion employers to search for union jobs).

SHIFTS IN LABOR DEMAND   Finally, recall that we discussed earlier the activities unions undertake to alter the demand for their members' labor services.

[40]See Jacob Mincer, "Unemployment Effects of Minimum Wages," *Journal of Political Economy* 84, pt. 2 (July/August 1976): S87–S104. Although Mincer discusses minimum wage effects, union-imposed "minimum wages" can be analyzed analogously.

In some cases these activities involve attempts to shift the product demand curve facing unionized firms (and hence their labor demand curve) to the right. If unions were successful in their efforts to increase product demand in the unionized sector, perhaps at the expense of the nonunion sector, the rightward shift in the union-sector labor demand curve—and the associated leftward shift in the labor demand curve in the nonunion sector—would again serve to lower wages in the nonunion sector below what they were originally.[41]

EVIDENCE OF UNION WAGE EFFECTS

The preceding discussion has highlighted a major point: because the presence of unions can influence both the union and the nonunion wage rate, it is not possible to observe the wage that would have existed in the absence of unions. Hence, estimates of a union's effects on the absolute level (A) of its members' real wages—see equation (13.3)—cannot be obtained. Care must be taken not to mistake the relative wage effects we can observe (equation 13.2) for the absolute effects.

Economists have expended considerable effort to estimate the extent to which unions have raised the wages of their members relative to the wages of comparable nonunion workers in the private sector. These studies have tended to use data on large samples of individuals and have attempted to separate wage differentials caused by unionization from wage differentials caused by differences in personal characteristics and differences in industry and occupation of employment. That is, these economists have sought to ascertain how much more union members get paid than nonunion workers, after controlling for any differences between the two groups in other factors that might be expected to influence wages. Most of the work has been done on the United States, where levels of unionization are so modest that it is relatively easy to find comparable nonunion workers.

Because the studies of union-nonunion wage differences have used various data sets and statistical methodologies, there is no single estimate of the gap upon which all researchers agree. Enough work has been done on the topic, however, for certain patterns to emerge.

1. The union relative wage advantage in the United States appears to fall into the range of *10 to 20 percent.* That is, our best estimate is that American union workers receive wages that are some 10 to 20 percent higher than those of comparable nonunion workers.[42]

---

[41]Our discussion of these four responses has assumed a partial equilibrium model. Once one considers a general equilibrium framework and allows capital to move between sectors, even more possibilities may exist. On this point, see Harry Johnson and Peter Mieszkowski, "The Effects of Unionization on the Distribution of Income: A General Equilibrium Approach," *Quarterly Journal of Economics* 84 (November 1969): 539- 561.

[42]For surveys of these estimates, see Richard Freeman and James Medoff, *What Do Unions Do?* (New York: Basic Books, 1984); H. Gregg Lewis, *Union Relative Wage Effects: A Survey* (Chicago: University of Chicago Press, 1986); Barry T. Hirsch and John T. Addison, *The Economic Analysis of Unions: New Approaches and Evidence* (Boston: Allen and Unwin, 1986); and Pencavel, *Labor Markets Under Trade Unionism.*

2. The *private sector* union wage advantage in the United States is larger than that in the *public sector.* For example, one study that used the same data and the same statistical methodology for both sectors estimated that the private sector wage gap was roughly 19 percent in the early 1990s, while in the public sector over the same period it was in the 10 to 12 percent range.[43]

3. The union relative wage advantage in the United States is larger than it is in other countries for which comparable estimates are available. One study that used the same data set and the same methodology for the United States and three other countries estimated the following wages gaps for 1985–1987: United States, 18 percent; United Kingdom, 10 percent; West Germany, 6 percent; Austria, 5 percent.[44] A study of Australia for the same time period also indicated smaller union wage effects there than in the United States.[45]

4. Unions everywhere tend to reduce the dispersion of earnings among workers.[46] They raise the wages of less-skilled workers relative to higher-skilled workers within the union sector, thereby reducing the payoff to human-capital investments. They "standardize" wages within and across firms in the same industry, and they reduce the earnings gaps between production and office workers. They also reduce the wage gap between white and black workers in the United States.[47]

5. The union relative wage advantage in the United States has historically tended to be larger during recessionary periods.[48] Studies suggest, for example, that the union-nonunion wage gap increased significantly during the early 1980s, when unemployment rates were relatively high. As we

---

[43]Barry T. Hirsch and David A. Macpherson, *Union Membership and Earnings Data Book 1993: Compilations from the Current Population Survey* (Washington, D.C.: Bureau of National Affairs, 1994), 11.

[44]David G. Blanchflower and Richard B. Freeman, "Unionism in the United States and Other Advanced OECD Countries," *Industrial Relations* 31, no. 1 (Winter 1992): 56–79.

[45]Robert Kornfeld, "The Effects of Union Membership on Wages and Employee Benefits: The Case of Australia," *Industrial and Labor Relations Review* 47, no. 1 (October 1993): 114–128.

[46]Blanchflower and Freeman, "Unionism in the United States and Other Advanced OECD Countries."

[47]James Peoples Jr., "Monopolistic Market Structure, Unionization, and Racial Wage Differentials," *Review of Economics and Statistics* 76, no. 1 (February 1994): 207–211; Richard Freeman and James Medoff, *What Do Unions Do?*, Chapter 5; David Card, "The Effect of Unions on the Distribution of Wages: Redistribution or Relabelling?" working paper no. 287, Industrial Relations Section, Princeton University, July 1991; Greg M. Duncan and Duane E. Leigh, "Wage Determination in the Union and Nonunion Sectors: A Sample Selectivity Approach," *Industrial and Labor Relations Review* 34 (October 1980): 24–35; Richard Freeman, "Union Wage Practices and Wage Dispersion Within Establishments," *Industrial and Labor Relations Review* 36 (October 1982): 3–21; and Thomas Hyclak, "The Effects of Unions on Earnings Inequality in Local Labor Markets," *Industrial and Labor Relations Review* 33 (October 1979): 77–84.

[48]Lewis, *Unionism and Relative Wages;* Peter Linneman and Michael Wachter, "Rising Union Premiums and Declining Boundaries Among Noncompeting Groups," *American Economic Review* 76 (May 1986): 103–108, and William Moore and John Raisian, "Union–Nonunion Wage Differentials in the Public Administration, Educational and Private Sectors," *Review of Economics and Statistics* 69 (November 1987): 608–615.

EXAMPLE 13.3

The Paradox of Large Wage Increases in Declining Sectors

The fact that union members' wages grew more rapidly in the 1970s and early 1980s appears paradoxical against the backdrop of a declining union employment share and the increased resistance to unions among nonunion employers. The ten manufacturing industries with the highest growth in wages between 1970 and 1980 had higher rates of union membership and lower output growth rates than the manufacturing sector as a whole. The increase in the pay of steelworkers was the highest of all, rising during the 1970s just as the steel industry was experiencing a wrenching decline in output of 16 percent! What explains the ability of unions to negotiate large wage increases from industries that are in relative, if not absolute, decline?

One possibility is that when industries that are capital-intensive experience declining demand for output (or at least not a growing one), their ability to substitute capital for labor in response to wage increases is diminished. Capital can be most easily substituted for labor when output is expanding and new capital is being purchased; once machinery and production processes are "in place," however, the substitution possibilities are substantially diminished. It is true that even with constant production levels substitution could occur when capital needed to be replaced, but much of the capital in manufacturing is long-lived and highly industry-specific (so that selling it "used" is not attractive). The result is that the demand for labor may be less elastic in contracting industries than in growing ones!

Rapidly rising wages exacerbate the contraction of output, however, and it is clear that when firms cannot cover their variable costs, plant closings become imminent. At this point (or when a majority of union members face the threat of permanent lay-off) unions have incentives to engage in an "end-game" strategy and to agree to wage concessions in an effort to preserve the firms for which their members work. For example, following their extraordinary wage gains in the 1970s, unionized steelworkers since 1982 have traded away wage gains for increased job security.

SOURCE: Colin Lawrence and Robert Z. Lawrence, "Manufacturing Wage Dispersion: An End Game Interpretation," *Brookings Papers on Economic Activity*, 1985–1, 47–106.

argue in Example 13.3, firms find it easier to substitute capital for labor when new capital investments are being made. Therefore, during periods when output and investements are not expanding, substitutions of capital for labor are more difficult and the union confronts a less elastic demand curve for labor.

6. Although the findings do not yet fit a pattern, researchers have attempted to discover whether greater levels of unionization tend to increase or decrease wages in the *nonunion* sector. In a word, these studies have tried to see whether the spillover or the threat effect dominates among nonunion employers. The evidence so far is ambiguous. A recent study found, for example, that threat effects dominated within *cities* (that is, in more highly unionized cities, the wages of nonunion workers were higher). It also found, however, that the spillover effect dominated within *industries* (in more

highly unionized industries, nonunion wages tended to be lower). These contradictory results mirror those of earlier studies.[49]

EVIDENCE OF UNION TOTAL COMPENSATION EFFECTS

Estimates of the extent to which the wages of union workers exceed the wages of otherwise comparable nonunion workers may prove misleading for two reasons. First, such estimates ignore the fact that wages are only part of the compensation package. It has often been argued that employee benefits, such as paid holidays, vacation pay, sick leave, and retirement benefits, will be higher in firms that are unionized than in nonunion firms. The argument states that, because tastes for the various benefits differ across individuals and because there is no easy way to communicate the preferences of the average employee to the employer in a nonunion firm, nonunion firms tend to pay a higher fraction of total compensation in the form of money wages. Recent empirical evidence tends to support this contention; employee benefits and the share of compensation that goes to benefits do appear to be higher in union than in nonunion firms.[50] Ignoring benefits may therefore understate the true union/nonunion total-compensation differential.

In contrast, ignoring *nonpecuniary* conditions of employment may cause one to overstate the effect of unions on their members' overall welfare levels compared to those of nonunion workers. For example, studies have shown that for blue-collar workers, unionized firms tend to have more-structured work settings, more-hazardous jobs, less-flexible hours of work, faster work paces, and less employee control over the assignment of overtime hours than do nonunion firms.[51] This situation may arise because production settings that call for more interdependence among workers and the need for rigid work requirements by employers also give rise to unions. That is, the decision to vote for unions may be heavily influenced by these nonpecuniary conditions of employment. While unions often strive to affect these working conditions, they do not always succeed. Part of the estimated union/nonunion earnings differential may be a premium paid to union workers to

[49]See David Neumark and Michael L. Wachter, "Union Effects on Nonunion Wages: Evidence from Panel Data on Industries and Cities," *Industrial and Labor Relations Review* 49, no. 1 (October 1995): 20–38; Richard B. Freeman and James L. Medoff, "The Impact of the Percentage Organized on Union and Nonunion Wages," *Review of Economics and Statistics* 63 (November 1981): 561–572; Lawrence Kahn, "The Effect of Unions on the Earnings of Nonunion Workers," *Industrial and Labor Relations Review* 31 (January 1978): 205–216; Casey Ichniowski, Richard Freeman, and Harrison Lauer, "Collective Bargaining Laws, Threat Effects, and the Determinants of Police Compensation," *Journal of Labor Economics* 7 (April 1989): 191–209.

[50]Richard Freeman, "The Effect of Trade Unions on Fringe Benefits," *Industrial and Labor Relations Review* 34 (July 1981): 489–509; William Alpert, "Unions and Private Wage Supplements," *Journal of Labor Research* 3 (Spring 1982): 179–190; and Kornfeld, "The Effects of Union Membership on Wages and Employee Benefits."

[51]Greg Duncan and Frank Stafford, "Do Union Members Receive Compensating Wage Differentials?" *American Economic Review* 70 (June 1980): 355–371, and J. Paul Leigh, "Are Unionized Blue-Collar Jobs More Hazardous Than Nonunionized Blue-Collar Jobs?" *Journal of Labor Research* 3 (Summer 1982): 349–357.

compensate them for these unfavorable working conditions. One study estimates that two-fifths of the estimated union/nonunion earnings differential reflects such compensation, suggesting that the observed earnings differential may overstate the true differential in overall levels of worker well-being.[52]

THE EFFECTS OF UNIONS ON EMPLOYMENT

If unions raise the wages and employee benefits of their members, and if they impose constraints on managerial prerogatives, we have seen that economic theory suggests their presence will have a negative effect on employment. In recent years, several studies have investigated this theoretical prediction, and the results suggest that unions do reduce employment growth. A study of plants in California during the late 1970s, for example, estimated that employment grew some 2 to 4 percentage points more slowly per year in union than in nonunion firms; in fact, the growth rates were so different that about 60 percent of the decline in California's unionization rate was attributed to slower employment growth in union jobs.[53] Other studies have found similar employment effects for the United States as a whole, as well as for Canada and the United Kingdom.[54] Finally, a recent study reminds us that even when employment is not much changed in the face of unionization, the total yearly hours of work might still fall.[55]

THE EFFECTS OF UNIONS ON PRODUCTIVITY AND PROFITS

There are two views on how unions affect labor productivity (output per worker). One is that unions *increase* worker productivity, given the firm's level of capital, by providing a "voice" mechanism through which workers' suggestions and preferences can be communicated to management.[56] With a direct means for expressing

---

[52]Duncan and Stafford, "Do Union Members Receive Compensating Wage Differentials?"

[53]Jonathan S. Leonard, "Unions and Employment Growth," *Industrial Relations* 31, no. 1 (Winter 1992): 80–94.

[54]Timothy Dunne and David A. Macpherson, "Unionism and Gross Employment Flows," *Southern Economic Journal* 60, no. 3 (January 1994): 727–738; Stephen G. Bronars, Donald R. Deere, and Joseph Tracy, "The Effects of Unions on Firm Behavior: An Empirical Analysis Using Firm-Level Data," *Industrial Relations* 33, no. 4 (October 1994): 426–451; Robert G. Valletta, "Union Effects on Municipal Employment and Wages: A Longitudinal Approach," *Journal of Labor Economics* 11, no. 3 (July 1993): 545–574; Richard J. Long, "The Impact of Unionization on Employment Growth of Canadian Companies," *Industrial and Labor Relations Review* 46, no. 4 (July 1993): 691–703; and David G. Blanchflower, Neil Millward, and Andrew J. Oswald, "Unions and Employment Behaviour," *Economic Journal* 101, no. 407 (July 1991): 815–834.

[55]William M. Boal and John Pencavel, "The Effects of Labor Unions on Employment, Wages, and Days of Operation: Coal Mining in West Virginia," *Quarterly Journal of Economics* 109, no. 1 (February 1994): 267–298.

[56]For a more complete statement of this argument, see Richard B. Freeman and James L. Medoff, *What Do Unions Do?* (New York: Basic Books, 1984). Note that there is another, more "mechanical" way in which unions can raise worker productivity. We have seen that unions raise wages, and theory suggests that the response by profit-maximizing employers will be to reduce employment and substitute capital for labor. Thus, as firms move up and to the left along their marginal product of labor curves, the marginal product of labor rises in response to the wage increase.

their ideas or concerns, workers may have enhanced motivation levels and be less likely to quit.[57] With lower quit rates, firms have more incentives to invest in firm-specific training, which should also raise worker productivity.

The other view on how unions affect worker productivity stresses the limits they place on managerial prerogatives, especially with respect to using cost-minimizing levels of the labor input. We argued earlier that if unions care about the employment, as well as the wages, of their members, they will put pressure on management to agree to staffing requirements, restrictions on work out of job title, cumbersome methods through which the disciplining of nonproductive workers must take place, and other policies that increase labor costs per unit of output.

Empirical analyses of union productivity effects have yielded conflicting results. One study that reviewed the results of many other studies concluded that no generalizations are possible, and that the effects of unions on workers' output depends very much on the quality of the relationship between labor and management in each particular collective bargaining setting.[58]

If unions raise wages, but do not clearly raise worker productivity, then we might expect them to reduce firms' profits. Some studies directly analyze unionization and profit levels, holding other things constant; these rather consistently estimate that profits in unionized firms are lower, both in the United States and in the United Kingdom.[59] Another way of studying unions' effects on profits, however, is to make use of evidence that the stock market quickly and accurately reflects changes in a firm's profitability. The stock-price studies that have been done to date also find evidence consistent with the hypothesis that unionization reduces the profitability of employers.[60]

NORMATIVE ANALYSES OF UNIONS

We have seen throughout this text that economic theory can be used in both its *positive* and its *normative* modes. The analyses of union effects in this section so far have been of a positive nature, in that we have summarized both theory and evidence on how unions affect various labor market outcomes. We turn now to a normative question that often underlies discussions of unions and the government

---

[57]Unionization appears to lower quit rates in the United States and elsewhere; see Blanchflower and Freeman, "Unionism in the United States and Other Advanced OECD Countries."

[58]Blanchflower and Freeman, "Unionism in the United States and Other Advanced OECD Countries."

[59]Bronars, Deere, and Tracy, "The Effects of Unions on Firm Behavior"; Blanchflower and Freeman, "Unionism in the United States and Other Advanced OECD Countries"; and Barry T. Hirsch, "Union Coverage and Profitability Among U.S. Firms," *Review of Economics and Statistics* 73 (February 1991): 69–77.

[60]Richard S. Ruback and Martin B. Zimmerman, "Unionization and Profitability: Evidence from the Capital Market," *Journal of Political Economy* 92 (December 1984): 1134–1157; and Becker, "Union Rents as a Source of Takeover Gains Among Target Shareholders."

policies that affect them: Do union enhance or reduce social welfare? As one might expect, opinions differ.

<u>**POTENTIAL REDUCTIONS IN SOCIAL WELFARE**</u>   We saw in Chapter 1 that that role of any market, including the labor market, is to facilitate mutually beneficial transactions by providing a mechanism for voluntary exchange. The ultimate goal of this exchange is to arrive at an allocation of goods and services that generates as much utility as is possible, given a society's resources, for the individuals in that society. If a market has facilitated *all* such transactions, then it can be said to have arrived at a point of *Pareto efficiency*. A requirement for the existence of Pareto efficiency is that all productive resources, including labor, be used in a way that generates maximum utility for society (this includes the utility of the workers themselves as well as that of the consumers who purchase the goods or services they produce).

One argument that unions reduce social welfare points to the production lost (the labor resources wasted) when workers go on strike. A second argument is similar: When labor and management agree to restrictive work rules (as noted in our discussion of the efficient-contracts model), the use of excess workers in the production process creates wastage--and therefore social loss--in the use of labor. A third argument is more subtle, however, and it is to this argument that we now turn.

Recall from Chapter 3 that profit-maximizing employers hire workers until their marginal revenue productivities are equal to their wage rates. Thus, when a worker leaves a lower-paying job for a higher-paying one, he or she is moving from a job in which marginal productivity is lower to one in which it is higher. If this move is made voluntarily, overall social welfare (utility) is clearly enhanced. The value to *others* of what the worker produces (as reflected by marginal revenue product) rises, and the fact that the worker moves voluntarily guarantees that his or her *own* utility is increased. Therefore, we can conclude that voluntary moves from lower- to higher-paying jobs are, from a social viewpoint, *Pareto-improving*.

Simple reasoning suggests that for Pareto efficiency to be achieved, resources that have the same *potential* productivity must have the same *actual* productivity. Consider, for example, a group of workers who are equally skilled, experienced, and motivated. If some of these workers are in jobs that produce $15 worth of goods or services per hour, while others in the group are in jobs that produce only $10, the value of society's output could be enhanced by the voluntary movement of members of the latter subset into the higher-paying jobs. Reducing the number of workers in the $10 jobs would serve to raise the marginal productivity of those who remain in those jobs, while increasing the number of workers in the $15 jobs would put downward pressure on the wage (and marginal productivity) in that sector. As long as the marginal productivities of workers in the skill group continue to differ, however, the value of society's output could be increased still further by having members of the lower-paid subset move into the higher-paying jobs. Only when all these Pareto-improving moves have been made--which will drive *the marginal productivities of all workers in the group toward equality*—can it be said that Pareto efficiency is reached.

The third argument that unions reduce social welfare, then, rests on two propositions. The first is that unions create wage (and therefore productivity) differentials among equivalent workers by raising wages in the union sector above those in the nonunion sector. The second is that, in the absence of unions, mobility across employers would ensure that equivalent workers would be paid the same wage (and therefore have the same marginal revenue productivity). Because wages in union jobs are not flexible enough to permit an expansion of jobs in the higher-paying sector, it is argued that union–nonunion wage differentials reduce society's output below its full potential (there are "too many" workers in lower-productivity jobs and "too few" in higher-productivity ones). Some economists have attempted to estimate these losses, and their estimates have generally been small—in the range of 0.2 to 0.4 percent of national output.[61]

POTENTIAL INCREASES IN SOCIAL WELFARE Arguments that unions reduce social welfare lose some of their force if, in the absence of unions, labor or product markets are not as competitive as assumed by standard economic theory. Suppose, for example, that the cost of mobility is so great that workers do not freely move to jobs in which their productivity (including their own utility) is maximized. If such barriers to mobility exist, one implication is that compensating wage differentials may fail to correctly guide the allocation of workers across jobs that have varying levels of unpleasant (or pleasant) characteristics. Recalling the discussion of Chapter 8, if a lack of information or choice impedes the movement of workers between jobs, wages will generally fail to reflect the value workers place on the nonpecuniary aspects (safety, for example) of their jobs. If so, too many workers may end up in dangerous or otherwise unpleasant jobs, which they would gladly leave (even for a lower-paying one) if they had the chance. The lack of information or choice prevents this movement, thereby allowing employers to continue offering jobs with characteristics workers otherwise would pay to avoid.

With respect to working conditions, there are two general means by which employer behavior can be influenced. The mechanism relied upon by the market, with its individual transactions, is one of *exit and entry.* If a worker is unhappy with certain conditions of employment, he or she is free to leave; if enough workers do so, the employer will be forced to alter the offending condition or else increase wages enough to induce the workers it has to remain. An alternative to the exit mechanism is the mechanism of *voice:* Workers can vocalize their concerns and hope that the employer will respond.

The voicing of requests by *individuals* is potentially very costly, for two reasons. First, many workplace conditions (such as lighting, scheduling, safety precautions, and the like) are examples of "public goods" within the plant. All workers are benefited by any improvements, whether or not they contributed to

[61]Freeman and Medoff, *What Do Unions Do?*, 57.

the campaign to secure them. Therefore, recalling our discussion of public goods in Chapter 1, the possibility of "free riders" inhibits individuals (acting alone) from bearing the costs of a campaign to change workplace conditions. Second, because the employer may respond to complaints by firing "troublemakers," an individual worker who uses the voice mechanism without some form of job protection must be prepared to suffer the costs of exit!

Those who hold the view that unions improve social welfare argue that, in the face of high mobility costs, unions offer workers the mechanism of *collective* voice in the establishment of their working conditions. By bargaining collectively with the employer about the various conditions of employment, they solve the free-rider problem and relieve their members of the risks and burdens associated with individual voice. Further, collective bargaining agreements almost always establish a grievance procedure through which certain employee complaints can be formally addressed by a neutral third party. In short, it can be argued that unions provide mechanisms of collective voice that substitute for an expensive-to-use exit mechanism in the determination of the workplace conditions that affect workers' utility. They therefore promote Pareto-improving transactions that otherwise would not have been induced because of the high costs of employee mobility.

Other arguments that unions enhance (or at least do not reduce) social welfare also rest on market conditions that call into question key assumptions underlying the standard economic model of employer behavior. For example, one possibility (mentioned earlier in this chapter) is that unionized employers have substantial monopoly power in their product markets, which yields them excess profits. If the efficient-contracts model of bargaining holds, and if the "contract curve" is vertical, then employment remains equal to its preunionization level, and the union and the employer end up simply splitting the employer's excess profits. In this case, income is transferred from owners to workers, but because total output is unaffected, there would be no social losses associated with higher union wages.

Another argument is that employers are not as knowledgeable about how to maximize profits as standard economic theory assumes. Because management finds it costly to search for better (or less costly) ways to produce, so the argument goes, we cannot be sure that it will always use labor in the most productive ways possible. (Clearly, this argument rests on the implicit assumption that entry into the product market is difficult enough that inefficient producers are not necessarily "punished" by competitive forces.) When unions organize and raise the wages of their members, firms may be "shocked" into the search for better ways to produce. Moreover, by establishing formal channels of communication between workers and management, unionization at least *potentially* provides a mechanism through which employers and employees can more effectively communicate about policies and procedures in the workplace.[62]

---

[62]For a fuller development of this argument, see Freeman and Medoff, *What Do Unions Do?*, 15.

REVIEW QUESTIONS

1. Suppose that a proposal for tax reductions associated with the purchase of capital equipment is up for debate. Suppose, too, that union leaders are called upon to comment on the proposal from the perspective of how it will affect the welfare of their members as workers (not consumers). Will they all agree on the effects of the proposal? Explain your answer.

2. The head of a large national union is trying to decide where he should concentrate his efforts at organizing a union. He perceives three options: firm A, firm B, or firm C. The three firms are identical except that:
    a. Firm A faces a perfectly elastic (horizontal) supply curve of labor and a rather inelastic demand curve for its output.
    b. Firm B behaves as a monopsonist (faces an upward-sloping supply curve of labor) and faces a perfectly elastic (horizontal) demand curve for its output.
    c. Firm C faces a perfectly elastic supply curve of labor and a perfectly elastic demand curve for its output.

    This union head would like to know where a new union will pay off most in terms of large wage gains with only small reductions in the numbers of workers. Rank the three options from best to worst, giving reasons for your ranking.

3. Is the following statement true, false, or uncertain? "The host of empirical studies indicating that unions raise the wages of their members by 10 to 20 percent relative to the wages of comparable nonunion workers imply that unions have a negative effect on national output." Explain your answer.

4. Consider the following quotation:
    "The theory of compensating wage differentials is based on the assumption that workers are able to command higher wages in higher-risk jobs. While I believe that this is true in such unionized sectors as ironworkers, construction workers, and lumber and sawmill workers, I have found the opposite to be true in nonunion, nonorganized industries. In the nonunion chemical industries, as well as in such industries as soap making, etc., it has been my experience that the most dangerous jobs were handled by the lowest-paid, least-educated, and usually minority workers. I am concerned about this because of the steady decline in the percentage of jobs that are covered by union contracts in this state over the past 20 years."

    Please answer the following two questions about the above quotation:
    a. Why might the presence of unions help to create compensating wage differentials for risk?
    b. If the lowest-paid, least-educated workers in the nonunion sector do the dangerous work, does this suggest that compensating wage differentials in the nonunion sector do not exist? Why or why not?

5. The Jones Act mandates that at least 50 percent of all U.S. government-financed cargo must be transported in U.S.-owned ships and that any U.S. ship leaving a U.S. port must have at least 90 percent of its crew composed of U.S. citizens. What would you expect the impact of this act to be on the demand for labor in the shipping industry and the ability of unions to push up the wages of U.S. seafarers?

6. Some collective bargaining agreements contain "union standards" clauses that prohibit the employer from subcontracting with firms that pay wages below those specified in the agreement. That is, the employer is prohibited from farming out

work normally done in the plant to other firms (the subcontractors) if the subcontractors pay less than the union wage.

a. What is the union's rationale for seeking a union standards clause?

b. Under what conditions will a union standards clause most likely be sought by a labor union?

7. A recent publication of the AFL-CIO stated, "There is accumulating evidence that unionized workers are more productive than nonunion workers and that unionization raises productivity in an establishment. This suggests that employers and American society generally should take a much more positive approach to unionism and collective bargaining." Comment on this quotation.

8. In the mid–1980s the teachers' union of a large American city was told that the city's financial difficulties made it necessary to cut payroll costs for teachers by 10 percent. The city gave the teachers' union a choice: it could accept a 10 percent cut in the salaries paid to teachers and suffer no employment losses, or it could keep salaries constant and accept a 10 percent cut in employment levels (and a corresponding 10 percent increase in class sizes). General-

izing from the political model of strike activity given in Chapter 13, in which the major actors are employers, workers, and union leaders (elected by majority rule), please perform the following tasks:

a. Predict and explain the union's decision, assuming that its collective bargaining agreement with the city specifies that any layoffs will occur among those teachers most recently hired.

b. Explain whether the decision in (a) would have been different if the collective bargaining agreement had specified that all layoffs would occur on a random basis, independent of seniority, teaching field, or any other teacher characteristics.

9. In Germany temporary layoffs and dismissals on short notice are often illegal. A dismissal is illegal if it is "socially unjustified," and it is considered "socially unjustified" if the worker could be employed in a different position or establishment of the firm, even one requiring retraining. Workers illegally dismissed may sue their employers. What are the likely consequences of this German law for the ability of German unions to raise wages?

SELECTED READINGS

Atherton, Wallace. *Theory of Union Bargaining Goals.* Princeton, N.J.: Princeton University Press, 1973.

Freeman, Richard B., and James L. Medoff. *What Do Unions Do?* New York: Basic Books, 1984.

Hirsch, Barry T., and John T. Addison. *The Economic Analysis of Unions: New Approaches and Evidence.* Boston: Allen and Unwin, 1986.

Kerr, Clark, and Paul D. Staudohar, eds. *Labor Economics and Industrial Relations: Markets and Institutions.* Cambridge, Mass.: Harvard University Press, 1994.

Lewis, H. G. *Union Relative Wage Effects: A Survey.* Chicago: University of Chicago Press, 1986.

Pencavel, John. *Labor Markets Under Trade Unionism.* Cambridge, Mass.: Basil Blackwell, 1991.

Arbitration and the Bargaining "Contract Zone"

What incentive do the parties to collective bargaining negotiations have to settle their negotiations on their own rather than go to arbitration and have an outside party impose a settlement? The answer may well be that the uncertainty about an arbitrator's likely decision imposes costs on both parties that give them an incentive to come to an agreement on their own. This appendix provides a simple model that illustrates this proposition; it highlights the roles of both *uncertainty* about an arbitrator's likely decision and the parties' *attitudes towards risk* in determining whether a negotiation will wind up in arbitration.[1]

Consider a simple two-party bargaining problem in which the parties, A and B, are negotiating over how to split a "pie" of fixed size. Each party's utility function depends only on the share of the pie that it receives. Figure 13A.1 plots the utility function for party A. When A's share of the pie is zero, A's utility (U_A) is assumed to be zero, and as A's share (S_A) increases, A's utility increases. Crucially, this utility function is also assumed to exhibit the property of *diminishing marginal utility*; equal increments in S_A lead to progressively smaller increments in U_A. As we shall show below, this is equivalent to assuming that the party is *risk averse*, which means that the party would prefer the certainty of having a given share of the pie to an uncertain outcome that, on average, would yield the same share.[2]

Now suppose party A believes that, on average, the arbitrator would award it one-half of the pie if the negotiations went to arbitration. If it knew with certainty

---

[1]The discussion here is a simplified version of some of the material found in Henry S. Farber and Harry C. Katz, "Interest Arbitration, Outcomes, and the Incentive to Bargain," *Industrial and Labor Relations Review* 33 (October 1979): 55–63.

[2]Refer to Appendix 8A, especially note 4, for an introduction to this use of cardinal utility functions.

FIGURE 13A.1

Utility Function for a
Risk-Averse Party:
Uncertainty About
Arbitrator's Decision
Leads to a Contract Zone

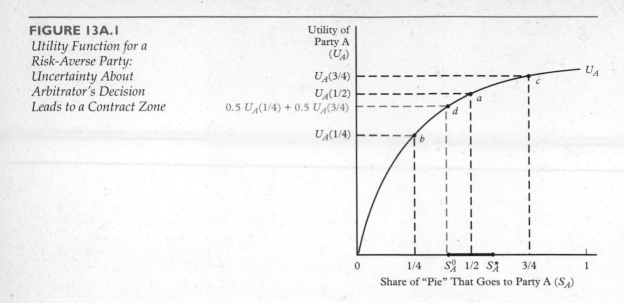

that the arbitrator would do this, party A's utility from going to arbitration would be $U_A(1/2)$, or point *a* in Figure 13A.1. Suppose, however, that party A is uncertain about the arbitrator's decision and instead believes the arbitrator will assign it one-quarter of the pie with probability one-half, or three-quarters of the pie also with probability one-half. Utility in these two states is given by $U_A(1/4)$, point *b*, and $U_A(3/4)$, point *c*, respectively. Although, on average, party A expects to be awarded one-half of the pie, its average or *expected* utility in this case is $0.5U_A(1/4) + 0.5U_A(3/4)$, which, as Figure 13A.1 indicates (see point *d*), is less than $U_A(1/2)$. This reflects the fact that party A is risk averse, preferring a certain outcome (point *a*) to an uncertain outcome (point *d*) that yields the same expected share.

Note that if party A were awarded the share S_A^0 with certainty, it would receive the same utility level it receives under the uncertain situation, where it expects, with equal probability, the arbitrator to award it either one-quarter or three-quarters of the pie. Indeed, it would prefer any *certain* share above S_A^0 to bearing the cost of the uncertainty associated with having to face the arbitrator's decision. The set of contracts it potentially would voluntarily agree to, then, is the set S_A such that

$$S_A^0 \leq S_A \leq 1; \quad S_A^0 < 1/2 \tag{13A.1}$$

Suppose party B is similarly risk averse and has identical expectations about what the arbitrator's decision will look like. It should be obvious, using the same logic as above, that the set of contracts, S_B, that party B potentially would voluntarily agree to is given by a similar expression:

$$S_B^0 \leq S_B \leq 1; \quad S_B^0 < 1/2 \tag{13A.2}$$

FIGURE 13A.2

*Increased Uncertainty
About Arbitrator's
Decision Increases Size of
the Contract Zone*

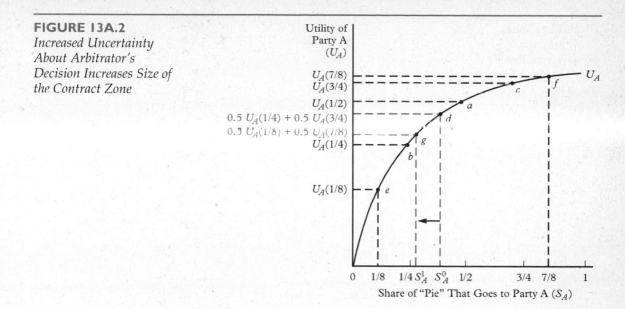

Now, any share that party B voluntarily agrees to receive implies that what B is willing to give party A is 1 minus that share. Since the minimum share B would agree to receive, S_B^0, is less than one-half, it follows that the maximum share B would voluntarily agree to give A in negotiations, S_A^* (which equals $1- S_B^0$), is greater than one-half. Party B potentially would be willing to voluntarily agree to any settlement that gives party A a share of less than S_A^*.

Referring to Figure 13A.1, observe that party A would be willing to voluntarily agree to contracts that offer it at least S_A^0, while party B would be willing to agree to contracts that give party A S_A^* or less. Hence, the set of contracts that *both* parties would find preferable to going to arbitration (and thus *potentially* would voluntarily agree to) is given by all the shares for A (S_A) that lie between these two extremes:

$$S_A^0 \le S_A \le S_A^* \qquad\qquad (13A.3)$$

This set of potential voluntary solutions to the bargaining problem is indicated by the bold-line segment on the horizontal axis of Figure 13A.1 and is called the *contract zone*. As long as both parties are risk averse and are uncertain what the arbitrator will do, a contract zone will exist.

The extent of the parties' *uncertainty* about the arbitrator's decision and the extent of their *risk aversion* are important determinants of the size of the contract zone. To see this, first suppose that party A continues to expect that, on average, the arbitrator will assign it one-half of the pie, but now believes that this will occur by receiving shares of one-eighth and seven-eighths with equal probability. Figure 13A.2 indicates its utility in each of these states (points *e* and *f*) and shows that, while its expected share is still one-half, the greater uncertainty (or "spread" of possible

FIGURE 13A.3

*Utility Function for a
Risk-Neutral Party:
Contract Zone Is
Reduced to a Single
Point*

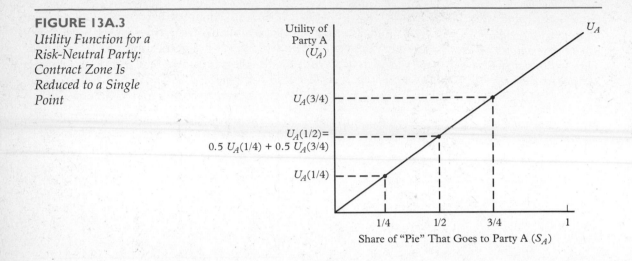

outcomes) has led to a reduction in its expected utility. Indeed, now party A would be as happy to receive the share S_A^1 with certainty as it would to face the risks associated with going to arbitration. Since S_A^1 is less than S_A^0, the size of the contract zone has increased. Hence, increased uncertainty about the arbitrator's decision leads to a larger contract zone.

Next consider Figure 13A.3, where we have drawn a utility function for a *risk-neutral* party. A risk-neutral party has a linear utility function because its utility depends only on its expected share, not the uncertainty associated with the outcome. So, for example, in Figure 13A.3 party A gets the same utility from having a share of one-half with certainty as it does from facing an arbitrated outcome in which there is equal probability that the arbitrator will award it either a share of one-quarter or a share of three-quarters. As a result, faced with the possibility of going to arbitration, there is no share less than one-half that party A would voluntarily agree to settle for prior to arbitration. If party B had similar expectations about the arbitrator's behavior and was similarly risk neutral, it also would refuse to settle for any share of less than one-half, which on average is what it expects to win from the arbitrator. Hence, the contract zone would reduce to one point, the point where both parties receive a share of one-half. The only voluntary agreement the parties will reach is what they expect to receive on average if they go to arbitration. (This illustrates how the arbitration process per se may influence the nature of negotiated settlements.)

More generally, one can show that as a party's risk aversion increases (the utility function becomes "more curved"), the size of the contract zone will increase. Hence, increases in either the parties' risk aversion or their uncertainty about the arbitrator's decision will increase the size of the contract zone.

Larger contract zones mean that there are more potential settlements that *both* parties would prefer to an arbitrated settlement, and some people have argued that this increased menu of choices increases the probability that the parties would settle on their own prior to going to arbitration.[3] An immediate implication of this argument is that, if one believes it is preferable for the parties to settle on their own, the arbitration system should be structured so that the arbitrator's behavior does *not* become completely predictable. As we discussed in the text (footnote 34), however, others argue that a *smaller* contract zone implies the parties have less to argue about, and that therefore *smaller* zones lead to more rapid voluntary settlements!

---

[3]Farber and Katz, "Interest Arbitration, Outcomes, and the Incentive to Bargain."

14

Inequality in Earnings

Workers as individuals, and society as a whole, are concerned with both the *level* and the *dispersion* of income in the economy. The level of income obviously determines the consumption of goods and services that individuals can enjoy, while concern about the distribution of income stems mainly from the importance people place on their relative standing in society (a subject touched on in Chapter 11). Our society attaches a great value to fairness, especially in the access to opportunities for self-improvement, and inequality of income is often thought to be the consequence of unfair treatment (as we saw in Chapter 12). Moreover, some individual benefits of consumption or human capital investments depend on the expenditure levels of *others.* For example, obtaining a high school diploma in an environment in which few attend means more than obtaining one where nearly all attend. Likewise, people often judge perceptions of their "worth" to (or status in) society in relative terms: earning $25,000 a year as a 22-year-old college graduate feels different from earning $25,000 a year as a 50-year-old college graduate.

For purposes of assessing issues of poverty and relative consumption opportunities, the distribution of *family incomes* is of interest. An examination of family incomes involves an analysis of unearned as well as earned income; thus, it must incorporate discussions of inheritance, welfare transfers, and tax policies. It must also deal with how families are defined, formed, and dissolved. Many of these topics are beyond the scope of a labor economics text.

Consistent with our examination of the labor market, the focus of this chapter is on the distribution of *earnings*. While clearly only part of one's overall income, earnings are a reflection of both marginal productivity (one's contribution to total output) and one's access to opportunities; therefore, the distribution of earnings is of critical importance to judgments about many of the individual and social concerns introduced above. (Ideally, the focus would be on total compensation, so that the analyses would include employee benefits. As a practical matter, however, data on the *value* of employee benefits are not widely available in a form that permits an examination of their *distribution* either over time or across individuals.)[1]

This chapter begins with a discussion of how to conceptualize and measure the equality or inequality of earnings. We then investigate the present earnings distribution and the recent trends toward greater inequality that have sparked so much public concern in the past decade. Finally, we review the factors, presented earlier in this text, that affect earnings in an attempt both to review some major concepts and to determine which seem to be related to the recent growth of inequality.

Measuring Inequality

To understand certain basic concepts related to the distribution of earnings, it is helpful to think in graphic terms. Consider a simple plotting of the number of people receiving each given level of earnings. If everyone had the same earnings, say $20,000 per year, there would be no dispersion. The graph of the earnings distribution would look like Figure 14.1.

If there *were* disparities in the earnings people received, these disparities could be relatively large or relatively small. If the average level of earnings were $20,000 and virtually all people received earnings very close to the average, the *dispersion* of earnings would be small. If the average were $20,000, but some made much more and some much less, the dispersion of earnings would be large.

---

[1]A recent study indicates that including private pensions with earnings affects measures of inequality only slightly in the United States, except in the union sector (where pensions are more unequally distributed than earnings). See Mary Ellen Benedict and Kathryn Shaw, "The Impact of Pension Benefits on the Distribution of Earned Income," *Industrial and Labor Relations Review* 48, no. 4 (July 1995): 740–757. Another study, however, analyzed pension *coverage* by gender, age, and education, and concluded that such coverage fell during the 1980s, especially among young, less-educated males; see David E. Bloom and Richard B. Freeman, "The Fall in Private Pension Coverage in the United States," *American Economic Review* 82 (May 1992): 539–545.

FIGURE 14.1
Earnings Distribution with
Perfect Equality

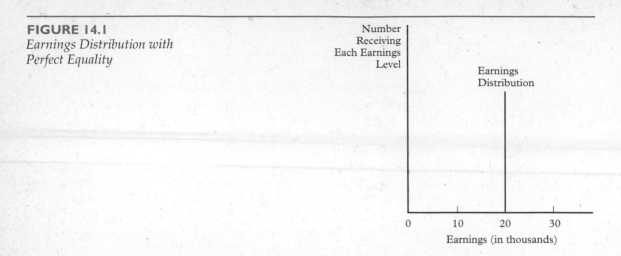

In Figure 14.2 two hypothetical earnings distributions are illustrated. While both distributions are centered on the same average level ($20,000), distribution A exhibits smaller dispersion than distribution B. Earnings in B are more widely dispersed and thus exhibit *a greater degree of inequality.*[2]

Graphs can help to illustrate the concepts of dispersion, but they are a clumsy tool for *measuring* inequality. Various quantitative indicators of earnings inequality can be devised, and they all vary in ease of computation, ease of comprehension, and how accurately they represent the socially relevant dimensions of inequality. The most obvious measure of inequality is the *variance* of the distribution. Variance is a common measure of dispersion, calculated as follows:

$$\text{Variance} = \frac{\sum_i (E_i - \bar{E})^2}{n} \tag{14.1}$$

[2]A summary of various inequality measures can be found in Frank Levy and Richard J. Murnane, "U.S. Earnings Levels and Earnings Inequality: A Review of Recent Trends and Proposed Explanations," *Journal of Economic Literature* 30 (September 1991): 1333–1381. While for most purposes the degree of dispersion is of key importance in judging inequality, it is also interesting to inquire whether the distribution of earnings is *symmetric* or not. If distributions are symmetric, as in Figure 14.2, then as many people earn $X less than average as earn $X more than average. Put differently, if the distribution is symmetric, the dispersion of earnings for the poorest half of society mirrors the dispersion for the richest half. If the distribution is not symmetric, we say it is *skewed*, meaning that one part of the distribution is bunched together and the other part is relatively dispersed. For example, many less-developed countries do not have a sizable middle class. Such countries have a huge number of very poor families and a tiny minority of very wealthy families. Thus, the distribution of income in these countries, normally considered unfair, is highly skewed to the right.

FIGURE 14.2

*Distributions of Earnings with
Different Degrees of Dispersion*

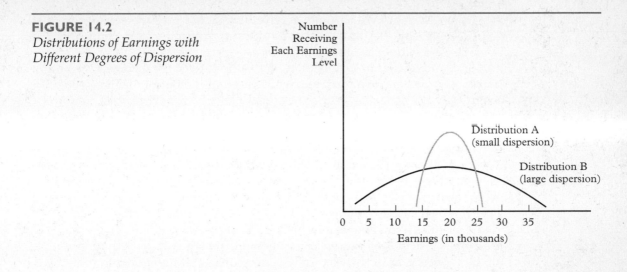

where E_i represents the earnings of person i in the population, n represents the number of people in the population, $\overline{E}$ is the mean level of earnings in the population, and the symbol $\sum$ indicates that we are summing over all persons in the population. One problem with using the variance, however, is that it tends to rise as earnings grow larger. For example, if all earnings in the population were to double, so that the ratio of each person's earnings to the mean (or to the earnings of anyone else, for that matter) remained constant, the variance would still quadruple. Variance is thus a better measure of the absolute than of the *relative* dispersion of earnings.

An alternative to the variance is the *coefficient of variation*: the square root of the variance (called the "standard deviation") divided by the mean. If all earnings were to double, the coefficient of variation, unlike the variance, would remain unchanged. Thus, when available, it is a useful tool for measuring dispersion; we use it later in Table 14.5. Because one must have access to the underlying data on each individual's earnings to calculate the coefficient of variation, however, it is impractical to construct it from published data. Unless the coefficient of variation is itself *published,* then, or unless the researcher has access to the *entire* data set, other more readily constructed measures must be found.

The most widely used measures of earnings inequality start with ranking the population by earnings level and establishing into which percentile a given level of earnings falls. For example, in 1992, men between the ages of 25 and 64 with yearly earnings of $26,934 were at the *median* (50th percentile), meaning that half of all men earned less and half earned more. Men with earnings of $12,622 were at the 20th percentile (20 percent earned less, 80 percent earned more), while those with earnings of $46,019 were at the 80th percentile.

Having determined the earnings levels associated with each percentile, one can either compare the earnings *levels* associated with given percentiles or compare the *share* of total earnings received by each. Comparing shares of total *income* received by the top and bottom fifth (or "quintiles") of families in the population is a widely used measure of *income* inequality. Using this measure we find, for example, that in 1992 families in the top fifth of the income distribution received 46.9 percent of all income, while those in the bottom fifth received 3.8 percent.[3]

Unfortunately, information on *shares* received by each segment of the distribution is not as readily available for individual *earnings* as it is for family income. Comparing the earnings *level* associated with each percentile is readily feasible, however. A commonly used measure of this sort is the ratio of earnings at, say, the 80th percentile to earnings at the 20th. Ratios such as this are intended to indicate how far apart the two ends of the earnings distribution are, and as a measure of dispersion they are easily understood and readily computed.

How useful is it to know that in 1992, for example, men at the 80th percentile of the earnings distribution earned 3.65 times more than men at the 20th? In truth, the ratio in a given year is not very enlightening unless it is *compared* to something. One natural comparison is with ratios for prior years. An increase in these ratios over time, for example, would indicate that the earnings distribution was becoming "stretched," so that the distance between the two ends was growing and earnings were becoming more unequally distributed.

As a rough measure of increasing distance between the two ends of the earnings distribution, the ratio of earnings at the 80th and 20th percentiles is satisfactory; however, this simple ratio is by no means a complete description of inequality. Its focus on earnings at two arbitrarily chosen points in the distribution ignores what is happening on either side of the chosen percentiles. For example, if earnings at the 5th percentile fell and those at the 20th percentile rose, while all other earnings remained constant, the above ratio would decline even though the very lowest end of the distribution had moved down. Likewise, if earnings at the 20th and 80th percentiles were to remain the same, but earnings in between were to become much more similar, this step toward greater overall earnings equality would not be captured by the simple 80:20 ratio.

These drawbacks notwithstanding, we present in the next section descriptive data on changes in earnings inequality based on comparisons of earnings *levels* at the 80th and 20th percentiles of the distribution. While crude, these measures indicate that during the decade of the 1980s there was a growing inequality of earnings among both men and women in the United States. The trend continued into the early 1990s for men, but was reversed for women.

---

[3]U.S. Bureau of the Census, *Money Income of Households, Families, and Persons in the United States: 1992*, Series P–60, no. 184 (October 1993), Table 29 and p. xviii. A more sophisticated measure would take into account the shares of income received by each of the five quintiles, and a way to quantify the deviation from strict equality (when the income share of each quintile is 20 percent) is discussed in Appendix 14A.

TABLE 14.1

The Dispersion of Earnings by Gender, Ages 25 to 64,
1975–1992 (expressed in 1992 dollars)

| | Earnings at | | |
	80th Percentile (a)	20th Percentile (b)	Ratio: (a) ÷ (b)
Men			
1975	$49,395	$19,117	2.58
1980	$49,227	$17,553	2.80
1985	$49,386	$15,350	3.22
1990	$46,892	$13,796	3.40
1992	$46,019	$12,622	3.65
Women			
1975	$25,313	$5,742	4.41
1980	$25,708	$6,331	4.06
1985	$29,185	$6,885	4.24
1990	$29,328	$6,382	4.60
1992	$29,905	$9,031	3.31

SOURCES: U.S. Bureau of the Census, *Money Incomes of Households, Families, and Persons in the United States*, Series P-60: no. 105 (1975, Table 49); no. 132 (1980, Table 54); no. 156 (1985, Table 38); no. 174 (1990, Table 29); no. 184 (1992, Table 29).

Earnings Inequality Since 1980: Some Descriptive Data

Table 14.1 displays, for men and women separately, the recent trends in the ratio of earnings at the 80th percentile to those at the 20th. Among men, earnings inequality grew steadily from 1975 to 1992, with the 80:20 ratio increasing by 41 percent. Interestingly, this growth in inequality took place in the context of generally falling real earnings at both points in the male earnings distribution. Clearly, then, the earnings of low-paid men fell substantially more than the earnings of those at the upper end of the distribution.

For women, the picture is very different in three ways. First, real earnings generally *rose* at both points in the female earnings distribution throughout the 1980s and into the early 1990s. Second, the 80:20 ratio rose only slightly from 1980 to 1990, but fell rather suddenly from 1990 to 1992. Third, earnings at the 20th percentile are so low that they are unlikely to be received by women who are working full-time (in 1992, 26.5 percent of women worked part-time); therefore the sizable increase in earnings at the 20th percentile from 1990 to 1992 may well reflect changes in the hours or the composition of part-time workers rather than an increase in wage rates for a given set of workers.[4] Indeed, once we turn to an analysis of earnings among full-time workers, we will see that similar trends in inequality prevail for both men and women.

Mathematically, earnings inequality could grow in two ways from one year to another. First, inequality could grow by moving people originally in the middle of the distribution to either end. For example, if middle-class jobs were disappearing and being replaced by highly technical jobs at one end of the distribution and by totally unskilled jobs at the other, then the earnings distribution would become more stretched. Second, the earnings of individuals originally at the upper end of the distribution might grow faster (or fall more slowly!) than the earnings of individuals originally in the lower tail. This rise in relative earnings could be caused by increases in relative wages or by relative changes in the hours of work. The different possible dimensions of change from 1975 to 1992 are explored below.

THE OCCUPATIONAL DISTRIBUTION

One possible cause of growing earnings inequality is the destruction of middle-income jobs and their replacement by both higher- and lower-paying occupations. Table 14.2 presents data, for men and women separately, on the occupational distribution in 1983 and again in 1990 and 1992 (unfortunately, changes in occupational definitions occurred in 1983, so earlier data are noncomparable). More specifically, Table 14.2 charts changes in the percentages of all workers who were in the highest-paying and lowest-paying occupations over those years. From the table one can see some slight shrinkage of jobs in the middle of the distribution, but only because of growth at the upper end of the distribution. The share of jobs in the lowest-paying occupations declined during this period.

Among men, executive and professional jobs increased slightly as a percentage of the total, from 24.5 percent in 1983 to 25.7 percent in 1992. The lowest-paying jobs, however, decreased as a percentage of the total (from 21.1 to 20.4 percent). Jobs in the middle of the male job distribution also shrank a bit, from 54.4 percent of the total to 53.9 percent over the nine-year period. These small changes could have contributed to growing inequality among men, but they were clearly not a major cause.

Jobs in the middle of the earnings distribution for women also decreased as a share of the total (from 41.6 to 39.0 percent) over this period but, as with men, so did jobs at the low end of the distribution. In contrast, the share of women in the highest-paying occupations grew by 5.5 percentage points in nine years, with most of this growth among executive and managerial workers. Among both women and men, then, the upper tail of the earnings distribution grew, with a tendency for

---

[4]From 1990 to 1992, there was a sharp decline in the number (and the share in total female employment) of teenagers who worked part-time. Teenagers, of course, have the lowest average wages, and teenagers who work part-time can therefore be expected to have the lowest earnings in the female earnings distribution.

TABLE 14.2
Changes in the Occupational Distributions of Men and Women, 1983–1992

	Median Weekly Earnings, 1983	Percent of Workforce in Occupation		
		1983	1990	1992
Men				
Highest-Paying Occupations		**24.5**	**25.8**	**25.7**
Executive, managerial, administrative	$530	12.8	13.8	13.5
Professional specialty	$506	11.7	12.0	12.2
Lowest-Paying Occupations		**21.1**	**20.8**	**20.4**
Machine operators, assemblers, inspectors	$319	7.9	7.5	7.1
Handlers, cleaners, helpers, laborers	$251	6.1	6.2	5.9
Service, except private household and protective workers	$217	7.1	7.1	7.4
All Other Occupations		**54.4**	**53.4**	**53.9**
Total		100.0	100.0	100.0
Women				
Highest-Paying Occupations		**21.9**	**26.2**	**27.4**
Executive, managerial, administrative	$339	7.9	11.1	11.4
Professional speciality	$367	14.0	15.1	16.0
Lowest-Paying Occupations		**36.5**	**34.9**	**33.6**
Sales occupations	$204	12.8	13.1	12.4
Machine operators, assemblers, inspectors	$202	7.4	6.0	5.6
Service, except private household and protective workers	$176	16.3	15.8	15.6
All Other Occupations		**41.6**	**38.9**	**39.0**
Total		100.0	100.0	100.0

SOURCE: U.S. Bureau of Labor Statistics, *Employment and Earnings*: 31 (January 1984), Table 21; 38 (January 1991), Table 21; 40 (January 1993) Table 21. Earnings data from U.S. Bureau of the Census, *Statistical Abstract of the United States 1991* (Washington, D.C.: U.S. Government Printing Office, 1991), Table 678.

this growth to pull jobs from both the middle and the lower end of the distribution. Thus, changes in the occupational distribution contributed, but probably only slightly, to growing inequality in the 1980s and early 1990s.

CHANGES IN RELATIVE WAGES

A second possible dimension of growing inequality is the increased disparity of earnings among those who remained in high- and low-paying jobs. This disparity could result from either an increase in the disparity of wage rates or from an increased disparity in hours worked. We first analyze changes in earnings among *full-time, full-year* workers, because eliminating part-time workers from the data represents a simple way to at least crudely control for hours of work, and it serves the purpose of moving the analysis from earnings to *wage rates*. In the subsection that follows, we look separately at changes in hours worked among full-time workers and at changes in part-time employment.

We know from Chapter 9 that, within age groups, those with four or more years of college tend to have the highest wages or salaries. Within educational groups, pay tends to be highest among older workers. Thus, patterns that could be associated with growing inequality are a rising payoff to a college education or a rising payoff to age or experience.

Table 14.3 summarizes some aspects of change in the returns to education and experience from 1975 to 1992. The top panel focuses on the returns to a four-year college education for full-time, year-round workers in mid-career (ages 35–44). The data clearly show, as did slightly different data in Chapter 9, that the salaries of college graduates rose relative to those of high school graduates after 1980. Among men, this increase was the product of roughly constant real earnings after 1980 for college graduates and rapidly *falling* real earnings for high school graduates. Among women, the real, "full-time" earnings of four-year college graduates grew by almost 25 percent from 1980 to 1992, while the earnings of high school graduates remained more or less constant.

The bottom panel of Table 14.3 summarizes changes in the returns to experience among full-time workers. In this panel we display the mean earnings of 45- to 54-year-olds relative to those of 25- to 34-year-olds. Among male and female college graduates the returns to experience stayed constant or fell, while among high school graduates, the returns to experience generally rose. For women, the rising returns to experience for high school graduates working full-time were the result of a 5 percent increase in the real earnings of 45- to 54-year-olds from 1980 to 1992, accompanied by a 2 percent fall in the real earnings of 25- to 34-year-olds. For men, the rising returns to experience resulted from an 8 percent fall in real earnings among the older group and a massive 17 percent decline among 25- to 34-year-olds.

In summary, one of the sources of greater earnings inequality within gender groups after 1980 was the rising returns to education, particularly to a college education. Changes in the returns to experience appear to have contributed, but only among less-educated workers, to the growth in earnings disparities during

TABLE 14.3

Returns to Education and Experience Among Full-Time, Year-Round Workers, Selected Ages, 1975–1992 (expressed in 1992 dollars)

A. Returns to Education

	Mean Earnings Men, Ages 35–44			Mean Earnings Women, Ages 35–44		
	College Grads (a)	High School Grads (b)	Ratio: (a)÷(b) (c)	College Grads (d)	High School Grads (e)	Ratio: (d)÷(e) (f)
1975	$55,152	$36,504	1.51	$27,534	$20,270	1.36
1980	$49,156	$34,884	1.41	$27,240	$19,996	1.36
1985	$49,598	$33,805	1.47	$29,162	$20,858	1.40
1990	$50,883	$31,052	1.64	$33,954	$21,347	1.59
1992	$49,733	$30,339	1.64	$33,616	$20,411	1.65

B. Returns to Experience
(Mean Earnings, Ages 45–54) ÷ (Mean Earnings, Ages 25–34)

	Men		Women	
	College Grads	High School Grads	College Grads	High School Grads
1975	1.54	1.24	1.15	1.06
1980	1.59	1.22	1.10	1.03
1985	1.54	1.30	1.06	1.06
1990	1.43	1.28	1.07	1.17
1992	1.40	1.37	1.10	1.10

SOURCES: U.S. Bureau of the Census, *Money Income of Households, Families, and Persons in the United States*, Series P—60: no. 105 (1975, Table 48); no. 132 (1980, Table 52); no. 156 (1985, Table 36); no. 174 (1990, Table 30), no. 184 (1992, Table 29).

the period. (For an example of how falling rates of return to education can generate *more* equality, see Example 14.1.)

RELATIVE CHANGES IN HOURS OF WORK

Do the changes in relative earnings noted in Table 14.3 really reflect changes in relative *wages* of full-time workers, or might they reflect changes in their *hours* of

EXAMPLE 14.1

Does Rapid Economic Growth Increase Inequality? The Korean Experience

Economic development has been so striking in Korea during the past two decades that per capita income (and labor productivity) is doubling every ten years. By way of contrast, recent per capita growth in Japan is half that fast, and growth in the United States, Canada, and Europe is proceeding at a pace that is about one-fourth as fast. Accompanying this change in Korea has been a rapid decline in the percentage of the workforce devoted to agriculture and a rapid increase in manufacturing. The real value of Korean manufacturing exports increased sevenfold from 1970 to the mid–1980s, and the percentage of the workforce in manufacturing (25 percent in 1990) is now larger than it is in the United States.

Some economists have hypothesized that wage inequality grows during the early stages of industrialization, as some workers adapt and do quite well while others are ill equipped for change and are "left in the dust." Korean data clearly contradict this hypothesis! The ratio of wages for men at the 90th to those at the 10th percentile, which was 5.38 in 1971, fell to 3.38 in 1989. During this period, the comparable 90:10 ratio in the United States rose from 3.19 to 4.31. Thus, the wages of Korean males are now more equally distributed than those of American workers. What caused this growth in equality within Korea?

Korean workers made heavy investments in human capital during this period. The percentage of the workforce ending their schooling at high school jumped from 27 to 47 percent during the 1972 to 1989 period, and the percentage with college degrees rose from 14 to 25 percent. This growing supply of college graduates drove down the percentage by which their wages exceed those of high school graduates, while the shrinking supply of workers with only an elementary education drove their wages up closer to those of high school graduates. The result was greater equality.

Source: Dae–Il Kim and Robert H. Topel, "Labor Markets and Economic Growth: Lessons from Korea's Industrialization, 1970–1990," *in Differences and Changes in Wage Structures*, ed. Richard B. Freeman and Lawrence F. Katz (Chicago: University of Chicago Press, 1995), 227–264.

work? Table 14.4 charts changes from 1983 to 1992 in the hours of work for full-time workers in high-paying jobs, usually requiring a college education, and for those in low-paying, less skilled jobs. Hours of work for *all* occupations listed rose over this time period, with no pronounced tendency for them to rise faster in the higher-paying occupations. Thus, the changes in relative earnings among full-time workers seen in Table 14.3 reflect relative changes in their salaries or wages, not relative changes in hours worked.

While it seems clear that a major cause of growing earnings inequality after 1980 was an increased gap between the wages or salaries of more-educated and less-educated workers, another possibility is that lower-paid workers saw their full-time jobs converted to part-time, or that they experienced rising unemployment. Put differently, another way in which the earnings distribution could have become more stretched is through the conversion of jobs in the lowest-paying sec-

TABLE 14.4
Average Weekly Hours of Work by Occupation, for Full-Time, Year-Round Workers, 1983–1992

	1983	1985	1990	1992
Men				
Highest-Paying Occupations				
Executive, managerial, administrative	46.4	47.1	47.5	47.1
Professional specialty	45.2	45.6	46.2	45.5
Lowest-Paying Occupations				
Machine operators, assemblers, inspectors	42.0	42.7	43.0	42.6
Handlers, cleaners, helpers, laborers	41.1	41.5	41.9	41.7
Service, except private household and protective workers	42.1	42.5	42.6	42.2
Women				
Highest-Paying Occupations				
Executive, managerial, administrative	42.4	43.0	43.2	42.9
Professional specialty	41.3	41.6	41.8	41.4
Lowest-Paying Occupations				
Sales occupations	41.5	42.0	42.2	42.3
Machine operators, assemblers, inspectors	40.0	40.3	40.7	40.4
Service, except private household and protective workers	40.6	40.8	41.2	41.2

SOURCE: U.S. Bureau of Labor Statistics, *Employment and Earnings*, vol. 31 (January 1984), Table 34; vol. 33 (January 1986), Table 34; vol. 38 (January 1991), Table 34; vol. 40 (January 1993), Table 34.

tors from full-time, year-round status into part-time or (through greater unemployment) part-year status.

Interestingly, there was no overall conversion of full-time to part-time or part-year jobs in the lowest-paid occupations during most of the 1980s. From 1983 to 1992, part-time employment in the lowest-paying occupations fell by 10 to 15 percent, and unemployment rates in those occupations fell even more. These declines reflected movement out of the 1982–83 recession, so they say nothing about long-run trends in either part-time work or unemployment. What is significant for our purposes here, however, is that the growth of earnings inequality that took place throughout the 1980s and early 1990s was not caused by a disproportionate decline in hours worked by low-paid employees. Changes in the relative wages or salaries of higher- and lower-paying occupations remain the most clearly identifiable dimension of growing inequality after 1980.

GROWTH OF EARNINGS DISPERSION WITHIN HUMAN CAPITAL GROUPS

While one factor in the growing diversity of earnings is the enlarged gap between the average pay of more-educated and less-educated workers, another possibility is that earnings *within* narrowly defined human capital groups became more diverse. If, for example, the distribution of earnings within groups of workers with the same age and education had become more stretched, the overall diversity of earnings would have grown. A greater diversity of earnings among 45- to 54-year-old college graduates, for example, could have raised earnings at the 80th percentile, while more diversity among younger workers with a high school degree or less would be likely to have reduced earnings at the 20th percentile.

Table 14.5 reports on the *coefficients of variation* for the earnings distributions of several groups of workers that are homogeneous in terms of education, age, and gender. Of the 16 groups shown, 11 experienced increased coefficients of variation between 1980 and 1992. Within-group earnings disparities grew across the board for those in the 55 to 64 age group, especially among the college-educated. As argued above, the growing disparities among older, better-educated workers could have pulled up earnings at the 80th percentile, although between 1990 and 1992 these disparities among men showed a decline. Disparities for 25- to 34-year-old high school graduates also grew for both men and women, which could have dragged down earnings in the lower percentiles.[5]

SUMMARIZING THE DIMENSIONS OF GROWING INEQUALITY

It can be concluded from our analyses in this section that the most important dimension of the growth in inequality after 1980 was the increased returns to a college education. These increases were observed among both women and men, and they were especially large in the period from 1985 to 1992. For men in midcareer, the increased returns to college were created by the sharply falling real earnings of high school graduates in an environment in which the real earnings of college graduates remained nearly constant. For women, however, the returns rose because the real earnings of college graduates grew quickly while those of high school graduates remained constant.

Three other dimensions of the growth in inequality were identified by our analyses, but their quantitative significance appears to be smaller. First, the disparity of earnings *within* narrowly defined human capital groups generally rose throughout the 1980s, especially among older workers. Second, among high

---

[5]A recent paper identifies another type of growing inequality in the 1980s: the instability in individuals' earnings year to year. See Peter Gottschalk and Robert Moffitt, "The Growth of Earnings Instability in the U.S. Labor Market," *Brookings Papers on Economic Activity*, 1994-2, 217–254.

TABLE 14.5
Coefficients of Variation by Age, Education, and Gender, 1975–1992, Full-Time, Year-Round Workers

	1975	1980	1985	1990	1992
Male College Graduates					
Ages 25–34	.015	.015	.015	.022	.016
35–44	.022	.021	.021	.021	.018
45–54	.023	.025	.029	.028	.026
55–64	.039	.031	.042	.048	.036
Male High School Graduates					
Ages 25–34	.009	.009	.010	.011	.011
35–44	.010	.012	.012	.013	.013
45–54	.016	.012	.014	.017	.018
55–64	.019	.017	.019	.021	.020
Female College Graduates					
Ages 25–34	.013	.017	.014	.016	.014
35–44	.028	.028	.023	.023	.022
45–54	.033	.042	.037	.033	.024
55–64	.042	.042	.050	.044	.053
Female High School Graduates					
Ages 25–34	.011	.011	.012	.012	.015
35–44	.014	.014	.013	.016	.014
45–54	.012	.014	.015	.016	.016
55–64	.017	.019	.019	.021	.020

Sources: U.S. Bureau of the Census, *Money Incomes of Households, Families, and Persons in the United States,* Series P-60: no. 105 (1975, Table 48); no. 132 (1980, Table 52); no. 156 (1985, Table 36); no. 174 (1990, Table 29); no. 184 (1992, Table 29).

school graduates the returns to experience increased, creating a bigger spread between the earnings of more-experienced and less-experienced workers. Third, changes in the occupational distribution among both men and women tended to increase the share of high-paying jobs, and this increase was at the expense of jobs both in the middle of the earnings distribution and at the lower end.

We also identified the presence of two developments that served to *reduce* earnings inequality after 1980. One was the reduced differential between older and younger male college graduates, which of course tended to mitigate the growing inequality among men. The other development was more widespread and socially significant: the earnings of women increased markedly relative to those of men. The data in Table 14.1 document trends in inequality *within* gender, but because women's earnings are substantially below those for men, the *overall* distribution of earnings exhibits more inequality than the male or female distributions separately. The increased relative earnings of women after 1980 was thus a force tending to reduce disparity in the overall distribution of earnings. Despite these two mitigating factors, there is a consensus among economists that wage inequality grew substantially in the United States after 1980. We now turn to an analysis of the causes of this growth.

The Underlying Causes of Growing Inequality

Identifying the forces that have caused growing inequality in recent years requires us to return to our basic economic model of the labor market. Market outcomes, in terms of wages and employment levels, are influenced by the forces of both demand and supply. Thus, changes in *market-clearing* wages or levels of employment result from shifts in the demand curve, shifts in the supply curve, or shifts in both. It is possible, of course, for wages and employment to be at levels *different* from their market-clearing levels owing to such institutional forces as minimum wage laws or unions. Thus, wage and employment levels could also change if the influence of institutional forces in the labor market were to change.

The major phenomenon we must explain is the widening gap between the wages of highly educated and less-educated workers, and our basic economic model suggests three possible causes. First, the *supply* of less-educated workers might have risen faster than the supply of college graduates, driving down the relative wages of less-skilled workers. Second, changes in *institutional* forces, such as the decline of unionism, might have reduced the wages of less-educated, production workers relative to the more highly educated. Third, the *demand* for more-educated workers might have increased relative to the demand for less-educated workers. We discuss these possibilities below.

CHANGES IN SUPPLY

In reality, shifts in supply and demand curves, and even changes in the influence of institutions, occur both simultaneously and continually. Sophisticated statistical studies can often sort through the possible influences underlying a change and estimate the separate contributions of each. For the most part, however, the details of these studies are beyond the scope of this text; instead, our focus will be on identifying the *dominant* forces behind the growth of wage inequality in recent years.

For the market-clearing wage rate of a particular group of workers to be reduced primarily by a shift in supply, that shift must be rightward and therefore accompanied by an increase in employment (see panel a of Figure 14.3 for a graphic

FIGURE 14.3

Changes in Supply as the Dominant Cause of Wage Changes

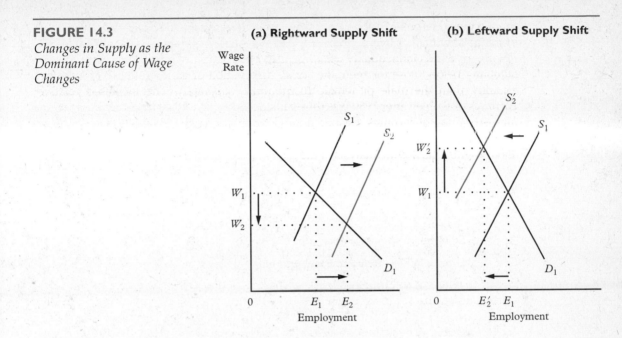

illustration). Conversely, if a (leftward) shift in the supply curve is the dominant cause of a wage increase, this wage increase will be accompanied by a decrease in the market-clearing level of employment (see panel b of Figure 14.3). Other things equal, the larger these shifts are, the larger will be the effects on the equilibrium wage.

The major phenomenon we are trying to explain is the increasing gap between the wages of highly educated and less-educated workers. If *supply* shifts are primarily responsible, we should observe that the employment of less-educated workers *increased* relative to the employment of the college-educated workforce. Table 14.6 contains data indicating that supply shifts could *not* have been the primary cause. It is clear from comparing rows A and B, respectively, with rows E and F of the table, that the groups with the larger wage increases also had larger *increases* in employment over the ten-year period! The shares of aggregate employment going to female and male college graduates both rose, while the corresponding shares of employment going to high school graduates both fell. Thus, shifts in supply cannot be the dominant explanation for the growing returns to education.

To say that shifts in supply were not the *dominant* influence underlying the increased returns to education is not to say, of course, that they had no effect at all. We saw in Chapter 10 that immigration to the United States rose during the 1980s, and that it was especially heavy among unskilled, less-educated workers—the very groups whose relative earnings fell most during that period. One study has estimated that one-third of the decreased relative wages of high school

TABLE 14.6

Employment Shares (Within Gender) of Groups Classified by Their Relative Change in Earnings, 1980 to 1992

	Share of Gender's Total Employment (%)		
	1980	1990	1992
Groups Whose Relative Earnings Rose:			
A. Women with four years of college, all ages	10.2	13.9	17.2
B. Men with four years of college, all ages	11.4	14.0	17.7
C. Female high school graduates, ages 45–54	7.5	7.5	8.4
D. Male high school graduates, ages 45–54	5.6	5.7	6.6
Groups Whose Relative Earnings Fell:			
E. Female high school graduates, all ages	46.4	42.1	36.8
F. Male high school graduates, all ages	38.2	38.1	33.6
G. Female high school graduates, ages 25–34	12.3	11.1	10.9
H. Male high school graduates, ages 25–34	10.7	11.9	11.7

SOURCE: U.S. Bureau of the Census, *Money Income of Households, Families and Individuals in the United States*, Series P– 60: no. 132 (1980, Table 52); no. 174 (1990, Table 30); no. 184 (1992, Table 29).

dropouts (a group that has done particularly poorly since 1980) was caused by immigration.[6] Because of immigration, then, the percentage of less-skilled workers in the labor force fell less than it would otherwise have fallen, and therefore the supply-related upward pressures on unskilled wages were smaller.

Could shifts in supply have been primarily responsible for the rising returns to *experience* observed among high school graduates? Among women, relative shifts in supply could not have been the primary cause; the share of aggregate employment among older high school graduates rose, while the share for younger high school graduates fell (compare rows C and G of Table 14.6). Among men, however, the picture is somewhat less clear. The employment shares of both older and younger high school graduates increased equally from 1980 to 1992, although the percentage increase was greater for the older group (compare rows D and H);

---

[6]See George J. Borjas, Richard B. Freeman, and Lawrence F. Katz, "On the Labor Market Effects of Immigration and Trade," in *Immigration and the Work Force*, ed. George J. Borjas and Richard B. Freeman (Chicago: University of Chicago Press, 1992), 213–244, for empirical estimates.

again, it seems unlikely that supply shifts played much of a role in the increased returns to experience.[7]

The analysis to this point has concentrated on *quantitative* shifts in labor supply. It is also possible that the *quality* of labor supplied changed in such a way that the gap between the wages of college and high school graduates grew in the 1980s. We mentioned in Chapter 9, for example, that there is a positive relationship between wage levels and performance on tests of cognitive achievement. There has also been a highly publicized decline in such test scores among American students. Did changes in cognitive achievement scores play a major role in the growing wage dispersion in the 1980s?

For changes in labor quality to have widened the gap between the wages of college and high school graduates in the 1980s, the scores of high school graduates would have had to *fall* relative to those of college graduates during that period. In fact, however, the scores of high school graduates *rose* relative to those of college graduates in the early 1980s, and scores of the two groups did not change relative to each other after that.[8] Thus, relative changes in labor *quality*, insofar as we can measure it, did not play a role in the growing disparity of wages during the 1980s.[9]

CHANGES IN INSTITUTIONAL FORCES

We know from Chapter 13 that the percentage of the labor force that is unionized fell during the 1980s. This decline was especially pronounced among less-educated workers in the private sector, the very group that had the highest union wage premiums. Thus fewer less-educated workers received the wage premiums union members have historically enjoyed, and correspondingly greater numbers earned lower, nonunion wages. Further, declining union influence also could have led to reduced wage premiums among those workers who remained unionized.

It can be argued, then, that the reduced role of unions in wage determination strengthened the importance of market forces. In the past, when unions took wage determination "out of the market" to a greater extent than they do now, the returns to education were relatively low in the union sector (it will be recalled from Chapter 13 that unions have tended to compress wage differentials across skill groups).

---

[7]The generally small role played by *supply* shifts in generating recent wage inequality is also found in more sophisticated studies: Lawrence F. Katz and Kevin M. Murphy, "Changes in Relative Wages, 1963–1987: Supply and Demand Factors," *Quarterly Journal of Economics* 107 (February 1992): 35–78; John Bound and George Johnson, "Changes in the Structure of Wages in the 1980s: An Evaluation of Alternative Explanations," *American Economic Review* 82 (June 1992): 371–392; McKinley L. Blackburn, David E. Bloom, and Richard B. Freeman, "The Declining Economic Position of Less Skilled American Men," *A Future of Lousy Jobs? The Changing Structure of U.S. Wages*, ed. Gary Burtless (Washington, D.C.: Brookings Institution, 1990) 31–76; and John Bound and George Johnson, "What Are the Causes of Rising Wage Inequality in the United States?" *Federal Reserve Bank of New York Economic Policy Review* 1, no. 1 (January 1995): 9–17.

[8]John Bishop, "Is the Test Score Decline Responsible for the Productivity Growth Decline?" *American Economic Review* 79 (March 1989): 190.

[9]This conclusion is supported by a different analysis reported in Blackburn, Bloom, and Freeman, "The Declining Economic Position of Less Skilled American Men."

Now that market forces have greater influence in the determination of wages, it is natural to expect that the returns to education should have risen.

There are three a priori reasons to doubt that the decline of labor unions has been a significant causal factor of the increased returns to education after 1980. First, as noted in Chapter 13, the declining share of unionized workers is a phenomenon that started in the 1950s and has continued unabated throughout each decade—even in the 1970s, when the returns to education *fell* (see Chapter 9). Second, women are less highly unionized than men (see Chapter 13), and yet increases in the returns to education were as large among women as among men, or larger, after 1980. Third, as also noted in Chapter 13, the wage premiums obtained by unions for their members actually rose in the early and mid–1980s, suggesting that *within* the union sector, at least, forces toward greater dispersion could not have started much before 1985.

Two empirical studies of growing wage dispersion among men in the 1980s concluded that, at most, one-tenth of the increased earnings gap between college and high school graduates could be attributed to declining unionization.[10] Both studies concluded that the effects on the relative wages of high school *dropouts* were somewhat larger, although in one study these effects were quantitatively insignificant. The only two studies that sought to explain the rising returns to education among women found that the decline of unions played no role at all.[11]

Another institutional factor that has been considered as a possible explanation for the rising returns to education is the declining real level of the minimum wage throughout the 1980s. As noted in Chapter 4 (Table 4.2), the nominal minimum wage rate was held constant at $3.35 from 1981 to 1990, a period during which the average nominal wage in manufacturing, for example, grew. Consequently, the minimum wage fell from 44 percent of the average hourly wage in manufacturing in 1981 to just 33 percent by 1991. While this decline could have reduced the relative wages of very poorly paid workers, it cannot have played a large role in the increased earnings gap between college and high school graduates, because few of the latter have earnings near the minimum. In fact, even the declining relative earnings of adult high school dropouts appear to have been little affected by the fall in the real minimum wage.[12]

---

[10]Bound and Johnson, "Changes in the Structure of Wages," and Blackburn, Bloom, and Freeman, "The Declining Economic Position of Less Skilled American Men." Also see Richard B. Freeman, "How Much Has De-Unionization Contributed to the Rise in Male Earnings Inequality?" in *Uneven Tides: Rising Inequality in America,* ed. Sheldon Danziger and Peter Gottschalk (New York: Russell Sage Foundation, 1993): 133–163, and David Card, "The Effect of Unions on the Distribution of Wages: Redistribution or Relabelling?" working paper no. 4195, National Bureau of Economic Research, Cambridge, Mass., October 1992.

[11]Bound and Johnson, "Changes in the Structure of Wages," and McKinley L. Blackburn, David E. Bloom, and Richard B. Freeman, "Changes in Earnings Differentials in the 1980s: Concordance, Convergence, Causes and Consequences," in *Poverty and Prosperity in the U.S.A. in the Late Twentieth Century,* ed. Dimitri B. Papadimitriou and Edward N. Wolff (New York: Macmillan, 1993).

[12]Blackburn, Bloom, and Freeman, "The Declining Position of Less Skilled American Men."

CHANGES IN DEMAND

Because changes in labor supply and institutional forces did not play dominant roles in the growing wage dispersion after 1980, shifts in labor *demand* must have been at the root of growing wage inequality. Recalling our introductory discussions of labor demand in Chapters 3 and 4, the demand for labor is a function of both *product* demand (which affects the *scale* of production) and decisions about the cost-minimizing *mix of capital and various kinds of labor* used to produce the profit-maximizing level of output. Thus, in looking for possible causes of shifts in the demand for labor, we must consider both product-demand shifts and the technological innovations that underlie changes in the mix of productive factors.

PRODUCT DEMAND   Over time, the demand for products produced in the United States shifts as incomes or preferences change, and as relative product prices increase or decrease. Moreover, developments in the international economy, from reductions in trade barriers to products newly produced abroad, also affect domestic demand. If the increased demand for college-trained workers relative to high school graduates were the result mainly of shifts in product demand, we would expect to observe a faster expansion of employment in industries that are heavily dependent on a highly educated workforce. The result would be an increased share of total employment among those industries that use the largest number of highly educated workers.

As shown in Table 14.7 (panel A), there were notable shifts in the distribution of employment across industries in the 1980s and early 1990s. The largest gains came in the private service sector, especially in such business services as advertising, computer and data processing, accounting, management consulting, and temporary-help agencies. The largest relative declines were in manufacturing, where the rising gap between imports and exports during the 1980s was most felt. The share of employment in retail and wholesale trade fluctuated modestly, while the percentage of total employment in government fell slightly. Were these shifts a dominant force in changing the relative demand for highly educated workers?

Panel B of Table 14.7 suggests that the biggest loser of employment, manufacturing, uses relatively few highly educated workers (managers and professionals) and relatively more workers in jobs requiring less education. In contrast, the service sector, which grew the most, uses more highly educated workers and fewer less-educated ones. One might think, then, that shifts in employment *across* industries played a dominant role in causing the earnings gap between educated and less-educated workers to grow after 1980.

Most studies of product demand shifts and wage inequality have concentrated on the effects of international trade. As restrictions on such trade were liberalized, imports as a fraction of all purchases in the United States rose from 7.7 percent in 1980 to 12.2 percent in 1992.[13] The most rapid growth of imports was in durable

---

[13]U.S. President, *Economic Report of the President* (Washington, DC: Government Printing Office, 1995), Table B–2.

manufactured goods, which are produced in the United States with the very workers whose relative earnings dropped most dramatically: less-educated men. The findings among economists who have analyzed the effects of trade on inequality are not unanimous, but the predominant conclusion is that the contributions of international trade to the changes in wage inequality after 1980 were rather small.[14] A survey of those who have studied the topic indicated that they believe, on average, that only 10 percent of the growth in wage inequality could be attributed to international trade.[15]

CHANGING THE MIX OF PRODUCTIVE FACTORS   A change in the mix of productive factors, perhaps by substituting highly educated labor for less-educated labor, will be manifest primarily in *intra*-industry changes in the distribution of employment across occupations. Table 14.7, panel B, contains some data pertinent to these intra-industry changes. Comparing the distribution of high- and low-education jobs within each industry in 1983 and 1992 indicates that, *within* each major industry displayed, the number of managers and professionals grew relative to those in jobs requiring less education. While the intra-industry percentage-point gains recorded by managers and professionals in panel B might appear modest compared with the percentage-point changes across industries in panel A, the former gains aggregate to a relatively large overall change in numbers because they apply to a base that equals *total* employment in the industry. In contrast, cross-industry effects on the number of managers and professionals are derived from a base that equals only the *change* in each industry's employment.[16]

The most plausible explanation for demand-side increases in the returns to education after 1980 is technological change. It has been widely observed that the introduction of new technology increased dramatically in the 1980s, as firms sought to become more competitive by adopting the use of advanced computers,

---

[14]A comprehensive review of various studies, by both labor economists and international trade specialists, is found in Gary Burtless, "International Trade and the Rise in Earnings Inequality," *Journal of Economic Literature* 33, no. 2 (June 1995): 800–816.

[15]Thomas Klitgaard and Adam Posen, "Morning Session: Summary of Discussion," *Federal Reserve Bank of New York Economic Policy Review* 1, no. 1 (January 1995): 33–34.

[16]To take a simple example, assume C = managerial/professional employment and that we want to explain the changes in this variable from 1983 to 1990; that is, we want to calculate $C_{90} - C_{83}$ in a certain industry. If E = total employment in the industry and k = the percentage of the total constituted by managers and professionals, then

$$C_{90} - C_{83} = E_{90}(k_{90}) - E_{83}(k_{83})$$

If $E_{90}(k_{83})$ is subtracted from the first term on the right-hand side and added to the second, the equation becomes

$$C_{90} - C_{83} = E_{90}(k_{90} - k_{83}) + k_{83}(E_{90} - E_{83})$$

Note that in the first expression on the right-hand side of the equation, the *intra*-industry changes in k are applied to total employment. Changes in C caused by growth or decline in the industry (the second expression) are based only on *changes* in employment; these latter changes form the basis for *inter*-industry effects. See Eli Berman, John Bound, and Zvi Griliches, "Changes in the Demand for Skilled Labor Within U.S. Manufacturing Industries: Evidence from the Annual Survey of Manufacturing," *Quarterly Journal of Economics* 109, no. 2 (May 1994): 367–397, for an empirical study that concludes the relative demand for skilled workers shifted more *within* industries than *between* them.

TABLE 14.7
The Distribution of Employment Across Industries, 1980 to 1992

A. Percentages of Employees in Major Industries

	1980	1983	1990	1992
Manufacturing	22.4%	20.4%	17.3%	17.0%
Trade (wholesale, retail)	22.4	23.1	23.7	20.7
Private services (business, health, personal, recreational, and social services)	20.6	23.0	26.5	26.8
Government	18.0	17.6	16.7	17.2
Others	16.6	15.9	15.8	18.3

B. Percentage of Employment by Selected Occupation, Major Industries

	Managerial, Professional			Operators, Laborers, Service Workers		
	1983	1990	1992	1983	1990	1992
Manufacturing	17.7%	20.5%	20.3%	43.5%	42.1%	41.4%
Trade	9.8	10.5	10.7	31.7	31.3	31.6
Private services (except household) and government	41.0	42.5	43.1	26.9	25.8	25.3

SOURCE: U.S. Bureau of Labor Statistics, *Employment and Earnings*: 38 (January 1991), Tables 25, 28; 31 (January 1984), Tables 25, 28; 40 (January 1993), Tables 25, 28, 13–1.

robots, more-flexible manufacturing systems, and new office technologies. Conventional technological improvements, such as larger or faster machines, were adopted at a slower pace, with the result that in manufacturing, for example, the new, high-tech capital rose from 9.5 percent of the total capital stock in 1976 to 25.7 percent in 1986.[17] The percentage of all workers who used computers in their jobs, to take another example, rose from 25 to 37 percent from 1984 to 1989.[18]

---

[17]Jerome Mark, "Technological Change and Employment: Some Results from BLS Research," *Monthly Labor Review* 110 (April 1987): 26–29, and Ernst R. Berndt, Catherine J. Morrison, and Larry S. Rosenblum, "High-Tech Capital, Economic Performance and Labor Composition in U.S. Manufacturing Industries: An Exploratory Analysis," National Bureau of Economic Research, working paper no. 4010, March 1992.

[18]Alan B. Krueger, "How Computers Have Changed the Wage Structure: Evidence from Microdata, 1984–89," *Quarterly Journal of Economics* 108 (February 1993): 33–60.

As noted in Chapter 4, technological change is equivalent to a decrease in the price of capital, and the effects on the demand for labor depend on the relative size of scale and substitution effects. If a category of labor is a complement in production with the capital whose price has been reduced, or if it is a substitute in production but a *gross* complement, then technological change will increase the demand for labor. If the category of labor is a gross substitute with capital, however, then technological change will reduce the demand for labor.

There are several reasons to suspect that the spread of high-tech capital, especially computers, played a key role in the growth of the earnings gap between more-educated and less-educated workers in the 1980s and early 1990s. First, it can be hypothesized that the relative demand for highly educated workers increases during periods of rapid technological innovation, because (as we argued in Chapter 9) those who invest in education tend to be those who have the greatest comparative advantage at learning. Rapid change requires rapid learning, and it can be argued that the better-educated are more adaptable.

Second, we know from Chapter 4 that, in general, capital and skilled labor tend to be gross complements, while capital and less-skilled labor are more likely to be gross substitutes. If these general patterns apply specifically to high-tech capital, then the falling price of such capital, and its consequent spread, would have shifted the demand curve for skilled labor to the right and the demand curve for less-skilled labor to the left.

Third, it has been estimated that those industries with the largest increases in high-tech capital were those with both the highest proportions of college-educated workers and the largest shifts away from the use of less-educated production workers.[19] Indeed, computer usage in 1989 was greater for the college-educated (59 percent) than for high school graduates (29 percent), and it was greater for women (43 percent) than men (32 percent).[20] One recent study, in fact, concludes that the greatest declines in the wages of less-educated men took place in regions that experienced the largest increases in the labor force participation rates of highly skilled women.[21]

Finally, it has been estimated that workers who used computers on their jobs in 1989 received 10 to 15 percent more in wages than they otherwise would have received, a larger differential than in 1984.[22] Thus, it appears that the widespread adoption of high-tech capital, especially the personal computer, increased the demand for highly educated workers relative to those with less education.

While a rightward shift in the demand for highly educated workers, which was associated with technological change, appears to have been a powerful force un-

---

[19]Berndt, Morrison, and Rosenblum, "High-Tech Capital, Economic Performance and Labor Composition"; David A. Brauer and Susan Hickok, "Explaining the Growing Inequality in Wages Across Skill Levels," *Federal Reserve Bank of New York Economic Policy Review* 1, no. 1 (January 1995): 61–75; and Berman, Bound, and Griliches, "Changes in the Demand for Skilled Labor Within U.S. Manufacturing."

[20]Krueger, "How Computers Have Changed the Wage Structure."

[21]Robert H. Topel, "Regional Trends in Wage Inequality," *American Economic Review* 84, no. 2 (May 1994): 17–22.

[22]Krueger, "How Computers Have Changed the Wage Structure."

derlying growing inequality, this rightward shift could only have raised relative wages if shifts in supply failed to keep pace. As will be recalled from Chapter 9, during the 1970s, when rates of return to college educations were low, there was a decline in the proportion of male high school graduates going to college. This decline slowed the growth of college graduates in the overall labor force during the 1980s, and even as the rate of return later rose rapidly, the supply response was relatively modest (the proportion of males enrolling in college actually fell a bit from 1985 to 1990 before rising in the early 1990s). Had the *supply* response to the increased demand for highly educated workers been larger, their wage growth would have been slower.

(This chapter analyzes inequality by comparing the earnings distribution in different years. Another way of looking at inequality, which relates to the accessibility of occupational training and higher education, is to analyze whether workers generally occupy the same spot in the earnings distribution as their parents. See Example 14.2 for a brief discussion of inequality from this perspective.)

TECHNOLOGICAL CHANGE AND THE RETURNS TO EXPERIENCE The introduction of new technology may also help to explain dimensions of growing inequality other than the increased returns to education. For example, the growing earnings gap between older and younger high school graduates may also be linked to the new technological change. It has been hypothesized that as industries cut back on their employment of less-educated workers, older workers, who are usually protected by seniority rules, were more likely to keep their jobs than younger ones. With the brunt of declining demand for less-educated workers being borne by younger workers, their real wages were bid down more than were those of older workers.[23] Some support for the hypothesis that the reduced demand for less-educated workers especially affected younger high school graduates comes from a regional analysis of the increased returns to education. In regions experiencing high unemployment and a loss of jobs in the aggregate, the gap between the earnings of recent college and high school graduates increased the most.[24]

TECHNOLOGICAL CHANGE AND WITHIN-GROUP DISPERSION The increased disparity of earnings *within* narrowly defined age/education groups possibly could be attributed to the adoption of new technology as well. It could be argued, for example, that rapid technological change, when combined with product demand shifts, created in the 1980s a greater than normal number of new job opportunities, on the one hand, and job loss on the other. Those in each human capital group lucky enough to obtain jobs in expanding sectors did well, while

---

[23]Bound and Johnson, "Change in the Structure of Wages," and Katz and Murphy, "Changes in Relative Wages, 1963–1987."

[24]Lawrence F. Katz and Ana L. Revenga, "Changes in the Structure of Wages: The United States vs. Japan," *Journal of Japanese and International Economies* 3 (December 1989): 522–553.

EXAMPLE 14.2

Do We Observe "Rags to Riches"? The Transmission of Inequality Across Generations

We have seen that earnings inequality grew after 1980, primarily because the returns to education rose dramatically. The increased importance of one's education in being able to reach the upper percentiles of the earnings distribution raises an interesting question: Given that children of higher-income parents tend to obtain more education (see Chapter 9), how great is the advantage enjoyed by children whose parents have higher earnings in reaching the upper percentiles of the earnings distribution? Research into how closely sons' earnings correlate with those of their fathers has produced findings that yield important insights into the extent to which one's spot in the earnings distribution is "inherited" from one's parents.

   If there were no economic mobility in a society, then the earnings a son could expect would be completely predicted by the earnings of his father. If one were to plot the earnings of sons and their fathers in such a society, the plots would generate a 45-degree

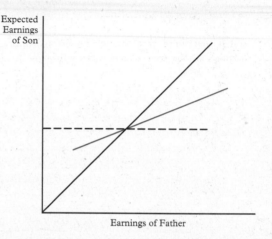

line, such as the solid black one shown in the diagram above. Thus, if the father's earnings were, say, continued on next page

those unfortunate enough to have lost jobs did poorly, with the result that disparities between the "lucky" and the "unlucky" grew.

   An alternative explanation that could tie growing within-group disparities to the new technology focuses on the willingness of workers to adapt to change. It might be argued that, within human capital groups, some workers are more adaptable and ready for new challenges than others. The adaptable ones profit most during periods of change, while the less adaptable fall behind.

   Both of the above explanations for greater within-group inequality suggest that the human capital groups facing the most difficult changes will exhibit the greatest growth in earnings inequality. Because younger workers, for example, are less established in careers and are more occupationally and geographically mobile anyway, *change* is not as difficult for them as it is for older workers; therefore, disparities in the willingness to adapt are probably smaller (and of less consequence) for younger workers. The implication of these arguments, then, is that within-group earnings dispersion might well grow faster for older workers during periods of

Continued...

50 percent greater than the earnings of other fathers, the son's earnings would be 50 percent higher than the earnings of other sons.

At the opposite extreme is a society with complete economic mobility, in the sense that a son's expected earnings are neither increased nor reduced by the earnings of his father. Knowing only what a father earns, the single best guess about the earnings of his son is that these earnings will be average (average earnings among sons are represented by the dashed line in the figure).

What researchers have found with data on American families is that the relationship of sons' and fathers' earnings is best described by a line such as the blue one in the figure, which is flatter than the 45-degree line of no mobility and steeper than the dashed line that represents complete mobility. Recent findings suggest that about 40 percent of the earnings advantage (or disadvantage) of fathers is transmitted to their sons. For example, if a father earns 50 percent more than average, his son can be expected to earn 20 percent more than average; likewise, if a father earns 50 percent less than average, his son can be expected to earn 20 percent less than average. With this father–son earnings correlation, a son whose father is in the bottom 5 percent of the earnings distribution would have something like a one-in-four chance of making it into the top half of the earnings distribution. Similarly, if a father's earnings are at the top 5 percent, the son has roughly a one-in-four chance of earning in the lower half of the distribution.

A reason for the *positive* correlation between the earnings of father and son is rooted in the fact, mentioned previously, that children in families with higher incomes tend to obtain more formal schooling than those in families with lower incomes; other reasons for the positive correlation relate to expectations, attitudes, and abilities that children are likely to "inherit" from their parents. One reason the correlation is not *perfect* is that random factors (elements of good or bad luck) play a role in a parent's being above or below average in earnings, and luck cannot be inherited. Of course, given the importance of education in determining one's earnings, policies or practices that enhance the abilities of low-income youth to invest in human capital will further reduce the child–parent earnings correlation.

SOURCE: Gary R. Solon, "Intergenerational Income Mobility in the United States," *American Economic Review* 82, no. 3 (June 1992): 393–408; and David J. Zimmerman, "Regression Toward Mediocrity in Economic Stature," *American Economic Review* 82, no. 3 (June 1992): 409–429.

---

great change. There is some evidence to support this hypothesis in Table 14.5. Among all four education/gender groups, coefficients of variation rose most consistently for the oldest workers.

The factors most likely to have caused increased within-group earnings dispersion after 1980 have yet to be fully researched. We do know that, *within occupations*, earnings disparities grew most for men and women in sales occupations. The next largest increases were among "salaried administrators and officials" in private industry: financial managers, human resource directors, advertising executives, and the like. In fact, one study estimated that the growth of within-group earnings dispersion was three times greater for sales workers and administrators/officials combined than for the aggregate of all other occupations.[25] Recalling the subject matter of Chapter 11 suggests one possible explanation.

---

[25]Paul Ryscavage and Peter Henle, "Earnings Inequality in the 1980s," *Monthly Labor Review* 113 (December 1990): 3–16.

Many sales workers are paid on a commission basis, and top executives often receive bonuses that tie yearly compensation to the profits of their firms. In an environment in which changes in product demand and technology created a great expansion of revenues for some firms and substantially reduced revenues for others, workers whose pay was tied most directly to their firms' revenues would have experienced the most immediate changes in earnings. Thus, the earnings dispersion of sales workers and officials might be expected to have grown most during the 1980s; however, because many workers in other occupations receive pay that is *indirectly* tied to the financial success of their employer, dispersion would have grown (although more slowly) among these other occupations as well.

There are potentially two versions of the hypothesis that the effects of "contingent pay" played a large role in the growth of within-group earnings dispersion, and both are echoes of our discussion just above. One could argue that contingent pay accentuates differences between the lucky and the unlucky. It could also be argued that such pay accentuates differences in adaptability, rewarding those who are more willing or able to accept change. While distinguishing between these two versions may not be possible, future research may indicate whether contingent pay played a significant role in the growth of earnings inequality.

International Comparisons of Changing Inequality

In the previous section, we analyzed the changes over *time* in the extent of wage inequality within the United States. It is also instructive to analyze these changes using a different point of reference: the experience of *other developed countries* during the same time period. After briefly describing trends in wage inequality elsewhere, we will analyze the contributions of demand, supply, and institutional forces toward explaining the different trends across countries.

We begin our international comparisons with Table 14.8, which compares the wages of full-time workers at the 90th and 10th percentiles across several countries for which comparable data are available (unlike those in Table 14.1, the data contained in Table 14.8 are only for full-time workers). As can be seen from the table, Canada and the United States have relatively high *levels* of wage inequality compared to the other advanced economies. Regardless of the level of such inequality, however, all but one of the countries shown exhibited *increases* in inequality during the 1980s.

The greatest increases in wage inequality throughout the 1980s were in the United Kingdom and the United States; the British 90:10 ratio grew slightly over 30 percent for both men and women, while the American ratios for men and women grew by 19 and 36 percent, respectively. Taking into account increases in the 90:10 ratios for both men and women, increases in the other countries were less than half as large. Thus, one question that arises is why inequality grew so much faster in Great Britain and the United States than elsewhere during the decade.

Another development is that, as we have seen, growing earnings disparities in the United States took place in the context of *falling real wages* for male workers.

TABLE 14.8
International Comparisons of Wage Inequality, Full-Time Workers, 1979 and 1990

Country	Men Ratio of Wages at 90th Percentile to Those at 10th			Women		
	1979	1990	Percentage Increase in 90:10 Ratio	1979	1990	Percentage Increase in 90:10 Ratio
United Kingdom	2.41	3.19	32	2.32	3.03	31
United States	3.42	4.06	19	2.61	3.56	36
Canada	3.49	3.97	14	3.74	3.97	6
Australia	1.99	2.22	12	1.75	1.95	12
Japan	2.59	2.83	9	2.20	2.34	6
Austria	2.64	2.75	4	3.35	3.53	5
France	3.29	3.42	4	2.61	2.77	6
Netherlands	2.75	2.75	0	na	na	na
Sweden	2.16	2.16	0	1.70	1.82	7

SOURCE: Richard B. Freeman and Lawrence F. Katz, "Introduction and Summary," *Differences and Changes in Wage Structures*, ed. Richard Freeman and Lawrence Katz (Chicago: University of Chicago Press, 1995), 13.

For American men, growing inequality arose from the fact that earnings near the top of the distribution fell less sharply than earnings at the bottom (the same was true for Canadian men, although differences in the rates of decline were somewhat smaller).[26] For American women, and more generally for workers in the comparison countries outside of North America, increased inequality was accompanied by at least modest real wage growth at the bottom of the earnings distribution—which means that workers near the top end had even more sharply increasing real wages. This latter pattern was especially evident in Great Britain, where men at the 10th percentile saw their real wages increase by some 12 percent from 1979 to 1989 (as compared to a 12 percent decrease for American men).[27] Thus, a second question that needs to be addressed concerns the causes and the consequences of the falling real wages for less-educated American men as compared to generally rising real wages elsewhere.

---

[26]David Card and Richard B. Freeman, *Small Differences That Matter: Labor Markets and Income Maintenance in Canada and the United States* (Chicago: University of Chicago Press, 1993), 49.

[27]Lawrence F. Katz, Gary W. Loveman, and David G. Blanchflower, "A Comparison of Changes in the Structure of Wages in Four OECD Countries," in *Differences and Changes in Wage Structures,* ed. Richard B. Freeman and Lawrence F. Katz (Chicago: University of Chicago Press, 1995), 30–31.

WHY DID INEQUALITY GROW MOST IN GREAT BRITAIN AND THE UNITED STATES?

We have seen that most economists who have studied the growth of inequality in the United States attribute it to what might be called *skill-biased technological change*—that is, technological change that increased the demand for skilled workers relative to that for less-skilled ones. The shifts in labor demand curves that resulted from this technological change were not accompanied by supply-curve shifts of equal magnitude in the United States; therefore, in an environment in which institutions did little to inhibit wage changes, the wages of skilled workers rose relative to those for unskilled workers.

Because the comparison countries have similar standards of living, and access to labor and capital of similar quality, it is quite likely that skill-biased technological change occurred in all these countries. It is also quite likely that these countries were also affected in roughly similar ways by international trade and the growing production of manufacturing durables elsewhere (especially by less-developed countries, as can be inferred from Example 14.1). Hence, it is unlikely that differences on the *demand* side of the labor market account for the different growth rates of earnings disparities across these countries.

The most notable feature of American wage inequality was the steeply rising returns to education during the 1980s, accompanied by increasing returns to experience among the less-educated. In Britain, the returns to a college education also rose throughout the decade, as did the returns to experience for both blue- and white-collar workers. Countries with smaller growth rates in inequality differed, with some (France, for example) showing no rise in the returns to education but steep increases in the returns to experience, and others (Japan, for example) exhibiting the reverse pattern.[28]

Analyses of trends in wage inequality within individual countries tend to identify country-specific conditions or developments that were especially relevant in each case.[29] However, economic theory leads us to expect some general patterns; most particularly, in the face of skill-biased technological change, the countries with smaller (or zero) increases in the returns to human capital investments must have experienced either (or both) of two phenomena. They must have had either relatively *large increases in the supply of highly skilled workers*, or very *strong institutional forces* that served to "prop up" the wages of the unskilled in the face of reduced demand.

INCREASES IN THE SUPPLY OF SKILLS   For reasons that have not yet been thoroughly analyzed, increases in the supply of college-educated workers were

---

[28]Katz, Loveman, and Blanchflower, "A Comparison of Changes in the Structure of Wages in Four OECD Countries," 36–46.

[29]The experiences of Australia, five European, and two Asian countries are analyzed in Freeman and Katz, eds., *Differences and Changes in Wage Structures*. Wage inequality in Canada is analyzed in Card and Freeman, *Small Differences That Matter*.

smaller in the United States during the 1980s than elsewhere.[30] Further, growth rates of the highly educated were smaller in the countries (such as Great Britain and Japan) that experienced rising returns to education than in the countries (such as France) that did not.[31] Thus, it appears that the rates at which the supply of college-educated workers increased in the various countries affected the returns to educational investments observed in each.

Another supply-side difference between the United States and other countries may well lie in the lower cognitive achievement levels of less-educated workers (see Chapter 9) and the lower levels of company training provided by American firms (see Chapter 5). Less-educated workers in the United States are relatively poor substitutes for the highly skilled, and the costs of upgrading their skills are apparently rather high; thus, in the face of technological change, these workers tended to be replaced (apparently by skilled women) rather than retrained. By way of contrast, consider Japan, where the educational and skills-training systems are both rigorous and widespread for nonuniversity students. Like the United States, Japan also experienced a sharp decline in the growth rate of its college-educated workforce in the 1980s (although its growth rate was still a bit higher than that in the United States). However, with production workers who are more readily retrained, the wage gap between university and high school graduates grew much more modestly in Japan than in the United States.[32]

INSTITUTIONAL FORCES We noted in Chapter 13 that unions tend to raise the wages of less-skilled workers relative to those of skilled workers, and that the United States is far less unionized than other developed countries. It is not surprising, then, that the *level* of American wage inequality is higher than elsewhere.[33] We are seeking to understand *changes* in wage inequality, however, so we must therefore look for changes (or the lack of them) in the power of unions to affect the structure of wages within other countries.

In some countries, such as Canada, unionization rates were not much changed throughout the 1980s.[34] In others, such as France, union membership fell sharply during the decade, but in France collective bargaining takes place at the industry level and the provisions bargained by unions are often extended to nonunion workers by the government (which also maintained a rather high minimum wage

---

[30]Katz, Loveman, and Blanchflower, "A Comparison of Changes in the Structure of Wages in Four OECD Countries," 48.

[31]Freeman and Katz, "Introduction and Summary," 16–17, 48.

[32]Katz, Loveman, and Blanchflower, "A Comparison of Changes in the Structure of Wages in Four OECD Countries."

[33]For an analysis of inequality and unionization in Canada and the United States, see Thomas Lemieux, "Unions and Wage Inequality in Canada and the United States," in *Small Differences That Matter*, ed. Card and Freeman.

[34]W. Craig Riddell, "Unionization in Canada and the United States: A Tale of Two Countries," in *Small Differences That Matter*, ed. Card and Freeman, 110.

during this period).[35] Thus, declining unionization in France was not associated with real wage declines for low-skilled workers.

In Great Britain and the United States, union membership *declined* in the context of bargaining structures that were relatively *decentralized* to begin with. That is, collective bargaining in these two countries was most significant at the firm and plant levels, where market forces are apt to be felt most keenly. (The student will recall from Chapters 4 and 13 that both product and labor demand curves are likely to be most elastic at the level of the firm.) Further, in both countries bargaining tended to become *more* decentralized throughout the decade.[36] Some analysts conclude that the twin phenomena of declining union membership and growing decentralization of collective bargaining contributed to the larger growth of inequality in Great Britain and the United States than elsewhere.[37] As the rates of unionization declined, and as collective bargaining agreements had to be increasingly responsive to market forces, unions in the United States and Britain lost some of their power to narrow the wage gap between skilled and less-skilled workers.

CAUSES AND EFFECTS OF DIFFERENT REAL WAGE CHANGES AMONG THE UNSKILLED

We should reiterate from the discussion immediately above that the effects of unions in a given country are a function of both the level of their membership and the centralization of the country's wage-determination process. Bargaining is tending to decentralize in many countries, a move that is probably a response to the dramatic technological changes taking place. It can be argued that in environments of rapid change local conditions are likely to vary widely, so centralized bargainers are especially ill informed about appropriate wage settlements (or the consequences of inappropriate ones). Thus, when the very rapid advances of high-technology capital were evident in the 1980s, many countries moved to decentralize their bargaining, at least to some degree.[38]

Despite this "market" response of collective bargaining in most advanced economies, the power of *institutions* to affect the wage structure is much stronger in European countries than in North America. European levels of unionization are relatively high, and beyond that, many European governments (as well as Australia's) tend to be quite active in the wage-setting process. The result is that, when faced with the same technological changes and very similar product market forces (for example, the decline of manufacturing), European institutions tended to ensure that the real wages of relatively unskilled workers did not fall. In Great

---

[35]Katz, Loveman, and Blanchflower, "A Comparison of Changes in the Structure of Wages in Four OECD Countries," 54.

[36]Harry C. Katz, "The Decentralization of Collective Bargaining: A Literature Review and Comparative Analysis," *Industrial and Labor Relations Review* 47, no. 1 (October 1993): 3–22.

[37]Freeman and Katz, "Introduction and Summary," 18–19.

[38]Richard B. Freeman and Robert S. Gibbons, "Getting Together and Breaking Apart: The Decline of Centralized Collective Bargaining," in *Differences and Changes in Wage Structures,* ed. Freeman and Katz, 345–370; and Katz, "The Decentralization of Collective Bargaining."

Britain, for example, where wage inequality grew rapidly, "wage councils" set industry-wide minimum wages up through the early 1990s. While the councils were weakened in the 1980s, which contributed to growing inequality, the real wages of unskilled workers were not allowed to fall as they did in the United States and Canada.[39]

Using the experience of the United States (which has the most market-dominated wage-determination process) as a point of reference, changes on the demand side of the labor market were apparently putting strong downward pressures on the market equilibrium wages of the unskilled. Unless the unskilled could be quickly trained for more-skilled jobs, the failure of their real wages to fall in Europe suggests that we will observe sharp increases in their unemployment rates. This is precisely what we do observe.

In Great Britain, the overall unemployment rate rose markedly in the early 1980s, and then fell after that; as we showed back in Chapter 2 (Table 2.4), overall British unemployment was higher in 1990 than in 1979 by some 1.4 percentage points. Unemployment among the least-skilled workers in Britain, however, rose much more steeply than among other groups. For example, from 1979 to 1987, when the unemployment rate of college graduates rose by 3.1 percentage points, the unemployment rate of the least-educated workers rose by 14 percentage points. Further, the least-skilled were overrepresented among the growing number of British workers who were unemployed for more than one year (again, see Table 2.4).[40]

In France and Germany, to take other examples, the decade of the 1980s also witnessed huge increases in unemployment among the least-skilled members of the workforce. As we noted at the end of Chapter 2, the unemployment rate among the lowest-paid workers in France jumped by some 6 percentage points in the decade, while in Germany it increased by over 9 percentage points. These increases were large relative to the 1.3 and 3 percentage-point increases (respectively) in American and Canadian unskilled unemployment rates; they were also large compared to the *overall* increases in France and Germany. In Australia, where the overall ratio of employment to the population was somewhat higher in 1990 than in 1980, the ratio among the least-skilled males fell by 14 percent.[41]

It is apparently the case, then, that in countries in which the real wages of unskilled workers did not fall in the 1980s, unemployment among the unskilled rose most precipitously. In other words, where the wages of unskilled workers did not fall, substitution and scale effects worked in the direction of reducing

[39]John Schmitt, "The Changing Structure of Male Earnings in Britain, 1974–1988," in *Differences and Changes in Wage Structures*, ed. Freeman and Katz, 203; Stephen Machin and Alan Manning, "The Effects of Minimum Wages on Wage Dispersion and Employment: Evidence from the U.K. Wage Councils," *Industrial and Labor Relations Review* 47, no. 2 (January 1994): 319–329. In 1992, when the wage councils were abolished, the United Kingdom became the only European Community country without a minimum wage system.

[40]Schmitt, "The Changing Structure of Male Earnings in Britain," 188–190.

[41]Robert G. Gregory and Francis Vella, "Real Wages, Employment, and Wage Dispersion in U.S. and Australian Labor Markets," in *Differences and Changes in Wage Structures*, ed. Freeman and Katz, 210, 218.

their employment rather sharply.[42] Beyond that, we noted back in Chapter 2 (Table 2.4) that the rates of *overall* unemployment in Europe rose quite markedly in the 1980s relative to those in North America. The failure of low-skilled wages to adjust to market conditions in Europe (and Australia) may well have contributed to a scale effect that served to reduce *total* employment opportunities, not just unskilled employment. That is, when unions or governments prevent wages from falling in some places (Europe) but not others (North America), production will tend to shift to the lower-cost sectors and the overall level of output in the places with rigid wages will experience relative decline.

REVIEW QUESTIONS

1. "The labor supply responses to programs designed to help equalize *incomes* can either narrow or widen the dispersion of *earnings*." Comment on this statement in the context of an increase in the subsidy paid under a "negative income tax" program to those who do not work. Assume that this program creates an effective wage that is greater than zero but less than the market wage, and assume that this effective wage is unchanged by the increased subsidy to those who do not work. (For a review of relevant concepts, see Chapter 6.)

2. Assume that the "comparable worth" remedy for wage discrimination against women will require governmental and large private employers to increase the wages they pay to women in female-dominated jobs. The remedy will not apply to small firms. Given what you learned earlier about wages by firm size and in female-dominated jobs, analyze the effects of comparable worth on earnings inequality among women. (For a review of relevant concepts, see Chapter 12.)

3. Analyze how increasing the investment tax credit given to firms that make expenditures on new capital affects the dispersion of earnings. (For a review of relevant concepts, see Chapter 4.)

4. Proposals to tax health and other employee benefits, which are not now subject to the income tax, have been made in recent years. Assuming that more highly paid workers have higher employee benefits, analyze the effects on earnings inequality if these tax proposals are adopted. (For a review of relevant concepts, see Chapter 8.)

5. One of organized labor's primary objectives in the 1990s is legislation forbidding employers to replace workers who are on strike. If such legislation passes, what will be its effects on earnings inequality? (For a review of relevant concepts, see Chapter 13.)

6. Discuss the role of geographic mobility in decreasing or increasing the dispersion of earnings. (For a review of the relevant concepts, see Chapter 10.)

7. Suppose a country's government is concerned about growing inequality of incomes and wants to undertake a program that will increase the total earnings of the unskilled. It is considering two alternative changes to its current payroll tax, which is levied on employers as a percentage of the first $50,000 of employee earnings.

   a. Extending employer payroll taxes to all earnings over $50,000 per year, **and** increasing the cost of capital by eliminat-

---

[42]See Francine D. Blau and Lawrence M. Kahn, "International Differences in Male Wage Inequality: Institutions versus Market Forces," *Journal of Political Economy* 104 (August 1996): 791–837.

ing certain tax deductions related to plant and equipment;

b. Reducing to zero employer payroll taxes on the first $20,000 of earnings but taxing employers on all employee earnings between $20,000 and $50,000 (there would be no taxes on earnings above $50,000).

Analyze proposal "a" and proposal "b" separately (one, but not both, will be adopted). Which is more likely to accomplish the aims of increasing the earnings of the unskilled? Why?

SELECTED READINGS

Bound, John, and George Johnson. "Changes in the Structure of Wages in the 1980s: An Evaluation of Alternative Explanations." *American Economic Review* 82 (June 1992): 371–392.

Burtless, Gary, ed. *A Future of Lousy Jobs? The Changing Structure of U.S. Wages.* Washington, D.C.: Brookings Institution, 1990.

Freeman, Richard B. and Lawrence F. Katz, eds. *Differences and Changes in Wage Structures.* Chicago: University of Chicago Press, 1995.

Katz, Lawrence F., and Kevin M. Murphy. "Changes in Relative Wages, 1963–1987: Supply and Demand Factors." *Quarterly Journal of Economics* 107 (February 1992): 35–78.

Levy, Frank, and Richard J. Murnane. "U.S. Earnings Levels and Earnings Inequality: A Review of Recent Trends and Proposed Explanations." *Journal of Economic Literature* 30 (September 1992): 1333–1381.

Lorenz Curves and Gini Coefficients

The most commonly used measures of distributional inequality involve grouping the distribution into deciles or quintiles and comparing the earnings (or income) received by each. As we did in the main body of this chapter, one can compare the earnings levels at points high in the distribution (the 80th percentile, say) with points at the low end (the 20th percentile, for example). A richer and more fully descriptive measure, however, employs data on the *share* of total earnings or income received by those in each group.

Suppose that each household in the population has the same income. In this case of perfect equality, each fifth of the population receives a fifth of the total income. In graphic terms, this equality can be shown by the straight line *AB* in Figure 14A.1, which plots the cumulative share of income (vertical axis) received by each quintile and the ones below it (horizontal axis). Thus, the first quintile (with a 0.2 share, or 20 percent of all households) would receive a 0.2 share (20 percent) of total income, the first and second quintiles (four-tenths of the population) would receive four-tenths of total income, and so forth.

If the distribution of income is not perfectly equal, then the curve connecting the cumulative percentages of income received by the cumulated quintiles—the *Lorenz curve*—is convex and lies below the line of perfect equality. For example, in 1992 the lowest fifth of U.S. households received 3.8 percent of total income, the second fifth received 9.4 percent, the third fifth 15.8 percent, the next fifth 24.2 percent, and the highest fifth 46.9 percent. Plotting the cumulative data in Figure 14A.1 yields Lorenz curve *ACDEFB*. This curve displays the convexity one would expect from the clearly unequal distribution of household income in the United States.

Comparing the equality of two different income distributions results in unambiguous conclusions if one Lorenz curve lies completely inside the other (closer to

FIGURE 14A.1

Lorenz Curves for 1980 and 1992 Distributions of Income in the United States

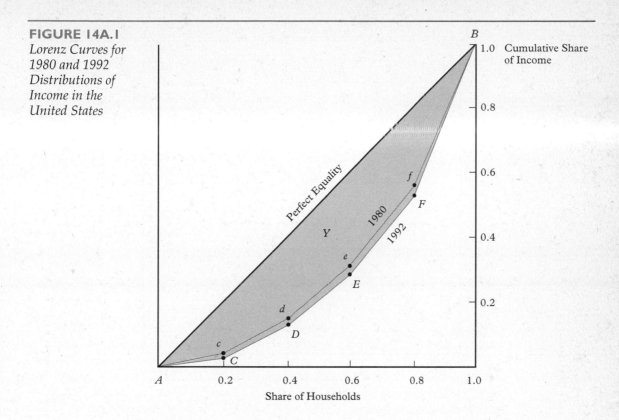

the line of perfect equality). If, for example, we were interested in comparing the American income distributions of 1980 and 1992, we could observe that plotting the 1980 data results in a Lorenz curve, *AcdefB* in Figure 14A.1, that lies everywhere closer to the line of perfect equality than the one for 1992.

If two Lorenz curves cross, however, conclusions about which one represents greater equality are not possible. Comparing curves *A* and *B* in Figure 14A.2, for example, one can see that the distribution represented by *A* has a lower proportion of total income received by the poorest quintile than does the distribution represented by curve *B*; however, the cumulative share of income received by the lowest two quintiles (taken together) is equal for *A* and *B*, and the cumulative proportions received by the bottom three and bottom four quintiles are higher for *A* than for *B*.

Another measure of inequality, which seems at first glance to yield unambiguous answers when various distributions are compared, is the *Gini coefficient*: the ratio of the area between the Lorenz curve and the line of perfect equality (the area labeled *Y* in Figure 14A.1) to the total area under the line of perfect equality. Obviously, with perfect equality the Gini coefficient would equal zero.

One way to calculate the Gini coefficient is to split the area under the Lorenz curve into a series of triangles and rectangles, as shown in Figure 14A.3 (which repeats the Lorenz curve for 1992 shown in Figure 14A.1). Each triangle has a base

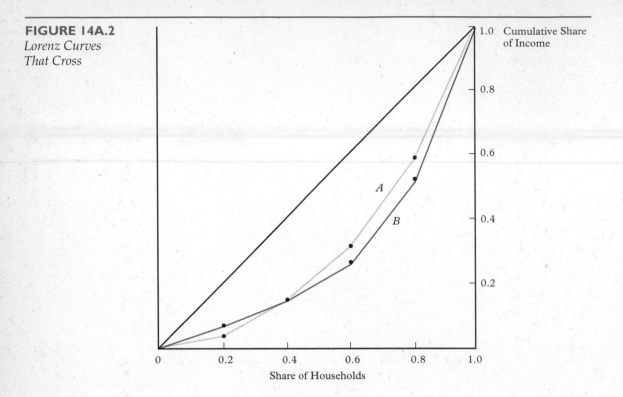

equal to 0.2—the horizontal distance for each of the five quintiles—and a height equal to the percentage of income received by that quintile (the cumulative percentage less the percentages received by lower quintiles). Because the base of each triangle is the same and their heights sum to unity, the *sum* of the areas of each triangle is always equal to 0.5 × 0.2 × 1.0 = 0.1 (one-half base times height).

The rectangles in Figure 14A.3 all have one side equal to 0.2 and another equal to the cumulated percentages of total income received by the previous quintiles. Rectangle $Q_1CC'Q_2$, for example, has an area of 0.2 × 0.038 = 0.0076, while $Q_2DD'Q_3$ has an area of 0.2 × 0.132 = 0.0264. Analogously, $Q_3EE'Q_4$ has an area of 0.0580 and $Q_4FF'Q_5$ an area of 0.1064; together, all four rectangles in Figure 14A.3 have an area that sums to 0.1984.

The area under the Lorenz curve in Figure 14A.3 is thus 0.1984 + 0.1 = 0.2984. Given that the total area under the line of perfect equality is 0.5 × 1 × 1 = 0.5, the Gini coefficient for 1992 is calculated as follows:

$$\text{Gini coefficient (1992)} = \frac{0.5 - 0.2984}{0.5} = 0.4032 \qquad (14A.1)$$

For comparison purposes, the Gini coefficient for the income distribution in 1980 can be calculated as 0.3768—which, because it lies closer to zero than the Gini coefficient for 1992, is evidence of greater equality in 1980.

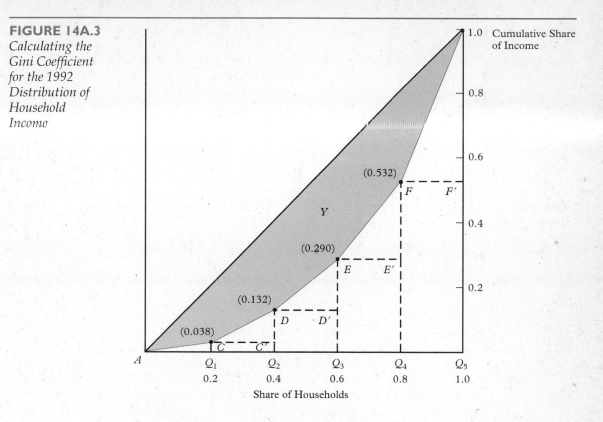

FIGURE 14A.3

Calculating the Gini Coefficient for the 1992 Distribution of Household Income

Unfortunately, the Gini coefficient will become smaller when the rich give up some of their income to the middle class as well as when they give up income in favor of the poor. Thus, the Gini coefficient may yield a "definitive" answer about comparative equality when none is warranted. As we saw in the case of Figure 14A.2, in which the Lorenz curves being compared cross, judging the relative equality of two distributions is not always susceptible of an unambiguous answer.

To this point in the appendix, we have analyzed the Lorenz curve and Gini coefficient in terms of *household income,* for the simple reason that published data permit these calculations. The underlying data on the *shares* of individual *earnings* are not published, but the Gini coefficients themselves that are associated with given earnings distributions have been published since 1988. For purposes of comparison it is interesting to note that the Gini coefficients for the *earnings* distribution of adult males who worked full-time year-round were 0.332 in 1988 and 0.347 in 1992; the corresponding coefficients for women who worked full-time were 0.293 and 0.296.[1] Both sets of coefficients suggest the presence of rising inequality in earnings over that period.

---

[1]U.S. Bureau of the Census, *Money Income of Households, Families, and Persons in the United States,* Series P–60: no. 124, Table 29 (1988); no. 184, Table 29 (1992).

15

Unemployment

As noted in Chapter 2, the population can be divided into those people who are in the labor force (L) and those who are not (N). The labor force consists of those people who are employed (E) and those who are unemployed but would like to be employed (U). The concept of unemployment is somewhat ambiguous, since in theory virtually anyone would be willing to be employed in return for a generous enough compensation package. Economists tend to resolve this dilemma by defining unemployment in terms of an individual's willingness to be employed at some prevailing market wage. Government statistics tend to take a more pragmatic approach, defining the unemployed as those who are on temporary layoff waiting to be recalled by their previous employers or those without a job who have actively searched for work in the previous month (of course, "actively" is not precisely defined).

Given these definitions, the unemployment rate (**u**) is measured as the ratio of the number of the unemployed to the number in the labor force:

$$\mathbf{u} = \frac{U}{L} \tag{15.1}$$

Much attention is focused on how the national unemployment rate varies over time and how unemployment rates vary across geographic areas and age/race/gender/ethnic groups.

It is important, however, to understand the limitations of unemployment rate data. They *do* reflect the proportion of a group that, at a point in time, actively want to work but are not employed. For a number of reasons, however, they *do not* necessarily provide an accurate reflection of the economic hardship that members of a group are suffering. First, individuals who are not actively searching for work, including those who searched unsuccessfully and then gave up, are not counted among the unemployed (see Chapter 7). Second, unemployment statistics tell us nothing about the earnings levels of those who are employed, including whether these exceed the poverty level. Third, a substantial fraction of the unemployed come from families in which other earners are present—for example, many unemployed are teenagers—and the unemployed often are not the primary source of their family's support. Fourth, a substantial fraction of the unemployed receive some income support while they are unemployed, in the form of either government unemployment compensation payments or private supplementary unemployment benefits.

Finally, while unemployment rate data give us information on the fraction of the *labor force* that are not working, they tell us little about the fraction of the *population* that are *employed*. Table 15.1 contains U.S. data on the aggregate unemployment rate, the labor force participation rate, and the *employment rate*—the last being defined as employment divided by the adult population—for 1994 and for two pairs of earlier years over which roughly equal changes in the unemployment rate were experienced. From 1948 to 1958, for example, the unemployment rate rose from 3.8 to 6.8 percent, and the employment rate fell from 56.6 to 55.4 percent. In contrast, from 1968 to 1991 the unemployment rate rose by a similar magnitude, from 3.6 to 6.7 percent, but the employment rate *rose* substantially! The reason for the opposite correlations between the unemployment and the employment rates for these two periods is that in the earlier period labor force participation grew only slowly, while in the latter period it was growing very rapidly.

TABLE 15.1

Civilian Labor Force Participation, Employment, and Unemployment Rates in the United States (in percentages)

Year	Unemployment Rate (U/L)	Labor Force Participation Rate (L/POP)	Employment Rate (E/POP)
1948	3.8	58.8	56.6
1958	6.8	59.5	55.4
1968	3.6	59.6	57.5
1991	6.7	66.0	61.6
1994	6.1	66.6	62.5

U = number of people unemployed.

L = number of people in the labor force.

E = number of people employed.

POP = total population over age 16.

SOURCE: U.S. Department of Labor, *Employment and Earnings*, January 1995, 162.

Nonetheless, the unemployment rate remains a useful indicator of labor market conditions. This chapter will be concerned with the causes of unemployment and with how various government policies affect, in an either intended or unintended manner, the level of unemployment.

We begin with a simple conceptual model of a labor market that emphasizes the importance of considering the *flows* between labor market states (for example, the *movement* of people from employed to unemployed status) as well as the *number* of people in each labor market state (for example, the *number* of the unemployed). Knowledge of the determinants of these flows is crucial to any understanding of the causes of unemployment.

A Stock-Flow Model of the Labor Market

Data on the number of people who are employed, unemployed, and not in the labor force are provided each month from the national Current Population Survey (CPS). As Figure 15.1 indicates, in May 1993 (when the overall unemployment rate averaged 6.9 percent) there were 119.2 million employed, 8.9 million unemployed, and 65.2 million adults aged 16 and over not in the labor force. The impression one gets when one traces these data over short periods of time is that of relative stability; for example, it is highly unusual for the unemployment rate to change by more than a few tenths of a percentage point from one month to the next.

Taking month-to-month "snapshots" of the number of people who are employed, unemployed, or out of the labor market misses a considerable amount of movement into and out of these categories *during* the month. Figure 15.1 contains data on the flows of workers between the various categories during a recent one-month period (April to May 1993) when the total number of workers unemployed was the same at the end as it was at the beginning. During this month, approximately 2.0 million unemployed individuals found employment (the flow denoted by UE in Figure 15.1), and 1.5 million of the unemployed dropped out of the labor force (the flow denoted by UN). These numbers represent the proportions 0.225 (P_{ue}) and 0.169 (P_{un}) of the stock of the unemployed, respectively; thus, one can conclude that approximately 40 percent of the individuals who were unemployed at the beginning of that month left unemployment by the next month. These individuals were replaced in the pool of unemployed by equivalent flows of individuals into unemployment from the stocks of employed individuals (the flow EU) and those not in the labor force (the flow NU).[1] The flow EU consists of individuals

---

[1] Joseph A. Ritter, "Measuring Labor Market Dynamics: Gross Flows of Workers and Jobs," *Review, Federal Reserve Bank of St. Louis* 75 (November/December 1993): 39–57. From the perspective of actual measurement, those who are classified as "unemployed" are distinguished from those considered "out of the labor force" only by self-reported information on job search. Thus, the empirical distinction between the two categories, as well as errors in recording movements between them, have attracted the attention of researchers. For a recent analysis of the former issue, see Füsun Gönsül, "New Evidence on Whether Unemployment and Out of the Labor Force Are Distinct States," *Journal of Human Resources* 27, no. 2 (Spring 1992): 329-361. On the latter topic, see Paul Flaim and Carma Hogue, "Measuring Labor Force Flows: A Special Conference Examines the Problems," *Monthly Labor Review* (July 1985): 7-15.

FIGURE 15.1
*Labor Market
Stocks and Flows:
May 1993*

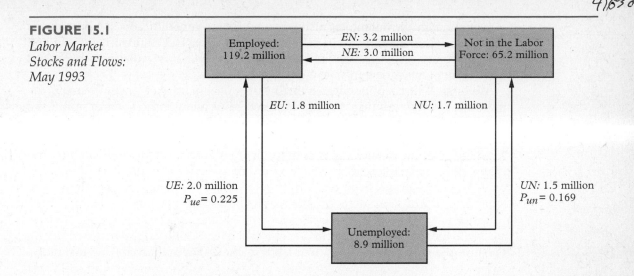

who voluntarily left or involuntarily lost their last job, while the flow *NU* consists of people entering the labor force. The fact that the flows *into* unemployment equaled the flows *out of* unemployment meant that the number of unemployed workers remained constant from April to May.

When one thinks of the unemployed, the image of an individual laid off from his or her previous job often springs to mind. However, the view that such individuals constitute all, or even most, of the unemployed is incorrect. Table 15.2 provides some data that bear on this point for years between 1970 and 1994, during which the unemployment rate varied between 4.9 and 9.7 percent. Only in the relatively high unemployment years, such as 1982, were more than half of the unemployed job losers. In each year, more than one-third of the unemployed came from out-of-labor-force status—that is, they were individuals who were either entering the labor force for the first time (*new entrants*) or individuals who had some previous employment experience and were reentering the labor force after a period of time out of the labor force (*reentrants*). Recent evidence suggests, though, that many reentrants are actually job losers who dropped out of the labor force for a short time. Finally, although the vast majority of individuals who quit their jobs obtain new jobs prior to quitting and never pass through unemployment status, in most years at least 10 percent of the unemployed were voluntary job leavers.[2]

Similarly, when one thinks of an individual on layoff, one may envision an individual who has permanently lost his or her job and who finds employment with a new employer only after an exhaustive job search and a long period of unemployment. However, the evidence suggests that a substantial fraction (approximately

---

[2]For evidence that most quits do not involve a spell of unemployment, see J. Peter Mattila, "Job Quitting and Frictional Unemployment," *American Economic Review* 64 (March 1974): 235–239. Evidence that many reentrants were job losers is found in Kim Clark and Lawrence Summers, "Labor Market Dynamics and Unemployment: A Reconsideration," *Brookings Papers on Economic Activity*, 1979–1, 13–60.

70 percent) of those individuals who *lost* their last job are on *temporary layoff* and ultimately return to their previous employer, many after only a relatively short spell of unemployment.[3] Why some individuals move between employed and unemployed status, maintaining attachment to a single employer, will be discussed below.

Although ultimately public concern focuses on the level of unemployment, to understand the determinants of this level one must analyze the flows of individuals between the various labor market states. A group's unemployment rate might be high because its members have difficulty finding jobs once unemployed, because they have difficulty (for voluntary or involuntary reasons) remaining employed once a job is found, or because they frequently enter and leave the labor force. The appropriate policy prescription to reduce the unemployment rate will depend upon which one of these labor market flows is responsible for the high rate.

Somewhat more formally, one can show that if labor markets are roughly in balance, with the flows into and out of unemployment equal, the unemployment rate (**u**) for a group depends upon the various labor market flows in the following manner:

$$\mathbf{u} = F(\overset{+}{P}_{en}, \overset{-}{P}_{ne}, \overset{-}{P}_{un}, \overset{+}{P}_{nu}, \overset{+}{P}_{eu}, \overset{-}{P}_{ue}) \tag{15.2}$$

In this equation,

F means "a function of,"
P_{en} = fraction of employed who leave the labor force,
P_{ne} = fraction of those not in the labor force who enter the labor force and find employment,
P_{un} = fraction of unemployed who leave the labor force,
P_{nu} = fraction of those not in the labor force who enter the labor force and become unemployed,
P_{eu} = fraction of employed who become unemployed, and
P_{ue} = fraction of unemployed who become employed.

So, for example, if there were initially 100 employed individuals in a group and 15 of them became unemployed during a period, P_{eu} would equal 0.15.

A plus sign over a variable in equation (15.2) means that an increase in that variable will increase the unemployment rate, while a minus sign means that an increase in the variable will decrease the unemployment rate. The equation thus asserts that, other things equal, increases in the proportions of individuals who voluntarily or involuntarily leave their jobs and become unemployed (P_{eu}) or leave the labor force (P_{en}) will increase a group's unemployment rate, as will an increase

---

[3]For evidence on the magnitude of temporary layoffs, see Martin Feldstein, "The Importance of Temporary Layoffs: An Empirical Analysis," *Brookings Papers on Economic Activity*, 1975–3, and Robert Topel, "Inventories, Layoffs and the Short-Run Demand for Labor," *American Economic Review* 72 (September 1982): 769–788. Since many of those who are temporarily laid off are rehired rather quickly, at any point in time most layoff unemployment is actually made up of individuals who will not be recalled. On this, see Lawrence Katz and Bruce Meyer, "Unemployment Insurance, Recall Expectations and Unemployment Outcomes," *Quarterly Journal of Economics* 105 (November 1990): 993–1002.

TABLE 15.2
Sources of Unemployment, United States, various years

Year	Unemployment Rate	Percent of Unemployed Who Were:			
		Job Losers	Job Leavers	Reentrants	New Entrants
1970	4.9	44.3	13.4	30.0	12.3
1974	5.6	43.5	14.9	28.4	13.2
1978	6.1	41.6	14.1	30.0	14.3
1982	9.7	58.7	7.9	22.3	11.1
1986	6.9	48.9	12.3	26.2	12.5
1990	5.5	48.3	14.8	27.4	9.5
1994	6.1	47.7	9.4	34.8	7.6

SOURCE: U.S. Department of Labor, *1982 Employment and Training Report of the President* (Washington, D.C.: U.S. Government Printing Office, 1982), Table A–36; U.S. Department of Labor, *Monthly Labor Review*, various issues.

in the proportion of the group that enter the labor force without first having a job lined up (P_{nu}). Similarly, the greater the proportion of individuals who leave unemployment status, either to become employed (P_{ue}) or to leave the labor force (P_{un}), the lower a group's unemployment rate will be. Finally, the greater the proportion of individuals who enter the labor force and immediately find jobs (P_{ne}), the lower a group's unemployment rate will be.[4]

Equation (15.2) and Figure 15.1 make clear that social concern over any given level of unemployment should focus on both the incidence of unemployment (on the fraction of people in a group who become unemployed) and the duration of spells of unemployment. Society is probably more concerned if small groups of individuals are unemployed for long periods of time than if many individuals rapidly pass through unemployment status. Until recently, it was widely believed that the bulk of measured unemployment could be attributed to the fact that many people

---

[4]The specific functional form for equation (15.2) is

$$u = \frac{1}{1 + \left[\dfrac{(P_{ne} + P_{nu})P_{ue} + (P_{ne})(P_{un})}{(P_{ne} + P_{nu})P_{eu} + (P_{nu})(P_{en})} \right]}$$

Its derivation is found in Stephen T. Marston, "Employment Instability and High Unemployment Rates," *Brookings Papers on Economic Activity* 1976–1, 169–203. An intuitive understanding of why each of the results summarized in equation (15.2) holds can be obtained from the definition of the unemployment rate in equation (15.1). A movement from one labor market state to another may affect the numerator or the denominator, or both, and hence the unemployment rate. For example, an increase in P_{en} does not affect the number of unemployed individuals directly, but it does reduce the size of the labor force. According to equation (15.1), this reduction leads to an increase in the unemployment rate.

were experiencing short spells of unemployment. However, evidence suggests that, while many people do flow quickly through the unemployed state, prolonged spells of unemployment for a relatively small number of individuals characterize those found in the *stock* of the unemployed at any given time.[5]

The various theories of unemployment discussed in the following sections all essentially relate to the determination of one or more of the flows represented in equation (15.2). That is, they provide explanations of why the proportions of individuals who move between the various labor market states vary over time or across geographic areas, including countries.

Types of Unemployment and Their Causes

FRICTIONAL UNEMPLOYMENT: THE THEORY OF JOB SEARCH

Suppose a competitive labor market is in equilibrium in the sense that, at the prevailing market wage, the quantity of labor demanded just equals the quantity of labor supplied. Figure 15.2 shows such a labor market, in which the demand curve is D_0, the supply curve is S_0, employment is E_0, and the wage rate is W_0. Thus far the text has treated this equilibrium situation as one of full employment and has implied that there is no unemployment associated with it. However, this implication is not completely correct. Even in a market-equilibrium or full-employment situation there will still be some *frictional unemployment*, because some people will be "between jobs."

Frictional unemployment arises because labor markets are inherently dynamic, because information flows are imperfect, and because it takes time for unemployed workers and employers with job vacancies to find each other. Even if the size of the labor force is constant, in each period there will be new entrants to the labor market searching for employment while other employed or unemployed individuals are leaving the labor force. Some people will quit their jobs to search for other employment (see Chapter 10). Moreover, random fluctuations in demand across firms will cause some firms to close or lay off workers at the same time that other firms are opening or expanding employment. Because information about the characteristics of those searching for work and the nature of the jobs opening up cannot instantly be known or evaluated, it takes time for job matches to be made between unemployed workers and potential employers. Hence, even when, in the aggregate, the demand for labor equals the supply, frictional unemployment will still exist.

The level of frictional unemployment in an economy is determined by the flows of individuals into and out of the labor market and the speed with which unemployed individuals find (and accept) jobs. The factors that determine this speed are captured in an analysis of the job search process, to which we now turn.

---

[5]Clark and Summers, "Labor Market Dynamics and Unemployment: A Reconsideration."

FIGURE 15.2

A Market with Full Employment Initially

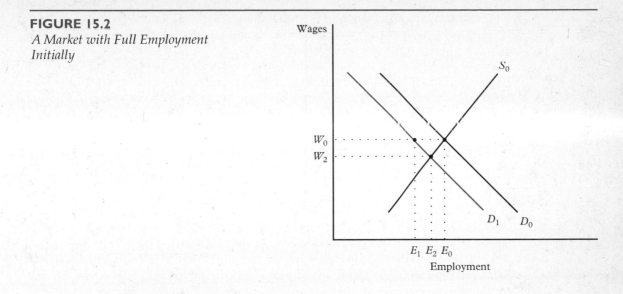

A MODEL OF JOB SEARCH   Workers who want employment must search for job offers, and because information about job opportunities and workers' characteristics is imperfect, it will take time and effort for matches to be made between unemployed workers and potential employers. Other things equal, the lower the probability that unemployed workers will become employed in a period (that is, the lower P_{ue} is), the higher will be their expected duration of unemployment and the higher will be the unemployment rate. To understand what can affect P_{ue}, we develop a formal model of job search, based on the key assumption that wages are associated with the characteristics of jobs, not with the characteristics of the specific individuals who fill them.[6]

Suppose that employers differ in the set of minimum hiring standards they use. Hiring standards may include educational requirements, job training, work experience, performance on hiring tests, etc. A very simple model of the hiring process assumes that this set of attributes can be summarized in a single variable, K, which denotes the minimum skill level a job requires. Associated with each job is a wage, $W(K)$—a wage that is assumed to be a function of the required skill level and not of the particular characteristics of the people hired. We also assume that the wage rate is an increasing function of the minimum required skill level and that two employers using the same standard will offer the same wage.

Because different employers have different hiring standards, our simple model implies that there will be a distribution of wage offers associated with job vacancies

---

[6]Our discussion here draws heavily on Dale T. Mortensen, "Job Search, the Duration of Unemployment, and the Phillips Curve," *American Economic Review* 60 (December 1970): 846–862. Dale T. Mortensen, "Models of Search in the Labor Market," in *Handbook of Labor Economics,* ed. Orley Ashenfelter and Richard Layard (Amsterdam: North-Holland, 1986), and Theresa Devine and Nicholas Kiefer, *Empirical Labor Economics: The Search Approach* (New York: Oxford University Press, 1990), provide surveys of the theoretical and empirical literature on job search models.

FIGURE 15.3
Choice of Reservation Wage in a
Model of Job Search

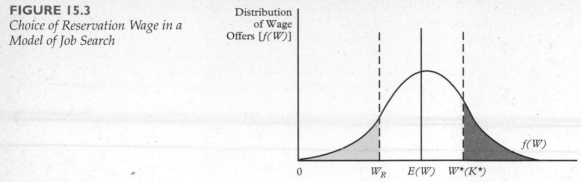

in the labor market. This distribution of wage offers is denoted by $f(W)$ in Figure 15.3. As one moves to the right in the figure, the minimum skill level and offered wage on a job increase. Since $f(W)$ represents a probability distribution of wage offers, the area under the curve sums to 1 (that is, the distribution contains 100 percent of all wage offers in the market). Each wage offer (on the horizontal axis) is shown in relation to that offer's share in the distribution (on the vertical axis).

Now suppose a given unemployed individual has skill level K^*. Since no firm will hire a worker who does not meet its hiring standards, the maximum wage this individual could hope to receive is $W^*(K^*)$. An individual who knew which firms had a hiring standard of K^* would apply to those firms and, since the individual meets their hiring standards, would be hired at a wage of W^*.

Suppose, instead, that job market information is imperfect in the sense that, while an applicant knows the shape of the distribution of wage offers, $f(W)$, he or she does *not* know what each particular firm's wage offer or hiring standard will be. One can conceptualize job search as a process in which the person randomly visits firms' employment offices. If the firm's hiring standard exceeds K^*, the person is rejected for the job, but if the hiring standard is K^* or less, the person is offered the job. While the individual might find it advantageous to accumulate a number of job offers and then accept the best, job seekers—especially those at the lower end of the skill ladder—are not always allowed such a luxury. Rather, they must instantly decide whether or not to accept a job offer, because otherwise the offer will be extended to a different applicant.

How does an unemployed worker know whether to accept a particular job offer? One strategy is to decide on a *reservation wage* and then to accept only those offers above this level. The critical question then is, "How is this reservation wage determined?"

To answer this question, suppose W_R is the reservation wage chosen (in Figure 15.3) by a person who has skill level K^*. Now observe that this individual's job application will be rejected by any firm that offers a wage higher than $W^*(K^*)$; the person will not meet its minimum hiring standards. Similarly, the person will reject any job offers that call for a wage less than W_R. Hence, the probability that he or she will find an acceptable job in any period is simply the unshaded area under the curve between W_R and W^*. The higher this probability, the lower the expected duration of unemployment. Given that the person finds a job, his or her *expected* wage is simply the weighted average of the job offers in the W_R to W^* range. This average (or expected) wage is denoted by $E(W)$ in Figure 15.3.

If the individual were to choose a slightly higher reservation wage, his or her choice would have two effects. On the one hand, since the person would now reject more low-wage jobs, his or her expected wage (once employed) would increase. On the other hand, rejecting more job offers also decreases the probability of finding an acceptable job in any given period, thus increasing the expected duration of unemployment. Put another way, higher reservation wages lead to the costs of longer expected spells of unemployment, but also to the benefits of higher expected wages once a job is found. Each unemployed individual will choose his or her reservation wage so that, at the margin, the expected costs of longer spells of unemployment just equal the expected benefits of higher postunemployment wages. That is, the reservation wage should be chosen so that the marginal benefit from a higher reservation wage just equals its marginal cost.

This simple model and associated decision rule lead to a number of implications. First, as long as the reservation wage is not set equal to the lowest wage offered in the market, the probability of finding a job will be less than 1 and hence some *search unemployment* can be expected to result. *Search unemployment* occurs when an individual does not necessarily accept the first job that is offered—a rational strategy in a world of imperfect information.

Second, since the reservation wage will always be chosen to be less than the wage commensurate with the individual's skill level, $W^*(K^*)$, virtually all individuals will be *underemployed* once they find a job (in the sense that their expected earnings will be less than W^*). This underemployment is a cost of imperfect information; better labor market information would improve the job-matching process.

Third, otherwise identical individuals will wind up receiving different wages. Two unemployed individuals with the same skill level could choose the same reservation wage and have the same *expected* postunemployment wage. However, the wages they actually wind up with will depend upon pure luck—the wage offer between W_R and W^* they happen to find. In a world of imperfect information, then, no economic model can explain all the variation in wages across individuals.

Fourth, anything that causes unemployed workers to intensify their job search (to knock on more doors per day) will reduce the duration of unemployment, other things equal. More efficient collection/dissemination of information on both jobs and applicants can increase the speed of the search process for all parties in the market; enhanced computerization among employment agencies is one example of an innovation that could reduce unemployment. The student will recall from Chapter 7, however, that even unemployed workers have alternative uses for their time (they can spend it in "household production"). Thus, the intensity of job search is also influenced by the value of their time in household production and the payoffs to job search that they expect; if the value of the former is high and the expected payoffs to the latter are low, unemployed workers may become "discouraged" and quit searching altogether—in which case they are counted as being "out of the labor force."

Finally, if the cost to an individual of being unemployed were to fall, the person should be led to increase his or her reservation wage (that is, the person would become more choosy about the offers deemed to be acceptable). A higher reservation wage, of course, would increase both the expected duration of unemployment and the expected postunemployment wage rate. One important influence on the cost of being unemployed, and hence on the reservation wages of unemployed workers, is the presence and generosity of governmental unemployment insurance (UI) programs.

THE EFFECTS OF UNEMPLOYMENT INSURANCE BENEFITS   Virtually every advanced economy offers its workers who have lost jobs some form of unemployment compensation, although these systems vary widely in their structure and generosity.[7] In the United States, the unemployment insurance system is actually composed of individual state systems and, although the details of the individual systems differ, one can easily sketch the broad outlines of how they operate.

When workers become unemployed, their eligibility for unemployment insurance benefits is based upon their previous labor market experience and reason for unemployment. With respect to their experience, each state requires unemployed individuals to demonstrate "permanent" attachment to the labor force, by meeting minimum earnings or weeks-worked tests during some base period, before they can be eligible for UI benefits. In all states, covered workers who are *laid off* and meet these labor market experience tests are eligible for UI benefits. In some states workers who voluntarily quit their jobs are eligible for benefits in certain circumstances. Finally, new entrants or reentrants to the labor force and workers fired for cause are, in general, ineligible for benefits.

After a waiting period, which is one week in most states, an eligible worker can begin to collect UI benefits. The structure of benefits is illustrated in Figure 15.4 where it can be seen that benefits are related to an individual's previous earnings level. As shown in panel (a), all eligible unemployed workers are entitled to at least a minimum benefit level, B_{min}. After previous earnings rise above a critical level, W_{min}, benefits increase proportionately with earnings up to a maximum earnings level (W_{max}), past which benefits remain constant at B_{max}. A few states also have dependents' allowances for unemployed workers, although in some of these

---

[7]Ronald Ehrenberg, *Labor Markets and Integrating National Economies* (Washington, D.C.: Brookings Institution, 1994), 62.

A more complete description of the characteristics of the American UI system is found in *Highlights of State Unemployment Compensation Laws, January 1995* (Washington, D.C.: National Foundation for Unemployment Compensation and Workers' Compensation, 1995).

FIGURE 15.4

Weekly Unemployment Insurance Benefits as a Function of Previous Earnings

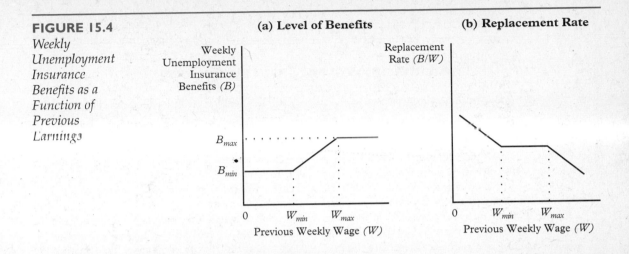

(a) Level of Benefits   (b) Replacement Rate

states the dependents' allowance cannot increase an individual's weekly UI benefits above B_{max}.

An implication of such a benefit structure is that the ratio of an individual's UI benefits to previous earnings varies according to his or her past earnings (see panel b). This ratio is often called the *replacement rate*, the fraction of previous earnings that the UI benefits replace. Over the range between W_{min} and W_{max}, where the replacement rate is constant, most states aim to replace around 50 percent of an unemployed worker's previous earnings.

Once UI benefits begin, an unemployed individual's eligibility for continued benefits depends upon his or her making continual "suitable efforts" to find employment; the definition of suitable efforts varies widely across states. In addition, there is a maximum duration of receipt of benefits that is of fixed length in some states (usually 26 weeks) and varies in other states with a worker's prior labor market experience (workers with "more permanent attachment" being eligible for more weeks of benefits). Congress has also passed legislation that allows states where the unemployment rate is high to extend the length of time unemployed workers can receive benefits; the typical extension is 13 weeks.

Our theory of job search outlined above leads to the expectation that, by reducing the costs associated with being unemployed, more generous UI benefits should cause an increase in the reservation wages of unemployed workers. Increased reservation wages will tend to reduce P_{ue} and P_{un}, which will lengthen the duration of unemployment. Longer durations, in turn, will increase the unemployment rate if other things remain equal. (One way to shorten durations is to offer workers a bonus if they accept offers more quickly. An analysis of some experiments along these lines is given in Example 15.1.)

Because the generosity of UI benefits varies widely across states, numerous studies have sought to empirically test the hypothesis that more-generous benefits

EXAMPLE 15.1

The Unemployment Insurance Bonus Experiments

Between mid-1984 and mid-1985 the state of Illinois conducted a *claimant bonus* experiment to test whether providing cash bonuses to unemployment insurance (UI) recipients who found a new job "quickly" would be an effective way to reduce their durations of unemployment without adversely affecting their postunemployment wages. The idea was that the promise of a cash bonus for rapid reemployment would cause UI recipients to increase the fraction of time they spent searching for new employment and that they would thus find acceptable jobs more quickly.

UI recipients in the experiment were randomly assigned to two groups. The first served as a control group and received regular UI benefits. Members of the second group were promised an additional cash bonus of $500 if they found a full-time job within eleven weeks and held that job for at least four months. Given that individuals were randomly assigned to the two groups, one would expect the two groups to exhibit, on average, roughly equivalent durations of unemployment and postunemployment wages in the absence of any "bonus effect."

It turned out that people eligible for the bonus experienced one less week of unemployment, on average, than did members of the control group. Further, their postunemployment wages were about the same as those among the control group. Thus, it appeared that offering the cash bonus to UI recipients achieved its goal. Policymakers were sufficiently interested in considering the possibility of reforming the UI system to include bonuses for rapid reemployment that further experiments involving the concept were conducted in the states of New Jersey, Pennsylvania, and Washington.

At the same time the claimant bonus experiment was undertaken, Illinois also undertook an *employer bonus* experiment. In this experiment, the UI recipients were again randomly assigned to two groups, and one group was told that if they found full-time employment within eleven weeks and held that job for at least four months, their *employers* would receive a $500 cash bonus. The intent here was to provide a subsidy to employers (see Chapter 3) in the hope that this would stimulate faster reemployment for unemployed workers. The results of this experiment suggested that the promise of an employer bonus did *not* significantly reduce the average duration of unemployment. Whether eligible recipients had difficulty explaining the potential subsidy to employers or whether their eligibility somehow made employers think they were less productive (see Example 3.3) is unclear.

SOURCE: Bruce D. Meyer, "Lessons from the U.S. Unemployment Insurance Experiments," *Journal of Economic Literature* 33, no. 1 (March 1995): 91–131.

serve to raise the unemployment rate beyond what it would otherwise be. Evidence from these studies suggests that higher UI replacement rates are indeed associated with longer durations of unemployment for recipients. Estimates differ, of course, on how responsive durations actually are to changes in the replacement rate, but one recent study estimated that if the United States had ended its UI program in 1976, the average duration of unemployment that year would have fallen from 4.3 to 2.8 months.[8] It is more realistic, of course, to consider how responsive durations are to more modest changes in UI benefits, and most estimates imply that a 10 percentage-point increase in the replacement rate would increase the length of unemployment spells by about one week.[9] Studies of the effects of unemployment compensation in other countries also support the hypothesis that more-generous UI benefits tend to increase the unemployment rate.[10]

Aside from benefit levels, the mere *eligibility* of workers for unemployment compensation benefits has also been found to influence workers' job search behavior. In the United States, for example, there is a huge jump in the probability of a worker's "finding" a job during the week his or her eligibility for UI benefits ends.[11] Further evidence concerning the eligibility for UI benefits is seen in an analysis of the differences between the unemployment rate in Canada and the United States. In 1981, an unemployed Canadian worker was 3 times more likely to qualify for UI benefits than was an unemployed worker in the United States, and by the end of the 1980s unemployed Canadians were 3.5 times more likely to be receiving benefits. Accompanying that change was a rise in the Canadian unemployment rate relative to that in the United States; in fact, one study concluded that the majority of the widening gap in unemployment between Canada and the United States was probably caused by differential eligibility for UI benefits.[12]

Do these findings imply that increasing the availability or generosity of unemployment compensation is unwise? Perhaps. Referring back to our theory of job search, the increased reservation wage accompanying more-generous UI benefits will tend to increase the duration of unemployment spells, but it should also raise the expected postunemployment wage; indeed, one purpose of unemployment compensation is precisely to permit workers to search for a suitable "match." Unfortunately, there is only weak evidence that higher UI benefits do raise the wages workers receive once they leave unemployment and find work. However, one study indicated that, as the UI replacement rate rises in the United States and UI

---

[8]James M. Poterba and Lawrence H. Summers, "Unemployment Benefits and Labor Market Transitions: A Multinomial Logit Model with Errors in Classification," *Review of Economics and Statistics* 77, no. 2 (May 1995): 207–216.

[9]See, for example, Ronald G. Ehrenberg and Ronald L. Oaxaca, "Unemployment Insurance, Duration of Unemployment and Subsequent Wage Gain," *American Economic Review* 66 (December 1976): 754–766. Anthony B. Atkinson and John Micklewright, "Unemployment Compensation and Labor Market Transitions: A Critical Review," *Journal of Economic Literature* 29 (December 1991): 1679–1727; and Gary Burtless, "Unemployment Insurance and Labor Supply: A Survey," in *Unemployment Insurance: The Second Half-Century*, ed. W. Lee Hansen and James Byers (Madison: University of Wisconsin Press, 1990), provide surveys of these studies.

[10]Jennifer Hunt, "The Effects of Unemployment Compensation on Unemployment Duration in Germany," *Journal of Labor Economics* 13, no. 1 (January 1995): 88–120; and David Card and W. Craig Riddell, "Unemployment in Canada and the United States: A Further Analysis," working paper no. 352, Industrial Relations Section, Princeton University, November 1995.

[11]Katz and Meyer, "Unemployment Insurance, Recall Expectations, and Unemployment Outcomes."

[12]Card and Riddell, "Unemployment in Canada and the United States."

recipients become more choosy, unemployed Americans who do *not* qualify for UI benefits are able to secure jobs more quickly![13]

STRUCTURAL UNEMPLOYMENT: OCCUPATIONAL AND REGIONAL UNEMPLOYMENT RATE DIFFERENCES

Structural unemployment arises when there is a mismatch between the skills demanded and supplied in a given area or an imbalance between the supplies of and demands for workers across areas. *If* wages were completely flexible *and* if costs of occupational or geographic mobility were low, market adjustments would quickly eliminate this type of unemployment. In practice, however, these conditions may fail to hold, and structural unemployment may result.

OCCUPATIONAL IMBALANCES   A two-sector labor market model, represented by Figure 15.5, can be used to illustrate this point. For the moment we shall assume the sectors refer to markets for occupational classes of workers; later we shall assume that they are two geographically separate labor markets. Suppose that market A is the market for production workers in the automobile industry and market B is the market for skilled computer specialists, and suppose that initially both markets are in equilibrium. Given the demand and supply curves in both markets, (D_{0A}, S_{0A}) and (D_{0B}, S_{0B}), the equilibrium wage/employment combinations in the two sectors will be (W_{0A}, E_{0A}) and (W_{0B}, E_{0B}), respectively. Because of differences in training costs and nonpecuniary conditions of employment, the wages need not be equal in the two sectors.

Now suppose that the demand for automobile workers falls to D_{1A} as a result of foreign import competition, while the demand for computer specialists rises to D_{1B} as a result of the increased use of computers. If real wages are inflexible downward in market A because of union contract provisions, social norms, or government legislation, employment of automobile workers will fall to E_{1A}. Employment and wages of computer specialists will rise to E_{1B} and W_{1B}, respectively. Unemployment of $E_{0A} - E_{1A}$ workers would be created in the short run.

If automobile employees could costlessly become computer specialists, these unemployed workers would quickly "move" to market B, where we assume wages are flexible, and eventually all the unemployment would be eliminated.[14] Structural unemployment arises, however, when costs of adjustment are sufficiently high to retard or even prevent such movements. The cost to displaced

---

[13]Ronald Ehrenberg, *Labor Markets and Integrating National Economies,* 64; and Phillip B. Levine, "Spillover Effects Between the Insured and Uninsured Unemployed," *Industrial and Labor Relations Review* 47, no. 1 (October 1993): 73–86.

[14]Actually, this statement is not quite correct. As noted in Chapter 13 when analyzing the effects of unions using a similar model, *wait unemployment* may arise. That is, as long as the wage rate in market A exceeds the wage rate in market B and unemployed workers in market A expect that normal job turnover will eventually create job vacancies in A, it may be profitable for them to remain attached to market A and wait for a job in that sector.

FIGURE 15.5
Structural Unemployment Due to Inflexible wages and Costs of Adjustment

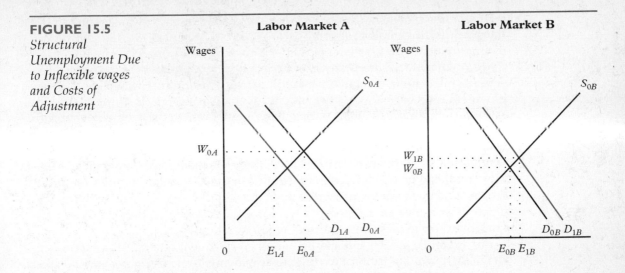

individuals, many in their fifties and sixties, may prove to be prohibitively expensive, given the limited time horizons they face until retirement. Moreover, it may be difficult for them to borrow funds to finance the necessary job training.

GEOGRAPHIC IMBALANCES   Geographic imbalances can be analyzed in the same framework. Suppose we now assume that market A refers to a Snowbelt city and market B to a Sunbelt city, both employing the same type of labor. When demand falls in the Snowbelt and unemployment increases because wages are not completely flexible, these unemployed workers may continue to wait for jobs in their home city for at least three reasons. First, information flows are imperfect, so workers may be unaware of the availability of jobs hundreds of miles away. Second, the direct money costs of such a move, including moving costs and the transaction costs involved in buying and selling a home, are high. Third, the psychological costs of moving long distances are substantial because friends and neighbors and community support systems must be given up. As noted in Chapter 10, such factors inhibit geographic migration, and migration tends to decline with age. These costs are sufficiently high that many workers who become unemployed as a result of plant shutdowns or permanent layoffs express no interest in searching for jobs outside their immediate geographic area.[15]

Structural factors can cause substantial variations in unemployment rates across geographic areas in the short run. In 1991, for example, when the U.S. national unemployment rate was 6.7 percent, individual state unemployment rates varied from 2.7 to 10.5 percent. However, there does not appear to be much persistence in

---

[15]A summary of the evidence on the losses workers suffer from plant shutdowns or permanent layoffs is found in Daniel Hamermesh, "What Do We Know About Worker Displacement in the U.S.?" *Industrial Relations* 28 (Winter 1989): 51–60, and Louis Jacobson, Robert LaLonde, and Daniel Sullivan, *The Cost of Worker Dislocation* (Kalamazoo, Mich.: W. E. Upjohn Institute, 1993).

relative unemployment rates across states over long periods of time. The fact that the unemployment rate in any individual state rarely exceeds the national average unemployment rate for a long period of time may strike one as surprising, given that employment in some states has persistently grown faster than the national average, while employment in other states has grown slower. The decline in unemployment rates back towards the national average in states whose unemployment rates are temporarily high appears to be primarily due to the eventual labor force *migration* of unemployed workers and potential new entrants to the labor force from these states to places where job opportunities are more plentiful.[16] (In terms of equation 15.2, when an area's relative unemployment rate is high, P_{un} becomes high, reducing its unemployment rate back to the national average.) Conversely, the increase in unemployment rates up to the national average in states whose unemployment rates are temporarily low appears to be due to the rapid growth of the labor force in these states caused by in-migration.

For example, in 1981 Indiana had an unemployment rate of 10.1 percent, substantially above the national average unemployment rate of 7.6 percent. Between 1981 and 1991, the civilian labor force grew by 6.5 percent in Indiana and by 10.4 percent nationwide. It is not surprising, then, that while the national unemployment rate was 6.7 percent in 1991, it was 5.9 percent in Indiana the same year. Similarly, New Hampshire's unemployment rate was 5.0 percent in 1981, substantially below the national average. However, between 1981 and 1991 New Hampshire's labor force grew by 31.5 percent and, again not surprisingly, its unemployment rose to 7.2 percent in 1991, which was slightly above the national average unemployment rate.

GOVERNMENT POLICIES   Structural unemployment can arise, then, because of changing patterns of labor demand that occur in the face of both rigid wages and high costs of occupational or geographic mobility.[17] In terms of equation (15.2), structurally unemployed workers have a low probability of moving from unemployed to employed status (low P_{ue}), and policies that increase this probability should reduce the level of structural unemployment (other things equal). Examples of such policies include the provision of subsidized training, the provision of information about job market conditions in other areas, the provision of relocation allowances to help defray the costs of migration and speed up the

---

[16]See Olivier Jean Blanchard and Lawrence F. Katz, "Regional Evolutions," *Brookings Papers on Economic Activity*, 1992–1, 1–75.

[17]For evidence on the magnitude of structural unemployment in the U.S. economy, see Katharine Abraham, "Structural/Frictional vs. Deficient Demand Unemployment," *American Economic Review* 73 (September 1983): 708–724; David Lilien, "Sectoral Shifts and Cyclical Unemployment," *Journal of Political Economy* 90 (August 1982): 777–793; and Katharine Abraham and Lawrence Katz, "Cyclical Unemployment: Sectoral Shifts or Aggregate Disturbances," *Journal of Political Economy* 94 (June 1986): 507–522. Lilien argues that shifts in employment growth rates across industrial sectors in the United States are responsible for a form of short-run structural unemployment and much of the apparent cyclical variation in unemployment rates. Abraham and Katz challenge this interpretation.

EXAMPLE 15.2

Advance Notice for Layoffs and Plant Shutdowns

In July of 1988, the Worker Adjustment and Retraining Notification Act (WARN) was enacted. WARN requires employers of 100 or more workers to give employees and local government officials 60 days' advance notice before they shut down or make large-scale layoffs. Most European nations and Canadian provinces enacted legislation relating to plant shutdowns and large-scale layoffs much earlier, and their legislation typically is more "protective" of workers (requiring in some cases that displaced workers also be given severance pay). Prior to the passage of WARN, very few workers in the United States actually received meaningful advance notice.

Advance-notice legislation is an attempt to reduce both frictional and structural unemployment. On the one hand, it gives workers an opportunity to search for new jobs prior to their displacement; this should facilitate their job search process and reduce frictional unemployment. On the other hand, it provides workers with time to try to prevent their displacement (by offering wage concessions, for example) and to consider the acquisition of new job skills prior to displacement, which should serve to reduce structural unemployment.

Studies undertaken prior to WARN show that workers whose employers voluntarily provided advance notice were less likely to suffer unemployment. Studies undertaken since the passage of WARN similarly suggest that advance notice decreases the chance that displaced workers will suffer any unemployment. These studies are inconclusive, however, as to whether advance notice reduces the wage loss workers suffer due to displacement.

Opponents of advance-notice legislation have argued that it increases the likelihood that troubled plants will have to close. If closing is a strong possibility, but not yet a certainty, such plants may still be required to give notice. Giving notice could encourage their best (most mobile) workers to quit, reduce morale, and lower the chances that buyers will place new orders, that banks will supply new credit, and that suppliers will continue to provide services. The legislation thus makes it more difficult for distressed firms to solve their problems or to sell their plants to potential buyers. Further, opponents argue that by effectively increasing the costs of closing, the legislation discourages new plants from opening and old ones from expanding, thereby inadvertently retarding employment growth.

SOURCES: Nancy Folbre, Julia Leighton, and Melissa Roderick, "Plant Closings and Their Regulation in Maine, 1971–1982," *Industrial and Labor Relations Review* 37 (January 1984): 185–197; Ronald Ehrenberg and George Jakubson, *Advance Notice Provisions in Plant Closing Legislation* (Kalamazoo, Mich.: W. E. Upjohn Institute for Employment Research, 1988); John Addison and Pedro Portugal, "Advance Notice and Unemployment: New Evidence From the 1988 Displaced Worker Survey," *Industrial and Labor Relations Review* 45 (July 1992): 645–664; Edward Lazear, "Job Security Provisions and Employment," *Quarterly Journal of Economics* 105 (August 1990): 696–726; and John T. Addison and McKinley Blackburn, "Advance Notice and Job Search: More on the Value of an Early Start," *Industrial Relations* 34, no. 2 (April 1995): 242–262.

adjustment process, and the requirement that employers planning to close plants issue advance notice to their employees (see Example 15.2).

Each of these policies is part of the Trade Adjustment Assistance Program, which was initiated by the United States under the Trade Expansion Act of 1962 and modified under several pieces of legislation during the 1970s and 1980s. This program was designed to aid individuals who became unemployed because of changes in product demand brought about by foreign competition, and it also provided for an expanded form of unemployment compensation benefits. The available evidence indicates, however, that, perhaps because of restrictive eligibility rules, this program has had little effect on increasing the probability that these structurally unemployed workers will find employment.[18]

At the international level, there is considerable disagreement about which government policies most effectively reduce long-term, structural unemployment. Many European countries, in an effort to combat structural unemployment by reducing the flow of workers from employment to unemployment, restrict employers' freedom to dismiss workers. In France, for example, dismissals involving ten or more employees require notification of the government, consultations with worker representatives, a relatively long waiting period, and severance pay.[19] France and other countries, such as Germany and the United Kingdom, also have relatively large publicly funded training programs for the unemployed, which are intended to reduce structural unemployment by speeding the flow of workers from unemployment to employment.

By way of contrast, the United States has relatively little government involvement with employer layoffs or worker training. As described in Example 15.2, advance notice of large-scale layoffs are required of some employers, but these requirements are mild by European standards. Further, whereas France, Germany, and the United Kingdom spend roughly 0.4 to 0.6 percent of national income on government training programs, the United States spends 0.1 percent.[20] The United States has far less long-term unemployment than most European countries, however, largely because geographic mobility is greater and the pace at which *new* jobs are created by employers is so much faster.

As was noted in earlier chapters (especially Chapters 2, 10, 13, and 14), many European countries have labor market institutions and other social policies (for example, subsidized housing) that inhibit interregional migration and prevent real wages from falling. These outcomes slow both the rate at which *workers* adapt to regional mismatches and the rate at which *employers* create new jobs. Further, the difficulties European employers face in dismissing workers, which reduce the rate of flow from employment to unemployment, also raise the costs of doing business and may reduce the rate at which *new* jobs are created—thereby reducing flows *out* of unemployment.

---

[18]See, for example, Walter Corson and Walter Nicholson, "Trade Adjustment Assistance for Workers: Results of a Survey of Recipients Under the Trade Act of 1974," in *Research in Labor Economics*, vol. 4, ed. Ronald Ehrenberg (Greenwich, Conn.: JAI Press, 1981).

[19]Katharine G. Abraham and Susan N. Houseman, "Does Employment Protection Inhibit Labor Market Flexibility? Lessons from Germany, France, and Belgium," in *Social Protection Versus Economic Flexibility: Is There a Trade-Off?* ed. Rebecca M. Blank (Chicago: University of Chicago Press, 1994), 59–93.

[20]Organisation for Economic Co-Operation and Development (OECD), *Employment Outlook: July 1993* (Paris: OECD, 1993): 45.

The consequences of relatively inflexible wage and employment levels in Europe are felt in the high rates of long-term unemployment that prevail there. We noted in Chapter 2 (Table 2.4) that the percentage of the *labor force* that has been unemployed for more than one year is much higher in Europe than in North America, where wages have been more flexible and employers are relatively uninhibited from dismissing workers. Put in different terms, about 6 percent of Americans who were *unemployed* in 1990 had been unemployed for more than one year, while in Germany, France, the United Kingdom, and the Netherlands, from *one-third to one-half of the unemployed* had been in that state for a year or more. What role government can play in reducing structural unemployment is thus a topic of ongoing debate.[21]

EFFICIENCY WAGES   It has also been argued that structural unemployment can arise if employers pay above-market, or *efficiency*, wages to increase worker productivity (refer back to Chapter 11, where this concept was introduced). To make the argument concrete, suppose that employers are unable to completely monitor the performance of their workers. One way to increase the chances that these workers will not shirk their duties is to pay them a wage above the market wage. That is, instead of paying workers the lowest possible wage that would attract them to the job, employers may choose to pay a wage above that, for two reasons.[22] First, by giving workers the "gift" of a generous wage, employers might expect that employees would reciprocate by giving them the "gift" of diligent work. Second, if an employee's effort is not diligent, the employee can be fired and faced with earning a lower wage or, as we argue below, with unemployment.

If all employers were to follow the above strategy and offer wages higher than the market equilibrium wage, then clearly supply would exceed demand and unemployment would result. If only *some* firms paid efficiency wages, then there would be a high- and a low-wage sector. Workers employed at lower-paying firms could not obtain employment at a high-wage firm by offering to work at some wage between the low (market-clearing) and the high (efficiency)

---

[21]See Rebecca M. Blank and Richard B. Freeman, "Evaluating the Connection Between Social Protection and Economic Flexibility," in *Social Protection Versus Economic Flexibility*, ed. Blank, 24. For a discussion of possible governmental programs which might avoid the long-term unemployment of Europe and the falling real wages in North America, see Lawrence F. Katz, "Active Labor Market Policies to Expand Employment and Opportunity," in *Reducing Unemployment: Current Issues and Policy Options* (Kansas City: Federal Reserve Bank of Kansas City, 1994), 239–322, including the associated comments by two discussants. Also see Anders Forslund and Alan B. Krueger, "An Evaluation of the Swedish Active Labor Market Policy: New and Received Wisdom," working paper no. 332, Industrial Relations Section, Princeton University, July 1994.

[22]Our argument here draws on, and abstracts from many of the complications discussed in, the articles in George Akerlof and Janet Yellen, eds., *Efficiency Wage Models of the Labor Market* (Cambridge, Eng.: Cambridge University Press, 1986), and Andrew Weiss, *Efficiency Wages: Models of Unemployment, Layoffs and Wage Dispersion* (Princeton, N.J.: Princeton University Press, 1990).

wage level, because the high-wage employers would want to maintain their wage advantage to discourage shirking. However, because jobs in the high-wage sector are preferable, and because such jobs will occasionally become available, some workers in the low-wage sector may quit their jobs, "attach" themselves to the high-wage sector, and "wait" for jobs to open up. That is, using reasoning similar to that used in Chapter 13, where a high-wage sector was created by unions, *wait unemployment* will tend to arise in the presence of an efficiency-wage sector.[23]

The wage premium that efficiency-wage employers must pay to discourage shirking depends upon the alternatives open to their employees. Other things equal, the higher the unemployment rate in an area, the poorer are the alternative employment opportunities for their workers and thus the less likely the workers are to risk losing their jobs by shirking. The employers, then, need not pay wage premiums that are as high as when alternative job opportunities are more plentiful. This leads to the prediction that, other factors held constant, there should be a negative association between average wage rates and unemployment rates across areas.

The efficiency-wage explanation of structural unemployment receives indirect support from a remarkable finding that has been recently published. An exhaustive study of data on wages and regional unemployment rates within 12 countries found that, after controlling for human-capital characteristics of individual workers (some 3.5 million of them), there was a strong negative relationship between regional unemployment rates and real wages in all countries. That is, in regions within these countries with *higher* rates of unemployment, wage levels for otherwise comparable workers were *lower.* This negative relationship between the region's unemployment rate and its real wage level, seen in Figure 15.6, has been called the *wage curve.*

The wage curve is remarkable on three accounts. First, it seems to exist in every country for which enough data are available to estimate it. Second, the curves for each country are surprisingly similar; a 10 percent increase in a

---

[23]Suppose that employees are *risk neutral* (that is, they do not lose utility if their earnings *fluctuate* over time around some mean value). In equilibrium, they would move from the low-wage to the high-wage sector and remain as unemployed job seekers as long as the expected wage from choosing to "wait" exceeds the expected wage of searching for work while employed in the low-wage sector. Put algebraically, a worker who is unemployed will "wait" for a high-wage job if

$$P_e W_e > P_0 W_e + (1 - P_0)\, W_0$$

where W_e and W_0 are the wages in the high- and low-wage sectors (respectively), P_e is the probability of finding a job paying W_e if one is unemployed, and P_0 is the probability of finding a high-wage job if one takes employment in the low-wage sector. Presumably P_e is greater than P_0 because individuals can search for work more intensively if they are not employed.

The above inequality can be rewritten as

$$(P_e - P_0) W_e > W_0 (1 - P_0)$$

and, as one can see from this latter expression, whether one chooses wait unemployment depends on the increased probability of finding a high-wage job if unemployed ($P_e - P_0$) as well as on the difference between W_e and W_0.

FIGURE 15.6
The "Wage Curve"

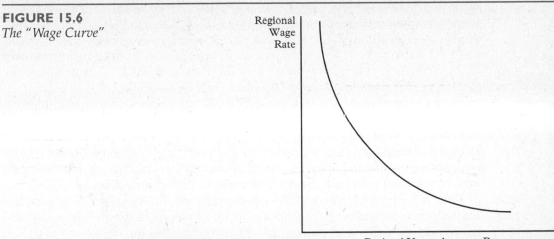

Regional
Wage
Rate

Regional Unemployment Rate

region's unemployment rate is associated with wage levels that are lower by 0.4 to 1.9 percent in eleven of the twelve countries studied.[24]

Finally, the wage curve is remarkable because it is a finding in search of an explanation. Using a standard demand-and-supply-curve analysis, one would think that higher unemployment and *higher* wages would be associated with each other (in other words, there would be a positively-sloped wage curve). Using this analysis, if wages were above market-clearing levels, supply would exceed demand, and the result would be workers who want jobs and cannot find them (unemployment); the higher that wages were above equilibrium, the more unemployment there would be. Thus, a downward-sloping relationship, such as depicted in Figure 15.6, is not what simple economic theory suggests.

Simple theory does suggest, of course, that when unemployment is relatively high, real wages will *fall*. The problem with this "explanation" for the wage curve is that the curve plots the relationship between unemployment and the wage *level*, not wage *changes*; thus, this implication of standard theory also fails to explain what we observe. If simple theory is not providing explanations for the wage curve, is there a more complex theory that does?

One reason why we might observe a negatively-sloped wage curve can be found in the efficiency-wage explanation of structural unemployment reviewed above. Suppose, for example, that one cause of long-term unemployment is the widespread payment of above-market wages by employers in an effort to reduce shirking among their employees. In regions where this and other causes happen to create higher levels of unemployment, the efficiency-wage premiums needed to reduce shirking would be lower—which would cause the negative association we

[24]See David G. Blanchflower and Andrew J. Oswald, "An Introduction to the Wage Curve," *Journal of Economic Perspectives* 9, no. 3 (Summer 1995): 153–167, and David Card, "The Wage Curve: A Review," *Journal of Economic Literature* 33, no. 2 (June 1995): 785–799.

observe between regional unemployment rates and wage levels. Put succinctly, while inconsistent with the implications of simple theory, a negatively sloped wage curve *is* consistent with the efficiency-wage explanation of structural unemployment.

DEMAND-DEFICIENT (CYCLICAL) UNEMPLOYMENT

Frictional unemployment arises because labor markets are dynamic and information flows are imperfect; structural unemployment arises because of long-lasting imbalances in demand and supply. *Demand-deficient unemployment* is associated with fluctuations in business activity (the "business cycle"), and it occurs when a decline in aggregate demand in the output market causes the *aggregate* demand for labor to decline in the face of downward inflexibility in real wages.

Returning to our simple demand and supply model of Figure 15.2, suppose that a temporary decline in aggregate demand leads to a shift in the labor demand curve to D_1. If real wages are inflexible downward, employment will fall to E_1, and $E_0 - E_1$ additional workers will become unemployed. This employment decline occurs when firms temporarily lay off workers (increasing P_{eu}) and reduce the rate at which they replace those who quit or retire (decreasing P_{ne} and P_{ue}). That is, flows into unemployment increase while flows into employment decline.

Unemployment, however, is not the inevitable outcome of reduced aggregate demand. Employers, for example, could cut the *hours* per employee as a substitute for reducing the level of *employment*. Alternatively, employers could reduce the wages they pay to their workers. If the latter response occurred, employment would move to E_2 and real wages to W_2 in Figure 15.2. Although employment would be lower than its initial level, E_0, there would be no measured demand-deficient unemployment, because $E_0 - E_2$ workers would have dropped out of the labor force in response to this lower wage. We will discuss these other possible responses to reduced aggregate demand as we analyze two features of the U.S. labor market thought to contribute to demand-deficient unemployment: (1) institutional and profit-maximizing reasons for rigid money wages, and (2) the way in which the U.S. unemployment compensation program is financed. We then briefly compare American and European reactions to cyclical changes in labor demand.

DOWNWARD WAGE RIGIDITY IN THE UNITED STATES   Stock and commodity prices fluctuate with demand and supply, and product market retailers have sales or offer discounts when demand is down, but do the wage rates paid to individual workers fall when the demand for labor shifts to the left? If such decreases are not very likely, what might be the reasons?

Wages, of course, can be measured in both nominal and real terms. Nominal wages (the money wages quoted to workers) may be rigid, yet the real wage (the nominal wage divided by an index of prices) can fall if prices are rising. It will come as no great surprise that the real wages received by individual workers quite commonly fall; all that needs to happen for one's real wage to fall is for the increase in his or her nominal wage to be less than the increase in prices. One study that followed individuals in the United States from 1976 to 1986 found that in a typical year, 43 percent of those who did not change employers took a real-wage cut.[25]

Despite evidence of downward flexibility of *real* wages, it is also important to see how common cuts in workers' *nominal* wages are. If real wages fall only when prices rise, they may not be able to fall fast enough to prevent an increase in unemployment during business downturns. In the study noted above, 17 percent of workers experienced a nominal-wage cut by their employer in a typical year. Similar estimates come from a study using different employee-provided data, although this latter study extended into the early 1990s, when some 18 to 20 percent of hourly paid workers experienced nominal-wage cuts.[26] These two studies, and another that used data obtained from employers,[27] suggest that nominal wages are not completely rigid in a downward direction. However, the studies also conclude that nominal wages are resistant to cuts, and as a result, employment adjustments during periods of downturn are larger and more common than they would be with complete nominal-wage flexibility.

Explanations for why employment levels are more likely to be reduced than nominal wages during business downturns must confront two questions: why do firms find it more profitable to reduce employment than wages, and why are workers who face unemployment not more willing to take wage cuts to save their jobs? The hypotheses concerning wage rigidity that have come to the forefront recently address both questions.

According to one explanation for rigid money wages, employers are not free to unilaterally cut nominal wages because of the presence of unions. This cannot be a complete explanation for the United States, because less than 15 percent of American workers are represented by unions (see Chapter 13), and unions could, in any case, agree to temporary wage cuts to save jobs instead of subjecting their members to layoffs. Why they fail to make such arrangements is instructive.

A temporary wage reduction would reduce the earnings of all workers, while layoffs would affect, in most cases, only those workers most recently hired. Because these workers represent a minority of the union's membership in most instances, because union leaders are elected by majority rule, and because these leaders are most likely drawn from the ranks of the more experienced workers (who are often immune from layoff), unions tend to favor a policy of layoffs rather than one that reduces wages for all members.[28] A variant of this explana-

---

[25]Kenneth J. McLaughlin, "Rigid Wages?" *Journal of Monetary Economics* 34 (1994): 383–414.

[26]David Card and Dean Hyslop, "Does Inflation Grease the Wheels of the Labor Market?" working paper no. 356, Industrial Relations Section, Princeton University, December 1995.

[27]Harry J. Holzer and Edward B. Montgomery, "Asymmetries and Rigidities in Wage Adjustments by Firms," *Review of Economics and Statistics* 75, no. 3 (August 1993): 397–408.

[28]See James Medoff, "Layoffs and Alternatives Under Trade Unions in United States Manufacturing," *American Economic Review* 69 (June 1979): 380–395, for evidence. This hypothesis suggests that unions are much more likely to bargain for wage reductions when projected layoffs exceed 50 percent of the union's membership. For evidence that this occurred in the early 1980s, see Robert J. Flanagan, "Wage Concessions and Long-term Union Flexibility," *Brookings Papers on Economic Activity*, 1984–1, 183–216.

tion is the *insider-outsider hypothesis*, which sees union members as "insiders" who have little or no concern for nonmembers or former members now on layoff ("outsiders"); these insiders gain from keeping their numbers small and may choose to negotiate wages that effectively prevent the recall or employment of outsiders.[29]

Layoffs do occur in *nonunion* firms, although perhaps less frequently than in unionized ones. There are several reasons why even nonunion employers may well prefer layoffs to wage reductions when demand falls. First, in the presence of firm-specific human capital investments, which often lead to structured internal labor markets (see Chapter 5), employers have incentives both to minimize voluntary turnover and to maximize their employees' work effort and productivity. Across-the-board temporary wage reductions would increase all employees' propensities to quit and could lead to reduced work effort on their part. In contrast, layoffs affect only the least-experienced workers, the workers in whom the firm has invested the smallest amount of resources. It is likely, then, that the firm will find choosing the layoff strategy a more profitable alternative.[30]

Second, employers with internal labor markets frequently promise, at least implicitly, a certain path of earnings to employees over their careers. As we saw in Chapter 11, firms may pay relatively low salaries to new employees with the "promise" (expectation) that if they work diligently these employees will be paid relatively high wages toward the end of their careers. The firm's promises are, of necessity, conditional on how well it is performing, but the firm has more accurate information on the true state of its demand than do its workers. If a firm asks its employees to take a wage cut in periods of low demand, the employees may believe that the employer is falsely stating that demand is low and, noting that the employer loses nothing by the wage cut, resist the request. If, instead, a firm temporarily lays off some of its workers, it loses the output these workers would have produced, and workers may therefore accept such an action as a *signal* that the firm is indeed in trouble. Put another way, the *asymmetry of information* between employers and employees makes layoffs the preferred policy.[31]

Third, firms with internal labor markets, and therefore long employer–employee job attachments, may be encouraged by the risk aversion of older employees to engage in seniority-based layoffs (last hired, first laid off) rather than wage cuts for all its workers. That is, the desire to have a constant income stream,

---

[29]Robert M. Solow, "Insiders and Outsiders in Wage Determination," *Scandinavian Journal of Economics* 87 (1985): 411–428.

[30]See, for example, Andrew Weiss, *Efficiency Wages: Models of Unemployment, Layoffs and Wage Dispersion.* Wendy L. Rayack, "Fixed and Flexible Wages: Evidence from Panel Data," *Industrial and Labor Relations Review* 44 (January 1991): 288–298, presents empirical evidence that the sensitivity of wages to unemployment is confined largely to workers with short job tenure.

[31]See, for example, Sanford Grossman, Oliver Hart, and Eric Maskin, "Unemployment with Observable Aggregate Shocks," *Journal of Political Economy* 91 (December 1983): 907–928; Sanford Grossman and Oliver Hart, "Implicit Contracts, Moral Hazard and Unemployment," *American Economic Review* 71 (May 1981): 301–307; and Costas Azariadis, "Employment with Asymmetric Information," *Quarterly Journal of Economics* 98 (Supplement, 1983): 157–172.

rather than a fluctuating one with the same average value over time, is something for which older, more-experienced workers may be willing to pay.[32] Thus, if the risks of income fluctuation are confined to one's initial years of employment, the firm may be able to pay its experienced workers wages lower than otherwise would be required. Of course, during the initial period, workers will be subject to potential earnings variability and may demand higher wages then to compensate them for these risks. However, if the fraction of the workforce subject to layoffs is small, on average employers' costs could be reduced by seniority-based layoffs.

Fourth, it will be noted that all three of the above "explanations" are centered on firms with internal labor markets, which may be roughly thought of as large employers. One is then tempted to ask why those laid off from large firms do not seek work in small firms. These firms pay lower wages and have few of the reasons cited above to avoid reducing them further when aggregate demand falls; hence, increased employment in these jobs would lower the average nominal wage paid in the economy and help reduce unemployment. Some theorists believe that the failure of unemployed workers to flock to low-wage jobs derives from their sense of status (their relative standing in society). These economists postulate that individuals may prefer unemployment in a "good" job to employment in an inferior one, at least for a period longer than the typical recession.[33] It is this sense of status that prevents the expansion of jobs and the further reduction of wages in the low-wage sectors during recessionary periods.

Finally, some analysts have stressed that prevailing market wages, even those paid by small, competitive firms, may be accepted as *social norms* that inhibit the unemployed from trying to undercut the wages of employed workers to find employment.[34] As explained below, that unemployed workers are apparently more willing to face unemployment than a reduced wage may have more to do with future considerations than with status.

Suppose there are many identical unemployed workers, each with the same "reservation wage," the minimum wage they will accept (which is influenced by the implicit monetary value each individual places on leisure time plus the unemployment benefits or other monetary payments each receives while unemployed). If each planned to remain in the labor force only for a single period, it would be rational to bid down wages in an effort to secure employment. As long as the wage ultimately received was greater than the workers' common reservation wage, unemployed workers would be better off working.

Suppose, however, that each unemployed worker planned to remain in the labor force for a number of periods. In this case, if workers offer to work for below the prevailing wage in the current period, they will reveal to employers that their

---

[32]This line of reasoning follows that in Costas Azariadis, "Implicit Contracts and Underemployment Equilibria," *Journal of Political Economy* 83 (December 1975): 1183–1202, and Martin Baily, "Wages and Employment Under Uncertain Demand," *Review of Economic Studies* 41 (January 1974): 37–50.

[33]See Alan S. Blinder, "The Challenge of High Unemployment," *American Economic Review* 78 (May 1988): 1–15.

[34]See Robert M. Solow, *The Labor Market as an Institution* (Cambridge, Mass.: Basil Blackwell, (1990), Chapter 2.

common reservation wage is lower than originally thought, and employers might decide to permanently cut wages in future periods as well. In this case individuals may be better off remaining unemployed until a job is ultimately found at the current wage. In fact, the individual's incentive not to undercut the current market wage is larger the greater the number of periods he or she plans to remain in the labor force and the greater the chance of finding work if the market wage is not undercut. Hence, this theory suggests that market wages are more likely to be inflexible in a downward direction when workers have more permanent attachment to the labor force and when increases in the unemployment rate are relatively small.

FINANCING U.S. UNEMPLOYMENT COMPENSATION   The incentives for employers to prefer temporary layoffs to fluctuations in real wages are affected by a key characteristic of the U.S. unemployment insurance system: *its methods of financing benefits.* As we will see, the way in which the government raises the funds to pay for UI benefits has a rather large effect on cyclical layoffs.

The benefits paid out by the UI system are financed by a payroll tax. Unlike the Social Security payroll tax, in all but four states the UI tax is paid solely by employers.[35] The UI tax payment (T) that an employer must make for each employee is given by

$$T = tW \qquad \text{if } W \leq W_B \qquad\qquad (15.3a)$$

and

$$T = tW_B \qquad \text{if } W > W_B \qquad\qquad (15.3b)$$

where t is the employer's UI tax rate, W is an employee's earnings during the calendar year, and W_B is the *taxable wage base*, the level of earnings after which no UI tax payments are required. In 1994 the taxable wage base ranged from $7,000 to $12,000 in about two-thirds of the states; thus, depending upon the state, employers had to pay UI taxes on the first $7,000 to $12,000 of each employee's earnings. The other one-third of the states had taxable wage bases that were somewhat higher.

The employer's UI tax rate is determined by general economic conditions in the state, the industry the employer is operating in, and the employer's *layoff experience*. The last term is defined differently in different states; the underlying notion is that since the UI system is an insurance system, employers who lay off workers frequently and make heavy demands on the system's resources should be assigned a higher UI tax rate. This practice is referred to as *experience rating*.

Experience rating is typically *imperfect* in the sense that the marginal cost to an employer of laying off an additional worker (in terms of a higher UI tax rate) is

---

[35]Recall from our discussion in Chapter 3 that this fact tells us nothing about who really bears the burden of the tax.

FIGURE 15.7
Imperfectly Experience-Rated Unemployment Insurance Tax Rates

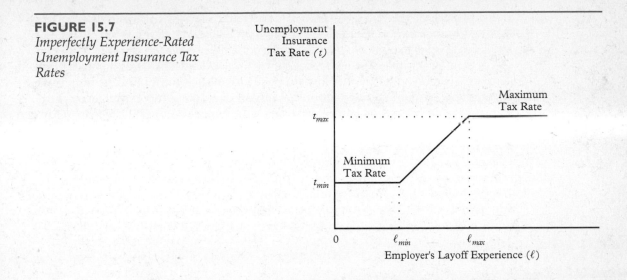

often less than the added UI benefits the system must pay out to that worker. Imperfect experience rating is illustrated in Figure 15.7, which plots the relationship between an employer's UI tax rate and that firm's layoff experience. (We shall interpret *layoff experience* to mean the probability that employees in the firm will be on layoff. Clearly, this probability depends both on the frequency with which the firm lays off workers and the average duration of time until they are recalled to their positions.)

Each state has a minimum UI tax rate, and below this rate (t_{min} in Figure 15.7) the firm's UI tax rate cannot fall. After a firm's layoff experience reaches some critical value (ℓ_{min}) the firm's UI tax rate rises with increased layoff experience over some range. In each state there is also a ceiling on the UI tax rate (t_{max}) and after this tax rate is reached additional layoffs will not alter the firm's tax rate.[36] The system is *imperfectly* experience-rated because for firms below ℓ_{min} or above ℓ_{max}, variations in their layoff rate have no effect on their UI tax rate.[37] Further, over the range in which the tax rate is increasing with layoff experience, the increase is not large enough in most states to make the employer's marginal cost of a layoff (in terms of the increased UI taxes the firm must pay) equal to the marginal UI benefits the laid-off employees receive.

The key characteristic of the UI system that influences the desirability of temporary layoffs is the *imperfect experience rating* of the UI payroll tax. To understand

---

[36]In actuality the UI tax rate changes discretely (as a step function) over the range ℓ_{min} to ℓ_{max}, not continuously as drawn in Figure 15.7. For expository convenience, we ignore this complication.

[37]Such a system of UI financing leads to interindustry subsidies, in which industries (such as banking) with virtually no layoffs still must pay the minimum tax, and these industries subsidize industries (such as construction) that have very high layoffs but pay only the maximum rate.

the influence of this characteristic, suppose first that the UI system were constructed in such a way that its tax rates were perfectly experience-rated. A firm laying off a worker would have to pay added UI taxes equal to the full UI benefit (50 percent of normal earnings) received by the worker, so it saves just half of the worker's wages by the layoff. Now suppose instead that the UI tax rate employers must pay is totally independent of their layoff experience (no experience rating). In this case, a firm saves a laid-off worker's *entire* wages because its UI taxes do not rise as a result of the layoff. Thus, compared to a UI system with perfect experience rating, it is easy to see that a system with incomplete experience rating will tend to enhance the attractiveness of layoffs to employers.

Empirical analyses of the effect of imperfect experience rating on employer behavior suggest that it is substantial. One study estimated that the unemployment rate would *fall by about one-fourth* if the UI system were perfectly experience-rated (so that employers engaging in added layoffs had to pay the full cost of the added UI benefits).[38]

CYCLICAL ADJUSTMENTS IN EUROPE   As we have discussed in this chapter and previous ones (notably Chapters 2 and 14), wages in Europe are much more rigid in a downward direction than wages in the United States and Canada. Perhaps because of the relative strength of European unions, not even the average *real* wage for unskilled European workers—a group for which demand had clearly shifted to the left—fell in the 1980s and early 1990s. Moreover, we have seen that many European governments place considerable restraints on the freedom of employers to adjust to changing demand conditions by laying off their workers. Yet the evidence indicates that European employers adjust their labor inputs over a business cycle almost as quickly as American employers do! How can this be? The answer appears to lie in the nature of the unemployment compensation systems in Europe.

In the United States, the typical state unemployment compensation system pays benefits only to those who are completely unemployed. Some seventeen states allow for partial benefits to those whose hours of work have been cut, but these partial-benefit provisions are rarely used. In most European countries, unemployment compensation systems have widely used provisions for "short-time" workers—workers who are still employed but whose hours have been cut. These provisions, when combined with the restraints on laying off workers, encourage employers to cut the *hours* of work rather than cutting the level of employment. Studies of short-time compensation in Europe have found that, while adjustments in *employment* levels were much more sluggish than in the United States during

---

[38]Robert H. Topel, "Financing Unemployment Insurance: History, Incentives, and Reform," in *Unemployment Insurance: The Second Half-Century*, ed. W. Lee Hansen and James F. Byers (Madison: University of Wisconsin Press, 1990), 108–135.

downturns, adjustments in the *total hours of work* were nevertheless very similar where short-time benefits are relatively generous.[39]

SEASONAL UNEMPLOYMENT

Seasonal unemployment is similar to demand-deficient unemployment in that it is induced by fluctuations in the demand for labor. Here, however, the fluctuations can be regularly anticipated and follow a systematic pattern over the course of a year. For example, the demand for agricultural employees declines after the planting season and remains low until the harvest season. Similarly, the demand for construction workers in Snowbelt states falls during the winter months. Finally, the demand for production workers falls in certain industries during the season of the year when plants are retooling to handle annual model changes; examples here include both the Detroit automotive industry (new car models) and the New York City apparel industry (new fashion designs).

The issue remains, why do employers respond to seasonal patterns of demand by laying off workers rather than reducing wage rates or hours of work? All the reasons cited for the existence of cyclical unemployment and temporary layoffs for cyclical reasons also pertain here. Indeed, one study has shown that the expansion (in the early 1970s) of the unemployment insurance system that led to the coverage of most agricultural employees was associated with a substantial increase in seasonal unemployment in agriculture. More recent studies of seasonal layoffs in nonagricultural industries also suggest that the imperfect experience rating of the U.S. unemployment compensation system significantly increases seasonal unemployment.[40]

One may question, however, why workers would accept jobs in industries in which they knew in advance they would be unemployed for a portion of the year. For some workers, the existence of UI benefits along with the knowledge that they will be rehired as a matter of course at the end of the slack-demand season may allow them to treat such periods as paid vacations. However, since UI benefits typically replace less than half of an unemployed worker's previous gross earnings and even smaller fractions for high-wage workers (see Figure 15.4), most workers will not find such a situation desirable. To attract workers to such seasonal industries, firms will have to pay workers higher wages to compensate them for being periodically unemployed. In fact, casual observation suggests that the hourly wages of construction workers are substantially higher than the hourly wages of

---

[39]Marc A. Van Audenrode, "Short-Time Compensation, Job Security, and Employment Contracts: Evidence from 10 OECD Countries," *Journal of Political Economy* 102, no. 1 (February 1994): 76–102, and Abraham and Houseman, "Does Employment Protection Inhibit Labor Market Flexibility?"

[40]Barry Chiswick, "The Effect of Unemployment Compensation on a Seasonal Industry: Agriculture," *Journal of Political Economy* 84 (June 1976): 591–602; Patricia M. Anderson, "Linear Adjustment Costs and Seasonal Labor Demand: Evidence from Retail Trade Firms," *Quarterly Journal of Economics* 108, no. 4 (November 1993): 1015–1042; and David Card and Phillip B. Levine, "Unemployment Insurance Taxes and the Cyclical and Seasonal Properties of Unemployment," *Journal of Public Economics* 53 (January 1994): 1–29.

comparably skilled manufacturing workers who work more hours each year. More formally, econometric studies confirm that, other things held constant (including workers' skill levels), wages are higher in industries in which workers' expected annual durations of unemployment are longer.[41] (For a more complete analysis of this issue, see Appendix 8A.)

The existence of wage differentials that compensate workers in high-unemployment industries for the risk of unemployment makes it difficult to evaluate whether this type of unemployment is voluntary or involuntary in nature. On the one hand, in an *ex ante* ("before the fact") sense, workers have voluntarily agreed to be employed in industries that offer higher wages *and* higher probabilities of unemployment than offered elsewhere. On the other hand, once on the job (*ex post,* or "after the fact"), employees prefer to remain employed rather than becoming unemployed. Such unemployment may be considered either voluntary or involuntary, then, depending upon the perspective one is taking.

When Do We Have "Full Employment"?

Governments constantly worry about the unemployment rate, because it is seen as a handy barometer of an economy's health. An unemployment rate that is deemed to be too high is seen as a national concern, because it implies that many people are unable to support themselves and that many of the country's workers are not contributing to national output. Often, governments will take steps to stimulate the demand for labor in one way or another when they believe unemployment to be excessive; indeed, the U.S. Full Employment and Balanced Growth Act of 1978 (also known as the Humphrey-Hawkins Act) "required" the federal government to pursue the social goal of an overall rate of unemployment equal to 4 percent.

Governments also worry about unemployment being "too low." Remembering that some frictional unemployment will exist even in the most robust labor markets, an unusually low rate of unemployment is thought by many to reflect a situation in which there is excess demand in the labor market. If labor demand exceeds supply, wages will tend to rise, it is argued, and wage increases will lead to price inflation. In addition, excessively low unemployment rates may increase shirking among workers and reduce the pool of available talent upon which new or expanding employers can draw.

If both too much and too little unemployment are undesirable, how much is "just right"? Put differently, what unemployment rate represents "full employment"? The *full-employment* (or *natural*) rate of unemployment is difficult to define

---

[41]John Abowd and Orley Ashenfelter, "Anticipated Unemployment, Temporary Layoffs, and Compensating Wage Differentials," in *Studies in Labor Markets,* ed. Sherwin Rosen (Chicago: University of Chicago Press, 1981), 141–170, and Robert H. Topel, "Equilibrium Earnings, Turnover, and Unemployment: New Evidence," *Journal of Labor Economics* 2 (October 1984): 500–522. Topel also shows that, other things equal, high UI benefits *reduce* the compensating wage differential paid for the risk of unemployment.

precisely, and there are several alternative concepts from which to choose. One defines the natural rate of unemployment as that rate at which wage and price inflation are either stable or at acceptable levels. Another defines full employment as the rate of unemployment at which job vacancies equal the number of unemployed workers, and yet another defines it as the level of unemployment at which any increases in aggregate demand will cause no further reductions in unemployment. A variant of the latter defines the natural rate as the unemployment rate at which all unemployment is voluntary (frictional and perhaps seasonal). Finally, a recent definition of the natural rate is that rate at which the level of unemployment is unchanging and both the flows into unemployment and the duration of unemployment are normal.[42]

All the various definitions above try to define in a specific way a more general concept of full employment as the rate that prevails in "normal" times. If we assume that frictional and seasonal unemployment exist even in labor markets characterized by equilibrium (i.e., markets having neither excess demand nor excess supply), it is clear that the natural rate of unemployment is affected by such factors as voluntary turnover rates among employed workers, movements in and out of the labor force, and the length of time it takes for the unemployed to find acceptable jobs. These factors vary widely across demographic groups, so the natural rate during any period is strongly influenced by the demographic composition of the labor force.

Table 15.3 presents data on actual unemployment rates for various age/race/gender/ethnic groups in 1994. The patterns indicated in Table 15.3 for 1994 are similar to the patterns for other recent years: high unemployment rates for teens and young adults of each race/gender group relative to older adults in these groups; black unemployment rates roughly double white unemployment rates for most age/gender groups, with Hispanic-American unemployment rates tending to lie between the white and black rates; and female unemployment rates roughly equal to, or lower than, male unemployment rates for each group (except Hispanics of prime age). The high unemployment rates of black teenagers, which ranged between 33 and 39 percent in 1994, have been of particular concern to policymakers.

Over recent decades, the age/race/gender/ethnic composition of the labor force has changed dramatically with the growth in labor force participation rates of females and substantial changes in the relative size of the teenage, black, and Hispanic populations. Between 1960 and 1994 the proportion of the labor force that was female grew from 33 to 46 percent. Similarly, between 1973 (when statistics were first collected) and 1994, the Hispanic-American labor force grew three times faster than average, going from 4.1 to 9.1 percent of the overall labor force. In contrast, while between 1960 and 1978 the proportion of the labor force that was black grew from 11.1 to 12.0 percent and the proportion that was teenage grew

---

[42]James Tobin, "Inflation and Unemployment," *American Economic Review* 62 (March 1972): 1–18, and John Haltiwanger, "The Natural Rate of Unemployment," in *The New Palgrave*, ed. J. Eatwell, M. Milgate, and P. Newman (New York: Stockton Press, 1987), 610–612.

TABLE 15.3

Unemployment Rates in 1994 by Demographic Groups

Age	White Male	White Female	Black Male	Black Female	Hispanic Male	Hispanic Female	All
16-17	18.5	16.6	39.3	32.9	33.3	29.7	
18-19	14.7	11.8	36.5	32.5	22.5	18.1	
20-24	8.8	7.4	19.4	19.6	10.8	13.5	
25-54	4.3	4.4	9.1	8.7	7.7	9.3	
55+	4.1	3.7	6.0	4.9	8.0	6.6	
Total	5.4	5.2	12.0	11.0	9.4	10.7	6.1

Source: U.S. Department of Labor, *Employment and Earnings* 42 (January 1995), Tables 3, 4. "Hispanic" refers to those of Hispanic origin; depending upon their races these individuals are also included in both the white and black population group totals.

from 7.0 to 9.5 percent, by 1994 the black proportion had fallen back to 11.1 percent and the teenage proportion to 5.7 percent.[43]

Until quite recently, women tended to have higher unemployment rates than men.[44] As a result, the increases in the relative labor force shares of women, blacks, Hispanics, and teenagers through 1978 were increases in the shares of groups that had relatively high unemployment rates; this led to an increase in the overall unemployment rate associated with any given level of labor market tightness. Indeed, one investigator concluded that demographic shifts in the composition of the labor force from the 1960s to the late 1970s probably raised the overall unemployment rate at least 1 percentage point for any given level of overall labor market tightness.[45] These demographic changes also led to an increase in the full-employment rate of unemployment, defined here as the unemployment rate that is consistent with a zero excess demand for labor.

Over the last decade and a half, however, a number of demographic forces have probably worked to reduce both the unemployment rate associated with any level of overall labor market tightness and the full-employment unemployment rate.[46]

---

[43]See U.S. Department of Labor, *Employment and Earnings* 42 (January 1995), Tables 1–4, and earlier years' issues.

[44]The fact that female unemployment rates now tend to be less than or equal to male rates is at least partially due to the growth of employment over the last decade in sectors such as services that employ proportionately many females, and to the "collapse" over the last decade of manufacturing, in which proportionately more males have historically been employed. See Barry Bluestone and Bennett Harrison, *The Great U-Turn: Corporate Restructuring, Laissez-Faire and the Threat to America's High Wage Society* (New York: Basic Books, 1988), for an extensive discussion of employment shifts in the U.S. economy.

[45]James Tobin, "Stabilization Policy Ten Years After," *Brookings Papers on Economic Activity,* 1980–1, 19–72.

[46]Richard Krashevski, "What Is So Natural About High Unemployment?" *American Economic Review* 78 (May 1988): 289–293.

The shares of both teenagers and blacks in the labor force have declined. In addition, while the share of women in the labor force has continued to expand, female unemployment rates have fallen relative to male rates because much of U.S. employment growth has occurred in sectors, such as the service sector, that employ proportionately more females.

While the goal of an overall unemployment rate of 4 percent was written into (an unenforceable) law in the late 1970s, it is doubtful that it was an appropriate "full employment" target at that time. Economists' estimates of the natural rate have varied over time, going from something like 5.4 percent in the 1960s, to about 7 percent in the 1970s, to 6 or 6.5 percent in the 1980s. As recently as late 1994, one economist advised the U.S. Federal Reserve Board that, in his opinion, the "natural rate" was 6 percent. However, with recent unemployment rates in the 6 percent range, and with continued downward pressures on wages in the United States, this economist revised his estimate of the natural rate in early 1995 to 5.5 or even 5 percent.[47] One must wonder, though, how useful estimates of the natural rate are for policy purposes if they keep changing; indeed, Milton Friedman, a Nobel-prizewinner in economics and a leader in the development of the natural-rate concept, disavows any attempts at forecasting it. He says, "I don't know what the natural rate is . . . and neither does anyone else."[48]

Is unemployment a serious problem? Certainly some level of frictional unemployment is unavoidable in a dynamic world fraught with imperfect information. Moreover, as we have seen, the parameters of the UI system encourage both additional-search unemployment and temporary-layoff (cyclical and seasonal) unemployment. Nonetheless, when unemployment rises above its full-employment or natural level, resources are being wasted. Some thirty years ago Arthur Okun pointed out that every 1-percentage-point decline in the aggregate unemployment rate was associated with a 3-percentage-point increase in the output the United States produces. More recent estimates suggest that the relationship is now more in the range of a 2-percentage-point increase in output. Even this last number, however, suggests the great costs a society pays for excessively high rates of unemployment.[49] Thus, while it is unlikely that zero unemployment would be an optimal rate, policies to reduce cyclical unemployment (in a noninflationary manner) are clearly desirable. Improving the functioning of labor markets would also reduce frictional and structural unemployment; however, the benefits of reduced unemployment must be weighed against the costs generated by the policies designed to accomplish this objective.

[47]Amanda Bennett, "Business and Academia Clash over a Concept: 'Natural' Jobless Rate," *Wall Street Journal*, January 24, 1995, A1, A8.

[48]Bennett, "Business and Academia Clash over a Concept," A8.

[49]Arthur Okun, "Potential GNP: Its Measurement and Significance," reprinted in *The Political Economy of Prosperity*, ed. Arthur Okun (Washington, D.C.: Brookings Institution, 1970), and Robert J. Gordon and Robert E. Hall, "Arthur M. Okun 1928–1980," *Brookings Papers on Economic Activity*, 1980–1, 1–5.

REVIEW QUESTIONS

1. A presidential hopeful is campaigning to raise unemployment compensation benefits and lower the full-employment target from a 6 percent to a 5.5 percent unemployment rate. Comment on the compatibility of these goals.

2. Government officials find it useful to measure the nation's "economic health." The unemployment rate is currently used as a major indicator of the relative strength of labor supply and demand. Do you think the unemployment rate is becoming more or less useful as an indicator of labor market tightness? What other measures might serve this purpose better?

3. The state of New York, in an effort to reduce job loss in the state, has approved the payment of unemployment insurance (UI) benefits to workers whose workweeks have been reduced from five eight-hour days to four. Specifically, workers are paid UI benefits (equal to about one-half of their normal daily pay) for the days each week they are off work. Please answer the following questions:

   a. How does this program differ from the normal UI program?

   b. How does this program affect the measured unemployment rate?

   c. How does this program affect hourly wage rates and average yearly earnings of workers in various age groups?

4. Is the following assertion true, false, or uncertain? "Increasing the level of unemployment insurance benefits will prolong the average length of spells of unemployment. Hence, a policy of raising UI benefit levels is not socially desirable." Explain your answer.

5. Recent empirical evidence suggests that unemployed workers' reservation wages decline as their spells of unemployment lengthen. That is, the longer they have been unemployed, the lower their reservation wages are. Explain why this might be true.

6. In the 1970s Sweden adopted several new labor market policies affecting layoffs. Three were notable: (1) Plants that provided in-plant training instead of laying off workers in a recession received government subsidies. (2) All workers had to be given at least one month's notice before being laid off, and the required time in the average plant was two to three months. (3) Laid-off workers had to be given first option on new jobs with the former employer. What probable effects would these policies, taken as a whole, have on wages, employment, and unemployment in the long run?

7. In recent years the federal government has introduced and then expanded a requirement that unemployment insurance beneficiaries pay income tax on their unemployment benefits. Explain what effect you would expect this taxation of UI benefits to have on the unemployment rate.

8. The present value of benefits in many pension plans is greater if a person retires before the normal retirement age. In short, there is a large inducement for many private sector workers to retire early. What effect will increasing the inducements to retire early have on the unemployment rate of older men? Fully explain your answer, making use of the assumption that retired workers withdraw from the labor force and do not seek or obtain other jobs.

9. The "employment-at-will" doctrine is one that allows employers to discharge workers for any reason whatsoever. This doctrine has generally prevailed in the United States except where modified by union

agreements or by laws preventing age, race, or gender discrimination. Recently, however, the courts and lawmaking bodies have begun to erode the employment-at-will doctrine by moving closer to the notion that one's job becomes a property right that the worker cannot be deprived of unless there is a compelling reason. If employers lose the right to discharge workers without "cause," what effects will this have on the unemployment rate?

SELECTED READINGS

Atkinson, Anthony, and John Micklewright. "Unemployment Compensation and Labor Market Transitions: A Critical Review." *Journal of Economic Literature* 29 (December 1991): 1679–1727.

Blanchflower, David G., and Andrew J. Oswald. *The Wage Curve.* Cambridge, Mass.: MIT Press, 1994.

Blank, Rebecca M., ed. *Social Protection Versus Economic Flexibility: Is There a Trade-off?* Chicago: University of Chicago Press, 1994.

Freeman, Richard, and Harry Holzer, eds. *The Black Youth Unemployment Crisis.* Chicago: University of Chicago Press, 1986.

Lang, Kevin, and Jonathan Leonard, eds. *Unemployment and the Structure of Labor Markets.* New York: Basil Blackwell, 1987.

Meyer, Bruce D. "Lessons from the U.S. Unemployment Insurance Experiments." *Journal of Economic Literature* 33 (March 1995): 91-131.

Reducing Unemployment: Current Issues and Policy Options. Kansas City, Mo.: Federal Reserve Bank of Kansas City, 1994.

Rees, Albert. "An Essay on Youth Joblessness." *Journal of Economic Literature* 24 (June 1986): 613–628.

Answers to Odd-Numbered Review Questions

Chapter 1

1. The basic value premise underlying normative analysis is that if a given transaction is beneficial to the parties agreeing to it and hurts no one else, then accomplishing that transaction is said to be "good." This criterion implies, of course, that anyone harmed by a transaction must be compensated for that harm (a condition tantamount to saying that all parties to a transaction must voluntarily agree to it). The labor market will reach a point of optimality when all mutually beneficial transactions have been accomplished. If there are mutually beneficial transactions remaining unconsummated, the labor market will not be at a point of optimality.

   One condition preventing the accomplishment of a mutually beneficial transaction would be *ignorance*. A party to a transaction may voluntarily agree to it because he or she is uninformed about some adverse effect of that transaction. Likewise, a party to a potential transaction may fail to enter into the transaction because he or she is uninformed about a benefit of the transaction. Informed individuals may fail to consummate a transaction, however, because of underlying *transaction barriers*. These may arise because of government prohibitions against certain kinds of transactions, imperfections in the market's ability to bring buyers and sellers together, or the nonexistence of a market where one could potentially exist.

3. The prohibitions of child labor laws would seem to violate the principle of mutual benefit by outlawing certain transactions that might be voluntarily entered into. However, there are at least two conditions under which such prohibitions would be consistent with the principles of normative economics. First, the children entering into an employment transaction may be uninformed of the dangers or the consequences of their decision to work in a particular environment. By their very nature children are inexperienced, and society frequently adopts legislation to protect them from their own ignorance.

   Second, society may adopt child labor legislation to protect children from their parents. A child forced by a parent to work in a dangerous or unhealthy environment has not voluntarily agreed to the employment transaction. Thus, a law prohibiting such a child from engaging in certain employment would not be violating the principle of mutual benefit when parental compulsion was present.

5. a. This behavior is entirely consistent with the model of job quitting described in the text. Workers are assumed by economic theory to be attempting to maximize utility (happiness). If all other aspects of two jobs are *similar*, this theory predicts that workers will prefer a higher-paying to a lower-paying job. However, two jobs frequently differ in many important respects, including the work environment, personalities of managers, and the stresses placed on employees. Thus, one way to interpret this woman's behavior is that she was willing to give up 50 cents an hour to be able to work in an environment free of stress.

   b. There is no way to prove that her behavior was grounded in "rationality." Economists define rationality as the ability to make considered decisions that are expected (at the time the decision is made) to advance one's self-interest. We cannot tell from any one individual act whether the person involved is being rational or not. Certainly, as described above, this woman's decision to quit could be interpreted as a move calculated to increase her utility (or level of happiness). However, it could also be that she became uncontrollably angry and made her decision without any thought of the consequences.

   c. Economic theory does not predict that everyone will act alike. Since economic agents are assumed to maximize utility, and since each person can be assumed to have a unique set of preferences, it is entirely consistent with economic theory that some workers would respond to a given set of incentives and that others would not. Thus, it could not be correctly concluded from the situation described that economic theory applied to one group of workers but not to another. It might well be that the other workers were less bothered by stress and that they were not willing to give up 50 cents an hour to avoid this stress.

7. Although a "draft" and a voluntary system of labor recruitment could conceivably result in the same number of employees working on the levee, the system of voluntary acceptance has one major normative advantage: It assures society that all employees working on the levee view the job as improving their welfare. When workers are drafted, at least some are being compelled to accept a transaction that they view as detrimental to their interests; allowing these workers to change employment would improve social welfare through simply reallocating (not increasing) resources. A system of voluntary recruitment, then, increases the welfare of society as compared to a system that relies on conscription.

Chapter 2

1. As shown in the figure at the top of the next page, the outflow of construction workers shifted the labor supply curve relevant to Egypt's construction sector to the *left* (from S_1 to S_2), while the demand curve for the services of construction workers shifted to the *right* (D_1 to D_2). Because both shifts, by themselves, tended to increase the equilibrium wage rate from W_1 to W_2, we would clearly expect wages in the Egyptian construction sector to have risen faster than average (in fact, they rose 200 percent from 1970–1975, as compared to a 53 percent increase in Egyptian manufacturing). However, the two shifts by themselves had opposite effects on employment, so the expected net change in employment is theoretically ambiguous.

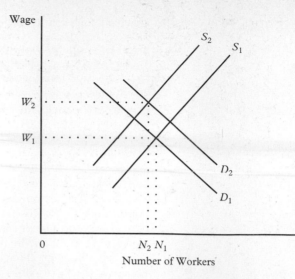

3. Many engineers are employed in research and development tasks. Therefore, if a major demander of research and development were to reduce its demand, the demand curve for engineers would shift left, causing their wages and employment to fall.

5. If the wages for arc welders are above the equilibrium wage, the company is paying more for its arc welders than it needs to and as a result is hiring fewer than it could. Thus, the definition of overpayment that makes the most sense in this case is one in which the wage rate is above the equilibrium wage.

   A ready indicator of an above-equilibrium wage rate is a long queue of applicants whenever a position in a company becomes available. Another indicator is an abnormally low quit rate as workers (in this case arc welders) who are lucky enough to obtain the above-equilibrium wage cling tenaciously to their jobs.

7. Proposal "a" increases the supply of teachers at any given wage, because college graduates can be compelled to enter the occupation at any wage the government chooses. This will tend to increase employment and reduce wages.

   The reduced wage may drive experienced teachers out of the profession, tending to reduce the average quality of teachers. The fact that many teachers will be conscripts who would rather be doing something else also reduces quality (and increases the costs associated with turnover). From a normative perspective, conscription violates the principle of encouraging mutually beneficial transactions.

   Proposal "b" increases average quality (presumably), but the licensing procedure reduces supply at any given wage. The leftward shift in the supply curve reduces employment and drives up the wage. Thus, proposal "a" increases employment but reduces the wage, while proposal "b" increases the wage but reduces employment.

9. This regulation essentially increases the cost of capital, and as such it will have an ambiguous effect on the demand curve for labor. On the one hand, the increased cost of capital will increase the cost of production and cause a scale effect that tends to depress employment. On the other hand, this regulation will increase the cost of capital relative to labor and could stimulate the substitution of labor for capital. Thus, the substitution effect will work to increase employment while the scale effect will work to decrease it. Which effect is stronger cannot be known a priori.

Chapter 3

1. This line of reasoning confuses the budgetary cost of achieving any desired force level with the social costs—the costs borne by society. Consider the figure below, where we have arbitrarily drawn a vertical demand curve to reflect the assumption that the military always wants F_1 soldiers regardless of the cost. The supply curve is drawn as an upward-sloping function of the military wage; this assumes that preferences for military service vary across the population and that as the military wage increases, more and more people find military service an attractive career alternative.

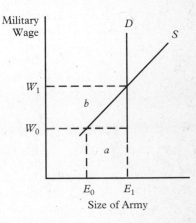

Suppose initially that the military wage is set at W_0, that only E_0 people volunteer, that the total military wage bill is W_0E_0, and that there is a perceived "shortage" of $E_1 - E_0$. If a draft system were instituted and $E_1 - E_0$ individuals were compelled to join the army, the *additional* budgetary cost (ignoring the cost of running the draft system) would be $W_0(E_1 - E_0)$, or rectangle a in the figure. If instead the military wage rate were allowed to rise to induce people to join voluntarily, it would have to rise to W_1 to eliminate the "shortage," and the additional budgetary cost would be $W_1E_1 - W_0E_0$ (the sum of rectangles a and b in the figure).

Obviously the budgetary cost is higher in the second case, but the true costs to society need not be. This is because, by forcing the $E_1 - E_0$ workers to join the armed forces in the draft-system case, but paying them less than they would require to voluntarily join, we are implicitly levying a tax on them. We are also levying an implicit tax on the E_0 workers, who would have been paid the wage of W_1 if the volunteer army were in effect but instead only receive W_0. The sum of these implicit taxes just equals rectangle b.

3. The potential employment effects of OSHA standards differ with the type of approach taken. If the standards apply to capital (machinery), they will increase the cost of capital equipment. This increase in cost has a scale effect, which will reduce the quantity demanded of all inputs (including labor). On the other hand, it also provides employers with an incentive to substitute labor (which is now relatively cheaper) for capital in producing any given desired level of output. This substitution will moderate the decline in employment.

In contrast, requiring employers to furnish personal protective devices to employees increases the cost of labor. In this case, employers have an incentive to substitute now relatively cheaper capital for labor when producing any given level of output (as above, the increased cost of production causes a scale effect that also tends to reduce employment).

Other things equal, then, the employment reduction induced by safety standards will be greater if the personal protective device method is used. However, to fully answer the question requires information on the costs of meeting the standards using the two methods. For example, if the "capital" approach increases capital costs by 50 percent while the "personal protective" approach increases labor costs by only 1 percent, the scale effect in the first method will probably be large enough that the greater employment loss will be associated with the first method.

5. The wage and employment effects in both service industries and manufacturing industries must be considered. In the service sector the wage tax on employers can be analyzed in much the same way as payroll taxes are analyzed in the text. That is, a tax on wages, collected from the employer, will cause the demand curve to shift leftward *if* the curve is drawn with respect to the wage that employees take home. At any given hourly wage that employees take home, the cost to the employer has risen by the amount of the tax. An increase in cost associated with any employee wage dampens the employer's appetite for labor and causes the demand curve to shift down and to the left.

The effects on employment and wages depend upon the shape of the labor supply curve. If the labor supply curve is upward-sloping, both employment and the wage employees take home will fall. If the supply curve is vertical, employment will not fall but wages will fall by the full amount of the tax. If the supply curve is horizontal, the wage rate will not fall but employment will.

The reduced employment and/or wages in the service sector should cause the supply of labor to the manufacturing sector to shift to the right (as people formerly employed in the service sector seek employment elsewhere). This shift in the supply curve should cause employment in manufacturing to increase even if the demand curve there remains stationary. If the demand curve does remain stationary, the employment increase would be accompanied by a decrease in manufacturing wages. However, the demand for labor in manufacturing may also shift to the right as consumers substitute away from the now more expensive services and buy the now relatively cheaper manufactured goods. If this demand shift occurs, the increase in employment would be accompanied by either a wage increase or a smaller wage reduction than would occur if the demand curve for labor in manufacturing were to remain stationary.

7. The imposition of financial penalties on employers who are discovered to have hired illegal immigrants essentially raises the cost of hiring them. The employers now must pay whatever the prevailing wage of the immigrants is, and they also face the possibility of a fine if they are discovered to have illegally employed workers. This penalty can be viewed as increasing the cost of hiring illegal workers so that this cost now exceeds the wage. This effect can be seen as a leftward shift of the demand curve for illegal immigrants, thus reducing their employment and wages.

The effects on the demand for skilled "natives" depend on whether skilled and unskilled labor are gross substitutes or gross complements. Raising the cost of unskilled labor produces a scale effect that tends to increase the cost of production and reduce skilled employment. If skilled and unskilled labor are *complements in production*, the demand for skilled labor will clearly shift to the left as a result of the government's policy. However, if they are *substitutes* in production, the increased costs of unskilled labor would stimulate the substitution of skilled for unskilled labor. In this case, the demand for skilled labor could shift either right (if the substitution effect dominated the scale effect) or left (if the scale effect dominated).

9. Profit maximization requires that firms hire labor until marginal revenue productivity equals the market wage. If wages are low, a profit maximizer will hire labor in abundant quantity, driving the marginal revenue productivity down to the low level of the wage. This statement, then, seems to imply that firms are not maximizing profits!

Chapter 4

1. While lower interest rates might well stimulate overall economic activity, thereby creating a scale effect that is beneficial to workers, they also lower the cost of buying capital (which could lead to a substitution effect that tends to shift the labor demand curve to the left).

3. All three options increase the costs of firms not already providing employees with acceptable health coverage. Since noncoverage is a characteristic mostly of small firms, all options would increase costs of small firms relative to costs in large firms. This would create a scale effect, tending to reduce employment in small firms relative to that in large ones. The magnitude of this scale effect will be greater the more elastic product demand is and (usually) the greater labor's share is in total cost.

Option A has, in addition to the scale effect, a substitution effect that tends to decrease the number of workers a firm hires. This substitution effect will be larger the more easily capital can be substituted for labor and the more elastic the supply of capital is.

Option B is a tax on a firm's revenues, so it would have just a scale effect on the demand for labor, not a substitution effect. It would increase total costs and cause downward pressures on employment and wages, but it does not raise the ratio of labor costs to capital costs. Thus, its effects on wages and employment would be smaller than under option A.

Option C raises the cost of capital, and if labor and capital are substitutes in production, it is possible that a substitution effect in favor of labor could mitigate, or even offset, the unfavorable scale effect. This option probably would have the smallest negative effects on employment and wages, and if the substitution effect were large enough it is possible that the effects on employment and wages could be positive. (Whether it makes sense to require capital to subsidize labor is another matter, however!)

5. The policies will generally lower the price of capital in one way or another. In terms of the demand for labor, this will create substitution and scale effects that work in opposite directions, so that as an overall statement, the effects on the demand for labor are ambiguous. Scale effects will tend to increase labor demand, and substitution effects will tend to reduce it. (If capital and labor are complements in production, then there is no substitution effect and labor demand will increase unambiguously.)

Investments in infrastructure will clearly increase demand for construction workers during the construction period. In the long run, better roads and cheaper transportation may lower the cost of production (lower transportation costs), and hence it will tend to increase labor demand of "transportation-intensive" firms through the scale effect.

Tax credits will make capital cheaper, and it could cause the substitution of capital for labor if the two are substitutes in production. This is more likely for unskilled than for skilled labor. Skilled workers are more likely to be gross complements with capital than unskilled labor, so skilled workers may face an increase in employment and wages.

Subsidizing research and development activities will increase the scale of such activities, and it will thus increase the demand for scientific workers. In the long run it may effectively reduce the price of capital, with the ambiguous effects on labor demand noted above. It could also generate new products and create a scale effect in some industries.

7. a. An increased tariff on steel imports will tend to make domestic *product* demand, and therefore the demand for domestic labor, more inelastic.

   b. A law forbidding workers from being laid off for economic reasons will discourage the substitution of capital for labor and therefore tend to make the own-wage elasticity of demand for labor more inelastic.

   c. A "boom" in the machinery industry will *shift* the product demand curve in the steel industry to the right, thereby shifting the labor demand curve to the right. The effects of this shift on the own-wage elasticity of demand for labor cannot be predicted (except that a parallel shift to the right of a straight-line demand curve will *reduce* the elasticity at each wage rate).

   d. Because capital and labor are most substitutable in the long run, when new production processes can be installed, a decision to delay the adoption of new technologies reduces the substitutability of capital for labor and makes the labor demand curve more inelastic.

   e. An increase in wages will move the firm *along* its labor demand curve and does not change the shape of that curve. However, if the demand curve happens to be a straight line, movement up and to the left along the demand curve will tend to increase elasticity in the range in which firms are operating.

   f. A tax placed on each ton of steel output will tend to shift the labor demand curve to the left, but will not necessarily change its elasticity. Again, however, if the demand curve happened to be a straight line this leftward shift would tend to increase the elasticity of demand for labor at each wage rate.

Chapter 5

1. What low-skilled workers and high-paid college professors have in common is that neither group receives much firm-specific training. The former group can be thought of as having received no training and the latter group as having received highly general training. In either case, we know that the workers' marginal productivity in their current firm is the same as their marginal productivity with other firms. In competitive labor markets, the latter will represent the wage other firms will be willing to pay them. As a result, if the wage at their current firm falls below their marginal productivity, both types of workers have an incentive to quit their jobs.

   One might contrast the behavior of these groups with the behavior of individuals who have received a good deal of firm-specific training. We know from the text that (*a*) by the definition of specific training, the marginal productivity of these individuals at their current firm exceeds their marginal productivity elsewhere, and (*b*) their wage at the current firm is less than their marginal productivity there. As long as this wage is greater than their potential marginal productivity elsewhere, these workers have reduced incentives to quit their jobs.

3. Because the level of investment in specific human capital is greater in Japan than in the United States, one would expect the temporary layoff rate in Japan to be lower. The specific training paid for by the employer creates a gap between workers' marginal productivities and their wage rates, with the result that temporary reductions in marginal productivity can be absorbed without creating incentives for the employer to reduce employment. The greater the level of investment, the greater is the decline in marginal productivity that can be absorbed in the short run without reducing employment.

   The broader scope of training in Japan suggests that workers are more interchangeable within the firm. Thus, if one division of a multiplant firm is closing down, Japanese workers have a good chance of finding employment in another division because they are broadly trained. Not surprisingly, Japan relies more on intraplant transfers than permanent layoffs as a means of adjusting to both temporary economic stress and permanent structural change in product and labor markets.

5. This change would convert a quasi-fixed labor cost to a variable one, inducing employers to substitute added workers for weekly hours (especially overtime hours) of work. Because this new financing scheme increases the cost of higher-paid workers relative to lower-paid ones, it also induces firms to substitute unskilled for skilled workers. (Both these effects emphasize labor–labor *substitution;* scale effects are minimal if total premiums are held constant.)

7. Employee benefits such as insurance impose *per-worker* costs on the employer, while wages impose *hourly* costs. If hourly costs of labor rise and per-worker costs remain the same or fall, employers will tend to substitute added workers for added hours per worker if they must increase labor input.

9. The effect of the wage subsidy will clearly be to increase the demand for labor, and depending on the shape of the supply curve this wage subsidy will increase employee wages or employment levels (or both) above what they would have been in the absence of such a subsidy. Another interesting aspect of the wage subsidy, however, is that only the first $12 a week of workers' wages are subsidized. If normal weekly earnings of full-time workers are $20 a week, then the $12 limit will tend to induce firms to expand labor hours by hiring part-time workers rather than working the ones they have for longer hours. Thus, this subsidy will tend to increase employment and reduce the average hours worked by employees. It subsidizes the marginal cost of hiring *workers* rather than the marginal cost of expanding *hours* per full-time worker.

Chapter 6

1. False. An inferior good is defined as one that people consume less of as their incomes rise (if the price of the good remains constant). A labor supply curve is drawn with respect to a person's wage rate. Thus, for a labor supply curve to be backward-bending, the supply curve must be positively sloped in some range and then become negatively sloped in another. A typical way of illustrating a backward-bending supply curve is shown on the following page.

   Along the positively sloped section of this backward-bending supply curve, the substitution effect of a wage increase dominates the income effect, and as wages rise the person increases his or her labor supply. However, after the wage reaches W_0 in the figure, further increases in the wage are accompanied by a reduction in labor

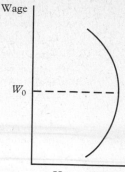

Hours of Work Supplied

supply. In this negatively sloped portion of the supply curve, the income effect dominates the substitution effect.

We have assumed that the income effect is negative and that, therefore, leisure is a normal good. Had we assumed leisure to be an inferior good, the increases in wealth brought about by increased wages would have worked *with* the underlying substitution effect and caused the labor supply curve to be unambiguously positively sloped.

3. The graphs for each option are shown below, with the new constraints shown as dashed lines. By mandating that 5 percent of each hour be worked for free, option A reduces lawyers' wages, creating income and substitution effects that work in opposite directions on their desired labor supply.

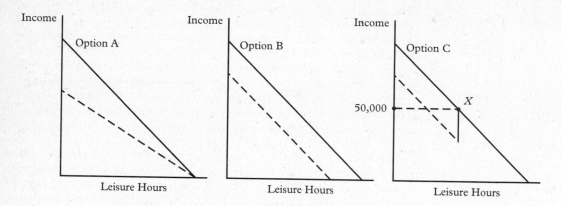

Option B essentially reduces the time lawyers have available for leisure and paid work, which shifts the budget constraint to the left in a parallel manner (keeping the wage rate constant). This creates an income effect that increases their incentives to work for pay.

Option C leaves the budget constraint of lawyers who work relatively few hours unchanged, but for those who work enough to earn over $50,000 there is an income effect that tends to increase work incentives. For some whose incomes were only slightly above $50,000, however, the $5,000 "tax" may drive them to reduce hours of work, thereby reducing their earnings to $50,000 and avoiding the tax. These lawyers find their utilities are maximized at point X in the graph of option C's budget constraint.

5. Absenteeism is one dimension of labor supply, so the proposals must be analyzed using labor supply theory. Both proposals increase worker income, because employees now have paid sick days; this increase in income will tend to increase absenteeism through the income effect. The first proposal also raises the *hourly wage*, however, because any unused sick leave can be converted to cash in direct proportion to the unused days. Thus, this first proposal will tend to have a substitution effect accompanying the income effect, so that the overall expected change in absenteeism is ambiguous.

    The second proposal raises the cost of the *first* sick day because, if absent, the worker loses the entire promised insurance policy. Thus, there is a huge substitution effect offsetting the income effect for the *first* day of absence. However, once sick leave is used at all, *further* days of absence cause no further loss of pay; thus, after the first day there is no substitution effect to offset the income effect, and this will tend to increase the incentives for absenteeism.

7. In the figure below, the straight line *AB* represents the person's market constraint (that is, the constraint in a world with no subsidies). *ACDEB* is the constraint that would apply if the housing subsidy proposal became effective.

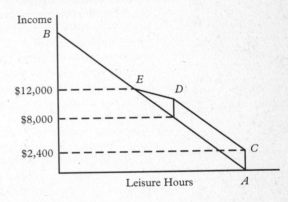

    The effects on labor supply depend upon which segment of *ACDEB* the person finds relevant. There are four possible cases. First, if the indifference curves are very steeply pitched (reflecting a strong desire to consume leisure), the housing subsidy proposal will not affect work incentives. The person strongly desiring leisure would continue to not work (would be at point *C*), but would receive the housing subsidy of $2,400. The second case occurs when the person has a tangency along segment *CD*. Along this segment the person's effective wage rate is the same as the market wage, so there is a pure income effect tending to reduce work incentives.

    If the person has a tangency point along segment *DE*, there are likewise reduced incentives to work because the income effect caused by the northeast shifting out of the budget constraint is accompanied by a *reduction* in the effective wage rate. Finally, those with tangency points along *EB* will not qualify for the housing subsidy program and therefore will not alter their labor supply behavior. (An exception to this case occurs when a person with a tangency point *near* point *E* before the initiation of the housing subsidy program now has a tangency point along segment *DE* and, of course, works less than before.)

Chapter 7

1. a. $6,000 - 5,600$, or 400.
   b. The labor force participation rate drops from 60 percent to 56 percent, a reduction of 4 percentage points.
   c. One implication of hidden unemployment is that the unemployment rate may not fully reflect the degree of joblessness. That is, some people who want to work but do not have work are not counted as unemployed because they place such a low probability on obtaining employment that they stop looking for work. While this observation may suggest that hidden unemployment should be included in the published unemployment figures, to do so would imperil the objectivity of the unemployment rate and call into question the theoretical underpinnings of our measure of unemployment. Economic theory suggests that unemployment exists if there are more people willing to work at the going wage than there are people employed at that wage. If economic conditions are such that at the going wage one decides time is better spent in household production, say, than in seeking market work, it can be argued that the person in question has in fact dropped out of the labor force.

3. Jimmy Carter's statement reflects the "additional-worker hypothesis." Stated briefly, this hypothesis suggests that, as the economy moves into a recession and some members of the labor force are thrown out of work, other family members currently engaged in household production or leisure will enter the labor force to try to maintain family income. While Carter's statement of the additional-worker hypothesis is an apt description of that hypothesis, his statement fails to reflect the fact that studies show the "discouraged-worker" effect dominates the added-worker effect (that is, as the economy moves into a recession and workers are laid off, the labor force shrinks, on balance).

5. To parents who already have small children, this subsidy of day care is tantamount to an increase in the wage rate. That is, each hour of work brings in more take-home earnings now than it did before. This increase in the take-home wage rate will cause both an income and a substitution effect, the net result of which is not theoretically predictable. If the substitution effect is dominant, then the change in policy would increase the labor supply (there is some evidence that the substitution effect is dominant for married women). If the income effect is dominant, then this increase in the take-home wage rate might cause a reduction in labor supply among parents with small children.

   However, the above changes in household *production* may also be accompanied by changes in household *consumption*. For younger families, the subsidy of day care may reduce the cost of having children enough that some may decide to increase the number of children they want to raise. Because the presence of small children tends to increase the productivity of at least one spouse in the home, an increase in the number of children per family could reduce the labor supply of at least one spouse over his or her life cycle. For example, a family with a six-year-old child may, in the absence of this federal policy, have planned on the mother's rejoining the labor force after a six-year absence and returning to full-time employment. However, if the new policy is implemented, this family may decide to have another child and have the mother work part-time.

   While the effects on parents with small children hinge on whether the substitution effect or the income effect dominates, the effects of this policy on other members of the population are a bit more complicated. For those past childbearing age or those who do not plan to have more children, this policy change would cause an increase in their taxes (some segment of society must pay for this program). Assuming the taxes that pay for this program are raised primarily through the individual income tax, this program would result in a decrease in take-home wages for those in the population who must bear the cost of the program without obtaining corresponding benefits. Thus, this segment experiences a net decrease in wage rates, and in mirror image of the above analysis, the effects on their labor supply depend on whether the income effect or the substitution effect dominates.

7. For workers close to retirement age this change in government policy creates a significant decrease in postretirement income. The basic postretirement pension has been cut in half, so these workers experience a substantial income effect that would drive them in the direction of more work (delayed retirement).

   For very young workers, the reduction in pension benefits facing them in their retirement years is offset by a reduction in payroll taxes (which, of course, acts as an increase in their take-home wage rate). Thus, if one assumes that these workers will pay for their retirement benefits through the payroll taxes they pay over their careers, this change in Social Security will leave their lifetime wealth unaffected. What it will do, however, is increase their wages during their working years, causing a pure substitution effect and an increase in labor supply. This increase in wages without any corresponding increase or change in lifetime wealth may well cause these people to delay retirement as they near the traditional retirement age.

9. a. The budget constraint facing this teenager is shown below, with line *ABC* representing the constraint associated with her job with the caterer, and *AD* the constraint as a babysitter (assuming she needs 8 hours per day for sleep and personal care).

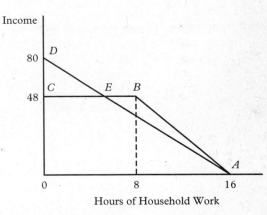

b. The value to her of studying and practicing would be shown by indifference curves, with more steeply sloped curves indicating a greater value. If she places a high value on her household activities, she will either not work (corner solution at point *A*) or choose to work as a caterer along constraint *AB*. In this case the state law has no effect. With a flatter indifference curve, however, she may maximize utility at point *B* (catering job) or along *ED*. In these cases, the state law reduces her earnings and her utility, but the effects on her hours at home are unclear. If she ends up at point B she spends more time at home than she would if unconstrained, but along ED the income and substitution effects of the law work in opposite directions and the effects on hours at home are ambiguous.

Chapter 8

1. False. Whether government policy is required in a particular labor market depends on how well that market is functioning. If the outcomes of the market take into account worker preferences (with full information and choice) and the preferences of other parties affected by coal-mine safety, then the labor market decisions will lead to utility maximization among workers. In this case, efforts by government to impose a level of safety greater than the market outcome could lead to a reduction in worker welfare. The reason for this, simply put, is that it is costly for employers to reduce injuries in environments that are "inherently dangerous." If a firm is to reduce injuries, it must invest resources toward that end, and it can remain competitive with other industries or firms only if it can sell its products at a price (which must at least cover costs) no higher than its competitors'. The increase in cost associated with increased safety must be offset either by cuts elsewhere (including cuts in labor costs) or by increases in product prices. In the latter case, of course, the downward-sloping nature of product demand curves suggests a reduction in employment. Thus, there is a good chance that workers will feel the effects of the increased investment in safety on their wages and/or employment levels. Whether these costs imposed on workers are outweighed by the benefits of greater safety is, of course, the central social question.

   If the market is functioning perfectly, then the costs and benefits of greater safety will have been weighed appropriately by private decision makers. If, however, the private decision makers do not weigh all the costs and benefits of greater safety, there is a very good chance that the market outcome will not be socially optimal. In this case, an appropriate setting of governmental standards could improve the utility of workers.

   Of course, if society does not trust workers' preferences or seeks to change those preferences, it would not want to rely on the market even if it were functioning perfectly, because the market would reflect worker preferences.

3. The demand curve shows how the marginal revenue product of labor (MRP_L) is affected by the number employed; if few workers are employed, they are placed in jobs in which their MRP_L is relatively high. The supply curve indicates the number of workers willing to offer their services at each wage rate. Because fewer construction workers are willing to offer their services at any given wage if working conditions are harsh (as in Alaska), construction wages will be higher than in the continental United States. Further, the higher wage that must be paid restricts employment in harsh conditions to the performance of projects that have a very high MRP_L.

5. A society unwilling to use force or trickery to fill jobs that are dangerous or otherwise have adverse working conditions must essentially "bribe" workers into these jobs. That is, workers must voluntarily choose these jobs over other alternatives they have. To induce workers to choose a dangerous or dirty job over a safer, cleaner one requires that the former be made more attractive than the latter in other dimensions, and one way is to have elevated compensation levels. These increased levels of compensation are what in this chapter we have called compensating wage differentials.

These compensating wage differentials will arise when job conditions differ *if* workers are well informed and can select from an adequate number of job choices. If workers are without *choice*, then society is using force. Workers are forced to take what is offered through the threat of being jailed or of not being able to obtain a means of livelihood. Thus, if choice is absent or severely restricted, society is in effect using force to allocate labor. (There is undoubtedly a fine line between being forced into something and voluntarily choosing an option, and the student is not here required to make this distinction.)

If, instead of lacking choice, workers lack *information* about working conditions in the jobs from which they have to choose, then society is in effect using trickery to allocate labor. That is, if workers are ignorant of true working conditions and remain ignorant of these conditions for a long period after they have taken a job, they have not made their choices with full information. They have been "tricked" into making the choices they have made.

7. Men and women who work in their homes do not have to bear the expenses of commuting and child care that factory workers do. Moreover, many prefer the flexibility of working at home to the regimen of a factory, because they can perform farming chores or do other household tasks that would be impossible to do during a factory shift. These intrinsically desirable or cost-saving aspects of working at home suggest that the same level of utility could be reached by homeworkers at a lower wage rate than factory workers receive. Thus, at least *part* of the higher wage paid to factory workers is a compensating wage differential for the cost and inconvenience of factory employment.

9. From the perspective of positive economics, banning Sunday work drives down the profits of employers, which will have a scale effect on employment, and drives up the cost of labor relative to capital (machines are not banned from running on Sunday). Overall, firms will tend to hire less labor.

Further, in the absence of government prohibitions, most workers presumably *preferred* to celebrate a Sabbath, and in Germany Sunday was most likely the typical choice. With most workers preferring Sunday off, employers who wanted to remain open had to hire from a small pool of workers who did not celebrate Sunday as a Sabbath. If this pool was small relative to the demand for Sunday workers, employers had to pay a compensating wage differential to lure workers into offering their services on Sundays. The workers most easily lured were those who cared least about having Sunday off. These workers will lose their premium pay (unless exempt from the law).

Normatively, this law prevents some voluntary transactions. It makes society worse off by preventing workers who are willing to work on Sundays (for a price) from transacting with employers who want Sunday workers, and it thus discourages some mutually beneficial transactions.

Chapter 9

1. Understanding why women receive lower wages than men of comparable age requires an analysis of many possible causes, including discrimination. This answer will explore the insights provided by human capital theory.

Women have traditionally exhibited interrupted labor market careers, thus shortening the period of time over which educational and training investments can be recouped. The shorter market-work lives of women have until recently been a factor causing women to acquire less formal education, on average, than men. Even recently, when educational attainment levels between relatively young men and women have equalized, women graduates are still bunched in occupations for which an interrupted working life is least damaging. Lower educational levels and "occupational bunching" are undoubtedly associated with lower wages.

The fact that female age/earnings profiles are relatively flat, while men have age/earnings profiles that are upward-sloping and concave, can also be explained by human capital analysis. If men acquire more education or on-the-job training in their early years than women do, their wages will be relatively depressed by these investments (this will cause wages of men and women at younger ages to be more equal than they would otherwise be). In their later years, those who have made human capital investments will be recouping them, and this will cause the wages of men and women to become less equal.

Thus, while human capital theory may not be the only explanation for the facts noted in this question, it can shed some light on them.

3. The commission of a crime like burglary is essentially the mirror image of human capital investment. With an investment, costs are incurred in the short run so that benefits may be obtained in the long run. With a crime like burglary, the benefits are obtained in the short run and costs may be borne in the long run. A person choosing criminal activity may well be one who is very present-oriented—that is, one who has a high discount rate and thus places a heavy discount on future costs and benefits. Thus, one's discount rate is probably a factor in decisions about crime. It is also likely that those who choose criminal activities are the least productive in noncriminal jobs. These people have the least to lose by being imprisoned and the most to gain by trying their hand at some criminal act.

Society might consider three general types of programs to reduce crime. One is to increase the earnings opportunities for less-advantaged citizens. Another is to undertake programs that would reduce the probability of a crime's being successful (programs to install burglar alarms, neighborhood watch groups, etc.). Finally, society might consider increasing the expected costs of a crime to the criminal. The theory in this chapter suggests that there are several ways the costs might be increased: increasing the *severity* of punishment, increasing the *likelihood* of apprehension and punishment, and *speeding up* the punishment by reducing the time between apprehension and punishment (this last will increase the expected present value of a crime's cost).

5. One cost of educational investment is related to the time students need to devote to studying in order to ensure success. People who can learn quickly are going to have lower costs of obtaining an education. If one assumes that learning ability and ability in general (including productive capacity in a job) are correlated, then the implication of human capital theory is that the most-able people, other things being equal, will obtain the most education.

7. Government subsidies will, of course, lower the costs to individuals of obtaining an education (of making a human capital investment). Reduced university costs will, from an individual perspective, raise the individual rate of return to making an investment in education. This will induce more people to attend college than would have attended otherwise. Students who would, in the absence of a college subsidy, have required a postcollege earnings differential (as compared to that of a high school graduate) of $2,000 per year may now be induced to attend college if the earnings differential is only $1,000 per year. From a social perspective, however, the increase in productivity of $1,000 per year may be insufficient to pay back society for its investments in college students.

Put differently, the subsidy may induce more investment in university education than is socially warranted (that is, the social rate of return on the human capital investment may be below the rate of return on nonhuman capital investments). Society, of course, could guard against this tendency toward overinvestment by restricting access to university positions and rationing the positions available so that they go to the abler students (those who would obtain the greatest net increase in productivity from a given human capital investment).

Chapter 10

1. a. State licensing increases the costs of interstate mobility among licensed professionals, thus tending to reduce the overall supply to these occupations and to drive up their wages. In addition, the flows from low- to high-earnings areas are inhibited, which slows the geographic equalization of wages among these professionals.

    b. The gainers from federalization would be licensed professionals who are in low-earnings areas, because their labor market mobility is enhanced. (One could also argue that *clients* in high-earnings areas similarly gain from the enhanced mobility of the professionals from whom they purchase services.) The losers are already licensed professionals in high-earnings areas, who face increased competition now because of enhanced mobility.

    Students who have yet to be licensed will find it less costly to acquire the ability to practice without geographic restrictions, but these gains may be offset by a lower wage attendant upon an increased supply of people to the licensed professions.

3. It is possible that Japanese workers do indeed have stronger preferences for loyalty (meaning that they are more willing to pass up monetary gains from mobility for the sake of "consuming" loyalty to their current employers). It is also true that quit rates are affected by *incentives* as well as preferences, and incentives for lower quit races can be altered by *employer* policies. Thus, quit rates do not by themselves allow us to measure differentials in inherent employee loyalties.

    Lower quit rates in Japan could result from poorer information flows about jobs in other areas, greater costs of changing jobs (employee benefits may be strongly linked to seniority within the firm so that when workers quit they lose benefits that are not immediately replaced by their new employer), smaller wage differentials among employers, or other employer policies adopted because of a greater reliance on firm-specific human capital investments by Japanese employers.

5. One factor inducing quit rates to be low is that the cost of job changing may be high (pension losses, seniority losses, and difficulties finding information about other jobs are examples of factors that can increase the cost of quitting). If there are cost barriers to mobility, then employees are more likely to tolerate adverse conditions within the firm without resorting to leaving.

    Firms also are more likely to provide their employees with firm-specific training if quit rates are low. Thus, if firms need to train their employees in firm-specific skills, they clearly prefer a low quit rate.

    Finally, firms prefer low quit rates because hiring costs are kept to a minimum. Every time a worker quits, a replacement must be hired, and to the extent that finding and hiring a replacement is costly, firms want to avoid incurring these costs.

From a social perspective, the disadvantage of having a low quit rate is related to the failure of the market to adjust quickly to shortages and surpluses. Changing relative demands for labor require constant flux in the employment distribution, and factors that inhibit change will also inhibit adaptation to new conditions.

Further, high costs of quitting will be associated not only with lower quit rates but also with larger wage differentials across firms or regions for the same grade of labor. Since firms hire labor until marginal productivity equals the wage they must pay, these large wage differentials will also be accompanied by large differentials in marginal productivities within the same skill group. As implied by our discussion of job matching, if marginal productivities differ widely among workers with the same skills, national output could be increased by reallocating labor so that marginal productivities of the low-paid workers are enhanced.

7. a. Immigrant workers create goods or perform services that have value to the rest of society. Thus, whether their presence enriches native-born Americans (in the aggregate) depends on the total value of these services, net of what they are paid. If immigrants receive no more than their marginal revenue product, the native-born cannot lose and in fact will reap inframarginal gains. If immigrants are subsidized by the native-born, so they are net *consumers* of goods and services, then the native-born could be worse off in the aggregate.

    b. There are two critical issues from a normative perspective. The first is whether immigrants are subsidized, on balance, by the native-born (as noted above). If they are not, then there is a second issue: Are there mechanisms whereby the native-born gainers from immigration can compensate the losers? Many economists argue that compensation of losers must take place for a potentially Pareto-improving policy to be socially defensible, so identifying whose wages are reduced and by how much is a critical social issue.

Chapter 11

1. If management *already* has power over workers because workers' ability to go to other jobs is severely limited by unemployment or monopsony, then low wages may result. However, paying low wages is definitely not the way to *acquire* power if management currently lacks it. Underpaid workers have no incentives to tolerate demanding requirements from management, because their current job is not better (and may be worse) than one they could find elsewhere. However, if workers are paid more by one firm than they could get elsewhere, they will tolerate heavy demands from their supervisors before deciding to quit. One way to acquire power over workers, therefore, is to *over*pay, not underpay, them.

3. Compensation schemes such as efficiency wages, deferred payments, and tournaments are made feasible by an expected long-term attachment between worker and firm. If small firms do not offer long enough job ladders to provide for career-long employment, long-term attachments will become less prevalent and the above three schemes less feasible. The growth of small firms, then, may mean more reliance on individual or group output-based pay schemes (or on closer supervision).

5. Layoffs become attractive to an employer only when marginal revenue product falls below the wage. That can never happen when workers are paid solely by commission, because they receive pay only when they generate a sale. Further, every time an agent receives a commission, so does the broker! Thus, if an agent generates no sales,

he or she receives no pay, but if the agent generates *any* sales at all, the broker's revenues (net of the agent's pay) increase. Brokers therefore gain nothing from laying off agents and stand to gain something if *any* sales are made by an agent.

7. a. Cutting the wages of all workers after age 65 reduces wages for both the productive and the nonproductive, with ambiguous retirement incentives (see Chapter 7). The nonproductive workers probably could not receive better offers elsewhere, but the productive ones who did not want to retire might quit to take better wages elsewhere.

    b. Retirement incentives increase (income effect), but for those who want to continue working, the lump-sum would induce more quits among the most-productive workers. The least-productive workers could not obtain a high-paying job elsewhere, so quitting employment at the firm would be less desirable for them than for productive workers.

    c. Increasing the monthly benefit of anyone who retired and did not work elsewhere would have ambiguous retirement incentives but would be at least neutral between productive and nonproductive workers. Both receive the same postretirement (at the firm) benefit, so incentives to quit employment at the firm are the same for both groups.

Chapter 12

1. a. Current labor market discrimination typically is said to exist when compensation levels paid to one demographic group are lower than those paid to another demographic group that is exactly comparable in terms of productive characteristics. Using this definition in the context of this question, there would be no discrimination because both men and women would receive equal yearly compensation while working. This equal yearly compensation would, in fact, result in a pension fund for each man and woman that would have exactly the same present value at retirement age. However, because women live longer than men on average, this retirement fund would be paid out over a longer period of time and thus would be paid out to retired women in smaller yearly amounts. The Supreme Court definition of discrimination would seem to stress the receipt of unequal yearly incomes by retirees who were comparable in productive characteristics but not comparable in terms of expected life spans. The Supreme Court decision would require employers to put aside more pension funds for women because of the requirement that women must receive equal yearly pension benefits over their longer life spans. Thus, the Supreme Court requires that working women have greater yearly compensation (while working) than comparable men.

    b. The *Manhart* decision essentially mandates greater labor costs for women than for men of comparable productive characteristics, and by raising the firm's costs of hiring women, it could give firms incentives to substitute male for female workers (or capital for female workers). This would tend to reduce the employment of women.

3. a. Firms frequently use marital status and gender to estimate how long a job applicant might be expected to remain with them. Those that offer specific training or find that hiring new employees requires substantial investments are especially sensitive to the expected tenure of workers in their firms. Thus, they are among the firms most affected by this ruling.

b. These firms have two general options open to them in adjusting to the antidis- crimination law. One is to undertake the implementation of alternative screening devices designed to estimate the expected length of employee tenure. The other is to essentially drop efforts to estimate expected employee tenure and adjust their behavior to the fact that those employees hired may now have shorter ex- pected tenures.

c. If a firm undertakes to use alternative screening devices, it may find that its costs of hiring have been increased. These alternatives presumably existed before and were rejected as more costly than the use of marital status and gender as indica- tors of expected tenure. If so, then the hiring investment in each worker must necessarily increase and, unless offset by a reduced wage rate, will cause labor costs of the firm to rise. If labor costs do rise, then there will be scale and substi- tution effects working in the direction of a smaller workforce within the firm. Be- cause it is the quasi-fixed labor costs that rise, however, firms will tend to increase hours per worker and reduce the number of workers.

If a firm decides to adjust its behavior to reflect the fact that new workers may have shorter expected tenures, then it may keep training investments the same but lower the posttraining wage (to recoup its training costs more quickly). However, it may also decide that training is not as profitable as it once was and reduce training of new employees. If this option is followed, there will be a smaller gap between marginal productivity and the wage rate, which could re- duce job stability over the business cycle. Finally, if neither wages nor training investments can be feasibly reduced, the firm will again face higher labor costs and would have to respond by reducing its workforce.

In general, if hiring investments are increased, if employment is reduced, or if wages are reduced, the gap between marginal productivity and wages will tend to rise, reflecting the more costly investments in workers, and job stability should be enhanced. If, however, as noted above, the firm decides to reduce in- vestments in employees, then job stability will be reduced.

5. Wage discrimination in the labor market is present when workers with the same pro- ductive characteristics are systematically paid differently because of the demo- graphic group to which they belong. The critical issue in judging discrimination in this case is whether male and female high school teachers have the same productive characteristics.

One area of information one would want to obtain concerns the human capital characteristics of level of education, major, and experience. Do male and female teachers have the same *level* of education? Is the male wage advantage associated with the *field* in which they teach? (If men are more heavily represented in fields in which there are shortages or better outside opportunities, their earnings could be higher for that reason.) Finally, if male teachers are more experienced their earnings will be relatively greater.

A second area of information concerns working conditions. Are male teachers working longer hours owing to such extra duties as coaching sports or sponsoring clubs? Are male teachers working in geographical areas that are associated with compensating wage differentials? (That is, are they working farther from home or in more dangerous areas of the city?)

7. When nursing wages are raised above market-clearing levels, a surplus of nursing applicants will arise. Because the supply of nurses at above-market wages is greater than the demand, the city will be facing a long queue of applicants each time it has a

nursing vacancy. The high wages, of course, will attract not only a large *number* of applicants but also a large number of *very high quality* applicants; the fact that applicants are so plentiful allows the city to select only the best. Therefore, comparable worth may reduce the number of nursing jobs available, but it will also tend to raise the demand for high-quality nurses.

Since the wages of nurses are tied to those of building inspectors, the city will be very reluctant to raise the wages of building inspectors even if there are shortages. Rather than raising wages as a recruiting device for building inspectors, the city may be tempted to lower its hiring standards and to employ building inspectors it would previously have rejected. Thus, employment opportunities for low-quality building inspectors may be enhanced by the comparable worth law.

9. a. A wage subsidy paid to employers who hire disadvantaged black workers will shift the demand curve for such workers (stated in terms of the employee wage) to the right. This shift can cause employment to increase, the wage rate paid to black disadvantaged workers to increase, or both. The mix of wage and employment changes will depend on the shape of the supply curve of these workers. The changes in wages and employment induced by the subsidy will tend to overcome the adverse effect on unskilled blacks of *current* labor market discrimination.

b. Increasing the wages and employment opportunities of unskilled black workers will reduce incentives of these workers to invest in the training required to become skilled. Thus, one consequence of a wage subsidy just for *unskilled* black workers is that the subsidy may induce more blacks to remain unskilled than would otherwise have been the case. Thus, while helping to overcome *current* labor market discrimination, the subsidy may increase premarket disparities between whites and blacks by reducing the incentives of blacks to acquire training for the skilled trades.

Chapter 13

1. Since a reduction in the price of capital equipment will stimulate the purchase of capital equipment, a union should be concerned whether its members are gross complements or gross substitutes with capital. In the former case, the proposed policy (reducing the price of capital) would cause the demand for union members to rise, while in the latter their demand would fall. Other things equal, the more rapidly the demand for labor is shifting out, the smaller will be the reduction in employment associated with any union-induced wage gain (assuming the collective bargaining agreement lies on the labor demand curve). Hence, unions representing groups that are gross complements (substitutes) with capital would benefit (lose) from the policy change.

Evidence cited in the text suggests that capital and skilled labor may be gross complements, but capital and unskilled labor are gross substitutes. This suggests that union leaders representing the latter type of workers will be opposed to the legislation, while union leaders representing the former may favor it.

3. The traditional neoclassical view is that union/nonunion wage differentials reflect marginal productivity differentials among similar workers, and thus (as discussed in the chapter's final section) their existence represents a misallocation of resources. To estimates of this output loss are typically added losses due to restrictive work practices and strike activity.

The alternative "neoinstitutionalist" viewpoint, associated most closely with Richard Freeman and James Medoff, stresses the productivity-enhancing effects of unions. These include reduced turnover, increased training, and increased morale. The net effect of unions on output is an empirical question. Some evidence is presented in the chapter.

Advanced students might also challenge the econometric evidence that produces union/nonunion wage differentials in the range of 10 to 20 percent. As noted in the text, such estimates do not always fully control for unobserved differences in "ability" between union and nonunion workers, and part of the observed wage differential may merely compensate unionized workers for their relatively unfavorable working conditions. To the extent that true union/nonunion wage differentials are smaller, the negative allocative effects of unions will be smaller.

5. The provisions of the Jones Act affect the demand for labor in the U.S. shipping industry in at least two ways. First, the provision that 50 percent of all U.S. government cargo must be transported in U.S.-owned ships makes the price elasticity of demand for U.S. shipping in the output market less elastic. Second, the restriction that at least 90 percent of the crews of U.S. ships must be U.S. citizens reduces the ability of ship owners to substitute foreign seamen for U.S. citizens. Both changes cause the wage elasticity of demand for U.S. seamen to be less elastic than it would otherwise be.

To the extent that the U.S. shipping industry is heavily unionized and there is little competition between union seamen and nonunion seamen (a reasonable assumption), the wage elasticity of demand for union seamen would become less elastic under the Jones Act. As stressed in the text, inelastic labor demand curves permit unions to push for increases in their members' wages without large employment losses, at least in the short run.

7. There are several reasons why unions may raise worker productivity. One of the more obvious is that, as wages are increased, firms cut back employment and substitute capital for labor. Both actions tend to raise the marginal productivity of labor. To survive in a competitive market, profit-maximizing firms must raise the marginal productivity of labor whenever wages increase.

Another reason unions raise productivity is that the high wages unionized employers offer attract a large pool of applicants, and employers are able to "cream" the best applicants. Moreover, the reduction in turnover that we observe in unionized plants increases firms' incentives to provide specific training to their workers, and the seniority system that unions typically implement encourages older workers to show younger workers the "ropes" (they can do so without fear that the younger workers will compete for their jobs when fully trained).

Because many of these sources of increased productivity are responses by firms to higher wages, they tend to mitigate the effects of unionization on costs. Some nonunion firms deliberately pay high wages to attract and retain able employees, and they often pursue this strategy even without the implicit threat of becoming unionized. However, the fact that firms generally pay the union wage only after their employees become organized suggests that they believe unions raise labor costs to a greater extent than they raise worker productivity.

What the quotation in question 7 overlooks is that increases in productivity must be measured against increases in costs. If unions enhance productivity to a greater extent than they increase costs of production, then clearly employers should take a much less antagonistic approach to unions. If, however, enhancements in labor productivity are smaller than increases in labor costs, employer profitability will decline under unionization.

9. This law makes it more difficult and more costly to substitute capital for labor. Any worker replaced by capital (or another substitute factor of production) must be retrained and employed elsewhere in the firm, which clearly raises the cost of this substitution. Thus, this law tends to reduce the elasticity of demand for union labor, and it increases the ability of unions to raise wages without reducing their members' employment very much.

Chapter 14

1. Increasing the subsidy guaranteed to those who do not work, but holding constant a nonzero effective wage rate, will clearly cause a reduction in labor supply. This reduction will take two forms: Some who worked before may decide to withdraw from the labor force, and some who worked before may reduce their hours of work. These two forms of labor supply reduction have quite different effects on the distribution of *earnings*.

   It is reasonable to suppose that the expected labor supply reductions will come mainly from workers with the lowest level of earnings. Thus, when labor force *withdrawal* takes place, those with the lowest earnings are leaving the labor force, and this withdrawal will tend to equalize the distribution of earnings (those at the lower end exit from the distribution).

   Reduced hours of work among those who continue in the labor force, however, will have the opposite effect on the distribution of earnings if this labor supply response is also focused among those with the lowest level of earnings. Reductions in working hours will lower the earnings of these low-wage workers further, which will tend to widen the dispersion of earnings. Therefore, while this increased generosity of the negative income tax program serves to equalize the distribution of *income* (which includes the subsidies), the labor supply responses can tend to either narrow or widen the dispersion of earnings.

3. Increasing the investment tax credit reduces the price of capital, and therefore has two possible effects on the demand for labor. If labor and capital are complements in production or are gross complements, then the tax credit will shift the labor demand curve to the right and tend to increase wages and employment. If, however, capital and labor are gross substitutes, then this tax credit could result in a decreased demand for labor.

   We learned from Chapter 4 that capital and unskilled labor are more likely to be substitutes in production than are skilled labor and capital; therefore, this investment tax credit is more likely to negatively affect the demand for unskilled labor than for skilled labor. If so, there will be more downward pressure on the wages of unskilled workers, and the resulting decline in the relative wages of the lowest-paid workers tends to widen the dispersion of earnings.

5. Forbidding employers to replace striking workers will have ambiguous effects on the dispersion of earnings. On the one hand, we know that forbidding striker replacement should increase the power of unions to raise the wages of their members, and we know that unions have historically raised the wages of less-skilled members relative to the wages of those who are more skilled. Thus, if union power is enhanced, the primary beneficiaries will be lower-skilled union workers, and this effect should tend to equalize the distribution of earnings.

   On the other hand, we need to consider the effects on those who would have worked as replacements. We know that unions are more prevalent in large firms, which pay higher wages anyway, and we can suppose that workers who wish to work as replacements are attracted to these jobs because they can improve their earnings. By encouraging higher wages in large, unionized firms, forbidding striker replacement could cause a spillover effect that reduces wages in the nonunionized sector. Thus, prohibiting striker replacement may actually drive down wages paid to those now in the small-firm, nonunion sector and create a greater dispersion in earnings.

7. Proposal "a" increases the cost of employing high-wage (skilled) labor and capital. This will have ambiguous effects on the demand curve for unskilled workers. On the one hand, it will tend to cause unskilled workers to be substituted for skilled workers and/or capital (assuming they are substitutes in production). On the other hand, the costs of production rise and the scale effect will tend to reduce both output and the demand for all workers (including the unskilled).

If the substitution effect dominates, the demand curve for the unskilled shifts to the right, tending to increase their employment and wage rate. If the scale effect dominates (or if the unskilled are complements in production with skilled labor and capital), then the demand curve for them shifts left, and their wage rate and employment level would decrease.

Proposal "b" cuts the cost of employing all labor, but the percentage decrease is greatest for the low-paid (unskilled). Thus, the proposal cuts the cost of unskilled labor relative to that of both capital and skilled labor. This will unambiguously shift the demand for unskilled labor to the right (keeping the employee wage on the vertical axis), because both the scale and the substitution effects work in the same direction. This will tend to increase both unskilled employment and the wages received by employees.

Proposal "b" is better for accomplishing the government's goal of improving the earnings of the unskilled, because the scale effect tends to increase, not reduce, the demand for their services.

Chapter 15

1. The two policy goals are not compatible in the short run. An increase in unemployment compensation benefits reduces the costs to unemployed workers of additional job search; this will lead them to extend their duration of unemployment and search for better-paying jobs. In the short run, increasing unemployment compensation benefits will increase the unemployment rate.

In the long run, however, the two policy goals *may* be compatible. If the prolonged durations of job search lead to better matches of workers and jobs, the chances that workers will become unemployed in the future will diminish. That is, the better matches will reduce both the probability that workers will quit their jobs and the probability that they will be fired. This reduced probability of entering unemployment will reduce the unemployment rate in the long run. Whether the reduction in the unemployment rate due to the smaller incidence of unemployment outweighs the increase due to the longer spells of unemployment is an open question.

3. a. Under the normal UI program, workers only receive benefits if they do not work at all. This new program in New York amounts to the payment of partial unemployment insurance benefits, for which workers need not be completely unemployed to be eligible.

b. This program should make it more attractive for workers to accept cuts in hours of work than was previously the case; therefore, employers should be more willing to cut weekly hours in times of economic distress. Because the measured unemployment rate includes as "unemployed" only those who have no paid employment at all, any tendency to reduce hours rather than lay off workers should serve to reduce the measured unemployment rate.

c. In an environment in which reductions in labor hours are taken mostly in the form of layoffs, it has been common for older workers to be protected. This practice has meant that during business slumps, the decline in yearly earnings among younger workers is much more dramatic than that among older workers. If younger workers in a highly volatile industry had realized their employment was likely to be interrupted by layoff, their *hourly* wages might have had to rise to compensate them for this risk. Conversely, older workers protected from layoff under a seniority system should have been willing to work for less per hour than they otherwise would have received. If, instead, layoffs are replaced by across-the-board cuts in hours, then these compensating wage differentials might disappear, with the result that there would be a somewhat greater spread between the hourly wages of younger and older workers. Thus, while hourly wages would tend to become more divergent between young and old, average yearly earnings would become less so (cutbacks in the labor input would not fall solely on younger workers).

5. There are a number of reasons why unemployed workers' reservation wages may decline as their spells of unemployment lengthen. One is that workers may have finite horizons and plan to be in the labor force for only specific time periods. As their durations of unemployment lengthen, the time they expect to work (once they find jobs) declines, and this shorter expected work life reduces the present value of the benefits obtained from searching longer. As a result, they tend to reduce their reservation wages.

   A second reason relates to their changing perceptions about the distribution of wage offers they face. When a worker first becomes unemployed, he or she may be optimistic about employment opportunities and set a high reservation wage. However, if over time only very low wage offers are received, the individual may realize that the distribution of wage offers is lower than initially assumed. This revision of expectations would also cause a downward revision of the reservation wage.

   In fact, even if workers' initial perceptions about the distribution of wage offers were correct, this distribution might systematically shift down over time. For example, employers might use the length of time an individual had been unemployed as a signal of the individual's relatively low productivity and might moderate wage offers accordingly. A systematically declining wage-offer distribution that arises for this reason would similarly cause reservation wages to decline as durations of unemployment lengthened.

7. This policy should have two effects on the unemployment rate. First, by reducing the value of benefits to unemployed workers, it should reduce the duration of their spells of unemployment. In other words, by taxing unemployment insurance benefits, the government is in effect reducing those benefits, and the reduction in benefits increases the marginal costs of remaining unemployed for an additional period of time. Thus, workers will tend to be less choosy about job offers they accept and should be induced to reduce the amount of time they spend searching for additional job offers. However, by reducing job search, the taxation of UI benefits may lead to

poorer "matches" between worker and employer, thus creating higher turnover (and more unemployment) in the long run.

Finally, because unemployed workers are now receiving less compensation from the government, those in jobs in which layoffs frequently occur will find them less attractive than they previously did. Employers who offer these jobs will have more difficulty attracting employees unless they raise wages (assuming workers have other job options). This compensating wage differential will act as a penalty for high layoff rates, and this penalty should induce firms to reduce layoffs to some extent. A reduced propensity to lay off workers, of course, should reduce the unemployment rate (other things being equal).

9. The level of unemployment is affected by flows into and out of the "pool" of unemployed workers. Restricting employers' ability to fire workers will reduce the flow of workers *into* the pool, thus tending to reduce unemployment. However, because these restrictions increase the costs of hiring workers (the costs of firing them are a quasi-fixed cost), firms will tend to reduce their *hiring* of labor. This reduction will slow the flows out of the unemployed pool, so that one cannot predict the overall effect of the restrictions on the unemployment rate.

Name Index

Abbott, Michael G., 362n
Abowd, John M., 125n, 138n, 281n, 285n, 393n, 490n, 592n
Abraham, Katharine G., 147(example), 578n, 580n, 591n
Abrams, Elliott, 353n
Abrams, Franklin S., 353n
Addison, John T., 508n, 579(example)
Aigner, Dennis J., 440n
Akerlof, George, 395n, 581n
Alchian, Armen, 77n
Allen, Steven G., 276n, 370n, 399n
Alpert, William, 511n
Alston, Lee J., 410n
Altonji, Joseph G., 178n, 296n, 305n, 323n
Anderson, C.A., 296n
Anderson, David A., 285n
Anderson, John, 183
Anderson, Patricia M., 361n, 367n, 591n
Andrews, Martyn, 488n
Angrist, Joshua D., 296n, 307n
Arai, Mahmood, 255n
Ashenfelter, Orley, 80n, 109n, 121n, 165n, 178n, 240n, 255n, 281n, 285n, 313n, 436n, 486n, 497n, 499n, 500n, 501n, 504n, 569n, 592n
Atkinson, Anthony B., 575n
Averett, Susan L., 216n
Azariadis, Costas, 586n, 587n

Badgett, M.V. Lee, 415n
Baily, Martin, 587n

Baker, George P., 382n, 389n, 394n, 396n, 402n
Baker, Joe G., 332n
Baldwin, Marjorie L., 415n
Baldwin, Robert E., 133n
Barrett, Nancy, 450n
Bartel, Ann P., 7n, 116n, 302n, 340n
Bassi, Lauri J., 163n, 166n, 302n
Baumol, William J., 331n
Bawden, Lee, 152(example), 377n
Bazerman, Max H., 503n
Beach, Charles M., 362n
Bean, Charles R., 88n
Becker, Brian E., 485n, 513n
Becker, Elizabeth, 162n
Becker, Gary S., 4n, 159n, 220n, 229n, 288n, 432n
Beller, Andrea H., 244n, 429n
Belzer, Michael H., 111(example)
Benedict, Mary Ellen, 277n, 499n, 525n
Benhabib, Jess, 331n
Bennett, Amanda, 595n
Bentham, Jeremy, 256n
Berg, Ivar, 320n
Bergmann, Barbara, 444n
Berman, Eli, 544n, 546n
Berndt, Ernst, 545n, 546n
Bernhardt, Dan, 405n
Betts, Julian R., 296n
Bhagat, S., 393n
Bhargava, Sandeep, 391n
Biddle, Jeff E., 188n, 255n

Things to Know

Particip rate

unempl

$POP = 12,000,000$

$Lab force = 8,000,000$

$unempl = 400,000$

4 kinds of unempl.
① Frictional ② Structural ③ Demand deficient
④ Seasonal

Reservation wage   efficiency wage

In the 30's was collective bargaining

Union inrl down 25% → 11% - 12%

20 out of 52 weeks to be eligible

Subject Index

TABLE 6.1 LABOR FORCE PARTICIPATION RATES OF FEMALES IN THE U.S. OVER 16 YEARS OF AGE, BY MARITAL STATUS, 1990–1994 (PERCENT)

Year	All Females	Single	Widowed, Divorced	Married
1900	20.6	45.9	32.5	5.6
1910	25.5	54.0	34.1	10.7
1920	24.0			9.0
1930	25.3	55.2	34.4	11.7
1940	26.7	53.1	33.7	13.8
1950	29.7	53.6	35.5	21.6
1960	37.7	58.6	41.6	31.9
1970	43.3	56.8	40.3	40.5
1980	51.5	64.4	43.6	49.8
1988	56.6	67.7	46.2	56.7
1994	58.8			59.6

TABLE 6.2 LABOR FORCE PARTICIPATION RATES FOR MALES IN THE U.S., BY AGE, 1900–1994 (PERCENT)

	Age Groups					
Year	14–19	16–19	20–24	25–44	45–64	Over 65
1900	61.1		91.7	96.3	93.3	68.3
1910	56.2		91.1	96.6	93.6	58.1
1920	52.6		90.9	97.1	93.8	60.1
1930	41.1		89.9	97.5	94.1	58.3
1940	34.4		88.0	95.0	88.7	41.5
1950	39.9	63.2	82.8	92.8	87.9	41.6
1960	38.1	56.1	86.1	95.2	89.0	30.6
1970	35.8	56.1	80.9	94.4	87.3	25.0
1980		60.5	85.9	95.4	82.2	19.1
1994		57.7	85.5	93.9	80.6	17.2